Handbook of Implementation Science
for Psychology in Education

Implementation science is the science of making programs and interventions effective in real-world contexts. This book is an indispensable, highly innovative, and evidence-based resource aimed at using implementation research findings in psychology to improve all aspects of education, from individual teaching programs to organizational development. It addresses the widespread confusion and disappointment about the lack of effectiveness of real-world psychology and provides 27 chapters offering proven policies, strategies, and approaches for designing, supporting, and improving interventions in schools. Collectively, the chapters go beyond the realm of psychology and education, tackling concerns about how to promote positive change in any context and covering topics from epistemology through statistics to examples of implementation approaches, frameworks, and protocols. This book creates an immensely relevant body of information and evidence for any practitioner or organization facing the challenges of change. It is essential reading for practitioners, policymakers, stakeholders, and funders in psychology, education, and beyond.

Barbara Kelly, Ph.D., is a graduate of Edinburgh, Glasgow, and Strathclyde Universities. She is currently Deputy Director (Research) of Post Graduate Professional Training in Educational Psychology, School of Psychological Sciences and Health, at the University of Strathclyde, Glasgow. She is also a Senior Educational Psychologist for Glasgow City Psychological Service. A former research fellow in the Departments of Education, Sociology, and Social Work at Glasgow University, her work has focused on the effectiveness of interventions and services designed to address children's needs. She has conducted research across a range of contexts, including innovative preschool education and interventions for child victims of sexual abuse. She has also carried out research for the Scottish government on interventions affecting juvenile offenders and on secure provision for juveniles. As both a practitioner and an academic, Barbara Kelly offers a unique perspective in exploring and developing innovative frameworks linking theory and epistemology to evidence and practice.

Daniel F. Perkins received his PhD from Michigan State University. He is currently Professor of Family and Youth Resiliency and Policy at Penn State University. His research interests include adolescent and family development; assets, risk, and protective factors; collaboration and community development; contextual influences on development; evaluation of prevention and intervention programs; civic engagement in youth; prevention science; risk behaviors and resiliency; theories of adolescence; and youth development. Professor Perkins is currently involved in two major prevention projects. The first involves assessing the effectiveness of a model for the diffusion of empirically validated prevention programs for adolescent substance abuse and mental health. The project is under way in 14 communities in Iowa and Pennsylvania. The second study focuses on strategies for strengthening the ability of after-school programs to promote citizenship, skills, and positive youth behavior in order to prevent delinquency and substance abuse.

Handbook of Implementation Science for Psychology in Education

Edited by

BARBARA KELLY

University of Strathclyde

DANIEL F. PERKINS

The Pennsylvania State University

CAMBRIDGE
UNIVERSITY PRESS

32 Avenue of the Americas, New York NY 10013-2473, USA

Cambridge University Press is part of the University of Cambridge.

It furthers the University's mission by disseminating knowledge in the pursuit of education, learning and research at the highest international levels of excellence.

www.cambridge.org
Information on this title: www.cambridge.org/9780521127028

© Cambridge University Press 2012

First published 2012
First paperback edition 2014

A catalogue record for this publication is available from the British Library

Library of Congress Cataloguing in Publication data
Handbook of implementation science for psychology in education / [edited by] Barbara Kelly, Daniel F. Perkins.
    pages cm
Includes bibliographical references and index.
ISBN 978-0-521-19725-0 (hardback)
1. Educational psychology.   2. School psychology.   I. Kelly, Barbara.
II. Perkins, Daniel F.
LB1051.H2355   2012
370.15–dc23   2012015674

ISBN 978-0-521-19725-0 Hardback
ISBN 978-0-521-12702-8 Paperback

To Richard, Adam, and Sarah – as always.

With very many thanks to Professor James Boyle for his invaluable input and to trainees and colleagues at Strathclyde University and Glasgow Psychological Service for their reflections and encouragement.

Contents

Contributors

GREGORY A. AARONS, Professor of Psychiatry, University of California, San Diego.

DR. NICK AXFORD, Senior Researcher, Social Research Unit, Social Research Centre, Dartington, United Kingdom.

FRANCES WALLACE BAILEY, MPH, Senior Management Consultant, Frank Porter Graham Child Development Institute, National Implementation Research Network, Chapel Hill, North Carolina.

PROFESSOR JUDITH BENNETT, Department of Education, University of York, United Kingdom.

DR. KAREN A. BLASE, Senior Scientist, Frank Porter Graham Child Development Institute, National Implementation Research Network, Chapel Hill, North Carolina.

PROFESSOR JAMES BOYLE, Director, Professional Training in Educational Psychology, School of Psychological Sciences and Health, University of Strathclyde, Glasgow, Scotland.

DR. TRACEY BYWATER, Reader in Enhancing Parental Input in Supporting Children's Success, Institute for Effective Education, University of York, and Director of Graduate Studies and Honorary Research Fellow, Bangor University, Wales.

LINDA L. CALDWELL, Distinguished Professor, Recreation, Park and Tourism Management and Human Development and Family Studies, and Director, College of Health and Human Development Global Leadership Initiative, Penn State University.

JEANNE CENTURY, Director of Science Education, Director of Research and Evaluation, Center for Elementary Mathematics and Science Education, The University of Chicago.

ANNE MICHELLE DANIELS, Associate Professor, Family Life Parenting and Child Care, Specialist, Department of Counseling and Human Development, College of Education and Human Sciences, University of South Dakota.

THOMAS J. DISHION, Professor, School of Psychology, University of Oregon, and Founder and Co-Director, Child and Family Center, University of Oregon, Eugene.

CELENE E. DOMITROVICH, Ph.D., Assistant Director, Penn State Prevention Research Center, Penn State University.

MORGAEN DONALDSON, Principal Researcher, Education Matters, Inc., Cambridge, Massachusetts.

GLEN DUNLAP, Ph.D., Professor of Research, University of South Florida and University of Nevada, Reno.

DR. CARL J. DUNST, Orelena Hawks Puckett Institute, Asheville, North Carolina.

DR. MELISSA VAN DYKE, LCSW, Investigator, Frank Porter Graham Child Development Institute, National Implementation Research Network, Chapel Hill, North Carolina.

DR. DEAN L. FIXSEN, Director, Frank Porter Graham Child Development Institute, National Implementation Research Network, Chapel Hill, North Carolina.

DR. TAMSIN FORD, Clinical Senior Lecturer in Child and Adolescent Psychiatry at Peninsula College of Medicine and Dentristry, Exeter, United Kingdom.

PROFESSOR LISE FOX, Department of Child and Family Studies and Director of the Florida Center for Inclusive Communities, University of South Florida Center for Excellence in Developmental Disabilities, University of South Florida.

CASSIE FREEMAN, Researcher, Center for Elementary Mathematics and Science Education, The University of Chicago.

PROFESSOR ROBYN M. GILLIES, School of Education, University of Queensland, Brisbane, Australia.

DR. AMY E. GREEN, Post Doctoral Scholar, Department of Psychiatry, University of California, San Diego.

MARK T. GREENBERG, Ph.D., Bennett Chair of Prevention Research, Director, Prevention Research Center, Penn State University.

PROFESSOR VIOLET H. HARADA, Department of Information and Computer Sciences, Library and Information Science Program, University of Hawaii.

TIM HOBBS, Ph.D., Researcher, Social Research Unit, Dartington, United Kingdom.

CINDY HUANG, Doctoral Student, Child and Family Center, University of Oregon, Eugene.

ROBERT J. ILLBACK, CEO, REACH of Louisville, Inc., Louisville, Kentucky, and Deputy CEO, Headstrong, The National Centre for Youth Mental Health, Dublin, Ireland.

DR. BARBARA KELLY, Deputy Director, Postgraduate Professional Training in Educational Psychology, School of Psychological Sciences and Health, University of Strathclyde, Glasgow, Scotland.

KATHRYN MARGOLIS, Doctoral Student, Child and Family Center, University of Oregon, Eugene.

DR. ELIZABETH MILLER, Post Doctoral Scholar, Department of Psychiatry, University of California, San Diego.

DANA T. MITRA, Associate Professor of Education, Education Theory and Policy, Penn State University.

JEREMY J. MONSEN, Executive Principal Psychologist, East London Consortium of Educational Psychologists, London Boroughs of Barking and Dagenham, Newham and Waltham Forest, United Kingdom.

JULIA E. MOORE, Ph.D., Researcher, Penn State Prevention Research Center, Penn State University.

LOUISE MORPETH, Co-Director, Social Research Unit, Dartington, United Kingdom.

BARBARA NEUFELD, President and Founder of Education Matters, Inc., Cambridge, Massachusetts.

COLLEEN K. REUTEBUCH, Ph.D., Director, The Reading Institute, The Meadows Center for Preventing Educational Risk, College of Education, The University of Texas at Austin.

MOLLIE RUDNICK, Researcher, Center for Elementary Mathematics and Science Education, The University of Chicago.

ROBERT SAVAGE, Professor, Department of Educational and Counselling Psychology, McGill University, Montreal, Canada.

ROBERT E. SLAVIN, Professor, Institute of Effective Education, University of York, United Kingdom and Director of the Center for Research and Reform in Education, John Hopkins University, Baltimore, United States.

ELIZABETH A. STORMSHACK, Professor, Associate Vice President for Research, College of Education, and Director, Child and Family Centre, University of Oregon, Eugene.

PROFESSOR PHILLIP STRAIN, Educational Psychology and Early Childhood, Director of PELE Center, School of Education and Human Development, University of Colorado, Denver.

PROFESSOR KEITH J. TOPPING, Education and Social Research, School of Education, University of Dundee, Scotland.

DR. CAROL M. TRIVETTE, Orelena Hawks Puckett Institute, Morganton, North Carolina.

SHARON VAUGHN, H.E. Hartfelder/Southland Corporation Regents Chair, Executive Director, The Meadows Center for Preventing Educational Risk, College of Education, The University of Texas at Austin.

JANET A. WELSH, Ph.D., Assistant Research Professor, Prevention Research Center for the Promotion of Human Development, Penn State University.

PROFESSOR LISA MARKS WOOLFSON, Head, School of Psychological Sciences and Health, University of Strathclyde, Glasgow, Scotland.

JOYCE YUKAWA, Assistant Professor, Communication and Information Sciences Ph.D. Program, Department of Information and Computer Sciences, Library and Information Science Program, University of Hawaii.

Foreword

Robert E. Slavin

Throughout the world, enlightened nations spend substantial amounts to improve the lives of children and vulnerable adults. Yet, until recently, government-sponsored programs were created, widely disseminated, or discontinued with little regard to their demonstrated effectiveness. Instead, programs have been enthusiastically instituted based on political or social factors. Then tastes or politics change, and programs are terminated in a pendulum of boom-to-bust change that fails to advance practice or research itself.

In recent years, this dynamic is beginning to change. In areas from education, to social services, to delinquency prevention, promising solutions to persistent problems are increasingly being put to the test, often in large-scale randomized, or quasi-experimental evaluations. These are not the small, brief, often artificial experiments of the past but sophisticated evaluations of realistic alternatives in practical settings on a scale that matters. As a result of these experiments, we are learning not only about "what works" but also about why various programs do or do not work, for whom and under what conditions they work, what is needed to scale up proven programs, and what policy supports are needed to scale them up without losing their effectiveness.

This book represents the current state of the art in this emerging implementation science. Investigators from many disciplines and several countries share their perspectives and findings on implementations and outcomes of a diverse set of interventions. This book could not have been written as recently as five years ago, so rapidly is this field developing.

The application of rigorous scientific methods to evaluate social programs has great potential to advance society. This volume makes an important contribution in assembling cutting-edge research and methods in one place to represent the potential and accomplishments of implementation science.

Part I

WHAT IS IMPLEMENTATION SCIENCE?

CHAPTER 1

Implementation Science for Psychology in Education

Barbara Kelly

What Is Implementation Science?

How to implement interventions effectively in educational contexts is the theme of this book. Essentially, the book aims to provide a resource for those involved in designing and delivering intervention in educational contexts. A range of applied and academic scientists, psychologists, educators, organisational consultants and practitioners from various domains explore the gap between the design and development of evidence-based programmes or interventions and the design and methodology required to ensure their successful transfer and application in real-world contexts. The book explores the topic of *implementation science*, a new area of scientific, academic and practitioner interest focussed on exploring and explaining what makes interventions work in real-world contexts.

Paradoxically, this new science has arisen mainly from the study of failure. Psychological interventions, or indeed any interventions involving people and resources in natural contexts, have notoriously unpredictable outcomes. This has been the case

for some considerable time, but implementation science is a remarkably new development. The scientific themes combining to create implementation science have materialised from a range of sources cutting across disciplines and practice contexts. The first academic journal dealing exclusively with this area appeared only as recently as 2006. The journal aimed to pull together the very disparate fields of epistemology, research protocols, practitioner methodology and experience that combine to create the implementation science focus and knowledge base. Before this, a wide-ranging evidence and interest base had begun to develop in pockets where failure to implement effectively was identified as underlying failure of interventions. A scientific focus on implementation provides the coherent perspective and accessibility urgently required by all applied scientists and practitioners, presenting evidence and direction for creating and supporting real-world change.

The application of psychology is well recognised, and it is influential in a wide range of contexts. Psychological programmes and interventions are applied globally in educational, health, organisational and therapeutic contexts with the over-arching objective of enhancing human well-being and potential. In education, psychological theory and empirical research have informed and continue to inform and develop many aspects of teaching and learning. For example, understanding and developing effectiveness in teaching style, literacy acquisition, behaviour management, social and emotional education, curricular design, school ethos and staff development and training are key areas derived directly from psychological theory and research.

In contrast, however, the effectiveness in general of applied psychological theory and intervention has proved very difficult to demonstrate with consistency, particularly in real-world contexts. Certainly, traditional, empirical approaches to design, measurement and evaluation of the effects of applied psychology have created a considerable range of what are rightly called 'evidence-based' programmes. However, problems have arisen in the transfer of these to real-world contexts that lack experimental control. These problems are mainly due to a scientific failure to anticipate and take into account factors and processes underlying variability and unpredictability in effectiveness. Variability effects arise from a range of sources but are related mainly to characteristics and attributes of practitioners who are asked to implement programmes and to surrounding contextual issues. Practitioners' understanding of the theory underlying the programme, their knowledge of how it should be implemented and why, their beliefs about the programme's potential to bring about change and the impact of external constraints such as time and resources have a profound effects on results.

Exploration of the nature of barriers to effectiveness and their impact on the delivery of effective evidence-based programmes in the real world is the major focus of implementation science. Implementation science is the study of the processes and methods involved in the systematic transfer and uptake of evidence-based practices into routine, everyday practice. Its central aims are to support the understanding of relevant, contextual processes and improve the quality and effectiveness of what is delivered as psychological intervention in applied contexts.

Scientific Paradigms and the Concept of Evidence Base

An important contemporary objective for practitioners is to make use of evidence-based practice. Evidence-based practice is practice that is based on robust research evidence of efficacy and effectiveness. Research on effectiveness is particularly salient where investment by government and other stakeholders is substantial and outcomes are intended to reflect and mobilise progressive policy. Directives to use evidence-based intervention have extended to education policies in the United States, where funding has been allocated specifically for schools to adopt proven, comprehensive reform models (American Psychological Association Presidential Task Force on Evidence-Based Practice, 2006; Slavin, 2002). In the United Kingdom, the demand for evidence-based intervention and practice is less explicit at the policy level but is expected of educational, psychology and other practitioners and is embedded in the leading concept of accountability (Friedman, 2005).

Evidence-based intervention is developed by rigorous, systematic scientific procedures. To be sure that a programme or intervention can be described as evidence-based, procedures commonly may involve the use of randomised, controlled trials (RCTs) at some point in the evolution of the intervention. RCT is an experimental design that involves the random allocation of participants either to an experimental group, which receives some form of treatment or intervention, or to a control group, which receives no such treatment or intervention (Robson, 2002). The RCT procedure is designed to ensure that there is an equal probability of the assignment of participants to the different conditions and to minimise bias by ensuring that there is comparability across groups. In this way, the impact of a programme or intervention can be measured by comparing the two groups before and after the intervention is applied. This type of research is considered to be essential in establishing the effectiveness of interventions, and therefore, it can be seen to underpin *directly* the development of effective, replicable programmes and practices that schools are encouraged to adopt. However, despite conviction that evidence-based intervention represents the 'gold standard' in practice contexts, ongoing attempts to assess the impact of any interventions applied in schools and in other contexts has highlighted substantial obstacles and challenges, not least of which are related to the complex processes of implementation. The traditional scientific approach, as Slavin (2002) points out, has largely been responsible for the transformation of society, guiding developments in medicine, technology and agriculture. However, he suggests that education has somehow avoided the classical scientific paradigm, and he points to the continuing haphazard adoption in schools of programmes and packages that are not scientifically verified. The situation remains similar in the United Kingdom. The realisation of contemporary aims and ideals in education does seem to rest to a large extent on psychological and social research, but educational policy and practice have not been so radically influenced and systematically transformed by scientific methodology and findings per se. The reasons for this are complex and related to the nature of the hitherto covert processes involved in enabling, demonstrating and measuring effectiveness. Evidence presented throughout this book indicates that although the traditional scientific approach is still accepted as critical to prove effectiveness, it is in fact highly unlikely to demonstrate statistically significant intervention effects from programme evaluation in uncontrolled and unprepared social contexts. However, while this information has been available for some time, it has not informed the development of methodologies more suited to the task (Boruch et al., 1975, 1978).

Identifying Barriers to Effectiveness

The processes operating in or around social contexts such as the classroom are elusive, intricate and unpredictable. It is these processes that have proved resistant to the rigours of the classical scientific paradigm, requiring a distinctive but complementary type of scientific methodology to measure and, in many instances, offset their influence. It is these processes that prevent or potentially support the transfer of scientifically developed, evidence-based approaches to real-world contexts, and they explain why it has not been possible to predict with accuracy how well a programme or approach will fare across a variety of real, as opposed to controlled, situations. The scientific approach to promoting change in human relational contexts has to take into account social, perceptual, attitudinal and value-based characteristics as well as existing frameworks for action, such as ethics, resources and policy directives. All these may support or hinder the intervention and change processes. It is clear now that these dimensions operate to a distinctive set of rules and that they are *additional* to those identified in classically controlled experimental paradigms. They require a distinctive systematic and scientific approach to understand and manage their effects.

It is a compelling fact that although psychological interventions may reflect rigorous standards of theory, development, design and methodology at the initial stages, and although they justifiably acquire the label 'evidence-based', variation across contexts is the norm. This has undoubtedly undermined confidence in the utility of psychology for educational or indeed any contexts. However, a greater degree of predictability is emerging steadily via the implementation perspective, illuminating processes and characteristics previously hidden but nevertheless critical in the gap between theory and practice. New design and methodology are providing a distinctive set of approaches involving innovative protocols and perspectives in scientific understanding and practice. Much of this relates to what is described as *implementation quality* and involves a network of integrated processes affecting staff training and selection, incorporation of interventions into school operations, organisational capacity and resourcing, principal and management support and readiness for change and progress embedded in specific practitioner values and attitudes. Implementation science can now provide frameworks for the preparation, execution, evaluation and sustainability of interventions in schools, organisations and communities. This information is proving to be decisive not only in supporting and sustaining the impact and effectiveness of programmes and interventions but also in influencing how they are conceived, designed and resourced.

The Emergence of Evidence-Based Implementation

The key question for implementation scientists has been: What is it about real-world contexts that makes measurable effectiveness so difficult to achieve? Although this particular question has taken a long time to emerge, it is central to the development of the concept of evidence-based practice in applied social contexts. Critically, the concept of evidence-based now has two elements, and the idea of an evidence base is not solely related to the nature of the evidence supporting a particular programme but applies *equally* to the way a programme is implemented in the field.

Researchers have always realised that what transpires in the field, especially in intervention research, does not reflect perfectly the conditions of scientifically controlled intervention trials. However, the powerful and decisive effects of contextual variables have been minimised to a large extent in research reports and in most cases completely overlooked in scientific explanations of variability. In a key paper illustrating this fundamental oversight, Dane & Schneider (1998) investigated the extent to which programme integrity – that is, the degree to which programmes were implemented as planned – was verified in studies of prevention programmes published between 1980 and 1994. Although a fair amount had been written by that stage about implementation processes and obstacles to programme integrity, the processes and variables involved were still not part of *scientific routine* in programme design, implementation and outcome evaluation. The authors selected articles for review in which an intervention focussed on the primary or early secondary prevention of behavioural, social and/or academic maladjustment in children. In total, 231 studies were examined in detail. Only 39 of 102 outcome studies specified features for the documentation of programme integrity. Of these, only 13 considered variations in integrity in analysing the *effectiveness* of the programme.

Dane & Schneider (1998) highlighted the importance of programme integrity in the context of preventative interventions. Some contemporary literature pointed out that interventions were often implemented in contexts presenting a range of identifiable *obstacles* to implementation and integrity. At that point, known obstacles mainly involved the feelings, values and attitudes of the programme recipients about the programme, the involvement of paraprofessionals in implementing programmes and limitations in resources to support programme delivery. Rohrbach and colleagues (1993) highlighted the fact that paraprofessionals might tend to feel uncomfortable or unfamiliar with the material they were being asked to deliver and, because of this, might prove less effective in delivering a programme exactly as it had been designed. Lack of appreciation of the impact of aspects of programmes also might result in spontaneous decisions by recipients to change the design or often, because of perennial resource problems, to cut or shorten an intervention. In addition, in schools, for example, where a large number of preventative interventions were taking place, a poor programme-context fit in terms of how much users saw the programme as useful and practical was found to have an impact on the integrity of the implementation and therefore on its measured impact and success.

A number of early studies involving attention to aspects of implementation indicate that as control over the implementation of interventions is relinquished by researchers, inconsistencies and distortions arise in delivery and therefore affect outcome. These tendencies emerge even in *effectiveness trials*, which involve testing interventions in naturalistic conditions using only the resources likely to be available in real-world contexts and thereby predicting and allowing compensation for the impact of less than optimal implementation (Rohrbach et al., 1993). Dane & Schneider's (1998) meta-analysis demonstrated that lowered adherence to programme or intervention protocol was significantly associated with poorer outcome. They found mixed evidence of dosage effects – effects related to how much of the programme recipients actually received. Crucially, they concluded that the omission of integrity data, particularly measures of adherence, would potentially compromise the internal validity of outcome studies.

The failure to consider programme implementation has had wide-ranging effects on the quality and usefulness of the scientific process of developing reliable evidence-based applied psychology. Knowledge about programme integrity enhances interpretation of effects. Significant programme effects can be hidden by inconsistencies in implementation. If programme integrity is not verified, evaluations may *under-represent* the potential of an intervention, putting programmes at risk of discontinuation that, in fact, are valuable and effective if implemented as designed (Felner et al., 1991).

Future Directions

Issues of control and measurement of contextual issues and implementation quality may be edging to the forefront for some social scientists and practitioners, but they are still considered optional in design, implementation and evaluation. For example, a number of relatively recent reviews explored whether depression can be prevented in children and adolescents. These included Durlak & Wells (1997), Gillham et al. (2007), and Merry et al. (2006). All argued that the evidence for prevention was inconclusive and highlighted the failure to evaluate programme integrity as a possible source of variation.

Implementation scientists can now offer model programmes that combine classical scientific paradigms with frameworks for implementation. For example, from the clinical perspective, Chambless & Hollon (1998) recommend rigorous experimental methods for treatment outcome research involving randomised assignment to condition, use of control groups, provision of a manual for delivery to allow faithful replication of the programme, consistent training for those delivering interventions and checks for programme adherence using a range of reliable and valid outcome measures. Spence & Short (2007) also suggest that programmes need a clear theoretical and conceptual basis and should be comprehensive, employ a variety of teaching methods, implement sufficient dosage and be based on the development of positive relationships. However, in recent evaluations of school-based interventions aimed at promoting social and emotional learning and skills and following implementation frameworks, Spence & Short (2007) noted ongoing and considerable variability in programme effectiveness. Greenberg et al. (2001) also noted additional factors within the child, family and school context likely to affect outcomes. Gillham et al. (2007) underline the complexity of developing an implementation science in finding that in their depression-prevention intervention, outcomes differed by school with *no identifiable variables* linked to different outcomes. They suggest that despite awareness of implementation effects and processes, subtle and complex school differences were affecting delivery and outcome of the programme.

It seems that implementation science has only begun to uncover the complexity of implementation and will continue to draw on eclectic perspectives, mixed models and wide-ranging evidence to create working models of reality and change.

Reviews of current programmes may give an unbalanced account of awareness and practice in the implementation field. Currently, an awareness of implementation and contextual issues may mitigate against large-scale prevention or intervention programmes that require wide dissemination and are beyond the immediate control of highly trained implementation support staff. Implementation evidence suggests a role for the interventionist field specialist who is able to build purposeful and effective relationships with clients and stakeholders and to work systematically to clarify highly specific contextual needs in individual organisations. Implementation science may define need currently in relation to overall *readiness for evidence-based programmes* – adequate resourcing, skills and capacity for effective delivery and ongoing evaluation. How to most effectively bring about the positive transformation of processes affecting implementation and development of the practitioner skills and ecological characteristics required to support change represents the cutting edge of implementation science.

If effective implementation is the key to intervention effectiveness, then all practitioners involved directly and indirectly in education and related professions are pivotal to its success. School psychologists as well as teacher educators and teachers themselves, and indeed all those who contribute by delivering programmes or services, are able to support or hinder implementation processes. Likewise, policymakers, research funders, stakeholders and advisors need to become aware of the central role played by implementation in the success of investment in programmes.

The Goals of This Book

Since the last millennium, the understanding and reporting of implementation effects have increased. Informed approaches for effective implementation draw on a substantial and growing evidence base about how best to support the application of psychology in education and elsewhere. However,

understanding of implementation processes is a separate, if related, discipline to the creation of evidence-based programmes per se. Slavin (2002) is undoubtedly correct in noting that schools do not currently select programmes because of their demonstrated evidence base. This issue has become very pressing. Knowledge is increasing about the evidential standards and effectiveness of programmes, and high-quality information is available about evidence base and how the selection of specific programmes should be made. The Collaborative for Academic, Social and Emotional Learning is a good example of initiative in this area and is a non-profit organisation that is advancing scientific methodology and evidence-based practice in social and emotional learning. The *Handbook of Implementation Science for Psychology in Education* offers an indispensable resource to all stakeholders in providing information about *how to* enhance impact from evidence-based programmes. This information is not yet disseminated as a discrete field of training or information for professionals in education, and this book makes unprecedented headway in clarifying concepts and setting out what information is available and how it can be used.

The boundaries of implementation science are currently drawn around the processes of implementing discrete programmes, but information on how to implement *any* aspect of teaching and learning comes under the same banner of promoting effectiveness. For this reason, this book contains chapters on work that is drawn from very different perspectives but which has been identified as supporting implementation of many different psychological and educational concerns. For example, there are chapters that explore frameworks for supporting implementation from a wide lens and in a range of contexts, and there are others that have a narrow focus, for example, on the elements of discourse or critical aspects of the teacher's role that have an impact on the quality of the learning experience and learning outcomes. By linking work from different and unrelated fields, this book highlights the intricate and potentially extensive role of implementation science in supporting all educational outcomes. However, its influence extends from the classroom to the home and the community, as well as to decision making and policy forums dealing with the appropriate allocation of resources, successful prevention of difficulties and effective evaluation of needs and outcomes. The use of evidence-based programmes and evidence-based practice supported by implementation science can strengthen the effectiveness of both psychology and education. This integrated approach fosters a shared purpose and a common vision.

The Plan of This Book

The chapters in this book are designed to reflect a wide and developing knowledge base about the influence of implementation effects and to allow an exploration of the implications for practice of an accumulation of useful and constructive findings. The chapters are organised into parts that focus on different areas of concern.

Part I begins with this chapter, and then, in Chapter 2, Karen Blase et al. discuss the role of implementation science in great depth and make a far-reaching, comprehensive contribution to promoting an understanding of implementation science. The authors draw on the work of the National Implementation Research Network and the Frank Porter Graham Child Development Institute, synthesising literature on implementation across a wide range of contexts. They outline a conceptual and practice-related framework of core implementation components related to key features of evidence-based practices and programmes.

Part II, 'Statistical Problems, Approaches and Solutions', covers epistemological, methodological and statistical issues that have a bearing on implementation science. This section is about exploring the potential and limitations of statistical methods in developing, applying and evaluating the impact of psychology in educational and related contexts. The aim is to describe methodologies and analytical approaches that fit

the demands of real-world effectiveness evaluation. Chapters tackle the epistemological, scientific and conceptual demands at the heart of evidence-based thinking and explore how new approaches may be developed, linking these with effective and useful scientific paradigms for real-world psychology. In Chapter 3, Tracey Bywater explores the complex methodology involved in ensuring that programme evaluations are rigorous and comprehensive. In Chapter 4, James Boyle considers the nature of experiments in real-world contexts, exploring how experimental paradigms can be incorporated into systematic *mixed-methods* approaches to contextual design and methodology. In Chapter 5, Carl J. Dunst and Carol M. Trivette explore information emerging via meta-analyses of the analysis of impact of implementation features in practice contexts. In Chapter 6, Judith Bennet provides an original and essential commentary that includes the rarely explored issue of the epistemology and its impact on interpretations of teaching practice, outcome assessment and evaluation.

Part III, 'Preparing for Effective Implementation: Frameworks and Approaches', focuses on methods *enabling* effective change. In Chapter 7, I explore how the implementation science evidence base can be accessed to enhance and integrate school psychology service delivery and practice at a range of levels from the conceptual to routine application. Chapter 8, by Jeremy J. Monsen and Lisa Marks Woolfson, looks at the role of problem-solving frameworks in educational psychology training and practice in the United Kingdom, linking the epistemology of critical realism to conceptual issues and key features of psychology in schools. The authors reflect on the implications and usefulness of this approach for implementation science in practice. They suggest that this type of innovative, overarching framework helps to ensure that readiness for change, programme fidelity and evaluation issues are tackled collaboratively in schools as a matter of course. This approach involves teachers and other professionals in collaborative development, design and evaluation of interventions. In Chapter 9, Gregory A. Aarons, Amy E. Green and Elizabeth Miller review the design and development of an instrument for assessing organisational readiness for change in practitioners, the Evidence-Based Practice Attitude Scale (EPAS). This instrument measures directly practitioner attitudes to accepting and implementing evidence-based change and is invaluable in highlighting where work *prior to* implementation may be required to enhance effectiveness.

Continuing the focus on enhancing organisational and practitioner effectiveness, Robert Illback in Chapter 10 offers a cutting-edge discussion and review of the elements of collaborative consultation processes, which are known to facilitate positive shifts in values, attitudes and practice in organisational contexts. Chapter 11, by Janet A. Welsh, looks afresh at pupil readiness for school context in relation to pressures for teacher accountability and implementation of successful teaching for student success.

Parts IV and V look in depth at the implementation of programmes and interventions with very specific goals and across very different contexts. Part IV, 'Successful Implementation of Specific Programmes and Interventions: Social, Emotional and Behavioural Change, Literacy Development and Leisure Education', looks at how implementation science can support directly a wide range of highly focused programmes and interventions in schools. These chapters are of great relevance for practitioners in particular who need detailed direction and support to develop high-quality implementation skills. In Chapter 12, Celene E. Domitrovich, Julia E. Moore, and Mark T. Greenberg review the practices and processes underlying maximum effectiveness in the implementation of social-emotional interventions for younger children. In Chapter 13, Keith Topping outlines a framework to support teachers and other school staff in improving the impact of school-based social competence programmes in general. In Chapter 14, Glen Dunlap, Phillip Strain and Lise Fox move beyond the school context and offer guidance on

implementing evidence-based strategies for managing seriously challenging behaviour in children with autism in the community. The authors review data and concepts related to the successful implementation of positive behaviour support, emphasising the precision of instructional delivery, dosage, ecological validity and importance of data-based decision making. In Chapter 15, Elizabeth Stormshack et al. outline the Ecofit Program, an evidence-based, integrated approach to parent intervention that is inspired by research indicating that successful interventions tackle multiple domains in reducing behavioural and academic problems. The project is implemented via school staff and resources and addresses misbehaviour in school via careful interventions tackling family interaction patterns.

Several chapters in this part deal specifically with the implementation of literacy programmes and the day-to-day effective teaching of literacy skills in schools. In Chapter 16, Robert Savage gives a comprehensive review of evidence-based reading interventions with a focus on the role and impact of implementation issues for the twenty-first century. The evidence base for *what works* is covered in detail, pursuing themes in research and evidence bases and exploring more technical issues in the teaching and learning dialogue. New perspectives are offered in quality implementation, methodology, scalability, sustainability and response to intervention. Chapter 17, by Colleen Reutebuch and Sharon Vaughan, also considers evidence-based literacy practices, but in relation to implementation, reading behaviour and the role of individual risk factors in compensatory literacy programmes for children who have English as an additional language. Part IV is completed by Chapter 18, in which Linda Caldwell explores the implementation of evidenced-based leisure education programmes.

In Part V, 'Improving the Implementation of Evidence-Based Programmes and Interventions via Staff Skills, Organizational Approaches and Policy Development', the intention is to shift the focus away from details of individual interventions and towards the evidence base that is developing on the impact of key staff skills, organisational approaches and policy and resourcing trends on effective implementation. These chapters flag areas of work that potentially have highly significant evidence to offer implementation science in a broad sense. In each chapter the subject matter may still be mobilised in the context of programmes and projects but can be seen to contribute in a pivotal way to the synthesis of knowledge and evidence in applying implementation science successfully. It is a sizable collection of chapters looking in considerable detail at critical features, dimensions and processes related to practitioner and organisational effectiveness in implementing evidence-based interventions and programmes. This section aims to be groundbreaking and innovative in helping to identify the specific training themes and skill requirements of professionals and organisations in building skills to develop and deliver effective policies, programmes and interventions.

In Chapter 19, Robyn M. Gillies outlines the critical features and dimensions of any class teacher's role in promoting effective group discourse. Effective discourse and dialogue can be seen to support learning across topics and contexts and clearly has wider implications for the support of implementation of *any* teaching and learning intervention. In Chapter 20, Mollie Rudnick, Cassie Freeman and Jeanne Century outline the *practical* applications involved in using a *fidelity-of-implementation* framework. This chapter documents the development and testing of important elements and processes in the application of fidelity components in real-world contexts and offers an in-depth study of the deeper processes involved in real-world implementation and their consequences. In Chapter 21, Dana Mitra describes the far-reaching role and potential of *student voice* in creating and enabling effective school reform. In this context and in many others, successful implementation can be seen to involve the building of genuine and transparent partnerships with students with measurable and meaningful outcomes.

Implementation science needs to know how to coach staff effectively for instructional improvement, and the evidence in this area is covered by Barbara Neufield and Morgaen Donaldson in Chapter 22. The authors investigate a form of coaching that may prove to be a potentially powerful training tool supporting enhanced implementation skills in delivering programmes and interventions. The authors describe a cascade model of training – *train the trainer* – in detail and in relation to the implementation of a project instigating a state-wide training system increasing the quality of infant toddler care via teacher effectiveness. In Chapter 23, Ann Michelle Daniels outlines the development of a training approach to improve the quality of the training and skills offered by child-care workers. The chapter reviews the problems facing those who need to evaluate the impact of professional qualifications and skills on child development and other specific measures of impact and outcome. In Chapter 24, the potential of action research is explored by Violet Harada and Joyce Yukawa as a method for reshaping and developing *depth of understanding* in the practice of educators through processes and skills in assessment and critical reflection in context. The authors focus on how this approach affects the ability to improve the implementation of evidence-based practice.

Chapter 25 focuses on the effective measurement of child well-being as a driver for appropriate selection and implementation of targeted intervention in school contexts. Tim Hobbs and Tamsin Ford review the suitability and potential of the *Strengths and Difficulties Questionnaire* for this purpose. This questionnaire has demonstrated a powerful evidence base over the last thirty years as a screening tool designed for the use of educational and school psychologists, and it is explored as a method for supporting the detailed direction, implementation and evaluation of well-being programmes in schools.

The Common Language method is explored and discussed in Chapter 26 by Nick Axford and Louise Morpeth. This chapter has a wide perspective, targeting collaborative approaches via the development of a common language across stakeholders and plays a crucial role in seeking to link science with implementation methodology overtly and in practice contexts. It has many points of contact with the problem-solving frameworks described by Jeremy J. Monsen and Lisa Marks Woolfson in Chapter 8. It also echoes some of the methodological issues raised by others, particularly Tim Hobbs and Tamsin Ford. It highlights the need for multilevel change, prioritising the need for systemic change to support impact.

In Chapter 27, I pull together the main themes emerging in this book, highlighting the need for concepts, evidence and practice emerging in implementation science to become integral and central to thinking and understanding of prevention, intervention and advancement of psychology in education.

References

American Psychological Association Presidential Task Force on Evidence-Based Practice (2006). Evidence-based practice in psychology. *American Psychologist* 61, 271–85.

Boruch, R. F. (1975). On contentions about randomizing field experiments. In R. F. Boruch and H. W. Riecken (eds.), *Experimental Testing of Public Policy*. Boulder, CO: Westview Press.

Boruch, R. F. (1978). Comments on Tallmadge's paper. In M. J. Wargo and D. R. Green (eds.), *Achievement testing of disadvantaged and minority students for educational program evaluation* (Based on the Proceedings of the U.S. Office of Education Invitational Conference). New York: CTB/McGraw-Hill.

Chambless, D. L., & Hollan, S. D. (1998). Defining empirically supported therapies. *Journal of Consulting Clinical Psychology* 66(1): 7–18.

Dane, A. V., & Schneider, B. H. (1998). Program integrity in primary and early secondary prevention: Are implementation effects out of control? *Clinical Psychology Review* 18(1), 23–45.

Durlack, J. A., & Wells, A. M. (1997). Primary prevention programmes for children and adolescents: A meta-analytic review. *American Journal of Community Psychology* 25(3), 115–52.

Felner, R. D., Philips, R. S. C., Dubois, D. & Lease, A. M. (1991). Ecological interventions and the process of change for prevention: Wedding theory and research to implementation in real world settings. *American Journal of Community Psychology* 19, 379–87.

Freidman, M. (2005). *Trying hard is not good enough: How to produce measurable improvement for customers and communities*. Victoria, BC: Trafford Publishing

Gillham, J. E., Reivich, K. J., Freres, D. R., Chaplin, T. M., Shatte, A. J., Samuels, B., Elkon, A. G. L., Litzinger, S., Lascher, M., Gallop, R. & Seligman, M. E. P. (2007). School-based prevention of depressive symptoms: A randomised control study of the effectiveness and specificity of the Penn Resiliency Programme. *Journal of Consulting and Clinical Psychology* 75, 9–19.

Gillham, J. E., Shatte, A. J. & Feres, D. R. (2000). Preventing depression: A review of cognitive behavioural and family interventions. *Applied and Preventive Psychology* 9, 63–8.

Greenberg, M. T., Domitrovich, C. & Bummbarger, B. (2001). The prevention of mental disorders in school-aged children: Current state of the field. *Prevention and Treatment* 4(1), 1–64.

Kelly, B., Woolfson, L. & Boyle, J. (2008). *Frameworks for practice in educational psychology: A textbook for trainees and practitioners*. London: Jessica Kingsley Publishers.

Merry, S., McDowell, H., Hettrick, S. & Muller, N. (2006). *Psychological and/or educational interventions for the prevention of depression in children and adolescents: A review*. Oxford, UK: Cochrane Library.

Robson, C. (2002). *Real-world research: A resource for social scientists and practitioner researchers*. Oxford, UK: Blackwell.

Rohrbach, L. A., Graham, J. W. & Hansen, W. B. (1993). Diffusion of a school-based substance abuse prevention program: Predictors of program implementation. *Preventative Medicine* 22, 237–60.

Slavin, R. E. (2002). Evidence-based educational policies: Transforming educational practice and research. *Educational Researcher* 31(7), 15–21.

Spence, S. H., & Short, A. L. (2007). Research reviews: Can we justify the widespread dissemination of universal, school based interventions for the prevention of depression among children and adolescents? *Journal of Child Psychology and Psychiatry* 35, 1191–228.

Sustainable School-Wide Social and Emotional Learning (SEL) (2010). CASEL (Collaborative for Academic Social and Emotional Learning) Resources and Publications; available at http://www.casel.org/pub/sel.php.

CHAPTER 2

Implementation Science

Key Concepts, Themes, and Evidence for Practitioners in Educational Psychology

Karen A. Blase, Melissa Van Dyke, Dean L. Fixsen, and Frances Wallace Bailey

Substantial investments are made in conducting and disseminating research to identify "what works" in education to produce desired academic, social, and behavioral outcomes. Research on intervention programs, prevention strategies, and instructional practices abound from journal articles to meta-analyses (Lipsey, 1995, Hattie, 2009). In addition, there is ready access to systematic reviews of research that assess the quality and impact of intervention and prevention research efforts (e.g., methodological rigor and effect size) (http://www.cochrane.org/; http://www.campbellcollaboration.org/). These reviews are readily accessible via the web, along with a number of registries that assess and categorize programs and practices based on research design and impact (http://www.colorado.edu/cspv/blueprints/; http://ies.ed.gov/ncee/wwc/) and, in some rare cases, readiness for dissemination (http://www.nrepp.samhsa.gov/). But developing new programs and practices, conducting rigorous research, assessing rigor and impact, and disseminating information about evidence-based practices and programs are only part of the equation.

This information helps us to choose what evidence-based program or practice in which to invest but does not tell us how to implement that program successfully to improve academic, social-emotional, and behavioral outcomes for children. Effective educational and behavioral approaches must be implemented successfully and sustained in very messy real-world settings. If research knowledge about "what works" is to be useful, not only must we assess the value and quality of the "what" (the intervention), but we also must understand "how" to implement, improve, sustain, and scale-up effective interventions.

As illustrated in Table 2.1, an effective "what" also requires careful attention to the effective "how" of implementation. The benefits of research in the real world can accrue only when effective practices are selected *and* effective implementation strategies are used.

Fortunately, there is a growing, though nascent, science of implementation to guide best practices related to implementation and organizational change, as well as the development of implementation-focused

Table 2.1. Relationship among Innovation, Implementation, and Outcomes

		Implementation: The "How"	
		Effective	Not effective
Innovation: The "What"	Effective	Improved student outcomes	Poor outcomes
	Not effective	Poor outcomes	Poor outcomes

research agendas. This chapter provides an overview of the science of implementation together with practical implementation frameworks and processes conceptualized through the work of the National Implementation Research Network (NIRN; http://nirn.fpg.unc.edu/). The recommendations for moving science to service are informed by a comprehensive review of the implementation evaluation and research literature across multiple domains (e.g., human services, health, and business) and the resulting synthesis of the literature by Fixsen et al. (2005) from extensive reviews of diffusion and dissemination literature (Greenhalgh et al., 2004; Rogers, 1995), as well as a specific review of the implementation literature in education (Wallace et al., 2008) and leadership (Waters, Marzano, & McNulty, 2003). This knowledge base is combined with NIRN's practical experience applying the frameworks in education (www.scaling.org), child welfare, and children's mental health to ground recommendations in both theory and practice.

Prerequisites for Using Science in the Real World

Before tackling the thorny issues related to implementation, organizational change, and systems transformation, it is important to note that there are certain prerequisite conditions for making good use of science in the real world. In addition to the quality and quantity of efficacy and effectiveness research, the evidence-based intervention also must be well operationalized, and there must be an active purveyor who can guide

implementing sites and schools through the implementation process.

Core Intervention Components

In order for an evidence-based intervention to be well operationalized, the core intervention components must be clearly specified. And there is some evidence that the more clearly identified the program components are, the more likely the program is to be implemented successfully (Bauman, Stein, & Ireys, 1991; Dale, Baker, & Racine, 2002; Winter & Szulanski, 2001). Knowing what is necessary to achieve results (e.g., dosage, activities, and therapeutic interactions) and how those components are linked to the theory base is important for real-world success. Identifying and validating core intervention components occurs as researchers conduct outcome studies and identify and validate fidelity measures. Fidelity measures that are highly correlated with positive outcomes provide strong indicators about what is required but are unlikely to tell the whole story with respect to necessary components and conditions. Efforts to more clearly specify core intervention components may require several iterative attempts to replicate the program with different groups of practitioners and in a number of different settings (e.g., different teachers in different classrooms in different schools or different therapists in different therapy groups in different agencies). Studying the conditions under which programs succeed and the conditions under which they falter brings into focus the core intervention components and the conditions necessary for success (Wolf et al., 1995; Huey et al., 2000; Korfmacher et al., 1999).

Active and Knowledgeable Purveyor

While clarity regarding the core intervention components is critical, so too is the advice and support from a qualified purveyor. Fixsen et al. (2005) define a *purveyor* as "an individual or group of individuals representing a program or practice who actively work to implement that practice or program with fidelity and good effect" (p. 14). Purveyors also have been referred to as *change agents* (Fairweather, Sanders, & Tornatzky, 1974; Havelock & Havelock, 1973), *linking agents* (Kraft et al., 2000), *site coordinators* (Blase, Fixsen, & Phillips, 1984) *site facilitators* (Datnow & Castellano, 2000), and *design-based assistance organizations* (Bodilly, 1996). The roles of purveyors are to help potential implementing sites assess their readiness to implement, help develop readiness where it does not yet exist, and provide a range of services to help develop the confidence and competence of practitioners and teachers. A number of evidence-based interventions have developed *purveyor organizations*, comprised of individuals who (1) know *interventions* from a practice point of view, (2) are skillful users of *implementation* methods, and (3) are thoroughly engaged in continuous quality *improvement* cycles in all aspects of their activities.

Over time, purveyors also have learned that they need to advise and guide at the systems level to promote administrative and system changes required to develop a more hospitable environment; otherwise, systems variables (e.g., funding, hiring practices, policies, and regulations) will overwhelm their program efforts. Some purveyors actively help to develop the local or state infrastructure needed for sustainability and/or scale-up of the intervention (Edwards et al., 2001; Slavin & Madden, 1999). Given the range of evidence-based programs and the variety of purveyor roles, it is not too surprising that not all purveyors are created equal. That is, some provide more support than others, and some are more knowledgeable about what it takes to implement with fidelity and maintain a high quality over time and across practitioners and teachers.

The advantage of having a well-organized and sustainable approach to implementation is that purveyors can accumulate knowledge, experience, and data over time to help improve their own efficiency and effectiveness (Fixsen & Blase, 1993; Fixsen Phillips, & Wolf, 1978; Winter & Szulanski, 2001). While a number of programs and practices have experienced and savvy purveyors, some programs are "implementation orphans" with only written and web-based material and journal articles to guide implementation efforts.

With programs and practices clearly operationalized and with support and clear guidance from purveyors, we can turn our attention to the variables and factors related to successful implementation endeavors. The following frameworks and processes for implementation and organizational change are based on current best evidence. Each is briefly defined below and then explored in more depth in the rest of the chapter.

Stages of Implementation

The implementation stages describe the essential activities that occur during the planning and execution of implementation efforts in education and other human service settings. Although the critical activities involved in each implementation stage often overlap with earlier and later stages, the "staging" of the activities is critical for successful implementation efforts and will be described in the more detailed discussion that follows. The stages are exploration and adoption, installation, initial implementation, and full implementation (Fixsen et al., 2005). In addition, while not strictly viewed as stages, literature and experience also indicate the need to attend purposefully to innovation and sustainability.

Implementation Drivers

Implementation drivers constitute the infrastructure for implementation because they are the processes required to implement,

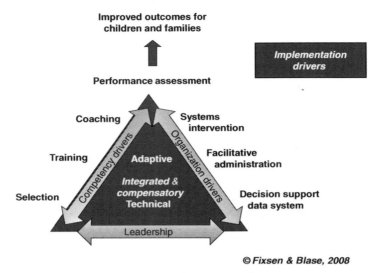

Figure 2.1. Implementation drivers.

sustain, and improve identified effective interventions. The implementation drivers are leverage points in a system to influence staff competency, to create enabling organization and systems conditions, and to guide appropriate leadership approaches. The drivers are grouped into three domains, as illustrated in Figure 2.1: competency drivers, organization drivers, and leadership. Collectively, the implementation drivers ensure that staff and teachers have the skills necessary to implement well, that policies and procedures are developed at multiple levels to create a more hospitable environment for the chosen intervention, and that the leadership strategies match the challenges faced during the process.

Implementation Teams

If the implementation drivers and stages constitute the frameworks and infrastructure for implementation, the structures for successful implementation lie in implementation teams. *Implementation teams* are defined as a core group of individuals who are well qualified and representative of the stakeholders and "system" and who are charged with guiding the overall implementation of the intervention from exploration

through to full implementation. For systems change and scale-up to occur, teams at multiple levels are required (e.g., school and community, district, technical assistance [TA] provider, and state) with interlocking communication and problem-solving protocols (Kaiser, Hogan, & Craig, 2008; Spoth et al., 2004).

Improvement Processes

Problem-solving protocols and improvement procedures are embedded in each implementation stage and each implementation driver and are used by leaders, managers, implementers, and implementation teams. They are purposeful processes to improve practice, test the usefulness of the intervention, and align policies, procedures, funding, and so on to support new programs and practices. At the core of each of the improvement processes is the plan, do, study, act (PDSA) cycle originally developed by applied researchers at the Bell Laboratories in the 1920s (Deming, 1986). The PDSA cycle is used by implementation teams to develop a more hospitable regulatory and funding environment for the evidence-based practice or program (e.g., new policies and procedures), and short- and longer-term improvement cycles (e.g., rapid-cycle problem solving and usability testing) are used by teams to improve the impact, fit, and sustainability of the program or practice.

The Frameworks in Action

The preceding frameworks and processes are not used in a linear, discrete, or siloed manner. All components of each framework are integrated at each point in the implementation process, from assessing behavioral and academic needs, to identifying useful and effective programs and practices, to fully integrating the intervention(s) into education or practice "as usual" with full benefits for all children. Unfortunately, words *are* linear – they follow one after the other – so the remainder of this chapter will review the salient features of the implementation stages and drivers with an attempt to weave in the integrated nature of the work to be done.

Stages of Implementation: The Big Ideas

Implementing an evidence-based program is not a quick fix, and the pathway is anything but lockstep or linear. Rather, a complex set of activities needs to occur over time and among stakeholders so that the program or practices are implemented with fidelity, are sustainable, and are able to be regenerated and improved on as new staff, leadership, and stakeholders appear on the scene. As mentioned earlier, Fixsen et al. (2005) identified six stages of implementation based on a review of the implementation evaluation and research literature. These stages include exploration and adoption, program installation, initial implementation, full implementation, innovation, and sustainability. The progression from exploration and adoption through to full implementation often takes two to four years and is characterized by progress, setbacks, and on-going problem solving. Moreover, while process and

outcome data should be collected during all stages, the summative decisions about the overall value and effectiveness of the program should not be made until the program is fully implemented. Premature decisions to abandon efforts can occur based on data that reflect programs that are not yet fully implemented (Dobson & Cook, 1980) rather than programs that are not able to achieve outcomes.

While the stages are reviewed in a linear fashion, in reality, they can overlap or may need to be repeated, or aspects of one stage may be infused into another. For instance, activities related to sustainability may be infused into any of the stages. Fiscal and programmatic sustainability issues first need to be considered during exploration and subsequently considered during every stage. And while there is a general progression through the first four stages, alert purveyors and implementation teams will recognize when a stage needs to be revisited or has reemerged. For example, significant turnover of skilled teachers and staff can move the work back to initial implementation, requiring more training and coaching. Or significant barriers during installation and initial implementation can result in a new round of exploration and adoption activities and decisions.

Given that implementation does not happen quickly and that the processes are complex and challenging, success is more likely when qualified purveyors work closely with implementation teams through the stages of implementation. This partnership can help in maintaining the focus and effort, problem solving effectively, and attending to the right issues relevant to the stage of implementation (Blase & Fixsen, 2003; Cheung & Cheng, 1997; Faggin, 1985; Feldman, Baler, & Penner, 1997; Fox & Gershman, 2000; Redmond et al., 2009; Rogers, 2002; Williams, 1975; Zins & Illback, 1995).

Overall, the stages and stage-based activities seem to be useful for those planning and carrying out implementation efforts in education and other human services. They are useful in ensuring that stage-based activities are taking place in a timely manner (e.g., buy-in occurs in exploration), in providing anticipatory guidance to stakeholders about the challenges ahead and outcomes related to each stage, and in interpreting evaluation outcomes.

Exploration and Adoption Stage

The exploration and adoption stage is critical to successful implementation. As Elias et al. (2003) note, "Long term dangers accrue when one bypasses the front-end time needed to build constituencies committed to the goals and process of change; to look honestly at the current state of conditions, services, and resources; and establish management capacities" (p. 309). Unfortunately, the time and effort required for careful exploration are not routinely included in efforts to implement evidence-based programs. In their research, Bodilly (1996), Cawelti & Protheroe (2003), and Slavin & Madden (1999) have found that administrators, teachers, districts, and schools may not be making informed choices when choosing programs to adopt and then implement.

In the exploration and adoption stage, the goals and activities associated with more successful implementation efforts include involvement of teachers, administrators, and stakeholders to improve buy-in, commitment, and understanding of the program or practices (Fashola & Slavin, 1997; Han & Weiss, 2005; & Kirby, Berends, & Naftel, 2001). Strategies to improve buy-in, commitment, and understanding include identifying a significant student need, selecting programs likely to address the need, examining the fit with current philosophy, the opportunity to fully understand the requirements for successful implementation, and a formal commitment to implement the program. To improve the process, Slavin & Madden (1999, p. 17) have suggested the use of "local brokers" (or purveyors) to provide administrators and teachers with the guidance they need about effective programs, organizational and change processes, and the match with the local needs and resources. Programs such as Success for All (SFA) and School-Wide Positive Behavior

Support (SWPS) require that teachers and administrators participate in an orientation process and then vote on whether or not to adopt and implement the program (Datnow & Castellano, 2000; Horner & Sugai, 2005; Slavin & Madden, 1999). Purveyors of these programs provide information about and rationales for the core elements of the intervention and the opportunity for staff to ask questions and raise concerns. If 80 percent of the teachers and administrators agree, the implementation efforts proceed with increased awareness of the requirements, the supports provided by the purveyor, and the accountability expected at the school and district level.

The interface with implementation drivers during this stage means that implementation teams are actively planning to install the competency drivers related to staff selection, skill-based training, data-driven coaching, and fidelity assessment. Implementation teams are also engaged with the organizational drivers and using improvement cycles as they work to create a more hospitable administrative, regulatory, and funding environment. And the leadership drivers are fully in play to hold the vision, guide the process, and choose the right leadership strategies for the challenges at hand.

The exploration and adoption stage transitions to the installation stage as the decision is made to proceed with implementation of an intervention in a given setting (Blase et al., 1984; Khatri & Frieden, 2002; Schoenwald & Hoagwood, 2001). It seems clear that effective practices and programs will not be implemented on any useful scale nor sustained over the long term without the support of teachers, staff, administrators, and the political, financial, and education systems at state and local levels (Schoenwald, 1997). That support is garnered during the exploration and adoption process and continues to be important throughout all implementation stages.

Installation Stage

Once a decision is made to adopt an evidence-based program, practice, or framework, there is work to be done before students can even begin to be exposed to the new intervention or curriculum. The goals of this stage are to install the implementation infrastructure (e.g., training, coaching, and data systems), make the necessary organizational changes (e.g., policy, procedures, form teams, and change schedules), and provide the instrumental supports needed to begin the work (e.g., computers, curricula, materials, and space). These activities and their associated "startup costs" are necessary first steps to begin operationalizing any new evidence-based program.

Experienced purveyors have a clear view of the preparatory steps that need to be taken during the installation stage and work closely with school, district, and state implementation teams. The implementation-related activities intensify, and resources are being expended, but "nothing is happening" yet with the students. Consequently, teachers, staff, and stakeholders can become impatient, especially when more complex interventions are being implemented and months may pass before there are changes in educational practices and behavioral interventions. Part of the purveyors' and teams' role is to provide anticipatory guidance about the importance of this stage; it is important to call attention to the work that is happening behind the scenes to "get ready" and to connect the current installation activities to the future success of the endeavor.

The installation stage often is overlooked, and there are few data in the human services and education literature about its role in successful implementation. In one of the few studies, Schaffer, Nesselrodt, & Stringfield (1997) conducted an analysis of issues that impede program implementation and sustainability with regard to ten promising education reform programs. The authors found that seed monies accepted by schools and districts for startup costs related to the reform programs often were not invested in implementation efforts. The same study also showed that when programs required a heavy investment up front for such things as computers and contracts, the program

was likely to continue to exist whether or not it was appropriate for the students and whether or not it was producing good outcomes for the students.

Many attempts to make use of evidence-based practices fail during the installation stage because those involved are not prepared to spend the time and resources required to accomplish the functions that are important at this stage, including the rapid-cycle problem solving required to move ahead. Similar to the exploration stage, the installation stage activities need to attend to the implementation drivers. This means thoughtfully installing the competency drivers (e.g., who and how will teachers be selected, trained, and coached). In addition, it will require attention to the organizational drivers to deal with the reality of altering or challenging the administrative and system status quo to actively support the new work. The leadership drivers as well are critical in this stage to maintain the focus on quality implementation and address the reality of challenging current values and paradigms that do not fit the new way of work.

Initial Implementation Stage

This stage begins as students first experience new instructional practices and/or new behavioral or social interventions or new school-wide approaches or reform. This is a time of vulnerability for the intervention because everyone is new to their roles, and feelings of incompetence and doubts about the decision are prevalent. Since changes are required at multiple levels (e.g., teacher, staff, administrator, and stakeholder) and do not occur simultaneously or evenly throughout the environment, the system is destabilized as new and fragile skills and processes are initiated. New skills, new instructional practices, changes in organizational capacity and culture, and new team functions and structures all require time to mature and move through the "initial awkward stage" (Joyce & Showers, 2002, p. 249). Fisher (1983) characterized "the real world...[as] an environment full of personnel rules, social stressors, union stewards, anxious administrators, political pressures, interprofessional rivalry, staff turnover, and diamond-hard inertia." Given these realities, the shift to new ways of work requires strong implementation teams, informed and committed leaders and key stakeholders, and the targeted supports to everyone involved in the change process.

Data from the evaluation of large-scale school reform indicate that there are significant challenges for the first year of implementation (Protheroe, 1998) or for implementation of new education management systems, as noted in the Rand evaluation of Edison schools (an education management organization). The evaluation findings emphasize that implementing large-scale reform or a new, comprehensive program takes time (a few years). A multiyear implementation process should be expected when implementing a comprehensive program (Gill et al., 2005).

What is required of educators, leaders, and the implementation teams during this stage? Attention to the competency drivers, with a particular emphasis on coaching (Joyce & Showers, 2002) and using data to make decisions, is critical to improving teacher, staff, and administrator confidence and competence. The organizational drivers will require attention to changing school administrative procedures (Felner et al., 2001) and may require changes in district expectations and supports. Implementation teams and/or purveyors engage in rapid-cycle problem solving and provide feedback at multiple levels (e.g., school, district, and state) to remove barriers and keep the implementation moving forward. Adaptive, or "second-order," leadership strategies (Daly & Chrispeels, 2008; Heifitz & Laurie, 1997) are needed to maintain focus, identify challenges, and collectively bring all stakeholders into the problem identification and solution process.

While the initial implementation stage can be rocky, preparing for and normalizing the process for all concerned and diligently attending to increasing competence, confidence, and administrative support and resources (McCormick, Steckler, & McLeroy, 1995; Panzano et al., 2005) can help

to ensure that the effort is not abandoned and that there is steady progress toward full implementation.

Full Implementation

Full implementation of the evidence-based practice or program occurs once the new skills, operating procedures, data systems, communication links, and often a new culture are integrated into classrooms, schools, district, and community. As confidence, competence, and support grow, the implemented program becomes fully operational and able to function and flourish in the context of the day-to-day realities of the education system. However, it should be noted that the day-to-day realities of the education system likely have been changed in order to support the new program. Full implementation and positive outcomes occur because the intervention does not change its core elements to fit the existing system, but the system changes to support the intervention.

Full implementation also means that teachers and staff carry out the intervention with confidence, proficiency, and skill; administrators support and facilitate the new practices; and parents and the communities who have participated in the process also have embraced and adapted to the new program. However, if there is significant teacher/staff turnover, then the issues and activities related to initial implementation will reemerge and need attention (e.g., increased coaching and leadership attention).

Measures of "fidelity" at the teacher and school level that are correlated with positive outcomes help in determining the degree to which the program is fully implemented (Kalafat, Illback, & Sanders, 2007). The anticipated benefits should be realized at this point as teachers and staff members become skillful and the procedures and processes are routinized. Once fidelity measures are above criterion levels most of the time, the effectiveness of the new site should approximate the effectiveness of the original program.

At this point, the competency drivers are monitored for quality and available in a timely fashion (e.g., training for new teachers, coaching and professional development, and use of data systems and routines). Implementation teams and administrators at multiple levels remain vigilant in using data to monitor program adherence and outcomes and continue to create a supportive host environment (e.g., attention to the organization drivers) for the evidence-based program or practice. The extraordinary becomes the ordinary as new expectations become "education as usual" (Faggin, 1985), but implementation functions and processes continue to require attention.

Sustainability

Typically, the term *sustainability* calls to mind the need for financial resources to sustain an effective program or practice, especially once grant or one-time funding ends. In reality, sustainability requires a two-pronged approach that addresses both financial and programmatic sustainability. And both should be addressed in every stage of implementation. Financial sustainability requires that time and resources (e.g., new staff functions, data systems, and program materials) are accounted for and built into budgets and funding streams. Programmatic sustainability requires that the infrastructure (e.g., implementation drivers) needed to train, coach, support, and supervise teachers and staff remains timely, accessible, of high quality, and functional in improving competence and fidelity and in maintaining and improving outcomes. Programmatic sustainability also requires ongoing attention to the impact of changes in leadership, champions, politics, funding streams, and mandates. These systems variables can trump program and practice effectiveness if they result in decreased fidelity or the lack of supports needed to create and maintain teacher and staff competencies. Education leaders, staff, parents, and the community must be aware of these challenges and adjust without losing the functional components of the program. Sustainability is an ongoing

and vigilant overlay at every point in the implementation journey. The goal is to ensure the long-term survival and improvement of the intervention and its continued benefits to students in the context of a changing organizational environment and fluctuating systemic conditions.

Innovation

A common assumption is that some adaptation of evidence-based programs and practices will be required to overcome a variety of implementation challenges (Datnow & Castellano, 2000; Denton, Vaughn, & Fletcher, 2003; Elias et al., 2003; Fashola & Slavin, 1997; Han & Weiss, 2005; and Slavin & Madden, 1999). However, cautionary tales abound. While a number of researchers discuss the necessity of adaptation, many of these same researchers have found that to achieve successful implementation of the program, the core components of the intervention must be defined and these components must *not* be adapted (Elias et al., 2003; Fashola & Slavin, 1997; Han & Weiss, 2005; Slavin & Madden 1999). Changes in core components at an implementing site or school constitute program drift that can have a negative impact on fidelity and outcomes (Adams, 1994; Mowbray et al., 2003; Washington State Institute for Public Policy, 2002; Yeaton & Sechrest, 1981). Purveyors and the original program developers can provide guidance to implementing sites about the wisdom of moving ahead with particular adaptations (Datnow & Castellano, 2000; Slavin & Madden, 1999).

Sound advice related to adaptation is first to implement with fidelity before attempting to innovate and then to engage the purveyor early in discussions about adaptation plans. Adaptation prior to achieving an acceptable level of fidelity makes interpreting program outcomes and engaging in program improvement particularly challenging. If results are not as expected and hoped for, then it is difficult to interpret the results and decide on improvement strategies. Was the program ineffective? Or were the disappointing outcomes due to poor fidelity?

Program strategies to improve fidelity are very different from strategies that add to or modify practices and procedures. Winter & Szulanski (2001) noted that adaptations made after an innovation had been implemented with fidelity were more successful than modifications made before full implementation. Changes in the evidence-based program protocols need to be evaluated to make sure that they are adding value to the effectiveness of the intervention or are able to produce comparable outcomes with reduced costs or investments of time. And once validated as useful, the changes need to be embedded in the implementation drivers. How will the improvements influence how staff and teachers are selected, trained, coached, and evaluated? What administrative, funding, policy, and data systems changes are needed to create and maintain a hospitable environment for the adaptation to become integrated? Adaptation is not doing things differently; it is doing things differently *and better*. At some point, if changes to the program or practice sufficiently change program operations, a new round of experimental outcome studies may be needed to test the overall benefits of the revamped program.

Implementation Drivers

The productive use of evidence-based programs in educational settings requires change in how teachers instruct and engage with students and parents, how community partners provide support services, how building administrators support teachers and manage schools, and how districts and states craft and modify policies, regulations, and funding streams. Implementation drivers are the core components that leverage and sustain change at the individual and organizational levels. As noted previously, the implementation drivers (Figure 2.1) are grouped into the following three domains: competency drivers, organization drivers, and leadership drivers.

- *Competency drivers* are mechanisms that help to develop, improve, and sustain one's ability and confidence to implement an intervention with fidelity and with benefits to students and families. They include staff selection, training, coaching for competence, and performance assessment.
- *Organization drivers* are mechanisms to create and sustain hospitable organizational and systems environments to support the effective use of an effective innovation. Organization drivers include decision-support data systems, facilitative administration, and systems intervention.
- *Leadership drivers* are leadership strategies to respond differentially to technical and adaptive challenges. *Technical challenges* are defined as those which are characterized by high levels of agreement about the problems at hand and relatively high levels of certainty about solutions. Adaptive challenges are characterized by less agreement about the definition of the problem and less certainty about the solutions that might be effective and require deeper change.

The implementation drivers are highly interactive, and when *integrated* well (Bernfeld, 2001) and focused on changing staff behavior and organizational culture, they can create robust implementation outcomes (e.g., competency, fidelity, and aligned and coherent policies) that lead to positive, sustainable outcomes. Purposeful integration means that all the drivers are focused on improving fidelity and achieving outcomes. The interactive nature of the drivers also means that they can *compensate* for one another. That is, a weakness in one implementation driver at the program level can be overcome by strengths in another (e.g., training and coaching can compensate for broad selection criteria required when there are few applicants for a position) or at the practitioner level (e.g., coaching can develop the skills of an individual teacher that are not present at hiring and/or not developed through training).

Competency Drivers

The competency drivers are focused on improving individual competency and confidence to implement effective practices well and with good effect. These drivers include staff selection, training, coaching, and consultation and staff performance assessment/fidelity assessment. The drivers function in an *integrated* way to support the core components of the intervention and to improve the overall quality and efficiency of the implementation process. Therefore, information produced by one driver can be used to improve other drivers. For example, information from training can be fed forward to coaches to target and improve staff skills (e.g., pre/posttraining) and back to interviewers about "coachability" of the new staff). Each competency driver is described briefly along with relevant research and evaluation findings.

STAFF SELECTION

Staff selection affects implementation outcomes and intervention effectiveness at every level (e.g., teachers, staff, and administrators). How will the recruitment and selection processes increase the likelihood that the evidence-based practice will be implemented well? How does selection compensate for the limitations of training, coaching, and data-driven feedback (e.g., performance assessment)? Beyond academic qualifications and experience, certain attributes and characteristics are difficult to compensate for through training and coaching, so they must be part of the selection process (e.g., content knowledge, ethics, and willingness to try new approaches). With respect to selection factors related to evidence-based programs, the ability to provide and accept feedback professionally and the willingness to use data to make decisions seem to be particularly important across evidence-based programs. Effectively implementing an evidence-based practice often requires coaching, feedback, and attention to data in order to develop competence and confidence. Therefore, receptivity to feedback and the ability and willingness to change one's behavior based on such feedback are keys to successful implementation.

Some evidence-based programs are designed to be fairly simple, thus minimizing the need for more careful selection. For example, the SMART reading tutoring program was designed to be staffed by volunteers who could read and who were willing to spend two days a week tutoring (Baker, Gersten, & Keating, 2000). When evidence-based programs require *new* skills and strategies, more specific requirements are integrated into the selection process (e.g., Chamberlain, 2003; Phillips, Burns, & Edgar, 2001; Schoenwald, Brown, & Henggeler, 2000), and specific competencies will need to be assessed during the interview (Blase, Fixsen, & Phillips, 1984; Maloney et al., 1975; Reiter-Lavery, 2004).

Staff selection procedures and opportunities in educational settings can be limited by several contextual variables such as union participation and contracts, teacher certification requirements, variability in courses of study offered through institutions of higher education, and teacher ability to transfer to another school (Bodilly, 1996; Denton, Vaughn, & Fletcher, 2003; Gill et al., 2005). Staff selection criteria and interviewing procedures can compensate for some of these systems-level limitations. For example, the opportunity to transfer to another school can be a respectful way of allowing current staff and teachers to choose whether or not to be part of a new initiative. As a corollary, if relevant staff selection criteria are in place and are focused on requirements related to implementation, then staff turnover can be an opportunity to hire staff who may be better aligned with program philosophy and prerequisites, and applicants can make an informed decision about working in that school (Datnow & Castellano, 2000). Another strategy to bolster selection is to engage in adequate exploration that leads to the majority of staff being willing to buy into a new program, with buy-in operationalized as a high percentage of staff voting to proceed (Slavin & Madden, 1996; Sugai & Horner, 2006). Not every candidate hired will be a perfect fit for the school's initiatives and reforms. However, knowledge of a new staff member's strengths and weakness gleaned from the interview process can be fed forward to those responsible for training and coaching, thus improving the efficiency and impact of these two drivers (e.g., the accepted candidate is willing to learn to use data as a part of the evidence-based programs but has little experience).

STAFF TRAINING

While there is some aversion to using the term *training* in relation to adult learners, use of the term keeps the activity focused on acquiring skills and abilities. It also requires that training staff be accountable for producing outcomes (e.g., increase in knowledge and skills). While broader professional development agendas are important, this implementation driver focuses on acquiring background knowledge and theory and on introducing required skills. Training, while ineffective when used alone as a strategy (Azocar et al., 2003; Schectman et al., 2003; Stokes & Baer, 1977) can be an efficient way to impart important information to participants. In addition, training coupled with coaching (Joyce & Showers, 2002) can effectively compensate for skills and abilities that are absent at the point of hire, as well as improve implementation outcomes.

Training content varies depending on the evidence-based program being implemented. However, effective training methods seem less variable. During training, participants learn about the theory, supporting data, and philosophy behind the program or practice. Training outcomes are related to increased knowledge, increased buy-in, and rudimentary skill acquisition. The skills needed to begin implementing the program effectively can be demonstrated and followed by behavior rehearsal to practice the skills, and trainees can receive feedback from qualified trainers and repractice to criteria (Blase et al., 1984; Joyce & Showers, 2002; Kealey et al., 2000). The posttraining outcomes can be fed forward to help coaches get a head start on targeting their feedback to individual teachers and staff. In summary, the training outcome data and observations can be fed back to inform the selection procedures (e.g., how amenable to feedback were training participants, and did their receptivity to feedback during training reflect the assessment during the selection process?).

COACHING AND CONSULTATION

Joyce and Showers (2002), after decades of research on the impact of teacher training, began to consider training and coaching as a continuous set of operations needed to produce changes in the classroom behavior of teachers. Their meta-analysis of research on training and coaching indicated that despite high-quality training (e.g., theory, demonstrations, and skill-based practice), it was not until coaching in the classroom setting was added that teacher behavior in the classroom changed. In a number of studies, training alone was insufficient to ensure the uptake of new ways of work or was inferior to training plus coaching in a variety of service settings (Harchik et al., 1992; Kelly et al., 2000) The value of observation, feedback, and support that are embedded in the work setting and provided by coaches who are content experts and skilled communicators seems to be key to improving implementation, adherence, and subsequent outcomes for students and children (Agar & O'May, 2001; Denton, Vaughn, & Fletcher, 2003; Schoenwald, Sheidow, & Letourneau, 2004).

Of course, installing a coaching system has its own set of implementation issues, and the implementation drivers need to be applied to the coaching function. The following questions about each of the implementation drivers, in relation to the coaching position, help to develop the infrastructure for the coaching system: Who is qualified to coach? How will coaches be trained, coached, and evaluated? Who monitors their adherence to the coaching plan? What outcomes are expected and monitored (e.g., fidelity or student outcomes)? And how will the administrative practices and the broader education system have to change to support the coaching function? Numerous published articles on coaching provide additional noteworthy guidance: McCormick & Brennan (2001) identified some characteristics of coaches that are important to the selection of coaches (e.g., supportive, encouraging, respectful, and patient); Joyce and

Showers (2002) noted the need for training and coaching of coaches; and McCormick & Brennan (2001), Kavanaugh et al. (2003), and Marks & Gersten (1998) noted a variety of administrative and systems issues that need to be attended to in providing successful coaching (e.g., adequate time, labor relations, staff resources, too much paperwork, and support from leadership). Without attention to all the implementation drivers, coaching is likely to suffer the same fate as any other poorly implemented intervention.

STAFF PERFORMANCE ASSESSMENT/ FIDELITY

Staff performance evaluation includes measures of fidelity and assessing the overall implementation of the evidence-based program, as well as the use of skills associated with the core intervention components. Through an implementation lens, these evaluation results are "owned" by everyone involved and reflect how well the other implementation drivers have been used to promote quality implementation efforts. These measures reflect how well individuals have been selected, trained, and coached (Blase et al., 1984; Schoenwald et al., 2004). They reflect how well the data are used to inform decision making at the student, classroom, and school levels. And they reflect the degree to which administrative policies internally and externally support the teachers' ability to implement the program (e.g., funding, policy, and resources). And, of course, a primary use of these data is to assist the teacher or staff member in building on his or her strengths and improving effectiveness in delivering the intervention or using the instructional practices. Evidence-based programs require a degree of rigor and adherence to specified criteria to be effective (Landenberger & Lipsey, 2005), and owing to the accountability for both process (fidelity) and outcomes, there can be concerns about the impact on staff autonomy and retention. A recent study, albeit in the child welfare arena, indicates that when fidelity monitoring is presented to staff in the context of ongoing, supportive consultation, staff retention is *positively* affected (Aarons et al., 2009).

Organization Drivers

The organization drivers include decision-support data systems, facilitative administration, and systems intervention. These drivers focus on strategies to create an informed and hospitable environment that supports the new way of work (e.g., resources, policies, and regulations) and promotes the use of data to inform decision making at many levels (e.g., student, classroom, school, district, and state). Organizational culture, climate, infrastructure, and policy can have a facilitative or deleterious impact on the implementation of an evidence-based program or practice. Attention to these areas is critical because the implementation of an evidence-based program generally requires organizational changes that affect expectations, how work is done, and subsequently, staff behavior and attitudes (Aarons & Sawitzky, 2006; Harris & Mossholder, 1996). And since current processes and results are supported and promoted by the current organizational practices, it is highly likely that organizational changes will be required if the new evidence-based program is to survive and achieve its promise. Each organization driver is described briefly along with relevant research and evaluation findings.

DECISION-SUPPORT DATA SYSTEMS

Process (e.g., fidelity data summaries and teacher and parent satisfaction data) and outcome data (e.g., reading scores, office discipline referrals, bullying incidents, and grade level performance) can be used to assess overall performance at the classroom, grade, and school levels. Data can be used to inform and support decision making that ensures implementation of the core intervention components over time and helps to evaluate efforts to improve both implementation strategies and intervention outcomes. For example, school implementation and leadership teams might find themselves engaged in data-driven discussion such as these: "Pre/post gains in teacher knowledge and skill indicate that our training program is not performing as well as last year. Why is that? What can we do about that?" or "Our reading scores in Grades 1–3 have dramatically improved and those gains are correlated with increased availability of skilled literacy coaches. Are we sure we want to cut back on coaching time?" Timely, valid, user-friendly reports provided at actionable units (e.g., by classroom) help to guide decision making at both policy and practice levels and help to ensure that the educational units (i.e., classrooms, districts, and regions) have the data they need to engage in continuous improvement processes (Hodges & Wotring, 2004; Horner & Sugai, 2005; Horner et al., 2004; Solomon et al., 2000).

FACILITATIVE ADMINISTRATION
The importance of this implementation driver is captured succinctly by Wallace et al. (2008, pp. 63–4):

> There is no such thing as an "administrative decision." They are all education decisions that affect how much time, energy, and skill teachers and others will bring to the educational experience of students. It is up to school and district administrators to ensure proper supports for teachers and others who are doing the skillful work of innovative education.

Teachers' and staff's interactions with students are the keys to successful evidence-based instructional and behavioral interventions. This means that building and district administrators must actively support integrated and effective use of the competency drivers (Bodilly, 1996; McGuire, 2001). In addition, educational leaders must provide facilitative administration, use data to make decisions, and proactively seek out ways to better align policies, procedures, resources, and structures to create a culture and climate that is hospitable to the new ways of work. (Mintrop et al., 2001; Rodgers, Hunter, & Rogers, 1993).

SYSTEMS INTERVENTION
Since the current systems (i.e., federal, state, county, and district) support the current processes, which, in turn, contribute to getting the current results, it stands to reason that implementing evidence-based practices will require change at multiple levels.

Systems interventions are strategies designed to inform and influence such external systems so that they are increasingly aware of the impact of external factors such as funding priorities, regulations, policy, federal and state laws, and human resources on the successful use of evidence-based practices and programs (Bernfeld, Farrington, & Leschied, 2001; Corrigan, 2001; Edwards et al., 2001; Kirby et al., 2001; Morton, 1991; Paine, Bellamy, & Wilcox, 1984; Zins & Illback, 1995). These strategies include designing feedback loops so that policies can enable evidence-based practice and so that the results of attempting to implement such policies can result in future and further improved policies and regulations (Fixsen et al., 2010; Sugai et al., 2010). Responding to and overcoming systemic barriers to implementation require attention by leadership at all levels. Other strategies include identifying and nurturing champions (Mihalic, Fagan, & Argamoso, 2008) and providing relevant and timely data to support concerns and celebrate success, as well as sharing success stories along with data. While it is never easy, Neufeld and Roper (2003, p. 255) noted: "Successful implementers carefully monitored entire change processes, regulating and controlling social and political issues as they arose."

Leadership Drivers

The leadership drivers in Figure 2.1 are depicted as the base or foundation of the implementation drivers. Tomes have been written about the importance of leadership to ensure success of large-scale reform, of school turnaround efforts, and in implementing new programs and practices (e.g., Bradley et al., 2005; Rowan, Barnes, & Camburn, 2004). Recent studies and meta-analyses are adding to our conceptualization and knowledge about the importance of leadership and the type of leadership needed in relation to the types of issues at hand. Leadership varies over time, requires different strategies for different challenges and matters at the classroom, school, and systems levels. For example, at the classroom level, Klinger et al. (2003) noted a linear relationship between implementation and administrative support for teachers learning new instructional methods for inclusive classrooms. When teachers perceived that the instructional practice was valued by their school leader, there was a greater likelihood that they would implement the practice. At the systems level, data also indicate that leadership functions and activities are not static, nor do they reside in a single person. Rather, leadership approaches vary across stages of implementation, and different leaders at different levels play diverse roles. Panzano et al. (2004; Panzano & Roth, 2006) provided data on the functions of leadership across the stages of implementation, and Rhim et al. (2007) provided detailed descriptions of leadership behavior under various conditions. Importantly, a meta-analysis of research on school leaders examined the relationship between student achievement and school-level leadership, finding a 0.25 correlation between leadership and student achievement or a 10 percentile point difference in a norm referenced test (Waters et al., 2003). Leadership matters in achieving implementation outcomes (e.g., willingness to implement) and in achieving student outcomes (e.g., academic and behavioral changes).

With respect to leadership, it is particularly useful to discriminate between the need for adaptive leadership and the need for technical leadership, as explicated by Heifitz et al. (Heifitz & Laurie (1997; Heifitz & Linsky, 2002). Both leadership approaches will be required given the lengthy and complex journey of implementation from exploration to full implementation and the need to align systems while using the implementation drivers effectively. Technical leadership is more appropriate when solutions exist within the current system, and there is greater certainty and more agreement about problem definition and greater certainty that the course of action will lead to a solution. Technical leadership under these more stable conditions can move projects forward and establish facilitating routines. For example, once defined and validated staff selection procedures are created, then the "technical" work of implementing new recruitment and interview protocols can occur. However, introducing a radically new staff selection procedure and hiring criteria that challenge the existing norms would require adaptive leadership.

Adaptive leadership requires second-order or deeper change because individuals are required to confront existing norms, values, and ways of work, calling into question their own competence and generating feelings of loss. Learning is required by all when the problem definition is not clear or not agreed on and there is less certainty that a given course of action will produce a solution. This is the uncomfortable position in which school staff and leadership, as well as broader education system leaders, can find themselves when, despite best efforts, academic gains and behavioral issues are not being addressed effectively. And, of course, purveyors will find themselves deeply involved in these adaptive challenges because they will be directly challenging many current ways of work. Adaptive leadership is highly interactive, involves multiple stakeholders and multiple "leaders," seeks to reconcile legitimate but competing interests, and relies on developing consensus among stakeholders rather than providing answers. Effective use of any of the implementation drivers can raise adaptive issues, but coaching, facilitative administrative practices, and systems interventions may require consistent use of adaptive leadership to determine and define challenges in new ways and then arrive at agreements on a course of action that is likely to challenge the existing order but result in closing the gap between current values and current reality. Balanced leadership that can flow from adaptive to technical and back again seems to be the hallmark of effective leaders (Daly & Chrispeels, 2008; Waters et al., 2003).

Implementation Teams

Large-scale implementation efforts at the system level or practice change at the individual school level fare much better with the establishment of implementation and leadership teams (e.g., Olds et al., 2003) to lead, coordinate, sustain, and evaluate the effort (Sugai & Horner, 2006, Fixsen et al., 2011). The number of teams at each level (e.g., school, district, and state) and linkages among teams depend on the degree to which the program is being taken to scale and the degree to which systems change is likely to be required. In general, the team members represent the stakeholders and the "system" involved, whether it is a school, a district, or a state team, and team members have knowledge about the innovation being implemented. In addition, teams are more likely to be functional if they have a framework for implementation (e.g., drivers, stages, and use of improvement cycles) and common commitment to change the system to support the intervention.

Critical to success for these teams is linking communication protocols and data-based decision making. Creating coherent and aligned systems is a new role for teams. Often they think and act on issues over which they have immediate control. This sometimes means that the structures and regulations promulgated at other levels are not informed about the impact their policies, procedures, and regulations have on implementation in the classroom. Therefore, functional practice and systems change is best accomplished when teams at multiple levels are integrated so that each team's information, knowledge, successes, and challenges are shared appropriately with other teams at other levels. Functionally, this means that communication pathways are transparent among and between teams and focused on solving problems, building capacity, ensuring implementation, and aligning policies, procedures, and funding to support new ways of work (Spoth et al., 2004; Sugai et al., 2010).

Each team needs to be purposeful in deciding its role and responsibility in installing, sustaining, and improving the implementation drivers, as well as mindful of the activities and challenges related to each implementation stage. And each team needs to engage its community, regardless of whether it is a school team, a district team, or a state team. Union representation, genuine parent engagement (including general and special education), school improvement, and community partners such as mental health will be critical to success.

Moreover, because teams need to make good decisions and monitor the impact of their decisions, they need to be comfortable and confident in using data to make a wide range of decisions, from selecting which interventions to support based on student need, to assessing the effectiveness of the intervention, to gathering data about the data (e.g., how reliable and valid are they?).

Implementation teams are focal points for accountability and for sustaining the challenging effort of high-quality implementation of evidence-based programs and practices. They are where the sense-making of a complex process comes together with attention to everything from strategies to create readiness, to ensuring that implementation occurs as intended, to monitoring and improving implementation outcomes and student outcomes.

Implementation and Implications for the Role of Educational Psychology

Educational psychologists and the field of educational psychology have many new and challenging roles to play to bring evidence-based practices and programs into everyday use in classrooms, schools, and communities. Not only do they need to assess the needs of students as individuals, but they also can play a significant role in using data to assess the overall needs of students in a school, the worth and feasibility of evidence-based and evidence-informed programs and practices to meet those needs, and the data needed to inform decisions about the degree to which new efforts are being implemented well and are achieving promised outcomes. Educational psychologists should be valued members of implementation teams at multiple levels, and their expertise and perspectives should be brought to bear on solving not only learning challenges for individual students but also implementation challenges for teachers and staff. Understanding the stages of implementation will allow educational psychologists to contribute productively by matching their contributions to the stage at hand and anticipating the work ahead. Educational psychologists can promote the uptake of evidence-based programs in the following ways: developing their ability and interest in assessing the quality of the competency drivers and contributing to their use to support implementation (e.g., providing coaching and summarizing data for decision making), understanding how and when to attend to the organization drivers to create a hospitable environment, and attending to the leadership drivers by recognizing and mastering technical and adaptive leadership approaches.

The "how" of implementation is critical to ensure that teachers and staff can make the "what" of science available and effective. As Seymour Sarason (1996, p. 78) noted:

> The way in which a change process is conceptualized is far more fateful for success or failure than the content one seeks to implement. You can have the most creative, compellingly valid, productive idea in the world, but whether it can become embedded and sustained in a socially complex setting will be primarily a function of how you conceptualize the implementation- change process.

Successful and sustainable implementation of evidence-based programs and practices clearly is possible. Attention to implementation science and best practices can help to embed the change in classrooms and schools so that all children can benefit from the findings of science in educational settings and in their communities.

References

Aarons, G. A., & Sawitzky, A. (2006). Organizational culture and climate and mental health provider attitudes toward evidence-based practice. *Psychological Services* 3(1), 61–72.

Aarons, G. A., Sommerfeld, D. H., Hecht, D. B., Silovsky, J. F., & Chaffin, M. J. (2009). The impact of evidence-based practice implementation and fidelity monitoring on staff turnover: evidence for a protective effect. *Journal of Consulting and Clinical Psychology* 77, 270–80.

Ager, A., & O'May, F. (2001). Issues in the definition and implementation of "best practice" for staff delivery of interventions for challenging behaviour. *Journal of Intellectual & Developmental Disability* 26(3), 243–56.

Adams, P. (1994). Marketing social change: The case of family preservation. *Children and Youth Services Review* 16, 417–31.

Azocar, F., Cuffel, B., Goldman, W., & McCarter, L. (2003). The impact of evidence-based guideline dissemination for the assessment and treatment of major depression in a managed behavioral health care organization. *Journal of Behavioral Health Services & Research* 30(1), 109–18.

Baker, S., Gersten, R., & Keating, T. (2000). When less may be more: A 2-year longitudinal evaluation of a volunteer tutoring program requiring minimal training. *Reading Research Quarterly* 35(4), 494–519.

Bauman, L. J., Stein, R. E. K., & Ireys, H. T. (1991). Reinventing fidelity: The transfer of social technology among settings. *American Journal of Community Psychology* 19, 619–39.

Bernfeld, G. A. (2001). The struggle for treatment integrity in a "dis-integrated" service delivery system. In G. A. Bernfeld, D. P. Farrington, & A. W. Leschied (eds.), *Offender rehabilitation in practice: Implementing and evaluating effective programs* (pp. 167–88). London: Wiley.

Bernfeld, G. A., Farrington, D. P., & Leschied, A. W. (2001). *Offender rehabilitation in practice: Implementing and evaluating effective programs.* New York: Wiley.

Blase, K. A., & Fixsen, D. L. (2003). *Evidence-based programs and cultural competence.* Tampa, FL: National Implementation Research Network, Louis de la Parte Florida Mental Health Institute, University of South Florida.

Blase, K. A., Fixsen, D. L., & Phillips, E. L. (1984). Residential treatment for troubled children: Developing service delivery systems. In S. C. Paine, G. T. Bellamy, & B. Wilcox (eds.), *Human services that work: From innovation to standard practice* (pp. 149–65). Baltimore: Paul H. Brookes Publishing.

Bodilly, S. (1996). *Lessons from the New American Schools Development Corporation's demonstration phase*. Santa Monica, CA: Institute on Education and Training, RAND Corporation.

Bradley, E. H., Webster, T. R., Baker, D., Schlesinger, M., & Inouye, S. K. (2005). After adoption: Sustaining the innovation. A case study of disseminating the Hospital Elder Life Program. *Journal of the American Geriatrics Society* 53(9), 1455–61.

Cawelti, G., & Protheroe, N. (2003). *Supporting school improvement: Lessons from districts successfully meeting the challenge*. Arlington, VA: Educational Research Service.

Chamberlain, P. (2003). The Oregon Multidimensional Treatment Foster Care Model: Features, outcomes, and progress in dissemination. *Cognitive and Behavioral Practice* 10, 303–12.

Cheung, W. M., & Cheng, Y. C. (1997). The strategies for implementing multilevel self-management in schools. *International Journal of Educational Management* 11(4), 159–69.

Corrigan, P. W. (2001). Strategies for disseminating evidence-based practices to staff who treat people with serious mental illness. *Psychiatric Services* 52(12), 1598–1606.

Datnow, A., & Castellano, M. (2000). *An inside look at Success for All: A qualitative study of the implementation and teaching and learning* (Report No. 45). Baltimore: Johns Hopkins University Center for Research on the Education of Students Placed at Risk.

Dale, N., Baker, A. J. L., & Racine, D. (2002). *Lessons learned: What the WAY program can teach us about program replication*. Washington: American Youth Policy Forum.

Daly, A. J., & Chrispeels, J. (2008). A question of trust: Predictive conditions for adaptive and technical leadership in educational contexts. *Leadership and Policy in Schools* 7, 30–63.

Deming, W. E. (1986). *Out of the Crisis*. Boston: MIT Press.

Denton, C. A., Vaughn, S., & Fletcher, J. M. (2003). Bringing research-based practice in reading intervention to scale. *Learning Disabilities Research & Practice* 18(3), 201–11.

Dobson, D., & Cook, T. J. (1980). Avoiding type III errors in program evaluation: results from a field experiment. *Evaluation and Program Planning* 3, 269–376.

Edwards, D. L., Schoenwald, S. K., Henggeler, S. W., & Strother, K. B. (2001). A multi-level perspective on the implementation of multisystemic therapy (MST): Attempting dissemination with fidelity. In G. A. Bernfeld, D. Farrington, & A. W. Lescheid (eds.), *Offender rehabilitation in practice: Implementing and evaluating effective programs*. New York: Wiley.

Elias, M. J., Zins, J. E., Graczyk, P. A., & Weissberg, R. P. (2003). Implementation, sustainability, and scaling of social-emotional and academic innovations in public schools. *School Psychology Quarterly* 32, 303–19.

Faggin, F. (1985). The challenge of bringing new ideas to market. *High Technology* 5(2), 14–16.

Fairweather, G. W., Sanders, D. H., & Tornatzky, L. G. (1974). Follow-up diffusion of the community lodge. In *Creating change in mental health organizations* (pp. 162–80). Elmsford, NY: Pergamon Press.

Fashola, O. S., & Slavin, R. E. (1997). Promising programs for elementary and middle schools: Evidence of effectiveness and replicability. *Journal of Education for Students Placed at Risk* 2(3), 251–307.

Feldman, S., Baler, S., & Penner, S. (1997). The role of private-for-profit managed behavioral health in the public sector. *Administration and Policy in Mental Health* 24, 379–90.

Felner, R. D., Favazza, A., Shim, M., Brand, S., Gu, K., & Noonan, N. (2001). Whole school improvement and restructuring as prevention and promotion: Lessons from STEP and the project on high performance learning communities. *Journal of School Psychology* 39(2), 177–202.

Fisher, D. (1983). The going gets tough when we descend from the ivory tower. *Analysis and Intervention in Developmental Disabilities* 3(2–3), 249–55.

Fixsen, D. L., & Blase, K. A. (1993). Creating new realities: Program development and dissemination. *Journal of Applied Behavior Analysis* 26, 597–615.

Fixsen, D. L., Phillips, E. L., & Wolf, M. M. (1978). Mission-oriented behavior research: The teaching-family model. In A. C. Catania & T. A. Brigham (eds.), *Handbook of applied behavior analysis: Social and instructional processes* (pp. 603–28). New York: Irvington Publishers, Inc.

Fixsen, D. L., Blase, K. A., Duda, M. A., Naoom, S. F., & Van Dyke, M. K. (2010). Implementation of evidence-based treatments for children and adolescents: Research findings and their implications for the future. In J. R. Weisz & A. E. Kazdin (eds.), *Evidence-based psychotherapies for children and adolescents*, 2nd ed. New York: Guilford Press.

Fixsen, D. L., Blase, K. A., Duda, M. A., Naoom, S. F., & Van Dyke, M. K. (2011). Sustainability of evidence-based programs in education. *Journal of Evidence-Based Practices for Schools* 11(1).

Fixsen, D. L., Naoom, S. F., Blase, K. A., Friedman, R. M., & Wallace, F. (2005). *Implementation research: A synthesis of the literature* (FMHI Publication No.231). Tampa, FL: University of South Florida, Louis de la Parte Florida Mental Health Institute, National Implementation Research Network.

Fox, J., & Gershman, J. (2000). The World Bank and social capital: Lessons from ten rural development projects in the Philippines and Mexico. *Policy Sciences* 33(3–4), 399–419.

Gill, B., Hamilton, L., Lockwood, J., Marsh, J., Zimmer, R., Hill, D., & Pribesh, S. (2005). *Inspiration, perspiration, and time: Operations and achievement in Edison schools*. Santa Monica, CA: RAND Corporation.

Greenhalgh, T., Robert, G., MacFarlane, F., Bate, P., & Kyriakidou, O. (2004). Diffusion of innovations in service organizations: Systematic review and recommendations. *Milbank Quarterly* 82(4), 581–629.

Han, S. S., & Weiss, B. (2005). Sustainability of teacher implementation of school-based mental health programs. *Journal of Abnormal Child Psychology* 33, 665–79.

Harchik, A. E., Sherman, J. A., Sheldon, J. B., & Strouse, M. C. (1992). Ongoing consultation as a method of improving performance of staff members in a group home. *Journal of Applied Behavior Analysis* 25, 599–610.

Harris, S. G., & Mossholder, K. W. (1996). The affective implications of perceived congruence with culture dimensions during organizational transformation. *Journal of Management* 22(4), 527–47.

Hattie, J. (2009). *Visible learning: A synthesis of over 800 meta-analyses relating to achievement*. New York: Routledge.

Havelock, R. G., & Havelock, M. C. (1973). *Training for change agents*. Ann Arbor, MI: University of Michigan Institute for Social Research.

Heifitz, R. A., & Laurie, D. L. (1997). The work of leadership. *Harvard Business Review* 75(1), 124–34.

Heifitz, R. A., & Linsky, M. (2002). *Leadership on the line*, Boston: Harvard Business School Press.

Hodges, K., & Wotring, J. (2004). The role of monitoring outcomes in initiating implementation of evidence-based treatments at the State level. *Psychiatric Services* 55, 396–400.

Horner, R. H., & Sugai, G. (2005). School-wide positive behavior supports: An alternative approach to discipline in schools. In L. Bambara & L. Kern (eds.), *Positive behavior support*. New York: Guilford Press.

Horner, R. H., Todd, A. W., Lewis-Palmer, T., Irvin, L. K., Sugai, G., & Boland, J. B. (2004). The School-wide Evaluation Tool (SET): A research instrument for assessing school-wide positive behavior support. *Journal of Positive Behavior Interventions* 6, 3–12.

Howard, J. L., & Frink, D. D. (1996). The effects of organizational restructure on employee satisfaction. *Group & Organization Management* 21(3), 278–303.

Huey, S. J., Henggeler, S. W., Brondino, M. J., & Pickrel, S. G. (2000). Mechanisms of change in multisystemic therapy: Reducing delinquent behavior through therapist adherence and improved family and peer functioning. *Journal of Consulting and Clinical Psychology* 68(3), 451–67.

Joyce, B., & Showers, B. (2002). *Student achievement through staff development*, 3rd ed. Alexandria, VA: Association for Supervision and Curriculum Development.

Kaiser, R. B., Hogan, R., & Craig, S. B. (2008). Leadership and the fate of organizations. *American Psychologist* 63, 96–110.

Kalafat, J., Illback, R. J., & Sanders, D. (2007). The relationship between implementation fidelity and educational outcomes in a school-based family support program: Development of a model for evaluating multidimensional full-service programs. *Evaluation and Program Planning* 30(2), 136–48.

Kavanagh, D. J., Spence, S. H., Strong, J., Wilson, J., Sturk, H., & Crow, N. (2003). Supervision practices in allied mental health: Relationships of supervision characteristics to perceived impact and job satisfaction. *Mental Health Services Research* 5(4), 187–95.

Kealey, K. A., Peterson, A. V., Jr., Gaul, M. A., & Dinh, K. T. (2000). Teacher training as a behavior change process: Principles and results from a longitudinal study. *Health Education & Behavior* 27(1), 64–81.

Kelly, J. A., Somlai, A. M., DiFranceisco, W. J., Otto-Salaj, L. L., McAuliffe, T. L., Hackl, K. L., et al. (2000). Bridging the gap between the science and service of HIV prevention: Transferring effective research-based HIV prevention interventions to community AIDS service providers. *American Journal of Public Health* 90(7), 1082–8.

Khatri, G. R., & Frieden, T. R. (2002). Rapid DOTS expansion in India. *Bulletin of the World Health Organization* 80(6), 457–63.

Kirby, S. N., Berends, M., & Naftel, S. (2001). *Implementation in a longitudinal sample of new American schools: Four years into scale-up.* Arlington, VA: RAND Education.

Klingner, J. K., Ahwee, S., Pilonieta, P., & Menendez, R. (2003). Barriers and facilitators in scaling up research-based practices. *Exceptional Children* 69(4), 411–29.

Korfmacher, J., O'Brien, R., Hiatt, S., & Olds, D. (1999). Differences in program implementation between nurses and paraprofessionals providing home visits during pregnancy and infancy: A randomized trial. *American Journal of Public Health* 89, 1847–51.

Kraft, J. M., Mezoff, J. S., Sogolow, E. D., Neumann, M. S., & Thomas, P. A. (2000). A technology transfer model for effective HIV/AIDS interventions: Science and practice. *AIDS Education and Prevention* 12(Suppl. A), 7–20.

Landenberger, N. A., & Lipsey, M. W. (2005). The positive effects of cognitive-behavioral programs for offenders: A meta-analysis of factors associated with effective treatment. *Journal of Experimental Criminology* 1, 451–76.

Lipsey, M. W. (1995). What do we learn from 400 research studies on the effectiveness of treatment with juvenile delinquents. In J. McGuire (ed.), *What works: Reducing reoffending* (pp. 63–78). Chichester, England: Wiley.

Maloney, D. M., Phillips, E. L., Fixsen, D. L., & Wolf, M. M. (1975). Training techniques for staff in group homes for juvenile offenders. *Journal of Criminal Justice and Behavior* 2, 195–216.

Marks, S. U., & Gersten, R. (1998). Engagement and disengagement between special and general educators: An application of Miles and Huberman's cross-case analysis. *Learning Disability Quarterly* 21(1), 34–56.

McCormick, K. M., & Brennan, S. (2001). Mentoring the new professional in interdisciplinary early childhood education: The Kentucky Teacher Internship Program. *Topics in Early Childhood Special Education* 21(3), 131–44.

McCormick, L. K., Steckler, A. B., & McLeroy, K. R. (1995). Diffusion of innovations in schools: A study of adoption and implementation of school-based tobacco prevention curricula. *American Journal of Health Promotion* 9(3), 210–19.

McGuire, J. (2001). What works in correctional intervention? Evidence and practical implications. In G. A. Bernfeld, D. P. Farrington, & A. W. Leschied (eds.), *Offender rehabilitation in practice: Implementing and evaluating effective programs* (pp. 25–43). London: Wiley.

Mihalic, S. F., Fagan, A. A., & Argamoso, S. (2008). Implementing LifeSkills Training drug prevention program: Factors relating to implementation fidelity. *Implementation Science* 3,5.

Mintrop, H., Gamson, D., McLaughlin, M., Wong, P. L., & Oberman, I. (2001). Design cooperation: Strengthening the link between organizational and instructional change in schools. *Educational Policy* 15, 520–46.

Morton, M. S. S. (1991). *The corporation of the 1990s: Information technology and organizational transformation.* New York: Oxford University Press.

Mowbray, C. T., Holter, M. C., Teague, G. B., & Bybee, D. (2003). Fidelity criteria: Development, measurement, and validation. *American Journal of Evaluation* 24(3), 315–40.

Neufeld, B., & Roper, D. (2003). *Coaching: A strategy for developing instructional capacity.* Cambridge, MA: Education Matters, Inc.

Olds, D. L., Hill, P. L., O'Brien, R., Racine, D., & Moritz, P. (2003). Taking preventive intervention to scale: The nurse-family partnership. *Cognitive and Behavioral Practice* 10, 278–90.

Paine, S. C., Bellamy, G. T., & Wilcox, B. L. (eds.). (1984). *Human services that work: From innovation to standard practice.* Baltimore: Paul H. Brookes.

Panzano, P. C., & Roth, D. (2006). The decision to adopt evidence-based and other innovative mental health practices: Risky business? *Psychiatric Services* 57, 1153–61.

Panzano, P. C., Roth, Crane-Ross, D., Massati, R., Carstens, C., Seffrin, B., & Chaney-Jones, S. (2005). The innovation diffusion and adoption research project (IDARP): Moving from the diffusion of research results to promoting the adoption of evidence-based innovations in the Ohio Mental Health System. In D. Roth & W. Lutz (eds.), *New research in mental health*, Vol. 16 (pp. 78–89). Columbus, OH: Ohio Department of Mental Health.

Phillips, S. D., Burns, B. J., & Edgar, E. R. (2001). Moving assertive community treatment into standard practice. *Psychiatric Services* 52, 771–9.

Protheroe, N. (1998). *School administration under attack: What are the facts?* Princeton, NJ: Educational Research Service.

Redmond, C., Spoth, R. L., Shin, C., Schainker, L. M., Greenberg, M. T., & Feinberg, M. (2009). Long-term protective factor outcomes of evidence-based interventions implemented by community teams through a community-university partnership. *Journal of Primary Prevention* 30(5), 513–30.

Reiter-Lavery, L. (2004). Finding great MST therapists: New and improved hiring guidelines. Paper presented at the Third International MST Conference, MST Services, Charleston, SC.

Rhim, L. M., Kowal, J. M., Hassel, B. C., & Hassel, E. A. (2007). *School turnarounds: A review of the cross-sector evidence on dramatic organizational improvement.* Lincoln, IL: Public Impact, Academic Development Institute.

Rodgers, R., Hunter, J. E., & Rogers, D. L. (1993). Influence of top management commitment on management on program success. *Journal of Applied Psychology* 78, 151–5.

Rogers, E. M. (1995). *Diffusion of innovations*, 4th ed. New York: The Free Press.

Rogers, R. W. (2002). White paper: The power of realization. Retrieved from http://www.ddiworld.com/research/publications.asp.

Rowan, B., Camburn, E., & Barnes, C. (2004). Benefiting from comprehensive school reform: A review of research on CSR implementation. In C. Cross (ed.), *Putting the pieces together: Lessons from comprehensive school reform research* (pp. 1–52). Washington: National Clearinghouse for Comprehensive School Reform.

Sarason, S. B. (1996). *Revisiting "The culture of the school and the problem of change."* New York: Teachers College Press.

Schaffer, E., Nesselrodt, P., & Stringfield, S. (1997). *Impediments to reform: An analysis of destabilizing issues in ten promising programs.* Arlington, VA: Educational Research Service.

Schectman, J. M., Schroth, W. S., Verme, D., & Voss, J. D. (2003). Randomized controlled trial of education and feedback for implementation of guidelines for acute low back pain. *Journal of General Internal Medicine* 18(10), 773–80.

Schoenwald, S. K. (1997). Rationale for revisions of medicaid standards for home-based, therapeutic child care, and clinical day programming. Technical Report prepared for the South Carolina Department of Health and Human Services, Columbia, SC.

Schoenwald, S. K., & Hoagwood, K. (2001). Effectiveness, transportability, and dissemination of interventions: What matters when? *Psychiatric Services* 52, 1190–7.

Schoenwald, S. K., Brown, T. L., & Henggeler, S. W. (2000). Inside multisystemic therapy: Therapist, supervisory, and program practices. *Journal of Emotional and Behavioral Disorders* 8(2), 113–27.

Schoenwald, S. K., Sheidow, A. J., & Letourneau, E. J. (2004). Toward effective quality assurance in evidence- based practice: Links between expert consultation, therapist fidelity, and child outcomes. *Journal of Clinical Child and Adolescent Psychology* 33(1), 94–104.

Slavin, R. E., & Madden, N. A. (1996). *Scaling up: Lessons learned in the dissemination of Success for All* (Report No. 6). Baltimore: Center for Research on the Education of Students Placed at Risk, Johns Hopkins University.

Slavin, R. E., & Madden, N. A. (1999). *Disseminating Success for All: Lessons for policy and practice* (Report No. 30). Baltimore: Center for Research on the Education of Students Placed at Risk, Johns Hopkins University.

Solomon, D., Battistich, V., Watson, M., Schaps, E., & Lewis, C. (2000). A six-district study of educational change: Direct and mediated effects of the Child Development Project. *Social Psychology of Education* 4, 3–51.

Spoth, R., Greenbert, Bierman, K., & Redmond, C. (2004). PROSPER community-university partnership model for public education systems: Capacity building for evidence-based, competence-building prevention. *Prevention Science* 5(1), 31–9.

Stokes, T. F., & Baer, D. M. (1977). An implicit technology of generalization. *Journal of Applied Behavior Analysis* 10, 349–67.

Sugai, G., & Horner, R. (2006). A promising approach for expanding and sustaining the implementation of school-wide positive behavior support. *School Psychology Review* 35, 245–59.

Sugai, G., Horner, R., Fixsen, D., & Blase, K. (2010). Developing systems-level capacity for RTI implementation: Current efforts and future directions. In T. A. Glover & S. Vaughn (eds.), *The promise of response to intervention: Evaluating the current science and practice.* New York: Guilford Press.

Sugai, G., Horner, R. H., Dunlap, G., Hieneman, M., Lewis, T. J., Nelson, C. M., et al. (2000). Applying positive behavior support and functional behavioral assessment in schools. *Journal of Positive Behavior Interventions* 2, 131–43.

Wallace, F., Blase, K., Fixsen, D., & Naoom, S. (2008). *Implementing the findings of research: Bridging the gap between knowledge and practice.* Washington: Education Research Service.

Washington State Institute for Public Policy. (2002). *Washington State's implementation of functional family therapy for juvenile offenders: Preliminary findings* (No. 02–08–1201). Olympia, WA: Washington State Institute for Public Policy.

Waters, J. T., Marzano, R. J., & McNulty, B. (2003). *Balanced leadership: What 30 years of research tells us about the effect of leadership on student achievement*, Aurora, CO: Mid-continent Research for Education and Learning.

Williams, W. (1975). Implementation analysis and assessment. *Policy Analysis 1*, 531–66.

Winter, S. G., & Szulanski, G. (2001). Replication as strategy. *Organization Science 12*(6), 730–43.

Wolf, M. M., Kirigin, K. A., Fixsen, D. L., Blase, K. A., & Braukmann, C. J. (1995). The teaching-family model: A case study in data-based program development and refinement (and dragon wrestling). *Journal of Organizational Behavior Management 15*, 11–68.

Yeaton, W. H., & Sechrest, L. (1981). Critical dimensions in the choice and maintenance of successful treatments: Strength, integrity, and effectiveness. *Journal of Consulting & Clinical Psychology 49*, 156–67.

Zins, J. E., & Illback, R. J. (1995). Consulting to facilitate planned organizational change in schools. *Journal of Educational and Psychological Consultation 6*(3), 237–45.

Part II

STATISTICAL PROBLEMS, APPROACHES, AND SOLUTIONS IN REAL-WORLD CONTEXTS

CHAPTER 3

Developing Rigorous Programme Evaluation

Tracey Bywater

The aim of this chapter is to discuss implementation science in relation to the process of evaluation of effects in social and educational interventions. Suggestions on how analysis and translation of results can be improved to reflect and evaluate the realities of social experimentation and intervention will be made.

What do 'evaluation' and 'process of evaluation of effects' actually mean? The Latin origin defines 'evaluation' as to *strengthen* or *empower*; more recently, it is defined as an *assessment of value*. What *process* must researchers follow to assess the value of an intervention in order to inform and empower? We should look not only to the end outcome of what *effect* an intervention has on the sample population in numerical or statistical terms but also to the equally important journey of how we reached the end point or outcome. Systematic investigation of working processes such as changing needs, resources, intervention application and delivery has an impact on intervention outcome (Gitlin & Smyth, 1989). At the end point we cannot be sure if it is the intervention, the process or both that influenced

outcome and effects without assessing both components. A recent review of the implementation of evidence-based programmes (Durlak & DuPre, 2008) found that high-quality implementation leads to improved prevention outcomes, with effects two to three times higher in cases where quality monitoring protocols were used.

Researchers, funders and service staff need to be clear on precisely *why* a certain intervention is being evaluated, *how* it will be evaluated, and *what* the evaluation will tell us. Evaluation can provide evidence of whether an intervention works and/or can improve process and practice (Rogers & Smith, 2006). Ideally, an evaluation will inform on strengthening practice, services, organisation, programme modification, enhancement of services or decommissioning of ineffective interventions or procedures. In the field of education, evaluation has been used to assess individual, small-group, class-wide, school-wide, county-wide and nation-wide approaches of academic or curriculum change, innovative literacy programmes, and interventions to target specific 'non-academic' areas such as social

> **Box 3.1. Selected Dimensions of Complexity According to Medical Research Council (2009) and Implications for Development and Evaluation**
>
> - *Number of components and interactions between them.* Theoretical understanding is needed of *how* the intervention causes change so that weak links in the causal chain can be identified and strengthened.
> - *Number and difficulty of behaviour changes required by those delivering or receiving the intervention.* Lack of impact may reflect implementation failure rather than genuine ineffectiveness; a thorough process evaluation is needed to identify implementation problems.
> - *Number of groups or organisational levels targeted by the intervention.* Variability in individual level outcomes may indicate a need for larger sample sizes to take account of the extra variability or cluster rather than individual randomised designs.
> - *Number and variability of outcomes.* A single primary outcome may not be most appropriate; a range of measures may be required.
> - *Degree of flexibility or tailoring of the intervention.* Ensuring strict fidelity to a protocol may be inappropriate; the intervention may work better if adaptation to the local setting is allowed.

and emotional literacy and child or teacher behaviour.

Many social policy interventions delivered in education, public health practice or family and children services can be viewed as 'complex interventions' (Medical Research Council, 2009). Complex interventions comprise several interacting components and present unique problems for evaluators in addition to usual practical and methodological difficulties. It is necessary to evaluate all dimensions outlined in Box 3.1 to fully assess any meaningful intervention and/or process effects. Additional problems may relate to the difficulty of standardising intervention delivery, adapting a programme for the local context, the logistical difficulty of applying experimental methods to service or policy change and the complexity of the causal chains linking intervention with outcome (Medical Research Council, 2009).

Developing, piloting, implementing, evaluating and reporting a complex intervention can be a lengthy, complicated process, and to skilfully negotiate these steps is an achievement for all key stakeholders regardless of whether outcomes are found to be clinically or statistically significant, that is, *successful* or *effective*. Adequate development and piloting work needs to be incorporated, with specific attention being paid to the practical issues of implementation. If development work is neglected, the main outcome results may be weak or, even worse, show that an evidenced-based intervention simply 'doesn't work', to the detriment of the proposed population and to the pocket of the funder. Box 3.2 highlights what can happen if development work is not carried out or is inadequate.

Box 3.3 draws together best research practices into an evaluation process model outlining eight key stages, including scale-up. The stages are very much interlinked with outcome effects and prospective scale-up being very much rooted in the interaction between stages one and seven. Owing to the nature of complex interventions effectiveness should not necessarily be based purely on the statistical analyses of an outcome measure.

This simplistic evaluation process model is presented diagrammatically in Figure 3.1, with the problem, or question, playing centre stage in a pivotal manner and with other

---

Box 3.2. The Importance of the Development Phase

In Masaka, Uganda, a school-based randomised, controlled trial in 31 schools with 2,000 pupils was shown to have no significant effect. It was discovered that the failure of the intervention was due to implementation failure, not design or intervention flaws. The intervention had been incompletely implemented owing to time constraints, teacher reticence and lack of skills (Kinsamn et al., 2001). A feasibility study would have saved money and time and highlighted any 'teething' problems, specifically with regard to fidelity assessment

---

Box 3.3. Evaluation Process Model for Complex Interventions

1. Identify basic issues/problems that need resolving.
2. Identify interventions or strategies shown to work for the specific problem.
3. Determine the target sample and identify key delivery and organisational staff.
4. Conduct necessary development work.
5. Design the main evaluation to assess outcome, implementation, processes and costs.
6. Conduct the evaluation and analyse data.
7. Disseminate findings.
8. Prepare for scale-up to include ongoing evaluation of service delivery and outcomes.

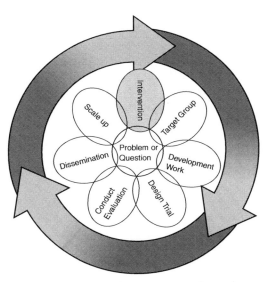

Figure 3.1. 'Growing' interventions for scale-up, a model for evaluating a complex intervention.

'growing interventions for scale-up (GIFS) model', and it forms the basis of the remainder of this chapter. Design and analysis issues will be the main focus, with a lighter touch being given to other stages because these are discussed at length elsewhere in this Handbook.

1. Identify the Problem

Research interests and questions vary according to what current policies, service managers, head teachers, funders or researchers are interested in. Attention may be focused on the prevalence rates of a certain 'problem', be it anti-social behaviour in young children, literacy levels or social or emotional difficulties, followed by the question of how to improve the situation by reducing or improving prevalence rates and, importantly, at what cost to the funders, services or government? Data from epidemiology studies, as well as prevalence rates, should be used to provide confirmatory evidence that

segments relating to each other via the question and each consecutive stage. The model appears 'flower-like' in form, the objective of which is to 'grow' interventions for possible scale-up. This model, then, will be called the a problem exists and is not based simply on conventional wisdom.

2. Identify the Intervention or Solution

Once an issue has been identified for resolution, the existing evidence base should be identified in order to select a programme or intervention with evidence of effectiveness for the target population. Systematic reviews might be conducted to establish *what* changes can be expected and *how* change can be achieved, thereby developing a theoretical understanding of the likely process of change. A word of warning: Trials with positive intervention effects tend to be more readily published than trials showing negative or no effect, thus implying that systematic reviews (reliant on published studies only) will be biased and (when used as evidence to inform the possible effectiveness of future trials) may give an unrealistic effect size (Torgerson & Torgerson, 2008).

Systematic reviews, including those undertaken for the National Institute for Clinical Health and Excellence (NICE) and the Cochrane Collaboration, assess the effectiveness of interventions such as parent training by pooling the results from many studies (published and unpublished) by meta-analysis. The aggregation of the effects of different programmes is a limitation of this method when used as a means of intervention identification because the analysis can dilute the effectiveness of the 'best' (most effective) programmes. Furthermore, reviews often fail to include highly relevant criteria for programme selection, such as whether it has long-term follow-up or adequate tools for replication and fidelity monitoring (Hutchings, Bywater & Daley, 2007). Existing evidence and theory therefore should be supplemented if possible with new primary research, such as epidemiology studies or interviews with key stakeholders, either those targeted by the intervention or those involved in its development or delivery.

3. Identify the Sample and the Staff

Complex interventions may include many different participant levels, such as individuals (e.g., pupils, teachers and parents), community units (e.g., children centres or schools), or whole populations. If an intervention is seeking to achieve change at more than one level, then processes and outcomes also need to be measured at each level to ensure that the new strategies have been effective. Intervention delivery staff, or facilitators, must possess the necessary background, experience, skills and personality to deliver complex interventions. Differences in these factors may lead to fidelity issues and treatment differentiation between intervention groups or participants. Heterogeneity of intervention delivery across groups or schools can be assessed by fidelity measures (Epstein, Kutash & Duchnowski, 2005).

4. Development Work

Development work must include assessing acceptability of the intervention to both delivery and support staff *and* the targeted sample. If staff is reticent, then the programme's or intervention's effectiveness most likely will be reduced or show no effect, as in the case highlighted in Box 3.2. Assessing staff attitude towards the intervention is part of 'process evaluation', an important stage in assessing complex interventions (see Box 3.1). Development work also should include undertaking feasibility or pilot studies to tease out any implementation barriers or recruitment issues.

Recruitment and retention are likely to be higher if the intervention is valued by potential participants such as teachers, children, parents and delivery staff. Potential service users of a parent programme in a multi-cultural city in the United Kingdom were asked their thoughts on the proposed implementation (Bywater & Axford, 2010). Common barriers to service engagement, according to parents' statements and beliefs, included

- There is no problem, so the service is irrelevant.
- Existing support is sufficient.
- The service will be too demanding in content and duration.
- There is uncertainty as to what the service involves owing to a lack of information;
- There is a lack of trust in the service, intervention or professionals involved.
- There are practical difficulties related to access and delivery (e.g., time or resource constraints).
- There are cultural and language barriers.

Although these beliefs are related specifically in this instance to attending a parent programme, similar beliefs and barriers could reflect potential barriers from schools when delivering a new intervention. If recruitment and retention are an issue, then the calculated sample size will not be achieved, and the trial will be underpowered, yielding almost meaningless findings. Research informs us that for interventions to be effective, we need to ensure the engagement and retention of service providers and participants by addressing three components: (1) the programme content, (2) the process of delivery and (3) barriers related to access and quality implementation (Hubble, Duncan & Miller, 1999).

Once acceptability of the programme or intervention has been achieved, appropriate staff should be identified and trained to deliver the intervention. Supervision or training support should be offered throughout initial delivery to ensure that deliverers possess equal skill bases in order to reduce possible bias in the trial. Thorough training has an impact on implementation fidelity and, again, on outcomes; it therefore is important to embed skills (wherever possible) before a main evaluation. It is essential to build *ongoing* training and support in the subsequent roll-out because the way in which programmes are delivered affects intervention outcomes across a range of fields, including health, education and industry (Bumbarger & Perkins, 2008; Lambert, 1992).

A feasibility, or pilot, study also should investigate and establish implementation and evaluation processes, particularly with regard to fidelity or replication issues. Factors to consider include adaptation of a programme to a local context, acceptability of outcome measures, translation requirements, service access/delivery issues and referral and recruitment strategy. The referral and recruitment strategy can serve to inform the main study on expected uptake rates and can be used (cautiously) to calculate appropriate sample sizes, bearing in mind that effects may be smaller or more variable and response rates lower when the intervention is rolled out across a wider range of settings. A mixture of qualitative and quantitative methods is likely to be needed to understand barriers to participation and to estimate response rates, for example. Depending on the results, a series of studies may be required to refine the design progressively before embarking on a full-scale evaluation (Medical Research Council, 2009).

5. Evaluation Design

The design of a main evaluation trial should be made on the basis of the proposed trial's characteristics, such as expected size of effect based on similar previous studies, type of intervention and the main question. There is a range of experimental and non-experimental approaches with many study designs to choose from; different designs suit different questions and different circumstances (McKee et al., 1999). In the field of education, interventions may be trialled to establish what is effective or 'what works' in improving teaching methods, classroom management, pupil learning, reading and social and emotional literacy and at what cost.

Chapter 4 in this Handbook discusses randomised, controlled trials (RCTs) in depth, including the pros and cons of this design; this chapter will briefly describe the design for context purposes. The RCT, although difficult to implement in a real-life or community setting, is the most rigorous evaluation design to establish an intervention's

Box 3.4. The Incredible Years (IY) Parent Programme and the Welsh Sure Start Study (Funded by the Health Foundation) (Hutchings et al., 2007)

The IY Parent Programme is one of only 11 programmes identified as a 'blueprint' for violence prevention in a review of 600 studies funded by the U.S. government (Mihalic et al., 2002).

Key components of effective behavioural family interventions include the following:

- New parenting skills must be actively rehearsed.
- Parenting programmes must offer principles rather than prescribed techniques.
- Programmes need to include both (non-violent) sanctions for negative behaviour and strategies to build positive relationships.
- Difficulties in the relationships between adults in the family need to be addressed.

The 12-week IY Parent Programme (Webster-Stratton, 1981) was evaluated in a pragmatic RCT with parents of 'at risk' pre-school children in 11 Sure Start areas in Wales, UK. Findings showed that perceived and observed child behavioural problems decreased after parents attended the programme compared to wait-list control parents six months after baseline. [For detailed short-term outcomes and cost-effectiveness, see Edwards et al. (2007) and Hutchings et al. (2007).]

Based on these positive findings, the Welsh Assembly Government (WAG) included the IY Parent Programme in their Parenting Action Plan (2005). WAG funding was provided subsequently to train staff from all 22 authorities across Wales and to provide them with programme materials. Long-term findings demonstrated maintained positive outcomes 18 months after baseline (Bywater et al., 2009). This research has provided the template for ongoing research in a large multi-cultural UK city and in Ireland's national evaluation of Incredible Years.

effectiveness because it can deal with the level of complex interventions inherent in health, social and educational fields.

In an RCT, individuals or units such as schools are randomly allocated to receive either an experimental intervention or an alternative such as standard treatment, a placebo or placement on a waiting list. Government bodies increasingly require evidence from rigorous RCTs before social interventions are implemented on a large scale, based on previous mistakes and experience. In England, Sure Start service providers were given UK government money to deliver support to families in disadvantaged areas. From its launch in 2001 to 2005, £3.1 billion was invested in the scheme (Meadows, 2006). Mistakenly, the support was provided

without direction from central government, and Sure Start providers delivered services or interventions that generally were not evidenced-based or previously trialled in a rigorous way. A wide variety of services was provided and implemented, with varying degrees of fidelity; hence the initial £20 million evaluation of Sure Start's first three years of operation in England failed to find significant evidence of its effectiveness in preventing or reducing conduct disorder (Belsky et al., 2006; Meadows, 2006).

In contrast, the Welsh Assembly Government (WAG) looked to evidence from an RCT of an evidenced-based parent programme to reduce conduct problems in pre-school children delivered in a community setting across 11 Sure Start areas in

Wales (see Box 3.4). The Incredible Years (IY) Parent Programme (Webster-Stratton, 1981) was found to be both clinically effective and cost-effective whilst also being acceptable to service providers and users (Bywater et al., 2009; Edwards et al., 2007; Hutchings et al., 2007). On completion of the trial, WAG included the programme in their Parent Action Plan (2005) and offered free training places for service staff to enable delivery of the programme in all 22 Welsh authorities.

The format of the RCT is simple yet very adaptable and yields results we can have confidence in if carried out well (Torgerson & Torgerson, 2008). Depending on what the research question is, we can randomise individuals or we can randomise institutions such as schools. RCTs can address questions in health, social policy and education by randomising individuals or groups to an intervention group (otherwise known as the 'experimental' or 'treatment' group) or a control group. By randomising, we can control for unknown variables so that a causal relationship between intervention and outcome can be established. Stratification can be used in the randomisation process to guard against 'known' variables likely to influence outcome, such as the size of the school or the level of disadvantage as assessed by the percentage of children qualifying for free school meals.

Randomisation controls for several confounding factors that can limit our confidence in interpreting the outcomes. Factors include selection bias, where those who receive the intervention differ systematically from those who do not (Collins & MacMahon, 2001; Eccles et al., 2003); regression to the mean, where extreme scores on first measurement will tend to be closer to the centre of the distribution on later measurement; and temporal changes. Randomisation therefore minimises the threat to internal validity – the extent to which we can accurately state that the intervention produced the observed effect.

Other forms of bias can occur following randomisation, possibly threatening the integrity of the trial, such as service staff offering services over and above 'service as usual' to the non-intervention condition because they felt it 'unfair' that the control group received 'less' than the intervention group. The offering of additional services to the control group may have a diluting effect on the intervention being offered (e.g., a parent programme, which ultimately may lead to results showing that the intervention is ineffective), thereby increasing the possibility of a type II error – whereby we could conclude mistakenly that there was no statistically significant difference between the intervention and control groups when there was.

Pragmatic RCTs are the most powerful in generalisability of findings, and this simply means that the trial is carried out in the context of where the intervention is intended to be rolled out, with a sample of the wider target population. If a school-based intervention were to be trialled in a controlled laboratory setting with psychologists delivering the intervention to pupils rather than in a school setting with everyday school staff delivering the intervention, then results may not be applicable to the real-life context, and the findings should be regarded with caution. A pragmatic RCT therefore has both internal and external validity. External validity relates to the generalisability of findings to or across target populations or environments.

Members of a particular group or classroom tend to be similar to members of another classroom within the same school. Because of homogeneity within schools, a cluster-randomised trial may be the most efficient way of assessing the effectiveness of school interventions across several schools. If a school-wide intervention, for example, is trialling curriculum changes or a social emotional literacy programme, then it makes sense to randomise some schools to the intervention condition and some schools to the control condition to avoid any possible introduction of contamination within the school. If individuals or sometimes classes within a school were randomised so that some were in an intervention group and some were in a control group, the control individuals or classes within that school may become aware of the intervention implementation processes and aims before they actually participate in the intervention by inadvertent knowledge transfer from the intervention group. This may happen through informal discussions among teachers in the staff room, children interacting on the playground and so on. By allocating whole schools, we guard against this scenario and the possible weakening or diluting of the intervention effects, giving us more confidence in the results.

Although it makes intuitive sense to randomise by schools, the downside to this is that a larger sample size will be needed to establish effectiveness in comparison to individually randomised trials. Possibly twice as many participants will be needed owing to the fact that children in a particular school or class will have similar outcomes from sharing a similar learning environment. This correlation between individuals within a cluster is called the 'intra-cluster correlation coefficient'. The coefficient needs to be taken in to account when calculating initial sample size. A cluster-randomised trial also requires more sophisticated statistics to assess multi-level characteristics, such as multi-level modelling (see Donner & Klar, 2000).

In trials with waiting-list control groups, the issue of how ethical it is to keep people waiting is often raised. Waiting-list control groups are similar to typical waiting lists, accepted (and expected) for any service; for example, we expect to wait to see our general practitioner or to attend a popular course. The service, or intervention, is not 'withheld' (a common misconception) but simply is offered at a later date than to the intervention group, so the argument against inclusion of a control group is a moot one.

If there are major concerns regarding control participants' access to the service/intervention, a randomised stepped-wedge design will overcome practical or ethical objections to evaluating an intervention experimentally for which there is some evidence of effectiveness or which cannot be accessed by the target population simultaneously. The stepped-wedge randomised trial design involves sequential roll-out of an intervention to participants (individuals or clusters) over a number of time points, whereby control participants act initially as a comparator group and then become part of the intervention group with assessments undertaken after the intervention. By the end of the study, *all* participants will have received the intervention, although in random order [for a review of the stepped-wedge design, see Brown & Lilford (2006)].

Sample Size

In order to be confident in our results, that is, that any differences between conditions is not due to chance, we must ensure that we have a large enough sample size. The sample size needs to be calculated as part of the initial trial design, based on findings from similar trials, such as a point estimate of a systematic review of evidence, or pilot studies. The likelihood of a chance finding is reduced with increased sample size. There are various statistical packages that can aid calculation.

Randomisation Ratios

RCTs do *not* have to use 1:1 randomisation with equal numbers in each condition; indeed, there are advantages to using a ratio of 2:1 intervention to control because this design can be ethically beneficial in that it reduces the number awaiting intervention and provides the opportunity to evaluate a larger intervention group than a 1:1 ratio with only a small loss of statistical power (Cohen, 1988). It is the design favoured in the field of parenting intervention research (Belsky et al., 2006; Webster-Stratton, 1998). Alternatively, if an intervention is very expensive, for example, in a medical drugs trial, it may be preferable to randomise participants 1:2 intervention to control to reduce costs.

What Should We Measure?

Outcomes for making informed decisions are tied to the original basic issue or problem to be resolved and form the basis for specific research questions. Typical examples include

- Is the intervention effective; that is, does it work (e.g., in reducing anti-social behaviour)?
- Is the intervention acceptable, and does it meet the needs and improve outcomes for children, families and/or schools who participate?
- Is the intervention implemented efficiently and effectively with fidelity?
- For which children/families/schools are the interventions effective?
- What are the environmental/contextual circumstances that improve the likelihood of success?
- Does the duration of time participating in an intervention affect the likelihood of success, that is, is there a dosage effect?
- What are the costs of implementing the intervention?
- Is the intervention cost-effective?
- What are the longer-term costs and benefits of intervention?

6. Analysis

On determining research questions, the issue of how to *assess* outcomes arises; that is, what measures will be administered or used, and how do we analyse and present them? As stated earlier, the Medical Research Council (MRC) guidelines for evaluation of complex interventions are clear in stating that both *intervention* and *process* outcomes should be assessed (see Box 3.1). The choice of outcome measures is a crucial aspect of an evaluation design. What are the primary and secondary outcome measures? A single primary outcome that is linked directly to the main evaluation question in combination with a small number of secondary outcomes is the most straightforward from the point of view of statistical analysis. Measures should be standardised, validated and reliable, and they need to be appropriate for the question. There needs to be a clear plan of when

data will be collected, from and by who and in what setting, for example, teachers in schools, parents in the home environment or children at a playgroup. Triangulation can be useful so that measures are completed from more than one source, yielding more than one perception of measured change; for example, child behaviour can be assessed by teacher and parent report or by child self-report or by independent, objective (blind to allocated condition) observation of child behaviour by a researcher. Measures can be used to assess (1) process effects, such as client engagement, dosage and attendance rates, client and facilitator satisfaction and implementation quality, and (2) outcome effects, which form primary and secondary measures to assess change over time, such as pre- and post-intervention and intervention versus control participants.

Process Evaluation

Having initially identified an evidence-based intervention with tools for effective replication (e.g., manuals, training support and standardised materials), successfully identified and trained suitable staff and tackled barriers to implementation, the final challenge is to ensure that the intervention is delivered with fidelity (Mihalic et al., 2002). Implementation fidelity is a topic of growing importance because evidenced-based programmes, shown to work in research trials, increasingly are being delivered within mainstream services.

The Network of Networks on Impact Evaluation (NONIE, 2009) offers guidance on impact evaluation, recommending that evaluators use mixed-method approaches to combine the strengths of both quantitative and qualitative methods, specifically for monitoring intervention implementation, to allow feedback on delivery and the possibility to adjust design or implementation to 'ground-level realities' (Bamberger, 2009).

Process evaluation is targeted on implementation, and effective monitoring could be argued as necessary for effective evaluation. Trial failure, relating to lack of (statistically) significant results, may be caused by

Box 3.5. Promoting Alternative Thinking Strategies (PATHS) (Greenberg et al., 1995)

PATHS is a school-based programme designed to promote social and emotional competence with a central emphasis on teaching pupils to identify, understand and self-regulate their emotions. In an RCT in the United States with 200 second and third grade regular education students, PATHS produced significant improvements in social problem solving and understanding of emotions post-test. Compared to control children (general education), intervention children showed improvements on social problem solving, emotional understanding, self-report of conduct problems, teacher ratings of adaptive behaviour and cognitive abilities related to social planning and impulsivity (Greenberg et al., 1995). These improvements were maintained at 1-year follow-up, and additional significant reductions in teacher and student reports of conduct problems appeared at 2-year follow-up.

Other PATHS findings:

- A reduction in teacher reports of students exhibiting aggressive behaviour by 32 per cent
- An increase in teacher reports of students exhibiting self-control by 36 per cent
- An increase in student vocabulary for emotions by 68 per cent
- An increase in student scores on cognitive skills tests by 20 per cent
- An improvement in students' ability to tolerate frustration
- A significantly decrease in conduct problems and the percentage of aggressive/violent solutions to social problems

design failure, intervention failure or implementation failure. A process evaluation will be less informative if conducted without reference to outcomes and may be misleading if perceptions differ from outcomes (Medical Research Council, 2009) – perhaps facilitators delivered the intervention well, it was acceptable to themselves and their clients, yet no significant findings for effectiveness were found. In this scenario, the implementation was successful, yet the intervention was a failure; if only the implementation data were presented, they would be misleading. Process evaluation can assess fidelity and quality of implementation, clarify causal mechanisms and identify contextual factors associated with variation in outcomes, such as differences across implementation sites (Bonell et al., 2006; Oakley et al., 2006). Process evaluation is critical when trialling an intervention programme, and it is important for the process evaluation to be ongoing throughout scale-up to provide a monitoring strategy that maintains the intervention's integrity and effectiveness and to ensure that programmes are not delivered by insufficiently trained staff with inadequate resources (Mihalic et al., 2002).

Intervention Outcome Effectiveness

Complex interventions typically involve multi-dimensional design and outcomes and, as such, present a range of options for analysis. Boxes 3.4 and 3.5 present social and educational trials with different designs; Box 3.4 presents an 'individual' and Box 3.5 a 'cluster' randomised trial. Individual and cluster-randomised trials use different methods of analysis. In the individual RCT highlighted in Box 3.4, analysis of covariance was applied to assess differences between the intervention and control conditions on follow-up scores, taking account of area (or sites), treatment (intervention or control) and baseline response value.

In Box 3.5 whole schools were randomised to intervention or control conditions as opposed to individuals. Cluster RCTs require more participants and more sophisticated statistical analyses than individual RCTs to account for any clustering effects. 'Clustering effects' refer to existing similarities between participants caused by the fact that they share a similar environment, for example, children who are in the same class with the same teacher will be more similar to each other than children from a different class. The same holds true for schools – children from a particular school will be more similar to each other than to children from a different school. Cluster trials yield data with multi-level characteristics (e.g., pupil, class and school levels), which require more sophisticated statistical techniques than individual RCTs.

Although cluster and individual RCTs are analysed using different methods, there are basic analyses and associated issues common to both designs, some of which are outlined below.

INTENTION-TO-TREAT (ITT)

Ideally, the trial will have been conducted in such a manner as to avoid biases that can affect the results; however, inappropriate analyses can introduce bias at the last stage. The most robust analytical method for analysing the results of RCTs is by ITT (Hollis & Campbell, 1999). This method requires participants to remain in their allocated randomised group for analytical purposes, even if they 'cross over' into the other intervention arm during the trial; for example, a school may have been allocated to the intervention group yet not take up or deliver the intervention. There may be a temptation to move the school into the control group for analytical purposes. If we exclude the school from intervention group analyses or, worse, include the school in control group analyses, we undermine the randomisation allocation.

ITT analysis may assume no change from baseline assessment for those lost to follow-up by using the 'last observation carried forward' technique, or an average score may be calculated and imputed as the missing value. There are a variety of methods to deal with missing data at the various levels (i.e., item, measure and time point). The trial statistician will be able to establish which method is most applicable for the data type and trial design.

If ITT analyses are applied, there is no need to conduct baseline characteristic comparisons across groups because participants are included in the analyses according to their allocation, with methods being applied to handle missing data.

Altman & Doré (1990) discourage baseline variable comparisons, stating that the randomisation process would make any differences across groups attributable to chance. If there is reason to believe that a certain variable, for example, gender of a child in conduct behaviour studies, may influence outcome, then this variable can be controlled for both at randomisation as a stratification variable and at the outcome analysis stage as a covariate. Torgerson & Torgerson (2008) suggest that it is acceptable to compare baseline characteristics only when attrition rates are thought to make randomised groups unbalanced and when a per-protocol analyses (analysis of only the participants with compliance/complete data) is to be undertaken.

ITT analyses is imperative in social science or education research because participants may move from school or area or change their minds about participation; it is a method that includes all participants, whether or not they received the allocated intervention. ITT avoids bias and in so doing dilutes the effects of the intervention to portray the 'real-life' effect of the trial.

ESTABLISHING EFFECTS: EFFECT SIZES

One issue facing government and service providers when presented with an evaluation report is to determine what processes and programmes or interventions qualify as 'effective'. Statistical tests are applied to establish whether 'statistically significant differences' are apparent between intervention and control groups after intervention.

When conducting a trial with a large sample, even a small difference may be statistically significant, as measured by the p value generated through statistical tests. The p value is the probability that the observed difference is 'true' and did not happen by chance. An 'effect size' may be a better measurement of meaningful effect. An effect size measures the *magnitude* of difference between the intervention and control group outcomes. Both the p value and the effect size should be reported, yet the effect size is probably the most meaningful for service managers or key decision makers.

A standardised effect can be calculated using a variety of measures, yet Cohen's d (1988) is used commonly. The mean difference (using adjusted means to take the differences in other variables into account, if possible) between the two conditions after intervention is divided by the pooled standard deviation or the control group standard deviation to obtain an effect size. What constitutes a valued difference or effect depends very much on what is being measured. As a guide, Cohen suggests 0.3 as a small but meaningful effect, 0.5 as a medium effect and 0.8 and above as a large effect. An effect size of 0.8 equates to an average 0.8 standard deviation improvement in the intervention group compared with the control group. Large effect sizes may occur only in trials where the intervention group is compared to a control group receiving no intervention and placed on a waiting list. In certain trials, for example, drug trials, an effect size of 0.2 may be regarded as meaningful because the effect of the drug may equate to saving thousands of people's lives when compared to an alternative or previously administered drug. Effect size therefore is relative to the research question, intervention type, trial design and expected outcome. As Torgerson & Torgerson (2008) state, an effect size is the likeliest, but not the definitive, estimate of the effect of the intervention. The effect size is the most likely estimate within a given range, that is, confidence intervals. Effect sizes should be reported with accompanying confidence intervals to highlight the range of uncertainty surrounding the result,

and it should be noted that the effect size is more likely to fall within the central range of the confidence intervals than the extremities. In addition, the smaller the sample size, the wider are the confidence intervals.

The reporting of effect size has been an important advance in health, social and educational research. However, the benchmark to interpret the size, or meaning, of these effect sizes to inform policy-making is lacking. Effect sizes can facilitate comparisons of effects across interventions using different measurement instruments, yet, owing to inconsistent interpretations and methods of analysis, such comparisons need to be approached with caution (Hill et al., 2007).

ESTABLISHING EFFECTS: NUMBER-NEEDED-TO-TREAT (NNT)

A more meaningful measure for service manager practitioners or key decision makers may be the *number-needed-to-treat* (NNT), where 'treat' refers to those prospectively participating in an intervention. The NNT tells us the number of people required to receive the intervention in order to get one person over a threshold; it could relate to passing a test, learning a second language, being more sociable and so on. Effect sizes can be translated into an NNT. An effect size of 0.3 could equate to an NNT figure of 8, which means that for every eight people put through the intervention, one will make a marked improvement on the measure of interest, such as pass an exam.

Although NNT may be more attractive than ITT, it is not without drawbacks. NNT needs to be based on *reliable* and *clinically significant* change. 'Reliable change' refers to whether people changed sufficiently that the change is unlikely to be due to simple measurement unreliability. 'Clinically significant change' is change that has taken the person from a score typical of a problematic, dysfunctional patient, client or user group to a score typical of the "normal" population [for more detail, see Evans, Margison & Barkham (1998)]. Presenting NNT can be misleading, and a figure of 50 NNT may be acceptable in some circumstances and not in others; that is, it cannot be universally accepted as a specified rate of improvement. An NNT of 50 will be more than acceptable if it is inexpensive medication yet is less than acceptable for an expensive one-to-one tuition strategy, for example. NNT has gone some way to bridge the gap to inform in a more meaningful way, yet the criteria used to define success or failure often are arbitrary (Evans, Margison & Barkham, 1998).

COST-EFFECTIVENESS

In addition to outcome effects and NNT, effect sizes can be used to ascertain the cost-effectiveness of an intervention (Harris, 2009). Levin & McEwan (2001) offer detailed discussions of basic issues associated with cost analyses. The cost-effectiveness of any intervention can be measured by the relationship between costs and effects.

Although of primary importance to policy-makers and service providers, economic evaluations are rarely conducted alongside randomised trials, with the majority of empirical educational research focusing on intervention effects, policies and programmes whilst ignoring costs (Rice, 2002). If an intervention in social or education services is to be seriously considered as an effective intervention to be scaled up into mainstream practice, costs need to be examined. These costs include those of implementation, cost-effectiveness, and long-term cost-benefits. It seems ludicrous to evaluate an intervention and find it extremely effective in achieving positive outcomes, yet later it is found not to be cost-effective and is abandoned through lack of resources, or worse, its delivery is continued, with various 'corners cut' without fidelity in an attempt to reduce the costs of implementation, which may yield the intervention useless.

As noted earlier, pragmatic RCTs are the best vehicle in which to establish the cost-effectiveness of interventions and possible scale-up and roll-out costs. It is understood that the costs of implementing an intervention for the first time, especially within an RCT, may be greater than when the intervention is rolled out subsequently, so ideally, economists should report two figures – one

to include initial setup costs, including material purchase costs, training costs and so on, and a second figure excluding non-recurrent costs – so that decision makers are aware of initial and (reduced) subsequent costs of implementing interventions. In addition to the resource costs, such as time, money and staff, economists can conduct an incremental cost-effectiveness ratio, which tells us whether an intervention is more or less cost-effective than a comparator or no intervention, for example, how much it costs to improve peer relations in schools by one point on an outcome measure such as the Strengths and Difficulties Questionnaire (Goodman, 1997).

A sensitivity analysis then can be conducted to test the economic analysis and to demonstrate at what point the intervention may no longer be cost-effective; for example, if the cost of implementation suddenly increased by 10 per cent, would the intervention still be cost-effective? With effective interventions, it is useful to know long-term cost-benefits. Most trials, however, are relatively short-lived, so economists supplement trial data with computer models in order to model any long-term benefits. If an intervention is found to be cost-effective in the shorter term, for example, through the duration of a trial, then modelling may not be useful because most likely it will confirm what we already know from the cost-effectiveness analysis based on 'real' data.

MEDIATOR AND MODERATOR ANALYSES

In addition to the main analyses outlined previously to establish intervention and process 'effectiveness', we also can assess secondary outcomes such as *who* the programme worked best (or least) for and what the mechanisms of change were using mediator and moderator analyses.

Questions about which subgroups of participants, for example, children or teachers, benefit most (or least) from an intervention are investigated through 'moderator analyses'. Moderator analyses are important for informing the next generation of trials and for informing practice directly (Gardner et al., 2010). They also may establish whether interventions meet the needs of girls versus boys or minority families or whether better outcomes are achieved by pupils when taught by male or female teachers. Within an intervention trial, the relevant question is whether a variable measured prior to randomisation influences or 'moderates' the relationship between treatment and outcome. The moderator is differentially associated with outcome, in the treatment compared with control groups, as shown by an interaction effect (Hinshaw, 2002; Kraemer et al., 2002).

Mediator analyses establishes the key mechanism, or active ingredient, of change for an intervention. There is a modest but growing literature in the parenting field based on secondary analysis of randomised trials (Forgatch & DeGarmo, 1999; Gardner, Burton & Klimes., 2006; Gardner et al., 2010; Reid, Webster-Stratton & Baydar, 2004) indicating that change in (independently observed) positive parenting skills mediates change in child outcome. Similar results have been found in teaching styles, whereby 'positive' teaching strategies such as labelled and proximal praise have predicted increased positive behaviour in pupils (Hutchings et al., 2008). Facilitators' key collaborative skills and strategies when delivering community-based parent programmes have been found to predict parent outcomes (Eames et al., 2008). Positive behaviour such as praise and reflective comments by facilitators delivering a parent group has been shown to predict positive parent behaviour, which, in turn, predicted positive behaviour change in children (Eames et al., 2008; Gardner et al., 2010).

7. Dissemination

A CONSORT (CONsolidated Standards of Reporting Trials) Statement offers guidelines to help authors improve reporting of RCTs by using a checklist and flow diagram (the most recent CONSORT Statement is downloadable at http://www.consort-statement.org/consort-statement/) and has been extended to cover cluster-randomised trials.

Publication in the research literature to inform the scientific community is only part of an effective implementation strategy. To translate findings into routine practice or policy, outcomes need to be made available using methods that are *accessible* and convincing to decision makers (Medical Research Council, 2009). Evaluation reports and research reports not only have different audiences, but their main objectives also are different. The goal of the research report is the enhancement of understanding and knowledge via publication to the scientific community. The main goal of the evaluation report is to inform decision makers. The relative emphasis of the two activities therefore is different.

Despite an increasing body of useful evidence in 'what works' in the field of education, initiatives and efforts to improve education research, there are still major challenges in the linking of research evidence to decision making at all levels. This is primarily due to practitioners' and researchers' differing needs and languages when discussing the 'effectiveness' of interventions and processes of implementation (Nutley & Davies, 2000). These differences need to be addressed, through appropriate dissemination, to encourage strategic collaboration amongst researchers, practitioners and decision makers and ultimate going-to-scale of worthwhile interventions in practice.

In the field of education, dissemination strategies are impeded by the lack of a guiding body to review research and inform educationalists. The National Institute for Clinical and Health Excellence (NICE) offers guidance and reviews recent research evidence to inform health-care professionals. For social care policy and practice, there is the Social Care Institute for Excellence (SCIE), which draws on evidence on key social care topics. As yet, there is no such equivalent for education research.

Conclusion

This chapter has discussed implementation science with regard to the process of evaluation of effects in social and educational interventions by establishing that social and educational interventions are *complex interventions* comprising many interacting components. The GIFS model provided the structure of this chapter, with reference to the Medical Research Council's (2009) dimensions of complex interventions. Intervention evaluation requires more than knowing *what* to do; it requires knowledge of *how* to do it effectively by paying attention to implementation processes, outcomes, mechanisms of change, costs and dissemination.

ITT analysis always should be carried out to portray real-life effects of the evaluation, alongside any per-protocol analyses. Analysis can be improved to reflect and evaluate better the realities of social experimentation and intervention by tailoring results to what is more meaningful to key stakeholders, such as service managers or decision makers, by offering effect sizes or NNT based on reliable or clinically significant change. Mediator and moderator analyses are also important to inform on who interventions work best for and under what conditions. Dissemination needs to be clear, understandable and accessible, and reports to decision makers may need to be quite different to the reporting of findings to the scientific community. Reporting on all components of the evaluation is essential to establish trial, intervention or implementation successes and failures; a 'full picture' is required to prevent misinformation from being presented within the public domain.

Oscar Wilde (1854–1900) once stated: "Success is a science: If you have the conditions, you get the results". This quote eloquently summarises complex intervention evaluation; that is, if all components of complex interventions are addressed to ensure strong interconnecting links between components, then success of evidence-based programmes should be assured.

References

Altman, D. G., & Doré, C. J. (1991). Randomisation and baseline comparisons in clinical trials. *Lancet* 335, 149–53.

Bamberger, M. (2009). Strengthening impact evaluation designs through the reconstruction of baseline data. *Journal of Development Effectiveness* 1(1), 37–59.

Belsky, J., Melhuish, E., Barnes, J., Leyland, A. H. & Romaniuk, H. (2006). Effects of Sure Start local programmes on children and families: Early findings from a quasi-experimental, cross-sectional study. *British Medical Journal* 332, 1476–8.

Bonell, C., Oakley, A., Hargreaves, J., Strange, V. & Rees, R. (2006). Assessment of generalisability in trials of health interventions: Suggested framework and systematic review. *British Medical Journal* 333, 346–9.

Brown, C. A., & Lilford, R. J. (2006). The stepped wedge trial design: A systematic review [doi:10.1186/1471-2288-6-54]. *BMC Medical Research Methodology* 6, 54.

Bumbarger, B., & Perkins, D. (2008). After randomised trials: Issues related to the dissemination of evidence-based interventions. *Journal of Children's Services* 3(2), 55–64.

Bywater, T., & Axford, N. (2010). Strategies for targeting and recruiting families to randomised controlled trials of evidenced based parent programmes in community settings. Paper presented at Society for Prevention Research, 18th Annual Meeting, 'Cells to Society: Prevention at All Levels', June 1–4, 2010, Denver, CO.

Bywater, T., Hutchings, J., Daley, D., Whitaker, C., Yeo, S. T., Jones, K., Eames, C. & Tudor Edwards, R. (2009). Long-term effectiveness of a parenting intervention in Sure Start services in Wales for children at risk of developing conduct disorder [doi:10.1192/bjp.bp.108.056531]. *British Journal of Psychiatry* 195, 318–24.

Cohen, J. (1988). *Statistical power for the behavioural sciences*. Hillsdale, NJ: Erlbaum.

Collins, R., & MacMahon, S. (2001). Reliable assessment of the effects of treatment on mortality and major morbidity. *Lancet* 357, 373–80.

Donner, A., & Klar, N. (2000). *Design and analysis of cluster randomization trials in health research*. London: Arnold.

Durlak, J. A., & DuPre, E. P. (2008). Implementation matters: A review of research on the influence of implementation on program outcomes and the factors affecting implementation. *American Journal of Community Psychology* 41, 327–50.

Eames, C., Daley, D., Hutchings, J., Hughes, C., Jones, K., Martin, P. & Bywater, T. (2008). The Leader Observation Tool (LOT): A process skills treatment fidelity measure for the Incredible Years Parenting Programme. *Child Care Health and Development* 34(3), 391–400.

Eccles, M., Grimshaw, J., Campbell, M. & Ramsay, C. (2003). Research designs for studies evaluating the effectiveness of change and improvement strategies. *Quality and Safety in Healthcare* 12, 47–52.

Edwards, R. T., Ó Céilleachair, A., Bywater, T., Hughes, D. & Hutchings, J. (2007). A parenting programme for children at risk of developing conduct disorder: A cost-effective analysis. *British Medical Journal* 334, 682.

Epstein, M. H., Kutash, K. & Duchnowski, A. J. (2005). *Outcomes for children and youth with emotional and behavioural disorders and their families: Programs and evaluation best practices*, 2nd ed. Dallas, TX: PRO-ED, Inc.

Evans, C., Margison, F. & Barkham, M. (1998). The contribution of reliable and clinically significant change methods to evidence-based mental health. *Evidence Based Mental Health* 1, 70–2.

Forgatch, M., & DeGarmo, D. (1999). Parenting through change: An effective parenting training program for single mothers. *Journal of Consulting and Clinical Psychology* 67, 711–24.

Gardner, F., Burton, J. & Klimes, I. (2006). Randomised controlled trial of a parenting intervention in the voluntary sector for reducing child conduct problems: outcomes and mechanisms of change. *Journal of Child Psychology and Psychiatry* 47, 1123–32.

Gardner F., Hutchings, J., Bywater, T. & Whitaker, C. (2010). Who benefits and how does it work? Moderators and mediators of outcome in an effectiveness trial of a parenting intervention. *Journal of Clinical Child and Adolescent Psychology* 39(4), 1–13.

Gitlin, A., & Smyth, J. (1989). *Teacher evaluation: Critical education and transformative alternatives*. Lewes, UK: Falmer Press.

Goodman, R. (1997). The Strengths and Difficulties Questionnaire: A research note. *Journal of Child Psychology, Psychiatry, and Allied Disciplines* 38(5), 581–6.

Greenberg, M. T., Kusche, C. A., Cook, E. T. & Quamma, J. P. (1995). Promoting emotional competence in school-aged children: The effects of the PATHS Curriculum. *Development and Psychopathology* 7, 117–36.

Harris, D. N. (2009). Toward policy-relevant benchmarks for interpreting effect sizes: Combining effects with costs. *Educational Evaluation and Policy Analysis* 31, 3–29.

Hill, C. J., Bloom, H. S., Black, A. R. & Lipsey, M. W. (2007), *Empirical benchmarks for interpreting effect sizes in research*. Washington: Manpower Demonstration Research Corporation.

Hinshaw, S. P. (2002). Intervention research, theoretical mechanisms, and causal processes related to externalizing behavior patterns. *Development and Psychopathology* 14, 789–818.

Hollis, S., & Campbell, F. (1999). What is meant by intention to treat analysis? Survey of published randomised, controlled trials. *British Medical Journal* 319, 670–4.

Hubble, M. A., Duncan, B. L. & Miller, S. D. (1999). *The heart and soul of change: What works in therapy*. Washington: American Psychological Society.

Hutchings, J., Bywater, T. & Daley, D. (2007). Pragmatic randomised, controlled trial of a parenting intervention in Sure Start services for pre-school children at risk of developing conduct disorder: How and why did it work? *Journal of Children's Services* 2, 4–14.

Hutchings, J., Bywater, T., Eames, C. & Martin, P. (2008). Implementing child mental health interventions in service settings: Lessons from three pragmatic randomised, controlled trials in Wales. *Journal of Children's Services* 13(2), 17–27

Hutchings, J., Bywater, T., Daley, D., Gardner, F., Whitaker, C., Jones, K., Eames, C. & Edwards, R. T. (2007). A pragmatic randomised, controlled trial of a parenting intervention in Sure Start services for children at risk of developing conduct disorder [doi:10.1136/bmj.39126.620799.55)]. *British Medical Journal*, March 7, 2007.

Kinsman, J., Nakiyingi, J., Kamali, A., Carpenter, L., Quigley, M., Pool, R. & Whitworth, J. (2001). Evaluation of a comprehensive school-based AIDS education programme in rural Masaka, Uganda. *Health Education Research* 16, 85–100.

Kraemer, H., Wilson, G., Fairburn, C. & Agras, W. (2002). Mediators and moderators of treatment effects. *Archives of General Psychiatry* 59, 877–83.

Lambert, M. J. (1992). Psychotherapy outcome research: Implications for integrative and eclectic therapists, in C. Norcoss & M. Goldfried (eds.), *Handbook of psychotherapy integration*. New York: Basic Books.

Levin, H. M., & McEwan, P. J. (2001). *Cost-effectiveness analysis*, 2nd ed. London: Sage.

McKee, M., Britton, A., Black, N., McPherson, K., Sanderson, C. & Bain, C. (1999). Interpreting the evidence: Choosing between randomised and non-randomised studies. *British Medical Journal* 319, 312–5.

Meadows, P. (2006). *Cost-effectiveness of implementing SSLPs: An interim research report* (NESS/2006/FR/015). London: Sure Start: Evidence & Research.

Medical Research Council (2009). *Developing and evaluating complex interventions: New guidance*. Retrievable at www.mrc.ac.uk/complexinterventionsguidance.

Mihalic, S., Fagan, M., Irwin, K., Ballard, D. & Elliot, D. (2002). *Blueprints for violence prevention replications: Factors for implementation success*. Center for the Study and Prevention of Violence, University of Colorado, Boulder.

Network of Networks on Impact Evaluation (NONIE) (2009). *Impact evaluations and development: NONIE guidance on impact evaluation*. Cairo International Evaluation Conference, Cairo, Egypt.

Nutley, S. M., & Davies, H. T. O. (2000). Making a reality of evidence-based practice: Some lessons from the diffusion of innovations. *Public Money and Management* 20(4), 35–42.

Oakley, A., Strange, V., Bonell, C., Allen, E. & Stephenson, J. (2006). RIPPLE Study Team. Process evaluation in randomised, controlled trials of complex interventions. *British Medical Journal* 332, 413–16.

Reid, M., Webster-Stratton, C. & Baydar, N. (2004). Halting the development of conduct problems in Head Start children: The effects of parenting training. *Journal of Clinical Child and Adolescent Psychology* 33, 279–91.

Rice, J. K. (2002). Cost analysis in education policy research: A comparative analysis across fields of public policy. In H. M. Levin & P. J. McEwan (eds.), *Cost-effectiveness in educational policy* (pp. 21–35), Larchmont, NY: Eye on Education.

Rogers, A., & Smith, M. K. (2006). *Evaluation: Learning what matters*. London: Rank Foundation/YMCA George Williams College. Retrievable as a pdf at www.ymca.org.uk/rank/conference/evaluation_learning_what_matters.pdf.

Torgerson, D. J., & Torgerson, C. J. (2008). *Designing randomised trials in health, education and the social sciences*. Hampshire, UK: Palgrave Macmillan.

Webster-Stratton, C. (1998). Preventing conduct problems in Head Start children: Strengthening parenting competencies. *Journal of Consultant Clinical Psychology* 66, 715–30.

Webster-Stratton, C. (1981). The incredible years: The parents and children series. Retrievable at http://www.incredibleyears.com/.

Welsh Assembly Government (2005). *Parenting action plan: Supporting mothers, fathers and carers with raising children in Wales* (DfTE Information Document No. 054–05). Swansea: Welsh Assembly Government.

CHAPTER 4

Understanding the Nature of Experiments in Real-World Educational Contexts

James Boyle

An experiment is always a study of change
—Abramson, 1990, p. 10

Overview

Experimental designs are used extensively by researchers to test hypotheses and predictions from theory, but in this chapter we shall consider the role of experiments in regard to evaluation and action research in determining whether change in educational contexts can be attributed to the introduction of an intervention approach or programme and in so doing establish the efficacy or effectiveness of the intervention. 'Experiments' traditionally are associated with deterministic, positivistic methodologies and, accordingly, may be viewed with suspicion by educationalists, psychologists and social scientists, whose interpretative paradigms emphasise the social construction of 'reality'. In terms of underlying epistemology and ontology, though, experimental designs can be accommodated within 'realist' and 'critical realist' positions. These positions are important because they

combine positivism, post-positivism and relativism as part of a systematic 'mixed-method' approach to the social sciences (Pawson & Tilley, 1997; Brewer & Hunter, 1989; Robson, 2002) which integrates quantitative data (e.g., to determine effectiveness of outcomes) and qualitative data (e.g., to investigate process variables, including acceptability of interventions to clients and stakeholders and overall feasibility).

Abramson & Abramson (2008, p. 13) define 'experiments' as 'studies of deliberate intervention by the investigators'. Using this definition, we will consider three classes of experimental design: 'true' experimental designs, such as randomised, controlled trials (RCTs), widely regarded as the 'gold standard' for intervention research; 'quasi-experimental' designs, where comparisons are drawn between non-randomised intervention and control groups that do not receive the intervention; and also 'small-n' experimental designs (formerly known as 'single-subject' designs), which compare the responses of individuals or groups to the systematic introduction of interventions following a series of baseline measures.

The rationale for each will be considered and examples discussed, together with implications for educationalists and other stakeholders as consumers of school-based interventions.

'True' Experiments and Quasi-Experiments

'True' and 'quasi-experiments' are 'studies of deliberate intervention by the investigators' (Abramson & Abramson, 2008, p. 13) and fall under the category of 'fixed' research designs (Anastas & MacDonald, 1994) which also include surveys (Robson, 2002). In an experimental design, the investigator makes decisions not only about the nature and delivery of an intervention but also about the participants: who they are and how they are allocated to an intervention group or non-intervention control group which does not receive the intervention. If the delivery of the intervention and the sampling of the participants are under the control of the investigator and the allocation of the participants to intervention or control groups is random, then the study is a 'true' experiment, such as an RCT (Abramson & Abramson, 2008). However, if the intervention is not under the direction of the investigator or if the allocation to intervention and control groups is not random to ensure that the groups are as equivalent as possible, then the study is a 'quasi-experiment' (Abramson & Abramson, 2008; Campbell & Stanley, 1963).

The importance placed on the investigator having control over both the intervention and the selection and allocation of the participants lies at the heart of experimental designs. They should be capable of determining causal relations between the intervention and other relevant independent variables systematically varied in the study and any observed change in the outcomes, or dependent variables. The ability to make inferences about causality in this way, what is referred to as 'internal validity' (Campbell & Stanley, 1963; Robson, 2002), addresses central questions of whether interventions make a difference.

Torgerson & Torgerson (2008, pp. 2–3) provide a useful summary of the key elements involved in an RCT:

1. The participants should be appropriate for the intervention being studied. There is little merit in studying the effects of an unsuitable intervention intended for younger or older participants, for example.

2. The sample size should be large enough not to be susceptible to type II statistical error (Robson, 2002). 'Type II' error refers to the probability that we might falsely reject the hypothesis that there is a difference between the intervention and control groups when in fact there is such a difference. This is likely to be a problem if the sample is too small (see Torgerson & Togerson, 2008, pp. 127–33).

3. The participants then should be allocated to groups of those receiving an intervention or to comparison or control groups that (a) do not receive the intervention or (b) might receive an alternative form of intervention in the area under investigation, such as a competing intervention to determine relative effectiveness.

4. In the case of a 'true' experimental design such as an RCT, allocation to groups must be random, for example, using random-number tables or computer programmes which produce random numbers. Systematic but non-random approaches such as alternation (e.g., using alternate names on a class list) may allow selection bias to occur and accordingly are problematic [see Torgerson & Torgerson (2008, pp. 25–28) for a discussion]. Such randomisation may be at the level of the individual but also could be at the level of groups such as classes or schools, referred to as 'cluster randomisation' (Jadad & Enkin, 2007).

5. Pre-intervention and post-intervention measures generally are obtained, the latter after the intervention has been delivered but at a point identified in

advance by the investigator. Note, however, that a post-intervention measure–only design still will meet the standards of an RCT if the groups have been randomised. A factorial design which investigates the effects of two or more independent variables also may be employed (Robson, 2002, pp, 127–8; Torgerson & Torgerson, 2008, pp. 114–18). For example, such a design could be used to investigate whether a spelling programme for primary school–aged pupils is delivered more effectively by parents than by teachers.

6. Additional follow-up measures also may be gathered to investigate whether any changes are maintained over time after the delivery of the intervention.

7. If there is a significant difference between the intervention and control groups, we can conclude that the intervention 'works'.

In contrast, quasi-experiments lack some of the important design elements of true experimental designs (Campbell & Stanley, 1963; Robson, 2002, pp. 133–46):

- Allocation of participants to intervention and control groups is not random, for example, where one group with severe problems receives an intervention and the control group consists of participants with less severe problems, perhaps on a waiting list for additional support or services. This can result in non-equivalent groups owing to selection bias (Torgerson & Torgerson, 2008) and can lead to further problems of interpretations of the findings due to regression to the mean (Zhang & Tomblin, 2003), which will be discussed below.
- Pre- and post-intervention measures on an intervention group are compared in the absence of a control group.
- This approach uses time-series designs where measures are obtained pre- and post-intervention over lengthy periods of time but without control phases such as withdrawal of intervention to observe whether this affects the dependent variable.

- This approach uses 'regression discontinuity designs' (Torgerson & Torgerson, 2008, pp. 40–1) where intervention effects are evidenced by changes or 'discontinuities' in the regression line of the plot of post-intervention scores against pre-intervention scores for two groups differing in terms of a pre-specified criterion which determines entry into a intervention programme or entry into a control group. These designs are not as efficient as RCTs and require a larger sample.

Randomisation and Bias

Randomisation of participants to groups either by simple randomisation or by stratified or blocked randomisation which balances any known confounders between groups (Abramson & Abramson, 2008; Torgerson & Torgerson, 2008) provides a means of attaining equivalence between intervention and control groups and of controlling for possible selection bias which may be the reason for the non-equivalence (Jadad & Enkin, 2007, pp. 31–3). It also controls for the confounding effects of regression to the mean, which is associated with measurement error and the reliability of any tests used (Zhang & Tomblin, 2003). 'Regression to the mean' refers to the tendency for extreme pre-intervention scores (e.g., of the kind associated with pupils with difficulties) to be higher on re-test as a result of measurement error. Thus test–re-test gain scores from such a population will be inflated by the effects of this regression to the mean and will tend to over-estimate the effects of an intervening intervention. If the intervention and control groups are from the same population and are randomised to their respective groups, then the investigator has controlled for the effects of regression to the mean. However, where the two groups are not equivalent in this way, the intervention group would be expected to have higher gain scores than a control group with even slightly higher pre-test scores, which makes it difficult to interpret the findings. Finally, randomisation also controls more generally for temporal effects associated with, for example, maturation, which might have a confounding effect on the results (Torgerson & Torgerson, 2008, p. 10).

Randomisation can control for these three sources of bias, but it should be noted that there are further sources of bias which come into play during the course of the study or during reporting and publication of the findings after randomisation has been carried out. These are discussed fully in the texts by Jadad & Enkin (2008, pp. 29–47) and Torgerson & Torgerson (2008, pp. 44–70), but two which are particularly relevant to educational research will be noted: attrition bias and ascertainment bias.

In general, intervention studies struggle to retain all the participants over the course of the study. If the drop-out, or 'attrition', rate is random across conditions, then there is less of a problem of bias. If there are differential attrition rates across independent variables or between groups, though, with, for example, more pupils in the intervention group dropping out than in the control group, then this could lead to the loss of equivalence between groups. The possibility of attrition bias is treated very seriously by journals specialising in publishing the findings from RCTs, and a flow-chart of participants through the study, a CONSORT diagram (from the 'Consolidation of the Standards of Reporting Trials') (Begg et al., 1996; Zwarenstein et al., 2008) is commonly required.

'Ascertainment bias' refers to the possibility that those who carry out the assessments or report the findings may favour positive effects for the intervention and thus may influence the results, perhaps unconsciously, by allowing more latitude to the scoring of post-intervention tests in the case of those receiving intervention, for example. Where possible, it is good practice to incorporate 'blinded assessments' in RCTs, where assessments are carried out by those who otherwise are not involved in the study and who are 'blind' to the groups to which the participants have been randomised.

External Validity and Generalisability of Findings

Thus far we have focused on internal validity. But consideration also should be given to 'external validity' (Cook & Campbell, 1979; Robson, 2002, pp. 106–8), the extent to which the findings can be generalised to a wider population. If such generalisability is important, then the participants also should be representative of that population and randomly sampled accordingly.

SMALL-*n* EXPERIMENTAL DESIGNS

'Small-*n*' experimental designs involve the manipulation of an independent (treatment) variable across a pre-intervention baseline phase, an intervention phase, and commonly a post-intervention phase (Barlow & Hersen, 1984; Kratochwill, 1978; Robinson & Foster, 1979; Robson, 2002; Todman & Dugard, 2001). They are 'true' experimental designs because the systematic introduction of the intervention is under the control of the investigator. They also provide repeated measures of the outcome over time from the same participants in regard not only to the effects of the introduction and continuation of an intervention but also to its alteration and withdrawal, depending on the specific design. The designs can involve more than one subject, and although traditionally referred to as 'single-subject' experimental designs, they are now more accurately referred to as 'small-*n*' designs.

Three small-*n* designs (withdrawal and reversal designs, multiple-baseline designs, and alternating-treatment designs) provide particularly high levels of experimental control (Barlow & Herson, 1984; Robson, 2002). Multiple-baseline (or 'multiple path') designs are of three types: (1) multiple baselines across participants, (2) multiple baselines across behaviours (where baselines for several behaviours are measured from one participant and then a treatment applied to each behaviour at a different time), or (3) multiple baselines across situations.

The multiple baseline across subjects design is illustrated in Figure 4.1. The first phase is the baseline, which extends

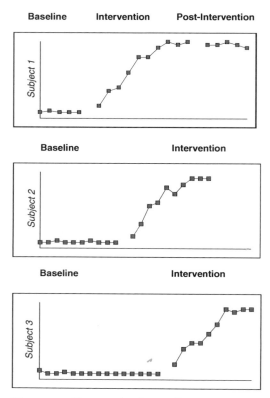

Baseline   **Intervention**   **Post-Intervention**

Baseline   **Intervention**

Baseline   **Intervention**

Figure 4.1. Illustration of a small-*n* experimental design (multiple baseline across subjects).

over a period of sessions, followed by the intervention, which is introduced once a stable baseline has been established. Intervention may be followed by a period of maintenance or follow-up, during which treatment is withdrawn. In the example here, the design is replicated across more than one subject, with treatment introduced to each subject sequentially with a time-lagged baseline, as shown in Figure 4.1. The treatment is assumed to affect only the behaviour targeted by the intervention, and other baseline or control behaviours hence should remain unchanged. The stability of the baselines for subjects 2 and 3 (after the onset of treatment for subject 1) and their subsequent changes in response to the introduction of treatment provide not only evidence that the observed changes in performance are the result of the treatment but also experimental control for the effects of maturation. Single-subject experimental designs provide data

regarding the generalisation of treatment to other settings and the maintenance of any gains after withdrawal of the treatment, two key issues underpinning the effectiveness of intervention. However, although the use of individual subjects as their own controls can reduce the variability in a study considerably, there are problems in generalising findings because of the small samples used. In general, single-subject experimental designs provide high internal validity but more limited external validity.

The analysis of data from small-*n* designs has long been the subject of debate, and many investigators have relied on visual inspection of graphical data as in Figure 4.1 to determine change of slope between baseline and treatment phases and hence the effects of intervention (Barlow & Hersen, 1984). A range of statistical procedures has been developed for analysing small-*n* designs (Kazdin, 1984), with randomisation tests which do not make assumptions about random sampling of participants or normality of underlying population distribution and are not affected by serial dependency of particular utility (Todman & Dugard, 2001).

Case Study 1: An RCT

Our first case study to illustrate the use of an experimental design in a school setting is an RCT carried out by Boyle et al. (2009). This was an investigation of the effectiveness of school-based language therapy for pupils with persistent severe expressive or mixed receptive-expressive language impairment. Severe expressive language impairment affects the verbal language that the pupils produce, for example, grammar and vocabulary. Mixed receptive-expressive language impairment, in contrast, affects not only expressive language but also understanding of vocabulary and grammar and inferring meaning and, in some cases, the use of language in social contexts.

The therapy delivered in the study by Boyle et al. was evidence-based, derived from meta-analyses of published studies which provided estimates of treatment-effect sizes that were used to identify the required sample size for the study. The therapy was manualised to ensure transparency and replicability of delivery: A manual detailing the intervention procedures to be carried out, together with additional materials and activities, was written for those delivering the language therapy.

The participants in the RCT were 161 children aged six to twelve years with persistent primary receptive and/or expressive language impairment. That is, they had no reported marked hearing loss and no moderate to severe articulation/phonology/dysfluency problems or otherwise requiring individual speech and language therapy work. The children all attended mainstream schools. Eighty-six of the children had mixed receptive-expressive impairment (defined using a threshold criterion on a standardised test of receptive language of $SS \leq 81$ and non-verbal IQ scores > 75), and seventy-five had specific expressive impairment. The RCT was a multi-centre investigation involving participants from two cities and surrounding areas to increase representativeness. A factorial design was used to investigate the benefits relative to a control group receiving the existing community-based therapy of (1) 1:1 language therapy in schools versus group-based therapy and (2) therapy delivered by speech and language therapists (SLTs) versus SLT assistants. The participants were allocated to one of five conditions using stratified randomization to ensure parity across groups in terms of city and gender:

- *Individual, direct project therapy:* SLT working individually with a child (N = 34, 20 with mixed receptive-expressive impairment and 14 with specific expressive impairment)
- *Group, direct project therapy:* SLT working with a small group of children (N = 31, 17 with mixed receptive-expressive impairment and 14 with specific expressive impairment)
- *Individual, indirect project therapy:* A trained SLT assistant working individually with a child (N = 33, 17 with mixed

receptive-expressive impairment and 16 with specific expressive impairment)
- *Group, indirect project therapy:* A trained SLT assistant working with a small group of children (N = 32, 18 with mixed receptive-expressive impairment and 14 with specific expressive impairment)
- *Control group:* The group which received existing community-based services (N = 31, 14 with mixed receptive-expressive impairment and 17 with specific expressive impairment)

There is an evidence base for each of these four modes of delivery [see Boyle et al. (2009) for full details], so equipoise exists between them (Jadad & Enkin, 2007); that is, there is no evidence that one mode is more effective or less effective than the others.

There were no significant differences between the five groups in terms of pre-intervention scores, so selection bias was not deemed to be a problem. Project therapy was delivered three times per week for fifteen weeks in thirty- to forty-minute sessions in the children's schools, and those in the control group received their on-going therapy regime. Project therapy focused on comprehension monitoring, vocabulary development, grammar, narrative, and developing language-learning strategies. All post-baseline measures were blind-assessed by qualified SLTs not otherwise involved with the project to minimize the effects of ascertainment bias. The children were reassessed at T_2, immediately after the end of the intervention programme, and again at T_3, a twelve-month follow-up.

The flow-chart of participants is shown in Figure 4.2, and details are given regarding attrition of participants over time. Statistical analyses were carried out using analyses of covariance (ANCOVAs) (Field, 2009), with pre-intervention standardised language test scores as covariates and post-intervention scores as the dependent variable. Analyses also were carried on an intention-to-treat (ITT) basis (Torgerson & Torgerson, 2008): Any participant who withdrew from the study had his or her pre-intervention scores

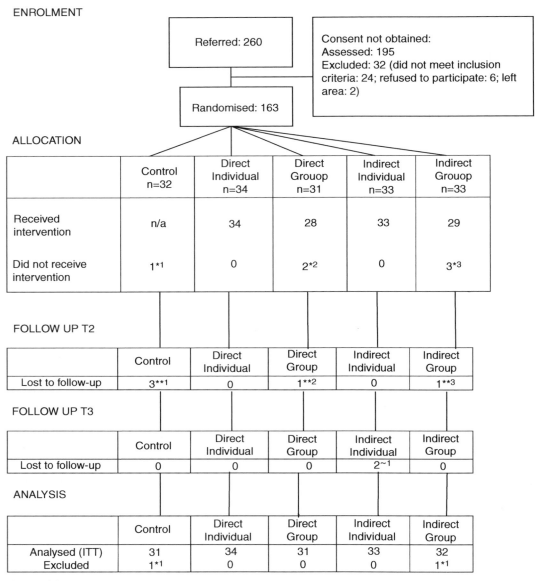

ENROLMENT

Referred: 260

Consent not obtained:
Assessed: 195
Excluded: 32 (did not meet inclusion criteria: 24; refused to participate: 6; left area: 2)

Randomised: 163

ALLOCATION

	Control n=32	Direct Individual n=34	Direct Grouop n=31	Indirect Individual n=33	Indirect Grouop n=33
Received intervention	n/a	34	28	33	29
Did not receive intervention	1*1	0	2*2	0	3*3

FOLLOW UP T2

	Control	Direct Individual	Direct Group	Indirect Individual	Indirect Group
Lost to follow-up	3**1	0	1**2	0	1**3

FOLLOW UP T3

	Control	Direct Individual	Direct Group	Indirect Individual	Indirect Group
Lost to follow-up	0	0	0	2~1	0

ANALYSIS

	Control	Direct Individual	Direct Group	Indirect Individual	Indirect Group
Analysed (ITT)	31	34	31	33	32
Excluded	1*1	0	0	0	1*1

Figure 4.2.

also used as post-intervention scores, making the conservative assumption of no progress. Although there were no differences between the groups in pre-intervention measures, the use of ANCOVA in this way increases the statistical power of the analysis by reducing error variance (Field, 2009).

There were no significant differences between the four modes of project therapy (all p values > 0.119), but children with specific expressive impairment made greater gains in both receptive and expressive language than those with mixed receptive-expressive impairment (all p values < 0.025). Further, while the children receiving project therapy made significant overall gains in expressive language (p = 0.031), there was only a modest and non-significant intervention effect for receptive language scores relative to the control group for the subgroup of children with mixed receptive-expressive impairment [SES = +0.25 (−0.32/+0.82)].

However, the impact of the small numbers involved on the statistical power of this comparison (fourteen in the control group and seventy-two receiving project therapy) should be noted. There were no differences between the modes of project therapy at T_3, twelve-month follow-up.

The power calculation to determine the required number of participants before the start of the study suggested a sample size of 250 (50 per group), but only 161 were recruited. Lower than intended sample size is a common problem in RCTs. An economic evaluation also was carried out (Dickson et al., 2009) which revealed the cost-effectiveness of indirect, group-based intervention delivery. Focus groups and questionnaires also were used to gather information about the acceptability of the models of intervention and about functional benefits. Such qualitative data are essential to determine acceptability and feasibility of interventions. The results revealed that all four modes of service delivery were acceptable to the children and their parents and teachers, and functional benefits in literacy and behaviour also were reported by the parents.

In conclusion, this study had high internal validity and determined the efficacy of the intervention (Abramson & Abramson, 2008) under the conditions of an RCT. However, additional studies to determine whether the intervention works in specific contexts with particular groups of clients under 'real-world' conditions would be helpful (Abramson & Abramson, 2008).

Case Study 2: A Quasi-Experimental Design

The next case study is an example of a quasi-experimental design which was used to determine the benefits of a nursery-based language outreach programme for young children attending local pre-school provision in a local authority.

Staff in participating nurseries were asked to nominate children who would benefit from additional support to encourage more effective use of language skills in nursery. Support teachers working with the project observed and assessed all the children thus referred and, following negotiation with nursery staff, identified a group of children for inclusion in the intervention programme. Priority was given to children in their final year in nursery who presented with marked difficulties in language, including children presenting with problems associated with developmental delay (particularly in language) or specific language difficulties and more able children who communicated fairly effectively but who might benefit from further opportunities to develop their information-related talk and use of language.

Each of these children was seen twice or, in nurseries where time-tabling was permitted, three times a week by a designated support teacher for twenty to thirty minutes in a small group of three or four. The number of sessions of support offered was not linked directly to the severity of the child's needs nor to specific teachers. In addition, contact was made with around 65 per cent of the parents of the children selected for additional support.

Two hundred and fifty-four children from a range of pre-five establishments (five nursery schools, two nursery classes and four community nurseries) received support over a four-year period. Fifty-five children referred in the first year of the project were randomly allocated to a non-intervention group and received no additional support. An equivalent number were randomised to the intervention group. However, in subsequent years, participants were recruited only to intervention groups. The children allocated to the non-intervention group served as a 'historical' control group for the pupils who followed, but the design is that of a quasi-experimental study, not an RCT. This comparison group provides some control over the effects of maturation, but there are other threats to validity that are not addressed (e.g., the effects of any more recent curricular changes in the nurseries and any changes to the entry criteria for the nurseries).

Table 4.1. Details of Participants

| Gender | N | Control Group | | N | Two Sessions per Week | | N | Three Sessions per Week | |
		Mean CA	SD (months)		Mean CA	SD (months)		Mean CA	SD (months)
Male	18	4y 0m	5.57	62	4y 0m	4.37	28	4y 2m	4.05
Female	27	4y 0m	4.13	50	4y 1m	4.30	22	4y 1m	4.70

Test–re-test data were available for 207 children (80 per cent of the total), with the details shown in Table 4.1. Complete data were available for only 45 of the children in the historical control group. The data for the remaining 20 per cent of the sample were incomplete because of absence from nursery during the pre- or post-intervention assessment phase. There thus was a considerable level of attrition which was a further source of bias. One of the key research questions was whether there were any differential benefits in receiving three sessions of support each week compared to only two. But the non-random allocation of children to the groups relating to numbers of sessions per week resulted in yet a further source of bias.

Intervention programmes were based on research into interactive learning and emphasised the need to encourage information-related talk in nursery settings by means of small group-work, practical activities and supportive adult interaction [see Boyle & McLellan (1998) for details]. Initial assessments were carried out at the end of the first term of the session. Following this, support programmes were carried out during twelve-week periods in the second term of the session. The outcomes were evaluated by means of further assessment carried out early in the third term.

At the end of the intervention, nursery staff were invited to complete an anonymous evaluation questionnaire, and their responses ($N = 33$, 100 per cent response rate) revealed that they felt that the children in their groups had benefitted from the additional support provided by the language support teacher. Qualitative data collected in this way provide information about the acceptability and feasibility of the intervention.

Parental views would have been helpful and would have informed an understanding of whether there was any generalisation of changes to the home setting.

Test–re-test data on a standardised language test were available for 207 children. The language test, the Preschool Language Assessment Instrument (PLAI) (Blank, Rose & Berlin, 1978), consisted of sixty items, fifteen for each of four 'levels', with each level measured on a zero to three scale. Level 1 measured skills such as labelling, matching and visual and auditory recall; level 2, use of language for description and recall of details; level 3, sequencing of ideas, following commands in the correct order, prediction and the ability to handle negatives; and level 4, use of language for inference, prediction and reflection.

Analyses of variance (ANOVAs) carried out on pre-intervention scores revealed statistically significant differences in favour of the historical control group, which achieved significantly higher pre-test scores than the participants receiving two sessions of support per week on levels 2, 3 and 4 of the PLAI and higher pre-test scores on level 4 than those receiving three sessions of support per week (all p values < 0.05). The groups thus were not equivalent, and in view of this, ANCOVAs were carried out with pre-intervention scores as covariate, number of sessions of support received each week as an independent variable and gain score (post-intervention − pre-intervention score) as the dependent variable. The resulting adjusted gain scores (co-varying initial test scores to statistically adjust for the differences between the groups in pre-intervention scores) for the three groups are shown in Figure 4.3.

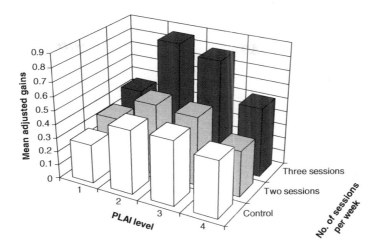

Figure 4.3. Mean adjusted gain scores × group.

The ANCOVAs revealed significant differences between the three groups in terms of gains on levels 2 and 3 of the PLAI ($p < 0.001$). Planned comparisons between the groups on level 2 and level 3 data (using Bonferroni-adjusted t tests) revealed that the group receiving three sessions of support per week made significantly greater gains than the group receiving two sessions or the control group ($p < 0.05$). Further, there was no significant difference between the gains made by the group receiving two sessions of support and the control group ($p > 0.05$). However, the interpretation of these findings is complicated by the lower internal validity of the quasi-experimental design arising from the non-equivalence of the historical control group as well as the non-random allocation of participants to the groups.

Case Study 3: Small-n Experimental Design

Rock's (2005) study of the effectiveness of a classroom-based self-monitoring programme provides an interesting example of a multiple baseline across subjects design which also incorporates a withdrawal of treatment phase. The aim of Rock's study was to support nine pupils in a mainstream school presenting problems with academic engagement, behaviour and performance in the curriculum. The programme combines elements of self-monitoring of attention and self-monitoring of academic performance in a novel strategy which incorporates goal setting and self-talk. The participants were organised into three groups with three participants in each. Two of the groups were located in the same grade four/five classroom and the third in a grade two classroom in the same school. The older pupils had a range of special needs including Asperger syndrome, floating harbour syndrome, learning disabilities and attention-deficit/hyperactivity disorder [see Rock (2005) for full details]. One was described as 'gifted and talented' but also was disengaged in class. Two of the younger group were developing but again were disengaged, and the third had attention-deficit/hyperactivity disorder. Dependent variables for the study were frequency data relating to academic engagement ('time on task') or academic disengagement ('time off task') and computer-generated measures of productivity and accuracy of academic work in mathematics in class. Inter-observer agreement for coding samples of the frequency data exceeded 80 per cent in all cases. The delivery of the intervention followed a similar pattern for each participant: a time-lagged baseline, followed by a period of intervention, followed by a period

Table 4.2. Results of Key-Word Searches from APA PsycNet for School Interventions for the 6- to 18-Year Age-Range Using Treatment Outcomes/Randomised, Controlled Trial (RCT) Designs

Years	N	RCT	Small-n
1980–9	2	0	1
1990–9	101	17	2
2000–9	558	171	12

of withdrawal of the intervention, followed by a second period of intervention. Overall, the results showed improvements following introduction of the intervention, then a decline in performance during the withdrawal of treatment, followed by a further improvement following the re-introduction of the intervention. However, there were differences between the groups. In contrast to participants in groups 2 and 3, the students in group 1 did not increase the accuracy of their academic work, for example. This may have been associated with some differences in the procedure followed by group 1 which included rewards for one participant. Overall, though, this study has high internal validity, with evidence for a causal relationship between the intervention and the observed changes in engagement, problem behaviours and academic performance which was evident for pupils with known special needs as well as more typically developing children. This highlights a strength of small-n designs: They can be used to explore whether an intervention has different outcomes for different subgroups within a population. However, results were reported using graphical displays and descriptive statistics (e.g., mean percentage rates during the different phases): The use of randomization tests may have strengthened the conclusions drawn further (Todman & Dugard, 2001).

The Impact of Experimental Designs on Real-World Educational Contexts

Experimental designs provide a means of determining the effects of intervention, with systematic reviews of RCTs and individual RCTs held to represent the highest levels of evidence in hierarchies of quality of research evidence (Sackett et al., 2000). But what is the impact of experimental designs on policy and practice in educational contexts?

Volumes such as those of McCall (1923) and Lindquist (1940) highlight the importance afforded to experimental designs in educational research in the first half of the last century. However, Campbell & Stanley (1963) note that thereafter they became less popular, although there was a resurgence of interest in the 1960s and 1970s in the United States at the time of evaluation of programmes such as Head Start (Robson, 2002).

The results of a key-word search of the American Psychological Association PsycNet computerized database shown in Table 4.2 is illustrative in this regard. Using the search terms 'school interventions', 'treatment outcomes' and 'randomized controlled trials' for the six- to eighteen-year age range, only two such published studies were identified for the period 1980–9, but 101 for the period 1990–9, rising to 558 for 2000–9, mirroring the prominence of evidence-based practice in health and the view of the RCT as the 'gold standard' for determining the effectiveness of interventions. Within these, it is possible to further distinguish RCT and small-n designs where these have been identified and to infer that most of the other studies are likely to be quasi-experimental designs or non-experimental designs, for example, correlational studies. Even acknowledging the flaws in this exercise, it is clear that there has been a marked increase in the number of published RCTs of interventions in schools over the last ten years and that small-n designs do not appear to be widely published in peer-reviewed journals. However, most published studies of the effectiveness of school-based interventions use quasi-experimental designs. Further support for this comes from two recent systematic reviews of the literature regarding the role of phonics in reading and spelling instruction (Ehri et al., 2001; Torgerson, Brooks & Hall, 2006) where of over 6,000 relevant studies, fewer than fifteen RCTs were identified in each study.

But is this a problem? There is a clear-cut case for carrying out an RCT if the funding body or sponsor requires it, for example, in the case of evaluations of complex interventions with high-stakes economic or policy implications where randomisation is crucial (Craig et al., 2008). However, as Mackenzie et al. (2010, p. 401) note, 'one size does not fit all' evaluations. There are particular merits in the use of small-n designs which, as in the case of Case Study 3, can lend themselves to the analysis of sub-groups of the kind advocated by Pawson & Tilley (1997). Audits of whether interventions of known efficacy are being implemented effectively may not even require a control group in cases where the participants are drawn from the same population as in an earlier RCT and the effect sizes and associated confidence intervals can be used to benchmark expected outcomes. Further, in cases where randomisation is not possible or feasible, a well-designed and focused quasi-experimental design may yet yield useful information, although, as we saw in Case Study 2, problems owing to selection bias or non-equivalence of groups may compromise the strength of the conclusions that can be drawn.

One further point is worth noting: It is important for educational researchers to be aware of the beliefs and values of participants and stakeholders and indeed of underlying policy contexts and political realities. 'Flexible' research designs (Anastas & MacDonald, 1994) can generate qualitative data which can inform an understanding of these issues, informed by approaches such as the critical incident technique (Flanagan, 1954; Butterfield et al., 2005; Davis, 2006). When combined with an experimental or quasi-experimental design as part of a 'mixed-model' approach, though, as in Case Study 1, qualitative data from interviews, questionnaires and focus groups can be triangulated with quantitative data from the study to cross-validate the findings and help in the interpretation of results. Threats to validity (e.g., differential attrition), specific elements of a process

model and the acceptability and feasibility of an intervention, for example, all could be investigated in this way and help to make studies more relevant to practitioners and policy-makers (Evans, 2003).

Conclusion

Torgerson & Torgerson (2008) report that educational researchers and social scientists in general carry out fewer RCTs than researchers in health-related disciplines, although the position is less clear regarding small-n designs. On one level, this may reflect funding patterns in health research and the needs of policy-makers in health, both of which may favour RCTs. However, on another level, it may reflect the concerns of educational researchers about the use of experimental designs, which include

- Philosophical objections: the view that RCTs and other experimental designs are positivist and deterministic in nature because they are based on the hypothetical-deductive model of science and alternative relativist and that interpreted approaches based on constructivism and social constructivism are more appropriate for educational research (Fox, 2003; Robson, 2002).
- Concerns about the feasibility of carrying out RCTs of practice in educational contexts in regard to training and resourcing issues (Fox, 2003; Robson, 2002).
- Concerns about how direct a role research in education may play in regard to policy and practice in regard to the dissemination of research evidence to education professionals and policy-makers and the integration of findings with experience as a practitioner to contribute to improvements in classroom practice (Hammersley, 2001).

With regard to philosophical concerns, Robson (2002, pp. 116–23) makes a spirited case for using RCTs and other fixed experimental designs from a realist/critical realist stance. Further, as we have seen, RCTs as well as quasi-experiments and small-*n* designs are being used to evaluate classroom activities and school-based interventions, so it is not impossible for researchers to use these methodologies.

Researchers must be mindful of the impact of their findings and make authoritative and accessible accounts of their work readily available. They also must ensure that processes of dissemination serve to make the work relevant to practitioners and policy-makers by directly addressing issues not only of effectiveness but also of acceptability and feasibility (Evans, 2003). Dissemination and knowledge transfer via consultation, training and evaluation lie at the heart of the challenge for implementation science. However, as Fixsen et al. (2009, p. 532) note, in settings such as education, social work and child welfare, 'the practitioner is the intervention'. It is the practitioner who has to address the key questions of 'What works, for whom, and in which contexts?' (Robson, 2002, p. 120), informed by an understanding of the nature of experiments and other methodologies and their application in real-world settings.

Acknowledgements

The study by Boyle et al. (2009) study was supported by a grant to the authors from the UK NHS Health Technology Assessment. The views and opinions expressed in this chapter do not necessarily reflect those of the sponsoring body.

References

Abramson, J. H. (1990). *Survey methods in community medicine*, 4th ed. Edinburgh: Churchill-Livingstone.

Abramson, J. H., & Abramson, Z. H. (2008). *Research methods in community medicine: Surveys, epidemiological research, programme evaluation, clinical trials*, 6th ed. Chichester: Wiley.

Anastas, J. W., & MacDonald, M. L. (1994). *Research design for social work and the human services*. Lexington, MA: Lexington Books.

Barlow, D. H., & Hersen, M. (1984). *Single case experimental designs: Strategies for studying behaviour change*, 2nd ed. London: Allyn & Bacon.

Begg, C., Cho, M., Eastwood, S., Horton, R., Moher, D., Olkin, I., Pitkin, R., Rennie, D., Schulz, K. F., Simel, D. & Stroup, D. F. (1996). Improving the quality of reporting randomised controlled trials: The CONSORT statement. *Journal of the American Medical Association* 276(8), 637–9.

Blank, M., Rose, S. A. & Berlin, L. J. (1978). *Preschool Language Assessment Instrument: The language of learning in practice*. Orlando, FL: Grune and Stratton.

Boyle, J., & McLellan, E. (1998). *The Early Language Skills Checklist: Observation-based assessment for early education*. London: Hodder & Stoughton.

Boyle, J., McCartney, E., O'Hare, A. & Forbes, J. (2009). Direct versus indirect and individual versus group modes of language therapy for children with primary language impairment. *International Journal of Language and Communication Disorders* 44(6), 826–46.

Brewer, J., & Hunter, A. (1989). *Multi-method research: A synthesis of styles*. Newbury Park, CA: Sage.

Butterfield, L. D., Borgen, W. A., Amundson, N. E. & Maglio, A. S. (2005). Fifty years of the critical incident technique: 1954–2004 and beyond. *Qualitative Research* 5, 475–97.

Campbell, D. T., & Stanley, J. C. (1963). Experimental and quasi-experimental designs for research on teaching. In N. L. Gage (ed.), *Handbook of research on teaching*. Chicago: Rand McNally.

Cook, T. D., & Campbell, D. (1979). *Quasi-experimentation: Design and analysis issues for field settings*. Boston: Houghton Mifflin.

Craig, P., Dieppe, P., Macintyre, S., Mitchie, S., Nazareth, I. & Petticrew, M. (2008). Developing and evaluating complex interventions: The new Medical Research Council guidelines. *British Medical Journal* 337, 979–83.

Davis, P. (2006). Critical incident technique: A learning intervention for organizational problem solving. *Development and Learning in Organizations* 20(2), 13–16.

Dickson, K., Marshall, M., Boyle, J., McCartney, E., O'Hare, A. & Forbes, J. F. (2009). Cost analysis of direct versus indirect and individual versus group modes of manual based speech and language therapy for primary aged school children with primary language impairment. *International Journal of Language and Communication Disorders* 44(3), 369–81.

Ehri, L., Nunes, S., Stahl, S. & Willows, D. (2001). Systematic phonics instruction helps students learn to read: Evidence from the National Reading Panel's meta-analysis. *Review of Educational Research* 71, 393–447.

Evans, D. (2003). Hierarchy of evidence: A framework for ranking evidence evaluating healthcare interventions. *Journal of Clinical Nursing* 12, 77–84.

Field, A. P. (2009). *Discovering statistics using SPSS: And sex and drugs and rock 'n' roll*, 3rd ed. London: Sage.

Fixsen, D. L., Blase, K. A., Naoom, S. F. & Wallace, F. (2009). Core implementation components. *Research on Social Work Practice* 19(5), 531–40.

Flanagan, J. C. (1954). The critical incident technique. *Psychological Bulletin* 51(4), 327–58.

Fox, M. (2003). Opening Pandora's box: Evidence-based practice for educational psychologists. *Educational Psychology in Practice* 19(2), 91–102.

Hammersley, M. (2001). Some questions about evidence-based practice in education. Paper presented at the symposium on 'Evidence-based practice in education' at the Annual Conference of the British Educational Research Association, University of Leeds, UK, September 13–15, 2001.

Jadad, A.R., & Enkin, M. W. (2007). *Randomised, controlled trials: Questions, answers and musings*, 2nd. ed. Oxford, UK: Blackwell Publishing/BMJ Books.

Kazdin, A. E. (1984). Statistical analyses for single-case experimental designs. In D. H. Barlow and M. Hersen (eds.), *Single case experimental designs: Strategies for studying behavior change*, 2nd ed. (Chap. 9, pp. 285–324). London: Allyn & Bacon.

Kratochwill, T. R. (ed.) (1978). *Single subject research: Strategies for evaluating change.* New York: Academic Press.

Lindquist, E. F. (1940). *Statistical analysis in educational research.* Boston: Houghton Mifflin.

Mackenzie, M., O'Donnell, C., Halliday, E., Sridharan. S. & Platt, S. (2010). Evaluating complex interventions: One size does not fit all. *British Medical Journal* 340, 401–3.

McCall, W. A. (1923). *How to experiment in education.* New York: Macmillan.

Pawson, R., & Tilley, N. (1997). *Realistic evaluation.* London: Sage.

Robinson, P. W., & Foster, D. F. (1979). *Experimental psychology: A small-n approach.* New York: Harper & Row.

Robson, C. (2002). *Real world research*, 2nd ed. Oxford, UK: Blackwell Publishing.

Rock, M. L. (2005). Use of strategic self-monitoring to enhance academic engagement, productivity, and accuracy of students with and without exceptionalities. *Journal of Positive Behavior Interventions* 7(1), 3–17.

Sackett, D. L., Strauss, S. E., Richardson, W. S., Rosenberg, W. & Haynes, R. B. (2000). *Evidence-based medicine: How to practice and teach EBM.* Edinburgh: Churchill-Livingstone.

Todman, J. B., & Dugard, P. (2001). *Single-case and small-n experimental designs: A practical guide to randomization tests.* Mahwah, NJ: Erlbaum.

Torgerson, C. J., Brooks, G. & Hall, J. (2006). *A systematic review of the research literature on the use of phonics in the teaching of reading and spelling.* London: DfES Research Report 711.

Torgerson, D. J., & Torgerson, C. J. (2008). *Designing randomised trials in health, education and the social sciences: An introduction.* Basingstoke, Hampshire: Palgrave Macmillan.

Zhang, X., & Tomblin, J. B. (2003) Explaining and controlling regression to the mean in longitudinal research designs: Tutorial. *Journal of Speech, Language and Hearing Sciences* 46(6), 1340–51.

Zwarenstein, M., Treweek, S., Gagnier, J. J., Altman, D. G., Tunis, S., Haynes, B., Oxman, A. D. & Moher, D., for the CONSORT and Pragmatic Trials in Healthcare (Practihc) Groups (2008). Improving the reporting of pragmatic trials: An extension of the CONSORT statement. *British Medical Journal* 337, 1–8.

CHAPTER 5

Meta-Analysis of Implementation Practice Research

Carl J. Dunst and Carol M. Trivette

Fixsen et al. (2005), in their review and analysis of the state of implementation science research, make a distinction between two types of evidence-based practices and outcomes: implementation and intervention practices and implementation and intervention outcomes. 'Intervention practices' include methods and strategies used by intervention agents (e.g., teachers, clinicians, parent educators, etc.) to effect changes or produce desired outcomes in a targeted population or group of recipients (e.g., students). In contrast, 'implementation practices' include a 'specific set of activities' (Fixsen et al., 2005, p. 5) used by implementation agents to promote the adoption and use of evidence-based intervention practices by intervention agents.

Figure 5.1 shows graphically the distinction between implementation and intervention practices and outcomes and the relationship between the two sets of activities (i.e., methods, procedures, strategies, etc.). Implementation practices include the methods (Donovan, Bransford & Pellegrino, 1999; Fixsen et al., 2005) used to teach or train others to use evidence-based intervention

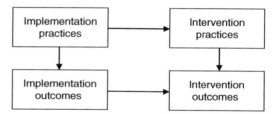

Figure 5.1. Relationship between implementation and intervention practices and outcomes.

practices (Dunst & Trivette, 2009b; Kazdin, 2008). It is important to recognize that 'no intervention practice, no matter what its evidence base, is likely to be learned or adopted if the methods and strategies used to teach or train students, practitioners, parents, or others are not themselves effective' (Dunst & Trivette, 2009a, p. 164). Accordingly, explicit attention to the characteristics of evidence-based implementation practices is essential to promote the adoption and use of evidence-based intervention practices.

Both implementation and intervention practices are amenable to investigation using any number of research methodologies (e.g., Bickman & Rog, 1998; Shadish,

Cook & Campbell, 2002), and studies of the same or similar implementation or intervention practices are amenable to integrative reviews using meta-analysis or another type of research synthesis (e.g., Cooper, Hedges & Valentine, 2009; Popay, 2006). This chapter includes a description of how meta-analysis can be used for synthesising findings from implementation practices research. The meta-analytical approach that is described goes beyond questions of efficacy or effectiveness to the identification of the key characteristics of implementation (or any other kind of) practice to isolate what matters most in terms of understanding which elements of implementation influence the adoption and use of evidence-based intervention practices. The goal of the chapter is to provide psychologists and educators with practical information for understanding how the findings from meta-analytical research syntheses can inform the adoption and use of evidence-based implementation practices.

The chapter is divided into five sections. The first includes a brief overview of implementation science, research and practice to place the content of the chapter in proper context. The second includes a framework for categorising different types of implementation and intervention studies. The third includes a description of different types of research syntheses and an expanded framework for categorising systematic and integrative reviews of different types of implementation and intervention research. The fourth includes a non-technical description of meta-analysis with a focus on a particular approach to conducting a research synthesis which attempts to unbundle (Leviton & Lipsey, 2007; Lipsey, 1993) and unpack and disentangle (Dunst & Trivette, 2009b; Dunst, Trivette & Cutspec, 2007) the characteristics of implementation practices that influence the adoption and use of evidence-based intervention practices. The latter type of meta-analysis is illustrated in the fifth section of the chapter using a research synthesis of adult learning methods (Dunst, Trivette & Hamby, 2010) to show the yield from this type of practice-

based translational research synthesis. The chapter concludes with a discussion of the implications of meta-analysis for informing advances in implementation research and practice.

Implementation Science, Research and Practice

As noted by Kelly (Chapter 1), 'implementation science is concerned with an understanding' of the processes that promote or impede the transferability of evidence-based intervention practices into real-world contexts and how the use of scientific methods can inform that understanding. Scientific methods include the theoretical, conceptual and operational frameworks for describing or hypothesising the relationships among variables of interest (e.g., Babbie, 2004). Accordingly, implementation science is concerned with the development and use of models that help to elucidate the processes associated with and the conditions under which evidence-based intervention practices can be exported and implemented as part of routine practice.

A better understanding of the processes that operate to promote adoption and use of evidence-based intervention practices is facilitated by implementation research. 'Implementation research' is the 'scientific study of methods to promote the systematic uptake of…research findings and other evidence-based practices to improve the quality…of health care', education, psychological treatments and other types of interventions (Eccles et al., 2009, p. 2). At least one major focus of implementation research ought to be identification of the features of implementation practices which are empirically associated with the use of evidence-based intervention practices with a high degree of fidelity (Carroll et al., 2007).

One of the desired outcomes of implementation research is identification of the active ingredients (Clark, 2009) or key characteristics (Dunst & Trivette, 2009b) of implementation practices that best explain the adoption and use of evidence-based intervention practices. Any implementation method or practice can be conceptualised as being 'made up' of many features and elements where certain characteristics or combinations of characteristics are likely to be more important than others as the determinants of adoption and use of evidence-based intervention practices. For example, a multi-component procedure for promoting teacher adoption of an innovative set of instructional practices could be disaggregated and evaluated in terms of which component or combination of components is related to differential teacher and student outcomes (Meehan et al., 2004). This cannot but lead to a better understanding of which practices under which conditions with which persons in which kinds of settings optimise the transferability, uptake and sustained use of intervention practices.

Implementation science is a relatively new field of inquiry, and the conduct of implementation research is relatively new as well. Nonetheless, implementation practice is now a major focus of many different kinds of research studies (see especially www.implementationscience.com). According to Davies (2006), research syntheses of implementation studies are important not only because they can help to identify what works with whom and how in different contexts and environments but also because research syntheses of implementation research are likely to uncover facilitators and barriers to adoption of evidence-based intervention practices which can to inform changes or improvements in implementation practices.

Types of Research Studies

Research in psychology and education historically has been characterised as either basic or applied research (e.g., Elmes, Kantowitz & Roediger, 1992) or basic, applied or evaluation research (e.g., Miller & Salkind, 2002). Implementation research is inherently applied in its purpose and function. Different types of research studies have been described which frame the purposes and goals of implementation (as well as other kinds of) studies.

Flay et al. (2005) made a distinction between efficacy and effectiveness studies which is often used to categorise or compare contrasting types of investigations (e.g., Brown et al., 2008; Glasgow, Lichtenstein & Marcus, 2003). 'Efficacy studies' evaluate the extent to which an intervention (i.e., technology, treatment, procedure, service or program) has hypothesised or expected effects when implemented under controlled conditions (e.g., van Doesum et al., 2008). 'Effectiveness studies' evaluate the extent to which interventions found effective under controlled conditions are effective when implemented in real-world contexts (e.g., Paul, Redman & Sanson-Fisher, 2004). Both efficacy and effectiveness studies typically involve comparisons between intervention and non-intervention study participants, but they also include comparative studies of contrasting types of interventions that are intended to have the same outcome (e.g., Fordis et al., 2005; Whitten et al., 1998).

Andrews (1999) and Marley (2000) describe a third type of study which they call 'efficiency research'. Efficiency studies evaluate the extent to which an intervention is considered worthwhile and acceptable to intended audiences (e.g., Metzger et al., 2000). Marley noted, for example, that even the most efficacious intervention implemented under controlled conditions may not be seen as acceptable by persons when implemented as part of routine practice. The acceptability and importance of an intervention, as well as its intended benefits, are determined, in part, by the extent to which a practice is judged socially valid by implementation and intervention agents (Foster & Mash, 1999).

A fourth type of study termed 'translational research' focuses on the extent to which research-generated knowledge, or the most important characteristics of evidence-based practices, inform the conduct of routine practices (Woolf, 2008). Spoth et al. (2008) made a distinction between two types of translational research based on recommendations by the U.S. Department of Health and Human Services, National Institutes of Health (National Institutes of Health, 2007). The first, called 'type 1 translational research', uses findings from other types of research (e.g., efficacy studies) to develop and test the effects of interventions in routine practice informed by that research (e.g., Dunning et al., 1999). The second, called 'type 2 translational research', employs findings from implementation research studies to inform interventions to promote the adoption, use and sustainability of evidence-based intervention practices in typical settings (e.g., Rohrbach et al., 2006).

The distinction made earlier between type of practice and the four types of studies just described is the basis for the framework shown in Figure 5.2. As shown in the figure, both implementation and intervention practices can be investigated in terms of their efficacy, effectiveness, efficiency or translational implications. Randomised, controlled trials (RCTs) of continuing-education practices (e.g., Sibley et al., 1982), the effectiveness of implementation practices used in typical programs or settings (e.g., Pazirandeh, 2000), comparisons of and preferences for different types of continuing education (e.g., Davis et al., 1999; Hobma et al., 2004) and the use research findings to inform continuing education (e.g., Cole & Glass, 2004) are examples of the four types of studies, respectively. Comparative studies of the efficacy, effectiveness, efficiency and evidence-informed implementation and

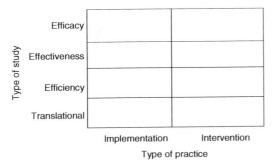

Figure 5.2. Framework for categorising different types of implementation and intervention studies.

intervention practices are also examples of the different types of studies (e.g., Fordis et al., 2005; Lacoursiere et al., 1997; Whitten et al., 1998).

The framework in Figure 5.2 expands on the distinction of Fixsen et al. (2005) between implementation and intervention practices by differentiating between two types of practice and four types of studies, each with their own goals, methods, procedures and outcomes. In principle, studies of practices in each of the eight cells in Figure 5.2 could be designed and carried out where each type of study leads to a better understanding of either or both implementation or intervention practices.

Research Syntheses of Implementation and Intervention Practices

Few studies provide such conclusive evidence that it is not necessary to further investigate a phenomenon of interest. More often than not, studies of the same phenomenon produce inconsistent and in many cases conflicting evidence. For these as well as other reasons, literature reviews are conducted to make sense of bodies of research on the same or similar phenomena. Literature reviews of empirical investigations have variously been called 'research syntheses' (Chalmers, Hedges & Cooper, 2002), 'integrative reviews' (Cooper, 1984), and 'systematic reviews' (Chalmers & Altman, 1995).

Research Synthesis

A 'research synthesis 'is an integrative or systematic review of studies which focus on the relationship between a target practice and the outcome(s) the practice is intended to effect. One goal of a research synthesis is establishing the extent to which there is consistency in the nature of the relationships between variables of interest in multiple studies.

Cooper, Hedges & Valentini (2009, p. 6) define a 'research synthesis' as the 'conjunction of a particular set of literature review characteristics....research syntheses

Table 5.1. Representative Categorisations of Different Types of Research Reviews and Syntheses

| Authors | Types of Reviews | | | | |
	Narrative Reviews	Descriptive Reviews	Vote Counting	Best Evidence Synthesis	Meta-Analysis
Davies (2000)	X		X	X	X
Kavale (2001)	X	X			X
King & He (2005)	X	X	X		X
Suri (2000)	X			X	X

attempt to integrate empirical research for the purpose of creating generalizations'. According to Davies (2000, p. 367), a 'research synthesis' includes 'methods for summarizing, integrating and, where possible, cumulating the findings of different studies on a topic or research question'. Similarly, Cooper (1984, p. 10) defined a 'research synthesis (integrative review)' as a set of procedures to 'summarize past research by drawing overall conclusions from many separate studies that are believed to address related or identical hypotheses'.

Most definitions of a research synthesis include descriptions of attempts to pool or summarise findings from different studies of the same phenomenon or practice with a focus on the replicability of the results across investigations (Thompson, 2005). Existing definitions of a research synthesis can be expanded to include literature reviews for discerning the efficacy of implementation or intervention practices ('efficacy syntheses'); the effectiveness of evidence-based practices when used in typical settings and programs ('effectiveness syntheses'); the acceptability of implementation or intervention practices by teachers, clinicians and so on ('efficiency syntheses'); the identification of the evidence-based characteristics of practices for informing implementation or intervention methods and strategies ('translational syntheses'); or any other type of implementation or intervention practice (e.g., relative effectiveness of two contrasting types of practices designed to have the same outcomes). Accordingly, a 'research synthesis' can be defined as the systematic review and

analysis of a literature where the focus of the studies included in the review permits identification of the relationships between variables of interest and a better understanding of the processes that operate to explain the nature of the relationship (Dunst et al., 2007; National Research Council, 2002).

Types of Research Syntheses

Research reviews and syntheses can be categorised along a qualitative-quantitative continuum that include narrative reviews, descriptive reviews, vote-counting reviews, best-evidence syntheses and meta-analyses. Table 5.1 shows several representative categorisations of research reviews and syntheses. The interested reader is referred to Blettner et al. (1999), Davies (2000) and Popay (2006) for descriptions of other types of reviews and syntheses.

NARRATIVE SYNTHESES
Narrative, or traditional, literature reviews 'attempt to identify what has been written on a subject or topic, using which methodologies, on what samples or populations, and what findings' (Davies, 2000, p. 367). Narrative reviews of research studies typically include summaries of the results from primary studies and interpretative statements about the nature of the relationships between variables of interest and the effects or impacts of an implementation or intervention practice (Hannes, 2010). These types of syntheses often employ a theoretical or conceptual framework for analysing the studies included in the synthesis. Spillane,

Resser & Reimers' (2002) analysis of the role that different kinds of cognitions (altitudes and beliefs) have on teacher adoption of new or innovative instructional practices is an example of a narrative review. Research syntheses of qualitative studies are a particular type of narrative review (e.g., Britten et al., 2002; Jones, 2004).

DESCRIPTIVE SYNTHESES

Descriptive reviews are similar to narrative reviews but include some type(s) of quantification, often in terms of patterns of findings according to, for example, type of intervention, setting, research designs or study participants. The findings from these types of reviews are often described as the 'state of the art' or 'state of the science' for a practice. Durlak & DuPre's (2008) analysis of factors associated with fidelity of implementation and the effects of fidelity on program outcomes is an example of a descriptive review. The outcome of descriptive reviews generally is a series of statements or conclusions about 'what is known' about a practice or intervention.

VOTE-COUNTING SYNTHESES

Vote counting is a particular approach to conducting a research synthesis that explicitly takes into consideration the statistical relationship between variables of interest using significance levels or other probability metrics for quantifying the results from different studies. Light & Smith (1971, p. 433), who first described the method some forty years age, noted that

> All studies which have data on a dependent variable and a specific independent variable of interest are examined. Three possible outcomes are defined. The relationship between the independent variable and the dependent variable is either significantly positive, significantly negative, or there is no specific relationship in either direction. The number of studies falling into each of these three categories is then simply tallied. If a plurality of studies falls into any one of these three categories, with fewer falling into the other two, the modal category is declared the winner.

As part of a research synthesis of student-centred, problem-based learning, Dochy et al. (2003) used the Light & Smith (1971) approach to vote counting to establish the effectiveness of student-centred compared to lecture-based instruction. Bushman & Wang (2009) describe advances in vote-counting methods that provide better ways of determining how tests of statistical significance can be used to evaluate the relationship between independent and dependent variables.

BEST-EVIDENCE SYNTHESES

Best-evidence research syntheses represent a middle ground between traditional literature reviews and meta-analyses (described below) by combining the quantification of study results with the systematic examination of better designed and implemented studies to identify the best evidence for a practice (Slavin, 1986). This type of research synthesis uses a priori standards to identify well-conducted and unbiased studies, examining each in considerable detail, and computing pooled or average sizes of effects for studies categorised as similar according to some study characteristic. According to Slavin (1995), studies that are best suited for identifying effective practices are ones that are judged as both internally and externally valid (Shadish et al., 2002) and therefore carry more weight in terms of determining the evidence for the practice. This type of research synthesis has been used by Slavin et al. for identifying the best evidence for a number of different implementation, instructional and teaching practices (e.g., Gutiérrez & Slavin, 1992; Slavin & Cheung, 2005).

META-ANALYTICAL SYNTHESES

Meta-analysis is not a single approach to research syntheses but rather a family of approaches which share one common feature, namely, the use of effect sizes for assessing the relationship between a practice and an outcome, where the combined results from a series of studies are used to evaluate the average effect of a practice. An 'effect size' is a measure of the strength of the relationship between two variables expressed in terms of a quantitative metric (Hedges, 2008).

Research syntheses that use meta-analytical methods rely on the statistical analysis of study results as the basis for integrating (i.e., synthesising) and interpreting findings from studies of the same or similar practice. Meta-analysis 'combines individual study treatment effects into a "pooled" treatment effect for all the studies combined, and for specific subgroups of studies' (Davies, 2000, p. 368). This approach to a research synthesis permits meta-analysts to determine the extent to which the results from many studies yield consistent results and thus provide empirical evidence for a practice. One of the more common effect size metrics is the post-test mean difference between experimental and control (or comparison) groups on an outcome measure divided by the pooled standard deviation of that measure. This standardised score, calculated for the results in each of the studies in the research synthesis, is combined (i.e., averaged) and used for substantive interpretation of the aggregated results.

A practice-based research synthesis, described in detail in the next section of the chapter, is a particular type of meta-analysis which focuses on identification of the characteristics of a practice most strongly associated with observed effects or outcomes. These types of syntheses involve the analysis of studies examining the same or similar practices where the different characteristics (i.e., elements, features, components, etc.) of the practices are coded and analysed so that the presence and absence of the characteristics can be related to variations in the study outcomes. For example, Clow et al. (2005) analysed studies of educational outreach to affect physician prescribing practices in terms of thirteen practice characteristics and found that five characteristics (i.e., baseline knowledge, message credibility, repeating a message, positive reinforcement and physician motivation) 'stood out' as most important in terms of affecting changes in prescribing practices.

Practice-based research syntheses are especially amendable to type 2 translational research syntheses because one goal of this type of integrative review is the identification of practice characteristics which can directly inform the ways in which research findings are used to promote or improve the adoption and use of evidence-based intervention practices (Rohrbach et al., 2006). A practice-based research synthesis, for example, can yield the kind of information needed to ensure that the most important characteristics of implementation practices are used to effect adoption of the evidence-based intervention in everyday, routine practice (National Institutes of Health, 2007; Tansella & Thornicroft, 2009).

Framework for Categorising Research Syntheses

The different types of research syntheses briefly described in this section can be incorporated easily into the framework introduced earlier (Figure 5.2) to include the review and analysis of different types of studies. Figure 5.3 shows such a framework that includes two types of practices, four types of studies and five types of research syntheses. Accordingly, different types of studies of either implementation or intervention practices are amendable to a research synthesis to the extent that enough studies of the same or similar practices can be located that also include investigation of the same or similar outcomes. The various cells in Figure 5.3 each represent different types of research syntheses that can yield answers to different kinds of questions (e.g., efficacy, effectiveness, etc.). The types of research syntheses shown in Figure 5.3 are illustrative, and any categorisation of different types of research syntheses can be accommodated (e.g., Blettner et al., 1999). The conduct of meta-analyses of implementation practice research, or a type 2 translational research synthesis, is the focus of the remainder of this chapter.

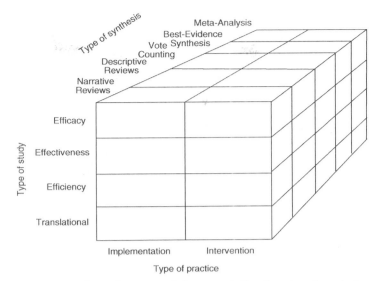

Figure 5.3. Three-dimensional framework for showing the relationships between different types of practices, studies and research syntheses.

A Proposed Approach to Meta-Analysis of Implementation Practice Research

The conduct of a meta-analysis is similar to the conduct of a primary study where a study rather than an individual participant is the unit of analysis. A meta-analysis of implementation practice research, or any other type of practice, requires attention to the same methodological considerations that are important as part of planning and carrying out a primary study. In addition, meta-analysis requires special attention to other procedural, methodological, statistical and data analysis procedures that are unique to this type of research syntheses. A detailed description of many of these considerations is beyond the scope of this chapter. The interested reader is referred to Cooper et al. (2009), Hunter & Schmidt (2004), and Lipsey & Wilson (2001) for a discussion of these matters. The purpose here is to outline a strategy to meta-analysis applicable to implementation practice research with an emphasis on unbundling (Lipsey, 1993) and unpacking (Dunst & Trivette, 2009b) the characteristics of

implementation methods which inform procedures for promoting the adoption and use of evidence-based intervention practices. The process of conducting a practice-based translational research synthesis is similar to that used in the conduct of most meta-analyses (e.g., Chalmers & Altman, 1995; Cooper, 1984) but includes a number of additional features that permit one to 'dig deeper' to identify the most important features of a practice.

Identifying the Practice of Interest

A meta-analysis of implementation practices research starts with identification and description of which practice or practices will be the focus of a research synthesis. This can be either a particular implementation practice (e.g., Eby et al., 2008) or two or more implementation practices that are designed to have the same or similar effects or consequences (e.g., Bero et al., 1998). Identification of the implementation practice(s) of interest helps to establish which methods and procedures for which purpose(s) will be the focus of analysis.

Problem Formation

The 'problem-formation phase' of a research synthesis of implementation practices research is concerned with the questions that one wants to answer from a synthesis of relevant studies. The four types of research studies described earlier can provide guidance: 'Is Implementation Method X effective when implemented under ideal or controlled conditions?' (efficacy), 'Is Implementation Method X effective when used in routine practice?' (effectiveness), 'To what extent is Implementation Method X adopted and used by implementation agents to promote practitioners' use of intervention practices?' (efficiency), and 'What are the key characteristics of Implementation Method X that have implications for informing adoption and use of evidence-based implementation practices?' (translational). The question or questions that guide the conduct of a research synthesis will determine the kinds of studies included in a systematic review. The problem-formation phase also will influence a better understanding of which kinds of studies will and will not be included in the research synthesis.

Identification of Relevant Studies

Once the practice or practices of interest have been identified and the question(s) to be answered about the practice have been identified, the next phase is to identify relevant studies. A search for studies should be systematic, comprehensive and exhaustive. A multi-faceted approach to identifying relevant studies more likely will locate the largest number of investigations of the practice of interest.

The sources for identifying studies include, but are not limited to, electronic reference databases (e.g., ERIC, PsychInfo and MEDLINE), author and journal article citation indexes (e.g., Social Science Citation Index), *Dissertation Abstracts International*, the Internet (e.g., Google Scholar), journals, books, book chapters, conference proceedings, bibliographies (e.g., *Sources of Information in the Social Sciences*),

unpublished studies or grey literature (e.g., Schöpfel & Farace, 2010) and contact with researchers who have investigated the practice that is the focus of the research synthesis. The reference sections of all retrieved material are also reviewed to identify additional studies.

Searches of electronic databases such as ERIC and PsychInfo are performed using controlled vocabulary as well as natural-language searches. Most electronic databases have a thesaurus of terms used to index entries. The use of these terms to identify studies is called a 'controlled vocabulary search'. Natural-language, or free-text, searching uses terms likely to be included in the title and the abstract or summary of a study. The interested reader is referred to Lucas & Cutspec (2007) for a description of the particular strategy for conducting a practice-based research synthesis search.

Coding the Studies

This phase of a research synthesis entails coding different study, participant, intervention, outcome and other variables of interest. Study characteristics include, but are not limited to, the type of study design or methodology (e.g., random versus non-random participant assignment), unit of assignment to groups (e.g., individual versus group), type of publication (e.g., published versus unpublished), year of publication and study quality. Participant characteristics include, but are not limited to, gender, age, socioeconomic status, ethnicity and sample size. Intervention characteristics include, but are not limited to, intervention agent (e.g., researcher versus teacher), setting (e.g., laboratory versus classroom), degree of intervention fidelity, duration of the intervention, dose and type of intervention (e.g., method X versus method Y). Outcome characteristics include, but are not limited to, outcome domain or construct, type of measure (e.g., standardised versus non-standardised), data source (e.g., observation versus self-report) and time of measurement. The use of as complete a coding scheme as possible permits more specific kinds of analyses of the research synthesis data. The reader is referred to Lipsey & Wilson (2001, appendix E) for a more detailed description of the variables that typically are included in a meta-analysis coding scheme.

A practice-based research synthesis differs from most other meta-analyses by the explicit coding of specific characteristics of an implementation method or practice to identify which characteristics are most important in terms of the strength of the relationship with the outcomes in the studies. The studies included in a practice-based research synthesis are coded using either some type of a priori or evolving coding scheme that permits as much specificity as possible in terms of the characteristics that make up the practice which is the focus of investigation. For example, Tornatzky & Klein (1982) used five a priori identified characteristics of innovations to discern which characteristics were associated with adoption of intervention practices. Durlak & DuPre's (2008) identification of factors associated with implementation fidelity and the intended benefits of innovative interventions is an example of an evolving or post hoc identification of characteristics and features of effective implementation practices.

Effect Size Coding

This phase of a meta-analysis involves calculation of the effect sizes for each of the outcomes included in a study and the aggregation of the sizes of effect. When calculating an effect, it is important to code the type of comparison or contrast that is the source of the size of effect. These can include, but are not limited to, the effect sizes for the post-test differences between an experimental and control group; pre-test–post-test differences for an experimental and comparison group, before and after comparisons of two contrasting types of interventions; or the pre-test–post-test differences for a single group of participants.

One needs to decide which type of effect size will be used for evaluating the strength of the relationship between variables. There are basically two families of effect sizes: the r family and the d family (Rosenthal, 1994). The r family includes the Pearson product moment correlation and its many variants (point–bi-serial, phi, etc.). The d family includes Cohen's d effect size for the difference between two mean scores divided by the pooled standard deviation for the two measures, as well as other between-group difference metrics (Glass' Δ, Hedges' g, etc.). The r effect size is useful in studies where variations in one variable are related to variations in another variable (e.g., observational studies). The d effect size is useful in studies where intervention versus non-intervention or contrasting condition comparisons are the focus of analysis. Rosnow, Rosenthal & Rubon (2000) describe how the two types of effect sizes are related (see also Rosenthal, 1994).

Once the effect sizes for all the outcomes are computed, they are then averaged. The average, or pooled, effect sizes in a meta-analysis are adjusted, giving more weight to studies with larger sample sizes. This is accomplished by weighting each individual effect size taking into consideration its variance (Lipsey & Wilson, 2001). This average effect size is considered the best estimate of the real effect between an independent or predictor variable and an outcome.

The extent to which the 'spread' in the effect sizes around the average is small (homogeneous) or large (heterogeneous) is determined by computing its 95 per cent confidence interval. A 'confidence interval' tells us the probability that the true or population average effect size is within a certain range. For example, an average effect size of 0.50 with a 95 per cent confidence interval of 0.40 and 0.60 tells us that there is a 95 per cent likelihood that the true effect size is somewhere between these two extremes.

Data Analysis and Interpretation

A number of different data analysis methods are used in meta-analysis to aid in interpretation of research synthesis results (see especially Hedges, 1994). Several of these are described briefly here.

The 'Z statistic' is used to determine if an average weighted effect size is statistically significant at the level specified by a confidence interval. The Z statistic is a measure of whether the average effect size differs significantly from zero (Shadish & Haddock, 1994). Parenthetically, a 95 per cent confidence interval that does not include zero is statistically significant at the 0.05 level.

The extent to which the individual effect sizes that contribute to the average effect size are homogeneous is assessed using the within-groups Q statistic (Lipsey & Wilson, 2001). Q is a measure of how much spread (variability) there is around the average. A significant Q indicates considerable variability in the sizes of effects contributing to the average effect size. This is one of the bases of further disaggregation of the data, as described below.

The extent to which the average effect sizes for two or more comparative conditions (e.g., implementation method X versus implementation method Y) differ significantly from one another is determined by the between-groups heterogeneity statistic Q_{BET}. The 'Q_{BET} test' is 'analogous to the omnibus F test for variation in group means in a one-way ANOVA' (Hedges, 1994, p. 290).

Effect Size Disaggregation

The unbundling (Lipsey, 1993) and unpacking (Dunst & Trivette, 2009b) of effect size data is accomplished through systematic analysis of the relationships between the various variables included in the coding protocol, with special attention to the practice characteristics coding. If, for example, a particular implementation method or approach was the focus of investigation, but several different types of practices were used to engage intervention agents in using a targeted practice, the average effect sizes for the different practices would be computed to determine if particular practices are more effective than others in terms of their relationships with the study outcomes. The process of unbundling and unpacking implementation methods is facilitated by using a framework for coding the practices

and analysing the results to identify 'what works best'. Durlak & DuPre (2008), for example, proposed a set of implementation characteristics that might influence the adoption and use of evidence-based intervention practices which could be used for disaggregation.

Effect size disaggregation is further aided by moderator and mediator analyses (Baron & Kenny, 1986; Shadish & Sweeney, 1991). A 'moderator' is a variable (e.g., dose) that influences the relationship between an independent and dependent variable. If, for example, the effects of an implementation practice is different depending on dose, then dose is said to 'moderate' the effects of the practice. A 'mediator' is a variable that accounts for the relationship between an independent and dependent variable. In the case where an implementation method is not related directly to an outcome but rather is related indirectly to the outcome through a third variable, the third variable is said to 'mediate' the relationship between the implementation practice and its consequences. In our meta-analytical research, for example, the effects of practitioner capacity building in helping to give practices on parenting confidence and competence have been found to be indirect mediated by parents' self-efficacy beliefs (Dunst, Trivette & Hamby, 2006, 2008).

Report Preparation

Cooper (1984) and Lipsey & Wilson (2001), as well as others (see, e.g., Cooper et al., 2009), recommend that different types of reports of the results from meta-analyses be prepared for researchers, practitioners and policy-makers. It is good practice to write plain-language (DuBay, 2007) descriptions of the implications of the findings for policy and practice. Practice-based translational research syntheses should include a report for implementation researchers or practitioners or both. In our own approach to meta-analysis and other research syntheses, we prepare both technical reports and non-technical (plain-language) summaries of both the findings and implications for

Table 5.2. Characteristics of the Adult Learning Methods that Were the Focus of Analysis

Features/Characteristics	Definition
Planning	
Introduce	Engage the learner in a preview of the material, knowledge or practice that is the focus of instruction or training.
Illustrate	Demonstrate or illustrate the use or applicability of the material, knowledge or practice for the learner
Application	
Practice	Engage the learner in the use of the material, knowledge or practice.
Evaluate	Engage the learner in a process of evaluating the consequence or outcomes of the application of the material, knowledge or practice
Deep understanding	
Reflection	Engage the learner in self-assessment of his or her acquisition of knowledge and skills as a basis for identifying 'next steps' in the learning process
Mastery	Engage the learner in a process of assessing his or her experience in the context of some conceptual or practical model or framework or some external set of standards or criteria

practice for different audiences depending on the practice constituting the focus of analysis (see, e.g., www.tracecenter.info/products.php).

An Illustrative Example

A recently completed meta-analysis of four adult learning methods (Dunst, Trivette & Hamby, 2010) is used to illustrate the conduct of a practice-based translational research synthesis. The four methods, taken together, constitute different types of implementation practices that were used by faculty, trainers and other implementation agents to promote learners' understanding and use of different kinds of knowledge or practice.

The meta-analysis was guided by findings reported in a narrative research synthesis of the science of learning (Bransford et al., 2000). Findings from this review were used to operationally define six adult learning method characteristics and to code the studies in the research synthesis in terms of use of the characteristics. Table 5.2 shows the characteristics. The three main features were 'planning', 'application' and 'deep understanding'. 'Planning' included the methods and procedures for both (1) introducing new

knowledge, material or practices to learners and (2) illustrating and demonstrating the use of the knowledge, material or practices. 'Application' included the methods and procedures for both (1) learner use of the knowledge, material or practices and (2) learner evaluation of the outcome or consequence of that experience. 'Deep understanding' included methods and procedures for (1) engaging the learner in reflection on his or her learning experience and (2) learner self-assessment of knowledge or practice mastery as a foundation for identifying new learning opportunities.

Practices of Interest

The four adult learning methods were accelerated learning, coaching, guided design and just-in-time training. The methods were selected for analysis because they have been used for both pre-service and in-service professional development in early childhood education, education and special education (e.g., Brown, 1986; Cain, Rudd & Saxon, 2007; Coscarelli & White, 1982; Craven, 1990; Davis, 2005; Ludlow, Faieta & Wienke, 1989), and the effectiveness of the learning methods has been evaluated using randomised, controlled design studies.

'Accelerated learning' is an adult learning method that includes procedures for creating a relaxed emotional state, an orchestrated and multi-sensory learning environment and active learner engagement in the learning process (Meier, 2000). 'Coaching is a…method of transferring skills and expertise from more experienced and knowledgeable practitioners…to less experienced ones' (Hargreaves & Dawe, 1990, p. 230) and includes procedures for joint planning and goal-setting, coach information sharing and modelling, learner information gathering and practicing, analysis of and reflection on the learner's experiences and coach feedback (Leat, Lofthouse & Wilcock, 2006). 'Guided design' is used to promote critical thinking and self-directed learning (Hancock, Coscarelli & White, 1983). The method is characterised by decision-making and problem-solving processes that include procedures for using real-world problems for mastering learning content using small-group or team processing and facilitator guidance and feedback (Wales & Stager, 1978). 'Just-in-time training' includes methods and strategies used in the context of real-life challenges in response to learner requests for guidance or mentoring (Beckett, 2000). This adult learning method provides individualised, tailored training in response to a request specific to an immediate concern or need (Redding & Kamm, 1999).

Problem Formation

The main focus of analysis was identification of the particular adult learning method characteristics and practices that were associated with optimal learner outcomes. The goal was to identify which practices had implications for informing the adoption and use of an evidence-informed approach to professional development (translational synthesis). The secondary goals were to evaluate the use of the adult learning methods with the experimental groups compared to the control or comparison conditions (efficacy synthesis) and the relative effectiveness of the four adult learning methods when used in typical settings (effectiveness synthesis).

Search Method

Studies that investigated the four adult learning methods were identified by four searches, one for each method. Both controlled vocabulary and natural-language searches were conducted (Lucas & Cutspec, 2007). The terms used to identify studies of each adult learning method were terms that at different times have been used interchangeably to describe the learning methods.

The Educational Resources Information Centre (ERIC), Psychological Abstracts (PsychInfo), Academic Search Elite, Business Source Elite, World CAT, Social Sciences Citation Index, InfoTRAC Expanded Academic ASAP, MEDLINE, OCLC PapersFirst and Dissertation Abstracts were searched. These were supplemented by searches of Ingenta, Google Scholar, ABI/IFORM Global, the Cochrane Databases and an extensive EndNote library maintained by our institute.

Hand searches of the reference sections of all retrieved journal articles, book chapters and books were conducted to identify additional studies. Journals and websites dedicated to the adult learning methods also were examined. We also conducted Social Science Citation Index author searches of seminal papers and studies by individuals who either developed one of the adult learning methods or are leaders in the use of such methods.

Search Results

Fifty-eight studies were located. Twenty-four studies investigated accelerated learning, fifteen investigated coaching, thirteen investigated guided design, and six investigated just-in-time training. Individual participants were the unit of randomisation in twenty-six investigations, and groups (e.g., university class) were the unit of randomisation in thirty-two studies.

The fifty-eight studies included 2,095 experimental group participants and 2,213 control group participants. The learners included classroom teachers, student teachers, undergraduate students, graduate students, medical personnel, counsellors and English-as-second-language learners. The settings in which the adult learning methods were implemented included college classrooms; elementary, junior and high schools; special education classrooms; hospitals and private physician practices and various work settings. The learner outcomes in the studies included teaching practices, early childhood intervention practices, nursing and medical procedures, foreign language learning, science and engineering, mathematics and statistics, economics and rare vocabulary.

Coding the Studies

The coding scheme included sample size, type of study (published versus unpublished), year of publication, participants (students versus practitioners), setting (classroom versus work), hours of training and the particular practices that were used for each of the six different characteristics shown in Table 5.2.

The studies differed from one another in terms of both the adult learning method characteristics used to effect learner outcomes and the particular practices for each characteristic. Both the characteristics and practices were coded and used to identify which were associated with the largest sizes of effects. The methods used to introduce new knowledge or practices were grouped into six categories: (1) class or workshop presentations, (2) warm-up exercises and pre-class quizzes, (3) self-instruction and out-of-class activities, (4) dramatic readings, (5) imagery, and (6) a combination of dramatic readings and imagery. The methods used to illustrate or demonstrate knowledge or practice were grouped into four categories: (1) real-life demonstrations and real-life demonstrations and role-playing, (2) role-playing (i.e., simulations, skits and plays), (3) instructional videos, and (4) learner-informed lecture content. The latter included instructor incorporation of learner experiences into lectures or presentations.

The methods used to engage learners in the application of newly acquired information or material were grouped into five categories: (1) real-life use of the knowledge or practice, (2) role-playing (i.e., simulations, skits and plays), (3) real-life demonstrations and role-playing, (4) problem-solving activities, and (5) games/writing exercises. Two methods were used to have learners evaluate the consequences of application: (1) instructor assessment, review and feedback on the learners' experiences and (2) learner review and self-assessment of their experiences. The latter included either individual or group reviews and assessment of learner use of the targeted information, material or practice.

The methods used to engage learners in reflection on knowledge acquisition and practice application were grouped into three categories: (1) performance-improvement reviews, (2) journaling and behavioural suggestions, and (3) group reflection on instructor feedback. Performance-improvement reviews involved joint learner and instructor discussions of learner application. Journaling and behavioural suggestions involved strategies for engaging learners in self-reflection on their learning experiences. Group reflection involved learner processing of instructor feedback on application to promote deeper understanding of the learning topic.

Learner mastery was determined by (1) self-assessment of personal strengths (and weaknesses) and (2) evaluation of learner performance using a set of standards or practice criteria. Self-assessment of learner strengths and weaknesses was done either individually or in a group in response to instructor feedback. Learner assessment of mastery used a priori identified standards or competencies (e.g., performance checklists) as criteria against which learner knowledge and performance were assessed.

Methods of Analysis

Cohen's d effect sizes for the mean difference on the post-test study outcomes between the experimental and control or comparison groups were used to evaluate the effectiveness of the adult learning methods. Multiple effect sizes for the same outcome in any one study were averaged so that there was no

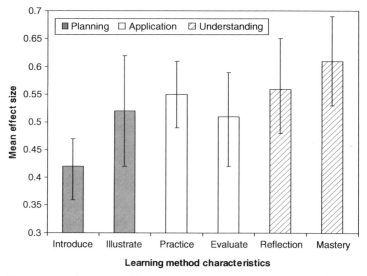

Figure 5.4. Average effect sizes and 95 per cent confidence intervals for the relationships between the adult learning method characteristics and learner outcomes.

more than one effect size for each of four types of outcomes (i.e., knowledge, skills, attitudes and self-efficiency beliefs). The weighted-average Cohen's *d* was computed for each of the six adult learning method characteristics, as well as the practices for each characteristic, to ascertain which characteristics and practices accounted for the largest between-group differences. The analyses included pre-planned comparisons or contrasts where indicated. Both the primary methods were supplemental by secondary analysis when interesting patterns emerged, and statistical analyses helped to clarify the nature of the results.

Synthesis Results

The efficacy of the adult learning methods was evaluated by comparing the post-test mean difference for the experimental versus control or comparison groups. The average effect size and 95 per cent confidence interval (CI) for all studies and outcomes combined was 0.42 (CI = 0.36–0.47). The average effect size was significant, $Z = 15.01$, $p < 0.00001$, indicating that the adult learning methods were effective in terms of influencing learner outcomes.

The relative effectiveness of the four different adult learning methods was evaluated by a between-method comparison. The average effects sizes and 95 per cent CIs for the four adult learning methods were 0.91 (CI = 0.78–1.04) for coaching, 0.52 (CI = 0.37–0.68) for just-in-time training, 0.49 (CI = 0.39–0.58) for guided design and 0.05 (CI = –0.04–0.14) for accelerated learning. The between-method comparison was significant ($Q_{BET} = 123.71$, $df = 3$, $p < 0.00001$), indicating that the four procedures were differentially effective. Coaching proved most effective, followed by both just-in-time training and guided design, whereas accelerated learning was not effective, as evidenced by a 95 per cent CI including zero.

The process of unbundling and unpacking the adult learning methods was begun by examining the average effect sizes for the six characteristics constituting the focus of analysis. The sizes of effects and 95 per cent CIs for the adult learning method characteristics are shown in Figure 5.4. Each of the six adult learning method characteristics was moderately to highly related to the study outcomes. Because the six characteristics represented a logical sequence of events, we determined the extent to which there was a

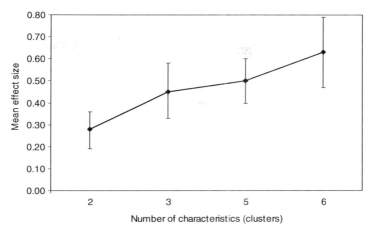

Figure 5.5. Average effect sizes and 95 per cent confidence intervals for the relationship between different combinations of adult learning method characteristics and learner outcomes.

discernible pattern in the sizes of effect by a test for a linear trend. The analysis produced a significant linear effect (χ^2 = 10.45, df = 1, p < 0.002), indicating that better learner outcomes were realised when events later in the learning process were used. We also determined if the two instructor-centred planning characteristics (i.e., introduction and illustration) differed from the four learner-centred application and understanding characteristics. The average effect sizes for the two sets of characteristics were 0.45 (CI = 0.38–0.51) and 0.55 (CI = 0.48–0.63), respectively. There was a significant difference between type of characteristics effect (Q_{BET} = 6.44, df = 1, p < 0.02), indicating the relative importance of active learner participation in the mastery of new knowledge or practice.

The extent to which different combinations of adult learning method characteristics was related to the study outcomes was determined by first performing a K-means cluster analysis (Dixon, 1992) of the six adult learning method characteristics and second by assessing the relationship between cluster membership and the sizes of effects for the study outcomes. A four-cluster solution showed that a combination of two, three, five or six characteristics was used in the different studies. Studies in cluster 1 introduced the learning topic to the learners and engaged

the learners in the use of the material or practice. Studies in cluster 2 used the same two characteristics and in addition instructor illustration of the material or practice. Studies in cluster 3 used all the characteristics except instructor illustration. Studies in cluster 4 used all six characteristics.

The relationship between cluster membership and average size of effects is shown in Figure 5.5. A between-cluster comparison was significant (Q_{BET} = 19.67, df = 3, p < 0.0002), indicating that the average sizes of effects differed from one another. A test for a linear trend also was significant (χ^2 = 14.38, df = 1, p < 0.0001), indicating that there was an incremental increase in the size of effects when more characteristics were used. The results showed that the more characteristics that were used by an instructor or trainer, the larger was the average effect size for the influence of the adult learning methods on learner outcomes.

Although the individual adult learning method characteristic (Figure 5.4) and different combinations of characteristics (Figure 5.5) were related to learner outcomes, there was considerable heterogeneity in the individual effect sizes contributing to the average effect sizes (Q_s = 177.89–566.35, df = 29–81, p_s < 0.00001). This was the basis for further effect size disaggregation. Table 5.3 shows the average effect sizes and 95 per

Table 5.3. Cohen's d Effect Sizes for the Different Adult Learning Method Characteristics and Practices

Characteristics/Practices	Number		Mean Effect Size	95% Confidence Interval	Z
	Studies	Effect Sizes			
Introduction					
Out-of-class activities/self instruction	9	11	0.64	.052–0.77	10.43**
Classroom/workshop lectures	21	31	0.63	0.53–0.72	13.14**
Pre-class exercises	5	5	0.54	0.38–0.71	6.44**
Dramatic readings/imagery	4	8	0.28	0.07–0.49	2.57*
Dramatic readings	15	21	−0.01	−0.14–0.12	0.15
Imagery	4	6	−0.02	−0.19–0.15	0.25
Illustration/Demonstration					
Role-playing/simulations	14	21	0.55	0.42–0.68	8.20**
Learner input	4	4	0.53	0.34–0.72	5.41**
Real-life example/real life + role-playing	3	4	0.45	0.14–0.76	2.85*
Instructional video	4	6	0.34	0.00–0.68	1.97
Practicing					
Real-life application	9	13	0.94	0.79–1.09	12.15**
Real-life application + role-playing	5	7	0.86	0.61–1.03	6.75**
Problem-solving tasks	13	19	0.49	0.39–0.58	10.10**
Learning games/written exercises	6	8	0.38	0.23–0.54	4.80**
Role-playing (skits, plays)	8	14	0.35	0.19–0.51	4.21**
Evaluation					
Assess strengths/weaknesses	7	9	0.94	0.65–1.22	6.49**
Review experience/make changes	16	24	0.47	0.38–0.56	10.19**
Reflection					
Performance improvement	4	6	1.27	0.89–1.65	6.56*
Journaling/behaviour suggestion	5	5	0.82	0.52–1.12	5.33**
Group discussion about feedback	13	19	0.49	0.39–0.58	10.10**
Mastery					
Standards-based assessment	8	11	0.86	0.72–0.99	12.47**
Self-assessment	13	19	0.49	0.39–0.58	10.10**

cent CIs for the practices associated with each adult learning method characteristics. All the practices except the use of dramatic readings and imagery for introducing new information and the use of instructional videos for illustrating learning content or practice were significantly related to the study outcomes. Although the largest majority of practices was related to the study outcomes, certain practices stood out as being more important.

Out-of-class activities on the learning topic or practice (including self-instruction) and classroom or workshop presentations proved most effective in terms of introducing

new knowledge or a practice. Instructor or trainer role-plays or simulations and the use of learner input and experiences for demonstrating a practice were most effective in terms of illustrating a learning topic or a practice.

Engaging learners is some type of real-life or applied use of new knowledge or practice, either as a primary method or in combination with role-plays, was far superior than the other practices for having learners apply and use new knowledge or practice. Learner direct assessment of his or her experiences proved most effective for having learners evaluate their experiences. Both practices more actively involved learners in applying and evaluating their experiences.

Two types of reflection were especially effective in terms of influencing learner outcomes: (1) joint instructor-learner discussions of learner performance with instructor-facilitated learner identification of 'next steps' in the learning process and (2) learner journaling and instructor-guided suggestions about a learner's experiences and which additional experiences would be most beneficial to the learner. Use of a standards-based assessment, performance checklist or a priori set of competencies that learners employed to judge their progress in learning new material or practice was a most effective practice for promoting learner mastery.

Whether the relationships between the adult learning methods and the study outcomes were influenced by setting, learner or intervention variables was assessed by moderator analyses. The learner variables were university students versus non-college students (e.g., teachers and English-language learners) and the number of learners (9–34, 35–75 or 76–300+). The effect of setting was examined by comparing the use of the adult learning methods in college classrooms versus work settings. The effects of length of the learning experience were assessed in terms of hours of instruction (1–10, 11–40 or 41+).

The adult learning methods were most effective when used with practitioners (Q_{BET} = 47.75, df = 1, p < 0.00001) and when implemented in applied settings and work environments (Q_{BET} = 25.55, df = 1, p < 0.00001). Both findings suggest that the adult learning methods had more positive effects when used to influence changes in participants' jobs and professions that had immediate applied relevance. The results also indicate that the adult learning methods were effective in terms of influencing learner outcomes as part of routine practice (Flay et al., 2005).

There was a significant between-group difference in the average effect sizes for the number of participants in each group (Q_{BET} = 31.45, df = 2, p < 0.00001). The average effect sizes for small (9–34), medium (35–75), and

large (76–300+) groups of learners were, respectively, 0.91 (CI = 0.71–1.11), 0.48 (CI = 0.38–0.58) and 0.33 (CI = 0.26–0.40). A test for a linear trend between the number of participants in each group and the sizes of effect also was significant (χ^2 = 29.32, df = 1, p = 0.00001). The smaller the number of learners, the larger was the average effect size. There also was a between-length-of-training difference in the average effect sizes (Q_{BET} = 42.51, df = 2, p < 0.0001). The average effect sizes for 1–10, 11–40 and more than 40 hours of training were, respectively, 0.21 (CI = 0.13–0.30), 0.55 (CI = 0.44–0.67) and 0.60 (CI = 0.51–0.70). A test for linear trend also was significant (χ^2 = 37.16, df = 1, p < 0.0001), indicating that the more hours of training, the larger was the average effect size.

Summary

The results showed that the six adult learning characteristics all were significantly related to the study outcome but that particular practices for each characteristic stood out as more important determinants of learner benefits. The more actively involved learners were mastering new knowledge or practice, and the more instructors or trainers supported and facilitated the learning process, the better were the learner outcomes. The findings also demonstrate that how instructors engage learners, provide guidance, orchestrate learner self-evaluation and reflection and encourage and support deeper learner understanding matters in terms of affecting learner outcomes. Taken together, the findings highlight the importance of active learner participation in as many aspects of the learning process as appropriate for the material or practice being taught, including opportunities to self-assess progress in learning and mastering new knowledge or practice. In addition, learner benefits were optimised when some type of a priori performance or standards-based assessment was used to have learners evaluate their progress in mastering new knowledge or practice, where the learning opportunities were used with a small number of participants for more than 10 hours on multiple occasions.

Report Preparation

The papers and reports that were the products of the research synthesis included a journal article (Dunst, Trivette & Hamby, 2010), a freely available technical report that includes a meta-analysis of both randomised and non-randomised studies (Trivette et al., 2009) and a journal article describing an evidence-based adult learning method based on meta-analysis findings (Dunst & Trivette, 2009a). In addition, a number of studies that used the practice characteristics framework for guiding the conduct of the meta-analyses have been published as journal articles, illustrating how the evidence-based adult learning method was effective as an implementation practice for promoting adoption of evidence-based pre-school classroom and family-systems intervention practices (Dunst & Raab, 2010; Dunst, Trivette & Deal, 2011). We also describe elsewhere the use of the adult learning method for promoting adoption of early literacy and language intervention practices (e.g., Raab, Dunst & Trivette, 2010). These kinds of materials, taken together, provide different audiences with different perspectives on the meta-analysis findings and their implications for implementation practice.

Discussion

The material in this chapter provides psychologists and educators with information for understanding how meta-analysis of implementation practice research would proceed and what the yield from such a synthesis would be. The particular meta-analytical approach described in the chapter goes beyond efficacy and effectiveness to include identification of the practice characteristics and conditions under which an implementation method most likely would effect adoption and use of an intervention practice (efficiency and translational implications). The process for conducting a practice-based translational research synthesis and the adult learning method research synthesis used to illustrate the process hopefully provides readers with the information for understanding how meta-analysis can inform implementation practice.

The use of meta-analysis for synthesising research on implementation methods and practices, and especially meta-analysis of type 2 translational research (Rohrbach et al., 2006; Spoth et al., 2008), could advance our understanding of which features of implementation practices account for the adoption and sustainability of evidence-based intervention practices. This, however, is most likely to occur if implementation and translational research, and the synthesis of that research, includes explicit attempts to identify what matters most in terms of the practices that are most effective in terms of promoting adoption and sustainability. This is in fact a major focus of a practice-based translational research synthesis. As was described earlier and reiterated here, this cannot but yield the kind of information needed to better inform how to promote practitioners' and other intervention agents' use of evidence-based interventions as part of routine practice.

Graham (2006), Glasgow (2003) and others (Rohrbach et al., 2006; Woolf, 2008) have described reasons and barriers to why we do not see more translation of research into routine practice in real-world settings. The Eccles et al. (2009) agenda for implementation research includes investigation of factors that move implementation practices out of the laboratory and into everyday practice and a call for a more systematic investigation of 'what it takes' to make this happen. The type of meta-analysis described in this chapter is at least one way that such an agenda can be brought to fruition.

References

Andrews, G. (1999). Efficacy, effectiveness and efficiency in mental health service delivery. *Australian and New Zealand Journal of Psychiatry* 33, 316–22.

Babbie, E. (2004). *The practice of social research*, 10th ed. Belmont, CA: Wadsworth.

Baron, R. M., & Kenny, D. A. (1986). The moderator-mediator variable distinction in social psychological research: Conceptual, strategic, and statistical considerations. *Journal of Personality and Social Psychology* 51, 1173–82.

Beckett, D. (2000). Just-in-time training as anticipative action and as inferential understanding. In C. Symes (ed.), *Proceedings [of the] International Conference on Working Knowledge: Productive learning at work* (pp. 15–20). Sydney, Australia: University of Technology, Research Centre for Vocational Education and Training.

Bero, L. A., Grilli, R., Grimshaw, J. M., Harvey, E., Oxman, A. D. & Thomson, M. A. (1998). Closing the gap between research and practice: An overview of systematic reviews of interventions to promote the implementation of research findings. *British Medical Journal* 317, 465–8.

Bickman, L., & Rog, D. J. (eds.). (1998). *Handbook of applied social research methods*. Thousand Oaks, CA: Sage.

Blettner, M., Sauerbrei, W., Schlehofer, B., Scheuchenpflug, T. & Friedenreich, C. (1999). Traditional reviews, meta-analyses and pooled analyses in epidemiology. *International Journal of Epidemiology* 28, 1–9.

Bransford, J. D., Brown, A. L., Cocking, R. R., Donovan, M. S., Bransford, J. D. & Pellegrino, J. W. (eds.). (2000). *How people learn: Brain, mind, experience, and school*. Washington: National Academy Press.

Britten, N., Campbell, R., Pope, C., Donovan, J., Morgan, M. & Pill, R. (2002). Using meta-ethnography to synthesize qualitative research: A worked example. *Journal of Health Services Research and Policy* 7, 209–15.

Brown, C. H., Wang, W., Kellam, S. G., Muthén, B. O., Petras, H., Toyinbo, P., Poduska, J., Ialongo, N., Wyman, P. A., Chamberlain, P., Sloboda, Z., MacKinnon, D. P., Windham, A. & The Prevention Science and Methodology Group (2008). Methods for testing theory and evaluating impact in randomized field trials: Intent-to-treat analyses for integrating the perspectives of person, place, and time. *Drug and Alcohol Dependence* 95, S74–104.

Brown, R. (1986). Suggestive-accelerative learning and teaching in special education. *Journal of the Society for Accelerative Learning and Teaching* 11, 13–22.

Bushman, B. J., & Wang, M. C. (2009). Vote-counting procedures in meta-analysis. In H. Cooper, L. V. Hedges and J. C. Valentine (eds.), *The handbook of research synthesis and meta-analysis* (pp. 207–20). New York: Russell Sage Foundation.

Cain, D. W., Rudd, L. C. & Saxon, T. F. (2007). Effects of professional development training on joint attention engagement in low-quality childcare centers. *Early Child Development and Care* 177, 159–85.

Carroll, C., Patterson, M., Wood, S., Booth, A., Rick, J. & Balain, S. (2007). A conceptual framework for implementation fidelity. *Implementation Science* 2, 40. Retrieved February 19, 2008, from http://www.implementationscience.com/content/pdf/17481–5908–2–40.pdf.

Chalmers, I., & Altman, D. G. (eds.). (1995). *Systematic reviews*. London: BMJ Publishing.

Chalmers, I., Hedges, L. V. & Cooper, H. (2002). A brief history of research synthesis. *Evaluation and the Health Professions* 25, 12–37.

Clark, R. E. (2009). Translating research into new instructional technologies for higher education: The active ingredient process. *Journal of Computing in Higher Education* 21, 4–18.

Clow, P., Dunst, C. J., Trivette, C. M. & Hamby, D. W. (2005). Educational outreach (academic detailing) and physician prescribing practices. *Cornerstones* 1(1), 1–9. Available at http://tracecenter.info/cornerstones/cornerstones_vol1_no1.pdf.

Cole, T. B., & Glass, R. M. (2004). Learning associated with participation in journal-based continuing medical education. *Journal of Continuing Education in the Health Professions* 24, 205–12.

Cooper, H., Hedges, L. V. & Valentine, J. C. (2009). *The handbook of research synthesis and meta-analysis*, 2nd ed. New York: Russell Sage Foundation.

Cooper, H. M. (1984). *The integrative research review: A systematic approach*. Beverly Hills, CA: Sage.

Coscarelli, W. C., & White, G. P. (1982). Applying the ID process to the guided design teaching strategy. *Journal of Instructional Development* 5(4), 2–6.

Craven, H. H. (1990). The relationship of peer coaching to the frequency of use of effective instructional behaviors in in-service teachers in three selected junior high schools (UMI No. 9028508). *Dissertation Abstracts International* 51(5), 1491A.

Davies, P. (2000). The relevance of systematic reviews to educational policy and practice. *Oxford Review of Education* 26, 365–378.

Davies, P. (2006). What is needed from research synthesis from a policy-making perspective? In J. Popay (ed.), *Moving beyond effectiveness in evidence synthesis: Methodological issues in the synthesis of diverse sources of evidence* (pp. 97–103). London: National Institute for Health and Clinical Excellence.

Davis, D., O'Brien, M. A. T., Freemantle, N., Wolf, F. M., Mazmanian, P. E. & Taylor-Vaisey, A. (1999). Impact of formal continuing medical education: Do conferences, workshops, rounds, and other traditional continuing education activities change physician behavior or health care outcomes? *Journal of the American Medical Association* 282, 867–74.

Davis, N. (2005). Just-in-time support for educational leadership. In T. J. van Weert (ed.), *Education and the knowledge society: Information technology supporting human development* (pp. 271–7). Boston: Kluwer Academic.

Dixon, W. (ed.) (1992). *BMDP statistical software manual*, Vol. 2. Berkeley: University of California Press.

Dochy, F., Segers, M., Van denBossche, P. & Gijbels, D. (2003). Effects of problem-based learning: A meta-analysis. *Learning and Instruction* 13, 533–568.

Donovan, M. S., Bransford, J. D. & Pellegrino, J. W. (eds.). (1999). *How people learn: Bridging research and practice*. Washington: National Academy Press.

DuBay, W. H. (2007). *Smart language: Readers, readability, and the grading of text*. Costa Mesa, CA: Impact Information.

Dunning, M., Abi-Aad, G., Gilbert, D., Hutton, H. & Brown, C. (1999). *Experience, evidence and everyday practice: Creating systems for delivering effective healthcare*. London: King's Fund.

Dunst, C. J., & Raab, M. (2010). Practitioners' self-evaluations of contrasting types of professional development. *Journal of Early Intervention*. (vol 32 no 4 239–254)

Dunst, C. J., & Trivette, C. M. (2009a). Let's be PALS: An evidence-based approach to professional development. *Infants and Young Children* 22(3), 164–75.

Dunst, C. J., & Trivette, C. M. (2009b). Using research evidence to inform and evaluate early childhood intervention practices. *Topics in Early Childhood Special Education* 29, 40–52.

Dunst, C. J., Trivette, C. M. & Cutspec, P. A. (2007). *Toward an operational definition of evidence-based practices* (Winterberry Research Perspectives Vol. 1, No. 1). Asheville, NC: Winterberry Press.

Dunst, C. J., Trivette, C. M. & Deal, A. G. (2011). Effects of in-service training on early intervention practitioners' use of family systems intervention practices in the USA. *Professional Development in Education*.(v37, no 2, 181–196)

Dunst, C. J., Trivette, C. M. & Hamby, D. W. (2006). *Family support program quality and parent, family and child benefits* (Winterberry Monograph Series). Asheville, NC: Winterberry Press.

Dunst, C. J., Trivette, C. M. & Hamby, D. W. (2008). *Research synthesis and meta-analysis of studies of family-centered practices* (Winterberry Monograph Series). Asheville, NC: Winterberry Press.

Dunst, C. J., Trivette, C. M. & Hamby, D. W. (2010) Meta-analysis of the effectiveness of four adult learning methods and strategies. *International Journal of Continuing Education and Lifelong Learning*. (Vol 3 No 1, 91–112)

Durlak, J. A., & DuPre, E. P. (2008). Implementation matters: A review of research on the influence of implementation on program outcomes and the factors affecting implementation. *American Journal of Community Psychology* 41, 327–50.

Eby, L. T., Allen, T. D., Evans, S. C., Ng, T. & DuBois, D. L. (2008). Does mentoring matter? A multidisciplinary meta-analysis comparing mentored and non-mentored individuals. *Journal of Vocational Behavior* 72, 254–67.

Eccles, M. P., Armstrong, D., Baker, R., Cleary, K., Davies, H., Davies, S., Glasziou, P., Ilott, I., Kinmonth, A.-L., Leng, G., Logan, S., Marteau, T., Michie, S., Rogers, H., Rycroft-Malone, J. & Sibbald, B. (2009). An implementation research agenda. *Implementation Science* 4, 18–25.

Elmes, D. G., Kantowitz, B. H. & Roediger, H. L., III. (1992). *Research methods in psychology*, 4th ed. St. Paul, MN: West Publishing.

Fixsen, D. L., Naoom, S. F., Blase, K. A., Friedman, R. M. & Wallace, F. (2005). *Implementation research: A synthesis of the literature*. Tampa, FL: University of South Florida. Retrieved October 8, 2007, from http://www.fpg.unc.edu/~nirn/resources/publications/Monograph/pdf/Monograph_full.pdf.

Flay, B. R., Biglan, A., Boruch, R. F., Castro, F. G., Gottfredson, D., Kellam, S., Moscicki, E. K., Schinke, S., Valentine, J. C. & Ji, P. (2005). Standards of evidence: Criteria for efficacy, effectiveness and dissemination. *Prevention Science* 6, 151–75.

Fordis, M., King, J. E., Ballantyne, C. M., Jones, P. H., Schneider, K. H., Spann, S. J., Greenberg, S. B. & Greisinger, A. J. (2005). Comparison of the instructional efficacy of Internet-based

CME with live interactive CME workshops: A randomized, controlled trial. *Journal of the American Medical Association 294*, 1043–51.

Foster, S. L., & Mash, E. J. (1999). Assessing social validity in clinical treatment research issues and procedures. *Journal of Consulting and Clinical Psychology 67*, 308–19.

Glasgow, R. E., Lichtenstein, E. & Marcus, A. C. (2003). Why don't we see more translation of health promotion research into practice? Rethinking the efficacy-to-effectiveness transition. *American Journal of Public Health 93*, 1261–7.

Graham, I. D., Logan, J., Harrison, M. B., Straus, S. E., Tetroe, J., Caswell, W. & Robinson, N. (2006). Lost in knowledge translation: Time for a map? *Journal of Continuing Education in the Health Professions 26*, 13–24.

Gutiérrez, R., & Slavin, R. E. (1992). Achievement effects of the non-graded elementary school: A best evidence synthesis. *Review of Educational Research 62*, 333–76.

Hancock, B. W., Coscarelli, W. C. & White, G. P. (1983). Critical thinking and content acquisition using a modified guided design process for large course sections. *Educational and Psychological Research 3*, 139–49.

Hannes, K. (2010, June). Qualitative evidence synthesis (QES). Presentation made at the Systematic Review Workshop of the Campbell Collaboration, Leuven, Belgium, June 2010.

Hargreaves, A., & Dawe, R. (1990). Paths of professional development: Contrived collegiality, collaborative culture, and the case of peer coaching. *Teaching and Teacher Education 6*, 227–41.

Hedges, L. V. (1994). Fixed effects models. In H. Cooper & L. V. Hedges (eds.), *The handbook of research synthesis* (pp. 285–99). New York: Russell Sage Foundation.

Hedges, L. V. (2008). What are effect sizes, and why do we need them? *Child Development Perspectives 2*, 167–71.

Hobma, S. O., Ram, P. M., vanMerode, F., vander Vleuten, C. & Grol, R. (2004). Feasibility, appreciation and costs of a tailored continuing professional development approach for general practitioners. *Quality in Primary Care 12*, 271–8.

Hunter, J. E., & Schmidt, F. L. (2004). *Methods of meta-analysis: Correcting error and bias in research findings*. Thousand Oaks, CA: Sage.

Jones, M. J. (2004). Application of systematic review methods to qualitative research: Practical issues. *Journal of Advanced Nursing 48*, 271–8.

Kavale, K. A. (2001). Meta-analysis: A primer. *Exceptionality 9*, 177–83.

Kazdin, A. E. (2008). Evidence-based treatment and practice: New opportunities to bridge clinical research and practice, enhance the knowledge base, and improve patient care. *American Psychologist 63*, 146–59.

King, W. R., & He, J. (2005). Understanding the role and methods of meta-analysis in IS research. *Communications of the Association for Information Systems 16*, 665–86.

Lacoursiere, Y., Snell, L., McClaran, J. & Duarte-Franco, E. (1997). Workshop versus lecture in CME: Does physician learning method preference make a difference? *Journal of Continuing Education in the Health Professions 17*, 141–7.

Leat, D., Lofthouse, R. & Wilcock, A. (2006). Teacher coaching: Connecting research and practice. *Teaching Education 17*, 329–39.

Leviton, L. C., & Lipsey, M. W. (2007). A big chapter about small theories: Theory as method: Small theories of treatments. *New Directions for Evaluation 114*, 27–62.

Light, R. J., & Smith, P. V. (1971). Accumulating evidence: Procedures for resolving contradictions among different research studies. *Harvard Educational Review 41*, 429–71.

Lipsey, M. W. (1993). Theory as method: Small theories of treatments. *New Directions for Program Evaluation 57*, 5–38.

Lipsey, M. W., & Wilson, D. B. (2001). *Practical meta-analysis* (Applied Social Research Methods Series Vol. 49). Thousand Oaks, CA: Sage.

Lucas, S. M., & Cutspec, P. A. (2007). *The role and process of literature searching in the preparation of a research synthesis* (Winterberry Research Perspectives Vol. 1, No. 10). Asheville, NC: Winterberry Press.

Ludlow, B. L., Faieta, J. C. & Wienke, W. D. (1989). Training teachers to supervise their peers. *Teacher Education and Special Education 12*, 27–32.

Marley, J. (2000). Efficacy, effectiveness, efficiency. *Australian Prescriber 23*, 114–15.

Meehan, M. L., Wood, C. L., Hughes, G. K., Cowley, K. S. & Thompson, J. A. (2004, November 3–6). Measuring treatment integrity: Testing a multiple-component, multiple-method intervention implementation evaluation model. Paper presented at the Annual Conference of the American Evaluation Association, Atlanta, GA, June 3–6, 2004.

Meier, D. (2000). *The accelerated learning handbook: A creative guide to designing and deliver-*

ing faster, more effective training programs. New York: McGraw-Hill.

Metzger, D. S., Koblin, B., Turner, C., Navaline, H., Valenti, F., Holte, S., Gross, M., Sheon, A., Miller, H., Cooley, P. & Seage, G. R., III. (2000). Randomized, controlled trial of audio computer-assisted self-interviewing: Utility and acceptability in longitudinal studies. *American Journal of Epidemiology* 152, 99–106.

Miller, D. C., & Salkind, N. J. (2002). *Handbook of research design and social measurement*, 6th ed. Thousand Oaks, CA: Sage.

National Institutes of Health (2007). *Dissemination and implementation research in health*. Rockville, MD: NIH. Retrieved September 13, 2010, from http://grants.nih.gov/grants/guide/pa-files/PAR-07-086.html.

National Research Council (2002). *Scientific research in education*. Washington: National Academy Press.

Paul, C. L., Redman, S. & Sanson-Fisher, R. W. (2004). A cost-effective approach to the development of printed materials: A randomized, controlled trial of three strategies. *Health Education Research* 19, 698–706.

Pazirandeh, M. (2000). Measuring continuing medical education effectiveness and its ramification in a community hospital. *Journal of Continuing Education in the Health Professions* 20, 176–80.

Popay, J. (ed.) (2006). *Moving beyond effectiveness in evidence synthesis: Methodological issues in the synthesis of diverse sources of evidence*. London: National Institute for Health and Clinical Excellence.

Raab, M., Dunst, C. J. & Trivette, C. M. (2010). Adult learning process for promoting caregiver adoption of everyday child language learning practices: Revised and updated. *Practically Speaking* 2(1), 1–8.

Redding, J. C., & Kamm, R. M. (1999). Just-in-time staff development: One step to the learning organization. *NASSP Bulletin* 83(604), 28–34.

Rohrbach, L. A., Grana, R., Sussman, S. & Valente, T. W. (2006). Type II translation: Transporting prevention interventions from research to real-world settings. *Evaluation and the Health Professions* 29, 302–33.

Rosenthal, R. (1994). Parametric measures of effect size. In H. Cooper & L. V. Hedges (eds.), *The handbook of research synthesis* (pp. 231–44). New York: Russell Sage Foundation.

Rosenthal, R., Rosnow, R. L. & Rubin, D. B. (2000). *Contrasts and effect sizes in behavioral research: A correlational approach*. New York: Cambridge University Press.

Schöpfel, J., & Farace, D. J. (2010). Grey literature. In M. J. Bates & M. N. Maack (eds.), *Encyclopedia of Library and Information Sciences*, 3rd ed. (pp. 2029–39). Boca Raton, FL: Taylor & Francis.

Shadish, W. R., Cook, T. D. & Campbell, D. T. (2002). *Experimental and quasi-experimental designs for generalized causal inference*. Boston: Houghton Mifflin.

Shadish, W. R., & Haddock, C. K. (1994). Combining estimates of effect size. In H. Cooper & L. V. Hedges (eds.), *The handbook of research synthesis* (pp. 261–81). New York: Russell Sage Foundation.

Shadish, W. R., Jr., & Sweeney, R. B. (1991). Mediators and moderators in meta-analysis: There's a reason we don't let dodo birds tell us which psychotherapies should have prizes. *Journal of Continuing and Clinical Psychology* 59, 883–93.

Sibley, J. C., Sackett, D. L., Neufeld, V., Gerrard, B., Rudnick, K. V. & Fraser, W. (1982). A randomized trial of continuing medical education. *New England Journal of Medicine* 306, 511–15.

Slavin, R. E. (1986). Best-evidence synthesis: An alternative to meta-analytic and traditional reviews. *Educational Researcher* 15(9), 5–11.

Slavin, R. E. (1995). Best evidence synthesis: An intelligent alternative to meta-analysis. *Journal of Clinical Epidemiology* 48, 9–18.

Slavin, R. E., & Cheung, A. (2005). A synthesis of research on language of reading instruction for English language learners. *Review of Educational Research* 75, 247–84.

Spillane, J. P., Reiser, B. J. & Reimer, T. (2002). Policy implementation and cognition: Reframing and refocusing implementation research. *Review of Educational Research* 72, 387–431.

Spoth, R., Rohrbach, L., Hawkins, D., Greenberg, M., Pentz, M., Robertson, E. & Sloboda, Z. (2008, May 19). *Type 2 translational research: Overview and definitions: Introduction to Mapping Advances in Prevention Science (MAPS) II*. Fairfax, VA: Society for Prevention Research. Retrieved May 23, 2010, from http://www.preventionscience.org/commlmon.php.

Suri, H. (2000). A critique of contemporary methods of research synthesis. *Post-Script* 1, 49–55.

Tansella, M., & Thornicroft, G. (2009). Implementation science: Understanding the translation of evidence into practice. *British Journal of Psychiatry* 195, 283–5.

Thompson, B. (2005). Replicability of results. In B. Everitt & D. C. Howell (eds.), *Encyclopedia of statistics in behavioral science*. Hoboken, NJ: Wiley.

Tornatzky, L. G., & Klein, K. J. (1982). Innovation characteristics and innovation adoption-implementation: A meta-analysis of findings. *IEEE Transactions of Engineering Management EM-29*, 28–43.

Trivette, C. M., Dunst, C. J., Hamby, D. W. & O'Herin, C. E. (2009). *Characteristics and consequences of adult learning methods and strategies* (Winterberry Research Syntheses, Vol. 2, Number 2). Asheville, NC: Winterberry Press.

vanDoesum, K. T. M., Riksen-Walraven, J. M., Hosman, C. M. H. & Hoefnagels, C. (2008). A randomized, controlled trial of a home-visiting intervention aimed at preventing relationship problems in depressed mothers and their infants. *Child Development* 79, 547–61.

Wales, C. E., & Stager, R. A. (1978). *The guided design approach*. Englewood Cliffs, NJ: Educational Technology Publications.

Whitten, P., Ford, D. J., Davis, N., Speicher, R. & Collins, B. (1998). Comparison of face-to-face versus interactive video continuing medical education delivery modalities. *Journal of Continuing Education in the Health Professions* 18, 93–9.

Woolf, S. H. (2008). The meaning of translational research and why it matters. *Journal of the American Medical Association* 222, 211–13.

CHAPTER 6

Using Evidence to Inform Practice in Science Teaching

The Promise, the Practice, and the Potential

Judith Bennett

Overview

This chapter considers the background against which evidence-based initiatives have been introduced into education and science education. Overviews of the findings of two contrasting reviews are presented, and the experience of conducting these is used to assess what the methods have to offer to science education policy and practice.

The Promise: The Use of Evidence in Educational Research

The last decade or so has seen much written about the use of evidence in education, set in the wider context of the need to make more use of evidence in informing decisions about policy and practice in a range of public service areas, including health, social welfare and education (see, e.g., Davies, 2000). One question that is frequently asked is, 'What works?'

Certainly, it would be difficult to argue against the use of evidence to inform educational interventions, and it is important

to know something about the likely effects of an intervention. However, underlying the question 'What works?' are a number of other questions:

- What constitutes good evidence?
- How might such evidence be gathered?
- How might such evidence be used to inform curriculum interventions?

At a time when increased emphasis was being placed on the role of evidence in informing decision making, there also was considerable debate over the usefulness of educational research in providing such evidence. In the United Kingdom, the debate was launched by David Hargreaves (1996). Hargreaves was critical of much educational research, arguing that schools would be more effective if teaching became a research-based profession, and he blamed researchers for failing to make this happen. Hargreaves argued that little of worth had emerged from half a century of educational research:

Given the huge amounts of educational research conducted over the past fifty years or more, there are few areas which have yielded a corpus of research evidence regarded as scientifically sound and as a worthwhile resource to guide professional action [p. 2].

He went on to pose the question:

…[J]ust how much research is there which (i) demonstrates conclusively that if teachers change their practice from x to y there will be a significant and enduring improvement in teaching and learning, and (ii) has developed an effective method of convincing teachers of the benefit of, and means to, changing from x to y? [p. 5].

Hargreaves also accused researchers of producing inconclusive and contestable findings of little worth and demanded an end to

…the frankly second-rate education research which has not made a serious contribution to fundamental theory or knowledge; which is irrelevant to practice; which is uncoordinated with any preceding or follow up research; and which clutters up academic journals which virtually nobody reads [p. 7].

These were very serious criticisms of educational research, questioning its purpose, its rigour, its quality and its relevance. Unsurprisingly, there were strong rebuttals from the education research community, leading to extensive discussion in the literature about the nature and purpose of educational research (e.g., Norris, 1990; Tooley & Darbey, 1998; Hillage et al., 1998; Davies et al., 2000; Evans & Benefield, 2001; Hammersley, 2001; Oakley, 2002; Vulliamy, 2004). Neither was the debate limited to the United Kingdom, because similar themes formed the bases of discussion in the United States (see, e.g., example, Shavelson & Towne, 2002; Slavin, 2002).

Underpinning the criticism of education research was the notion that it was 'unscientific' because it failed to draw on the experimental approaches of the natural sciences, thus failing to yield recommendations for practice that could be implemented with confidence. The solution was seen to lie in the undertaking of 'high-quality' research rather than basing decisions on 'poor-quality' research, current 'whims', tradition or

professional wisdom. Such research would be more scientific in design and provide a much more rigorous means of testing any educational intervention to assess its effectiveness. Hargreaves was one of a number of people who encouraged the educational research community to look to the medical research model for procedures and practices which would allow much more definite conclusions to be reached about 'what works'.

At the heart of evidence-based medicine is the desire to ensure that a particular treatment offered to a patient is based on scientific evidence which suggests that the treatment is likely to be more effective than any alternative. The key features of evidence-based medicine are the randomised, controlled trial (RCT), in which people (patients in health-care situations) are randomly allocated to groups receiving different treatments, with the outcomes being subjected to tests of statistical significance. Included in the treatments may be an option of no treatment or the use of a placebo, where the patient is unaware that the treatment will have no effect. In medical research, systematic reviews are used to synthesise the findings of series of interventions, allowing knowledge to be built up cumulatively. Such reviews have been used in medical research for some years, emerging from the setting up of the Cochrane Collaboration in Oxford in 1993. The Cochrane Collaboration draws on the principles described by its founder, Professor Archibald Cochrane, then president of the Faculty of Community Medicine of the Royal Colleges of Physicians in the United Kingdom, in his very influential book *Effectiveness and Efficiency: Random Reflections on the Health Services* (Cochrane, 1972). The Cochrane Collaboration advocates the use of quantitative research studies based on experimental methods, supported by systematic reviews of the findings of studies, to generate evidence on which decisions can be made.

In response to the criticisms of educational research, initiatives were made in the early 2000s to introduce aspects of the evidence-based medical model into education. The first of these initiatives was the setting up of the Campbell Collaboration in Philadelphia in the United States to review evidence from RCTs in education, criminology and other social sciences (see, e.g., Petrosino et al., 2000). Others include the establishing of the What Works Clearinghouse (What Works Clearinghouse, 2002; http://ies. ed.gov/ncee/wwc/) and the *Best Evidence Encyclopedia* (BEE; www.bestevidence.org) in the United States to review and summarise research for policy and practice and the Evidence for Policy and Practice Initiative Centre (EPPI-Centre; www.eppi.ioe.ac.uk) in the United Kingdom, with its associated electronic Research Evidence in Education Library (REEL; accessible from the EPPI-Centre homepage) to focus on systematic reviews of research evidence in key areas of education.

In summary, there has been considerable debate over the last fifteen years about the nature of educational research and a drive to improve its quality through adoption of a more scientific approach. The promise is that this will provide a much sounder evidence base to inform decision making. How does the practice live up to the promise?

What Are Systematic Reviews?

Reviews of research are undertaken for a variety of purposes. They may be an entity in themselves, such as an expert review paper in a journal, or they may form part of a bid for research funding or a section of a research thesis. Most research reviews are not currently 'systematic' in that they do not follow the procedures normally associated with systematic reviews.

Systematic review methods involve developing systematic search strategies for reports of research studies based on specific criteria, coding the studies against pre-specified and agreed characteristics, generating an overview or map of the area and then looking in detail at specific aspects of studies. As such, systematic reviews are undertaken with reference to a rigorous protocol for identifying and including research studies and synthesising the findings. Depending on the nature of the evidence reviewed, systematic

reviews also may involve meta-analysis of the findings.

Conventional reviews, sometimes referred to as 'narrative reviews', differ from systematic reviews in several ways. The most obvious of these are that the authors of a narrative review have much more latitude in determining the search strategy, structure and scope of what is included in the review and the way in which findings are presented. Advocates of the systematic review (see, e.g., Cooper, 1998) see narrative reviews as having the potential for a high degree of personal preference and selectivity which lays them open to the criticisms of bias in reporting, discussion and emphasis, whereas systematic reviews provide a much sounder evidence base for decisions about policy and practice.

Systematic reviews have been proposed as a key early step that can be taken towards improving educational research. The idea is to review systematically the nature and quality of what already exists. This section looks at systematic review methods applied in the United Kingdom in the context of educational research.

The EPPI-Centre

The EPPI-Centre has been funded by the U.K. government for over a decade now to support systematic reviews of research evidence in areas concerned with schools and students up to eighteen years of age. The EPPI-Centre is based in the Social Science Research Unit at the Institute of Education in London and works in partnership with review groups located around the United Kingdom. The review groups for the three core curriculum subjects in England and Wales, English, science and mathematics, were established in the Department of Educational Studies at the University of York in the period 2001–3.

The provision of significant funding grants from the central government in the United Kingdom was one indicator of the level of interest in and aspirations for systematic review work in education. The work also has the support of the Organisation for

Economic Co-operation and Development. In reviewing educational research in the United Kingdom (OECD, 2002), the report commented that

> The review team emphasises the value of the EPPI-Centre. Building up the methodologies for scientific reviews and exploiting the results for future research are the most important efforts currently needed for accumulating knowledge on educational research [p. 21].

As such, there was considerable political impetus to fund a series of systematic reviews in a number of areas of education, including assessment and learning, citizenship education, English, mathematics, post-sixteen education, school leadership, science and thinking skills.

EPPI-Centre Review Methods

The EPPI-Centre aims to produce high-quality reviews of research findings that provide evidence accessible to a range of different user groups, including teachers, researchers and policy-makers. Each review is undertaken by a review group, which is a form of steering group whose membership includes policy-makers, teachers, school inspectors, academic researchers, teacher trainers and those involved in curriculum development work.

In essence, a systematic review carried out under EPPI-Centre methodology comprises seven main phases, as detailed in Table 6.1.

The in-depth review involves extracting a range of data from the study (termed 'data extraction') through answering over 100 questions. These enable the study to be evaluated in terms of the study aims and rationale, the research questions, the design methods, the methods used to collect and analyse the data, the results and conclusions and the quality of the reporting. These features are used to make an overall quality judgement about the study of high, medium or low, and these judgements underpin the final synthesis of the quality of the research evidence in answering the review question. The review reports generated, detailing the steps in the process and the substantive findings, are substantial

Table 6.1. Phases of a Systematic Review

Phase	Main Activity
1	Identification of review research question and development of inclusion/exclusion criteria
2	Producing the review protocol
3	Searching and screening for potentially relevant research studies
4	Coding research studies against the inclusion/exclusion criteria
5	Producing an overview of research in the area – the systematic map
6	Conducting the in-depth review via data extraction of key features in the study
7	Production of the review report

documents, being some 20,000 words in length. A detailed account of the detail of the review methods may be found in Bennett et al. (2005), and details of the review tools may be found on the EPPI-Centre website (www.eppi.ioe.ac.uk).

The Practice: Examples of Systematic Reviews in Science Education

The Science Review Group at York has undertaken systematic reviews in three areas: the impact on students of the use of context-based and science-technology-society (STS) approaches to the teaching of science (Bennett et al., 2003, 2007; Lubben et al., 2004), the use and effects of small-group discussion work in science teaching (Bennett et al., 2004a, 2004b, 2010; Hogarth et al., 2004) and the impact of information and communication technology (ICT) on science teaching (Hogarth et al., 2006). In addition to the review reports, a number of journal articles on aspects of the reviews also have been published (Bennett et al., 2005, 2007, 2010). This chapter focuses on the findings of the reviews undertaken in the first two of these areas because the nature of the work means that they provide contrasting examples of reviews. The review of context-based/STS approaches encompasses a number of experimental studies, whilst the review of the use of small-group discussions contains a much higher proportion of studies that are predominantly qualitative in nature. Thus the two reviews present a good opportunity to explore the review methodology in two different contexts.

The key aspects of each review are summarised below, followed by discussion of the findings and their implications for the use of evidence.

Use of Context-Based/Science-Technology-Society (STS) Approaches

The first set of reviews explored the effects of the use of context-based/STS approaches on student understanding of science and attitudes towards science. This area was seen as important because the use of such approaches in science teaching has been one of the more significant shifts in science teaching over the last two decades, particularly in the eleven- to eighteen-year age range. In the classroom, the use of such approaches might mean, for example, that students study medical diagnostic techniques in order to develop their understanding of electromagnetic radiation and atomic structure or look at a range of different fabrics and their uses to introduce ideas about materials and their properties. Advocates of context-based approaches believe that there are improvements in both understanding of science and attitudes towards science as a result of their use. Those who are less persuaded of the benefits believe that the use of context-based approaches means that students do not acquire a good grasp of underlying scientific ideas – in other words, understanding is adversely affected. The review wished to test these claims.

The review research question was: What evidence is there that teaching approaches that emphasise placing science in context and promote links between science, technology and society (STS) improve the understanding of science ideas and the attitudes towards science of eleven- to eighteen-year-old students?

Three reviews were conducted within this overall question. The first focused on attitudes and understanding and the second and third on gender and ability effects, respectively.

THE REVIEW FINDINGS

The searches yielded some 2,500 studies, of which sixty-one met the inclusion criteria for the review. The chief characteristics of the work are as follows: Fifty of the studies in the systematic map were carried out in the United States, the United Kingdom, the Netherlands and Canada. Forty-one studies were undertaken with students in the eleven- to sixteen-year age range and eighteen with students in the seventeen- to twenty-year age range. The emphasis on students in the eleven- to sixteen-year age range is likely to reflect the perception of this age group being very critical in terms of the decline in interest in science.

All sixty-one studies were evaluations (this was a criterion for inclusion in the review), with twenty-four employing experimental research designs, that is, using some form of control group. The remainder explored effects only on students experiencing the context-based/STS materials. Forty-four of the studies reported on attitudes and 41 on understanding. Of these, twenty-four reported on both these aspects.

Just over half the studies (thirty-five) focused on initiatives characterised as science. Where there was a single-subject focus, thirteen related to chemistry, ten to physics and three to biology. It is likely that the focus on chemistry and physics in the individual science disciplines reflects the motives for developing context-based materials in the first instance, with chemistry and physics being seen as subjects with a lower appeal than biology.

Test results, unsurprisingly, were the most commonly used measure in experimental studies and were used in almost two-thirds of the cases. Questionnaires and interviews featured more prominently in non-experimental studies. The most common outcome measures employed in studies were test results (twenty-seven studies), open questionnaires (twenty-seven studies), agree/disagree scales (twenty-one studies) and interviews (twenty studies).

The data extraction and judgements about quality indicated that seventeen studies were of medium quality or better, and the evidence presented below is based on these seventeen studies.

Making judgements about the quality of studies is not easy, particularly when they involve complex interventions, such as context-based/STS approaches. A set of criteria therefore was developed against which studies could be judged. These related to the focus of the study (understanding and/or attitude, with these as explicit independent variables), research design, the reliability and validity of the data-collection methods and tools (including the measures to assess understanding and/or attitude, the reliability and validity of data analysis, the sample size and the matching of control and experimental groups, the nature of the data collected (before and after intervention or post-intervention), the range of outcome measures and the extent to which the situation in which the data were collected was representative of normal classrooms.

EVIDENCE ON UNDERSTANDING OF SCIENCE IDEAS

The evidence on understanding of science ideas came from the findings of twelve studies, and seven of the twelve studies reported evidence that indicates that context-based/STS approaches develop a level of scientific understanding comparable to that of conventional courses. Four studies indicated that context-based/STS approaches lead to a better understanding of science ideas than conventional courses and one to poorer understanding.

The findings of two studies pointed to a particular issue related to the assessment of understanding when comparing context-based/STS courses with conventional courses which concerns the nature of the items used to provide measures of understanding. In the United Kingdom, in addition to external examinations at age eighteen+, the Royal Society of Chemistry (a prestigious scientific body) has a test bank of standard chemistry questions which it makes available to teachers to use if they so wish

to assess their students' knowledge. One of the studies reported that students taking a context-based chemistry course got lower scores on this national test than students taking a conventional course. However, the same students did better than students taking the conventional course in their final external examinations. The overall standard of these final examinations is regulated by an external body, but students taking the context-based course sit examinations with context-based questions rather than more conventional questions. The standard assessment items in the national test more closely resemble questions on more conventional examination papers. One of the other studies reports a similar finding. The implication is that students on different types of courses are likely to perform better on assessment items that resemble the style of course they are following.

HOW BIG ARE THE EFFECTS?

There has been considerable emphasis on 'effect size' in recent research literature on evaluation studies as a means of quantifying the size of the difference in performance between two groups. Effect sizes tend to be described as 'small' if less than 0.2 and 'large' if greater than 0.4 (see, e.g., Cohen, 1969). Typically, educational interventions tend to have small effect sizes.

Of the four studies that report improved understanding, none reported effect sizes per se. Two studies presented sufficient statistical analysis for effect sizes to be calculated, and both had 'large' effects. Of these, one study had a particularly large effect. It is worth noting here that the instrument used to test levels of understanding was developed by the researchers themselves as part of an ongoing research and development programme on STS education, and the issues concerning style of assessment items mentioned earlier also may be of relevance here.

In summary, the review findings on understanding of science ideas appear to provide good evidence that context-based/STS approaches provide as good a development of understanding as more conventional approaches. There is more limited evidence to suggest that understanding may be enhanced. There is some evidence to suggest that performance on assessment items is linked to the nature of the items used; that is, students following context-based/STS courses perform better on context-based questions than on more conventional questions.

THE EVIDENCE ON ATTITUDES TOWARDS SCIENCE AND SCHOOL SCIENCE

The evidence on attitudes towards school science and science comes from the findings of nine studies. By far the most common approach to gathering data on attitude was the use of inventories involving agreement/disagreement scales (Likert-type questionnaires). In all but one of the cases where these were employed, the instruments were developed by the researchers specifically for the study.

Seven of the nine studies reported evidence that indicates that context-based/STS approaches improve attitudes towards school science (or aspects of school science) and/or science more generally. Of these studies, three presented data that had been subjected to statistical analysis, and each indicated that the effects were statistically significant at the 0.05 level. In one case, there were sufficient data to calculate an effects size, and this was 0.67 – a large effect. (This evaluation tools used here had been designed by the developers of the intervention.) The remainder of the studies either employed simple descriptive statistics or gathered data for which statistical analysis was inappropriate.

One study reported evidence that indicates that context-based/STS approaches promote attitudes towards school science comparable to those promoted by conventional courses, and one study reported evidence that indicates that context-based/STS approaches have a negative effect on attitudes towards school science.

Three studies also collected data relating to subject choices beyond the compulsory period and/or career intentions because these are seen as important indicators of attitude towards the subject. Here, the evidence is mixed. Two studies reported increases in

numbers electing to study science subjects, and one reported no change.

In summary, the review findings on attitudes towards school science and science appear to provide very good evidence that context-based/STS approaches foster more positive attitudes towards school science than conventional courses. There is more limited evidence to suggest context-based/STS approaches foster more positive attitudes towards science more generally than conventional courses and mixed (and limited) evidence on the impact of context-based/STS approaches on science subject choices in the post-compulsory period.

GENDER AND ABILITY EFFECTS

Five medium- to high-quality studies explored gender effects. Three of these suggested that gender differences in attitudes are reduced through the use of a context-based approach. Two studies suggested that girls in classes using a context-based/STS approach held more positive attitudes towards science than their female peers in classes using a conventional approach. There also was some evidence from one study to suggest girls following context-based/STS courses were more positive than their peers following conventional courses towards pursuing careers involving science, with results being significant at the 0.01 level. Taken together, these findings suggest that there is moderate evidence to indicate that context-based/STS approaches promote more positive attitudes towards science in both girls and boys and reduce the gender differences in attitudes.

Only one study, though of high quality, explored ability effects and reported that lower-ability students in classes using a context-based/STS approach developed a better conceptual understanding of science and held significantly more positive attitudes towards science than their lower-ability peers taking conventional courses. They also developed a better conceptual understanding of science and held significantly more positive attitudes towards science than their higher-ability peers in the same classes. All results were significant at the 0.01 level. With only one study reporting on ability effects, it is not possible to reach any general conclusions.

Use of Small-Group Discussions in Science Teaching

The second set of reviews focused on the use of small-group discussions in science teaching. Many people involved in teaching and curriculum development in science believe that small-group discussions are an important tool in science teaching, motivating students and enhancing their learning in science. This is set in the context of wider aspirations for science teaching that include the promotion of scientific literacy (e.g., Millar and Osborne, 1998) and the use of constructivist approaches in science teaching (e.g., Driver and Bell, 1985). There is also a growing body of evidence that teachers would welcome support and guidance on running small-group discussions (see, e.g., Osborne et al., 2002; Levinson & Turner, 2001) because their introduction into science lessons challenges the established pedagogy of science teaching and places new demands on teachers. The review area had additional interest for the review group in that a high proportion of the research studies in the area were almost qualitative studies, thus testing a review methodology that seemed to group members to be more suited to quantitative experimental studies.

The review research question was: How are small-group discussions used in science teaching with students aged eleven to eighteen years, and what are their effects on students' understanding of science or attitude towards science?

Within this context, three reviews were conducted, focusing on the nature of small-group discussions in science, the effect of small-group discussions on students' understanding of evidence in science and the effect of different stimulus materials on understanding of evidence in science.

THE REVIEW FINDINGS
The searches yielded some 2,290 studies, of which ninety-four met the inclusion criteria for the review. Some of the chief characteristics of the work are as follows: Most of the studies report work that has taken place in the United States, the United Kingdom and Canada. The majority of work (sixty-nine studies) focused on small-group discussions in relation to student understanding. A substantial amount of the work (fifty-seven studies) also focused on the nature of the communication itself and collaborative skills associated with the discussion tasks given to student groups. Typical small-group discussions involved groups of three to four students emerging from friendship ties and lasted for at least thirty minutes. They also had individual sense making as their main aim (as opposed to, for example, leading to a tangible product such a as as a poster or group presentation) and use prepared printed materials as the stimulus for discussion. Most of the work focused on biology or physics topics, with very little on chemistry topics. This appeared to reflect their use in addressing the difficulty of some physics topics, with small-group discussions being used as a means of students exploring their understanding of particular ideas, and the more issues-based of some biology topics, for example, genetic engineering.

Methodologically, the most common research strategy was that of the case study, which was employed in just over half the studies. Twenty-eight studies reviewed used experimental designs seeking to explore the effects of small-group discussions compared with other approaches.

The most popular techniques for gathering data were observation, video- and audio-tapes of discussions and interviews. Questionnaires and test results also were used.

It is not surprising that more than half the studies employed case studies, because a characteristic of work in the area is a desire to gather detailed information about the nature of discussions. One outcome of the case-study approach and the very labour-intensive nature of much of the data collection and analysis was that sample sizes tended to be small – very often one class or one or two groups of students within a class. Studies involving several classes or classes in more than one school were comparatively rare.

In contrast to the review of context-based/STS approaches, the studies included in the in-depth review were not limited to experimental studies but focused on the medium- to high-quality studies, of which there were twenty-five. In reaching decisions about quality in a review that encompassed a substantial number of qualitative studies, the Review Group for Science drew on the work of Spencer et al. (2003), who had developed a framework for assessing qualitative research evidence in response to some of the criticisms of EPPI-Centre review methods. This area is explored in more detail in the next section of this chapter.

EVIDENCE ON THE NATURE OF SMALL-GROUP DISCUSSIONS

Nineteen studies addressed the nature of small-group discussions, and the evidence reported here is based on the fourteen studies rated as medium quality or better.

The review revealed a number of features of particular interest in relation to the use of small-group discussion work in science. It is clear from the studies that a complex and interacting set of factors is involved in enabling students to engage in dialogues in a way that could help them to draw on evidence to articulate arguments and develop their understanding. Thus a particular characteristic of such studies is very detailed description of student interactions.

Although the studies in the in-depth review shared a number of similar characteristics at the broad level, there are considerable differences at the detailed level. There was considerable variety in the specific research questions, the topics used for the discussion tasks and the use and interpretation of the term 'small-group discussion'. It was apparent that small-group discussions were being used in a variety of ways in science lessons, with many of the studies wrapping up small-group discussions within other activities, often characterised as 'collaborative learning'. This term itself was used in a variety of ways, often loosely, and on occasion, it appeared to include most activities

which did not involve teacher exposition. Despite this variety, there is a high degree of consistency in the findings and conclusions. In general, students often struggle to formulate and express coherent arguments during small-group discussions and demonstrate a low level of engagement with tasks.

The review presents very strong evidence of the need for teachers and students to be given explicit teaching in the skills associated with the development of arguments and the characteristics associated with effective group discussions. Indeed, five of the seven highest-quality studies in the review make this recommendation.

The review presents good evidence that groups function better when the stimulus used to promote discussion involves both internal and external conflict, that is, where a diversity of views and/or understanding is represented within a group (internal conflict) and where an external stimulus presents a group with conflicting views (external conflict).

There is good evidence on group structure. Groups functioned better when they were specifically constituted such that differing views were represented. There is also evidence to suggest that assigning managerial roles to students (e.g., reflector, regulator, questioner or explainer), as suggested in collaborative learning theory, is likely to be counter-productive for poorly structured tasks.

Some evidence also was presented which suggests that single-sex groups may function better than mixed-sex groups, although overall development of understanding was not affected by the group gender composition. Group leaders emerged as having a crucial role: Those who were able to adopt an inclusive style, and one which promoted reflection, were the most successful in achieving substantial engagement with the task. An alienating, overly assertive leadership style generated a lot of 'off-task' talk and low levels of engagement.

Finally, little systematic data have been gathered on the effects of small-group discussions on students' attitudes towards science. Methodologically, the review also helped to provide information on the research strategies adopted to explore aspects of small-group discussion work. A number of similarities emerged in the approaches adopted in the studies. They tended to make use of opportunistic samples, drawing on the researchers' personal contacts. Experimental designs were not used often, although studies often made comparisons between discussion groups in the same class or within a discussion group. Data-collection methods typically involved audio and/or video recordings, with analysis and reporting drawing heavily on extracts from recorded dialogue. Whilst approaches to gathering data were seldom justified in any detail by the authors, sound procedures appeared to have been introduced to check the reliability of the data analysis and present the findings in a way which made them trustworthy. A key difference that emerged concerns the two contrasting approaches to data analysis, with some studies developing grounded theory from the data and others drawing on existing models to structure their analysis.

EVIDENCE ON THE EFFECTS OF SMALL-GROUP DISCUSSIONS ON STUDENTS' UNDERSTANDING OF EVIDENCE

Fourteen studies were included in the in-depth review, of which twelve were medium quality or better. The review suggested that there is reasonable evidence that use of small-group discussions based on a combination of internal conflict (i.e., where a diversity of views and/or understanding are represented within a group) and external conflict (where an external stimulus presents a group with conflicting views) resulted in a significant improvement in students' understanding of evidence. Where there was either internal or external conflict, there was some improvement in students' understanding.

Improvement in students' understanding of evidence correlated with the initial *dissimilarity* of the group members in terms of their understanding of the science content of the discussion task; that is, student groups were constructed such that they contained students with as wide a range of understandings as possible.

Improvements in understanding were independent of gender composition of groups, although single-sex groups functioned more purposefully.

Students' understanding of evidence improved when they were provided with specific guidance on how to engage in small-group discussions and/or construct arguments. There also was some evidence to suggest that the use of small-group discussions (together with specific instruction in argumentation skills) improved students' ability to construct more complex arguments.

The review of the effects of different stimulus materials on understanding of evidence did not suggest that any particular stimulus materials were more effective than others. Rather, it affirmed the findings of the other reviews about the need for guidance on how to engage in the task and that tasks involving internal and external conflict tended to be more successful.

The Possibilities: What Evidence Might Have to Offer to Science Education

Engaging in the process of undertaking systematic reviews has raised a number of issues and questions relating to the review process, to the dissemination of review findings and to the implications of systematic review work for several more general aspects of educational research. This section draws on the experience of the EPPI-Centre Review Group for Science to explore the more conceptual issues and assess the potential of systematic reviews for science education.

General Methodological Issues Associated with Systematic Reviews

There have been a number of challenges associated with the undertaking of systematic reviews in science education. The EPPI-Centre systematic review process is, in the view of the Review Group for Science, relatively non-contentious up to and including the point of developing the systematic map. For the science reviews themselves, many aspects of the review process were fairly straightforward. There was consensus in the review group over the priority areas for review. There were few problems identifying studies in the areas reviewed, with over two-and-a-half thousand emerging from initial searches and some several dozen meeting the inclusion criteria in each case. (These figures were typical of reviews carried out in other areas of education.) The principal problem encountered in screening the studies was the quality of many of the abstracts: In a substantial number of cases, insufficient information was provided in the abstract to decide if the study met the inclusions criteria, necessitating obtaining and reading the whole paper to make a decision, adding substantially to the time taken to undertake the review. There is certainly a message here for the compiling of good-quality abstracts. The review process was reassuring in that there was a high degree of consensus in the quality-assurance steps incorporated into the review process, whereby more than one member of the review team conducted the same task (e.g., coding the studies or extracting the data). However, it is worth noting here that a much greater consensus was obtained when the quality assurance was undertaken by subject specialist than, for example, by a subject specialist and a non-specialist, although with review experience, with discrepancies arising from the non-specialist's lack of knowledge of the area. This points to the desirability of reviews being undertaken by people with specialist knowledge.

The main problems with the review process have been in working with the coding tools developed by the EPPI-Centre such that they encompass the full range of work in the field and in synthesising the results. Unsurprisingly, given the background against which they were developed, the systematic review tools, coding schemes and processes provided a better 'fit' when applied to quantitative experimental studies than to more qualitative studies. Thus, in the case of the two areas reviewed by the Review Group for Science, the EPPI-Centre methods were easier to apply to the review of the effects of context-based approaches than to the review of the use of small-group discussion work. Clearly, at one level, this issue could be addressed without too much difficulty by making revisions to the tools used in the review. However, problems arise if the underlying philosophy of the review methods is one that places a premium on experimental studies and their findings. Certainly, proponents of systematic reviews have argued that this should be the case (see, e.g., Oakley, 2000; Torgerson & Torgerson, 2001).

There is a sense in which the debate over the sorts of research that should be included in systematic reviews and the value of RCTs and experimental research designs are reminiscent of that of the 1970s on the relative merits of experimental approaches and 'illuminative evaluation' (Parlett and Hamilton, 1972). Now, as then, there are those who believe that experimental research is the principal means by which the 'what works' question can be answered, whilst there are others who feel that it is largely inappropriate for research in educational contexts, much of which is carried out in an environment where the researcher cannot control all possible variables and therefore needs to draw on a wider range of strategies to offer insights and explanations. Now, as then, it is unlikely that a consensus will be reached, and the debate will continue. It is worth noting that current systematic review work appears to be establishing that there are comparatively few examples of RCTs in educational research. Certainly there appear to be very few in science education, where, arguably, the nature of the focus might lead one to expect more in the way of experimental approaches to research.

Paradoxically, an emphasis on experimental studies as higher-quality studies has the effect of distorting systematic reviews in a number of ways. First, it can steer those conducting review to formulate review research questions which are likely to yield experimental studies in the searches. Second, and as a consequence of embarking on reviews more likely to yield experimental studies, the reviews run the risk of generating findings that are not context-sensitive, where such sensitivity might be important.

For example, the United States has a much stronger tradition of experimental research than many other countries. There are examples of reviews conducted in the United Kingdom which have reviewed only studies undertaken in the United States. Whilst is some cases this might not be important, there are contextual features of the educational system in the United States that are very different from the United Kingdom. 'What works' in one country may not work or may work in different ways in another. Third, systematic reviews become unsystematic if only certain types of studies are seen as high quality when findings are synthesised.

Implications of the Review of Context-Based/STS Approaches in Science Teaching

The evidence presented in the review of context-based/STS approaches supports the notion that the use of contexts as a starting point in science teaching is an effective way to improve attitudes towards school science whilst, at the same time, not resulting in any drawbacks in the development of understanding of science ideas. However, the process of conducting the review suggests that there is a range of contextual information within which this very general finding needs to be interpreted.

The review focused on evaluations with experimental designs, and the review group was interested to see how many RCTs emerged, given that these have been described as the 'gold standard' (Torgerson & Torgerson, 2001) of research design and provide the strongest evidence of 'what works' (Oakley, 2000). It is interesting that only one of the studies in the review was an RCT, and this poses the question, Why was this approach so seldom employed?

Certainly, there are practical constraints which may make RCTs less feasible in educational contexts, particularly in relation to the evaluation of large-scale curriculum interventions. Decisions on participation in such interventions rarely can be made by researchers, making it difficult to allocate students or classes randomly to groups that will or will not receive an intervention. Most often, the research design has to be built around existing class sets in schools. In the review of context-based approaches, the sampling often was opportunistic in that schools and classes using a new intervention were identified, and then other schools using more conventional course were identified to create a comparison group of roughly similar size. Practical constraints also frequently made it necessary to gather data from intact classes, and this raises issues to do with the construction of matched samples for control and experimental groups.

The constraints just outlined point towards the use of 'design experiments' as being potentially fruitful (see, e.g., Brown, 1992; Collins, 1993; Cobb et al., 2003). A 'design experiment' in educational contexts involves evaluating the effects of an intervention in a limited number of settings. For example, this might involve selecting teachers who teach roughly comparable groups but who have different teaching styles and exploring the effects of the intervention on each group of students. The design experiment then yields information on the circumstances in which the intervention is likely to be most successful. Design experiments have the advantage of being able to encompass the complexity of educational settings whilst enabling the aims of interventions to be tested systematically.

A more fundamental point about the use of RCTs concerns the 'What works?' question, which is not as simple as it first appears in the context of the evaluation of an educational intervention. Before it is possible to decide 'what works', it is necessary to decide what 'working' means – and 'working', quite legitimately, may mean different things. This can be illustrated with reference to the study mentioned earlier in which students following the context-based course performed significantly less well on standard test items of chemical knowledge and understanding than students following more conventional courses. However, students in both groups achieved similar grades in their final examinations, where standards are rigorously monitored to ensure comparability, but students are examined through styles of questions that most closely resemble the teaching and learning approaches, that is, context-based questions for student following a context-based course and conventional questions for students following conventional courses. Thus, if 'what works' means getting similar marks on traditional-style questions, the context-based course clearly does not 'work'. However, if it means getting similar grades on external examinations judged to be of the same standard, then it does 'work'. It seems perfectly reasonable to suggest that if the aims of an intervention are different, the way that it is evaluated will need to be different such that judgements are reached as declared aims and not by comparisons with another approach. In this specific case, most context-based/STS interventions involve a shift in the intended outcomes for science teaching, and the old and the new therefore cannot be compared directly, making the 'What works?' question more problematic to answer.

Three weaknesses were most apparent in the research on context-based approaches. These were lack of standardisation of instruments, the matter of who collected the data and for what purpose and the nature of the resources.

Each of the studies reviewed employed different instruments to gather data on attitudes and/or understanding. This variety meant that it was not feasible to make direct comparisons between studies or to undertake any meta-analysis of the data. This raises the question of how feasible it might be to make use of standardised instruments in the evaluation of context-based approaches when such approaches are developed and used in a number of countries. There would appear to be scope for the development of a standardised instrument to measure attitudes, although research in the area has been characterised for several decades by a tendency for new instruments to be developed for specific studies or existing instruments to be adapted for use. However, there would be considerable merit in trying to put together a small bank of well-validated instruments on which researchers might draw when wanting to assess attitudes towards science or have a common 'core' of items to be included. Cross-national tests of understanding are more problematic. Those developing items for use in international assessments of understanding in science (and other areas), such as The International Mathematics and Science Survey (TIMSS) and the Programme for International Student Assessment (PISA), have encountered a number of challenges. Countries differ in their educational frameworks in relation to when students start school, to the number of years of compulsory schooling, to the ages that students sit national tests and examinations and in the curriculum students have experienced by these points. All these factors mitigate against the validity of using some form of cross-national measure of scientific understanding, although the problems would appear to diminish as pupils reach their final years of schooling and are more likely to have covered the full range of areas common to school science curricula.

The matter of who collects the data and for what purposes also raises issues to do with the quality of the research. It was very noticeable that this information was difficult to identify in the studies and, in almost all cases, had to be drawn by inference. Two particular patterns emerged. The most common situation was for study authors to have been involved in the development of the intervention as well as evaluation its effects. Although it was not clarified, such studies appeared to be undertaken for personal interest rather than to satisfy any funders/ sponsors. In other cases, the study authors were users of the intervention and collected their data for personal interest as part of their studies for a higher degree. However, there was an absence of independent, external evaluation. The involvement of developers and users in the evaluation does raise ethical issues about introducing possible bias into the evaluation findings because it could be argued that developers have a vested interest in demonstrating that their intervention has been successful. However, this appears to be less of an issue than might be the case because detailed examination of the studies during the review process suggested that the appropriate steps were taken to minimise such bias.

Turning to the nature of the resources, the information in the studies included in this review focused on the evaluation data, and very few, if any, examples of the resources were included. It is clear from the studies that the terms 'context-based approaches' and 'STS approaches' can be interpreted quite broadly. This suggests that some caution is needed in interpreting the findings of the review because it seems difficult to imagine that all contexts have the same effects on all students. However, this caveat can be set against a background of the consistency of the evidence yielded by the studies taken as a whole.

Implications of the Review of Small-Group Discussions in Science Teaching

The review suggests that small-group discussion work can provide an appropriate vehicle for assisting students in the development of ideas about using evidence and constructing well-supported arguments. As with the review of context-based approaches, this general finding needs to be interpreted within a range of contextual information.

Two particularly striking features emerge from the work undertaken for the review in relation to the nature of the research and the approaches to analysis. First, it is very apparent that there is considerable variation in the nature of research into small-group discussion work, particularly in relation to its focus, the clarity with which any variables being investigated are specified and the techniques used to analyse data. Second, two very contrasting approaches to data analysis emerged, with some studies developing grounded theory from the data and others drawing on existing models to structure their analysis. This finding suggests that research into small-group discussions in science teaching would benefit from a consideration of discourse analysis techniques developed in other subject areas, such as

English, to establish what they might have to offer work in science.

The review also revealed considerable uncertainty on the part of teachers as to what they are required to do to implement good practice. Given that current policy strongly advocates the use of small-group discussion work, both these factors point to a pressing need for a medium- to large-scale research study which focuses on the use and effects of a limited number of carefully structured small-group discussion tasks aimed at developing various aspects of students' understanding of evidence and that such a study should be linked to a coherent analysis framework. This work then could very usefully inform the nature of guidance offered to teachers and students on the development of the skills necessary to make small-group discussions work effectively. This, in turn, points to the desirability of professional development training for teachers.

Methodologically, the review of small-group discussions also demonstrated some of the limitations of the EPPI-Centre review process when extracting data from studies. As noted earlier, the review contained a high proportion of descriptive studies. Such studies were felt by the Review Group for Science to be a valuable source of information in an area of work in its infancy in science education. The review group therefore decided to enhance the EPPI-Centre data-extraction process by drawing on the guidance for assessing research evidence in qualitative research studies developed by Spencer et al. (2003). This enhanced data extraction addressed such matters as details of data-collection methods (including the rationale for their development), measures taken to increase the trustworthiness of the data, information provided about descriptive analytical categories generated and used, diversity in the data, trustworthiness of the analysis process, information provided about the generation of criteria for effectiveness or impact and the relatability of findings. The review group felt that the addition of these questions greatly enhanced the data-extraction process and the quality of the information yielded.

Full details of this process may be found in Bennett et al. (2004b).

Summary and Conclusions

In terms of the substantive findings of the reviews, the Review Group for Science has concluded that the reviews it conducted have provided insights into effects rather than concrete evidence of 'what works'. Reviews are based on a limited number of studies, many of which are small scale and unrelated to other studies. Taken together, these three factors mean that the evidence base is unlikely to be extensive, and any recommendations made would need to be seen as tentative hypotheses to be tested through the gathering of empirical data. Thus review findings cannot currently form a particularly secure basis on which to make recommendations for evidence-informed policy and practice. Rather, the reviews clear the ground by providing a picture of the current state of work and set an agenda for further research which could inform decisions about policy and practice.

There are a number of benefits associated with the review process and products. The systematic map of work in the field, based on all the studies that meet the inclusion criteria, represents a very valuable resource in terms of both systematically identifying and characterising research undertaken in an area and pointing to under-researched areas. There are also considerable benefits to be had from following systematic review methods in any review of research, although the full review process is very resource intensive. The Review Group for Science does not believe, as proposed by Torgerson (2003), that every piece of primary research should be preceded by a systematic review. The inherent resource implications would appear to make this largely impractical in many situations. However, streamlined reviews are possible, and the experience of members of the Review Group for Science has demonstrated that the ability to offer such reviews is attractive to research funders.

More widely, there is a positive outcome from the systematic review/RCT debate, which is to encourage the educational research community to look more closely at the possibility and desirability of undertaking RCTs in educational research. What seems to be important here is not to see RCTs as some 'gold standard' of research design but to ask the question, *When* is such a technique appropriate? It will be interesting to see in the next few years the extent of the impact of RCTs on the design of research studies in education.

The Review Group for Science has considered the 'objectivity' of the review process, particularly in relation to comments about the relative merits of systematic and narrative reviews. The experience of the review group suggests that reviews are less objective than they purport to be. Value judgements, many of which are rooted in professional experience, are inherent in several aspects of the review process, including specification of the inclusion criteria and differences in interpretation of material in abstracts and studies, not all of which are simply related to depth and breadth of knowledge of the field. Certainly the final synthesis of quality is a far from mechanical process, drawing very heavily on knowledge and expertise in the field. Thus the *process* is transparent and replicable, but the *products*, including the systematic map and the in-depth review, depend on the values held and judgements made by those involved in the review process.

The Review Group for Science also has given some thought into what the process of engaging in the reviews has suggested about the quality of educational research. Based on their experience, review group members would support some of the criticisms made by Hargreaves (1996). There is a sense of much research not drawing on previous work or being cumulative in nature. The review of small-group discussion work in particular suggested that disparate approaches were being adopted by studies which were ostensibly addressing similar questions, resulting in a fragmented picture of the overall findings in an area rather than a cohesive evidence base from which suggestions and recommendations for policy and practice could be made. Whilst these messages may not reflect the situation in all areas of research in science education, they would seem important for the science education community to consider.

In conclusion, systematic review methods appear to have much to offer educational research and research in science education. They may not yet have reached a point where they can answer existing questions about learning and 'what works' except in certain limited areas. However, they have the potential to make a very valuable contribution to research through providing a firmer foundation for decisions about future empirical research; through improving the comprehensiveness, clarity and rigour of research studies; through contributing to the establishment of a culture of evidence-enriched practice; through stimulating informed debate about the nature, purpose and quality of educational research; and ultimately through contributing to the accumulation of reliable evidence on educational practice.

References

Bennett, J., Hogarth, S., Lubben, F., Campbell, B. & Robinson, A. (2010). Talking science: The research evidence on the use of small group discussions in science teaching. *International Journal of Science Education* 32(1), 69–95.

Bennett, J., Lubben, F. & Hogarth, S. (2007). Bringing science to life: A synthesis of the research evidence on the effects of context-based and STS approaches to science teaching. *Science Education* 91(3), 347–70.

Bennett, J., Lubben, F., Hogarth, S. & Campbell, B. (2005). Systematic reviews of research in science education: Rigour or rigidity? *International Journal of Science Education* 27(4), 387–406.

Bennett, J., Lubben, F., Hogarth, S., Campbell, B. & Robinson. A. (2004a). A systematic review of the nature of small-group discussions in science teaching aimed at improving students' understanding of evidence. In *Research evidence in education library.* London: EPPI-Centre, Social Science Research Unit, Institute of Education.

Bennett, J., Lubben, F., Hogarth, S. & Campbell, B. (2004b). A systematic review of the use of small-group discussions in science teaching with students aged 11–18, and their effects on students' understanding in science or attitude to science. In *Research evidence in education library.* London: EPPI-Centre, Social Science Research Unit, Institute of Education.

Bennett, J., Lubben, F. & Hogarth, S. (2003) A systematic review of the effects of context-based and Science Technology-Society (STS) approaches to the teaching of secondary science. In *Research evidence in education library.* London: EPPI-Centre, Social Science Research Unit, Institute of Education.

Brown, A. (1992). Design experiments: Theoretical and methodological challenges in creating complex interventions in classroom settings. *Journal of the Learning Sciences* 2(2), 141–78.

Cobb, P., Confrey, J., diSessa, A., Leherer, R. & Scauble, L. (2003). Design experiments in educational research. *Educational Researcher* 32(1), 9–13.

Cochrane, A. (1972). *Effectiveness and efficiency: Random reflections on the health services.* London: Nuffield Provincial Hospitals Trust.

Cohen, J. (1969). *Statistical power analysis for the behavioral sciences.* New York: Academic Press.

Collins, A. (1993). Toward a design science of education. In E. Scanlon and T. O'Shea (eds.), *New directions in educational technology.* New York: Springer-Verlag.

Cooper, H. (1998). *Synthesizing research: A guide for literature reviews*, 3rd ed. Thousand Oaks, CA: Sage.

Davies, P. (2000). The relevance of systematic reviews to educational policy and practice. *Oxford Review of Education* 26, 365–78.

Davies, H., Nutley, S. & Smith, P. (eds.) (2000). *What works? Evidence-based policy and practice in public services.* Bristol, UK: Policy Press.

Driver, R., & Bell, B. (1985). Students' thinking and the learning of science: A constructivist view. *School Science Review* 67(240), 443–56.

Evans, J., & Benefield, P. (2001). Systematic reviews of educational research: Does the medical model fit? *British Educational Research Journal* 27(5), 527–41.

Hammersley, M. (2001). On 'systematic' reviews of research literature: A 'narrative' response to Evans and Benefield. *British Educational Research Journal* 27(5), 543–54.

Hargreaves, D. (1996). Teaching as a research-based profession: Possibilities and prospects. Teacher Training Agency Annual Lecture. Teacher Training Agency (TTA), London.

Hillage, L., Pearson, R., Anderson, A. & Tamkin, P. (1998). *Excellence in research on schools*. Brighton, UK: Institute for Employment Studies.

Hogarth, S., Bennett, J., Lubben, F. & Robinson, A. (2006). The effect of ICT teaching activities in science lessons on students' understanding of science ideas. In *Research evidence in education library*. London: EPPI-Centre, Social Science Research Unit, Institute of Education.

Hogarth, S., Bennett, J., Campbell, B., Lubben, F. & Robinson, A. (2004). A systematic review of the use of small-group discussions in science teaching with students aged 11–18, and the effect of different stimuli (print materials, practical work, ICT, video/film) on students' understanding of evidence. In *Research evidence in education library*. London: EPPI-Centre, Social Science Research Unit, Institute of Education.

Levinson, R., & Turner, S. (2001). *Valuable lessons: Engaging with the social context of science in schools*. London: The Wellcome Trust.

Lubben, F., Bennett, J., Hogarth, S. & Robinson, A. (2004). A systematic review of the effects of context-based and Science-Technology-Society (STS) approaches in the teaching of secondary science on boys and girls, and on lower ability pupils. In *Research evidence in education library*. London: EPPI-Centre, Social Science Research Unit, Institute of Education.

Millar, R., & Osborne, J. (eds.) (1998). *Beyond 2000: Science education for the future*. London: King's College/The Nuffield Foundation.

Norris, N. (1990). *Understanding educational evaluation*. London: Kogan Page.

Oakley, A. (2000). *Experiments in knowing*. Cambridge, UK: Polity Press.

Oakley, A. (2002). Social science and evidence-based everything: The case of education. *Educational Review* 54(3), 21–33.

OECD (2002). Educational research and development in England: examiners' report.

Organisation for Economic Co-operation and Development. Retrievable at www.oecd.org/dataoecd/17/56.

Osborne, J., Duschl, R. & Fairbrother, R. (2002). *Breaking the mould? Teaching science for public understanding*. London: Nuffield Foundation.

Parlett, M., & Hamilton, D. (1972). Evaluation as illumination: A new approach to the study of innovative programmes (Occasional Paper No. 9). Centre for Research in the Educational Sciences, University of Edinburgh, Edinburgh, Scotland.

Petrosino, A., Boruch, R., Rounding, C., McDonald, S. & Chalmers, I. (2000). The Campbell Collaboration: Social, Psychological, Educational and Criminal Trials Register (C2-SPECTR). *Evaluation and Research in Education* 14(3), 206–19.

Shavelson, R., & Towne, L. (eds.) (2002). *Scientific enquiry in education*. Washington: National Academy Press.

Slavin, R. (2002). Evidence-based educational policies: Transforming educational practice and research. *Educational Researcher* 31(7), 15–21.

Spencer, L., Ritchie, J., Lewis, J. & Dillon, L. (2003). *Quality in qualitative evaluation: A framework for assessing research evidence*. London: The Strategy Unit.

Tooley, J., & Darbey, D. (1998). *Educational research: A critique. A survey of published educational research*. London: Office for Standards in Education (Ofsted).

Torgerson, C., & Torgerson, D. (2001). The need for randomised controlled trials in educational research. *British Journal of Educational Studies* 49(3), 316–28.

Torgerson, C. (2003). *Systematic reviews*. London: Continuum.

Vulliamy, G. (2004). The impact of globalisation on qualitative research in comparative and international education. *Compare* 34(3), 261–84.

What Works Clearinghouse (2002). A trusted source of evidence of what works in education. Retrievable at http://ies.ed.gov/ncee/wwc/.

Part III

PREPARING FOR EFFECTIVE IMPLEMENTATION: FRAMEWORKS AND APPROACHES

Implementation Science and Enhancing Delivery and Practice in School Psychology Services

Some Lessons from the Scottish Context

Barbara Kelly

Introduction

This chapter explores the potential of implementation science to support the development of school psychology[1] services. It makes use of a case-study approach, focusing on the evolving and distinctive role of the school psychologist in Scotland to investigate key parallel issues in school psychology and implementation science. Finally, it looks at the implications of the findings of implementation science for the development and future of school psychology.

The Role, Status and Concerns of School Psychology Today

The International School Psychology Association (ISPA) Research Committee developed and piloted the International School Psychology Survey (ISPS) in 2002 (Jimerson et al., 2006).The survey reflected the fact that although school psychology services around the world were undergoing a period of rapid development, little comparative information was then available about the training, roles and responsibilities of school

psychologists or the contrasting contexts in which they worked. This survey was piloted initially in five countries but extended to include many more. The information confirmed previous research on roles and responsibilities and in many respects confirmed the shared nature and consistency of current challenges facing school psychology. Most school psychologists around the world report engaging primarily in assessment of child-related and organisational problems and devising interventions to prevent or counteract these. In addition, consultation increasingly is cited as a core activity, as is psycho-educational evaluation and counselling. Challenges to school psychology remain familiar (Jimerson et al., 2006):

- Lack of research and evaluation of the impact of work done either by themselves or by external researchers
- Lack of effective leadership and meaningful setting and enforcing of professional standards
- Lack of money and resources to fund school psychology services adequately and the low status of school psychology

Challenges were noted almost universally and seemed to defy the wealth of countries involved. Amongst school psychologists, concerns are mainly about their own effectiveness and value. In considerable contrast, recent consumer surveys report the value and esteem in which school psychology actually is held. Consumer views from around the world confirm that school psychologists are seen to make an important contribution to the lives of children and young people and their parents, teachers and other professions who work with them (Farrell & Kalambouka, 2000; Gavrilidou et al., 1994; Gilham & Gabriel, 2004).

Similarly, discussion of future directions for school psychology tends to focus on themes which are long-standing and share similar and consistent strands globally. Concerns are linked to tensions within and about the role itself and about the distinctiveness of the school psychologist's contribution. Underlying these concerns is the central and fundamental challenge of bringing about demonstrable change. This has remained over-riding despite school psychology's shift in perspective from a child-deficit model concerned with within-child problems to one encompassing ecological, systemic and organisational issues as central to child development (Gilham, 1978; Bronfenbrenner, 1979).

Barriers to change continue to evoke incomplete responses from practitioners and from academic researchers engaged in intervention research (Lambert, 1993; Stobie, 2002; de Jong, 2000; Bradley-Johnson & Dean, 1999; Conoley & Gutkin, 1995; Fagan, 2000). For example, Norwich (2005) drew the conclusion that school psychology in the United Kingdom is mainly an advisory support service that arguably might be filled by teachers suitably trained in psychology. To be more effective, it was suggested that psychological theory as well as practice needs to be given to practitioners and that the school psychologist needs to link with academic researchers to develop knowledge of contemporary trends and evidence to be in a position to give these ideas to teachers.

Implementation science would endorse this advice and places the training and evaluation of those who deliver interventions directly very high on the agenda of implementation strategies. However, this is only one requirement in making school psychology distinctive and effective, and the implementation science evidence base suggests that comprehensive, integrated approaches to the implementation of change are required for effective school psychology. Some relatively recent approaches to training in school psychology in facilitating change and measuring impact provide examples of integrated and innovative approaches, anticipating and reflecting areas highlighted by implementation science and pulling together various theories, concepts and practice frameworks for more effective intervention (Kelly et al., 2008; Woolfson et al., 2008; Hatzichristou, 2002).

The application of psychology in schools is widespread, and its main recipients continue to be children. But contemporary school psychology also aims to influence and support the skills and capacities of teachers, managers, policy-makers and related professionals in enabling children to reach their potential. Legislation relating to the education of children is increasingly holistic, encompassing, for example, broad concepts such as 'well-being' and encouraging the development of new ways to teach children to reach personal goals in social development and responsibility (De Jong, 2000). Psychology seems to have much to offer children and education, and much of the new educational vocabulary is derived directly from developments such as positive psychology.

Parallel to the development of holistic perspectives in education, legislation empowers children and parents to access psychological input particularly for assessment and intervention for a range of educational needs (Boyle, MacKay & Lauchlan, 2008). World-wide, the involvement of school psychologists is guided by codes of practice outlining ethical and legal issues for practitioners (Lindsay, 2008; American Psychological Association, 2002, 2005; British

Psychological Society, 2006). Collectively, these directives lend weight to the power of psychology. They leave no doubt that the school psychologist is both valued and accountable. Currently, the concept of 'evidence-based practice' is central to the idea of practitioner accountability, suggesting that what is offered by psychologists is rigorously designed and tested. It seems incongruous, then, to find that applied psychology has many unanswered questions about impact and that the evidence base is far from straightforward in scientific terms. Rather, school psychology is unexpectedly unpredictable and operates within high levels of variability in relation to impact and outcomes, the reasons for which often exceed current understanding. Despite the obvious influence of psychology in schools, and indeed in any live context, it cannot be described as scientific in the traditional sense. This has been the case since psychology first appeared in schools, but scientific understanding of its role and effects is now emerging and is the focus of implementation science.

Linking Implementation Science and School Psychology

Ironically, perhaps, over the last forty years, school psychology practitioners have anticipated much of the evidence now emerging from implementation science. They have highlighted contextual barriers to change experienced in schools but arguably have lacked sufficient scientific influence and the large-scale evidential basis required to create scientific impact. Now, a shift in perspective and a clear scientific focus on social contexts and how they operate in relation to processes of change have begun to clarify what needs to happen to make school psychology more predictable, effective and measurable.

For the school psychologist, defining a distinctive role and promoting and evidencing effective change are enduring and significant challenges. Clarity about role and effectiveness can be greatly enhanced by the contribution made by implementation

science. Both school psychology and implementation science deal directly with challenges presented by real-world contexts, in particular, contextual reactions and responses to the introduction of psychological concepts and interventions. The discoveries of implementation science about the social and contextual processes impeding change mirror those experienced and reflected in school psychology practice and literature throughout the world. Both share key objectives which are fundamental in promoting change. These are:

- The development of a sound academic and scientific evidence base concerning the nature of real-world barriers to change
- Corresponding real-world epistemologies, methodologies and practice frameworks

Developing conceptual, theoretical and evidential foundations will substantiate practice in all applied psychology and improve the effectiveness of interventions.

What Does Implementation Science Offer School Psychology?

Implementation science perspectives and evidence base provide essential information for effective school psychology service delivery. The evidence base is indispensable in many areas of work routinely addressed by school psychologists. Throughout this book, studies substantiate the type of school psychology required to support effectiveness in interventions. Beyond immediate practice and service delivery protocols, the implementation science evidence base has profound implications for the epistemology underpinning school psychology, for the development of the science of psychology itself and especially for the concepts of 'evidence-based' and 'impact' in both academic and practice contexts. It can help to develop methodology for effective practice protocols and offer strategies for improving design and impact. It can help to create broad directions for development of school psychology services world-wide and more focused practice across all school psychology core activities, summarised, for example, in Scotland as consultation, assessment, intervention, training and research (Scottish Executive, 2002). It can help to develop and populate already existing self-evaluation and professional performance measures with evidence-based developments targeted at fostering professional excellence.

In common with other professional and academic contexts, the development of evaluation processes for school psychology services by internal and external processes remains unclear (MacKay, 1999). Globally, leadership is seen to be insufficient and to lack focus. Processes of self-evaluation link directly to measuring impact and favourable stakeholder reviews, but school psychology still seeks to identify and clarify exactly *which processes and which outcomes* to measure and why (Jimerson et al., 2006; MacKay, 1999, 2006; Hatzichristou, 2002). A persistent, unanswered question about the nature of evidence required to demonstrate change is: Do stakeholder perceptions of change constitute valid school psychology data, or are more and different types of evidence required before robust claims can be made for success? Evaluation of the effects of school psychology is also subject to variability in evidence; for example, in comparing outcomes across different contexts, practitioners and evaluators are unable to specify confidently which variables will be worth examining or strengthening to demonstrate consistency of positive effects. As we have seen, these fundamental questions and uncertainties about the role and effectiveness of school psychologists are reiterated globally. The constructive and meaningful design and measurement of psychological and other interventions and of applied services themselves are now recognised to be urgent challenges.

The Impact of Uncertainty on Ethics and Accountability

The lack of scientific clarity and clearly defined evidence base in much of psychology in real-world contexts makes the role of legislation and ethics in effective practice a challenging one and one which requires careful integration into theory, practice, training and evaluation of impact (Lindsay, 2008).The role of ethics linked to school psychology practice requires that school psychologists in the United Kingdom and elsewhere be aware of the rights of the child and parent to quality interventions which are both in their best interests and reflect an accurate evidence base to support decisions about appropriateness and effectiveness (Bersoff, 2003). Implementation science can help to inform and support ethical and effective practice by providing evidence on both the effectiveness of interventions and the *support of effectiveness* via implementation processes and effective service delivery. It seems crucial to ask:

- How has it come about that evidence and effectiveness of school psychology are unclear and yet school psychology is embedded and growing within education systems world-wide?
- How has it emerged that ethics and legislation can set demands for excellence in school psychology given the unpredictability of its evidence base?
- What underlies the value and repute in which school psychology is held globally?
- How have the themes of change and impact influenced the history and evolution of school psychology, and how can they be carried forward by implementation science?

A Case Study of the Development of School Psychology

In the United Kingdom, the term 'educational psychology' is preferred. It is a relatively small profession which is entered via doctoral or doctoral-equivalent training (British Psychological Society, 2006/2011). Educational psychology in the United Kingdom reflects global trends and is largely one of identifying the nature of issues and problems presented by children, clients and stakeholders mostly within educational contexts and of devising interventions and solutions, usually collaboratively, to effect positive change (Boyle, 2011). The history of educational psychology in the United Kingdom is complicated and diverse. Scottish educational psychology services in particular have distinctive features relating on the whole to the unique statutory nature and breadth of the educational psychologist's role (Boyle & MacKay, 2010). The historical roots of U.K. educational psychology and Scotland's position are important to throw light on its current stage of development, particularly in terms of relations between theory and practice and in relation to parallels and shared imperatives emerging in implementation science.

The development of educational psychology as an academic discipline followed a similar path in most parts of the United Kingdom, emerging initially from the work of academics in philosophy and logic. They were instrumental in establishing the significance of the new science of experimental psychology for education (Boyle & MacKay, 2010). In Scotland, educational psychology as a profession emerged from an experimental movement linking psychological theory in teacher training and teacher practice in demonstration schools applying experimental approaches. Compulsory classes in psychology in teacher training programmes resulted in the development of educational psychology as a distinctive field of educational research in Scotland and, ultimately, in the development of a distinctive educational psychology profession. Early interest in applying experimental psychology in the classroom context in relation to assessment and teaching methods was widened by a growing interest in child mental health. This was encouraged by the emergence of psychoanalysis and the Child Guidance Movement (Stewart, 2006). From the 1920s onward, professional focus developed and changed to encompass an eclectic array of practice interests, including mental hygiene, experimental psychology and mental testing (Sharp, 1980). In 1962, the first degree in educational psychology in Scotland was set up

but retained a powerful educational element in the experience of graduating professionals, requiring teacher training to gain access. Even those with honours degrees in psychology as late as 1969 were not eligible for educational psychology training unless they also were teacher trained. Crucially, the formal requirement of teacher training was finally waived in Scotland but as late as the 1980s. This decision can be seen to represent a shift away from the dominance of education thinking in educational psychology and a move towards incorporating contemporary ideas of psychology as an 'applied science' in education (Boyle & MacKay, 2010).

Arguably, in Scotland, the legislative and statutory grounds for educational psychology have been influential in making educational psychology more psychological and in encouraging a wider focus (MacKay, 1996; Boyle & MacKay, 2010). Although currently schools and other educational organisations remain the major focus of the educational psychologist's work, the five functions of the educational psychologist in Scotland are unique in being statutory and involving consultation, assessment, intervention, training and research. However, in Scotland, the role moves beyond the scope of the school and education into the community and has been formalised in the Scottish government review of educational psychology services (Scottish Executive, 2002). In Scotland, the educational psychologist has a broad statutory focus on child well-being and development and not principally in educational contexts. Boyle & Mackay (2010) point out that Scottish educational psychology is distinctive in combining breadth of remit with statutory duties. They argue that it demonstrates a *coherent* range of professional roles, of which research is one; that it is the first in the international context to have a framework of self- evaluation performance indicators; and that it is the only statutory psychological service in the world to make universal provision of post-school educational psychological services (MacKay, 1999, 2006).

In the context of global trends, this account of the development of educational psychology in Scotland highlights its unique history and profile, describing the emergence of the role of the educational psychologist as a distinctive, contextual, scientific practitioner who is committed to understand and apply research paradigms, conduct research and evaluate the effects of psychology. The role in Scotland is very wide and potentially highly influential because it extends to individual children, schools and communities and, with the advent of post-school services, to young people until they are twenty-four years of age. Its research role implies evidence-based consultation and advice for stakeholders, communities, resource managers and policy-makers. In addition, the evaluation of educational psychology in Scotland is highly innovative in terms of both self-evaluation and external evaluation. Self-evaluation processes are applied consistently across educational psychology services and relate closely to its role and perceived effectiveness. In addition, external and compulsory evaluation by Her Majesty's Inspectorate in Education (HMIE) is a collaboratively developed and evolving process, with educational psychologists leading this service (Scottish Executive, 2011). Interestingly, current concerns with the evaluation process are related to the understanding and measurement of impact on children, families and stakeholders (Kelly, 2008b).

Epistemological, Conceptual and Practical Developments in Reconstructing Educational Psychology

Diversity in origins and scope is clearly influential in the context of the development of the role of educational psychology day to day. In Scotland and across the United Kingdom since the late 1980s, the principal concern of demonstrating effectiveness has edged to the fore in training and practice. 'Epistemology' (which refers to the understanding we have of reality and how we define it) research paradigms and the basic theoretical frameworks and practical tools to move psychological theory into practice have become prominent concerns in training educational

psychologists. In Scotland in particular, practitioner frameworks have emerged focused primarily on creating explicit links between epistemology and methodology in practice contexts (Woolfson, 2008; Kelly et al., 2008a). In Scotland, it can be said that these developments are being fuelled by direct experience of a range of real-world contexts as multifaceted and complex recipients of psychological science and interventions. Educational psychology training and practice in Scotland and elsewhere in the United Kingdom are addressing via theory-into-practice protocols many of the major and often over-riding conceptual and practical constraints which are currently a major focus of implementation science.

Why Epistemology Is Central to School Psychology: The School Psychologist as Researcher and Practitioner

Accounts of the history of the role of educational psychologists in the United Kingdom, at least until the late 1960s, suggest that it was narrow and one demanded by a particular epistemology, that is, by a particular scientific understanding of the nature of reality. The profession was focused largely on the interpretation of individual differences and appropriate responses to these differences educationally (Gilham, 1978). Within this particular perspective which was reflected in legislation of the period, children were seen to conform to or deviate from psychometric or other measurement related to norms and consequentially required to be educated with those who showed similar norms or deviations (Department of Education and Science, 1968). Because of a focus on *individual* child measurement, within norms based on interpretations of psychometric testing and outcomes related clearly to the categorising of child deficit, the advent of U.K. educational psychology was bound initially to a medical perspective. This perspective had a primary focus on deficits or deviations as *evidence of insufficiency within the child* to meet the challenges presented by ordinary education. This evidence was a means to direct action and intervention towards the child.

The psychometric perspective was not exclusive in U.K. educational psychology and certainly in Scotland educational psychology, it included therapeutic intervention which was practiced in the child guidance clinics of the 1940s and 1950s. But the central difficulties addressed were identified as *within child*. The profession did incorporate child development and psychoanalytical approaches prevalent at the time and based child intervention on individual assessments and observational frameworks derived from these areas (Stewart, 2006). In terms of theoretical models within educational psychology, the approach adopted in Scotland generally was experimental or treatment-oriented and interventionist but without the rigour associated with scientific, experimental or strictly medical perspectives and paradigms. However, changing epistemological and theoretical perspectives in the social sciences had a profound impact on the shape and evolution of educational psychology, particularly in the 1960s and early 1970s (Gilham, 1978).

The Social Constructionist Movement in Educational Psychology in the United Kingdom

Over the last five decades, educational psychology in the United Kingdom has committed to a shift towards an immensely challenging and innovative focus which places child development and educational processes in complex epistemological, theoretical and methodological contexts. The main shift in orientation came from the emergence of the social constructionist movement in modern social science. For Educational Psychology in particular, a specific goal emerged in the early 1970s reflecting the emergence in the social sciences of new epistemologies redefining the parameters of *measurable* reality and the fundamental role of *meaning* (Gergen, 1985). This approach opened up the investigation of social and psychological processes as *central* to child development but also challenged the traditional foundations of educational psychology in Scotland and the United

Kingdom. Social constructionism[2] itself is radical in challenging not only the nature of reality but also any theoretical and conceptual bases of scientific knowledge. Basically, it argues that reality does not exist as a static and objective entity. A 'social construct' is, for example, a construct or a practice which, although it may appear to be natural, objective and valid to those who accept it, may be seen equally as an artefact or an invention of a particular culture or society. This radical position is also known as 'relativism' (Fletcher, 1996). Constructionist paradigms contributed to an epistemological and conceptual evolution in the social *and* natural sciences. Evidence for this position is provided by the differing historical and cultural bases of various forms of perception, descriptions of reality and psychological processes (Heelas & Lock, 1981; Lutz, 1982; Rosaldo, 1980; Aries, 1962). Gergen (1985) was one of the few constructionist theoreticians to consider the role of the constructionist practitioner, suggesting that social constructionism would engender and support a move towards social and cultural emancipation. His views of the social constructionist practitioner are echoed by Gilham (1978) discussing the reconstruction of educational psychology in the United Kingdom to incorporate constructionist theory. He commented that new *theoretical tools* would be required to mobilise concepts lying between the problematic, explanatory domains of psychology and sociology.

In educational psychology in the United Kingdom, the need for a very different epistemology and methodology to that offered by purely experimental paradigms or child-deficit and medical models was clearly identified in the late 1960s. In 1968, the Summerfield Report reviewed the practice of psychologists in education services in the United Kingdom. This review reflected quite clearly intolerance and the shift in thinking amongst educational psychologists away from the traditional within-child-deficit practice model. Educational psychologists were unwilling to continue to apply a range of narrow, child-focused procedures which they felt had no sound scientific rationale and which now caused them academic and professional embarrassment. Social constructionist epistemology and research derived from it made the educational psychologist's traditional, clinic-based child-deficit approach more or less untenable. At this stage, educational psychology was improvised and transitional. Although their first degrees in psychology alerted potential practitioners to the negotiable nature of reality and issues of social control and social emancipation, post-graduate courses preparing educational psychologists did not yet set out to create social constructionist practitioners. As we have seen, their role was very much tied to the educational context and to teaching at that stage, albeit experimental and research-led in Scotland. There were as yet no course texts on how to apply social constructionist epistemology to implement change. At the same time, it was impossible for educational psychologists to ignore the crucial contributions of context and ecology of which school effectiveness research, for example, was a particularly powerful reflection (Reynolds, 1976; Rutter et al., 1979). The critical and decisive role of educational, political, social, cultural, organisational and interpersonal factors and how these processes influenced childrens' developmental trajectories for better or for worse were becoming central to social and psychological thinking. In particular, ecological theory was very well documented and effectively undermined the medical and child-deficit approaches previously characteristic of educational psychology (Bronfenbrenner, 1979). For educational psychology in Scotland and elsewhere in the United Kingdom, systemic approaches provided an interim solution to interpreting and mobilising social constructionist–derived perspectives and evidence. Systemic work is intervention provided by the educational psychologist which targets whole-school or organizational issues via training, research and project work as opposed to work which is targeted directly at the resolution of individual and casework-related issues (Boyle and MacKay, 2007).

This move anticipated the evidence currently provided by implementation science about the crucial role played by practitioner training to support effectiveness in psychological interventions. Initially, educational psychologists hoped that this approach would be a panacea and would deliver social constructionist psychology in action by shifting the focus from child deficits to the school environment, aiming to reshape values and practices to support optimal child development in context. Unsurprisingly, perhaps in the light of implementation science evidence, systemic approaches have proved limited; teachers, education managers, children and parents failed to act predictably and did not on the whole implement change as expected on the basis of training and whole-school project work. This approach fell short of a much wider task which was, and still is, to develop and articulate distinctive and comprehensive 'theory-into-practice' frameworks and to create a linked evidence base about effective implementation. Gilham (1978), whose work encapsulates the constructionist crisis in U.K. educational psychology, had prophetic insight in finding that educational psychology knew where it was going but suspected problems in implementation. There were indeed very major problems in implementing social constructionism as it stood then, which, had they been given more careful examination theoretically and practically, might have led to considerable apprehension regarding the nature of the related professional role. This did not happen in any clearly scientific way, and as a result, the development of educational psychology in Scotland and the United Kingdom has focused on exploratory approaches to developing effectiveness in real-world contexts. Considerable tensions still exist today reflecting increasing demand for practice and intervention which is evidence-based, accountable and ethical but which remains difficult to substantiate and demonstrate (Kelly 2006; Kelly, Woolfson & Boyle, 2008).

Although arguably the pure social constructionist position is yet to be applied in practitioner contexts, it has proved impossible to ignore. In the research context, Robson (2002) outlined the emergence of theoretical and conceptual tools which led eventually to the partial merging of both social constructionist and traditional, empirical positions to form a class of differentiated epistemological models which acknowledge the role of *both* the objective and the subjective in co-creating reality. These mixed models are known as 'realist models'. Realist epistemology and related scientific paradigms and research have obvious relevance and usefulness for the applied practitioner and real-world researcher and are discussed later.

School Psychology and Implementation Science: Shared Paradigms and Perspectives

School psychologists and a wide range of other applied psychologists and researchers are acutely aware of shortfalls in defining and achieving change in real-world contexts. However, they are also increasingly alert to pressures to develop evidence-based practice and to measure their impact (Jimerson, Oakland & Farrell, 2006). Although longstanding, their particular dilemmas in dealing with social and contextual reality as practitioners are only now being clearly reflected, highlighted and explored as central in intervention and prevention research which is experiencing the same barriers to the effective implementation of evidence-based programmes and interventions.[3] Investigation of these barriers by implementation scientists indicates that, by and large, barriers may be defined principally in relation to the *social reality and more objective measures* of real-world contexts. Arguably, implementation science has emerged in direct response to the need to combine realist as well as traditional empirical epistemology in live, real-world contexts. In advance of implementation science, realist epistemology and methodology have been used explicitly to influence and rationalise practice and measure effectiveness in a variety of real-world research and professional contexts, for example, criminology (Young & Mathews, 1992), education (Scott, 2000), health (Williams, 1999), social work (Kazi & Ward 2001) and organisational analysis

(Reed, 1997). Critical realism in particular reflects a need to combine and collate data sources to include the impact of social, perceptual and value-based processes with more directly observable and quantifiable data. Viewed as a development in understanding and explaining the complexity, meaning and influence of social processes and as an attempt to locate social processes in an analytical framework designed to promote and measure positive change, this perspective is creating new shared meta-theories about real-world scientific change (Manicas and Secord, 1983).

Epistemology, Educational Psychology and Implementation Science: Some Parallel Issues

The development of implementation science mirrors the same problems encountered by school psychology world-wide and other applied psychology professions – those of incorporating real-world social and contextual issues within a scientific frame of reference which allows change to be created and evaluated effectively. The main concern experienced by school psychology and by implementation scientists is: What prevents people and systems from achieving positive change? This question is dealt with in considerable depth and detail throughout this book. Implementation science is a recent but fast-developing science providing a much-needed evidence base. The journal *Implementation Science* appeared as recently as 2006. The editors of the journal described implementation science as originating across disciplines, and the fact that it was slow to have any dedicated journal was attributed to the wide-ranging disciplines currently conducting implementation research. Articles describing implementation processes often are difficult to locate, and the breadth of the field is not easily understood. Attempts to create a single scientific focus on this area are proving extremely valuable (Eccles and Mittman, 2006). The evidence base for implementation science has evolved more specifically from the failure to transfer empirically designed and controlled evidence-based interventions to real-world contexts, and it aims to explore and resolve barriers to making these interventions effective. This book offers testament to the wide range of areas, both academic and practice-related, which now need to draw primarily on an implementation science evidence base to develop increasing effectiveness and to help conceptualise ideas about impact. Implementation science now provides practitioners and academics with detailed guidance about core processes which support effective intervention in the real world and about specific contexts where particular approaches will be required and are known to enhance positive change and development. Implementation science is creating an evidence base of effective social constructions and social conditions.

What Is Evidence, and What Do We Mean by 'Evidence-Based'?

Evidence drawn from implementation science and from practitioner accounts finds that there are two distinct types of evidence base required to implement psychology in real-world contexts: (1) the evidence that programmes or interventions designed to transfer psychology into practice will be effective in highly controlled experimentally designed contexts and (2) the evidence base about barriers to implementing these programs and interventions in real, less controlled contexts. The latter is the more challenging to establish.

What we understand by the concept of evidence base and the distinctive nature of evidence base in the real world is explored fully in the introductory, statistical and experimental chapters of this book and tangentially in all of them. For example, researchers consistently find that although the experimental paradigm which traditionally relies on RCTs is still considered to have a central role in developing effective interventions in psychology in education, this approach has proved weak and insufficient to guaranteeing transfer and effectiveness to real-world contexts. Intervention studies based on isolated measures of impact

involving outcome data alone have drawn heavily on public funding only to demonstrate inexplicable variability across live contexts. This situation was ignored or minimised for many years by the academic and scientific community world-wide, although researchers did begin in the late 1980s and in some cases much earlier to ask questions about the lack of acknowledgement, exploration and control of social processes as possible sources of variation in real-world intervention studies (Dane & Shneider, 1998; Durlak & Dupres, 2008). It is now possible to substantiate a radical statement in terms of experimental design, relevance and efficiency: High-quality implementation of a poor programme may be more effective than low-quality implementation of evidence- based programmes (Gottfredson & Gottfredson, 2002). The overwhelming relevance and complexity of implementation processes have emerged remarkably slowly, and as has been suggested, this slow realisation may be seen to be due to some extent to the need for a different epistemology and methodology to explain and investigate real-world situations, an epistemology which is different but essential and complementary to the empiricism which underlies RCT design.

Overarching Principles: The Key Role of Epistemology and Existing Practice Frameworks in Helping to Develop High-Impact Psychological Services

In the historical development of educational psychology in the United Kingdom and Scotland in particular, there are parallels between the recognition of the need to have distinctive epistemologies for different purposes in implementation science and the need to have particular epistemological approaches embedded in frameworks for practice in educational psychology (Kelly et al., 2008). The discovery of the need for a range of design approaches, interventions and measurement for tackling the covert processes affecting change in implementation science reflects the process of identifying and working with the indistinct forces of social and contextual processes within educational psychology. Applying psychological interventions from a strictly positivist position would and still does support the application of RCTs but offers no explanation as to why these have uncertain and highly variable outcomes in real-world contexts. The epistemological position underlying RCTs, in isolation, is experimental and positivist. Arguably, this position and associated methodology have driven and underpinned unparalleled progress in, for example, the major health and agricultural advances of the twentieth century (Slavin, 2002). However, where social situations, interpersonal processes, beliefs and attitudes impinge on how an intervention is delivered, the empiricist paradigm is of more limited use.

As we have seen, critical realist epistemology finds that reality may be usefully construed as both *objective* and *socially constructed* and that we need to acknowledge and work with both types of related data to create positive change. These ideas allow school psychologists to work within a mixed methodological approach to defining and describing problems and issues within contexts, designing interventions and evaluating change. Implementation science offers an evidence base which is wholly in tune with the critical realist perspective; for example, it acknowledges the role of RCT design in providing crucial information about the objective impact of an intervention but also requires assessment, preparation, support and evaluation of the social constructions within the target ecology involved in delivering the intervention to improve the chances of positive impact.

In educational psychology in the United Kingdom, training and practice frameworks are used which reflect critical realist epistemology and are based directly on related mixed methodological paradigms. These can be described as executive frameworks, and examples include the problem-solving framework (Monsen & Frederickson, 2008), the integrated practice framework (Woolfson, 2008), both of which are described in detail in this text, and the constructionist model of informed and reasoned action (COMOIRA)

(Gameson and Rhydderch, 2008). These frameworks bridge the gap coherently and transparently between the epistemology, methodology and practice steps for creating change effectively. Implementation science can be seen to provide a further *evidential framework* of applied psychological service delivery priorities and practice steps based on similar, compatible epistemology and methodology. In addition and crucially, implementation science also *substantiates* unresolved questions about what actually works and why in terms of intervention protocols. These questions have been very difficult for any applied psychologies or other human service professions to verify without the necessary large-scale, rigorous scientific and academic exploration of the social and contextual reasons behind success and failure. Emergence of shared epistemology, methodology and evidence in both academic and practice contexts is timely.

Linking Scientific Rationale, Effective Implementation and Practitioner Roles

Educational psychology now has conceptual and practice frameworks for description, enquiry, analysis and evaluation of interventions. In terms of role, these require the school psychologist to make use of a broad evidential basis and to look into various processes at various levels: micro and macro, individual, group and organisational. Robson (2002) gives the example of measuring the effectiveness of a new curricular development in literacy in school. The school psychologist would not limit assessment to effects on individual children alone, though this is one essential level of enquiry. We know the curriculum is delivered via *interactive* processes within complex classroom *contexts* and that these will inevitably vary across classrooms and schools. Teachers and pupils are seen to bring their own *values and experiences* to school. In addition, any innovation or intervention will have *variable* impact in a school under varying *circumstances*.

A critical realist practitioner interested in the *effects* of innovation will look for *mechanisms* at various levels within these contexts. It is understood that these mechanisms are unlikely to be universal but are specific to the contextual dynamics of each school. Currently, we know that understanding these mechanisms can be used to optimise effects by directing and supporting appropriate contextual change. Whilst this describes the role of the social scientist and researcher, this is essentially the role of the contemporary educational psychologist globally and has clear parallels with the role of implementation scientist.

Critical realist epistemology very much suits working with the challenging blend of facts, processes, negotiations, value systems and legislative and ethical imperatives which represent the scientific aims of implementation science and the professional field of contemporary school psychology. The problem-solving frameworks (Monsen et al., 2008; Woolfson, 2008) integrate and address the complexities of social reality by describing and defining both what they are and how to evaluate them. This involves using qualitative and quantitative approaches interwoven alongside each other to make sense of reality. Interestingly, this is also the epistemology currently used to evidence and drive emancipation and social change research (Tesch, 1990). Emancipation is a key goal in education, and school psychology is expected to challenge barriers to education and to support developments for those needing enhanced or differentiated teaching (Scottish Executive, 2008, 2009). The scientist or practitioner with an emancipation role might do the following: Design and carry out work which questions value systems via exploring experiences, interpretations and impacts of social reality across individuals and contexts; further progressive social change by linking results to social progress and individual development and embed change via ethical, legislative and welfare systems (Lindsay, 2008; Boyle, MacKay & Lauchlan, 2008). Examples of wider change using realist paradigms are found in relation to racial equality, feminism and childrens' rights. Epistemology and practice frameworks already exist in educational psychology in Scotland and elsewhere to support the findings and implement practices reflecting the implementation science evidence base.

Implementation Science: Broad Directions for Improving the Delivery of Psychology

The term 'epistemology' is rare in implementation science literature, but the role of epistemology may need to become central to the shared thinking and shared frameworks required for academics, implementation scientists and psychology practitioners to work effectively. It has been argued that constructionist and in particular critical realist epistemology reflects the goals, evidence and discoveries of implementation science and the practice experience of school psychologists in education and elsewhere. The evidence base clarifying and supporting this approach has been as slow to emerge in educational psychology as in implementation science. As in implementation science, educational psychology has engaged in debate about the need for a genuine evidence base describing what is really required to make applied psychology work *and why*. Within Scotland, recent development has focused more on the relative importance of different *types* of epistemology to real-world contexts and to devising approaches to psychological service delivery based on these but without an evidence base for creating a fully fledged change-related science (Kelly & Woolfson, 2008). Implementation science likewise has begun to identify the need for systems-supporting core processes *affecting* adoption of evidence-based approaches and, in the process, has become a science of social change. Interestingly, Fixsen et al. (2009) called for implementation science to become a profession, the focus of which is the design and implementation of change. School psychologists are searching for answers to similar questions to those posed by implementation science: What do we need to do to improve the direction and effectiveness of evidence-based interventions in the real world? Essentially, this is the job of the school psychologist world-wide and, of course, to different degrees and with variable emphasis. Implementation science, arising from the same issues challenging school psychology, gives greater weight and focus to frameworks for action and to mobilising and measuring the concept of impact by providing evidence on which approaches support positive impact. By inference, this evidence suggests how to design and customise effective interventions, and it offers an immense range of continuing professional development topics to help enhance the training of school psychologists in effective practice protocols.

Beyond this, implementation science can be shown to provide an invaluable *operational perspective*, reducing uncertainty and increasing accountability and supporting ethical intervention. It can guide school psychology in considerable detail towards evidence with sound implications for effectiveness across core functions of consultation, assessment, intervention, training and research. It can boost knowledge and guide the development of specific adaptations where psychology can be influential, for example, within the many practice- and policy-related contexts such as establishing cost-effective individual therapeutic approaches and advising on preventative programme implementation.

School psychologists are aware that real-world change relies on contextual processes and that certain contexts present barriers to achieving and sustaining change. Education authorities might struggle to match demands to provide evidence-based interventions for children in schools and often well designed and evidence-based approaches purchased in good faith and delivered to schools are not implemented with awareness of crucial aspects of evidence-based implementation practice. This results in fragmented, inappropriate and unsustainable interventions which are difficult or impossible to evaluate. In some instances, the key role of evaluation is missed altogether or the probability of variable impact across cultures and contexts neglected. Although the best of school psychology training and practice already reflects considerable understanding of principles of effectiveness in real-world

contexts, well documented and integrated change-related evidence and tools are only now beginning to emerge. In terms of the need for implementation tools for practice, research and design of interventions, these may well become a key aspect of the school psychologist's role and are already emerging in educational psychology services in Scotland.

Implementation science is complex and wide ranging and requires integrated systems and approaches to be designed for practitioner and scientific use. Blase et al. in this book (Chapter 2) outline seven core components or processes which affect implementation. These are to some extent already reflected in key processes underlying the delivery of effective psychology in education, but incompletely, and their relative importance and specific methods which may be most efficient are not clear. The Scottish context in particular lends itself very well to implementation science evidence and frameworks. Its research basis within a very broad statutory focus beyond school contexts has highlighted the ubiquitous and complex nature of barriers to change. Its innovative and unique self-evaluation processes and experience of professional practice frameworks create a powerful substrate and readiness for applying the findings of implementation science. The core implementation components and processes of Blase et al. (Chapter 2) are embedded in the following practice and policy areas:

- The recruitment and selection of those who will deliver interventions in schools
- The provision of pre- and in-service training prior to implementation
- Ongoing consultation and coaching for those involved in providing programmes and interventions
- The monitoring and evaluation of staff skills and practice in delivering the programmes and interventions
- The collaborative development of a decision-support data system to evaluate the effects of the intervention and support for effective decision making about its impact

- The provision of facilitative administrative supports which offer clear leadership and reinforcement to keep staff skilled and motivated
- The provision of systems interventions to ensure the availability of financial, organisational and human resources required to implement the intervention effectively

These are the key areas where implementation science evidence indicates that psychological intervention in education will need a focus and understanding before educational practice itself can be described as evidence-based or evaluated in terms of accountability or effectiveness. These core components provide an *integrated system* of evidence-based processes, supports and checks which effectively support change. They highlight where and how school psychology might focus or redirect efforts in relation to aspects of the core functions of consultation, assessment, intervention, training and research. Overall, integrated approaches to increasing effectiveness tend to suggest that *impact* may be conceived of as a product of using the existing and developing evidence base to *actively* direct perspective, policy and practice at all levels of service delivery. This integrated and evidence-based *direction of travel* also would guide the rationale for internal evaluation and external inspection and evaluation of school psychology in terms of measuring practice compatibility with the evidence base provided by implementation science.

The evidence base provided by implementation science often is directly transferable to school psychology contexts, particularly in Scotland, where, as we have seen, role and remit are wide, and evaluation processes are well developed and have priority. However, the implications of implementation science are broad and need *interpretation* and in some instances *transformation* to make good use of the evidence base. Importantly, the executive problem-solving frameworks automatically resolve challenging areas highlighted in implementations science, such as collaboration with stakeholders, establishing stakeholders' commitment, understanding

and ownership of problems and issues, gathering an accurate breadth of evidence for decision making, measuring and fostering client willingness to accept intervention, effective consultation and collaborative processes, evaluation of impact and a reflective feedback loop (Monsen & Woolfson, 2012). Practitioners using this approach are already more effective implementers.

This book offers a very detailed overview of many key aspects of effective implementation processes. These aspects relate to *over-arching key themes*, one of the most important of which is *fidelity*, that is, the extent to which key processes in implementation reflect an original programme or intervention design. Implementation science focuses on the implementation of evidence-based programmes. The school psychologist's role is also to focus on providing appropriate evidence-based consultation and intervention to address a wide range of needs from those of an individual child to school or organisational system development. Regardless of whether a programme or customised intervention is to be offered, fidelity to planned intervention remains central to success. Dane & Shneider (1998) considered four primary components to ensuring greater programme fidelity:

- *Adherence*, which refers to the extent to which the intervention is being delivered as it was designed, with all core aspects being delivered to the intended population; staff trained appropriately, using the right protocols, techniques and materials and in the contexts prescribed
- *Exposure*, which involves the number, length or frequency of sessions of a programme or intervention delivered
- *Quality*, which is defined as the manner in which a teacher, staff member, parent or other delivers an intervention in terms of the techniques, skills and methods required and in terms of enthusiasm, preparedness and attitude
- *Participant responsiveness*, which is the extent to which participants are engaged by and involved in the activities and content of the intervention or programme

Fidelity may be assessed *alongside outcomes as a process evaluation* which in applied practice terms means investigating and supporting practitioners, parents, teachers and others in all the preceding areas. Process evaluation is crucial to effective change, and emphasis on these areas in psychological service delivery is fully justified. Research indicates that process evaluations almost consistently show superior outcomes when the programme or intervention is implemented with high fidelity (Gottfredson, Gottfredson & Hybl, 1993; Flay, 2000). Some evidence-based programmes show significant effects only in high-fidelity samples (Botvin et al., 1990), and, for example, studies looking at educational strategies designed to promote educational achievement and school bonding demonstrate that it is only through thorough and careful implementation of *teachers' practices* that student change was achieved (Abbott et al., 1998).

Conclusion

The evidence base of implementation science is extensive and has many points of contact with school psychology. In Scotland in particular, systems and frameworks exist in school psychology that provide a substrate for the effective incorporation of evidence-based implementations: The historical and statutory requirement to carry out research; the development of training and practice frameworks which link epistemology, theory and methodology for real-world contexts; the development self-evaluation processes linked transparently to consultation and collaboration with users; and the extension of work beyond educational contexts to the community and post-sixteen populations anticipate many of the broad concerns of implementation science. The scientific evolution of both implementation science and school psychology is linked via issues about the processes involved in creating change effectively in all real-world contexts. For school psychology, the development of realist epistemology has proved central to understanding, defining,

focusing and measuring the processes which govern change in real-world contexts. Much of the information offered by implementation science is directly transferable to school psychology delivery. For example, training of staff is essential to support change, but it needs to be differentiated according to emerging evidence about the needs of teaching practitioners to deliver intervention which is transparent, shared and with an obvious relevance to their context. Table 7.1 highlights a number of areas where implementation science offers evidence and direction in school psychology service delivery. These areas are not exhaustive but give examples of how the evidence base can be implemented. For example, in terms of consultation approaches, the evidence supports extending and elaborating training of school psychologists in theory and practice related to specific evidence in *organisational consultative skills* necessary to facilitate full and effective implementation of innovation in schools. Raising *awareness of epistemology* in training and in practice is also highlighted in helping both school psychologists and participants to understand the reasoning behind what is put in place and how. The same applies to wide-ranging assessments of interventions; the reasoning behind covering ecology and perceptions as well as quantifiable data has to be explained to those delivering interventions to improve adherence. Measures of readiness are likely to be central to effectiveness building and need to be developed in practitioner contexts in ways which allow those involved to accept and develop their key role in innovation and change.

School psychology has done much to expand knowledge about the influences operating in social and organisational contexts which present barriers to change, and in Scotland in particular, this has been driven historically by a statutory investment in research and constructionist paradigms but without reference to large-scale scientific evidence bases. The emergence of implementation science and the forging of close links between school psychology globally and implementation science through

Table 7.1

Delivery and Practice in Educational Psychology Core Functions	Contributions of Implementation Science Evidence Base	Examples of Evidence-Based Focus in Related Training and Practice in Educational Psychology
Consultation approaches	Skilled *organisational consultation* is an essential ingredient in implementation and change processes	Extend and elaborate training of educational psychologists in theory and practice related to specific evidence in *organisational consultative skills* necessary to facilitate full and effective implementation of innovation in schools
Conceptual and theoretical approaches to assessment and intervention	Shared epistemology with educational psychology	Raise *awareness of epistemology* in training and in practice
	Endorsement of the *ecological* evidential basis for assessment and intervention	Understand the complementary and crucial nature of *scientific paradigms in real-world* practice and evidence
	Supports processes of *engagement* with stakeholders' and clients' values and views in the change processes	Clarify the need for *wide-ranging assessment* covering ecology and perceptions as well as quantifiable data to clarify the problem
		Make use of appropriate *executive practice frameworks* that complement implementation science evidence bases
Processes of assessment and intervention	Evidence supports the engagement and collaboration of stakeholders in *understanding the approach taken in* assessment and intervention	Provide training for stakeholders on the *concepts behind assessment* processes and their role in the process
Nature and range of consultation about assessment		Engage stakeholders in the *ownership of evidence* about problems and about change
Engagement in designs for change	Evidence supports the identification of *key individuals in* the change process and their active involvement in the process of *evidence gathering and design of interventions for* change	Raise practitioner awareness of the role of careful needs analysis in effective implementation to *avoid ineffective training and intervention*
	Evidence supports *customising input* via a full assessment of the real, specific needs presented by that ecology	Make use of *readiness for evidence-based practice measures* to guide levels of need for highly specific implementation input
		Develop *whole-school assessment and self-assessment processes* related to school climate and engage in collaborative change processes that are driven by the stakeholder organisation

	Evidence	Recommendations
Self-evaluation and external evaluation Review and evaluate impact: fidelity of delivery Delivery and practice in educational psychology	Evidence points to checking via self-evaluation and external evaluation of no the *fidelity, development and impact of intervention* Adherence at a range of levels to programme design is crucial to success	Build in reviews of progress and checks on *client views* on use of any intervention Combine *external and collaborative* evaluations Check adherence and innovation to processes of intervention via interview, teacher diary or observation of practice Coaching and one-to-one *skills teaching* boosts effectiveness of skill acquisition *Mentoring and accreditation* will support skill development and endorse success
Training Link training to real needs and pressing contextual issues Promote self-training and evaluation Build in sustainability strategies at the outset	Evidence indicates that training needs to be linked to *real needs* and that *conceptual understanding* of interventions and agreement on their rational and usefulness enhances compliance Evidence suggests that stakeholder *self-training and self-evaluation* are likely to boost impact of interventions Evidence suggests that *sustainability* requires ongoing support and evaluation	Avoid a menu approach and develop training as a *staged, highly contextualised approach to effective intervention* *Measuring readiness* and using collaborative, staff-led approaches such as teacher researcher and working parties enhances stakeholder commitment and sustainability Revisit the need for training and build stakeholder *capacity for review, research and self-evaluation* *Coaching and One-to-one skill teaching booss* effectiveness of skill acquisition *Mentoring and accreditation* support skill development and endorse success
Research and policy development Understand underlying scientific paradigms Make use of evidence bases appropriately Design and evaluation of school-based research Inform managers and policy developers about implementation science evidence base	Evidence supports the *use of critical realist epistemology and mixed methodology* Implementation science and prevention science literature offers *evidence-based information* on how to effectively support change Evidence supports awareness-raising of policy makers, funders and stakeholders about theory and implementation issues in designing change, purchasing expertise and using evidence-based material and approaches. Boost awareness of effective research	Train educational psychologists on implementation science processes and findings Encourage skill development in implementing intervention research in schools using appropriate, linked methodology Educational psychologists need to articulate the centrality of implementation science evidence base in their service delivery and research findings

shared and complementary epistemology and evidence bases represent a new era for school psychology and one where the perennial questions of 'how' and 'why' will have clearer answers.

Notes

1. The term 'school psychology' is used in most countries, but in others such as the United Kingdom, the preferred title is 'educational psychology', reflecting wider remits which can be community-based as well as school-based.
2. Although the term 'constructivism' is also used in referring to the same movement, this term is also used in referring to aspects of Piagetian theory, to perceptual theory and to a movement in twentieth-century art. The term 'constructionism' avoids confusion and is the term used by Berger and Luckman (1966).
3. 'Evidence-based' refers here to the RCT experimental design, which currently confers the status of evidence-based to interventions. The topic of transfer of this status to programs or interventions in real-world contexts is a focus of implementation science.

References

Abbott, R. D., O'Donnell, J., Hawkins, J. D., Hill, K. G., Kosterman, R. & Catalano, R. F. (1998). Changing teaching practices to promote achievement and bonding in school. *American Journal of Orthopsychiatry* 68, 542–52.

American Psychological Association (2002). *Ethical principles of psychologists and code of conduct.* Washington: APA.

American Psychological Association (2005). *Report of the American Psychological Association Presidential Task Force.* Washington: APA.

Anastas, J. W., & MacDonald, M. L. (1994). *Research design for social work and the human services.* Lexington, MA: Lexington Books.

Aries, P. (1962). *Centuries of childhood: A social history of family life.* New York: Vintage Books.

Bamberger, M., & White, H. (2007). Using strong evaluation designs in developing countries: Experience and challenges. *Journal of Multidisciplinary Evaluation* 4(8), 58–73.

Berger, P., & Luckmann, T. (1966). *The social construction of reality.* Garden City, NY: Doubleday.

Bersoff, D. N. (1999). *Ethical conflicts in psychology,* 2nd ed. Washington: American Psychological Association.

Blase, K., Van Dyke, M., Fixsen, D. L. & WallaceBailley, F. (2011). Implementation science: Key concepts themes and evidence for practitioners in educational psychology. In B. Kelly and D. Perkins (eds.), *Cambridge handbook of implementation science for psychology in education.* New York: Cambridge University Press.

Botvin, G. J., Baker, E., Dusenbury, L., Tortu, S. & Botvin, E. (1990). Preventing adolescent drug abuse through a multi-modal, cognitive-behavioural approach: Results of a three-year study. *Journal of Consulting and Clinical Psychology* 58, 437–46.

Boyle, J. (2011). Educational psychology: Professional issues. In G. Doray (ed.), *Introduction to applied psychology.* Oxford, UK: BPS Blackwell.

Boyle, J., & MacKay, T. (2007). Evidence for the efficacy of systemic models of practice from a cross-sectional survey of schools' satisfaction with their educational psychologists. *Educational Psychology in Practice* 23(1), 19–31.

Boyle, J., & MacKay, T. (2010). The distinctiveness of applied educational psychology in Scotland and early pathways into the profession. *History and Philosophy of Psychology* 12(2), 37–48.

Boyle, J., MacKay, T., & Laughlan, F. (2008). The legislative context and shared practice models. In B. Kelly, L. Woolfson, and J. Boyle (eds.), *Frameworks for practice in educational psychology: A textbook for trainees and practitioners.* London: Jessica Kingsley Press.

Bradley-Johnson, S., & Dean, V. J. (1999). Role change for school psychology: The challenge continues. *Psychology in the Schools* 37(1), 1–5.

British Psychological Society (2006). *Code of ethics and conduct.* Leicester, UK: British Psychological Society, Division of Educational and Child Psychology Training Committee.

British Psychological Society (2006/2011). *Core curriculum for initial training courses in educational psychology.* Leicester: British Psychological Society, Division of Educational and Child Psychology Training Committee.

Bronfenbrenner, Y. (1979). *The ecology of human development.* Cambridge, MA: Harvard University Press.

Conoley, J. C., & Gutkin, T. B. (1995). Why didn't, why doesn't school psychology realize its promise? *Journal of School Psychology* 33, 209–17.

Department of Education and Science (1968). *Psychologists in education services: Summerfield report.* London: HMSO.

Dane, A. V., & Shneider, B. H. (1998). Program integrity in primary and early secondary prevention: Are implementation effects out of control? *Clinical Psychology Review* 18, 23–45.

DeJong, T. (2000). The role of the school psychologist in developing a health promoting school: Some lessons from the South African context. *School Psychology International* 12(4), 337–57.

Durlak, J. A., & DuPres, E. P. (2008). Implementation matters: A review of research on the influence of implementation on program outcomes and the factors affecting implementation. *American Journal of Community Psychology* 41, 327–50.

Eccles, M. P., & Mittman, B. S. (2006). Welcome to implementation science. *Journal of Implementation Science* 1, 1–12.

Fagan, T. (2000). Practicing school psychology: A turn of the century perspective. *American Psychologist* 55(7), 754–57.

Farrell, P., & Kalambouka, A. (2000). Teachers views of school psychologists in different countries. *International School Psychology Association – World Go Round* 27(5):8–9.

Fixsen, D., Blase, K., Naoom, S., & Wallace, F. (2009). Core implementation components. *Research on Social Work Practice* 19(5), 531–40.

Fletcher, G. J. O. (1996). Realism versus positivism in psychology. *American Journal of Psychology* 109(3), 409–29.

Flay, B. R. (2000). *An intensive case study of the of the Positive Action Program as a comprehensive school reform demonstration program.* Chicago: The University of Illinois Health Research and Policy Centers.

Gameson, J., & Rhydderch, G. (2008). The constructionist model of informed and reasoned action. In B. Kelly, L. Woolfson and J. Boyle (eds.), *Frameworks for practice in educational psychology.* London: Jessica Kingsley Press.

Gavrilidou, M., deMesquita, P. B. & Mason, E. J. (1994). Greek teachers' perceptions of school psychologists in solving classroom problems. *Journal of School Psychology* 32, 293–304.

Gergen, K. J. (1985). The social constructionist movement in modern psychology. *American Psychologist* 40, 266–75.

Gilham, B. (1978). *Reconstructing educational psychology.* London: Croom Helm.

Gilham, R., & Gabriel, S. (2004). Perceptions of school psychologists by educational professionals: Results from a multi-state survey pilot study. *School Psychology Review* 33, 271–87.

Gottfredson, D. C., & Gottfredson, G. D. (2002). Quality of school-based prevention programs: Results from a national survey. *Journal of Research in Crime and Delinquency* 39, 3–35.

Gottfredson, D. C., Gottfredson, G. D. & Hybl, L. G. (1993). Managing adolescent behavior: A multi-year, multi-school study. *American Educational Research Journal* 30, 179–215.

Hatzichristou, C. (2002). The future of school psychology: A cross-national approach to service delivery. *Journal of Educational and Psychological Consultation* 15(3), 313–33.

Heelas, P., & Locke, A. (eds.) (1981). *Indigenous psychologies.* London: Academic Press.

Jimmerson, S., Oakland, T. & Farrell, P. (eds.) (2006). *International handbook of school psychology.* London: Sage.

Jimerson, S. R., Graydon, K., Yuen, M., Lam, S. F., Thurm, J., Klueva, N., Coynre, J., Loprete, L. J. & Phillips, J. (2006). The International School Psychology Survey. *School Psychology International* 27(1), 3–5.

Kazi, M. A. F., & Ward, A. (2001). Service-wide integration of single subject designs and qualitative methods: A realist evaluation. Paper presented at the Social Work and Research Conference, Atlanta, GA, January.

Kelly, B. (2006). Exploring the usefulness of the Monsen problem solving framework for applied practitioners. *Educational Psychology in Practice* 22(1), 1–17.

Kelly, B. (2008a). Frameworks for practice in educational psychology: Coherent perspectives for a developing profession. In B. Kelly, L. Woolfson and J. Boyle (eds.), *Frameworks for practice in educational psychology: A textbook for trainees and practitioners.* London: Jessica Kingsley Press.

Kelly, B. (2008b). Proving it. Keynote address to the Her Majesty's Inspectorate in Schools in Educational Psychology Conference, Stirling, Scotland.

Kelly, B., & Woolfson, L. (2008). *Developing a system of complementary frameworks.* In B. Kelly, L. Woolfson and J. Boyle (eds.), *Frameworks for practice in educational psychology.* London: Jessica Kingsley Press.

Kelly, B., Woolfson, L. & Boyle, J. (2008). *Frameworks for practice in educational psychology: A textbook for trainees and practitioners.* London: Jessica Kingsley Press.

Lambert, N. (1993). Historical perspective on school psychology as a scientist-practitioner: Specialization in school psychology. *Journal of School Psychology* 31(1), 163–93.

Lindsay, G. (2008). Ethics and value systems. In B. Kelly, L. Woolfson & J. Boyle (eds.), *Frameworks for practice in educational psychology*. London: Jessica Kingsley Press.

Lutz, C. (1982). The domain of emotion words in Ifaluk. *America Ethnologist* 9, 113–28.

MacKay, T. (1996). The statutory foundations of Scottish educational psychology services. *Educational Psychology in Scotland* 3, 3–9.

MacKay, T. (1999). *Quality assurance in education authority psychological services: Self-evaluation using performance indicators*. Edinburgh: Scottish Executive Education Department.

MacKay, T. (2006). *Evaluation of post school psychological services: Pathfinders in Scotland (2004–2006)*. Edinburgh: Edinburgh University Press.

Manicas, P. T., & Secord, P. F. (1983). Implications for psychology of the new philosophy of science. *American Psychologist* 38, 399–413.

Monsen, J., & Frederickson, N. (2008). Problem framework ten years. In B. Kelly et al. (eds.), *Frameworks for practice in educational psychology: A textbook for trainees and practitioners*. London: Jessica Kingsley Press.

Monsen, J., & Woolfson, L. (2012). The role of executive practice frameworks in preparing for effective change. In B. Kelly and D. Perkins (eds.), *Cambridge handbook of implementation science for psychology in education*. New York: Cambridge University Press.

Norwich, B. (2005). Future directions for professional educational psychology. *School Psychology International* 26(4), 387–97.

Reed, M. I. (1997). In praise of duality and dualism: Rethinking agency and structure in organisational analysis. *Organisational Studies* 18, 21–42.

Reynolds, D. (1976). The delinquent school. In P. Woods (ed.), *The process of schooling*. London: Routledge and Keegan Paul.

Robson, C. (2002). *Real world research: A resource for social scientists and practitioner researchers*. Oxford, UK: Blackwell.

Rosaldo, M. (1980). *Knowledge and passion: Ilongot notions of self and social life*. Cambridge, UK: Cambridge University Press.

Rutter, M., Maughan, B., Mortimore, P., Ouston, J. & Smith, A. (1979). *Fifteen thousand hours*. Cambridge, MA: Harvard University Press.

Salomon, G. (1996). Transcending the qualitative-quantitative debate: The analytical and systemic approaches to educational research. *Educational Researcher* 20(6), 10–18.

Sameroff, A. J., & MacKenzie, M. J. (2003). Research strategies for capturing transactional models of development: The limits of possible. *Development and Psychopathology* 15(3), 613–40.

Sayer, A. (2000). *Realism and social science*. London: Sage.

Scott, D. (2000). *Realism and educational research: New perspectives and possibilities*. London: Routledge.

Scottish Executive (2002). *Review of provision of educational psychology services in Scotland: Currie report*. Edinburgh: HMSO.

Scottish Executive (2011). *Educational psychology in Scotland: Making a difference: An aspect report on the findings of inspections of local authority psychological services 2006–2010*. Edinburgh: Scottish Executive Publications.

Scottish Government. (2008). *Getting it right for every child*. Edinburgh: Scottish Government.

Scottish Government (2009). *Education (additional support for learning) act*. Edinburgh: Scottish Government.

Sharp, S. A. (1980). Godfrey Thomson and the concept of intelligence. In J. V. Smith and D. Hamilton (eds.), *The meritocratic intellect: Studies in the history of educational research*. Aberdeen, UK: Aberdeen University Press.

Slavin, R. E. (2002). Evidence-based educational policies: Transforming educational practice and research. *Educational Researcher* 319(7), 15–21.

Spence, S. H., & Short, A. L. (2007). Research reviews: Can we justify the widespread dissemination of universal, school-based interventions for the prevention of depression among children and adolescents? *Journal of Child Psychology and Psychiatry* 35, 1191–228

Stewart, J. W. (2006). Child guidance in interwar Scotland: International influences and domestic concerns. *Bulletin of the History of Medicine* 80(3), 513–39.

Stobie, I. (2002). Processes of change and continuity in educational psychology, Part 1. *Educational Psychology in Practice* 18(3), 214–37.

Tesch, R. (1990). *Qualitative research: Analysis types and software tools*. London: Falmer.

Williams, S. J. (1999). Is anybody there? Critical realism, chronic illness and the disability debate. *Sociology of Health and Illness* 21, 797–819.

Weimer, W. B. (1979). *Notes on the methodology of scientific research*. Hillsdale, NJ: Erlbaum.

Woolfson, L. (2008) The Woolfson et al integrated framework: An executive framework for service wide delivery. In B. Kelly, L. Woolfson, and J. Boyle (eds.), *Frameworks for Practice in Educational Psychology*. London: Jessica Kingsley Press.

Young, J., & Matthews, R. (eds.) (1992). *Rethinking criminology: The realist debate*. London: Sage.

CHAPTER 8

The Role of Executive Problem-Solving Frameworks in Preparing for Effective Change in Educational Contexts

Jeremy J. Monsen and Lisa Marks Woolfson

Introduction

The past twenty years have witnessed a period of far-reaching educational reform within the United Kingdom and in other countries. Politicians, policy-makers, researchers and practitioners alike have come to the reluctant conclusion that the impact of the majority of this reform on children and young people, in terms of, for example, academic attainments, has been marginal. Such marginalisation is particularly apparent within the most vulnerable groups in society (e.g., those from lower socio-economic backgrounds and those in public care). Fullan (2010a, 2010b) aptly illustrates this in his evaluations of the United Kingdom's Literacy and Numeracy Hour initiatives. Such a bleak scenario has emerged despite significantly increased expenditure on education – on its staffing, on its infrastructure, on lowering class sizes and on new polices, curricula and programs – on an unprecedented scale and scope (e.g., Every Child Matters, Sure Start, Social Emotional Aspects of Learning, Common Assessment Framework and so on; Fullan, 2010b).

One of the key issues stressed in this chapter is that money has been spent on programs which have no evidence base to show that they work. Critical evaluation does not seem to have influenced policy initiatives and certainly not applied practice. This paradox is described within this chapter, which is written primarily for practitioners[1] who are motivated to make sure that their efforts actually do make a real and sustained difference for children and young people and those who care for and work with them. The main conclusion reached is that an important part of improving the implementation and evaluation of effective applied interventions within educational settings is the need to build teacher capacity by emphasising the development of more rigorous problem-solving and decision-making processes and practices. Teaching staff require the ability to think about complex work-related problems in a more scientific and structured way, emphasising the need for practitioners to develop more of a 'new scientist-practitioner' stance. Finally, problem-analysis methodology (Monsen & Fredrickson, 2008; Monsen et al., 1998) is presented as an example of an executive framework within which teachers can conceptualise the phases of critical thinking involved in the process of embedding sound research and theory into effective and sustainable applied practice which actually makes a difference for children and young people and those close to them.

The Research to Policy to Practice Paradox

The Centre for Social Justice (2007) in the United Kingdom was one of the first agencies to clearly point out a disturbing quandary in education: that despite a 50 per cent increase in government direct spending on education since 1997, there continued to be significant educational failure within the most disadvantaged and marginalised groups within society. Indeed, the United Kingdom has the highest level of educational inequality in the Western world (Centre for Social Justice, 2007; Hills, 2010; Save the Children, 2010; UNICEF, 2007). For example, pupil referral units were designed as special part-time settings for short-term placements for pupils who have been excluded or suspended from mainstream school, with the aim of enabling re-integration back into mainstream school. In practice, these units are the least successful in improving pupil academic, behavioural and social-emotional outcomes when compared with other initiatives, such as on-site day and residential units, and this at an annual cost of about £228 million (Centre for Social Justice, 2007). This finding is concerning because a large sum of money is being spent on an intervention which clearly has been shown to be ineffective. However, a cynic might argue that actually pupil referral units have been 'very successful' in allowing mainstream schools to 'get rid' of their most problematic pupils.

There is surprisingly little research evidence to support a number of other key government policy initiatives which had been given a high public profile. These included providing schools with more resources, reducing class sizes or streaming groups within classes. Instead, research concludes that it is the effectiveness of the leadership and management of existing classroom resources, including personnel, which can be achieved through a focus on quality teaching (Duckworth et al., 2009; Pont, Nusche & Hopkins, 2008; West-Burnham, 2009).

When the Department for Education and Skills (DfES, 2004) found that the national literacy and numeracy strategies promulgated by the then New Labour Government were not effective in improving performance across all schools because fewer than 50 per cent of pupils achieved level 4 at key stage 2 in many schools (Fullan, 2010a, 2010b), a pilot initiative was devised. The Intensifying Support Program was designed to raise the quality of teaching and, as a result, pupil achievement. One component involved targeting pupils who should be achieving more than they were, and the program attempted to help them 'catch up' to their expected level of achievement (DfES, 2004). The quality of teaching was addressed within the program through a focus on sharing objectives and reflecting on learning, questioning, modelling and problem solving. Another area focussed on improving the teaching and learning environment (e.g., making better use of resources, including web-based, additional adults in the classroom, and providing an emotionally secure environment for learning; DfES, 2004). Interestingly, all these components sound very much like long-standing and accepted aspects of effective pedagogy which have been researched and detailed for many years in the literature on effective classroom practice (e.g., Brophy, 1988; Brophy & Good, 2002; Good & Brophy, 1990). Evaluations conducted by the DfES (2004) indicated that the package was effective in raising both the quality of teaching practice and student achievement.

This research to policy to applied practice paradox was first described by Robinson (1993). (It is also referred to as the 'science to service dilemma'; see Fixen et al., 2009). Robinson observed that many academic researchers want their work to make a difference to applied practice, but it rarely does.

Politicians and policy-makers, certainly at an espoused level, also want to make a difference to people's lives, but research often plays a small or non-existent role within policy and practice discussions. The naive assumption is that once practitioners are aware of new 'truths', they will dutifully put them into practice consistently and coherently. Researchers often frustratingly say that if only people implemented all their recommendations, then outcomes would improve. Equally, educators and other applied practitioners often ask why researchers and policy-makers do not focus on the problems that they are *actually* dealing with on a day-to-day basis and offer them something focussed, practical and doable. Clearly, there is a need for processes and structures which enable more of a co-worker relationship between researchers who want their work to have an impact on applied practice, policy-makers and practitioners. This is the very dilemma that this book as a whole is trying to clarify, namely, the need to better understand the community, organizational and interpersonal conditions that encourage or discourage the selection and implementation of effective interventions and programmes.

Building Teacher and School Capacity: Developing Teachers' Problem-Solving and Decision-Making Skills

An important component in what is acknowledged to be a complex multi-faceted task is the view that it is the quality of teacher problem solving and decision making that is a key variable in linking sound research to effective practice and thus supporting the raising of pupil standards and attainments. The Department for Children, Schools and Families (DCFS, 2008) alluded to this when it emphasised the importance of the quality of teacher-learner interactions and their impact on both academic, behavioural and social-emotional success (Brown et al., 2010; Palardy & Ramberger, 2008).

The DCFS (2008) provided a practical guide on how to implement a Quality First Teaching program. This approach involves supporting less able pupils to enable them to keep up with the pace of the class and make improved progress in their learning. This replaces the emphasis on teachers differentiating work according to ability by providing less able children with 'easier work'. The DCFS (2008) argued that this method could reduce expectations and subsequent level of performance. Instead, the DCFS (2008) suggested differentiating according to the level of support required, setting mixed-ability tasks and offering extension activities. Furthermore, high and demanding yet realistic challenges should be set for pupils, with children expected to articulate their thoughts and ideas. Quality First Teaching requires teachers to develop effective strategies in questioning, modelling and explaining, each of which require adjusting according to the skills, prior learning and interests of pupils within the class. For instance, effective questioning promotes higher-order thinking skills and knowledge generation, whilst effective explanations help pupils to understand concepts which are beyond their own experiences (DCFS, 2008).

Quality First Teaching implements the following key characteristics: highly focussed lesson design with concrete objectives; high demands of pupil involvement and engagement with their learning; high levels of interaction for all pupils; appropriate use of teacher questioning, modelling and explaining; an emphasis on learning through dialogue, with regular opportunities for pupils to talk both individually and in groups; an expectation that pupils will accept responsibility for their own learning and work independently; regular use of encouragement and specific praise to engage and motivate pupils (DCFS, 2008).

An important component implicit within the whole Quality First Teaching rhetoric is the rigor of teacher problem solving and decision making. Four pieces of work now will be examined to add weight to the argument that directly training teachers to be better problem solvers can improve both the quality of teaching and, as a consequence, student outcomes.

In the first study, Bahr & Kovaleski (2006) were troubled by the number of pupils who had not acquired basic skills, including core literacy and numeracy, and suggested that one solution would be to implement problem-solving teams for members of staff to enable them to better help their pupils to develop these skills. They suggested that these problem-solving teams not only would be beneficial in terms of support whilst dealing with problems in the classroom but also would help teachers in the implementation of new strategies required of them.

In the second study, Farouk (2004), employing the Staff Sharing Scheme (a problem-solving group for school staff and others set up after training in core skills including problem solving; Gill & Monsen, 1995, 1996), attempted to evaluate the success of a group consultation approach using a structured collaborative problem-solving model. This work provided some evidence that training in problem solving helped teachers to offer more support to the pupils in their classrooms, which, in turn, led to improved outcomes. As part of the study, Farouk (2004) implemented group consultations with teachers working with children with emotional and/or behavioural difficulties. The intervention consisted of four phases: First, a named teacher describes their current problem in behavioural terms with data; second, reflection, in which the teacher was asked questions about the issue, home, classroom and other environmental aspects, including their contribution, with other teachers providing similar examples; third, group members discussed their theories about the situation; and fourth, strategies were generated through teachers collaboratively suggesting solutions that could be implemented and looking at intended and unintended consequences. The situation then was reviewed at the next meeting, and the cycle repeated.

Farouk (2004, p. 218) reported this intervention to be 'constructive and effective' and suggested that staff who felt emotionally contained in their school were more likely to have a positively supportive role within the classroom because they had the opportunity to reflect on their relationship with their pupils. However, this study did not identify either the measures taken to assess the effectiveness of this intervention or the basis on which the intervention was judged 'constructive and effective'.

Monsen & Graham (2002), in reflecting on the Staff Sharing Scheme, concluded that unless all staff had prior training in core skills (such as having a shared problem-solving model, shared language and concepts with which to talk about and structure thinking and issues and observation and interviewing skills including meeting management), problem solving within the Staff Sharing Scheme meetings reverted quickly to advice giving and largely 'within-child' conceptualizations. To address issues of behavioural drift, they ran yearly 'booster' training and had on-going quality assurance procedures built in (e.g., templates for meeting structure and written discussion summaries using ideas from Synectics, Rees & Monsen, 2000, 2010).

In the third study, Gregory (2010) considered teachers' attitudes towards problem-solving groups which aimed to address particular issues through exploring solutions and implementing these with students. This process has the potential to provide teachers with greater self-efficacy for managing problems. However, not all teachers reported problem-solving groups as being useful. Gregory (2010) suggested that teacher expectations affected the extent to which they implemented the solutions addressed within the problem-solving team. She further argued that this can lead to self-defeating beliefs and practices developing in which low expectations of students lead to subsequent low achievement. She proposed that these expectations can be affected by a range of factors, including previous negative experiences with problem-solving teams and a lack of perceived benefits of the intervention.

Finally, in the fourth study, Santangelo (2009) suggested that the expectation of the impact of collaborative problem solving has an influence on the actual outcome. For instance, teachers who entered collaborative problem solving with an attitude of 'referring' a child for special education screening were likely to use the group as an opportunity to confirm their negative expectations of that child, whilst those who viewed collaborative problem solving as a means to prevent unnecessary referrals were more likely to make effective and meaningful use of the groups. Santangelo (2009) highlighted that the types of interventions developed were affected by where participants attributed causation. If the problem is viewed internally to the student (i.e., largely 'within-child' causation), interventions will focus on the individual and to some extent his or her family, whilst if the problem is viewed more holistically (i.e., more eco-systemically and using circular rather than linear causation; Bronfenbrenner, 1979; Lave & Wenger, 1990), interventions will be implemented at both the classroom and school levels. The findings of this study revealed that the collaborative problem-solving groups were beneficial to teachers and led to the implementation of interventions for most children referred to the group. Staff were unanimous in describing these interventions as beneficial and demonstrating 'concrete progress'.

This was a longitudinal research study, and disappointingly, it showed that by year two, frequency of the collaborative problem-solving groups had dropped off dramatically, meetings were less structured than the previous year and few or inadequate meeting minutes and notes were taken. The joint collaborative feel of the group was lost through one individual mainly dominating discussions, and very few interventions were discussed and proposed. As a result, year two of the intervention had little impact on the children who were referred, and teachers expressed frustration that the second year of the approach was not as successful as the first year.

Teachers as 'New Scientist-Practitioners'?

Research, data and applied practice within education are often perceived as being quite separate from each other, even as 'different worlds' (Beycioglu, Ozer & Ugurlu, 2009; Carter & Wheldall, 2008). Results of the study by Beycioglu et al. (2009) indicated that 68 per cent of teachers had 'considered' empirical research findings as part of their on-going professional development, although the remaining 32 per cent had not. Of the 68 per cent who did say that they referred to research, the majority focussed on teacher development (31 per cent), followed by information communication technology and education (13.6 per cent), teacher-pupil interaction (12.8 per cent) and subject knowledge and effective teaching (10.8 per cent). This study found no significant differences between males and females, nor years of teaching experience, in those who considered empirical research. Although this study indicated that teachers did consider research findings to a certain extent, it did not investigate whether teachers actually implemented the findings in their classroom practice.

Teachers do not consistently consider research or data to be of great applied value and, as a result, do not seek to remain informed of current research practices, approaches and outcomes. Instead, some educationalists would argue that researchers do not have the insight of teachers because they do not have first-hand experience in schools, and thus their research findings are irrelevant to teaching practice (Beycioglu et al., 2009). In addition, since teachers do not actively engage with research after completing their own education and training, they lose their familiarity with the style of research reports, which thus become inaccessible to them (Beycioglu et al., 2009).

It may be that research is perceived as failing to address the individual situations teachers experience, and as a consequence, research findings are not seen as being relevant and therefore not implemented in their specific classrooms, that 'one size does not fit all' (Miretsky, 2007). Learning new ideas can be viewed by some teachers as threatening their 'expert' status, and finally, within the research community, teachers felt unaccepted as co-researchers amongst academic researchers (Miretsky, 2007; Vogrinc & Zuljan, 2009)

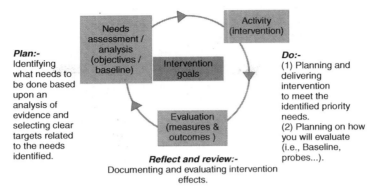

Plan:-
Identifying
what needs to
be done based
upon an
analysis of
evidence and
selecting clear
targets related
to the needs
identified.

Do:-
(1) Planning and
delivering
intervention
to meet the
identified priority
needs.
(2) Planning on how
you will evaluate
(i.e., Baseline,
probes...).

Reflect and review:-
Documenting and evaluating intervention
effects.

Figure 8.1. The plan, do, reflect, review cycle.

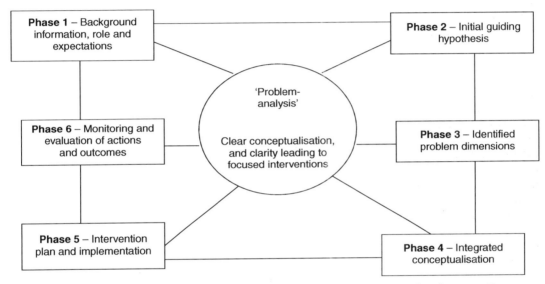

Figure 8.2. The six phases of the problem-analysis framework (Monsen & Frederickson, 2008).

This chapter argues that for quality teaching to be achieved, teachers must engage in professional training and development, which involves formulating and developing theories of their applied practice based on research and experience and which includes a critical reflection of actual data (e.g., including their own behaviour and the outcomes compared to baseline levels following implementation of a particular program, strategy or approach). Such an approach informs systematic changes in teacher practice and that of others which is evaluated, reviewed and used to inform future action. These actions can be conceptualised within a simple plan, do, reflect, review cycle which links well with later discussions around executive frameworks, such as the problem-analysis methodology (Figures 8.1 and 8.2).

Hemmeter and Fox's (2010) Teaching Pyramid provides a useful approach to aid teachers in putting research into practice in the classroom by offering a framework for interventions for social-emotional development and problem behaviour prevention. In order to succeed, the Teaching Pyramid assumes that teachers are willing to implement teaching practices that have been supported by empirical research. Teachers may not be able to implement each level of the Teaching Pyramid without support because they are not usually trained in research methods, including problem solving, or in implementing intensive and individual support to at-risk children. Hemmeter & Fox (2010) therefore proposed a professional training and development approach to support teachers in implementing the Teaching Pyramid in the classroom. This included training in the practices of the Teaching Pyramid, along with on-going classroom input that includes feedback and support in developing plans for individual children. Initially, teachers attend a training program of four non-consecutive days covering relationships, environment, social-emotional teaching strategies and intensive interventions for individuals. Additionally, researchers work alongside teachers to help them implement the Teaching Pyramid in their classroom practice. To do this, the researchers use data-based feedback to highlight the teachers' areas in which extra support is required, as well as helping teachers to plan how to implement the practices. On-going and comprehensive training practices are emphasized, and the teachers who undertook extensive training were most successful in implementing the Teaching Pyramid.

In a timely and challenging paper, Carter & Wheldall (2008) made a distinction between scientific and pseudo-scientific educators based on whether they actively evaluated the effectiveness of interventions using evaluative approaches such as triangulating different sources of information to inform and evaluate applied practice or whether they simply relied on non-verifiable testimonials and untested opinion to support their claims. They concluded that the teaching profession is still largely relying on opinions over quantified data, and as a result, the profession may be viewed as pre-scientific, although they note that an observable shift towards a more scientist-practitioner stance is evolving gradually.

The 'scientist-practitioner approach' as used in this chapter involves a conceptual stance by practitioners in which teaching methods and practices are informed according to valid and reliable evidence, either derived from the research literature or developed rigorously through the use of the scientific method within 'real-world' situations [see problem-based methodology (Robinson, 1993) as one way this process can be structured). Indeed, teachers who consider research findings and direct their teaching according to empirical evidence sometimes are referred to as 'data-based teachers' (Hattie, 2009). Nonetheless, implementation of evidence-based research into the classroom is very low, with one study indicating that only 17 per cent of teachers used methodologically sound techniques to implement programs (Forman et al., 2009).

In their research, Forman et al. (2009) sought to investigate the factors that influence graduates to implement either evidence-based interventions or approaches with no empirical backing. Participants attended a 15-week course on school-based interventions in which they were taught about the research literature regarding each approach, along with related issues around implementation. Participants were taught how to select appropriate interventions, how to implement them and how to evaluate them. Participants completed a questionnaire reflecting their use of the different interventions taught, both evidence-based and non-evidence-based, as well as on factors which had affected their use and implementation. Disappointingly, results indicated no significant difference in the use of evidence-based and non-evidence-based interventions. Forman et al. (2009) found that the use of an intervention included the belief that the approach would be effective for students, that the participant was able to implement the intervention successfully based on his or her knowledge and skills, that the intervention was consistent with the participant's general approach and the belief that the intervention was culturally specific to the students.

The Role of Executive Problem-Solving Frameworks

There is a small but growing body of research which suggests that the quality of teacher problem solving and decision making[2] (including the adoption of a more scientist-practitioner stance), whether undertaken individually with support or within collaborative groups, can lead to improved teaching practices (e.g., the systematic linking of research/data to informing applied practice) and subsequently positive impacts on a range of student outcomes. However, there are real questions about the sustainability of such approaches because teacher problem-solving groups are seen to slowly drift away from core principles, procedures and practices. This dilemma underpins much of this book, namely, how do effective approaches get embedded within systems which are sustainable and keep true to their core purposes? To do this, schools need to create systems and processes that encourage the regular use of research (whether generated internally or externally) data to inform problem solving, decision making and applied practice. DuFour, DuFour & Eaker (2008) refer to this as 'developing learning communities within collaborative learning environments'. Teacher capacity building, of which problem-solving efficacy is a core component, is vital for such a community to grow and develop (Pont, Nusche & Hopkins, 2008).

School leaders, teachers and other practitioners need help to do this complex task. They need a thinking framework which incorporates processes that enable clarity to be brought to the often complex and confusing situations with which practitioners work. Such a framework not only would have a structure to guide logical thinking but also would stress the importance of theory, research and data in the formulation, intervention planning and evaluation tasks. One type of executive framework which can be used by practitioners at either an individual, group or systems level to guide integrative practice is a 'problem-analysis framework' (Monsen & Frederickson, 2008; Monsen et al., 1998; Woolfson, 2008; Woolfson et al., 2003). It is argued that such a meta-conceptual framework can help with teacher capacity building by enabling practitioners, individually and collectively, to navigate the complexities inherent in working with 'real-world messes', to critically reflect on their actions

by using data to inform this process, to make alterations based on this evidence and to evaluate the effectiveness of new actions and so on in a purposeful developmental cycle. In this way, intervention approaches are designed after a careful analysis of the child or young person within a meaningful context bounded by the set of initial concerns. This would include consideration of individual, family, teacher, school and wider systemic factors. An intervention then is designed based on best current thinking and implemented and evaluated. The outcomes then inform a critical review of the efficacy of the approach, and changes are made in response to these. The cycle then continues until an agreed exit point is reached.

The problem-analysis cycle fits very much within the new scientist-practitioner model advocated by Lane & Corrie (2006) because it incorporates many of the core features of the scientific method. It also links very clearly with the five phases of research underpinning the translational research agenda, as detailed in this book [e.g., (1) identification of the problem and a critical review of information, (2) identification of both assets and areas of concern, (3) designing and piloting an intervention, (4) assessing effectiveness, and (5) disseminating outcomes; Mrazek & Haggerty (1994)].

Although it is beyond the scope of this chapter to delineate different problem-analysis frameworks [for a more comprehensive explanation of these, see Monsen et al. (1998, 2008), Woolfson et al. (2003), and Woolfson (2008)]. The remainder of this chapter will focus on one particular framework, that described by Monsen & Frederickson (2008), and in so doing aims to provide an understanding of some of the key conceptual and operational processes inherent in problem-analysis frameworks in general

The problem-analysis methodology was developed originally in New Zealand in the early 1980s by Robinson (1987) to help structure trainee educational and child psychologist thinking and decision making when working with complex cases, and it was developed further in the United Kingdom over the past twenty years by Monsen et al. (1998,

2008). The problem-analysis framework is now taught in an increasing number of training programmes for educational and child psychologists across a number of countries (Kelly, 2006; Kelly, Woolfson & Boyle, 2008; Woolfson, 2008; Woolfson et al., 2003). One of the main assumptions underpinning a problem-analysis approach is that the complex and ill-structured problems of practice with which practitioners are routinely involved can be seen to represent a set of conceptual and interpersonal interactions between the practitioner and others involving the explicit management of a range of information-processing and problem-understanding strategies and tasks. This position sees all those joining to solve problems as being involved in an active inquiry-based process as both 'meaning seekers' and 'problem solvers'. This view is informed by theoretical models of how experts and novices go about solving complex and ill-structured real-life problems and associated research into the constraints of human working memory, cognition and information processing (Anderson, Reder & Lebiere, 1996; Anderson, Spiro & Anderson, 1978; Argyris, 1993a, 1993b, 1993c; Argyris & Schön, 1974; Chi, Glaser & Farr, 1988; Dewey, 1933; Eraut, 1994; Elstein, Shulman & Sprafka, 1990; Frederickson, Webster & Wright, 1991; Glaser, 1984; Newell & Simon, 1972; Rose, 1999; Schraagen, 1993; Schwartz, Mennin & Webb, 2001; Shin, Jonassen & McGee, 2003; Simon, 1978).

The Problem-Analysis Cycle

This section delineates the six phases involved in the current problem-analysis framework (Monsen & Frederickson, 2008) as used in work with both trainee educational and child psychologists and, more recently, in developmental work with teacher-practitioners (see Figure 8.2).

Phase 1: Background Information, Role and Expectations

The first phase involves clarifying the presenting issue, problem or dilemma and checking out the need for more detailed practitioner[3] engagement and involvement. 'Clarification' involves making an objective appraisal of whether the issues are ones the practitioner (working with others and within his or her zone of professional competency) can deal with or whether the involvement of other agencies/practitioners is required given the nature of the initial concerns expressed.

If the practitioner considers that he or she is best placed to start work initially on the presenting issues, he or she needs to be clear about what the scope of his or her involvement will be (e.g., what his or her role, brief and purpose are – *the practitioner needs to negotiate and contract a clear role which includes a starting point and an exit point*). Such a tacit contract details the aspects of the problem situation which will be focussed on initially, along with tentative working performance targets (e.g., the goal would be that in six to eight weeks' time, Tim's attendance at the residential centre has increased to 95 per cent; see Dunsmuir et al., 2009). In each case, explicit rationales are provided for decisions made. The practitioner needs to give a clear indication of the scope and parameters of the investigative process, including how he or she and others (e.g., parents/care-givers and the students themselves) will be included, their role and how information will reported back and intervention plans negotiated, monitored and reviewed, including confidentiality.

Phase 2: Initial Guiding Hypotheses

PART I: INITIAL GUIDING HYPOTHESES
On the basis of the information collected so far, the practitioner begins to generate tentative 'initial guiding hypotheses' which help to focus and direct subsequent investigations and aid in the collection of additional information. Initial guiding hypotheses are formulated with direct reference to the unique details of the presenting problem context – to the theoretical, research and applied knowledge bases within the discipline of education and the social sciences. Initial guiding hypotheses are framed as 'if-

so, then-what' propositions (e.g., if Stewart had glue ear as an infant, it would be likely that he suffered from intermittent hearing loss, and so early phonological processing skills could have developed inconsistently, thus having a negative impact on his ability to decode words and so on).

While the initial guiding hypotheses define manageable sub-problems that are likely to be relevant, a holistic overview of the problem situation is maintained through the development of a visual 'problem map' in the form of an 'interactive factors framework' (Morton & Frith, 1995). All the initial guiding hypotheses are represented with arrows linking hypothesised cognitive and affective influencing factors with tentatively recorded behavioural level–specific descriptions of student behaviour and with information about systemic, home, school and biological-based factors (e.g., obtained from parent/care-giver interviews, records and other workers). Over the course of the problem-analysis cycle, the interactive factors framework (IFF) will be altered many times as new information is identified and processed conceptually. It is useful to represent 'assets/strengths' (both within individuals and in their environments) on the IFF because this information can assist in ruling out some hypotheses, generating new ones and providing insights into what interventions might be effective in later phases.

PART II: ACTIVE INVESTIGATION (DATA COLLECTION AND ASSESSMENT)
Having formulated a range of within-child and broader eco-systemic initial guiding hypotheses about what could be going on to perpetuate difficulties and how improvements might be effected, the practitioner is now in a position to systematically investigate these various lines of inquiry (i.e., collect information which may support or disconfirm these initial guiding hypotheses). The practitioner may draw on the full range of direct and indirect assessment techniques at his or her disposal. In seeking to 'triangulate' key conclusions, it is important that confirmatory information is sampled from more than one source and that a sound (e.g.,

reliable, valid and culturally appropriate) range of approaches has been drawn on.

Phase 3: Identified Problem Dimensions

On the basis of the investigations undertaken as part of phase 2, the practitioner sorts and combines the information obtained to identify at a conceptual level what aspects in the problem situation are currently problematic. These conceptual categories are called 'problem dimensions'. Each problem dimension is given a clear and unambiguous title or label. The main dimensions isolated need to cover the key conceptual areas of the problem situation for which there is triangulated evidence, and they must be linked (e.g., same titles or labels are used) throughout any written or oral presentation.

A critical task for the practitioner is to make sure that all relevant problem dimensions are covered and that supporting information is presented for all dimensions (i.e., a mini-integration is provided which clearly argues why a given area is 'problematic'. Specific supporting information, derived from tests, observation and interviews can be located in the appendices in the form of tables and/or summaries). It is important to note that dimensions are presented in terms of *behaviours* (e.g., for literacy, a student may present with 'limited self-correction skills') and/or relevant *constructs* (e.g., limited impulse control), not by the assessment devices used (e.g., the Neale Analysis of Reading Ability II) or by un-integrated data (e.g., child's views or parent's/care-giver's views).

Phase 4: Integrated Conceptualisation/ Formulation

PART I: INTEGRATING STATEMENT
The main task during this part of phase 4 is to formulate an over-arching integrating statement which argues for possible interconnections, influences and 'causal relationships' between problem dimensions and priorities for action which will inform intervention planning. The integrating hypotheses chosen are based on logic and sound

research and must help to make sense of the information collected and lead to a clear rationale for subsequent intervention recommendations and actions. The second task is for the practitioner to give reasons for the selection of one or more of the dimensions as being a priority for intervention rather than targeting all dimensions. Some dimensions may be selected as priorities because they are hypothesised as contributing to others, or it may be predicted that by focussing on X dimension(s), changes in the other problem areas are likely. Dimensions also may be prioritised because they require immediate intervention (e.g., child safety, socio-emotional and well-being issues) or because they are the only accessible dimensions.

In undertaking this conceptual task, the practitioner must be mindful that his or her integrating or linking hypotheses are consistent with the evidence presented in previous phases and that his or her reasoning is clear and coherent (e.g., why have selected dimensions been chosen as priorities, or equally, why have all dimensions been selected?) Whilst constructing his or her statement, the practitioner must evaluate other plausible alternative conceptualisations for 'goodness of fit' and, if discounted, provide reasons. It is also important that arguments are supported with reference to sound contemporary research.

PART II: INTERACTIVE FACTORS FRAMEWORK DIAGRAM

In this part of phase 4, a coherent working version of the IFF is completed. The IFF displays all the problem dimensions identified, together with other relevant aspects of the problem situation for which there is evidence. The integrating hypotheses will be shown via arrows indicating the connections between the behavioural, cognitive, affective, environmental and biological level variables as argued in the integrating statement.

Influences between problem dimensions (and other elements) in the IFF diagram are sometimes mutual, leading to vicious or virtuous cycles. Where this is thought to be happening, the factors concerned can be connected by double-headed arrows which represent bi-directional interactions. In these cases, a decision may be taken at phase 5 to change whichever of the two factors is easiest to alter. However, in most cases, one of the factors will be conceptualised as exerting a stronger influence on the other, and a uni-directional arrow should be used for conceptual clarity.

Phase 5: Intervention Plan and Implementation

AGREED ACTION PLAN, FEEDBACK AND AGREED PROBLEM ANALYSIS AND CREATION OF AN INTERVENTION PLAN

During this phase, the practitioner uses his or her 'working' conceptualisation of the problem situation (phase 4) and the reasons for the intervention approach(es) being considered in the form of a menu with which to negotiate and agree on a 'final' action plan with relevant co-workers, including parents/care-givers and the students themselves. An important skill for the practitioner is to be able to detach from his or her own working conceptualisation so that he or she can actively listen to others' views. In this way, valid new perspectives and insights can be discussed and integrated into plans. One of the skills practitioners need to develop is the ability to carefully critique arguments for or against particular courses of action and locate them firmly back to the agreed logic of the working conceptualisation. During these 'critical dialogues' (Cameron & Monsen, 1998; Robinson, 1993), it is vital that the practitioner considers the manageability of any proposed plan as well as the detail of target setting and monitoring arrangements (both internal and external).

An outcome of phase 5 is that the integrating statement and IFF are reviewed and revised as necessary, with the final intervention plan being developed in active consultation with those directly involved in the situation: other teachers, carer-givers and children/young people. This said, interventions must be consistent with the agreed core principles outlined in the integration statement, efficacy evidence, relevant theory and research, logic and/or best-practice guidance, with the rationale for the intervention being made explicit to all parties. Once an intervention has been agreed on, the practitioner guides the discussion towards the details of implementation: the who, what, when and where and procedures for recording, target setting, monitoring and evaluating. It is important to check out, rather than assume, that those involved have the skills and key resources needed to implement the intervention successfully and that they are realistic about the commitment of time and effort involved.

Phase 6: Monitoring and Evaluation of Outcomes

This phase involves a joint critical evaluation with all those who have been involved in trying to improve the problem situation. The participants evaluate the status of the problem (as framed by the performance targets negotiated at the outset of the process) following their efforts (this may involve consideration of the on-going records being kept by teachers/care-givers and/or the students themselves, or it may involve further data collection, such as a post-intervention reading test or behaviour-monitoring checklists to allow pre/post-intervention comparisons). The participants decide whether satisfactory progress is apparent in relation to the evaluation criteria (agreed-on targets) confirmed in phase 5 and consider further actions that may be needed (from further investigations to regular reviews of progress). If progress is judged to be satisfactory, maintenance procedures may be identified to ensure that the problem situation does not recur, and systemic implications of what has been learned that may be relevant to other similar problems in the future may be discussed. If progress has not been judged to be satisfactory, participants would critically review the problem-solving cycle undertaken and make amendments and changes as required. This may involve going back to the beginning or earlier phases and revising the intervention and re-running the process.

Reflective Commentary

Practitioners are asked to critically reflect on their own involvement in considering how effective they were at each of the phases in the problem-analysis cycle. Specific performance criteria for each phase have been developed based on earlier work undertaken by Robinson (1987) to guide this process. For example, practitioners are asked to consider the following when judging problem-analysis quality: At phase 3, were the problem dimensions accurate, complete and clear? At phase 4, did the integrating statement make clear the relative importance of the problem dimensions and the 'causes' of the priority problem? At phase 5, were the intervention plans specific, appropriate and complete? And at phase 6, did the criteria for evaluation enable clear pre/post-intervention comparisons and enable the use of both qualitative and quantitative information?

Practitioners are encouraged to identify factors across phases which supported or constrained their functioning. Great emphasis is placed on tutor and/or peer consultation to provide a 'critical' perspective not only on the efficacy of the actual intervention negotiated and implemented but also on practitioner performance and quality of analysis and formulation (e.g., from listening to or viewing interview tapes or reviewing the logic and clarity of written and oral work and feedback from problem owner, parents/care-givers, students, supervisor, tutors, other practitioners and so on).

Working with Teacher-Practitioners

In recent developmental work, three cohorts of elementary classroom and specialist teachers within a large local authority in England were directly taught a modified version of the problem-analysis framework of Monsen et al. (2008). One of the main research questions was to see whether a problem-solving framework that was designed originally for trainee psychologist practitioners also could be applicable to teacher-practitioners. Such practitioners need to develop their critical-thinking and decision-making skills around identifying, investigating, analyzing, designing, implementing and evaluating interventions within classrooms, and it was argued that problem-analysis methodology could assist these tasks greatly.

The outcomes for teacher-practitioners were positive when compared to control group results. Before and after training, both teacher-practitioner and control groups were given a written task [writing an abridged problem analysis under prescribed headings in response to a standardised video case study based on the methodology first used by Monsen & Frederickson (2002)]. The subsequent scripts then were compared to a model problem analysis based on this case study using a number of criteria. In addition, an assessment was made of an actual written case study, following the six phases of the modified version of the problem-analysis approach and undertaken by participants over a term. The results of this study are currently being written up (Monsen, Eberlien & Soan, forthcoming).

The problem-analysis framework used in this study with teacher-practitioners was based on the various theoretical, conceptual and practical considerations detailed in previous publications (see Monsen & Frederickson, 2008; Monsen et al., 1998). Problem managers and their collaborators are helped to conceptualise 'the facts of the situation' derived from the 'real-world problems' with which they are involved in ways which facilitate understanding by themselves, other practitioners, parents/care-givers and the children and young people themselves. The assumption is that because subsequent actions and a uniquely tailored intervention are based on a sound analysis of the situation's assets, difficulties and constraints, client outcomes will be more successful.

The problem situations with which school staff and other practitioners work can appear overwhelming initially. It is not surprising that unless trained directly in the rigor of an executive framework such as problem analysis, problem managers and their collaborators can lose sight initially of the problem situation as a whole in an attempt to 'contain the situation' by focussing too early on what seems to be the most relevant aspects, the 'priority problem' (Robinson, 1987). On the other hand, order does need to be established from the morass of information available before a clear path of action can be clarified, negotiated and implemented.

The problem-analysis framework demands that the problem manager does more than record actions taken, the data obtained and agreed-on outcomes; information is organized *conceptually*. One way to manage such a complex task is for the problem manager and his or her key partners to be clear about what the issue(s) actually is and who they need to involve. Such clarification of the *role, purpose and brief* assists not only the problem-solving task but also communication (phase 1). Next, the problem manager and his or her key partners use their content knowledge (derived from their core discipline – education, psychology or social sciences) and their own experiences to formulate 'initial guiding hypotheses' (phase 2, which is linked clearly with the relevant research literature) to focus their thinking and subsequent actions. The problem manager and partners then systematically investigate the efficacy of these various lines of initial inquiry, culminating in the development of a model which transforms the details of the situation into a 'problem map' (this can be presented visually using the IFF, which structures the facts of the case, the assets which are important in developing interventions and the identified problem dimensions, including systemic, organizational, environmental and with-in client, which were found to be problematic (this is phase 3 – and at phase 5, an overlay is provided which clearly shows how intervention strategies and approaches will address all or some of the identified problem dimensions). Then the problem manager and partners present an argued conceptualisation/formulation (this is phase 4, integrating hypotheses, which again is linked clearly with the research literature on the efficacy of various approaches to deal with the issues identified as priorities for intervention). It describes the key 'problem dimensions' (aspects of the situation found to be problematic) and their interconnections and leads to a clear plan for focussed action (i.e., the unique intervention; this is phase 5, where intervention strategies are overlaid onto the IFF). Embedded throughout the cycle is critical evaluation not only of the intervention itself but also of the problem manager's own actions at each phase, in the form of a 'reflective commentary' (this is phase 6 and facilitates supervision sessions).

In working with teachers, as opposed to trainees or practicing educational psychologists, although the conceptual framework is essentially the same, the following elements need to be taught directly and reinforced in parallel to presenting the framework itself: being able to read research papers critically, including library skills; introduction to research methods, including being able to interpret basic statistical data; practicing core skills, such as classroom observation, interviewing and assessment; and so on. There is an additional need for supervision to help develop the discipline of critical reflection around applying the framework to the actual practice. This was carried out within both one-to-one and small groups.

In learning problem analysis, the phases needed to be made explicit, and teacher-practitioners learned whilst they worked on a 'real-life' case within a classroom over the course of a term. The level of detail and writing required would be much more streamlined after training and in subsequent practice. For example, one specialist teacher used the problem-analysis approach to re-structure her assessment reports, using the following headings – 'Background and Brief' (phase 1), 'Themes Emerging from Investigations' (phase 3), 'Integration' (phase 4), and 'Agreed Actions and Next Steps' (phase 5).

Concluding Comments

This chapter has argued that one important component greatly overlooked in the research to policy to practice dilemma [also referred to as the 'science to service dilemma' (Fixen et al., 2009)] is the quality and rigor of practitioner problem solving and decision making. The recent re-discovery that it is the quality of teaching which makes the most difference in terms of the fidelity of intervention implementation goes a long way towards reinforcing the need to develop rigorous individual and organisational thinking (DuFour et al., 2008).

Executive frameworks such as the problem-analysis methodology described in this chapter provide a conceptual structure within which practitioner thinking and action can be guided and made explicit and therefore open to challenge, debate and review. Such an approach is one way of structuring both the stages of intervention implementation (e.g., exploration, installation, initial implementation, full implementation, innovation and sustainability) and some of the more specific core components of implementation (e.g., staff selection, pre-service and in-service training, on-going training and consultation, staff evaluation, decision-support data systems, facilitative administrative support and systems intervention) which have been shown to increase the effectiveness of intervention implementation (Fixen et al., 2009).

The deployment of an executive framework would greatly assist in the pragmatic task of structuring the complex processes involved in moving practitioners away from so-called cook book approaches to intervention thinking and implementation. Executive frameworks would enable practitioners to become more active thinking partners in the process rather than merely delivering core components without any real awareness or understanding of why an approach has to be done in a particular way to ensure the increased likelihood of positive change.

Within the problem-analysis executive framework described in this chapter are a set of task demands built into each of the six phases in the cycle. For example, phases 2 and 3 move practitioner thinking towards seeing problems of practice as occurring within a complex ecology rather than simply emanating from 'within-person' causes. Phases 1, 4, 5 and 6 stress the need for practitioners to take much more responsibility for evaluating the impact of their plans and actions in systematic ways (i.e., adopting a 'new scientist-practitioner' stance) in quality assuring the implementation of plans and interventions (e.g., ensuring the fidelity of programs in terms of both quality and quantity) and in on-going monitoring and review.

Fixen et al. (2009) argue that teacher-practitioners and school leaders cannot do these tasks on their own and need skilful external assistance and support. Fixen et al. (2009) refer to the role of 'purveyors' (e.g., an individual or group of individuals who actively work to implement a practice or programme with fidelity and good effect) and the importance of collaborative coaching as a means of achieving this. These roles and approaches need much more delineating as we grapple with the tasks of embedding relevant evidence-based research into sound applied practice.

Acknowledgements

We wish to thank Donna Ewing (research consultant to the Kent Educational Psychology Service Research Group) for her help and assistance in the preparation of this chapter.

Notes

1. Although examples are drawn from educational research and practice, many of the ideas will have applicability to others working with children and young people.
2. It is beyond the scope of this chapter to detail other equally important aspects for effective practice, such as practitioner interpersonal skills and level of content knowledge and expertise. It is argued that unless these aspects are also developed, problem solving and decision making are less effective.
3. The term 'practitioner' has been used in this section as a generic term to cover anyone who is in a problem-solving co-ordination role.

References

Allen, J. M. (2009). Valuing practice over theory: How beginning teachers re-orient their practice in the transition from the university to the workplace. *Teaching and Teacher Education* 25, 647–54.

Annan, J. (2005). Situational analysis: A framework for evidence-based practice. *School Psychology International* 26(2), 131–46.

Anderson, J.R., Reder, L. M. & Lebiere, C. (1996). Working memory: Activation limitations on retrieval. *Cognitive Psychology* 30, 221–56.

Anderson, R. C., Spiro, R. J. & Anderson, M. C. (1978). Schemata as scaffolding for the representation of information in connected discourse. *American Educational Research Journal* 15, 433–39.

Argyris, C. (1993a). *Knowledge for action: A guide to overcoming barriers to organizational change.* San Francisco: Jossey-Bass.

Argyris, C. (1993b). On the nature of actionable knowledge. *The Psychologist* 16, 29–32.

Argyris, C. (1999). *On organisational learning*, 2nd ed. Oxford, UK: Blackwell.

Argyris, C., & Schön, D. A. (1974). *Theory in practice.* San Francisco: Jossey-Bass.

Bahr, M. W., & Kovaleski, J. F. (2006). The need for problem-solving teams: Introduction to the special issue. *Remedial and Special Education* 27(1), 2–5.

Beycioglu, K., Ozer, N. & Ugurlu, C. T. (2009). Teachers views on educational research. *Teaching and Teacher Education* 26, 1088–93.

Bronfenbrenner, U. (1979). *The ecology of human development.* Cambridge: MA: Harvard University Press.

Brophy, J. E. (1988). Research linking teacher behavior to student achievement: Potential implications for instruction of Chapter 1 students. *Educational Psychologist* 23(3), 235–86.

Chi, M. T. H., Glaser, R. & Farr, M. J. (eds.) (1988). *The nature of expertise.* Hillsdale, NJ: Erlbaum.

Good, T. L., & Brophy, J. E. (2002). *Looking in classrooms*, 9th ed. Boston: Allyn & Bacon.

Good, T. L., & Brophy, J. E. (1990). *Educational psychology: A realistic approach*, 4th ed. Reading, MA: Addison-Wesley.

Brown, J. L., Jones, S. M., LaRusso, M. D. & Aber, J. L. (2010). Improving classroom quality: Teacher influences and experimental impacts of the 4Rs programme. *Journal of Educational Psychology* 102(1), 153–67.

Cameron, R. J., & Monsen, J. J. (1998). Coaching and critical dialogue in educational psychology practice. *Educational and Child Psychology* 15(4), 112–26.

Carter, M., & Wheldall, K. (2008). Why can't a teacher be more like a scientist? Science, pseudoscience and the art of teaching. *Australasian Journal of Special Education* 32(1), 5–21.

Centre for Social Justice (2006). *The state of the nation report: Educational failure*. London: Educational Failure Working Group.

Centre for Social Justice (2007). *Breakdown Britain: Ending the costs of social breakdown*, Vol. 3. London: Educational Failure Working Group.

Department for Children, Schools and Families (DCSF) (2008). *Personalised learning: A practical guide*. London: DCSF.

Department for Children, Schools and Families (DCSF) (2009). *The children's plan: Two years on a progress report*. London: DCSF.

Department for Education and Skills (DfES) (2004). *Intensifying support programme*. London: DfES, Primary National Strategy.

Dewey, J. (1933). *How we think: A restatement of the relation of reflective thinking to the educative process*. Boston: D.C. Heath (originally published 1910).

Duckworth, K., Ackerman, R., MorrisonGutman, L. & Vorhaus, J. (2009). *Influences and leverages on low levels of attainment: A review of literature and policy initiatives*. London: Centre for Research on the Wider Benefits of Learning, Institute of Education, University of London.

DuFour, R., DuFour, R. & Eaker, R. (2008). *Revisiting professional learning communities at work: New insights for improving schools*. Bloomington, IN: Solution Tree Press.

Dunsmuir, S., Brown, E., Iyadurai, S. & Monsen, J. J. (2009). Evidence-based practice and evaluation: From insight to impact. *Educational Psychology in Practice* 25(1), 53–70.

Efran, J. S., & Clarfield, L. E. (1992). Constructionist therapy: Sense and nonsense. In S. McNamee and K. J. Gergen (eds.), *Therapy as social construction*. London: Sage.

Eisenhauer, L. A., & Gendrop, S. (1990). *Review of research in nursing education*, Vol. 3. New York: National League for Nursing.

Elstein, A. S., Shulman, L. S. & Sprafka, S. A. (1990). Medical problem-solving: A ten-year retrospective. *Evaluation and the Health Professionals* 13(1), 5–36.

Eraut, M. (1994). *Developing professional knowledge and competence*. London: The Falmer Press.

Frederickson, N., Webster, A. & Wright, A. (1991). Psychological assessment: A change of emphasis. *Educational Psychology in Practice* 7(1), 20–9.

Farouk, S. (2004). Group work in schools: A process consultation approach. *Educational Psychology in Practice* 20(3), 207–20.

Fixen. D., Blasé, K. A., Naoom, S. F. & Wallace, F (2009). Core implementation components. *Research on Social Work Practice* 19(5), 531–40.

Forman, S. G., Fagley, N. S., Steiner, D. D. & Schneider, K. (2009). Teaching evidence-based interventions: Perceptions of influences on use in professional practice in school psychology. *Training and Education in Professional Psychology* 3(4), 226–32.

Fullan, M. (2010a). *Motion leadership: The skinny on becoming change savvy*. Thousand Oaks, CA: Corwin/Sage.

Fullan, M. (2010b). *All systems go: The change imperative for whole system reform. Motion leadership: The skinny on becoming change savvy*. Thousand Oaks, CA: Corwin/Sage.

Gill, D. W., & Monsen, J. J. (1996). The staff sharing scheme: A school-based management system for working with challenging child behaviour. In E. Blyth and J. Milner (eds.), *Exclusion from school: Inter-professional issues for policy and practice* (pp. 185–207). London: Routledge.

Gill, D. W., & Monsen, J. J. (1995). The staff sharing scheme: A school-based management system for working with challenging child behaviour. *Educational and Child Psychology* 12(2), 71–80.

Glaser, R. (1984). Education and thinking: The role of knowledge. *American Psychologist* 39(2), 93–104.

Gregory, A. (2010). Teacher learning on problem-solving teams. *Teacher and Teacher Education* 26, 608–15.

Hattie, J. (2009). *Visible learning: A synthesis of over 800 meta-analyses relating to achievement*, London: Routledge.

Hemmeter, M. L., & Fox, L. (2010). The teaching pyramid: A model for the implementation of classroom practices within a program-wide approach to behavior support. *National Head Start Association Dialogue* 12(2), 133–47. Retrieved 24 April 2010, from http://nationalstrategies.standards.dcsf.gov.uk/node/156775?uc%20=%20force_uj.

Hills, J. (Chair) (2010). *An anatomy of economic inequality in the UK*. London: National Equality Panel.

Jones, V., & Jones, L. (2006). *Comprehensive classroom management: Creating communities of support and solving problems*, 6th ed. Boston: Allyn & Bacon.

Kelly, B. (2006). Exploring the usefulness of the Monsen problem-solving framework for applied practitioners. *Educational Psychology in Practice* 22(1), 1–17.

Kelly, B., Woolfson, L. & Boyle, J. (eds.) (2008). *Frameworks for practice in educational psychology: A textbook for trainees and practitioners.* London: Jessica Kingsley Publishers.

Lane, D. A., & Corrie, S. (2006). *The modern scientist-practitioner: A guide to practice in psychology.* London: Routledge.

Lave, J., & Wenger, E. (1990). *Situated learning: Legitimate peripheral participation.* Cambridge, UK: Cambridge University Press.

Miretsky, D. (2007). A view of research from practice: Voices of teachers. *Theory into Practice* 46(4), 272–80.

Monsen, J. J., & Frederickson, N. (2008). The Monsen et al problem-solving model ten years on. In B. Kelly, L. Woolfson, and J. Boyle (eds.), *Frameworks for practice in educational psychology: A textbook for trainees and practitioners* (pp. 69–93). London: Jessica Kingsley Publishers.

Monsen, J. J., & Frederickson, N. (2002). Consultant problem understanding as a function of training in interviewing to promote accessible reasoning. *Journal of School Psychology* 40(3), 197–212.

Monsen, J. J., & Graham, B. (2002). Developing teacher support groups to deal with challenging child behaviour: The staff-sharing scheme. In P. Gray (ed.), *Working with emotions: Responding to the challenges of difficult pupil behaviour in schools* (pp. 129–49). London: Routledge.

Monsen, J. J., Graham, B., Frederickson, N. & Cameron, S. (1998). Problem analysis and professional training in educational psychology: An accountable model of practice. *Educational Psychology in Practice* 13(4), 234–49.

Morton, J., & Frith, U. (1995). Causal modelling: A structural approach to developmental psychopathology. In D. Cilchette and D. J. Cohen (eds.), *Manual of developmental psychopathology*, Vol. 1 (pp. 357–90). New York: Wiley.

Newell, A., & Simon, H. A. (1972). *Human problem-solving.* Englewood Cliffs, NJ: Prentice-Hall.

Palardy, G. J., & Rumberger, R. W. (2008). Teacher effectiveness in first grade: The importance of background qualifications, attitudes and instructional practices for student learning. *Educational Evaluation and Policy Analysis* 30(2), 111–40.

Pont, B., Nusche, D. & Hopkins, D. (eds) (2008). *Improving school leadership*, Vol. 2: *Case studies on systems leadership.* Paris: OECD.

Rees, R., & Monsen, J. J. (2010). Using pieces of synectics to enhance applied practice within a large children's services: An ever evolving jigsaw. In V. Nolan (ed.), *Imagine that! 50 years of synectics* (pp. 160–4). London: Synectics Education Initiatives.

Rees, R., & Monsen, J. J. (2000). Perspectives on using ideas from synectics to contribute to creativity, innovation and organisational change within a large local authority. In V. Nolan (ed.), *Educating a nation of innovators* (pp. 199–222). London: Synectics Education Initiatives.

Reis-Jorge, J. (2007). Teachers' conceptions of teacher-research and self-perceptions as enquiring practitioners: A longitudinal case study. *Teaching and Teacher Education* 23, 402–17.

Robinson, V. (1987). A problem-analysis approach to decision-making and reporting for complex cases. *Journal of the New Zealand Psychological Service Association* 8, 35–48.

Robinson, V. (1993). *Problem-based methodology: Research for the improvement of practice.* Oxford, UK: Pergamon Press.

Robinson, V., & Halliday, J. (1987) A critique of the micro-skills approach to problem understanding. *British Journal of Guidance and Counselling* 15(2), 113–24.

Robinson, V., & Halliday, J. (1988). Relationship of counsellor reasoning and data collection to problem-analysis quality. *British Journal of Guidance and Counselling* 16(1), 50–62.

Rose, S. (ed.) (1999). *From brains to consciousness? Essays on the new sciences of the mind.* London: Penguin Books.

Schraagen, J. M. (1993). How experts solve a novel problem in experimental design. *Cognitive Science* 17, 285–309.

Schwartz, P., Mennin, S. & Webb, G. (eds.) (2001). *Problem-based learning: Case studies, experience and practice.* London: Kogan Page.

Shin, N., Jonassen, D. H. & McGee, S. (2003). Predictors of well-structured and ill-structured problem-solving in an astronomy simulation. *Journal of Research in Science Teaching* 40(1), 6–33.

Santangelo, T. (2009). Collaborative problem-solving successfully implemented, but not sustained: A case for aligning the sun, the moon and the stars. *Exceptional Children* 7(2), 185–209.

Save the Children (2010). *Measuring severe child poverty in the UK: Policy briefing*. London: Save the Children.

Smith, C., Blake, A., Curwen, K., Dodds, D., Easton, L., McNally, J., Swierczek, P. & Walker, L. (2009). Teachers as researchers in a major research project: Experience of input and output. *Teaching and Teacher Education* 25, 959–65.

Simon, H. A. (1978). *The sciences of the artificial*, 2nd ed. Cambridge, MA: MIT Press.

UNICEF (2007). *Child poverty in perspective: An overview of child well-being in rich countries* (Innocenti Report Card 7). Florence: UNIEF Innocenti Research Centre.

Vogrinc, J., & Zuljan, M. V. (2009). Action research in schools: An important factor in teachers' professional development. *Educational Studies* 35(1), 53–63.

West-Burnham, J. (2009). *Rethinking educational leadership*. London: Network Continuum.

Wilden, S., & LaGro, N. (1998). New frameworks for careers guidance: Developing a conceptual model of the interview. *British Journal of Guidance and Counselling* 26(2), 175–93.

Woolfson, L. (2008). The Woolfson et al integrated framework: An executive framework for service-wide use. In B. Kelly, L. Woolfson, and J. Boyle (eds.), *Frameworks for practice in educational psychology: A textbook for trainees and practitioners*. London: Jessica Kingsley Publishers.

Woolfson, L., Whaling, R., Stewart, A. & Monsen, J. J. (2003). An integrated framework to guide educational psychologist practice. *Educational Psychology in Practice* 19(4), 283–302.

CHAPTER 9

Researching Readiness for Implementation of Evidence-Based Practice

A Comprehensive Review of the Evidence-Based Practice Attitude Scale (EBPAS)

Gregory A. Aarons, Amy E. Green, and Elizabeth Miller

Introduction

There is increasing momentum in the United States and abroad for the dissemination and implementation of evidence-based practices into real-world service settings. This momentum is bringing pressure on service systems, organizations, and service providers to adopt evidence-based practices (Burns, 2003; Essock et al., 2003; Glisson, 2002; Hoagwood, 2005; Ringeisen & Hoagwood, 2002). There are many sources of such pressure, including federal, state, and local government agencies, mental health authorities, agency directors, health management organizations, insurance companies, supervisors, peers, and consumers (Essock et al., 2003). However, the recent proliferation of promising and empirically tested interventions and protocols has not been matched by widespread and effective implementation of such practices in

community settings. Concern about this "knowledge-practice" gap has focused attention on identifying and testing mechanisms that facilitate or inhibit evidence-based practice dissemination and implementation (Aarons, 2005; Greenhalgh et al., 2004; Simpson, 2002). In considering initiatives that support the "push" of evidence-based practices into community-based settings, it is important to take into account provider attitudes toward adopting evidence-based practices in order to better tailor implementation efforts to meet the needs and/or characteristics of providers and to increase their motivations for evidence-based practice use. Understanding and increasing the market for evidence-based practices, as represented by service provider perspectives, can contribute to increasing the "pull" for evidence-based practice by tailoring strategies to increase the demand for these practices.

Attitudes and Implementation

Attitudes toward innovation can be a facilitating or limiting factor in the dissemination and implementation of new technologies (Damanpour, 1991; Frambach & Schillewaert, 2002). Attitudes can be a precursor to the decision of whether or not to try a new practice, and the affective component of attitudes can have an impact on decision processes regarding innovation adoption (Candel & Pennings, 1999; Frambach & Schillewaert, 2002; Rogers, 1995). Attitudes, along with behavioral intention and self-efficacy, often precede behavior and can predict behavior change (Bandura, 1982, 2002; Fishbein & Ajzen, 1975; Fishbein et al., 2003). Hence there is a need to better understand the relationship of provider beliefs, attitudes, and behavior (Jaccard et al., 1995) toward adoption of evidence-based practice.

Providers' attitudes toward change and innovation may influence the implementation of evidence-based practice at several stages. First, provider attitudes toward innovation in general can be a precursor to the decision of whether to try a new practice or not. Second, if providers do decide to try a new practice, the affective or emotional component of attitudes can affect decision processes regarding the actual implementation and use of the innovation (Aarons, 2005; Candel & Pennings, 1999; Frambach & Schillewaert, 2002). Third, attitudes can and do change with experience, and it is important to be able to gauge these changes over time (Rydell & McConnell, 2006).

Evidence suggests that the dissemination and implementation of an innovation such as evidence-based practice must take into account the complexity inherent in real-world service settings (Fraser & Greenhalgh, 2001; Hasenfeld, 1992; Henggeler, Lee, & Burns, 2002; Jankowicz, 2000; Simpson, 2002). For example, service providers often work in programs that are subject to federal, state, and county policies and regulations. In regard to contracting, programs may have to compete for contracts, and service provision is often subject to the terms of such contracts that may or may not mandate the use of evidence-based practices. Services also take place within organizational contexts that vary in regard to the quality of leadership and supervision, organizational norms and expectations, organizational climate (Glisson, 2002), and climate for implementation (Aarons, Dlugosz, & Ehrhart, forthcoming). Common methods of social service technology transfer (e.g., treatment manuals, off-site training sessions) often fail to take into account the many complexities inherent in practice change and hence may lack effectiveness (Addis, 2002; Backer, David, & Soucy, 1995; Backer, Liberman, & Kuehnel, 1986; Henggeler & Schoenwald, 2002; Strupp & Anderson, 1997). Thus it is important to understand and consider the attitudes of clinicians and providers embedded within such complex organizational systems (Burns, Hoagwood, & Mrazek, 1999; Garland, Kruse, & Aarons, 2003; Hoagwood et al., 2001).

The existing literature suggests at least four potentially important domains of provider attitudes toward adoption of evidence-based practice. First, the intuitive appeal of innovation is important to consider in organizational change. This notion is supported by studies of persuasion processes and provider efficacy (Cialdini, Bator, & Guadagno, 1999; Tormala & Petty, 2002; Watkins, 2001). For example, studies have shown that providers are more at ease with information derived from colleagues in contrast to research articles or books (Cohen, Sargent, & Sechrest, 1986; Morrow-Bradley & Elliott, 1986) and that attitudes toward adoption of evidence-based practices likely will be influenced by the appeal of an evidence-based practice, including the information source (Frambach & Schillewaert, 2002).

Second, requirements to provide services in a specified way based on organizational policies or funding exigencies may or may not be followed by service providers. For example, there is variability in the degree to which providers adopt and comply with new practices even when "required" by supervisors or agency mandates (Garland et al., 2003). Although some providers may be more or less compliant with required changes, individual and organizational variability can affect the degree to which innovations are adopted and sustained in practice (Glisson, 2002). Compliance with requirements differs from openness (i.e., willingness to try new experiences or consider new ways of doing things) in that it denotes how employees respond to organizational rules and regulations. For example, an employee may be high on the characteristic of openness but also may resist authority.

Third, openness to change in general has been identified as an important component of workplace climate that can affect innovation in mental health service programs (Anderson & West, 1998). Individual differences in openness are related to both organizational characteristics and job performance (Barrick & Mount, 1991). Business and organizational literatures have shown that openness to innovation may be important in developing the characteristics of "learning organizations" that are more responsive and adaptive to internal and environmental contingencies (Anderson & West, 1998; Birleson, 1999; Fiol & Lyles, 1985; Garvin, 1993).

Finally, divergence may occur when there is a perceived difference between current and new practices. For example, mandated use of evidence-based assessment protocols is often perceived as incongruent or unneeded in clinical practice (Garland et al., 2003). Even where systems are in place to make the use of an evidence-based practice relatively seamless, there may be skepticism with regard to the use of such practices when perceived by providers to come from the culture of research and evaluation or when imposed by mandate. Similar "process resistance" has been documented in business-sector studies (Garvin, 1993).

The Evidence-Based Practice Attitude Scale (EBPAS) was developed to address the aforementioned provider-level attitudes in the domains of intuitive *appeal* of empirically supported treatments, attitudes toward organizational *requirements*, general *openness* to innovation, and perceived *divergence* of research-based innovation with usual practice (Aarons, 2004).

Development of the Evidence-Based Practice Attitude Scale (EBPAS)

The Evidence-Based Practice Attitude Scale (Aarons, 2004) is a brief fifteen-item measure developed to assess mental health provider attitudes toward adoption of innovation and evidence-based practice in mental health service settings. The scale items were developed based on literature review, discussions with providers and researchers, item generation, data collection, and exploratory and confirmatory factor analyses. To date, three articles have been published by the scale author et al. detailing (1) the initial validation and factor structure of the EBPAS, (2) cross-validation of the factor structure and psychometric properties of the EBPAS, and (3) U.S. national validation and norms and examination of the second-order factor structure of the EBPAS.

Initial Validation and Factor Structure of the EBPAS

An initial pool of items was generated based on a literature review and consultation with mental health service providers and child and adolescent services researchers, including several with extensive experience working with clinicians to implement evidence-based protocols. A total of eighteen items were identified for use in the initial survey. The items assessed openness to innovation, rigidity related to academic training, perceptions of the utility of research-based interventions and manualized interventions, consistency in therapeutic practices over time, interest in using new interventions, perception of the importance of requirements to use particular practices, empirical support for interventions, and divergent attitudes toward adoption of evidence-based practices. Respondents were asked to indicate their agreement with the items about their attitudes toward adopting new or different types of therapy/interventions. Response options were as follows: 0 = "Not at all"; 1 = "To a slight extent"; 2 = "To a moderate extent"; 3 = "To a great extent"; and 4 = "To a very great extent." It is important to note that this is an increasing-magnitude scale with no neutral midpoint. Owing to a possible lack of familiarity with the concept of evidence-based practice among those providing care in public mental health systems, the EBPAS questions are prefaced with the following statement: "The following questions ask about your feelings about using new types of therapy, interventions, or treatments. Manualized therapy refers to any intervention that has specific guidelines and/or components that are outlined in a manual and/or that are to be followed in a structured/predetermined way."

The initial scale development and validation sample consisted of mental health service providers (i.e., clinicians and case managers) in one large California county. Based on a random split, half the sample (n = 159) was used to conduct an exploratory factor analysis (EFA) and the other half (n = 163) to conduct a confirmatory factor analysis (CFA) (Aarons, 2004). The EFA suggested a four-factor solution in accordance with examination of the scree plot, simple structure criteria, item-total correlations, Chronbach's alpha analysis of internal consistency reliability, parallel analyses, and interpretability of the factors. Fifteen of the original eighteen items were retained, and the EFA model accounted for 63 percent of the variance in the data. Cronbach's alphas ranged from 0.90 to 0.59, with an overall scale alpha of 0.77. The factors represented four subscales of attitudes toward evidence-based practice in keeping with hypothesized dimensions. *Appeal* (four items, α = 0.80) is the extent to which the provider would adopt a new practice if it is intuitively appealing, makes sense, could be used correctly, or is being used by colleagues who are happy with it. *Requirements* (three items, α = 0.90) is the extent to which the provider would adopt a new practice if it is required by an agency, supervisor, or state. *Openness* (four items, α = 0.78) is the extent to which the provider is generally open to trying new interventions and would be willing to try or use new types of therapy. *Divergence* (four items, α = 0.59) is the extent to which the provider perceives research-based interventions as not clinically useful and less important than clinical experience. Item analyses showed that the reliability coefficient for the divergence scale would not have been improved by removing items from the scale. For the CFA using data from the other half of the sample, items were constrained to load only on the primary factor indicated in the EFA, thus providing a highly stringent test of the factor structure. As in the EFA, factor intercorrelations were allowed. CFA factor loadings confirmed the EFA-based a priori factor structure, and the model demonstrated good fit [χ^2 (84) = 144.92, CFI = 0.93, TLI = 0.92, RMSEA = 0.067, SRMR = 0.077], further supporting the EBPAS factor structure.

Cross-Validation of the EBPAS

A second study was conducted to further examine the psychometric properties of the EBPAS using a new, independent, more geographically diverse (seventeen states) sample (Aarons et al., 2007). Participants were mental health professionals providing services to children and adolescents with severe emotional disturbance (SED) and their families identified through a list of agencies affiliated with communities funded under the federal Comprehensive Community Mental Health Services for Children and Their Families (CCMHS) Program. Providers in this study were surveyed about their attitudes toward evidence-based practice using web-based surveys rather than pen-and-paper methods used in the previous study. A CFA was conducted specifying the factor structure identified in the original EBPAS scale-development study (Aarons, 2004). The CFA results indicated that the model demonstrated very good fit, supporting the original EBPAS factor structure [χ^2 (83) = 183.51; CFI = 0.92; TLI = 0.90; RMSEA = 0.07; SRMR = 0.07; χ^2/df = 2.21]. All factor loadings were statistically significant, and the model supported the a priori factor structure of the EBPAS. Interestingly, internal consistency reliabilities were better than in the original scale-development study (Aarons, 2004). Specifically, Cronbach's alphas for the EBPAS in this sample ranged from 0.93 to 0.66, with an overall scale alpha of 0.79, and individual scale reliabilities were as follows: appeal (α = 0.74), requirements (α = 0.93), openness (α = 0.81), and divergence (α = 0.66).

National Validation and Norms for the EBPAS

The most recent study examining psychometric characteristics and validity of the EBPAS evaluated national norms for the EBPAS in a sample of 1,089 mental health service providers from 100 outpatient mental health clinics in twenty-six states sampled to be representative of social service agencies in the United States (Aarons et al., 2010). Participants were part of the national survey of service providers in mental health clinics (Glisson et al., 2008) included in the Clinical Systems Project (Schoenwald, Kelleher, & Weisz, 2008) of the MacArthur Research Network on Children's Mental Health that began with the counties sampled in the National Survey of Child and Adolescent Well-Being (Burns et al., 2004; Dowd et al., 2004). In addition to providing national norms for the EBPAS, this study also examined whether a higher-order factor structure might describe the EBPAS more appropriately than a first-order factor structure because all first-order EBPAS factors are, in theory, indicators of a more global higher-order factor representing attitudes toward adoption of evidence-based practices.

Evidence of content validity also was obtained by asking an expert panel of six mental health services researchers to rate each item of the EBPAS in terms of (1) *relevance* in assessing attitudes toward evidence-based practices, (2) *importance* in assessing attitudes toward evidence-based practices, and (3) *representativeness* of the particular factor that the item is attempting to assess on a five-point Likert scale (0 = "Not at all relevant"; 1 = "Relevant to a slight extent"; 2 = "Relevant to a moderate extent"; 3 = "Relevant to a great extent"; and 4 = "Relevant to a very great extent"). For individual items, the mean rating across panel members ranged from 3.33 to 4.67 for relevance,

3.17 to 4.67 for importance, and 3.17 to 4.67 for representativeness. This result supports EBPAS content validity because every item, on average, was rated as at least moderately relevant, important, and representative of the factor it was purported to assess.

CFA was used to evaluate the factor structure of the EBPAS, with model specification based on preliminary findings from the two previous EBPAS scale-development studies (Aarons, 2004; Aarons et al., 2007). Acceptable fit indices were found for both the first-order and higher-order factor structures. Based on the interpretability of conceptualizing attitudes toward evidence-based practices as representing a more global higher-order construct and the likelihood that future use of this scale in structural models may involve use of the higher-order factor as an independent or dependent variable, preference was given to the higher-order factor structure. The established norms using this national sample are as follows: appeal (M = 2.91, SD = 0.68, α = 0.80), requirements (M = 2.41, SD = 0.99, α = 0.91), openness (M = 2.76, SD = 0.75, α = 0.84), divergence (M = 1.25, SD = 0.70; α = 0.66), and total EBPAS score (M = 2.73, SD = 0.49, α = 0.76). Thus the psychometric characteristics as reflected in these later studies are better than in the original scale-development study and are consistent with one another supporting the internal consistency of the EBPAS.

Use of the EBPAS

Although the EBPAS is relatively new, it is being used across the United States and internationally, as evidenced by requests for the measure from the first author. More than 150 requests for permission to use the EBPAS have been made by researchers in the United States and abroad. Requests for the EBPAS have come from investigators in other countries, including Iran, Israel, Japan, Korea, Norway, Romania, and Sweden. Translations have been completed in eight languages (Iranian, Japanese, Korean, Norwegian, Romanian, Swedish, Icelandic, and Spanish). With the exception of the Spanish translation, translations were completed by investigators in the countries listed. In order to better understand how the EBPAS is being cited in the literature and being used in researcher studies, a comprehensive literature review was conducted and is described next.

Literature Search Strategy

A search of the literature identified 118 publications (articles, n = 114; book chapters, n = 4) citing the EBPAS. This search was conducted using the "cited by" feature for the three EBPAS validation studies (Aarons, 2004; Aarons et al., 2007, 2010) and searching for the terms "EBPAS" and "Evidence Based Practice Attitude Scale" in six popular databases (Scopus, PsychInfo, PubMed, Google Scholar, Science Direct, and ERIC). Each article was reviewed to determine whether the EBPAS was cited only or cited and used as a measurement instrument in the study. Ninety-four articles and book chapters cited the EBPAS but did not use the measure for data collection, whereas twenty-four articles used the EBPAS to collect data regarding attitudes toward adopting evidence-based practices. Literature citing the EBPAS spanned the fields of psychology (n = 45), social work (n = 16), psychiatry (n = 8), substance abuse (n = 6), child welfare (n = 6), implementation science (n = 6), medicine (n = 3), education (n = 2), nursing (n = 1), and criminology (n = 1). We focus here on use of the EBPAS for research purposes. Thus the following sections describe use of the EBPAS in the twenty-four peer-reviewed articles identified in our search and its association with provider characteristics, organizational characteristics, and service delivery in mental health, substance abuse, education, and social work settings.

Associations with EBPAS Scores and Related Findings

Provider Characteristics

Several demographic and professional characteristics of providers have been found to be related to attitudes toward evidence-based practice, as measured by the EBPAS. Female gender has been associated with higher scores on the appeal subscale (Aarons, 2006; Aarons et al., 2010) and the requirements subscale (Aarons et al., 2010), as well as with higher total EBPAS scores (Aarons et al., 2010). In a national sample, Caucasian ethnicity was associated with higher scores on the appeal subscale (as compared with African American, Latino, and "other" ethnicity), lower scores on the divergence subscale (as compared with African American and "other" ethnicity), and higher total EBPAS scores (as compared with African American, Latino, and "other" ethnicity) (Aarons et al., 2010).

Factors related to education, including level of education, field of study, and training model, have been examined in relationship to attitudes toward evidence-based practice. Higher levels of education consistently have been associated with higher scores on the appeal subscale (Aarons, 2004, 2006; Aarons et al., 2010; Stahmer & Aarons, 2009), and level of education has been negatively associated with the requirements subscale (Aarons et al., 2010). Aarons (2004) did not find any difference in EBPAS scores by discipline (e.g., social work or psychology), but a later study found that providers with their highest degree in social work had higher total EBPAS scores and openness subscale scores than those with their highest degree in psychology, and those with a degree in psychology scored lower on the divergence subscale than those with a degree in social work (Aarons et al., 2010).

The EBPAS has also been examined in relation to provider training models. In a sample of trauma professionals, no significant differences were found by training model (e.g., clinical scientist, practitioner-scholar) (Gray, Elhai, & Schmidt, 2007). The divergence subscale of the EBPAS also was examined in relation to psychology graduate training (reverse scored and combined with a measure of esteem for and utilization of research) and was found to be related to research emphasis in graduate training. This combined measure of "pro-research attitudes" was not related to provider sex, age, or experience (Stewart & Chambless, 2007).

Gray et al. (2007) examined attitudes toward evidence-based practices among trauma professionals of different theoretical orientations and found a number of differences. Respondents identifying as cognitive-behavioral practitioners scored higher on the EBPAS than those selecting psychodynamic, eclectic, or "other" as their orientation but did not differ from those identifying as client-centered practitioners. Psychodynamic practitioners scored the lowest on the EBPAS but were still above what the authors considered a "neutral midpoint," indicating that they do not hold negative attitudes toward evidence-based practice (Gray et al., 2007). It is important to clarify here that there is no "neutral midpoint" on the EBPAS. The scores are of increasing magnitude, as described earlier. Stewart & Chambless' (2007) measure of pro-research attitudes also was related to theoretical orientation, with a similar pattern of results. Respondents identifying as cognitive-behavioral practitioners scored higher on the measure than those identifying as eclectic or dynamic practitioners, whereas eclectic practitioners scored higher than dynamic practitioners.

While most research using the EBPAS has focused on mental health providers, additional studies have examined attitudes toward evidence-based practice among practitioners in different areas of practice. Stahmer & Aarons (2009) found that autism early-intervention providers (i.e., in-home and center-based providers working with at least one child with an autism spectrum disorder) reported more positive attitudes toward evidence-based practice than did mental health providers, scoring higher on the appeal, openness, and requirements subscales and lower on the divergence subscale. Another study administered the EBPAS to drug abuse and mental health providers but did not provide comparisons between the two groups (Henggeler et al., 2007).

EBPAS scores also have been found to vary by age, job tenure, and work experience. Age has been found to be negatively related to attitudes toward evidence-based practice, with younger respondents scoring higher on the EBPAS (Gray et al., 2007), but this relationship may be affected by job tenure. Aarons & Sawitzky (2006) found that providers with longer job tenure scored lower on the openness subscale, but older providers scored higher on the same scale. However, older providers scored higher on the divergence subscale, indicating that they perceived more divergence between evidence-based practice and their usual practice. In a national sample of mental health providers, older practitioners scored higher on the requirements subscale, indicating that they were more likely to adopt an evidence-based practice if required to do so (Aarons et al., 2010).

Stahmer & Aarons (2009) found that years of both general and specialty experience were related to increased divergence subscale scores for autism early-intervention providers and decreased openness and total EBPAS scores for child and family mental health providers. Years of specialty experience for mental health providers also was negatively associated with the requirements subscale, indicating a lower likelihood of adopting even when required to do so. In another sample, professional experience was negatively related to the openness, divergence, and requirements subscales, indicating that providers with more years of professional experience were less open to evidence-based practice, perceived greater divergence between evidence-based practice and their usual care, and were less likely to adopt an evidence-based practice even if required to do so (Aarons et al., 2010). Providers who are interns, with little professional experience, tend to endorse more positive attitudes toward evidence-based practice. Intern status has been associated with higher scores on the appeal and openness subscales, lower scores on the divergence subscale, and higher total EBPAS scores (Aarons, 2004, 2006; Aarons & Sawitzky, 2006).

Organizational Characteristics

In addition to relationships with provider characteristics, EBPAS scores have been associated with measures of staff and organizational characteristics related to implementing new technologies. Saldana et al. (2007) found that several subscales of the organizational readiness for change scale related to the EBPAS. Specifically, the staff attributes (e.g., growth, efficacy, influence, and adaptability) scale was positively related to the appeal, openness, and divergence subscales. A scale measuring training exposure and utilization was positively related to the appeal, openness, and requirements subscales. Motivational readiness for change was positively related to the appeal and openness subscales, and adequacy of resources was negatively related to the appeal subscale, with high resources associated with low appeal of evidence-based practice.

Organizational culture and climate both have been found to be related to providers' attitudes toward evidence-based practice. Positive climate measured by the organizational readiness for change scale was negatively related to divergence scores on the EBPAS (Saldana et al., 2007), and demoralizing or negative organizational climate has been found to be positively related to divergence scores (Aarons & Sawitzsky, 2006). These results indicate that providers in organizations with positive climates perceive less divergence between evidence-based practice and their usual care, whereas organizations with poor climates perceive more divergence. Constructive organizational culture that promotes achievement and mutual encouragement has been positively associated with higher scores on appeal and openness subscales, as well as higher total EBPAS scores, whereas defensive culture, emphasizing rules and orders over personal beliefs and ideas, has been positively associated with divergence scores and marginally positively associated with requirements subscale scores (Aarons & Sawitzky, 2006).

Leadership behaviors in an organization, specifically transformational (charismatic) and transactional (effective management) leadership, have been related to attitudes toward evidence-based practice. *Transformational leadership* refers to a leader's ability to inspire, motivate, and intellectually stimulate each staff member. *Transactional leadership* refers to the extent to which a leader monitors staff behavior and rewards staff for achieving goals. Aarons (2006) found that transformational leadership was positively associated with the requirements subscale and negatively associated with the divergence subscale. Transactional leadership was positively associated with the openness subscale and marginally positively associated with the requirements subscale. Both transformational leadership and transactional leadership were positively associated with total evidence-based-practice AS scale scores, indicating that more positive supervisor leadership (as rated by mental health providers) is associated with more positive attitudes toward adopting evidence-based practice. In addition to leadership, organizational support for evidence-based practice has been positively related to provider attitudes as measured by the EBPAS (Aarons, Sommerfeld, & Walrath-Greene, 2009).

Additional agency characteristics such as the level of bureaucracy and the use of written practice policies (i.e., policies specifying the use of particular interventions for particular mental health problems) also have been related to EBPAS scores (Aarons, 2004). Specifically, lower levels of bureaucracy were associated with higher openness and requirements subscale scores, as well as with higher total EBPAS scores, indicating that providers in less bureaucratic programs are more open to evidence-based practice use, are more likely to adopt an evidence-based practice if required, and have more positive attitudes toward evidence-based practice overall. The use of written practice policies is also associated with higher scores on the appeal and openness subscales, as well as the overall EBPAS.

Program type, agency type (public or private), and agency location (rural versus nonrural) also have been examined in relationship to attitudes toward evidence-based practice. To examine differences among program type, Aarons (2004) compared providers in inpatient, day treatment, outpatient, case management, and wraparound programs and found that EBPAS scores were related to program type. Providers in wraparound programs scored higher on the openness subscale and the total EBPAS than those in outpatient programs, whereas providers in day treatment programs scored higher on the requirements subscale than those in outpatient programs. Outpatient providers scored higher on the appeal subscale than those in case management programs. Additionally, providers within private agencies have been found to report more positive attitudes toward evidence-based practice than those in public agencies. Private agencies also exhibited higher levels of organizational support for evidence-based practice than public agencies, and organizational support was associated with higher EBPAS scores (Aarons et al., 2009). In regard to agency location, Jameson et al. (2009) examined attitudes toward evidence-based practice in a sample of clinical directors (or their designees) in rural and nonrural mental health clinics and found that EBPAS scores did not differ between rural and nonrural respondents.

Service Delivery

Several studies have examined how attitudes toward evidence-based practice, measured by the EBPAS, are related to how services are delivered by providers. In a sample of drug abuse and mental health practitioners eligible to attend an evidence-based practice workshop, workshop attendance was not related to EBPAS scores (Henggeler et al., 2008); however, the requirements subscale predicted increased future probability of evidence-based practice use (Henggeler et al., 2008). Additionally, while Gray et al. (2007) did not find a relationship between EBPAS scores and self-reported evidence-based practice behaviors (e.g., frequency of literature searches), Pignotti & Thyer (2009) found that EBPAS scores in a sample of social

workers were positively correlated with the number of unsupported interventions used, possibly because providers who are open to evidence-based practice and find it appealing are also open to and find unsupported interventions appealing. One study found some evidence for a link between EBPAS scores and clinician adoption of evidence-based practice; however, that link became nonsignificant in the final analytical model, likely owing to the low statistical power and small sample size in the study (Aarons et al., 2009).

EBPAS Scores over Time

To date, two studies have examined changes over time of EBPAS scores, with both reporting little variation over time. Lopez et al. (2010) administered the EBPAS to a sample of providers before evidence-based practice training, one month after training, and six months after training. Generally, little change was found over time, with the exception of a small increase in the appeal subscale from baseline to the one-month follow-up. Gioia (2007) also found that EBPAS scores varied little over a two-year implementation period; however, the first administration occurred after participants were recruited and received information on evidence-based practice, so some contamination may have occurred. Gioia (2007) suggested that practitioners actively using evidence-based practices may report more positive attitudes toward evidence-based practice; however, Weist et al. (2009) administered the EBPAS to clinicians involved in a school-based evidence-based practice implementation project and found no differences between those implementing the evidence-based practice and those implementing another intervention. However, higher starting scores for the EBPAS may account for difficulties in detecting change over time because these studies reported higher means than those presented by Aarons (2004). Schurer et al. (2010) also found EBPAS scores higher than those found by Aarons (2004); however, no significance testing was conducted. Given the limitations of these studies, it will be important to examine changes in EBPAS scores over time in a large representative sample of providers over the course of evidence-based-practice implementation (before training, immediately after training, and longer-term follow-up with evidence-based-practice–trained providers) to determine whether these attitudes may change over time in response to direct experience with an evidence-based practice.

EBPAS Scale Modifications and Expansion

Several researchers have adapted the EBPAS or used it as a basis for developing related measures. Researchers in Belgium used the EBPAS to develop a semistructured questionnaire for use with Belgian substance abuse treatment agencies. Most respondents reported a positive attitude toward evidence-based practice, and although most respondents reported no differences in attitudes between various disciplines and professions in the agency, some reported that physicians and nurses had more positive attitudes toward evidence-based guidelines than psychologists, particularly compared with those with a psychodynamic background or orientation. Other researchers have used the EBPAS to develop related quantitative measures, but no associations have yet been reported between these measures and other variables (Bernal & Rodríguez-Soto, 2010; Kurth, 2009).

While acknowledging the importance of measuring attitudes toward evidence-based practice, Borntrager et al. (2009) expressed concerns that the EBPAS does not effectively differentiate attitudes toward evidence-based practice with attitudes toward manualized treatments. To address this concern, the researchers developed the Modified Practice Attitudes Scale (MPAS) a measure of attitudes toward evidence-based practice similar to the EBPAS but without any references to manualized treatment, and administered both the MPAS and the EBPAS to a sample of clinicians being trained in either standard manual treatment or modular

manual treatment before and after training. No significant differences were found in EBPAS scores by training group or over time. However, a significant interaction between time and condition was found for the MPAS, indicating that attitudes of therapists in the modular condition became more positive from before to after training. These results reflect some movement from more strictly manualized interventions to new models that modularize interventions or use specific treatment elements approaches toward evidence-informed practice (Chorpita et al., 2004; Chorpita, Becker, & Daleiden, 2007). As such, there is a need to continue to refine measures of attitudes toward evidence-based practice to reflect innovations in intervention development.

EBPAS-50

Most recently, an attempt was made to expand the measurement of attitudes toward evidence-based practice and identify additional dimensions by generating new items and content domains (Aarons et al., 2010). For this study, sixty-three items representing twelve potential content domains of attitudes toward evidence-based practice were created based on review of the literature, experience with previous studies of provider attitudes toward adopting evidence-based practice (Aarons, 2004, 2005; Aarons & Sawitzky, 2006), and experience with the fifty-one mental health programs in the previous scale-development study (Aarons, 2004). Additionally, focus groups were conducted with mental health program managers ($n = 6$) and clinicians ($n = 8$) to obtain feedback on the preceding items and generate additional potential items. A total of thirty-three additional items based on the program managers' focus group and thirty-seven items from the clinicians' focus group were added to the item pool. No new domains were identified, indicating conceptual saturation. These items then were reviewed by the research team for redundancy. Next-card sorting methods were used by the investigative team to sort items into piles based on similarity, resulting in

127 items sorted into eight broad domains, including (1) attitudes toward supervision (monitoring/supervision, feedback/ongoing clinical support), (2) evidence-based practice fit with work responsibilities (workload, time, organizational support), (3) balancing professional growth and the status quo (adequate skills, learning, job rewards, status quo), (4) arguments against evidence-based practice (evidence-based practice fit with real-world clients, art versus science, common factors, stigma, characteristics of evidence-based practice), (5) training and education (evidence-based practice fit with education/training, training), (6) research practice partnership, (7) evidence-based practice effectiveness, and (8) consumer preference.

Next, a sample of 422 mental health service providers from sixty-five outpatient and day treatment programs in a large California county completed a survey that included the new items. An iterative exploratory factor analysis process was employed using parallel analysis and the Minimum Average Partial (MAP) Test to the correct number of factors (Zwick & Velicer, 1986). After four iterations, thirty-three items remained, representing eight EBPAS factors (limitations, fit, monitoring, balance, burden, job security, organizational support, and feedback). The identified factors correspond to several of the subdomains originally conceived by the research team and community clinicians and program managers. The data-reduction process, however, also resulted in identification of additional domains that were not proposed originally. Generally, internal consistencies were high, ranging from 0.77 to 0.92, and factor correlations were small to moderate, ranging from 0.01 to 0.56 in absolute value. The convergence of these factors with the four previously identified evidence-based practice attitude factors (fifteen items) was small to moderate, suggesting that the newly identified factors represent distinct dimensions of provider attitudes toward adopting evidence-based practice. The combination of the original fifteen items with the thirty-five new items comprises the EBPAS fifty-item version (EBPAS-50), which can add to our understanding of provider attitudes toward adopting evidence-based practices.

Conclusions and Future Directions

Although the study of attitudes toward evidence-based practice is in its infancy, there is accumulating evidence that such attitudes are related to a number of individual and organizational characteristics and factors. The factor structure and psychometric characteristics of the EBPAS have undergone rigorous evaluation, and the most recent studies converge to demonstrate good scale internal consistency reliability, factor structure, and validity.

Studies have found that individual provider characteristics such as job tenure, years of experience, theoretical orientation, and type and level of education all may affect provider attitudes. Whether an organization is private, public, or nonprofit may affect the attitudes of those who work in the organization. In addition, organizational culture and climate and the type and quality of leadership can influence staff attitudes toward and willingness to adopt evidence-based practices. There are also differences in those working in mental health and early-education settings. Taken together, these findings suggest that greater attention should be paid to improving the organizational context for evidence-based practices.

New models and approaches to evidence-based practice are also changing how we conceptualize and assess attitudes. For example, while there are many highly structured and manualized psychosocial interventions, some clinician/researchers are developing modularized or systematic approaches combining elements of manualized interventions into more flexible approaches that may be better able to meet the needs of clients with multiple or very discreet problems that don't require a full manualized intervention.

We did not identify, nor do we know of, any studies where an intervention was developed specifically to change attitudes toward evidence-based practice and to promote the uptake of evidence-based practice by practicing clinicians. While some studies have examined change in attitudes as a function of participating in training or other activities, in order to really determine the impact of attitudes on behavior, specific studies should be designed to address this issue. For example, studies could be designed based on the social psychology of persuasion and influence in order to directly affect attitudes. Then studies could be conducted to identify the links among attitudes, mediating or moderating factors, and uptake or use of evidence-based practices. Such studies are needed to expand the nomologic net and enhance our understanding of what leads to and what follows from attitudes toward adopting evidence-based practices.

It is important to remember that the overall goal of this line of research is to improve care for those in need of the most effective and proven interventions. This can be in the arenas of health care, educational instructional approaches, early intervention, developmental services, mental health, substance abuse, and social services. There is a vast literature on the nature of attitudes and their operation. The purpose here was to review the literature on attitudes toward evidence-based practice in order to move the study of such attitudes forward. It is not enough to identify attitudes – but rather to take what we are learning and parlay this new knowledge to learn how to most effectively disseminate, implement, and sustain evidence-based practices in real-world settings. By doing so, we can improve the lives of those in need of effective intervention by providing access to the best interventions available.

References

Aarons, G. A. (2004). Mental health provider attitudes toward adoption of evidence-based practice: The Evidence-Based Practice Attitude Scale (EBPAS). *Mental Health Services Research* 6, 61–74.

Aarons, G. A. (2005). Measuring provider attitudes toward evidence-based practice: Organizational context and individual differences. *Child and Adolescent Psychiatric Clinics of North America* 14, 255–71.

Aarons, G. A. (2006). Transformational and transactional leadership: Association with attitudes toward evidence-based practice. *Psychiatric Services* 57, 1162–9.

Aarons, G. A., & Sawitzky, A. C. (2006). Organizational culture and climate and mental health provider attitudes toward evidence-based practice. *Psychological Services* 3, 61–72.

Aarons, G. A., Dlugosz, L., & Ehrhart, M. (forthcoming). The role of organizational process in dissemination and implementation research: A look at leadership, culture, climate, readiness for change, and improvement strategies. In R. Brownson, G. Colditz, and E. Proctor (eds.), *Dissemination and implementation research in health: Translating science to practice*. Oxford, UK: Oxford University Press.

Aarons, G. A., Sommerfeld, D. H., & Walrath-Greene, C. M. (2009). Evidence-based practice implementation: The impact of public vs. private sector organization type on organizational support, provider attitudes, and adoption of evidence-based practice. *Implementation Science* 4, 1–13.

Aarons, G. A., Cafri, G., Lugo, L., & Sawitzky, A. (2010). Expanding the domains of attitudes towards evidence-based practice: The Evidence Based Practice Attitude Scale-50. *Administration and Policy in Mental Health and Mental Health Services Research* 50, 1–10.

Aarons, G. A., Glisson, C., Hoagwood, K., Landsverk, J., & Cafri, G. (2010). Psychometric properties and United States national norms of the Evidence-Based Practice Attitude Scale (EBPAS). *Psychological Assessment* 22, 356–65.

Aarons, G. A., McDonald, E. J., Sheehan, A. K., & Walrath-Greene, C. M. (2007). Confirmatory factor analysis of the Evidence-Based Practice Attitude Scale (EBPAS) in a geographically diverse sample of community mental health providers. *Administration and Policy in Mental Health* 34, 465–9.

Addis, M. E. (2002). Methods for disseminating research products and increasing evidence-based practice: Promises, obstacles, and future directions. *Clinical Psychology: Science and Practice* 9, 367–78.

Anderson, N. R., & West, M. A. (1998). Measuring climate for work group innovation: Development and validation of the Team Climate Inventory. *Journal of Organizational Behavior* 19, 235–58.

Backer, T. E., David, S. L., & Soucy, G. E. (1995). *Reviewing the behavioral science knowledge* base on technology transfer (NIDA Research Monograph 155, NIH Publication No. 95–4035). Rockville, MD: National Institute on Drug Abuse.

Backer, T. E., Liberman, R. P., & Kuehnel, T. G. (1986). Dissemination and adoption of innovative psychosocial interventions. *Journal of Consulting & Clinical Psychology. Special Issue: Psychotherapy Research* 54, 111–18.

Bandura, A. (1982). Self-efficacy mechanism in human agency. *American Psychologist* 37, 122–47.

Bandura, A. (2002). Growing primacy of human agency in adaptation and change in the electronic era. *European Psychologist* 7, 2–16.

Barrick, M. R., & Mount, M. K. (1991). The big five personality dimensions and job performance: A meta-analysis. *Personnel Psychology* 44, 1–26.

Bernal, G., & Rodríguez-Soto, N. (2010). Development and psychometric properties of the Evidence-based Professional Practice Scale (EBPP-S). *Puerto Rico Health Sciences Journal* 4, 385–90.

Birleson, P. (1999). Turning child and adolescent mental-health services into learning organizations. *Clinical Child Psychology & Psychiatry* 4, 265–74.

Borntrager, C. F., Chorpita, B. F., Higa-McMillan, C., & Weisz, J. R. (2009). Provider attitudes toward evidence-based practices: Are the concerns with the evidence or with the manuals? *Psychiatric Services* 60, 677–81.

Burns, B. J. (2003). Children and evidence-based practice. *Psychiatric Clinics of North America* 26, 955–70.

Burns, B. J., Hoagwood, K., & Mrazek, P. J. (1999). Effective treatment for mental disorders in children and adolescents. *Clinical Child & Family Psychology Review* 2, 199–254.

Burns, B. J., Phillips, S. D., Wagner, H. R., Barth, R. P., Kolko, D. J., Campbell, Y., & Landsverk, J. (2004). Mental health need and access to mental health services by youths involved with child welfare: A national survey. *Journal of the American Academy of Child & Adolescent Psychiatry* 43, 960–70.

Candel, M. J., & Pennings, J. M. (1999). Attitude-based models for binary choices: A test for choices involving an innovation. *Journal of Economic Psychology* 20, 547–69.

Chorpita, B. F., Taylor, A. A., Francis, S. E., Moffitt, C., & Austin, A. A. (2004). Efficacy of modular cognitive behavior therapy for childhood anxiety disorders. *Behavior Therapy* 35, 263–87.

Chorpita, B. F., Becker, K. D., & Daleiden, E. L. (2007). Understanding the common elements of evidence-based practice: Misconceptions and clinical examples. *Journal of the American Academy of Child & Adolescent Psychiatry 46,* 647–52.

Cialdini, R. B., Bator, R. J., & Guadagno, R. E. (1999). Normative influences in organizations. In L. Thompson, D. Messick, and J. Levine (eds.), *Shared cognition in organizations: The management of knowledge* (pp. 195–212). Mahwah, NJ: Lawrence Erlbaum.

Cohen, L. H., Sargent, M. M., & Sechrest, L. B. (1986). Use of psychotherapy research by professional psychologists. *American Psychologist* 41, 198–206.

Damanpour, F. (1991). Organizational innovation: A meta-analysis of effects of determinants and moderators. *Academy of Management Journal* 34, 555–90.

Dowd, K., Kinsey, S., Wheeless, S., Thissen, R., Richardson, J., Suresh, R., Lytle, T., et al. (2004). *National Survey of Child and Adolescent Well-Being (NSCAW): Combined waves 1–4, data file user's manual, restricted release version.* Ithaca, NY: Cornell University Press.

Essock, S. M., Goldman, H. H., Van Tosh, L., Anthony, W. A., Appell, C. R., Bond, G. R., Drake, R. E., et al. (2003). Evidence-based practices: Setting the context and responding to concerns. *Psychiatric Clinics of North America* 26, 919–38.

Fiol, C. M., & Lyles, M. A. (1985). Organizational learning. *Academy of Management Review* 10, 803–13.

Fishbein, M., & Ajzen, I. (1975). *Belief, attitude, intentions, and behavior: An introduction to theory and research.* Reading, MA: Addison-Wesley.

Fishbein, M., Hennessy, M., Yzer, M., & Douglas, J. (2003). Can we explain why some people do and some people do not act on their intentions? *Psychology, Health & Medicine* 8, 3–18.

Frambach, R. T., & Schillewaert, N. (2002). Organizational innovation adoption: A multilevel framework of determinants and opportunities for future research. *Journal of Business Research* 55, 163–76.

Fraser, S. W., & Greenhalgh, T. (2001). Complexity science: Coping with complexity: Educating for capability. *British Medical Journal* 323, 799–803.

Garland, A. F., Kruse, M., & Aarons, G. A. (2003). Clinicians and outcome measurement: What's the use? *Journal of Behavioral Health Services and Research* 30, 393–405.

Garvin, D. A. (1993). Building a learning organization. *Harvard Business Review* 71, 78–91.

Gioia, D. (2007). Using an organizational change model to qualitatively understand practitioner adoption of evidence-based practice in community mental health. *Best Practices in Mental Health: An International Journal* 3, 1–15.

Glisson, C. (2002). The organizational context of children's mental health services. *Clinical Child and Family Psychology Review* 5, 233–253.

Glisson, C., Landsverk, J., Schoenwald, S., Kelleher, K., Hoagwood, K. E., Mayberg, S., & The Research Network on Youth Mental Health (2008). Assessing the organizational social context (OSC) of mental health services: Implications for research and practice. *Administration and Policy in Mental Health and Mental Health Services Research* 35, 98–113.

Gray, M., Elhai, J., & Schmidt, L. (2007). Trauma professionals' attitudes toward and utilization of evidence-based practices. *Behavior Modification* 31, 732–48.

Greenhalgh, T., Robert, G., Macfarlane, F., Bate, P., & Kyriakidou, O. (2004). Diffusion of innovations in service organizations: Systematic review and recommendations. *Milbank Quarterly* 82, 581–629.

Hasenfeld, Y. (1992). *Human services as complex organizations*. Newbury Park, CA: Sage.

Henggeler, S. W., & Schoenwald, S. K. (2002). Treatment manuals: Necessary, but far from sufficient: Commentary. *Clinical Psychology: Science & Practice* 9, 419–20.

Henggeler, S. W., Lee, T., & Burns, J. A. (2002). What happens after the innovation is identified? *Clinical Psychology: Science and Practice* 9, 191–4.

Henggeler, S., Chapman, J., Rowland, M., Halliday-Boykins, C., Randall, J., Shackelford, J., & Schoenwald, S. K. (2007). If you build it, they will come: Statewide practitioner interest in contingency management for youths. *Journal of Substance Abuse Treatment* 32, 121–31.

Henggeler, S., Chapman, J., Rowland, M., Halliday-Boykins, C., Randall, J., Shackelford, J., & Schoenwald, S. K. (2008). Statewide adoption and initial implementation of contingency management for substance abusing adolescents. *Journal of Consulting and Clinical Psychology* 76, 556–67.

Hoagwood, K. (2005). Family-based services in children's mental health: A research review and synthesis. *Journal of Child Psychology and Psychiatry* 46, 690–713.

Hoagwood, K., Burns, B. J., Kiser, L., Ringeisen, H., & Schoenwald, S. K. (2001). Evidence-based practice in child and adolescent mental health services. *Psychiatric Services* 52, 1179–89.

Jaccard, J., Radecki, C., Wilson, T., & Dittus, P. (1995). Methods for identifying consequential beliefs: Implications for understanding attitude strength. In R. E. Petty, and J. A. Krosnick (eds.), *Attitude strength: Antecedents and consequences* (pp. 337–59). Mahwah, NJ: Lawrence Erlbaum Associates.

Jameson, J., Chambless, D., & Blank, M. (2009). Empirically supported treatments in rural community mental health centers: A preliminary report on current utilization and attitudes toward adoption. *Community Mental Health Journal* 45, 463–7.

Jankowicz, D. (2000). From "learning organization" to "adaptive organization." *Management Learning* 31, 471–90.

Kurth, J. (2009). Introducing evidence-based practice to an inpatient child and adolescent psychiatry unit. *Academic Psychiatry* 33, 400–3.

Lopez, M., Osterberg, L., Jensen-Doss, A., & Rae, W. (2010). Effects of workshop training for providers under mandated use of an evidence-based practice. *Administration and Policy in Mental Health and Mental Health Services Research* 38, 1–12.

Magnabosco, J. L. (2006). Innovations in mental health services implementation: A report on state-level data from the U.S. evidence-based practices project. *Implementation Science* 1(13), 1–13.

Morrow-Bradley, C., & Elliott, R. (1986). Utilization of psychotherapy research by practicing psychotherapists. *American Psychologist* 41, 188–97.

Pignotti, M., & Thyer, B. (2009). Use of novel unsupported and empirically supported therapies by licensed clinical social workers: An exploratory study. *Social Work Research* 33, 5–17.

Ringeisen, H., & Hoagwood, K. (2002). Clinical research directions for the treatment and delivery of children's mental health services. In D. T. Marsh and M. A. Fristad (eds.), *Handbook of serious emotional disturbance in children and adolescents* (pp. 33–55). New York: Wiley.

Rogers, E. M. (1995). *Diffusions of innovations*, 4th ed. New York: The Free Press.

Rydell, R., & McConnell, A. (2006). Understanding implicit and explicit attitude change: A systems of reasoning analysis. *Journal of Personality and Social Psychology* 91, 995–1008.

Saldana, L., Chapman, J., Henggeler, S., & Rowland, M. (2007). The Organizational Readiness for Change scale in adolescent programs: Criterion validity. *Journal of Substance Abuse Treatment* 33, 159–69.

Schoenwald, S. K., Kelleher, K., & Weisz, J. (2008). Building bridges to evidence-based practice: The MacArthur Foundation child system and treatment enhancement projects (Child STEPs). *Administration and Policy in Mental Health* 35, 66–72.

Schurer, J., Kohl, P., & Bellamy, J. (2010). Organizational context and readiness for change: A study of community-based parenting programs in one Midwestern city. *Administration in Social Work* 34, 178–95.

Simpson, D. D. (2002). A conceptual framework for transferring research to practice. *Journal of Substance Abuse Treatment* 22, 171–82.

Stahmer, A., & Aarons, G. (2009). Attitudes toward adoption of evidence-based practices: A comparison of autism early intervention providers and children's mental health providers. *Psychological Services* 6, 223–34.

Stewart, R., & Chambless, D. (2007). Does psychotherapy research inform treatment decisions in private practice? *Journal of Clinical Psychology* 63, 267–81.

Strupp, H. H., & Anderson, T. (1997). On the limitations of therapy manuals. *Clinical Psychology: Science & Practice* 4, 76–82.

Tormala, Z. L., & Petty, R. E. (2002). What doesn't kill me makes me stronger: The effects of resisting persuasion on attitude certainty. *Journal of Personality and Social Psychology* 83, 1298–313.

Watkins, M. (2001). Principles of persuasion. *Negotiation Journal* 17, 115–37.

Weist, M., Lever, N., Stephan, S., Youngstrom, E., Moore, E., Harrison, B., Stiegler, K., et al. (2009). Formative evaluation of a framework for high quality, evidence-based services in school mental health. *School Mental Health* 1, 196–211.

Zwick, W. R., & Velicer, W. F. (1986). Comparison of five rules for determining the number of components to retain. *Psychological Bulletin* 99, 432–42.

CHAPTER 10

Change-Focused Organizational Consultation in School Settings

Robert J. Illback

Introduction

Psychologists who practice in schools are often asked to become active in facilitating organizational and systems-level changes (Curtis & Stollar, 2002; Illback & Zins, 1995). Some do so as staff members embedded in the school system working with change-focused teams or as internal change leaders. Others may serve as external change facilitators empowered to work with organization members as they implement change-oriented programs. As organizational boundary role professionals who cross physical, social, and normative boundaries within school communities, psychologists are uniquely positioned to engage in system-enhancing activity (Illback & Maher, 1984).

When engaged in organizational change activities, psychologists rely heavily on a range of consultation skills that connect the theoretical and conceptual underpinnings of interventions with the implementation challenges in real-world settings. Consultation can be conceived as a type of helping process within which strategic, targeted, and collaborative interactions occur between the consultant and key people (consultees) necessary to bring about change. As opposed to the management role of directing and controlling human, programmatic, and financial resources, consultation is a voluntary problem-solving process that involves the application of particular techniques in a skilled manner at critical points to move the change process forward.

Psychologist-facilitated consultative activities in schools have included support of wide-ranging innovation and change strategies such as instructional support teams (Rosenfield & Gravois, 1999), school-wide positive behavioral interventions and supports (Sugai & Horner, 2002), social and emotional learning (SEL) programs (Zins et al., 2004), effective special services teams (Illback & Fields, 1992), school health and mental health (Adelman & Taylor, 2000; Carlson et al., 1996; Talley & Short, 1996), integrated services (Illback, 1994), reduction of teacher stress (Huebner, Gilligan, & Cobb, 2002), inclusion of students with disabilities (Fuchs & Fuchs, 1988), developing full-service schools (Kalafat & Illback, 1998, 2007), program planning and evaluation (xxIllback,

Maher, & Zins, 1999), improving student health and nutrition (Suarez-Balcazar et al., 2007), and forming school-community partnerships (Sheridan, Napolitano, & Swearer, 2002). Psychologists also have contributed to whole-school change initiatives that center on broad restructuring of how schools operate (Maher & Illback, 1983; Miles & Schmuck, 1971; Zins & Illback, 1995).

The content of and evidence for these innovations have been well specified. What is less clear are the consultative skills necessary to facilitate full and effective implementation of such innovations in schools. This chapter therefore explores what is known about effective organization-level consultation, much of which is found in the management and business literature, but a portion of which relates specifically to school change efforts. It then considers the deployment of specific consultation skills in the context of comprehensive school reform (CSR) efforts and examines the challenges and complexities involved at each stage of the change process.

Effective Organizational Consultation

General Findings

Organization development and related fields are rich with respect to theories and strategies, but research about the actual facilitating behavior of organization-level consultants in implementing change is limited (Wooten & White, 1989). In early writing about the subject, Warwick & Donovan (1979) described skills associated with organization consultant effectiveness within four broad categories: knowledge, consulting skills, conceptual skills, and human skills. Neilsen (1984) subsequently suggested that project management skill also was crucial to effective consultation. Carey & Varney (1983) perceived that self-awareness and interpersonal awareness; conceptual, analytic, and research skills; and influence skills were essential. Esper (1990) interviewed key informants about core organizational consultant competencies, finding that process skills (i.e., individual, group, and organizational dynamics), conceptual

ability, communication, and management of the consulting process emerged as most salient for consultants.

More recently, Worley & Varney (1998) conducted surveys of organizational consultants to determine their views of both foundational and advanced competencies and skills practitioners should be trained to perform. This research identified entry-level knowledge and skills in areas of group dynamics, management and organizational theory, research methods and statistics, management principles, and development of interpersonal communication, collaboration, coaching, and teamwork skills. It further suggested that more advanced organization consultant skills included organizational design, organization-level research, system dynamics, process consultation, and change management.

O'Driscoll & Eubanks (1993) studied a sample of 45 organizational consultants from the United States and Canada. This creative investigation focused on the conduct of an organizational intervention by the consultant and explored the perspectives of both the consultant and members of the consultee organization. A critical-incident scale assessed six clusters of behavioral competence: contracting, using data, implementing the intervention, displaying interpersonal skills, managing group processes, and maintaining client relations. Respondents (clients and consultants) were asked about consultation and intervention goals. They also completed questionnaires to estimate the impact of the consultation on organizational processes (e.g., communication, leadership, and power distribution) and outcomes (e.g., organizational effectiveness, profitability, and satisfaction). Finally, they rated the flexibility of the consultation, amount of support and acceptance it received, extent of collaboration, and the relative value of the consultation to the organization.

Predictably, consultants tended to rate themselves more favorably than clients, but both groups indicated that consultant interventions were worthwhile. Stepwise multiple regression explored the association between perceived consultant competencies and

Table 10.1. Eighteen Essential Skills for School Organization Consultants

- *Interpersonal ease* – relating simply and directly to others
- *Group functioning* – understanding group dynamics, able to facilitate team work
- *Training/doing workshops* – direct instruction, teaching adults in a systematic way
- *Educational general (master teacher)* – wide educational experience, able to impart skills to others.
- *Educational content* – knowledge of school subject matter
- *Administrative/organizational* – defining and structuring work, activities, time
- *Initiative taking* – starting or pushing activities, moving directly toward action
- *Trust/rapport building* – developing a sense of safety, openness, and reduced threat on part of clients; good relationship building
- *Support* – providing nurturant relationship, positive affective relationship
- *Confrontation* – direct expression of negative information, without generating negative effect
- *Conflict mediation* – resolving or improving situations where multiple incompatible interests are in play
- *Collaboration* – creating relationships where influence is mutually shared
- *Confidence building* – strengthening client's sense of efficacy, belief in self
- *Diagnosing individuals* – forming a valid picture of the needs/problems of an individual teacher or administrator as a basis for action
- *Diagnosing organizations* – forming a valid picture of the needs/problems of a school as an organization (including its culture) as a basis for action
- *Managing/controlling* – orchestrating the improvement process; coordinating activities, time, and people; direct influence on others
- *Resource bringing* – locating and providing information, materials, practices, and equipment useful to clients.
- *Demonstration* – modeling new behavior in classrooms or meetings

Source: Miles, Saxl, & Lieberman (1988).

outcomes. For consultants, data utilization and goal-setting skills accounted for the most variance (56 percent). For clients, the addition of perceived measurable goals, interpersonal skills, and group process management accounted for 76 percent of the variance in terms of outcome. In synthesizing their findings, the authors stressed that (1) data collection is a proxy for gathering and interpreting information about the language and culture of the organization, (2) listening to and understanding the client's perspective, providing feedback, and breaking problems down into manageable elements are core skills of the consultation process, and (3) setting specific and measurable goals in collaboration with management creates the foundation for effective organizational consultation.

The most recent analysis to emerge in the organizational consultation literature involved a data reduction through exploratory factor analyses to derive a more coherent and more elegant model of consultant competencies (Worley, Rothwell, & Sullivan, 2010). After reviewing all the items derived from previous studies (many of which the authors had conducted), a large group of relatively discrete skill descriptions ($n = 175$) was edited, examined by experts, and then factor analyzed in two different ways. When the final clusters of items were compared, judgments were made about their fit, and a final conceptual framework was derived by the authors. Table 10.1 shows the domains, brief item descriptions, and number of items that supported each. In essence, the final list could be categorized around stages of the consultation processes plus items that were more cross-cutting and issue-specific.

Organizational Consultation in Educational Settings

The application of organizational consultation principles and practices in school settings is especially challenging, as documented by Fullan, Miles, & Taylor (1980). Their seminal review considered the state of the art of organization development in education, highlighting unique aspects of schools that made this work difficult (e.g., overpermeable boundaries, diffuse goal orientation, lack of accountability, and inadequate outcome data). These contextual and organizational factors likely account, at least in part, for the fact that many school improvement strategies have failed to achieve their aims (Chatterji, 2002; Elmore, 1991; Sarason, 1990).

In this context, Fullan (1991) noted that much of the change in school reform is of the first order, wherein goals are altered, different materials are used, and new behaviors are imitated, but what is lacking is a fundamental understanding of the principles and rationale behind the recommended change. The result is that the intended change is not sustained. For Sarason (1990, pp. 2–3):

> ...the failure of educational reform derives from a most superficial conception of how complicated settings are organized: their structure, their dynamics, their power relationships, and their underlying values and axioms.

These findings imply that organizational consultants working in schools must have a deep understanding of the nature and culture of school environments.

Not linking organizational change efforts to teaching and learning processes is likely to be another contributor to failure of change efforts. Peterson, McCarty, & Elmore (1993) analyzed restructuring experiments in three elementary schools over a two-year time frame. They found that all the schools did restructure, as evidenced by changes in grouping and time allocation, teacher collaboration, shared decision making, and access to new ideas. Nonetheless, teachers struggled to integrate what they were learning into instructional practices. The researchers concluded that changing structure can provide opportunities for changes in teaching practices but that teacher learning is the critical variable for instructional changes to occur.

This finding is reinforced by the work of Wang, Haertel, & Walberg (1993), who synthesized 270 research reviews and meta-analyses using content analysis, expert opinion, and meta-analytic techniques. A large number of variables found to influence learning were categorized into 30 scales within 6 broad categories based on distance from the actual teaching and learning transaction in the classroom. System-level policies (e.g., reform guidelines) were considered the most distal, whereas time on task, discipline, and other classroom variables were the most proximal. The presumed strength of association with learning outcomes then was assessed, leading to a model of influence on learning that suggested that proximal variables were more closely associated with learning than more distal variables. The order of influence that resulted, from most to least influential, was (1) instructional design (i.e., the direct instructional process), (2) nonschool contextual variables (e.g., home environment), (3) classroom management and climate, (4) student-specific variables (e.g., motivation), (5) school building variables (e.g., parent involvement), and (6) system-level variables (e.g., organizational structure and policies). These findings imply that school organizational consultants must take a multisystem perspective that incorporates and integrates change elements at several levels.

Most central to the present discussion is recognition that school organizational consultation processes must be carried out in a skillful and timely manner. School change efforts can flounder when consultants do not have the skills to mobilize people around the change process both initially and over the long term (Zins & Illback, 1995).

Perhaps the most comprehensive (and creative) analysis of school organizational consultant skills was completed by Miles, Saxl, & Lieberman (1988). Using qualitative methodology, they studied 44 "assisters" (i.e., experienced consultant/facilitators with specialized training) working in school improvement projects in New York City over a period of three years. Their investigation began with a conceptual framework that portrayed the role of "assisters" (consultants) in the context of change processes. As shown on the left side and lower portion of Figure 10.1, consultants were conceived as bringing

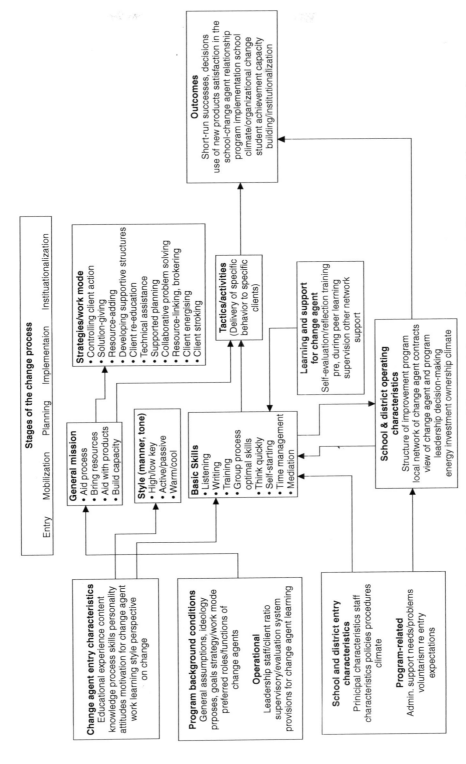

Figure 10.1. Miles, Saxl, & Lieberman's conceptual framework for successful assistance (Reprinted with permission.)

their own unique skills and characteristics to the process, which also was influenced by certain features of school programs and personnel and by system-level variables. In the middle of the diagram, stages of the change process are articulated, as are the consultant behaviors presumed to contribute to meaningful organizational change. These are defined as mission, style, skills, strategies, and tactics. Outcomes associated with effective consultation practices are shown on the right portion of the diagram.

In this study, extensive and multiple semistructured interviews were conducted with the consultants, their clients in schools (i.e., teachers, principals, and parents, but not students), and their program managers. These were coded using qualitative methods with reference to the preceding conceptual framework and then sorted within clusters using six interrelated data sets (i.e., vignettes of incident-linked skills, skills of outstanding versus average assisters, frequently used skills, skills listed as strengths, skills ranked as typical, and skills recommended for training). The result was a list of 18 essential skills for school organization consultants (shown in Table 10.2).

In a more recent synthesis, Duffy (2009b) proposed that jurisdictions adopt research-based change leadership standards and license school professionals who engage in change leadership based on those standards (see Table 10.3). While not specifically consultation-focused, it can be seen that many of the same competencies suggested in other lists are present, demonstrating that consultation and change leadership roles can overlap to a significant extent.

In sum, the literature on organizational consultation skills and competencies reflects the complexity of the work. There is general agreement across the available studies that foundational knowledge is needed in areas such as systems and organizational theory, group dynamics, and management approaches. Some degree of knowledge about the core content of the host organization (e.g., school) is also deemed vital. There is agreement that relationship building and interpersonal skills are necessary

prerequisites for success, as is the ability to use data in a problem-solving process. Higher-order skills such as organizational diagnosis, problem conceptualization, managing the change process, and dealing with conflict, while more difficult to define, are also seen as vital. But this brief overview of the current state of knowledge also highlights the extent to which successful organizational consultation practice is as much a craft as a systematic application of a set of evidence-based activities.

With this in mind, the remainder of this chapter describes the application of core consultation skills within a hypothetical whole-school (comprehensive) reform effort. Emphasis is placed on the need for thoughtful, targeted actions at key leverage points in the change process. To set the stage, a brief history and research summary of the comprehensive school reform movement in the United States are offered, with particular reference to the role of external support and assistance (consultation).

Applying Organizational Consultation within Comprehensive School Reform

The term *comprehensive school reform* (CSR), sometimes called *whole-school reform*, has come to connote a range of evidence-based strategies available for adoption by school districts in the United States. The approach emerged from decades of school improvement research and was predicated on the belief that comprehensive and integrated strategies were more likely to result in lasting achievement gains than fragmented and narrowly targeted approaches. This new paradigm for school improvement can be traced to the formation of demonstration projects by the New American Schools Development Corporation in 1991 (Bodilly et al., 1996) and the RAND Corporation's evaluation of its efforts (McLaughlin, 1990). By the late 1990s, this idea had taken hold, and there was an explosion of such initiatives across the country, many of which were funded by the U.S. Department of Education Comprehensive School Reform Demonstration (CSRD)

Table 10.2. A National Framework of Professional Standards for Change Leadership in Education

Performance Standards, Criteria, and Rubrics for Graduate-Level Change Leadership in Education Programs

Standards of Performance	*Sample Knowledge, Skills, and Dispositions for Each Standard*
Standard 1.0 – Systems Thinking: A change leader perceives school districts as intact, organic systems and explains how districts function as systems.	**Knowledge** – explains in detail the key features of school district as a system **Skill** – analyzes in detail the functional properties of school districts as systems **Disposition** – fully accepts that school districts are intact, organic systems
Standard 2.0 – Focus of Systemic Transformational Change: A change leader understands that transforming an entire school district requires improvements in student, faculty, and staff and whole-system learning.	**Knowledge** – describes the importance of whole-system improvement in rich detail **Skill** – Collects and interprets data about the need for change **Disposition** – accepts the importance of whole-district learning and can explain that importance in rich detail
Standard 3.0 – Initiating Change: A change leader creates the case for systemic transformation within school districts and in communities by providing data to support the both the *need* for change and the *opportunities* that can be seized by engaging in change.	**Knowledge** – explains in rich detail a strong rationale for creating and sustaining whole-district change **Skill** – explains in rich detail tools and processes for gaining and sustaining internal and external political support for change **Disposition** – enthusiastically endorses the concept of whole-system change.
Standard 4.0 – Assessing the Impact of Change: A change leader assesses the breadth, depth, sustainability, and anticipated positive outcomes of a systemic transformational change strategy.	**Knowledge** – can explain in rich detail the breadth, depth, sustainability, and expected returns from engaging in whole-system change **Skill** – able to conduct an in-depth analysis of the breadth, depth, sustainability, and expected returns from engaging in whole-system change **Disposition** – accepts the fact that whole-system change is complex and requires careful planning and acts on this acceptance
Standard 5.0 – Facilitating Change: A change leader helps colleagues and community members to gain insight into the human dynamics of system transformation and develops their confidence to achieve transformation goals.	**Knowledge** – possesses advanced level of knowledge of facilitation skills **Skill** – possesses advance level of skill for facilitating interpersonal and group behavior **Disposition** – is a strong advocate for helping people understand the nature of change prior to launching a change effort

Table 10.2. (cont.)

Performance Standards, Criteria, and Rubrics for Graduate-Level Change Leadership in Education Programs

Standard	Criteria
Standard 6.0 – Developing Political Support for Change: A change leader develops political support for systemic transformational through effective change leadership.	**Knowledge** – explains in rich detail strategies and tactics for building political support **Skill** – demonstrates sophisticated skills for developing political support **Disposition** – is a staunch advocate for acting in a political way to gain political support for change
Standard 7.0 – Expanding Mind-sets: A change leader engages in and shares with colleagues personal learning to deepen and broaden personal mind-sets about why systemic transformation of school districts is necessary and about the best strategy for creating and sustaining transformational change.	**Knowledge** – provides a detailed and cogent rationale for engaging in personal learning **Skill** – develops a detailed and feasible plan to engage in personal learning **Disposition** – is a strong advocate for engaging in personal learning
Standard 8.0 – Planning Systemic Transformational Change: A change leader formulates and leads the implementation of a plan to create and sustain systemic transformation in school districts.	**Knowledge** – understands the complexity of planning for change and describes the key elements of change plans **Skill** – possesses advanced skills for planning for system-wide change **Disposition** – is a powerful advocate for engaging in good planning for change
Standard 9.0 – Demonstrating Disposition for Change Leadership: A change leader demonstrates high personal emotional intelligence while leading transformational change.	**Knowledge** – provides a powerful rationale for leading with a high level of emotional intelligence **Skill** – demonstrates advanced skills for emotional intelligence **Disposition** – is a strong advocate for the importance of leading change with a high level of emotional intelligence and teaches others how to develop their emotional intelligence.
Standard 10.0 – Mastering the Art and Science of Systemic Transformational Change: A change leader is familiar with and skillful in using a variety of change theories, tools, and methodologies derived from interdisciplinary perspectives on change leadership and systemic transformation.	**Knowledge** – can explain in great detail at least one methodology for creating and sustaining whole-system change, including tools and processes that are part of that methodology **Skill** – can apply at least one methodology for creating and sustaining whole-system change, including tools and processes that are part of that methodology. **Disposition** – is a vocal advocate for the importance of change leaders knowing, understanding, and applying change theories and tools.

program (1998–2001) and its derivatives in Part F of the "No Child Left Behind" legislation and, more recently, Title I, Part A, of the Elementary and Secondary Education Act. Rowan, Camburn, & Barnes (2004) estimated that as many as 20 percent of all elementary schools in the United States were at that time engaged in a whole-school reform effort. (*Note:* As of fiscal year 2009, the CSRD program was unfunded.)

The core attributes promoted by CSR advocates included (1) use of evidence-based methods and strategies, (2) deployment of a comprehensive design with aligned components, (3) ongoing high-quality professional development for teachers and staff, (4) measurable goals and benchmarks for student performance, (5) support within the school from teachers, administrators, and staff, (6) support for staff members, (7) meaningful parent and community involvement in planning and implementing school improvement activities, (8) high-quality external technical support and assistance from an external partner with experience and expertise in school-wide reform and improvement, (9) evaluation strategies for the implementation of school reforms and for student achievement, (10) coordination of financial and other resources to support and sustain the school's reform effort, and (11) scientific research to demonstrate the effectiveness of the approach in participant schools when compared with nonparticipating schools.

The list of validated comprehensive school reform models is extensive, but some of the most commonly adopted models include the Accelerated Schools Program (Levin, 2005), America's Choice (May & Supovitz, 2006), the Comer School Development Program (Comer, 1996), Core Knowledge (Datnow, Borman, & Stringfield, 2000), Modern Red Schoolhouse (Kilgore & Jones, 2003), and Success for All (Slavin & Madden, 2001). Some (e.g., Accelerated Schools and Comer School Development) are more focused on changing organizational processes in schools, such as planning and decision making, assuming that these will translate into changes in instructional

processes. Others (e.g., Core Knowledge) concentrate on modifications to the curriculum, assuming that school organization and management will follow. Some seek to facilitate change at both instructional and organizational levels with complex interventions targeted on curriculum, grouping, assessment, staffing, and instruction but focus only on particular areas (e.g., elementary school literacy instruction in Success for All). And then some are comprehensive in scope (e.g., Modern Red Schoolhouse).

A meta-analysis summarizing the specific effects of 29 widely implemented models on student achievement (Borman et al., 2003) found that schools that implemented CSR models for over five years had consistently positive (although modest) effects. Three models had demonstrably higher effect sizes across varying contexts and study designs: the Comer School Development Model, Direct Instruction, and Success for All.

Unfortunately, follow-up research in CSR schools five years subsequent to the award of federal funding found that, in the aggregate, schools receiving awards did not demonstrate larger achievement growth than matched comparison schools (Orland, Hoffman, & Vaughn, 2010). To a significant extent, this was attributed to the fact that CSR schools typically implemented fewer than 5 of the required 11 components (4.6 at the elementary level, 4.1 at the middle school level). Moreover, only one-third of the CSR schools selected reform models with a strong scientific base. Clearly, implementation fidelity was of major concern. In contrast, an identifiable subset of schools demonstrated significant positive gains relative to matched comparisons, some in rapid and dramatic fashion and others more slowly but steadily. Exploratory substudies within these successful schools identified leadership, school climate, instruction and data use, and external support (i.e., consultation) as central to support (Aladjem et al., 2010). Thus, while design considerations, including content, complexity, target, and sequencing of activities, play an important role, a key factor in success appears to be the extent to which schools work productively with external assistance providers (consultants) to bring change to fruition (Desimone, 2002).

In studies of the Accelerated Schools Program, America's Choice, and Success for All, Rowan, Cambron, & Barnes (2004) found that the depth and breadth of consultation assistance were vital to the level of implementation. Within these widely disseminated programs, consultants often provided additional training in specific design components, observed during site visits, offered ad hoc assistance via e-mail and phone, facilitated connections to larger networks for implementation support, and enriched information provided in curricular documents through media.

Case Illustration

For the purposes of illustrating the application of consulting skills to a CSR initiative, it may be useful to embed the discussion that follows in a hypothetical consultancy. The illustration that follows relates to implementing Success for All (SFA) in an elementary school. SFA was developed in the mid-1980s by Robert Slavin et al. at Johns Hopkins University. As of 2009, it was implemented in 1,300 mostly high-poverty schools within more than 500 school districts in 48 states in the United States (plus Guam and the Virgin Islands), as well as in Canada, Mexico, England, Israel, and Australia. More than 100 research studies have been conducted on SFA-related components.

SFA focuses on reading, writing, and oral language development for students in prekindergarten through eighth grade. Implementing sites purchase a comprehensive package from the Success for All Foundation that provides materials, training, ongoing professional development, a blueprint for delivery of the model, and ongoing external support. As a prevention and early-intervention model, SFA targets classroom reading instruction, in which students are continuously regrouped by reading skill level for daily 90-minute blocks of instruction. The reading curriculum is provided by SFA and includes lessons in phonics, phonemic

awareness, vocabulary, and comprehension. Using benchmark measures and a structured data system to drive instruction, teachers assess student reading performance in eight-week intervals and regroup accordingly. Individual tutoring is provided to students who experience difficulty. The model makes extensive use of cooperative learning, in which heterogeneous groups of students ($n \approx 5$) work together on learning tasks to facilitate engagement and social support. Other components of SFA include a solutions team designed to increase parental participation and mobilize integrated family and community services for certain children, 26 days of training for school staff in the first year geared toward mastering the curriculum and instructional techniques, classroom visits by specialists, and mentoring by a full-time school facilitator who coordinates the various components of the program.

Envision an organizational consultant who is approached to provide support for the process of implementing SFA. The request comes from a school superintendent and relates to a failing urban school in her district. This school has a long and troubled history of low academic achievement and is embedded in a community that is economically disadvantaged, with high rates of unemployment and crime. It has been designated recently by the state department of education as a failing school based on lack of test score improvement and is under threat of takeover by the state. There has been a succession of principals at the school, and the level of conflict between prior principals and the central office staff has been high. There also has been a great deal of conflict within the community and a demand for greater investments to support school improvement efforts. Partly owing to high turnover rates, the current teaching staff is young and inexperienced, but they are eager to be part of a change effort. They are led by a new and enthusiastic principal with a history of leading "turnarounds." The school has just completed comprehensive needs assessment and change planning, the result of which was to adopt SFA as the vehicle for comprehensive change. The school board has approved a three-year project and fully funded the initiative.

In addition to these resources to support full adoption of the model as disseminated by SFA, the superintendent is seeking help from the organizational consultant to provide hands-on management of the change process in close consultation with the principal and other external supports. As justification, she cites research demonstrating that not all schools implement SFA fully and that partial SFA implementation is associated with diminished outcomes (Datnow & Castellano, 2000, 2001; Klingner, Cramer, & Harry, 2006; Nunnery et al., 1997; Slavin & Madden, 2001). Implementation challenges cited in these and related studies (see, e.g., Glazer, 2009) include school and community politics, inhospitable school cultures, difficulties involving parents and the community, low levels of teaching capability, teacher reservations about loss of autonomy and creativity in teaching reading, grouping and scheduling difficulties, and stagnation of students at lower levels.

The discussion that follows highlights the consultation processes and issues that the organizational consultant is likely to negotiate as the SFA implementation unfolds.

Contracting, Entry, and Mapping

On receipt of the request to engage in the school change consultancy, a number of issues and challenges emerge immediately, the successful resolution of which will determine the effectiveness of the consultation and shape project outcomes. The threshold issue is *contracting*, which relates to the initial exploratory process leading to a decision to engage with a consultancy. Contracting is not just about the establishment of a written agreement that specifies what the parties are agreeing to (although this is advisable). Rather, it relates to the process of achieving a shared and mutually satisfactory understanding of the relationship that is to be established and clarity about expectations.

Before deciding to take on the task, the prospective organizational consultant must engage in initial explorations with the consultee (in this case, multiple consultees, including the superintendent, principal, school facilitator, teaching staff, and SFA consultant/trainers). This exploration can take a variety of forms, including reviews of documentation, data, and other current and historical information. The most important, of course, is the need to conduct face-to-face exploratory interviews with a representative group of individuals and groups with whom the consultant will collaborate.

Initially, the consultant should explore the multiple perspectives that will come into play as the process evolves. For example, teachers and principals often have strongly held views about the nature of teaching and learning, and in some instances, these may be in direct conflict with the approach taken by SFA. Teachers may be invested in locally developed methods and materials and may have been given freedom to use a variety of approaches in the past. But SFA is quite specific and detailed about the nature and scope of reading instruction, and participation requires use of SFA-sanctioned curricula. The result could be "pedagogical dissonance" (Meyers, 2002).

It is also essential to discern whether the school has a history with innovation and what its experiences with external interveners and consultants have been. These experiences are likely to shape the consultant's ability to formulate a role within the initiative that has *acceptability* for key participants (if not for all). This has been described as "goodness of fit" [Margulies and Raia (1979) call this a "goodness-of-fit assessment," similar to what occurs in other helping processes (e.g., counseling).] The basic question is: Can we work together? Openness to having consultants and external interveners in and out of classrooms, for example, may be a new and troubling experience for some teachers. Similarly, not all principals enjoy or benefit from executive coaching.

The prevailing mood and circumstances within the organization often are apparent at this exploratory stage. In failing schools, teachers may experience feelings of blame and inadequacy as a function of external criticisms leveled at the school (and perhaps more personally). In the course of initial interactions, one can almost sense the mood of the school environment, based on physical and psychological cues that are immediately apparent (e.g., brightness of the environment and interactiveness of the staff). The extent to which school personnel feel disheartened or disempowered also may become obvious to the prospective consultant.

It is also advisable to sense the school's climate and culture. Each school organization is unique, and one forms impressions about the school's psychological "atmosphere" quickly. Some consultants may have great difficulty operating within a school that is run in highly autocratic ways or a school where the atmosphere is somewhat negative. Also, given that many failing schools are located within communities and neighborhoods that are disadvantaged and may have high proportions of minority students, consideration of goodness of fit with respect to racial and ethnic compatibility is an important dimension to assess [see Meyers (2002) for a thoughtful discussion of this issue in contract negotiation].

Ultimately, contracting is about understanding what is to be accomplished, what expectations the organization has for the consultant (and vice versa), what activities will occur and in what sequence, how much effort and energy will be required of the parties, and not least, what the compensation arrangement will be. Successful contracting establishes the foundation for the collaborative process and sets the tone for the relationships that will be built over time. Contracting, like other elements of consultation, is not a static or linear process. It is recursive and requires continuous reexamination.

It is useful to remember at this stage that contracting is not a unidirectional process. In this early stage, consultees are also attending to the behavior and style of the consultant and making judgments about competence and goodness of fit.

Entry is another term used by consultants to describe a complex preliminary process. Gaining entry into the school organization is not merely obtaining access to the building or having a physical presence. Entry is about the social and psychological features of relationship building with and becoming accepted by various constituencies. The subtle aspects of entry are often overlooked and can lead to later difficulties. Thinking through how to gain entry is an important strategic consideration in which the consultant must ask where to enter, with whom to interact in the initial stages, and what method to use. For example, the manner in which the consultant is introduced initially to others and by whom and the impression created by the language and content (messages) that the consultant projects in individual and group circumstances (e.g., faculty meetings) can be consequential and influence consultees' perceptions of the consultant and his or her work.

Given that there are multiple constituencies when whole-school reform is underway, being careful not to become aligned with any particular group and maintaining a sense of objectivity and neutrality are advisable. Entry is facilitated by the skills of interpersonal ease, building trust, and gaining rapport, as described earlier. Recognition that there are multiple perspectives on problems and solutions in any organization argues for expending substantial effort on active, nonjudgmental listening.

Another consultation term of art, *mapping*, signifies reaching a detailed understanding of the characteristics and interconnections among the multiple systems that make up the school community. These characteristics may include staffing patterns, roles, and responsibilities; personalities; history and issues; programs and funding streams; terminology; policies and procedures; and the norms of behavior. This knowledge will be especially useful when designing the implementation of SFA because issues of acceptability, compatibility, and readiness for change come into play.

Engaging with Planning

Once the decision has been made to engage with the change initiative, events begin to move more swiftly. Relevant consultation skills and knowledge at the planning stage include systems thinking, goal setting,

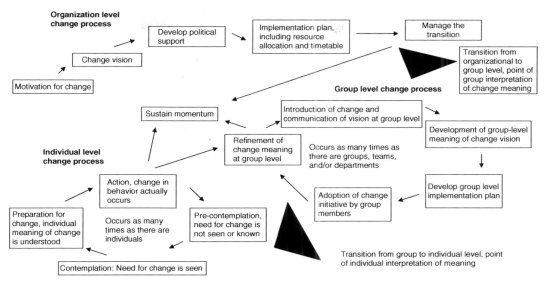

From: Whelan-Berry, K., Gordon, J., & Hingings, C. (2003). Reprinted with permission.

Figure 10.2. Nested change processes in organizational consultation.

knowledge about innovation diffusion, content knowledge (e.g., about reading instruction and SFA in this instance), team-building and small-group work, structuring tasks and time lines, information systems design, and implementation planning.

Kotter (2001), a leading theorist and researcher on organizational change processes, has written persuasively about why change initiatives fail. A primary cause is lack of a shared vision. As an organizational consultant entering a process that is well underway, spending time determining the extent to which people in the school community share the same vision and expectations is a sound investment. Meyers (2000) describes a school reform consultancy that imploded, in part, owing to assuming that the entire school community was fully engaged and empowered. In that instance, teachers were privately highly skeptical about the instructional design but did not voice their reservations in deference to the principal. With respect to SFA, it is important to know, for example, whether everyone understands that implementation of the program involves cross-age grouping and continuous assessment strategies. These strategies have significant implications for scheduling and teacher planning time.

Gathering data about these kinds of questions can be accomplished with various methods, including brief informal interviews with key informants (e.g., principal and head teachers), anonymous surveys, focus groups, and other participatory planning tools. The object is to obtain a more fine-grained sense of what information led to the decision to adopt the innovation, how and when the information was provided, what the decision-making process encompassed, the extent to which all were in agreement, and by extension, what potential problems are likely to emerge at the point of implementation.

Another activity that suggests itself during the planning stage of the consultancy is to engage with the leaders of the effort (e.g., principal, school facilitator, and the planning committee) to explore their understanding of the SFA program design, the logic model and goals that underlie it, and more broadly, the systems thinking that is embedded in comprehensive school reform. While it may be second nature for organizational consultants to think systemically and conceptualize systems change, not everyone will have this perspective. Figure 10.2 presents a visual representation of how systems change can be conceived as a multidimensional and multilevel process (Whelan-Berry, Gordon,

& Hingings, 2003). Talking through a model such as this can help leaders to take a broader and longer-term view.

Helping the leadership team to develop an implementation plan in close consultation with all constituencies builds collaboration and teamwork. In addition, it strengthens the potential for the project to be implemented in a coordinated and integrated manner. Project management at its most basic is about organizing information about tasks, time lines, resources, responsibilities, and intended products or deliverables. It anticipates and plans for implementation questions such as what, who, when, where, why, and how. Organizational consultants can facilitate delineation and sequencing of these elements by teaching and modeling development of a *work breakdown structure* (Lanford & McCann, 1983), perhaps enhanced by software designed to accomplish this task. (See http://en.wikipedia.org/wiki/Comparison_of_project_management_software for a comprehensive analysis of available tools.)

In constructing the plan, specifying the activities that are required is critical. In the case of SFA, these will include acquisition of materials, training, preparation, teambuilding, and the like. The more important contribution of this part of the consultation will be thinking through issues such as the development of plans for communication, internal and external; for the development of information and use of data at key decision points; for stakeholder engagement; and for risk management.

Setting the Stage and Mobilizing Resources

As the preparatory activities come to a close, the momentum begins to accelerate, there is a sense of being about to launch, and the planning team begins to communicate with others in the school environment about what is to be done. Knowledge acquired in the entry and mapping processes can help in making decisions about what to communicate, how to do so, and who should be the initial targets of the information. In

general, the consultant should adhere to basic principles of adult learning, such as providing succinct overviews coupled with examples and narratives that help staff to feel comfortable with the ideas. Early communications should subtly address questions such as: How hard is this likely to be? How much am I going to have to change? How will students profit in ways that they do not now? What's in it for me?

In particular, consultants can help consultees (e.g., the principal) to guard against common problems such as providing too much information at once, becoming too theoretical or using language that is off-putting, and not giving sufficient time for open dialogue. Given the history of this particular school, a degree of skepticism may lie just below the surface, so it will be important to help consultees to frame the work in positive terms that communicate commitment tempered by realism. Rather than revisiting all the events that led up to the current state of affairs, describing how SFA has worked in similar schools can help, or better yet, elicit personal testimonials from teachers and principals who have been successful in implementing the approach.

Facilitating the development of self-directed work teams to carry out project components is another contribution consultants might make toward effective implementation. Activities might involve modeling how to plan and carry out a meeting (e.g., about instructional grouping decisions), how to identify problems (e.g., with logistics and scheduling) and resolve them, how to plan work (e.g., collaborating on instructional content over a specified period), how to communicate effectively in a blame-free environment (e.g., when classroom management problems emerge), how to share resources, how to set goals for continuous improvement, and how to celebrate successes. If these teams are to work, they must be given sufficient authority and sanction by administrators, and the consultant can mentor managers in empowerment techniques.

"Political" hurdles can derail implementation. Anticipation of such issues in the early stages can go a long way toward minimizing their effects. A primary source of conflict in schools is related to internal competition for limited resources. It is entirely plausible that in a failing school, staff members who do not benefit directly from the additional resources and supports provided by SFA could be resentful and obstruct the process. Moreover, the politics of the community can spill over into the school environment (e.g., divisions along racial or socioeconomic lines around issues of equity, representation, and trust). Facilitation of frank and open discussions regarding political factors can help to attenuate their effect.

Another of the predictors of change failure referenced by Kotter (2001) is the lack of a sense of urgency. Because change opportunities emerge out of a specific set of circumstances that are not always present, the window of opportunity for implementation can be limited. If planning processes become too long and drawn out, or if staff become distracted by other issues, the opportunity for transformative change can be lost. Consultees may need help with "keeping their eyes on the prize," motivating and reinforcing staff, and activating behavior throughout the process. While one hopes that work teams would act on the empowerment they have been given, there is no guarantee that they will. Innovation and change are not self-executing, and consultants can be more objective about the need for and timing of additional encouragement and confidence building.

A major obstacle to full and sustained implementation of whole-school reform models is overdependency on the external model and the experts promulgating it. This can result in lack of a sense of ownership on the part of school staff (Fullan, 1993). The organizational consultant can play a significant role by ensuring that change leaders take the time to talk through the knowledge and skills that are being imparted through training and initial experience. The immediate goal is to help staff to internalize ideas and methods, but an overarching goal is also to promote a culture of organizational learning that can sustain the change

initiative. Peter Senge, a leader in thinking about organizational change, calls this the "fifth discipline" (Senge et al., 2000), comprising elements of systems thinking, personal mastery, mental models, shared vision, and team learning.

Change Program Management

Once the change initiative has gotten underway, consultation challenges multiply, and the organizational consultant must make strategic decisions about where to focus consultative effort. Several areas derived from what is known about successful change implementations suggest themselves. Initially, the need to define and engineer visible performance improvements (short-term wins) is paramount because innovations are fragile in the early stages and need bolstering (Kotter, 2001). In the case of SFA, this may involve encouraging the school principal to recognize and reward teachers who are enthusiastic early adopters and have been able to organize their classrooms to accommodate multigrade grouping strategies. Or the leadership team also might be encouraged to highlight student groupings that achieve the greatest achievement gains in a given eight-week interval.

On a broader level, as the instructional innovation grows and develops, continuous mentoring and coaching of the leadership team likely will become an indispensable ingredient of the organizational learning process. As the staff accumulates experience with the innovation, successes will occur, but frustrations and failures also will emerge. The leadership team's ability to manage both successes and failures determines whether momentum is built or the process gets bogged down. The consultant can help leaders to obtain perspective on the change process, which is by its nature nonlinear. Taking the long view can be difficult in high-stakes change efforts, but maintaining resolve and persistence in the face of barriers and setbacks is one of the strongest predictors of success (Duffy, 2006).

Lip service is often paid to the critical nature of effective communication in change efforts, but the reality is often that insufficient or inaccurate information is communicated and or what is transmitted is not timely or is uninspiring. Organizational consultants can help the leadership team to become clear about what information needs to be transmitted through which channels so that everyone in the school community feels fully informed about how the process is unfolding. Framing clear messages in creative and engaging formats is vital. Managing the "mood" of the organization during the change process through communication processes also has been suggested as a core consulting task (Garvin & Roberto, 2005). This can involve being sensitive to and acknowledging the frustrations and fears people may have about changing roles and responsibilities, but primarily it should be about helping leaders to set a tone of optimism and support. Effective communication also helps to maintain enthusiasm and commitment, manage expectations, control rumors and misunderstandings, and provide opportunity for dialogue between and among the various stakeholders and systems.

The notion of *paradigm shifting* has received considerable attention in both the popular and management press to the extent that it has become clichéd. Nonetheless, at the center of virtually all school reform efforts is a desire to promote new ways of thinking and behaving. For Duffy (2009a), *paradigms, mental models,* and *mind-sets* are the determinative variables of concern in whole-school reform. Dominant educational concepts to be overcome for learner-centered innovations to work include the following: (1) teaching students in classroom groups is the necessary delivery system for instruction, (2) teaching can and should be standardized, (3) students should be grouped according to age and grade level, (4) there is a fixed amount of material to be covered in a specified time frame, and (5) teachers must work center stage in classrooms for learning to occur.

The way people in schools think about teaching and learning does not shift automatically when they acquire and deploy new skills or competencies, such as through SFA training. The process takes longer and is more subtle. Paradigms, mental models, and mind-sets begin to shift when educators experience simple and cogent explanations accompanied by concrete examples, observe others (especially high-status models) implementing the innovation successfully, and are sufficiently engaged with the idea on an emotional level that it becomes part of a meaningful narrative (i.e., it is connected to a broader and more meaningful goal). In addition to helping change leaders attend to what teachers do while implementing the innovation, the organizational consultant can help change leaders support paradigm shifting by ensuring that they recognize and reinforce subtle changes in thinking and teaching and learning.

Managing change is also about problem solving. The organizational consultant, as a more objective party to the change process than those engaged with it on a daily basis, is in a unique position to recognize when the process has slowed or particular barriers have emerged. In the instance of SFA implementation, available literature suggests several kinds of difficulties that can occur (see earlier discussion). A key and obvious role for the consultant is to surface these and enable data-based problem exploration and solution seeking.

Finally, sustaining and institutionalizing change is a challenge for organizational consultants. To some extent, the robustness of the organizational change process as it evolves dictates whether change is fundamental and lasting. Consultants can help to conceive and establish policies and procedures that create a supportive framework for the changes that have transpired. They also can establish information systems that ensure periodic measurements in support of the innovation, perhaps moving away from static achievement scores and toward more functional measurement. Finding ways to connect people to the changes that have occurred and helping them take pride in their accomplishments help. More generally, consultants can help leaders to attend to the maintenance and enhancement of a desirable school culture in which continuous learning is paramount. Perhaps most important, consultants can foster the identification and development of new leaders who personify the vision of change that guided the undertaking.

Summary

Skilled organizational consultation is an essential ingredient of implementation and change processes. Research evidence indicates that when effective consultation is deployed in the service of school change, the likelihood of achieving meaningful and lasting outcomes is enhanced. The literature regarding what consultative skills and competencies are necessary and sufficient to ensure effective implementation of change initiatives is somewhat undifferentiated and comprised mostly of domain-based listings of core and advanced attributes. Moreover, most studies of school change do not describe or measure the specific contributions skilled consultation makes to implementation processes. Through a hypothetical case example, this chapter sought to explicate the points at which timely consultative intervention can help leaders to move the change process forward.

References

Adelman, H. S., & Taylor, L. (2000). Shaping the future of mental health in schools. *Psychology in the Schools* 37, 49–60.

Aladjem, D. K., Birman, B. F., Orland, M., Harr-Robins, J., Herredia, A., Parrish, T. B., & Ruffini, S. J. (2010). *Achieving dramatic school improvement: An exploratory study.* Washington: U.S. Department of Education.

Bodilly, S. J., Purnell, S. W., Ramsey, K., & Keith, S. J. (1996). *Lessons from New American Schools Development Corporation's demonstration phase.* Santa Monica, CA: RAND Corporation.

Borman, G. D., Hewes, G. M., Overman, L. T., & Brown, S. (2003). Comprehensive school reform and achievement: A meta-analysis. *Review of Educational Research* 73(2), 125–230.

Carey, A., & Varney, G. (1983). Which skills spell success in OD? *Training and Development Journal* 37(4), 38–40.

Carlson. C., Tharinger, D., Bricklin, P., DeMers, S., & Paavola, J. (1996). Health care reform and psychological practice in schools. *Professional Psychology: Research & Practice* 27, 14–23.

Chatterji, M. (2002).Models and methods for examining standards-based reforms and accountability initiatives: Have the tools of inquiry answered pressing questions on improving schools? *Review of Educational Research* 72, 345–86.

Comer, J. P. (ed.) (1996). *Rallying the whole village: The Comer process for reforming education.* New York: Teacher's College Press.

Curtis, M. J., & Stollar, S. A. (2002). Best practices in system-level change. In A. Thomas and J. Grimes (eds.), *Best practices in school psychology IV* (pp. 223–34). Bethesda, MD: National Association of School Psychologists.

Datnow, A., & Castellano, M. (2000). Teachers' responses to Success for All: How beliefs, experiences and adaptations shape implementation. *American Educational Research Journal* 37, 775–99.

Datnow, A., Borman, G., & Stringfield, S. (2000). School reform through a highly specified curriculum: Implementation and effects of the core knowledge sequence. *Elementary School Journal* 101, 167–92.

Desimone, L. (2002). How can comprehensive school reform models be successfully implemented? *Review of Educational Research* 72, 433–79.

Duffy, F. M. (2009a). *Paradigms, mental models, and mind-sets: Triple barriers to transformational change in school systems.* Retrieved on June 28, 2010, from the Connexions website: http://cnx.org/content/col10723/1.1/.

Duffy, F. M. (2009b). *National framework of professional standards for change leadership in education.* Retrieved on June 29, 2010, from the Connexions website: http://cnx.org/content/col10638/1.2/.

Duffy, F. M. (2006). *Step-up-to-excellence: A change navigation protocol for transforming school systems.* Retrieved June 29, 2010, from the Connexions website: http://cnx.org/content/m13656/1.1/.

Elmore, R. (1991). Paradox of innovation in education: Cycles of reform and the resilience of teaching. Unpublished manuscript, Harvard University, Cambridge, MA.

Esper, J. (1990). Organizational change and development: Core practitioner competencies and future trends. *Advances in Organization Development* 1, 277–314.

Fuchs, D., & Fuchs, L. S. (1988). Mainstream assistance teams to accommodate difficult-to-teach students in general education. In J. Graden, J. E. Zins, and M. J. Curtis (eds.), *Alternative educational delivery systems* (pp. 49–70). Washington: National Association of School Psychologists.

Fullan, M. G. (1991). *The new meaning of educational change*. New York: Teachers College Press.

Fullan, M. G. (1993). *Change forces: Probing the depths of educational reform*. Bristol, PA: Falmer Press.

Fullan, M. G., Miles, M. B., & Taylor, G. (1980). Organizational development in schools: The state of the art. *Review of Educational Research* 50, 121–83.

Garvin, D.A. and Roberto, M.A. (2005) Change Through Persuasion. Harvard Business Review (February), 1–5. (no vol number)

Glazer, J. L. (2009). How external interveners leverage large-scale change: The case of *America's Choice*, 1998–2003. *Educational Evaluation and Policy Analysis* 31, 269–97.

Huebner, E. S., Gilligan, T. D., & Cobb, H. (2002). Best practices in preventing and managing stress and burnout. In A. Thomas and J. Grimes (eds.), *Best practices in school psychology IV* (pp. 173–82). Bethesda, MD: National Association of School Psychologists.

Illback, R. J. (1994). Poverty and the crisis in children's services: The need for services integration. *Journal of Clinical Child Psychology* 23, 413–24.

Illback, R. J., & Fields, T. (1992). Building effective teams and groups: Common themes and future directions. *Special Services in the Schools* 6, 195–205.

Illback, R. J., & Maher, C. A. (1984). The school psychologist as an organizational boundary role professional. *Journal of School Psychology* 22, 63–72.

Illback, R. J., & Zins, J. E. (1995). Organizational intervention in educational settings. *Journal of Educational and Psychological Consultation* 6, 217–36.

Illback, R. J., Maher, C. A., & Zins, J. E. (1999). Program planning and evaluation. In T. R. Gutkin and C. R. Reynolds (eds.), *Handbook of school psychology*, 3rd ed. New York: Wiley.

Kalafat, J., & Illback, R. J. (1998). A qualitative evaluation of school-based family resource and youth service centers. *American Journal of Community Psychology* 26, 573–604.

Kalafat, J., Illback, R. J., & Sanders, D. (2007). The relationship between implementation fidelity and educational outcomes in a school-based family support program: Development of a model for evaluating multidimensional full-service programs. *Evaluation and Program Planning* 30, 136–48.

Kilgore, S. B., & Jones, J. D. (2003). Leadership in comprehensive school reform initiatives: The case of the Modern Red School House. In J. Murphy and A. Datnow (eds.), *Leadership for school reform: Lessons from comprehensive school reform designs* (pp. 52–84). Thousand Oaks, CA: Corwin Press.

Klingner, J. K., Cramer, E., & Harry, B. (2006). Challenges in the implementation of Success for All by four urban schools. *Elementary School Journal* 106(4). 333–349.

Kotter, J. P. (2001). *What leaders really do: Best of HBR*. Boston: Harvard Business School Press.

Lanford, H. W., & McCann, T. M. (1983). Effective planning and control of large projects using work breakdown structure. *Long Range Planning* 16, 38–50.

Levin, H. M. (2005). Accelerated schools: A decade of evolution. In M. Fullan (ed.), *Fundamental change* (pp. 137–60). Amsterdam: Springer.

Maher, C. A. & Illback, R. J. (1983). Planning for organizational change in schools: Alternative approaches and procedures. *School Psychology Review* 12, 460–6.

Margulies, N., & Raia, A. P. (1979). *Conceptual foundations of organizational development*. New York: McGraw-Hill.

May, H., & Supovitz, J. A. (2006). Capturing the cumulative effects of school reform: An 11-year study of the impacts of America's Choice on student achievement. *Educational Evaluation and Policy Analysis* 28, 231–57.

McLaughlin, M. (1990). The RAND change agent study revisited: Macro perspectives and micro realities. *Educational Researcher* 19, 11–16.

Meyers, B. (2002). The contract negotiation stage of a school-based, cross-cultural organizational consultation: A case study. *Journal of Educational and Psychological Consultation* 13, 151–83.

Miles, M. B., & Schmuck, R. A. (1971). Improving schools through organizational development: An overview. In *Organization development in schools*. Palo Alto, CA: National Press.

Miles, M. B., Saxl, E. R., & Lieberman, A. (1988). What skills do educational "change agents" need?: An empirical view. *Curriculum Inquiry* 2, 157–93.

Neilsen, E. (1984). *Becoming an OD practitioner*. Englewood Cliffs, NJ: Prentice-Hall.

Nunnery, J., Slavin, R. E., Madden, N.A., Ross, S., Smith, L., Hunter, P., & Stubbs, J. (1997). Effects of full and partial implementations of Success for All on student reading achievement in English and Spanish. Paper presented at the Annual Meeting of the American Educational Research Association, Chicago.

O'Driscoll, M. P., & Eubanks, J. L. (1993). Behavioral competencies, goal settings, & OD practitioner effectiveness. *Group & Organizational Management* 18(3), 308–27.

Orland, M., Hoffman, A., & Vaughan, E. S., III (2010). *Evaluation of the Comprehensive School Reform Program implementation and outcomes: Fifth-year report.* Washington: U.S. Department of Education.

Peterson, P. L., McCarthey, S. J., & Elmore, R. F. (1993). Learning from school restructuring. *American Educational Research Journal* 33, 119–53.

Rosenfield, S., & Gravois, R. A. (1999). Working with teams in the school. In C. R. Reynolds and T. B. Gutkin (eds.). *The handbook of school psychology*, 3rd ed. (pp. 1025–40). New York: Wiley.

Rowan, B., Camburn, E., & Barnes, C. (2004). Benefiting from comprehensive school reform: A review of research on CSR implementation. In C. Cross (ed.), *Putting the pieces together: Lessons from comprehensive school reform research* (pp. 1–52). Washington: National Clearinghouse for Comprehensive School Reform.

Sarason, S. B. (1990). *The predictable failure of educational reform.* San Francisco: Jossey-Bass.

Senge, P., Cambron-McCabe, N., Lucas, T., Smith, B., Dutton, J., & Kleiner, A. (2000). *Schools that learn: A fifth discipline fieldbook for educators, parents, and everyone who cares about education.* New York: Doubleday.

Sheridan, S. M., Napolitano, S. A., & Swearer, S. M. (2002). Best practices in school-community partnerships. In A. Thomas and J. Grimes (eds.), *Best practices in school psychology IV* (pp. 321–36). Bethesda, MD: National Association of School Psychologists.

Slavin, R. E., & Madden, N. A. (2001). *Success for All: Research and reform in elementary education.* Mahwah, NJ: Lawrence Erlbaum.

Suarez-Balcazar, Y., Redmond, L., Kouba, J., Hellwig, M., Davis, R., Martinez, L., et al. (2007). Introducing systems change in the schools: The case of school luncheons and vending machines. *American Journal of Community Psychology* 39, 335–45.

Sugai, G., & Horner, R. (2002). The evolution of discipline practices: School-wide positive behavior support. *Child & Family Behavior Therapy* 24, 23–50.

Talley, R. C., & Short, R. J. (1996). Schools as health service delivery sites: Current status and future directions. *Special Services in the Schools* 10, 37–55.

Wang, M., Haertel, G., & Walberg, H. (1993). Toward a knowledge base for school learning. *Review of Educational Research* 63, 249–94.

Warwick, D., & Donovan, T. (1979). Surveying organization development skills. *Training & Developmental Journal* 33(9), 22–5.

Whelan-Berry, K., Gordon, J., & Hingings, C. (2003). Strengthening organizational change processes: Recommendations and implications from a multilevel analysis. *Journal of Applied Behavioral Science* 39, 186–207.

Wooten, K., & White, L. (1989). Toward a theory of change role efficacy. *Human Relations* 42, 651–69.

Worley, C., & Varney, G. (1998). A search for a common body of knowledge for master's level organization development and change programs. *Academy of Management OD Consultants Newsletter*, pp. 1–4.

Zins, J. E., & Illback, R. J. (1995). Consulting to facilitate planned organizational change in schools. *Journal of Educational and Psychological Consultation* 6, 237–45.

Zins, J. E., Weissberg, R. P., Wang, M. C., & Walberg, H. J. (eds.) (2004). *Building academic success through social and emotional learning: What does the research say?* New York: Teachers College Press.

CHAPTER 11

Implementation of Interventions to Promote School Readiness

Janet A. Welsh

School Readiness: Definition and Importance

What Is School Readiness?

The past decade has seen an increase in accountability for students' educational performance, along with recognition that the skills that children demonstrate at school entry are often predictive of their later achievement and adjustment. This, in turn, has led to increased interest in the school readiness of young children and the most appropriate ways to promote it, particularly for children at risk. Although there is no universally accepted definition of exactly what constitutes school readiness, there is general consensus that *school readiness* refers to a constellation of cognitive, behavioral, and social-emotional competencies mastered by the time children enter school that allow them to adjust well to the school setting and to acquire academic skills. Where there is less agreement, however, is regarding specific skills that indicate readiness. Parents and teachers, for example, often have different ideas about which "readiness" skills are the most important; parents often say that

their children should know how to count, name letters, and write, whereas kindergarten teachers tend to emphasize social and behavioral skills such as following directions, paying attention, getting along with other children, and performing self-help tasks such as zipping a jacket (Dockett & Perry, 2003; Heaviside & Farris, 1993). Although some definitions of school readiness are focused primarily on child characteristics and abilities, others emphasize the importance of considering child skills within the context of the developmental challenges present in the school environment. For example, the importance of specific skills may vary as a function of class size, instructional practices, and the educational priorities of schools (Blair et al., 2007).

The belief that school readiness is important is supported by longitudinal research indicating that children's skills in various domains at the time of school entry (kindergarten or first grade) are often predictive of their school adjustment, achievement, and other significant outcomes years later. As schools have come under increasing pressure to demonstrate good academic progress for students, the following questions have been raised:

> What are the specific components of school readiness?
> Which students are not ready for school?
> What does research say about the effectiveness of school readiness interventions?
> What are the challenges involved with implementing school readiness programs in real-life settings?

COMPONENTS OF SCHOOL READINESS

Among the component skills that comprise school readiness are cognitive, behavioral, and social-emotional competencies, as well as organizational and motivational capacities that affect children's functioning in multiple domains. Cognitive contributions to school readiness include expressive and receptive language abilities, emergent reading and math skills, and general knowledge of the world (e.g., birds live in nests, food is purchased in a grocery store, etc.). Social-emotional aspects of school readiness include the ability to actively engage in learning, follow directions, get along well with other children, and manage emotions (McClelland, Acock, & Morrison, 2006). Bridging these two domains are a subset of skills often referred to as *executive functions*, which involve several capacities related to learning, including working memory, impulse control, and the ability to attend to important aspects of the school environment (Blair et al., 2007). Additionally, current models of school readiness consider how the skills of various children interact with the demands of a particular school environment.

WHICH CHILDREN ARE NOT READY FOR SCHOOL?

Most developmental researchers and educational practitioners are particularly concerned with children who arrive at school lacking the requisite readiness skills. Children may show deficits in school readiness for a variety of reasons that often overlap. Children with delays in various aspects of cognitive and social-emotional development may start school at considerable disadvantage compared with their nondelayed peers. Characteristics of the child, the family, and the school environment all influence children's subsequent school adjustment, with many children experiencing risks in multiple domains.

CHILD CHARACTERISTICS

A number of child characteristics, including general intelligence, language development, temperament, and executive function are related to both children's skills at school entry and their later school adjustment. Probably best documented is the relationship between academic achievement and intelligence quotient (IQ). While IQ is also related to other life outcomes, such as behavioral adjustment and vocational attainment, the impact of IQ is strongest for academic achievement (Massoth & Levensen, 1982; Sattler, 2001). Although related to IQ, factors such as language development and social competence make their own unique contributions to school readiness. Children's early vocabulary and expressive language skills are strongly related to later reading comprehension (Wagner, Muse, & Tannenbaum, 2007), and language delay during the preschool years is often a predictor of subsequent reading disability (Rescorla, 2009).

Recent developmental and educational research has examined the relations between children's temperament and social-emotional competence and school readiness. Children who are consistently oppositional and noncompliant with teachers and who are aggressive and irritable with peers may have chronic difficulty with school adjustment. Poor self-regulation at school entry is associated with poor achievement, repeated discipline referrals during elementary school, and eventually with dropout and delinquency during adolescence (Kellam, Brown, & Fleming, 1983; Moffitt, 1993; Patterson, Reid, & Dishion, 1998). In particular, children who exhibit high rates of inattention, poor impulse control, and poor working memory may be unable to profit from learning opportunities available in the school environment (Blair & Diamond, 2008).

FAMILY INTERACTIONS

Research on the relations between family factors and school readiness has revealed a number of important characteristics of both the home environment and the quality of parent-child interaction patterns. First, a large body of research with infants and toddlers indicates a central role for sensitive, responsive caregiving in the development of both cognitive and social-emotional competence. *Sensitive/responsive caregiving* refers to parent-child relationships characterized by high levels of affection and emotional warmth, along with a high degree of contingent responsiveness to children's signals and needs (Ainsworth et al., 1978; Darling & Steinberg, 1993). Additionally, researchers sometimes expand the definition of *sensitive/responsive parenting* to include rich linguistic input and parent behaviors that facilitate children's attention and task persistence (Akhtar, Dunham, & Dunham, 1991; Smith, Landry, & Swank, 2000).

Given the link between early language development and later reading achievement, it is no surprise that the quality of language and social interactions between children and adults during the preschool years has a powerful effect on school readiness (Brooks-Gunn & Markman, 2005; Hart & Risley, 1992). Children who have many opportunities to engage in rich conversations with adults during early childhood demonstrate advanced vocabulary and syntactic skills at school entry; these, in turn, have an impact on early reading acquisition. Additionally, early cognitive stimulation in the form of access to literacy materials, toys, and life experiences such as trips to the zoo all contribute to children's competence at school entry (Hart & Risley, 1995).

Parent discipline style also affects school readiness. Children whose parents adopt a more "authoritarian" style or use harsh, punitive, or inconsistent discipline strategies show lower levels of social-emotional readiness skills than those whose parents are more sensitive and child-centered in their management approaches (Moilanen et al., 2010).

Classroom Environment and Teacher-Child Relationship

Research has revealed that the quality of young children's early relationships with their teachers can be very important for their long-term adjustment to school. Warm, supportive relationships with kindergarten teachers facilitate the behavioral, academic, and social adjustment of young children (Birch & Ladd, 1997; Hamre & Pianta, 2001; Hughes, Cavell, & Jackson, 1995; Ladd & Burgess, 2001). Children with close teacher relationships have fewer behavioral problems, are more positive about school, and are less likely to be referred for special education or grade retention. Close child-teacher relationships in kindergarten also predict later academic success (Palermo et al., 2007). Conversely, kindergartners with highly conflicted teacher relationships were more likely to be aggressive and less likely to show positive behavior in first grade (Birch & Ladd, 1998). In some cases these effects appear to be very long lasting; in the Hamre & Pianta (2001) study, children's relationships with their kindergarten teachers were predictive of behavioral adjustment and academic achievement through the eighth grade.

Teacher-child closeness is associated with young children's reading skills (Burchinal et al., 2002), whereas dependency and conflict in the teacher-child relationship are associated with school avoidance and poor achievement (Birch & Ladd, 1997). Children who experience responsive teacher interactions in preschool displayed stronger vocabulary and decoding skills at the end of first grade, demonstrating a crossover between social-emotional and academic aspects of school functioning (Connor, Son, & Hindman, 2005). Positive relationships with teachers appear to be particularly important for children who demonstrate behavior problems at school entry (Pianta & Walsh, 1998) and help to reduce the "achievement gap" for high-risk children (Hamre & Pianta, 2005).

POVERTY

Perhaps the largest single factor accounting for differences in school readiness is economic disadvantage. Delays in school readiness are part of the larger issue of health and mental health disparities associated with poverty (Ritsher et al., 2001). Children from low-income families consistently enter school far behind their more affluent peers in every aspect of school readiness, and this "achievement gap" widens as children progress through school (Ryan, Fauth, & Brooks-Gunn, 2006). Furthermore, poverty rates are significant, affecting approximately 20 percent of children in the United States. Poverty is linked to school readiness by a variety of mechanisms. Most significantly, the quality of the home environment and parent-child interaction is strikingly different between low- and middle-income children. Low-income homes have fewer books, cognitively stimulating toys, and opportunities for experiential learning. Additionally, low-income parents tend to talk and read less to their children and to use fewer vocabulary words and complex sentences (Berlin et al., 1995; Hart & Risley, 1999). Finally, low-income parents experience elevated rates of stress and are more likely to be harsh and negative in their interactions with their children (Lengua, Honorado, & Bush, 2007; Ritsher et al., 2001). These differences are substantial and have an immediate and significant effect on school readiness; discrepancies between middle- and low-income children's cognitive skills are apparent by age two (Klebanov, Brooks-Gunn, & Duncan, 1994). Children from impoverished homes demonstrate significant delays in language and emergent literacy skills (Zill et al., 1995) and show elevated rates of depression and anxiety disorders, peer problems, conduct disorders, and attention deficit/hyperreactivity disorder (ADHD) (Franz, Lensche, & Schmitz, 2003; Ritsher et al., 2001).

Beyond the quality of parent-child interactions, poverty exposes children to other hardships that may contribute to their school readiness deficits. Children from poor families are more likely to experience health issues such as low birth weight (Klebanov, Brooks-Gunn, & Duncan, 1994), nutritional deficiencies (Looker, 2002), and exposure to neurotoxins such as lead (Meyer et al., 2003), all of which have implications for learning and behavior. Poor families experience more chronic stress, conflict, and mental illness than middle-income families, all of which diminish the support available for young children's acquisition of readiness skills (Ryan, Fauth, & Brooks-Gunn, 2006). Once they enter school, low-income children are more likely to experience less supportive and lower-quality school environments, which further compound their difficulties (Knitzer & Lefkowitz, 2005; Lee & Loeb, 1995). Although poverty has global negative effects on children's development, verbal ability and academic achievement appear to be the most directly and persistently affected (Duncan & Brooks-Gunn, 2000).

Interventions to Enhance School Readiness: The Evidence Base

A great deal of research on the effectiveness of early childhood programs at enhancing school readiness was initiated in the 1960s, during Lyndon Johnson's "War on Poverty." School readiness interventions vary in a number of ways. First, the target population of the interventions can differ. While some programs are *universal*, that is, intended to benefit all children regardless of risk level, many others are *selective*, meaning that they are designed to address the needs of specific high-risk groups. Because of the multiple risks associated with poverty, poor children are often the target of selective school readiness interventions. However, interventions also have focused on other risk factors, such as premature birth or adolescent motherhood. The developmental focus and timing of the intervention also vary. For example, programs that emphasize children's emergent academic skills often focus directly on preschoolers (ages three to five), whereas those which target mothers' sensitivity and responsiveness toward their children usually are designed for parents of infants and toddlers.

While the goal of virtually all early childhood interventions is to promote children's competence in one or more domains, not all interventions target children directly. Some may focus on changing the behaviors of parents and teachers as a way of improving children's outcomes. Thus child-focused interventions strive to affect children's competencies directly, whereas teacher- or parent-focused programs attempt to affect child competence indirectly through improvements in the quality of adult-child interactions. Some multicomponent interventions target both parent and child skills, whereas others simultaneously target both children and teachers. Some interventions are narrowly focused on improving one specific aspect of child functioning (e.g., attachment security), whereas others are more comprehensive and target multiple domains (e.g., cognitive and social-emotional), multiple settings (e.g., home and school), or multiple family members (e.g., parent and child).

Finally, in the era of increased accountability for students' educational performance, it has become important to consider whether an intervention is *evidence-based*. This means that the program has been rigorously evaluated under scientific conditions and found to be effective at strengthening one or more aspects of children's school readiness. Most educational interventions and approaches being used in real-life settings lack an empirical basis; that is, most programs implemented with young children are not evidence-based. However, a number of key programs have strong longitudinal designs, in which child participants are followed for many years after the program ends to determine its long-term effects. Below I discuss several key evidence-based approaches to school readiness.

School-Based Preschool Programs

HEAD START AND EARLY HEAD START

Head Start is the most well-known and enduring program designed to promote school readiness and reduce the achievement gap in disadvantaged children. Head Start was initiated in 1965 and is currently widely implemented throughout the United States, although only about a third of eligible children participate (Lee et al., 1990). Head Start is federally funded and targets three- and four-year-olds from low-income families, providing a half-day center-based program that includes intensive language and cognitive stimulation along with an emphasis on nutrition, preventive health care, and parent outreach. Longitudinal investigations on the effectiveness of Head Start have yielded mixed results.

On the one hand, children attending Head Start typically demonstrate immediate and significant gains in cognitive skills and achievement compared with children who do not attend the program, and effects seem particularly strong for the children with the greatest initial delays (Lee et al., 1991). Unfortunately, in long-term research evaluations, most of these differences, particularly those related to IQ, disappear by the time the children are in first grade, casting doubts regarding the long-term value of Head Start. However, subsequent follow-up of these children reveals more general long-term benefits for program participants, including reduced placement in special education and higher high school graduation rates (McKey et al., 1985).

Early Head Start was initiated in 1995 as a downward extension of Head Start, serving infants, toddlers, and pregnant women. The rationale behind Early Head Start was that children from deprived environments would benefit from very early intervention rather than waiting until age three or four. Early Head Start programs vary in terms of their format. Some are primarily center-based, others primarily home-based, and others use a combination of center- and home-based services. Early Head Start targets maternal and child health, infant development, and sensitive parenting, with the recognition that these factors in infancy and toddlerhood contribute to school readiness and general competence later in childhood (Davidov & Grusec, 2006; Landry et al., 2008; Olds, 2007). Because Early Head Start is a relatively recent program, longitudinal data on its effectiveness such as those available for traditional Head Start are currently unavailable. However, preliminary research has shown favorable outcomes in a number of child and parenting domains, with the mixed center/home-based format yielding the best results.

ABECEDARIAN PROJECT AND PROJECT CARE

The Abecedarian Project was an intensive intervention for infants and young children from low-income minority families in North Carolina. The goal of the project was to prevent the cognitive deficits often seen in poor children. In the Abecedarian Project, children were identified prenatally and enrolled in full-time, five-day-per-week day care beginning at six months of age. The program continued until children were five years old and provided intensive cognitive and language stimulation at all age levels. Early comparisons between the children who received the program and a control group of children revealed significant differences in IQ beginning at age 18 months and continuing through age five, with peak differences in IQ occurring at age four (Ramey & Ramey, 2004). Long-term follow up of Abecedarian participants revealed that significant differences in cognitive and academic performance remained at age twenty-one. Furthermore, when compared with the control group, young adults who received the intervention had completed more years of school, were more likely to be enrolled in college and employed in skilled occupations, and were less likely to be adolescent parents or to engage in health-risk behaviors such as smoking (Campbell et al., 2002).

Project CARE replicated the Abecedarian Project but added a third condition that included weekly home visits to encourage active participation of parents in their children's education. Long-term follow-up indicated that Project CARE participants had outcomes similar to the Abecedarian group, with most of the effects driven by the early center-based care received by the children and few additional benefits found for the parent-education component (Campbell et al., 2008).

PERRY PRESCHOOL PROJECT

The Perry Preschool Project was initiated in 1962 in Ypsilanti, Michigan, and involved the High/Scope curriculum, which is widely implemented in preschools today, including many Head Start programs. Like Head Start and the Abecedarian Project, the Perry Preschool Project included children from disadvantaged families; unlike the others, the participants in the Perry Project were all African American and had IQ scores below ninety. Children were randomly assigned to receive or not receive the preschool program. Longitudinal follow-up showed that the children in the preschool group demonstrated significant improvements in IQ and academic achievement in kindergarten; however, many of these effects faded across the early elementary grades. Nonetheless, children who received the program demonstrated significant long-term benefits, including more investment and involvement in education, more years of schooling completed, and for the girls, fewer adolescent pregnancies (Weikart, 1998). Program effects seemed particularly strong for girls. Subsequent analyses of the outcomes of Perry Preschool participants strongly underscored the importance of school readiness. Children's cognitive competence and academic motivation in kindergarten were related to achievement in the later grades and influenced how long they remained in school (Luster & McAdoo, 1996).

THE INCREDIBLE YEARS

The Incredible Years Dina Dinosaur School (Webster-Stratton & Hammond, 1997; Webster-Stratton & Reid, 2003; Webster-Stratton, Reid, & Stoolmiller, 2008) is a classroom-based program designed to improve the school readiness of young children with aggressive and oppositional behavior problems. Unlike some of the other school-based programs described here, the Incredible Years program primarily targets social-emotional development, and many of the child effects are driven by changes in teachers' classroom management practices and interactions with children. Goals of the program include the establishment of more positive and responsive classroom management, reduction in harsh or critical discipline, an increase in the amount of instruction in social-emotional skills, and increased involvement of parents in young children's education. Teachers receive extensive training and support in implementing lessons in the following areas: learning school rules, how to be successful in school, emotional literacy, empathy and perspective taking, emotional self-regulation, anger management, communication, interpersonal problem solving, and social skills. These lessons are implemented in the preschool or early elementary classroom at least twice per week, and in the research trial, a member of the research staff co-led many classroom activities to ensure fidelity. Teachers in schools implementing the Incredible Years program were found to be significantly more affectionate with their students, less harsh, more consistent, and provided more instruction in social-emotional learning than teachers in comparison classrooms. Furthermore, children in Incredible Years classrooms had fewer conduct problems, improved social competence, and better self-regulation than those in the comparison group. Finally, teachers in the Incredible Years program reported feeling closer to their students' parents and made greater efforts to include them in children's learning (Webster-Stratton, Reid, & Stoolmiller, 2008). Although long-term effects of the Incredible Years program are unknown, research is currently under way to determine whether young children's improvements in social competence and self-regulation are maintained throughout elementary school and beyond.

PATHS

The Preschool Promoting Alternative Thinking Strategies (PATHS) program was developed for use in regular preschool settings, with the goal of improving classroom climate and strengthening the social-emotional competencies of young children. In contrast to the previously described programs, PATHS was designed as a universal curriculum targeting skills of both teachers and students, with the goal of improving classroom climate and children's social competence and behavior. PATHS was developed originally for elementary school children and later extended down to preschoolers (Greenberg et al., 1995). PATHS lessons are implemented by classroom teachers at least once per week, and each lesson has associated extension activities that provide practice and generalization of the targeted skill. The curriculum targets emotional understanding, self-control, positive peer relations, interpersonal problem solving, and better classroom management by teachers. It is designed to be integrated into already-existing preschool curricula, such as High/Scope. A recent evaluation of PATHS revealed that children in Head Start classrooms who received the program in addition to their usual curriculum showed improvements in social-emotional competence compared with children in regular Head Start classrooms (Domitrovich, Cortes, & Greenberg, 2007).

Home-Based Programs to Improve Parenting Quality

NURSE-FAMILY PARTNERSHIPS

Nurse-Family Partnerships (NFP) is a program that provides home visitation services from nurses to young, first-time mothers, most of whom are also single and of low income (Olds, 2006). The program begins during the second trimester of pregnancy and continues until the child's second birthday. Like Early Head Start, the short-term program goals involve health outcomes and sensitive-responsive parenting, with the idea that these, in turn, will affect children's school adjustment. Additionally, the program targets the life-course development of the mother by encouraging her to pursue educational and vocational opportunities and to delay subsequent childbearing (Olds et al., 1998).

Longitudinal research on NFP has revealed substantial long-term benefits for both children and their mothers that include school readiness as well as other positive life outcomes. Relative to controls, program children had fewer emergency room admissions, better developmental scores in infancy and toddlerhood, and better school adjustment (including higher academic attainment and fewer behavioral problems) at school entry. As adolescents, youth who received the intervention were more likely to complete high school and less likely to become delinquent (Olds, 2007). Additionally, mothers of the target children also experienced substantial benefits, including increased educational attainment, greater vocational stability, and fewer subsequent births (Olds, 2007). Owing to its strong evidence of long-term effectiveness, the NFP program has been disseminated widely throughout the United States, with sites in more than thirty states.

THE PALS PROGRAM

While the NFP program targets multiple aspects of parent and child functioning, the Playing and Learning Strategies (PALS) program (Landry et al., 2008) focuses more narrowly on increasing maternal responsiveness in mothers of infants and toddlers, with the expectation that these changes, in turn, will yield subsequent improvements in children's cognitive and social-emotional competencies. In the PALS studies, *responsiveness* was defined as emotionally warm, positive, and contingent responding to child signals; rich linguistic input; and support for children's focus of attention. Increases in these maternal behaviors then were expected to have a positive effect on children's emergent readiness skills, including vocabulary and syntactic development, sustained attention, and cooperativeness. During PALS intervention home visits, mothers and their coaches review and discuss videotapes of other parents and infants and then create their own videos of parent-child interaction, which they then review. Mothers are encouraged to reflect on their interactions and ways in which they might be enhanced. Home visitors offer suggestions about how mothers might increase their responsiveness. Although not specifically designed for high-risk families, PALS has been evaluated using a largely low-income sample, including a subsample of children at risk owing to low birth weight. In one evaluation of the PALS project, Landry et al. (2008) found that children whose parents received the program were more competent in terms of their language and social-emotional development than were children whose parents did not receive the intervention. As anticipated, the positive effects on children's development occurred as a result of changes in parents' responsiveness and language use (Landry & Smith, 2007). A subsequent study examined the relationship between maternal responsiveness in infancy with children's later literacy skills and found that responsiveness predicted reading comprehension at age eight, especially for children with lower cognitive ability (Taylor et al., 2008). This study made an important link between the quality of early parenting and later academic skills.

The PALS program evaluation was particularly helpful in highlighting the importance of developmental considerations for the timing and duration of early interventions. Landry et al. (2008) investigated whether parents and children who received a toddler intervention in addition to the infant program would show greater benefits than those who received the infant intervention alone. Interestingly, this study revealed that the effects were specific to certain types of parenting behaviors and child outcomes. The infant intervention (PALS I) increased mothers' warmth and positive affect toward their babies, whereas the toddler intervention (PALS II) did not result in further gains in this area. On the other hand, contingent responsiveness, or mothers' ability to notice their children's signals and respond in an appropriate manner, and maintaining children's attention and focus were enhanced when mothers received both the PALS I and PALS II programs. Furthermore, children's language development was most positively affected by the toddler program, whereas joint attention seemed to benefit most from exposure to both interventions. This study highlights the importance of different intervention targets (e.g., maternal warmth versus verbal stimulation) for different developmental periods.

To summarize, interventions to promote school readiness target a variety of developmental levels (e.g., infancy, toddlerhood, preschool, early elementary) and skill domains (e.g., cognitive, social-emotional, behavioral). Additionally, programs can focus directly on child skills or affect children's outcomes indirectly through changing the behaviors and interaction patterns of parents or teachers. Interventions use a variety of modalities, with some providing center-based services, others home-based services, and some comprehensive programs providing both. Finally, early interventions target a variety of child populations, with some being universals designed for all children, whereas many others are focused on specific high-risk populations, particularly children in poverty.

There is some research evidence to suggest that center-based programs are most effective at improving cognitive skills and academic achievement and are more appropriate for preschool or elementary-aged children (Barnett, 1995). Although some of the gains of preschool programs disappear over time, others endure, including reduced grade retention, reduced special education placement, increased high school graduation rates, and better vocational outcomes in adulthood (Barnett, 1995). These effects are often strongest for the children with the greatest delays or deficits. Alternatively, home-based, parent-focused programs are most effective at changing parent responsiveness and are most appropriate for infants and toddlers. As the NFP program demonstrates, children may experience long-term benefits indirectly, through improved parenting skills and through the changing life circumstances of their parents, particularly in the areas of improved health and emotional well-being (Olds et al., 2007).

Universal classroom-based programs are designed specifically to strengthen social-emotional aspects of school readiness and target both child and teacher skills. Although high-risk children may benefit substantially from these universal approaches, they often require additional support or skill training in order to be maximally successful in school.

While social-emotional programs such as PATHS show good immediate effects on children's behavior and social development, their long-term impact and their relations to the cognitive and academic aspects of school readiness remain to be seen. One study using the PATHS curriculum found improvements in reading skills for deaf children (Greenberg & Kusche, 1998), but academic effects of PATHS have not yet been investigated for preschool children.

Despite the generally positive long-term findings associated with these and similar programs designed to promote school readiness in children from disadvantaged homes, the achievement gap persists for many high-risk children. While children who receive early interventions are better off than their counterparts who do not, they still often end up behind low-risk children in terms of school readiness. A number of barriers limit the potential promise of early childhood intervention programs. Below, two of the major barriers are discussed: (1) limited attention to quality of program implementation and (2) restricted access to evidence-based interventions.

Issues in Implementing School Readiness Interventions in Real-World Settings

Costs and Benefits

Evidence-based early childhood interventions to promote school readiness are often not adopted in real-world settings because of perceptions that they are ineffective or too costly. The research reviewed earlier indicates that school readiness interventions for high-risk children can produce substantial benefits to participants in terms of both their educational outcomes and their overall life adjustment. Nonetheless, these programs require substantial financial investment, and the first challenge that communities may encounter as they address school readiness issues involves securing stable funding for early childhood initiatives. Comprehensive programs for vulnerable children that may yield the greatest benefits are particularly expensive. Advocacy for early childhood programming has been greatly assisted by recent research that includes cost-benefit analyses, in which the savings generated by program effects such as reduced special education placement, higher wage earning, and reduced rates of delinquency are calculated and contrasted with the costs of implementing the programs. Consistently, these cost-benefit analyses indicate that early childhood readiness interventions save money in the long run because participants require fewer costly health and social services across the course of their lives. In the Perry Preschool Project, for example, estimates of savings increased as participants grew older: When participants were twenty-seven years old, it was estimated that $7 was saved for every dollar invested in the program, but when they were forty years old, the ratio had increased to $17 (Schweinhart & Wahlgren, 1993; Nores et al., 2005). Cost-benefit data can be of great value to communities as they identify educational and social-service priorities and make decisions regarding which school readiness programs to adopt; evidence of potential savings associated with these programs may boost stakeholder commitment and investment.

Matching Programs and Goals to Child Populations

As discussed previously, school readiness interventions vary somewhat with regard to their particular goals and strategies; therefore, specific interventions may be appropriate for slightly different child populations. Although many high-risk children share common risk factors, different eligibility criteria will yield target populations that vary in their risk status and educational needs. For example, children can be identified based on sociodemographic factors such as family income level (Head Start) or single parenthood (Nurse-Family Partnerships) or by child skill domain such as aggressive behavior (Incredible Years) or IQ (Perry Preschool Project). These various criteria will yield child populations with somewhat different needs, and program adopters need to be

aware that different programs may produce somewhat different benefits. For example, low-IQ children may benefit most from an intervention designed to bolster cognitive development, whereas children with aggressive behavior problems may show the most improvement with interventions that emphasize social-emotional competencies. Many high-risk families and children appear to benefit most from a continuum of services beginning in infancy and following through the elementary school years. Additionally, when choosing an evidence-based program, it is important to make sure that the target population is similar to the group on which the program was originally tested. A program developed for rural families may not have the same effects in an urban setting; similarly, programs evaluated with white, English-speaking families may not be appropriate for children from other cultural groups. Finally, measurement limitations and the low stability of young children's test scores mean that it may be challenging to correctly identify children and families who are appropriate for the intervention. This is particularly true when the program targets long-term outcomes such as school dropout or delinquency. It is easy in this situation to overidentify (i.e., include children who would have adjusted well without the program) or underidentify (i.e., fail to include children who later go on to develop difficulties). For example, only about half the children who display aggressive and disruptive behavior problems in early childhood go on to have significant adjustment difficulties later in life (Coie & Dodge, 1998).

Adherence and Its Relation to Program Outcomes

Adherence refers to the degree to which programs are actually done the way they were originally designed and evaluated, and research has shown that low adherence can interfere substantially with a program's effectiveness. One disappointing finding that emerged from widespread community adoption of Head Start and other early childhood programs was that they often failed to yield the impressive benefits found in the original research trials (Barnett, 1995). In many cases, these failures can be traced back to low adherence (Lee et al., 1990). Poor implementation quality often occurs in real-world settings when critical program elements are deleted or modified in a way that diminishes or completely eliminates the program's effects (Greenberg et al., 2005).

Poor implementation quality can occur for a myriad of reasons. First, characteristics of the program itself may affect adherence. Programs that are expensive or cumbersome to implement, that do not provide materials that are easy to understand and use, or that do not provide a clear rationale for their approach are unlikely to be well implemented. Alternatively, programs that are manualized and provide clear, simple instructions are more likely to be implemented well (Gottfredson & Gottfredson, 2002; Mihalic, 2002).

Second, even when programs are well designed for dissemination, adherence can be low if the people implementing the program are unmotivated, lack the necessary skills, or fail to understand the program. Additionally, support from administrators or other key stakeholders is critical (Dariotis et al., 2008). By illustration, an evaluation of the PATHS program in six inner-city classrooms found that children's skills improved in some classrooms but not in others and that the differences could be attributed to both support received from the building principal and the degree to which the teachers actually delivered the lessons correctly (Kam, Greenberg, & Walls, 2003). In this case, both organizational and implementer characteristics influenced the outcome.

Third, adherence can be affected by pressures to "adapt" a program to local circumstances. For example, schools may lack the time or financial resources to fully implement a program and choose to implement in a piecemeal fashion (e.g., deliver some activities or lessons while abbreviating or excluding others) or make substantial changes to the way in which the program is delivered (e.g., change the order in which program elements are presented or have a different person delivering the program than is recommended by the developer). As an illustration of the potential hazards associated with program adaptation, an NFP evaluation of the impact of different program delivery systems and found that when implemented by paraprofessionals rather than nurses, the positive effects of the program on mother and child outcomes were substantially diminished (Olds & Kitzman, 1993). The adherence-adaptation balance is a difficult one to achieve when implementing evidence-based programs in real-world settings. While some degree of local adaptation may be both necessary and desirable, implementers should work closely with program developers to identify adaptations that may boost or increase the program's impact or uptake versus those which detract from its effectiveness.

Finally, program implementation can be substantially improved and maintained through the provision of high-quality training and ongoing supervision and technical assistance (Gottfredson & Gottfredson, 2002; Mihalic, 2004). High-quality training can help program implementers to develop both the skills required to implement the program effectively and a clear understanding of the program's rationale and potential as well. Proactive technical assistance can help teachers, home visitors, or other implementers to anticipate and find solutions to barriers that otherwise effectively result in low implementation quality or even termination of the program. Even when implementation quality is high initially, many programs implemented in community settings experience "drift" over time as adaptations creep in and erode program quality; ongoing supervision that includes observations, consultation, and feedback to program implementers can reduce this problem substantially (Sheidow et al., 2008).

Implementation quality is closely related to the issue of *sustainability*, which refers to the long-term adoption of a program past a period of initial funding. Often this involves programs that initially receive short-term grants or startup money but then transition to more stable or renewable resources such as local school, mental health, or human services funding. Sustainability requires long-term planning and preparation and is aided by attention to implementation quality and program evaluation that provides feedback on the program's impact to stakeholders. Evidence-based programs that are well implemented and demonstrate local impact are likely to generate enthusiasm from stakeholders and to be sustained over time (Scheirer, 2005).

Although research clearly indicates that program quality can be established and maintained through the use of high-quality training, technical assistance, and ongoing monitoring, funding for this type of program support is often overlooked or unavailable in real-world settings. Sources of funding for school readiness may only be willing to cover program costs, or implementers and stakeholders may attempt to reduce costs by eliminating this support. Unfortunately, this may result in the potential of the program remaining unrealized. In addition to poor-quality implementation, programs lacking technical support and quality monitoring may be at risk of being discontinued altogether (Scheirer, 2005). Therefore, stakeholders considering the adoption of an evidence-based school readiness intervention should allocate resources for program support as well as for the programming itself.

Barriers to Access

Currently, many children and families who would benefit from high-quality readiness interventions fail to access those services. Owens et al. (2002) identified a number of access barriers for children and families in need of mental health services, including structural barriers such as lack of availability of providers, long waiting lists, insurance issues, inability to afford services, and pragmatic difficulties such as transportation, beliefs and perceptions on the part of parents, teachers, and health care providers that the services are not necessary or worthwhile, and stigma associated with help seeking around issues of parenting or child development. Prinz & Sanders (2007)

estimated that a high percentage of children with early behavioral problems received no mental health services, and for those who did, services often were not evidence-based. Lack of access to services is related to a number of factors, including inadequate financial resources and difficulty engaging the target population. In the educational realm, lack of resources is a chronic reason for the underfunding of early childhood school readiness programs. For example, in the United States, Head Start programs serve only about a third of the eligible child population (Lee, 1990).

In recent years, several innovative attempts to remedy the situation of limited access have emerged. The Positive Parenting Program (Triple P) (Sanders, 1999; Sanders, Turner, & Markie-Dadds, 2002) was developed as a system of tiered interventions designed to prevent and remediate child behavioral problems along a continuum of severity. The overarching goal of Triple P is to increase access to evidence-based preventive interventions and to decrease the prevalence of disorders at the population level. Triple P has five levels of intervention ranging from components appropriate for all families up to highly selective interventions for families with significant problems. At the universal level, Triple P provides general information on parenting to all interested parents, sometimes using mass-media outlets that reach a broad base of parents and help to remove the stigma associated with help seeking. The second level targets mild behavior problems common to most families, including bedtime or toilet training issues, whereas levels three through five are increasingly selective and target the relatively few families experiencing more serious behavioral problems, including those in which child behavioral issues co-occur with other problems, such as marital discord (Sanders & Turner, 2005). Interventions at the lower levels are both low intensity and low cost, whereas those at higher levels are more intensive and expensive. Triple P uses a variety of modalities, including self-study materials for parents, phone consultation with clinicians, and brief individual and family therapy for particularly serious problems. The overarching goal of all the activities is to reduce child behavior problems through improvements in parenting. Many of the Triple P outcomes involve older children and youth, and none of the current research examines its impact on school readiness specifically. However, one evaluation of the Triple P approach in the United States. found that Triple P had a population-level impact on rates of substantiated child maltreatment, out-of-home placements of children, and injuries related to maltreatment (Prinz et al., 2009). Additionally, several small-scale studies have demonstrated the utility of the Triple P approach at reducing behavior problems in preschool children at risk for conduct disorders and school difficulty (Boyle et al., 2009). Triple P's multiple innovations (e.g., tiered system, careful attention to cost-effectiveness and dissemination) suggest that it has much promise for the dissemination and sustainability of evidence-based prevention and for accessing previously underserved child and family groups.

In another example of an innovation designed to boost access to services, Bagett et al. (2010) adapted the PALS program for Internet use and tested the effectiveness of this mode of service delivery with a small sample of low-income mothers of infants. Parents completed eleven online sessions that included modeling videotapes, questions that checked understanding and use of the material, a computerized videotaping of actual parent-child interaction, and a weekly phone call with a coach who monitored the parents' use of the session materials and reviewed the parent-child interaction video in consultation with the parent. Results indicate that parents completed over 90 percent of the program sessions and that they found the materials easy to use and understand. Additionally, the intervention yielded several significant effects on parent and infant behavior, including increased child social engagement and reduced rates of parent-reported depression. Although these findings involved a small sample of families and thus must be regarded as preliminary, they also suggest another potential modality for increasing the access and thus the impact of evidence-based early childhood services.

School Readiness: Successes, Challenges, and Future Directions

Emerging Research on School Readiness Interventions

Longitudinal research from a variety of projects has documented consistent, positive effects of school readiness interventions for both high-risk and general preschool populations. Despite these impressive findings, high-risk children, and particularly those from disadvantaged families, remain substantially behind middle-income children in terms of school readiness and subsequent school attainment. Thus developmental and educational experts continue to seek ways to refine and enhance school readiness interventions so that they provide the maximum benefits to children in poverty and other risk groups. One approach has been to suffuse already existing high-quality programs such as Head Start with additional evidence-based practices. For example, the Preschool PATHS trial described earlier infused the PATHS program into already existing Head Start programs, with positive effects for children's social-emotional learning above and beyond those accomplished with Head Start alone. Similarly, the Head Start Research Based, Developmentally Informed (REDI) Project (Bierman et al., 2008) provided evidence-based enhancements to Head Start programs that targeted specific aspects of children's school readiness. In addition to Preschool PATHS, Head Start REDI included cognitive elements targeting early phonemic awareness, alphabet knowledge, and language development. Mindful of recent research on the importance of high-quality staff development for achieving the desired outcomes, the Head Start REDI Project included both curricular elements targeting children's skills directly and intensive training, supervision, and feedback for teachers. Particular attention was paid to supporting high-quality implementation of the program as well as program sustainability. Early findings revealed that children in Head Start REDI classrooms experienced benefits in both social-emotional and cognitive development relative to children in "regular" Head Start programs (Bierman et al., 2008) and that these were largely related to improvements in teaching practices, including the use of PATHS lessons and concepts and teachers' increased use of dialogic reading and enriched language (Domitrovich et al., 2009).

The preliminary findings from the Head Start REDI Project suggest that research-based enhancements to already existing quality intervention programs can result in improved outcomes for children. In a second wave of research, a parenting home visitation component was added to the Head Start REDI intervention with the goal of improving support for learning within the home. An evaluation is currently under way to determine whether the combination of a school-based and a home-based program can lead to additional improvements in children's school readiness.

Another new approach to enhancing children's school readiness, the Tools of the Mind Program (ToM) (Bodrova, & Leong, 2009; Diamond et al, 2007), focuses primarily on the development of self-regulation. ToM is based on recent research in neuroscience that indicates a central role for executive functions such as impulse control, cognitive flexibility, working memory, and planning in the development of school readiness (Blair & Diamond, 2007; Welsh et al., 2010). In the ToM program, preschool children participate in complex fantasy play sequences that emphasize following rules, planning, and language development (Barnett et al., 2008). A recent evaluation of ToM found effects on both students and teachers. First, ToM classrooms were rated higher in support for literacy, enriched language, and teacher sensitivity than comparison classrooms using "regular" preschool curricula. Second, children in ToM classrooms had lower rates of behavioral problems, improved language development, and better scores on measures of social-emotional development than

children in comparison classrooms (Barnett et al., 2008). Although no significant differences in children's academic readiness were found in this trial, further research on the ToM program is under way to determine its long-term impact on school adjustment.

Attention to Implementation Issues

As discussed previously, advances in evidence-based preventions to enhance school readiness increasingly have included attention to issues related to implementation quality and sustainability. This makes it easier for program adopters to maintain high quality and overcome the inevitable barriers they encounter as they implement programs in real-world settings. Programs such as PATHS and Nurse-Family Partnerships provide extensive training and ongoing technical assistance to sites implementing these programs. The Triple P also includes careful attention to training and implementation issues in its large-scale public health trials (Seng, Prinz, & Sanders, 2006). This helps to ensure that program implementers will be well prepared and that they will have access to assistance when they encounter challenges or difficulties. When programs must be modified to align with local circumstances, technical assistance providers can ensure that these adaptations are made in a way that preserves program quality and effectiveness. Many evidence-based programs have moved toward *manualization* of their materials, in which program activities are described and delineated in a clear and user-friendly manner that diminishes the likelihood that implementers will "improvise." Both these developments increase the likelihood that programs will be implemented as designed. However, implementation quality and sustainability also can be enhanced when stakeholders (including teachers and other implementation staff, supervisors, school administrators, and program funders) are highly committed to and supportive of the program and provide resources for ongoing quality monitoring and feedback to implementers.

To summarize, developmental and educational research conducted over the past 40 years indicates that a number of programs are available to enhance children's school readiness and that high-risk children and their families often can experience substantial long-term benefits from such programs. Furthermore, in many cases, cost-benefit analyses have confirmed the economic value of school readiness interventions because they reduce the costs associated with difficult problems such as school drop-out and delinquency. Finally, these programs are most likely to yield a maximum benefit when they are well matched to the target population and carefully implemented and supported by stakeholders. Even the best designed and implemented programs do not entirely eliminate the achievement gap created by economic disadvantage; therefore, researchers continue to seek innovative ways to broaden access to services and further enhance the readiness of vulnerable children. As the era of accountability for student performance continues in education, the trends toward refinement, adoption, and high-quality implementation of evidence-based practices in school readiness interventions will help to guide many more young children down the path of school success.

References

Ainsworth, M. S., Blehar, M.C., Waters, E., & Wall, S. (1978). *Patterns of attachment: A psychological study of the strange situation.* Oxford, UK: Lawrence Erlbaum.

Akhtar, N., Dunham, F., & Dunham, P. J. (1991). Directive interactions and early vocabulary development: The role of joint attentional focus. *Journal of Child Language* 18, 41–9.

Baggett, K. M., Davis, B., Feil, E. G., Sheeber, L. L., Landry, S. H., Carta, J. J., & Leve, C., (2010). Technologies for expanding the reach of evidence-based interventions: Preliminary results for promoting social-emotional development in early childhood. *Topics in Early Childhood Special Education* 29, 226–38.

Barnett, W. S. (1995). Long term effects of early childhood programs on cognitive and school outcomes. *The Future of Children*, 5, 25–50.

Barnett, W. S., Jung, K., Yarosz, D. J., Thomas, J., Hornbeck, A. Stechuk, R., & Burns, S. (2008). Educational effects of the Tools of the Mind curriculum: A randomized trial. *Early Childhood Research Quarterly* 23, 299–313.

Berlin, L. J., Brooks-Gunn, J., Spiker, D., & Zaslow, M. J. (1995). Examining observational measures of emotional support and cognitive stimulation in black and white mothers of preschoolers. *Journal of Family Issues* 16, 664–86.

Bierman, K. L., Domitrovich, C. E., Nix, R. L., Gest, S. D., Welsh, J. A., Greenberg, M. T., Blair, C., Nelson, K. E., & Gill, S. (2008). Promoting academic and social-emotional school readiness: The Head Start REDI program. *Child Development* 79, 1802–17.

Birch, S. H., & Ladd, G. W. (1997). The teacher-child relationship and children's early school adjustment. *Journal of School Psychology* 35, 61–79.

Birch, S. H., & Ladd, G. W. (1998). Children's interpersonal behaviors and the teacher-child relationship. *Developmental Psychology* 34, 934–46.

Blair, C., & Diamond, A. (2008). Biological processes in prevention and intervention: The promotion of self-regulation as a means of preventing school failure. *Development and Psychopathology (Special Issue: Integrating biological measures into the design and evaluation of preventive interventions)* 20, 899–911.

Blair, C., Knipe, H., Cummings, E., Baker, D. P., Gamson, D., Eslinger, P., & Thorne, S. L. (2007). A developmental neuroscience approach to the study of school readiness. In R. C. Pianta, M. J. Cox, and K. L. Snow (eds.), *School readiness and the transition to kindergarten*. Baltimore: Brookes.

Bodrova, E., & Leong, D. J. (2009). Tools of the mind: A Vygotskian-based early childhood curriculum. *Early Childhood Services: An Interdisciplinary Journal of Effectiveness* 3, 245–62.

Bolger, K. E., Patterson, C. J., Thompson, W. W., & Kuperschmidt, J. B. (1995). Psychosocial adjustment among children experiencing persistent and intermittent family economic hardship. *Child Development* 66, 1107–29.

Boyle, C. L., Sanders, M. R., Lutzker, J. R., Prinz, R. J., Shapiro, C., & Whitaker, D. J. (2009). An analysis of training, generalization, and maintenance effects of primary care Triple P for parents of preschool aged children with disruptive behavior. *Child Psychiatry and Human Development* 41, 114–31.

Brooks-Gunn, J., & Markman, L. B. (2005). The contribution of parenting to ethnic and racial raps in school readiness. *The Future of Children* 15(1), 138–67.

Brooks-Gunn, J., Rouse, C. E., & McLanahan, S. (2007). Racial and ethnic gaps in school readiness. In R.C. Pianta, M. J. Cox, and K. L. Snow (eds.), *School readiness and the transition to kindergarten*. Baltimore: Brookes.

Burchinal, M. R., Peisner-Feinberg, E., Pianta, R. C., & Howes, C. (2002). Development of academic skills from preschool through second grade: Family and classroom predictors of developmental trajectories. *Journal of School Psychology* 40, 415–36.

Campbell, F. A., Ramey, C. T., Pungello, E., Sparling, J., & Miller-Johnson, S. (2002). Early childhood education: Young adult outcomes from the Abecedarian Project. *Applied Developmental Science* 6, 42–57.

Campbell, F. A., Wasik, B. H., Pungello, E., Burchinal, M., Barbarin, O., Kainz, K., Sparling, J., & Ramey, C. T. (2008). Young adult outcomes of the Abecedarian and CARE early childhood educational interventions. *Early Childhood Research Quarterly* 23, 452–66.

Coie, J. D., & Dodge, K. A. (1998). Aggression and antisocial behavior. In W. Damon and N. Eisenberg (eds.), *Handbook of child psychology*, Vol. 3: *Social, emotional and personality Development*, 5th ed. (pp. 779–862). New York: Wiley.

Connor, C. M., Son, S., & Hindman, A. H., (2005). Teacher qualifications, classroom practices, family characteristics, and preschool experience: Complex effects on first graders' vocabulary and early reading outcomes. *Journal of School Psychology* 43, 343–75.

Currie, J. (2005). Health disparities and gaps in school readiness. *The Future of Children* 15, 117–38.

Dariotis, J. K., Bumbarger, B. K., Duncan, L. G., & Greenberg, M. T. (2008). How do implementation efforts relate to program adherence? Examining the role of organizational, implementer, and program factors. *Journal of Community Psychology* 36, 744–60.

Darling, N., & Steinberg, L. (1993). Parenting style as context: An integrative model. *Psychological Bulletin* 113, 487–96.

Davidov, M., & Grusec, J. (2006). Untangling the links of parental responsiveness to distress and warmth to child outcomes. *Child Development* 77, 44–58.

Diamond, A., Barnett, W. S., Thomas, J., & Munro, S. (2007). Preschool program improves cognitive control. *Science* 318, 1387–8.

Diamond, K. E., Reagan, A. J., & Bandyk, J.E. (2000). Parents' conceptions of kindergarten readiness: Relationships with race, ethnicity, and development. *Journal of Educational Research* 94, 93–100.

Dockett, S., & Perry, B. (2003). The transition to school: What's important? *Educational Leadership* 60, 30–3.

Domitrovich, C. E., Cortes, R. C., & Greenberg, M. T. (2007). Improving young children's social and emotional competence: A randomized trial of the preschool "PATHS" curriculum. *Journal of Primary Prevention* 28, 67–91.

Domitrovich, C. E., Gest, S. D., Gill, S., Bierman, K. L., Welsh, J. A., & Jones, D. (2009). Fostering high-quality teaching with an enriched curriculum and professional development support: The Head Start REDI Program. *American Educational Research Journal* 46(2), 567–97.

Duncan, G. J., & Brooks-Gunn, J. (2000). Family poverty, welfare reform, and child development. *Child Development* 71, 188–96.

Franz, M., Lensche, H., & Schmitz, N. (2003). Psychological distress and socioeconomic status in single mothers and their children in a German city. *Social Psychiatry and Psychiatric Epidemiology* 38, 59–68.

Gottfredson, D. C., & Gottfredson, G. D. (2002). Quality of school-based prevention programs: Results from a national survey. *Journal of Research in Crime and Delinquency* 39, 3–35.

Greenberg, M. T., & Kusche, C. A. (1998). Preventive interventions for school-aged deaf children: The PATHS curriculum. *Journal of Deaf Studies and Deaf Education* 3, 49–63.

Greenberg, M. T., Domitrovich, C. E., Graczyk, P. A., & Zins, J. E. (2005) *The study of implementation in school-based preventative interventions: Theory, research and practice*, Vol. 3. Rockville, MD: Center for Mental Health Services, Substance Abuse and Mental Health Services Administration, DHHS.

Greenberg, M. T., Kusche, C. A., Cook, E. T., & Quamma, J. T. (1995). Promoting emotional competence in school-aged children: The effects of the PATHS curriculum. *Development and Psychopathology (Special Issue: Emotions in developmental psychopathology)* 7, 117–36.

Gunnar, M. (2000). Early adversity and the development of stress reactivity and regulation. In C. A. Nelson (ed.), *The effects of adversity on neurobehavioral development: Minnesota* symposium on child psychology, Vol. 31 (pp. 163–200). London: Routledge Taylor Francis.

Hamre, B. K., & Painta, R. C. (2001). Early teacher-child relationships and the trajectory of children's school outcomes through eighth grade. Child Development 72, 625–38.

Hart, B., & Risley, T. R. (1992). American parenting of language-learning children: Persisting differences in family-child interactions observed in natural home environments. Developmental Psychology 28, 1096–105.

Hart, B., & Risley, T. R. (1995). Meaningful differences in the everyday experience of young American Children. Baltimore: Brookes.

Hart, B., & Risley, T. R. (1999). The social worlds of children learning to talk. Baltimore: Brookes.

Heaviside, S., & Farris, S. (1993). Public school kindergarten teachers views on children's readiness for school. Washington: National Center for Educational Statistics.

Hernandez, D. J., Denton, N. A., & McCartney, S. E. (2007). Child poverty in the U.S.: A new family budget approach with comparison to European countries. In H. Winterburger, L. Alanen, T. Olk, and J. Qvortrup (eds.), Children's economic and social welfare. Odense: University Press of Southern Denmark.

Hughes, J. N., Cavell, T. A., & Jackson, T. (1995). Influence of the teacher-student relationship on childhood conduct problems: A prospective study. Journal of Clinical Child Psychology 28, 173–84.

Kam, C., Greenberg, M. T., & Walls, C. T. (2003). Examining the role of implementation quality in school-based prevention using the PATHS curriculum. Prevention Science 4, 55–63.

Kellam, S. G., Brown, C. H., & Fleming, J. P. (1983). Relationship of first-grade social adaptation to teenage drinking, drug-use, and smoking. Digest of Alcoholism Theory & Application 2, 20–4.

Klebanov, P. K., Brooks-Gunn, J., & Duncan, G. J. (1994). Does neighborhood and family poverty affect mothers' parenting, mental health and social support? Journal of Marriage and the Family 56, 441–55.

Knitzer, J., & Lefkowitz, J. (2005, November). Resources to promote social and emotional health and school readiness in young children and families: A community guide. Retrieved October 5, 2010, from Columbia University Mailman School of Public Health, National Center for Children in Poverty website: http://www.nccp.org/pub_pew.html.

Ladd, G. W., & Burgess, K. B. (2001). Do relational risks and protective factors moderate the linkages between childhood aggression and early psychological and school adjustment. Child Development 72, 1579–601.

Landry, S. H., & Smith, K. E. (2007). Parents' support of children's language provides support for later reading competence. In R. K. Wagner, A. E. Muse, and K. R. Tannenbaum (eds.), Vocabulary acquisition: Implications for reading comprehension. New York: Guilford Press.

Landry, S. H., Smith, K. E., Swank, P. R., & Guttentag, C. (2008). A responsive parenting intervention: The optimal timing across early childhood for impacting maternal behaviors and child outcomes. Developmental Psychology 44, 1335–53.

Lee, V. E., & Loeb, S. (1995). Where do Head Start attendees end up? One reason why preschool effects fade out. Educational Evaluation and Policy Analysis 17, 62–82.

Lee, V. E., Brooks-Gunn, J., Schnur, E., & Liaw, F. (1990). Are Head Start effects sustained? A longitudinal follow-up comparison of disadvantaged children attending Head Start, no preschool, and other preschool programs. Child Development (Special Issue: Minority children) 61, 495–507.

Lee, V. E., Brooks-Gunn, J., Schnur, E., & Liaw, F. (1991). Are Head Start effects sustained? A longitudinal follow-up comparison of disadvantaged children attending Head Start, no preschool, and other preschool programs. In Annual Progress in Child Psychiatry & Child Development (pp. 600–18). New York: Brunner/Mazel.

Lengua, L. J., Honorado, E., & Bush, N. R. (2007). Contextual risk and parenting as predictors of effortful control and social competence in preschool children. Journal of Applied Developmental Psychology 28, 40–55.

Looker, A. C., Cogswell, M. E., & Gunter, E. W. (2002). Iron deficiency – United States, 1990–2000. Morbidity and Mortality Weekly Report 51, 897–9.

Luster, T., & McAdoo, H. (1996). Family and child influences on educational attainment: A secondary analysis of the High Scope/Perry Preschool data. Developmental Psychology 32, 26–39.

Massoth, N. A., & Levenson, R. L. (1982). The McCarthy scales of children's abilities as a predictor of reading readiness and reading achievement. Psychology in the Schools 19, 293–6.

McClelland, M. M., Acock, A. C., & Morrison, F. J. (2006). The impact of kindergarten learning-related skills on academic trajectories at the end of elementary school. *Early Childhood Research Quarterly* 21, 471–90.

McKey, R. H., Condelli, L., Granson, H., Barrett, B., McConkey, C., & Plantz, M. (1985). *The impact of Head Start on children, families, and communities* (Final report of the Head Start Evaluation, Synthesis, and Utilization Project). Washington: CSR, Inc.

McWayne, C. M., Fantuzzo, J. W., & McDermott, P. A. (2004). Preschool competency in context: An investigation of the unique contributions of child competencies to early academic success. *Developmental Psychology* 40, 633–45.

Meyer, P. A., Pivetz, T., Dignam, T. A., Homa, D. M., Schoonover, J., Brody, D., et al. (2003). Surveillance for elevated blood lead levels among children – United States, 1997–2001. *Morbidity and Mortality Weekly Reports Surveillance Summary* 52, 1–21.

Mihalic, S. (2004). The importance of implementation fidelity. *Emotional & Behavioral Disorders in Youth* 4, 83–105

Moffitt, T. E. (1993). Adolescence-limited and life course persistent antisocial behavior: A developmental taxonomy. *Psychological Review* 100, 674–701.

Moilanen, K. L., Shaw, D. S., Dishion, T. J., Gardner, F., & Wilson, M. (2010). Predictors of longitudinal growth in inhibitory control in early childhood. (2010). *Social Development* 19, 326–47.

NICHD Early Child Care Research Network (2003). Do children's attentional processes mediate the link between family predictors and school readiness? *Developmental Psychology* 39, 581–93.

Nores, M., Belfield, C. R., Barnett, W. S., & Schweinhart, L. (2005). Updating the economic impacts of the High/Scope Perry preschool program. *Educational Evaluation and Policy Analysis* 27, 245–61.

Olds, D. L. (2006). The nurse-family partnership: An evidence-based preventive intervention. *Infant Mental Health Journal. Special Issue: Early Preventive Intervention and Home Visiting* 27, 5–25.

Olds, D. L. (2007). Preventing crime with prenatal and infancy support of parents: The Nurse-Family Partnership. *Victims & Offenders (Special Issue on Early Intervention)* 2, 205–25.

Olds, D. L., & Kitzman, H. (1993). Review of research on home visiting. *The Future of Children* 3, 51–92.

Olds, D. L., Henderson, C., Kitzman, H., Eckenrode, J., Cole, R., & Tatelbaum, R. (1998). The promise of home visitation: Results of two randomized trials. *Journal of Community Psychology (Special Issue: Home Visitation II)* 26, 5–21.

Olds, D. L., Kitzman, H., Hanks, C., Cole, R., Anson, E., Sidora-Arcoleo, K., Luckey, D. W., Henderson, C. R., Holmberg, J., Tutt, R. A., Stevenson, A. J., & Bondy, J. (2007). Effects of nurse home visiting on maternal and child functioning: Age-9 follow-up of a randomized trial. *Pediatrics* 120, e832–40.

Owens, P. L., Hoagwood, K., Horwitz, S. M., Leaf, P. J., Poduska, J. M., Kellam, S. G., & Ialongo, N. S. (2002). Barriers to children's mental health services. *Journal of the America Academy of Child and Adolescent Psychiatry* 41(6), 731–8.

Palermo, F., Hanish, L. D., Martin, C. L., Fabes, R. A., & Reiser, M. (2007). Preschoolers' academic readiness: What role does the teacher-child relationship play? *Early Childhood Research Quarterly* 22, 407–22.

Patterson, G. R., Reid, J. B., & Dishion, T. J. (1998). Antisocial boys. In J. M. Jenkins, K. Oatley, and N. L. Stein (eds.), *Human emotions: A reader.* Malden, MA: Blackwell.

Phillips, M., Brooks-Gunn, J., Duncan, G., Klebanov, P., & Crane, J. (1998). Family background, parenting practices, and the black-white test score gap. In C. Jencks and M. Phillips (eds.), *The black-white test score gap.* Washington: Brookings Institution.

Pianta, R. C., & Walsh, D. J. (1998). Applying the construct of resilience in schools: Caution from a developmental systems perspective. *School Psychology Review* 27, 407–17.

Prinz, R. J., & Sanders, M. R. (2007). Adopting a population-level approach to parenting and family support interventions. *Clinical Psychology Review* 27, 739–49.

Prinz, R. J., Sanders, M. R., Shapiro, C. J., Whitaker, D. J., & Lutzker, J. R. (2009). Population based prevention of child maltreatment: The U.S. Triple P system population trial. *Prevention Science* 10, 1–12.

Raikes, H., Pan, B. A., Luze, G., Tamis-LeMonda, C. S., Brooks-Gunn, J., Constantine, J., et al. (2006). Mother-child book reading in low income families: Correlates and outcomes during the first three years of life. *Child Development* 77, 924–53.

Ramey, C. T., & Ramey, S. L. (2004). Early learning and school readiness: Can early intervention make a difference? *Merrill-Palmer Quarterly: Journal of Developmental Psychology (Special Issue: 50th Anniversary Issue, Part II: The Maturing of the Human Developmental*

Sciences: Appraising Past, Present, and Prospective Agendas) 50, 471–91.

Raver, C. C., Garner, P. W., & Smith-Donald, R. (2007). The roles of emotion regulation and emotion knowledge for children's academic readiness. In R. C. Pianta, M. J. Cox, and K. L. Snow (eds.), *School readiness and the transition to kindergarten*. Baltimore: Brookes.

Rescorla, L. (2009). Age 17 language and reading outcomes in late-talking toddlers: Support for a dimensional perspective on language delay. *Journal of Speech, Language, and Hearing Research* 52, 16–30.

Rimm-Kaufman, S. E., Pianta, R. C., & Cox, M. J. (2000). Teachers' judgments of problems in the transition to kindergarten. *Early Childhood Research Quarterly* 15, 147–66.

Ritsher, J. E., Warner, V., Johnson, J. G., & Dohrenwend, B. P. (2001). Intergenerational longitudinal study of social class and depression: A test of social causation and social selection models. *British Journal of Psychiatry* 178, s84–90.

Ryan, R. M., Fauth, R. C., & Brooks-Gunn, J. (2006) Childhood poverty: Implications for school readiness and early childhood education. In B. Spodek and O. N. Saracho (eds.), *Handbook of research on the education of young children*, 2nd ed. (pp. 323–46). Mahwah, NJ: Lawrence Erlbaum.

Sanders, M. R. (1999). The Triple P – Positive Parenting Program: Towards an empirically validated multilevel parenting and family support strategy for the prevention of behavior and emotional problems in children. *Clinical Child and Family Psychology Review* 2, 71–90.

Sanders, M. R., & Turner, K. M. T. (2005). Reflections on the challenges of effective dissemination of behavioral family intervention: Our experience with the triple P – Positive Parenting Program. *Child and Adolescent Mental Health* 10, 158–69.

Sanders, M. R., Turner, K. M. T., & Markie-Dadds, C. (2002). The development and dissemination of the Triple P – Positive Parenting Program: A multilevel, evidence-based system of parenting and family support. *Prevention Science* 3, 173–89.

Sattler, J. M. (2001) *Assessment of children: Cognitive applications*, 4th ed. La Mesa, CA: Jerome M. Sattler Publisher.

Schierer, M. A. (2005). Is sustainability possible? *American Journal of Evaluation* 26, 320–47.

Schweinhart, L. J., & Wallgren, C. R. (1993). Effects of a follow through program on school achievement. *Journal of Research in Childhood Education* 8, 43–56.

School Readiness Act (2005).

Seng, A. C., Prinz, R. J., & Sanders, M. R. (2006). The role of training variables in effective dissemination of evidence based parenting interventions. *International Journal of Mental Health Promotion* (Vol 8,issue 4 pages 20–8).

Sheidow, A. J., Donohue, B. C., Hill, H. H., Henggler, S. W., & Ford, J. D. (2008). Development of an audiotape review system for supporting adherence to an evidence-based treatment. *Professional Psychology: Research and Practice* 39, 553–60.

Smith, K. E., Landry, S. H., & Swank, P. R. (2000). Does the content of mothers' verbal stimulation explain differences in children's development of verbal and nonverbal cognitive skills? *Journal of School Psychology (Special Issue: Developmental perspectives in intelligence)* 38, 27–49.

Snow, K. L. (2006). Measuring school readiness: Conceptual and practical considerations. *Early Education and Development* 17, 7–41.

Taylor, H. B., Anthony, J. L., Aghara, R., Smith, K. E., & Landry, S. H. (2008). The Interaction of early maternal responsiveness and children's cognitive abilities on later decoding and reading comprehension skills. *Early Education and Development* 19, 188–207.

Wagner, R. K., Muse, A. E., & Tannenbaum, K. R. (2007). Promising avenues for better understanding implications of vocabulary development for reading comprehension. In R. K. Wagner, A. E. Muse and K. R. Tannenbaum (eds.), *Vocabulary acquisition: Implications for reading comprehension*. New York: Guilford Press.

Webster-Stratton, C., & Hammond, M. (1997). Treating children with early-onset conduct problems: A comparison of child and parent training interventions. *Journal of Consulting and Clinical Psychology* 65, 93–109.

Webster-Stratton, C., & Reid, J. (2003). Treating conduct problems and strengthening social and emotional competence in young children: The Dina Dinosaur Treatment Program. *Journal of Emotional and Behavioral Disorders* 11, 130–43.

Webster-Stratton, C., Reid, J., & Stoolmiller, M. (2008). Preventing conduct problems and improving school readiness: Evaluation of the Incredible Years teacher and child training programs in high-risk schools. *Journal of Child Psychology and Psychiatry* 49, 471–88.

Weikart, D. P. (1998). Changing early childhood development through educational intervention. *Preventive Medicine: An International Journal Devoted to Practice and Theory* 27, 233–7.

Werthamer-Larsson, L., Kellam, S. G., & Wheeler, L. (1991). Effect of first-grade classroom environment on shy behavior, aggressive behavior, and concentration problems. *American Journal of Community Psychology (Special Issue: Preventive intervention research centers)* 9, 585–602.

Welsh, J. A., Nix, R. L., Blair, C., Bierman, K. L., & Nelson, K. E. (2010). The development of cognitive skills and gains in academic school readiness for children from low-income families. *Journal of Educational Psychology* 102, 43–53.

West, J., Denton, K., & Germino Hausken, E. (2000). *America's kindergartners* (NCES 2000–070). Washington: National Center for Education Statistics.

West, J., Denton, K., & Reaney, L. (2001). *The kindergarten year* (NCES 2001–023). Washington: National Center for Education Statistics.

Zill, N., Moore, K. A., Smith, E. W., Stief, T., & Coiro, M. J. (1995). The life circumstances and development of children in welfare families: A profile based on national survey data. In P. L. Chase-Lansdale and J. Brooks-Gunn (eds.), *Escape from poverty: What makes a difference for children?* (pp. 38–59). New York: Cambridge University Press.

Part IV

SUCCESSFUL IMPLEMENTATION OF SPECIFIC PROGRAMMES AND INTERVENTIONS: SOCIAL, EMOTIONAL, AND BEHAVIOURAL CHANGE; LITERACY DEVELOPMENT; AND LEISURE EDUCATION

Maximizing the Effectiveness of Social-Emotional Interventions for Young Children Through High-Quality Implementation of Evidence-Based Interventions

Celene E. Domitrovich, Julia E. Moore, and Mark T. Greenberg

Introduction

The majority of research on the impact of preschool has been with disadvantaged populations, where this early educational experience was conducted as part of a comprehensive early intervention strategy (Manning, Homel, & Smith, 2010). However, in many countries, preschool is now a more common educational experience that is attended by children representing a broader portion of the population. In the United States, the number of states with publically funded preschool programs has grown steadily over the past several years (Barnett et al., 2009). In the United States and other countries, preschool and interventions that include early education have expanded under large-scale government-funded initiatives (Sylva et al., 2004; Vargas-Barón, 2009). Evaluations of these programs have shown that even with more diverse populations, exposure to quality educational experience early in life facilitates the growth of cognitive skills, behavioral adjustment, and early academic achievement (Gormley et al., 2010; Sylva et al., 2004; Curby, Rimm-Kaufman, & Ponitz, 2009).

The quality of education provided in preschools varies, and higher-quality programs are more effective at improving the school readiness of participants (Curby et al., 2009; Howes et al., 2008). Current guidelines for developmentally appropriate practice in early childhood education settings suggest that there are key structural and process features that define high quality (National Association for the Education of Young

Children). *Structural features* are those aspects of preschool programs that can be regulated. Factors such as teacher-child ratios and teacher qualifications are the most frequently cited, although the research linking them to student outcomes is inconclusive (Early et al., 2007, Pianta et al., 2005). *Process features* of high-quality preschools refer primarily to the nature of interactions between teachers and students and the instructional content within the classroom (La Paro, Pianta, & Stuhlman, 2004). Research on this aspect of quality suggests that the quality of instruction, the degree of warmth and support provided by the teacher, and the nature of the behavior management strategies used by the teacher in the classroom all influence children's academic learning as well as their social development (Hamre & Pianta, 2007; Howes et al., 2008; Pianta et al., 2005).

Current models of school readiness emphasize social competence and behavioral readiness as much as early academic skills (Blair, 2002; Ladd, Herald, & Kochel, 2006, National School Readiness Indicators Initiative, 2005; Shonkoff & Phillips, 2000). This reflects the growing recognition of the role that social-emotional, self-management, and behavioral skills play in enabling young children to manage the demands of school entry. A recent content analysis of the early learning standards in the United States indicated that those developed by state-level government agencies differed from those developed by nongovernmental organizations in that the former placed a heavier emphasis on language and cognitive skills than on social skills and approaches to learning (Scott-Little, Kagan, & Frelow, 2006). The emphasis of the former on early academic skills reflects the current political climate in the United States and the school reform movement, which includes policies (e.g., No Child Left Behind Act) designed to ensure that schools are held accountable for students who are not performing adequately. However, surveys conducted with kindergarten teachers reflect their concern that children need both early academic and social-behavioral competencies to be successful (Rimm-Kaufman, Pianta, & Cox,

2000; Lin, Lawrence, & Gorrell, 2003) and early childhood interventions that improve these nonacademic skills are also showing impacts on cognitive outcomes (Raver et al., 2011; Bierman et al., 2009).

In the last two decades, research regarding how children acquire social and behavioral skills has fostered a new generation of early interventions aimed at improving these aspects of child development. Most of social-emotional curricula that target young children are appropriate for use with all students in that they foster skills included in general definitions of school readiness. However, these interventions are especially important for students at risk for school failure or mental health problems owing to poverty, problem behavior, or poor peer relationships.

Social-emotional learning is the process of acquiring skills to develop emotion recognition and management, a positive sense of self, compassion for others, healthy relationships, and effective decision making (Zins et al., 2004). High-quality interventions are largely based on models of social and emotional learning and target malleable factors that have been identified through research (Institute of Medicine, 2010). The individual child skills that comprise the building blocks for social competence and behavioral adjustment can be organized into four broad domains: emotional knowledge, self-management, social-cognitive, and relationship skills. Skills in these four domains are the basis for children's behavioral styles that have a direct effect on academic and social success and therefore are important targets for interventions with young children.

In the United States, there has been growing demand for accountability regarding children's academic success, and these demands have resulted in increased requirements at the state and federal levels for schools and communities to use evidence-based interventions (EBIs). EBIs are empirically validated, which means that they have been tested in a randomized clinical trial or a rigorous quasi-experimental trial that includes a control group and assessments at both the beginning and end of the intervention (Kellam & Langevin, 2003). In the past decade, numerous EBIs have been identified, and registries of these programs have been developed. In the United States, examples of registries include the Substance Abuse and Mental Health Services Administration's (SAMHSA) National Registry of Evidence-based Programs and Practices (NREPP), Blueprints for Violence Prevention, the Education Department's What Works Clearinghouse (WWC), and the Rand Corporation's Promising Practices Network.

The use of universal, evidence-based social-emotional curricula in early educational settings is expanding. Although these programs have the potential to enhance target outcomes, their success depends on the quality with which they are conducted in community settings. The purpose of this chapter is to provide guidelines to practitioners who are planning to implement these types of interventions to ensure quality implementation and maximize effectiveness. Before presenting these guidelines, we summarize the most effective intervention models that are currently available for communities to enhance the social competence of young children and define the core process components of social-emotional interventions because these reflect high-quality implementation and are the primary mechanisms responsible for behavior change in participants.

Overview of Effective Social-Emotional Interventions

Preventive interventions differ in terms of the level of risk in the audience they target (Institute of Medicine, 2010). Table 12.1 provides a list of some of the most rigorously evaluated universal social-emotional interventions that have undergone a quasi-experimental or randomized evaluation and have been found to produce positive outcomes in preschool-age children. It should be noted that few have undergone independent replications. These EBIs include both child- and teacher-focused interventions. Universal child-focused interventions

typically are curricula that include explicit lessons for teachers to deliver and practices to be used throughout the day to reinforce children's understanding and application of core concepts. Teacher-focused interventions share the same goal of improving children's level of social competence and overall adjustment but are designed to promote skill development indirectly by changing the nature of interactions between teachers and students and between children and peers in the classroom.

All the interventions included in the table are theory-based, in that they have a logic model that specifies a set of research-based features or practices that account for the mechanism of change (Institute of Medicine, 2010). Most of the child-focused interventions are skill-focused. Several, such as the Emotions Course or I Can Problem Solve, target primarily one domain, but the majority of programs are comprehensive, fostering skills in multiple domains. The comprehensive approach is more common because of the interconnectedness of social-emotional competencies and the lack of empirical evidence regarding the relative importance of individual skills for long-term adjustment.

The evaluation findings of these interventions suggest that as a group, they effectively improve children's emotion knowledge, executive functioning, and social-cognitive skills. Most of the interventions assessed global social competence and showed a positive impact on this outcome (Bierman et al., 2008; Domitrovich, Cortes, & Greenberg, 2007; Driscoll & Pianta, 2010; Izard et al., 2008; Lynch, Geller, & Schmidt, 2004; Webster-Stratton, Reid, & Stoolmiller, 2008). In addition, most included measures of the specific skills that were targeted by the program and demonstrated significant effects on these outcomes. For example, several programs (e.g., I Can Problem Solve, Preschool PATHS, REDI, and Incredible Years Dinosaur School) use lessons focuses on promoting children's problem-solving skills. The studies of these interventions assessed this skill, and all but one demonstrated positive impacts in this domain

Table 12.1. Early Childhood Programs Targeting Social-Emotional Skills

Program Name	Target Population	Program Outcomes	References
Child-focused interventions			
Al's Pals: Kids Making Healthy Choices	Preschool to third grade	Behavior problems (reducing aggression); social competence; independent functioning; coping strategies	Lynch, Geller, & Schmidt, 2004
Banking Time	Preschool	Frustration tolerance; task orientation; social competence; teacher-child relationship; conduct problems	Driscoll & Pianta, 2010
Child School Readiness Project (CSRP)	Preschool	Internalizing behavior; externalizing behavior; self-regulation (attention/impulsivity); vocabulary; letter naming; early math ; executive function	Raver et al., 2009, 2010
Emotions Course	Preschool	Emotion knowledge; emotion regulation; emotion expression; interpersonal relationships; compliance	Izard et al., 2004, 2008
I Can Problem Solve (ICPS)	Preschool	Social problem solving; frustration tolerance; impulsivity; task engagement	Feis & Simons, 1985; Shure & Spivack, 1982
Incredible Years Dinosaur School	Preschool to first grade (universal & indicated)	Emotional self-regulation; social competence; conduct problems	Webster-Stratton et al., 2008
Learning with Purpose: A Life Long Learning Approach to Self-Determination	Preschool	Adaptive behavior	Serna & Lau-Smith, 1995; Serna et al., 2000
Preschool PATHS (Promoting Alternative THinking Strategies	Preschool to 5th grade	Emotion understanding; social problem-solving; social behavior; learning engagement	Domitrovich et al., 1999, 2007
Tools of the Mind	Preschool	Executive functioning	Bodrova & Leong, 2007; Diamond et al., 2007
Teacher-focused Interventions			
Head Start REDI	Preschool teachers	Teacher communication; positive classroom climate; behavior management	Domitrovich et al., 2009
Incredible Years Teacher Training Module	Preschool teachers	Teacher use of praise; effective discipline; fewer harsh techniques; positive classroom climate; teacher sensitivity; behavior management in classroom; child internalizing behavior; child externalizing behavior	Raver et al., 2008, 2009; Webster-Stratton, Reid, & Hammond, 2004
MyTeaching Partner	Preschool teachers	Teacher sensitivity; communication; behavior management; instructional learning formats	Pianta et al., 2008
Parent-focused interventions			
Getting Ready	Parents with preschool-aged children	Child interpersonal competence; initiative; attachment; anxiety-withdrawal	Sheridan et al., 2010
Incredible Years Basic	Parents with children aged three through six	Child aggression; parent responsiveness; nurturing parenting; harsh parenting; providing stimulating environment	Brotman et al., 2008; Webster-Stratton & Reid, 2008

(Bierman et al., 2008; Schure & Spivak, 1982; Webster-Stratton et al., 2008). Three interventions (i.e., Emotions Course, REDI, and Preschool PATHS) included lessons that were designed to enhance children's emotion knowledge. Positive effects were found on this domain in all three evaluations (Bierman et al., 2008; Domitrovich et al., 2007; Izard et al., 2008). Several interventions were found to be effective at reducing externalizing behavior problems (Bierman et al., 2008; Izard et al., 2008; Raver et al., 2011; Shure & Spivak, 1982). However, it should be noted that few programs have assessed impacts greater than one year after preschool.

Most evaluations of universal social-emotional interventions also have not included assessments of academic or cognitive skills. When these have been included, the findings are inconsistent. The REDI program had a positive impact on language quality, vocabulary, and phonemic awareness, but this is not surprising given that this model also included evidence-based language and literacy interventions. The Chicago School Readiness Project (Raver et al., 2011), which is a teacher-focused intervention that includes teacher training on stress reduction and positive discipline, also enhanced children's emergent literacy skills. The authors attribute this to improvements in children's attention and impulse control that resulted from changes in teacher behavior that improved the level of structure and reduced the amount of conflictual interactions in the classroom (Raver et al., 2011). Both the Emotions Course and Tools of the Mind programs included academic assessments but found no effects in this domain (Diamond et al., 2007; Izard et al., 2004). In most cases, the evaluation studies of the social-emotional curricula were conducted in preschools that also were using a base curriculum or language and literacy interventions, which may explain the comparable findings on academic outcomes across conditions in these studies.

Most of the studies included in Table 12.1 relied on teacher reports of children's social competence and behavior problems. Teacher ratings are more subject to bias because they are completed by the individuals delivering the program. Although teacher reports were the most commonly used forms of measurement, parent reports and direct child assessments also were used in some of the evaluations. Observations are the most reliable form of assessment and tend to be the source of evaluation data in teacher-focused intervention trials, but these measures are used less frequently in child-focused intervention evaluations. Social-emotional interventions are rarely compared with one another within the same study, and each uses a unique measurement battery that emphasizes measurement of the outcomes relevant to that intervention model, so it is almost impossible to determine their relative strengths.

Core Process Components of Evidence-Based Social-Emotional Interventions

Research on teaching quality suggests that there are specific types of interactions between students and teachers in preschool classrooms that foster children's social and cognitive learning (Hamre & Pianta, 2007; Mashburn & Pianta, 2006; NICHD Early Child Care Research Network, 2000a, 2000b). Based on the work of Pianta et al., these interactions can be organized into three categories: emotion supports, classroom organization, and instructional supports (Hamre & Pianta, 2007). Most universal social-emotional interventions foster these types of interactions but also include other unique practices that elicit specific types of adult and peer interactions that promote the affective-cognitive building blocks of social competence (Bierman & Erath, 2006). These techniques and the types of interactions they elicit will be described in addition to the characteristics of high-quality teaching.

EMOTION SUPPORTS
Teachers who are warm and caring, express genuine and positive regard for their students, and enjoy the time they spend in the classroom provide a level of emotional support in their interactions with students

that facilitates positive adjustment and engagement in learning (Hamre & Pianta, 2007). Teachers who are emotionally supportive also create this kind of atmosphere in the classroom by responding with sensitivity to the needs of their students and maintaining a child-centered classroom environment. These behaviors, in combination with warmth and caring, help children to experience a secure and predictable environment (Howes & Smith, 1995; Kontos & Wilcox-Herzog, 1997; NICHD Early Child Care Research Network, 1998). Security fosters mastery motivation, which is a positive emotional state that promotes engagement in learning through feelings of interest and exploration and experiences of success (Connell & Wellborn, 1991).

Most school-based interventions for young children assume that the teachers delivering the intervention are providing emotional support as part of their standard practice. However, interventions that include emotion-focused components build on this pattern of interaction by also encouraging teachers to be purposeful when emotions arise in the classroom and to see these as opportunities for learning (Greenberg, Kusche, & Speltz, 1991). Teachers are encouraged to be aware and accepting of children's feelings, to respond to emotional expressions rather than ignore or dismiss them, and to engage children in active problem solving regarding how to manage their emotions in constructive ways. This approach is drawn from the developmental literature on maternal-child interactions (Dunn, Bretherton, & Munn, 1987) and is based in part on the work of Gottman et al., who identified a specific pattern of emotion responding by parents (i.e., emotion coaching) that fosters emotion regulation (Gottman, Katz, & Hooven, 1997). Emotional validation by the teacher simply can involve labeling the emotion that is being observed or including a more extensive reflection that communicates understanding about why the child feels the way he or she does. In this process, teachers can expand children's emotional understanding by labeling the emotion strategically.

For example, a child may report that she feels angry in a situation when she is actually jealous of a peer. If that child is not familiar with this word *jealous*, she will be more likely to learn the concept when it is presented in this situation as opposed to being introduced abstractly in the context of a lesson. This type of reflection, which is more accurate and easily managed compared with the original emotion, also lays the groundwork for more effective problem solving. Given the central role of language in self-regulation (Raver, Blackburn, & Bancroft, 1999), providing children with labels for their emotional experiences also helps to promote self-regulation because it increases the likelihood that the child will be able to communicate his or her emotional experience (Greenberg & Snell, 1997). This often results in diffusion of the emotional intensity. Related to this is the process of emotion modeling by teachers. Both psychoanalytic education and social-learning theory and research suggest that a significant amount of children's behavior is the result of modeling what they observe in the environment (Kusche, Riggs, & Greenberg, 1999). Given this process, teachers have the opportunity to promote children's emotional understanding and provide them with an adaptive model of emotion regulation by explicitly labeling their own emotional experiences, pointing out how children's behavior affects them (and others), and demonstrating positive emotion coping strategies in naturally occurring situations.

CLASSROOM ORGANIZATION

In the teaching quality literature, classroom organization includes teaching behaviors that engage students, promote self-regulation, and provide productive opportunities for learning. It also includes behavior management because these positive processes are undermined when students are disruptive. Teachers who are skilled at behavior management have clear expectations, are proactive, redirect low-level misbehavior, and rely primarily on positive strategies (e.g., praise) as opposed to using harsh or punitive discipline techniques (Emmer

& Stough, 2001; Pianta, La Paro, & Hamre, 2008). *Classroom organization* refers to how the environment supports student behavior and also how the teacher organizes the learning process. Teachers who are efficient and manage transitions efficiently keep students engaged in productive activities most of the time (Cameron, Connor, & Morrison, 2005). Student engagement depends on the learning format employed by the teacher and the skill with which it is used (Rimm-Kaufman et al., 2005). There are a number of instructional methods and techniques in the educational literature that teachers draw from, but what is most important is that they are varied, tailored to the individual needs of students, and involve them as active participants. Teachers promote self-regulation when they establish a predictable classroom environment and use routines to reduce wasted time. These routines also enable students to act independently, regulate their own behavior, and develop a sense of autonomy. However, classroom organizational models do not explicitly teach self-regulation skills.

Self-regulation is a competency that is central to both academic and social success, so many universal social-emotional interventions target this domain, but they differ in the techniques that are used to facilitate this skill. Young children are often taught through the use of a story and with an analogy to an animal (e.g., turtle or snail) that is calm and slow-moving. Preschool PATHS and Incredible Years Dinosaur School programs both draw on the work of Robin, Schneider, & Dolnick (1976), who developed the "Turtle Technique" to help children develop the ability to stop and calm down independently. As part of this technique, children learn to follow a sequence of steps that include self-talk (e.g., "Tell myself to stop") and tension reduction through nasal breathing. The first step is essential to the strategy given research on the role of language in self-regulation. The authors of the Emotion Course describe a similar technique referred to as "Hold Tight," which is also designed to reduce arousal in emotionally charged situations.

Theoretically, these self-control techniques are designed to promote neural connections between the parts of the brain and replace automatic responses with those which are the result of cognitive evaluation. Both Hold Tight and the PATHS version of the Turtle Technique include an important element as a first step that should be a part of any calming-down technique that is taught to young children. This is a motor action (e.g., crossing the arms across the chest in the PATHS version of the Turtle Technique) that serves as a replacement for the automatic action that accompanies emotional reactions in situations of perceived threat. The calming-down technique and the replacement action in particular should be practiced and reinforced so that they become extremely salient to the children. Doing so at naturally occurring times also will help children to understand the appropriate times to apply the strategy. Prompting or cuing children at lower levels of arousal also promotes learning and is less likely to be met with resistance. When interventions include a self-control technique, they also should include emotion communication as the final step of the calming-down process in order to prepare the child to engage in problem solving.

Teachers' discipline practices can promote or undermine self-regulation. The term *inductive discipline* has been used to describe a pattern of parental discipline based on the theory of Hoffman (1963), which involves providing information regarding the emotional effect their behavior has on others (Krevans & Gibbs, 1996). As described by Bierman (2004) and Bierman & Erath (2006), this work is similar to the coaching approach used in several social skills training interventions with children (Cartledge & Kleefeld, 1991; Guglielmo & Tyron, 2001; Mize & Ladd, 1990). It was adapted by Bierman & Erath as a strategy for teachers participating in the REDI program to provide reminders, cues, and feedback to children in a way that allows them to monitor and self-correct their own behavior, promoting self-regulation and prosocial behavior (Domitrovich et al., 2009). The use of induction or coaching is favorable over more controlling behavior management techniques because when the child responds by self-correcting his or her own behavior or by engaging in a positive social behavior, the child's experience is that he or she made the choice to do so rather than responding to a potential negative consequence. This is intrinsically more rewarding and more likely to be internalized and repeated over time.

INSTRUCTIONAL SUPPORTS

In the teaching-quality framework developed by Pianta et al., instructional supports include the nature and quality of interactions related specifically to the academic learning process. Both general and content-specific interactions are considered in this framework, but only the former will be discussed in this section because they are most relevant to the promotion of social-emotional learning. General instructional supports include the strategies that teachers use to promote children's higher-order thinking skills (Pianta, LaParo, & Hamre, 2008). This is reflected in children's ability to flexibly apply their knowledge in new situations, not in how much children know or are able to recite. Teachers promote these skills by helping children to analyze and evaluate information, understand information by building on what children already know, and apply knowledge in new and creative ways (Hamre & Pianta, 2007). This process requires teachers to be skilled at noticing and taking advantage of "teachable moments" that arise during the day when the conditions are optimal for making these kinds of connections for students. In addition to strategic timing, research has shown that the provision of feedback is also important. This comes in various forms, including praise, reinforcement, and attributions.

Related to the general provision of instructional support is the specific social-emotional promoting strategy of *dialoguing* (Shure, 1981), which is associated with social-cognitive intervention effectiveness (Denham & Almeida, 1987). When adults engage in this process, they provide in vivo information to children regarding their emotional experiences in problem situations, and they scaffold self-regulation and problem solving by encouraging children to calm down, identify the problems, generate solutions, and select a solution (Denham & Burton, 2003; Shure & Spivak, 1978). Skilled teachers dialogue with children in a way that is nonhierarchical and communicates collaboration between all parties involved. They also adjust the amount and type of support they provide to meet children's developmental needs and challenge them enough to promote learning and advance their level of competence.

SUMMARY

Research suggests that universal preventive interventions that are designed to change the nature of teacher-student interactions through professional development alone or in combination with explicit, scripted lessons are effective at improving student outcomes. In the case of curricular interventions, it is the interactions between the students and the teacher facilitated by the core process features of the intervention in addition to the content of the lessons that are the likely mechanism of change responsible for those outcomes. As a result, both the delivery of the lessons and the quality of the teaching in the classroom should be reflected in implementation assessments.

Implementation of Social-Emotional Interventions

As literature documenting the effectiveness of preventive interventions accumulates and policy support for the use of EBIs grows, the number of communities interested in adopting these models is expanding. A positive association between implementation quality and program outcomes has been documented in community replications (Domitrovich et al., 2010; Hamre et al., 2010; Durlak & Dupree, 2008). While it is more challenging to achieve high-quality implementation in community settings (Durlak, 2010), it is possible (Spoth et al., 2007). Less is known about the replication of EBIs in community-based early childhood education settings compared with elementary schools, but even in a recent set of effectiveness trials evaluating a variety of preschool curricula, there was variation in levels of implementation, with 5 to 10 percent of implementers failing to conduct 50 percent of the intervention (Knoche et al., 2010; Odom et al., 2010). This implementation failure has the potential to undermine the impact of the intervention because if participants are not exposed to key components or the quality of what is delivered is substandard, they may not receive the essential elements that are needed to result in behavior change. This undermines the intervention's effectiveness and the investment made by the community in the intervention.

Defining and Measuring Implementation

There are a number of ways to assess implementation quality, but the most common approach is to measure fidelity or dosage (Dusenbury et al., 2005; O'Donnell, 2008). Measurement of either dimension requires the specification of the core components of the intervention. EBIs include specific content and process features that are the mechanisms through which outcomes in participants are achieved. These core components should be theoretically based and verified with intervention studies, although the latter is rare (Collaborative for Academic, Social, and Emotional Learning, 2003; Institute of Medicine, 2010). Specifying the core components of an intervention is critical for accurately assessing fidelity or dosage because this defines the model against which the actual replication is compared. *Fidelity* is the extent to which the content of the core components is adhered to when replicated. Often this dimension is assessed by coding the extent to which scripts or lesson guides are adhered to or the objectives are achieved. *Dosage* is the amount of the intervention to which participants are exposed. Depending on the program model, dosage can be assessed in terms of the frequency or duration of the intervention. Low levels of either fidelity or dosage of core components

have the potential to reduce intervention impact.

Additional dimensions of implementation have been identified and used in the literature (Dane & Schneider, 1998). One that is particularly important to social-emotional interventions is quality of delivery. This process-oriented dimension varies in the way it has been conceptualized, but in the most general sense, it refers to how well a program is enacted (Dusenbury et al., 2003; O'Donnell, 2008). Quality of delivery depends on the actions of the individual implementing the intervention, the characteristics of the participants, and the nature of the interactions that evolve between the implementer and the participants. Many early childhood social-emotional interventions are curricular enhancements that are delivered through lessons integrated into existing classroom practices. High-quality delivery depends on the teacher's ability to maintain student engagement, and in some studies, ratings of this are included as a more distal indicator of implementation quality (Odom et al., 2010). Maintaining the interest and attention of young children during a lesson requires sensitivity, affective engagement, teaching skill, and flexibility (Dusenbury et al., 2005; Greenberg et al., 2005). In some cases, teachers must adapt the pacing of lessons. It is difficult to make these adjustments and still achieve a high degree of fidelity without having an in-depth understanding of a program's theory and primary objectives. This information is often included in the training of EBIs, most likely for this purpose.

In the case of universal intervention models delivered by teachers, quality of delivery also should be defined as the extent to which the implementer generalizes the intervention throughout the day (Greenberg et al., 2005). This is important because simply providing social-emotional instruction is not enough to improve children's actual social and behavioral skills. Young children's learning depends heavily on experience, so they benefit from observing models and being prompted to use new skills in naturally occurring situations. *Generalization* involves proactively creating opportunities to revisit concepts through modeling or the use of extension activities and taking advantage of teachable moments throughout the day to help children master key program concepts. An example of this technique is prompting a child to stop and calm down when he or she is starting to show signs of frustration as he or she works on a challenging task in the classroom. While the child may have experienced a lesson on the topic of calming down, his or her understanding and mastery of the concept is limited when his or her only experience with the behavior up that point was hearing it described or seeing pictures of it. Generalization helps children to learn the appropriate time to use a behavior and provides practice in using the skill and an opportunity for the adult to use reinforcement and feedback to refine the children's behavior. This and other key process interactions involved in social-emotional learning are described in the first half of this chapter in order to provide guidance for the development of process-related ratings of quality.

In a recent paper describing methods to assess fidelity of implementation of elementary math and science instructional programs, Century, Rudnick, & Freeman (2010) distinguish *structural* critical components from *instructional* critical components. Within *structural* critical components, the authors suggest identifying both the *procedural* and the *educative* dimensions of the program model as a first step toward developing a fidelity of implementation (FOI) framework and assessment strategy. *Procedural* critical components are the organizing elements of the intervention that tell the user what to do (e.g., scripted lessons), whereas the *educative* critical components reflect what the user is expected to know in order to implement the intervention with fidelity. Parallel to the structural critical components are the process-oriented, *instructional* critical components, which include the *pedagogic* and *student engagement* dimensions. *Pedagogic* critical components are the behaviors and practices that are essential for the implementer to conduct when delivering an

intervention, whereas those which reflect what the participants are expected to demonstrate during the intervention are referred to as *student engagement* critical components (Century et al., 2010).

Curriculum-focused social-emotional interventions are designed to facilitate children's mastery of specific skills by supplying learning objectives and instructional activities to teachers based on a scope and sequence of skill acquisition and helping teachers to organize learning activities in a systematic and strategic way that is validated in developmental research (Justice & Pullen, 2003; Joseph & Strain, 2003). For these interventions, the number of lessons delivered is a common assessment of dosage used to determine the level of implementation that is being achieved. In most evidence-based models of these interventions, teachers not only are provided with scripted materials and instructions regarding how to conduct the intervention but also are also provided with training and support designed to support high-quality teaching or the *instructional core components* of that intervention, which are best judged by the level of quality with which they are executed.

As reviewed in preceding sections, instructional core components of social-emotional interventions include general teaching practices and specific promotion strategies. Ideally, the curriculum lessons or activities promote these types of interactions. However, research has shown that conducting lessons or following procedures does not automatically result in high-quality interactions. In one naturalistic study of preschool classrooms in which all participants of the project implemented an evidence-based language and literacy intervention, the authors distinguished procedural fidelity from quality of implementation (Justice et al., 2008). *Procedural quality* (i.e., fidelity) was defined as adherence to the step-by-step procedures of the lesson plans as written and was coded from videos submitted by teachers every two weeks. *Quality of implementation*, also coded from the videos, was defined as the core relational processes that were expected to take place in the context of instruction as a result of the intervention. The two indicators of implementation were not correlated with one another, and ratings of procedural quality did not explain any of the variance in the ratings of instructional quality. This research suggests that ratings of dosage or fidelity alone fail to capture all the important dimensions of implementation and that including an assessment of quality is critical.

SUMMARY

There are a number of ways to assess implementation, but the most common approaches include indicators of fidelity, dosage, and quality of delivery. Little is known about which implementation dimensions are the most important to assess, but recent studies of early academic interventions for preschool-age children suggest that quality of deliver may be one of the most important (Hamre et al., 2010). Communities implementing universal social-emotional interventions should follow an approach such as the one described in Century et al. (2010) to identify the structural and process core components of the intervention being implemented and attempt to monitor both with measures of all three dimensions. Practitioners should pay particular attention to the delivery quality of the process features of the intervention that hopefully are made explicit in the curriculum materials or intervention training but, if not, are described in this chapter.

Maximizing the Effectiveness of Evidence-Based Interventions

There are several phases that communities must negotiate to establish the effective and sustained use of an EBI. The first, referred to as the *adoption phase*, is the process of selecting which intervention is going to be used and preparing for its implementation. The second, referred to as the *implementation phase*, is the period in which the intervention is first conducted. This is followed by the *sustainability phase*, in which the intervention is maintained over time. Suggestions of ways in which community leaders and practitioners can navigate these phases successfully by addressing critical factors that influence the process are provided in the sections that follow.

Adoption Phase

PROMOTE ACCEPTABILITY

Interventions vary in terms of their outcomes goals, the levels they target (e.g., individuals, systems, and the environment), and the methods through which they operate. Given the unique features of each community and the particular needs of specific early childhood programs, certain interventions may work better in some settings than others. As interventions are being considered, it is important to evaluate their fit to the existing needs of the program, the children being served, available resources, and the organizational capacity of the institution. Key stakeholders (i.e., administrators, teachers, and parents) should be involved early on, when the school or program is in the process of selecting an intervention and planning its implementation. Having implementers involved in the decision-making process is a way to increase motivation and buy-in that is essential because research has shown that implementer attitudes and perceptions of an intervention are associated with their implementation. Specifically, studies have shown that program acceptance is associated with higher levels of implementation (Rohrbach, Graham, & Hansen, 1993) and that one effective strategy to promote this attitude toward EBIs is to disseminate them in an organization through key opinion leaders who are the well-respected and influential individuals in the setting (Atkins et al., 2008).

Establishing positive perceptions of the intervention is important for increasing the likelihood of high-quality implementation by those charged with conducting the intervention. If a program is viewed as being necessary and better than the current practice, it is more likely to be implemented well (Elias et al., 2003; Pankratz, Hallfors, & Cho, 2002; Parcel et al., 1991; Ringwalt, et al., 2003). Given the variation in staff and setting characteristics across communities, interventions also will vary in the extent to which users view them as compatible with the overall mission of the organization or the particular needs for which they are being used. Closer alignment between the setting and the intervention is associated with higher levels of acceptance and implementation quality (Pankratz et al., 2002; Rogers, 2003). Given that a history of failed intervention attempts is associated with difficulty implementing and sustaining innovations, it is important to consider how to differentiate new interventions being introduced in a community from any in the past that were unsuccessful (Gottfredson & Gottfredson, 2002).

BE PREPARED AS AN ORGANIZATION
High-quality implementation is not simply a function of the implementer's attitude or motivation. The characteristics of the settings in which interventions are conducted also influence whether they are done well (Domitrovich et al., 2008). Much of the research literature on organizational factors associated with the implementation of preventive interventions has been done in schools, but it is also relevant for early childhood education and care settings. Findings from studies in these settings suggest that a positive work climate in which individuals are open to change and trust one another facilitates positive student outcomes (Bryk & Schneider, 2002). Open communication and effective problem solving allow for the discussion and resolution of implementation challenges that might be encountered (Kallestad & Olweus, 2003; Parcel et al., 2003), whereas settings characterized by low morale or a sense of resignation are less effective at implementing interventions (Gottfredson & Gottfredson, 2002). Providers need to be realistic about their expectations when introducing an innovation into a low-functioning system and consider addressing the systemic issues simultaneously.

A critical but often omitted step in the adoption process is to have those involved in the decision making contact others who are currently using an intervention. This enables the new user to be fully informed regarding the requirements for successful implementation and determine whether it is viable to use in his or her particular community. It also highlights issues that might be encountered when replicating the intervention. Universal interventions often require an annual investment for disposable materials in addition to the initial cost of purchasing curriculum kits, but this is not always evident at the time of purchase. Although gathering this information can be accomplished by phone, there is no substitute for a site visit in which a program coordinator or planning committee can see the program in action and discuss issues with staff who are actually using the intervention. On-site visits are extremely helpful for administrators as well because these individuals must develop a vision and action plan for how any new programs or practices fit and are prioritized within the organization. As those with authority over financial as well as programmatic decisions, administrators are often critical for providing practical support that is needed for high-quality implementation.

Implementation Phase

Evidence-based interventions are unlikely to be implemented well without a support system that establishes the context for the delivery of the intervention. This includes the infrastructure and resources necessary to deploy the intervention, the training that is necessary to prepare implementers, and the ongoing support that ensures high-quality replication (Greenberg et al., 2001). The goal of the support system is to ensure high-quality replication and reduce variability in implementation of the intervention across individuals and settings.

PROVIDE ADEQUATE TRAINING
One of the most common forms of professional development for early childhood educators are preservice trainings, which are often the mode of training associated with preventive interventions. These workshops are designed to provide those responsible for implementing the intervention with the

skills and knowledge necessary to conduct the intervention properly (Fixsen et al., 2005). Participation in training is an important element for effective implementation, so providers should not underestimate the importance of this investment (Parcel et al., 1991; Perry, Murray, & Griffin, 1990; Ross et al., 1991). Most developers of EBIs offer training delivered by certified staff with extensive experience and expertise regarding the program model. Practitioners in community settings should follow the guidelines and not try to save money by sending one representative to be trained and then expect that person to disseminate his or her knowledge to colleagues. It is likely that this type of informal "train the trainer" model dilutes the impact of the training, which undermines program effectiveness.

One strategy for community replications that is likely to reduce unanticipated implementation challenges and increase acceptability by staff is to have a small group of motivated individuals pilot the intervention within their program or school. Having this group discuss their experiences when the remainder of the staff is trained allows participants to hear from colleagues they trust who have been using the model with children who are similar to their own. A staggered rollout of any new innovation allows a program or school to work through implementation challenges and avoid large-scale problems that are more difficult to resolve. Involving the most motivated staff first also ensures that if there are problems, they will be experienced by individuals who are probably more understanding and flexible.

INTEGRATE WITH EXISTING PRACTICE

As stated previously, it is important that providers take the time to fully investigate an intervention prior to implementation. This includes how much preparation is involved, the time that is needed for delivery, and how frequently the intervention is conducted. The goals of most universal interventions are consistent with those of early childhood education programs. If the intervention involves explicit lessons or activities, these should be integrated with ongoing practice. Teachers benefit from seeing how an innovation fits both conceptually and practically with what they are already doing. This can be accomplished by providing them with conceptual crosswalks (e.g., alignment of intervention practices with the program's base curriculum or with early learning standards) and implementation pacing guides. Providing a pacing guide that reflects the program calendar also makes teachers feel that the expectations for program delivery are realistic, which, in turn, increases buy-in. It also provides an explicit structure that helps to keep the program on track. Finally, the more integrated an intervention is with existing practice, the more likely it is that it will be sustained.

PROVIDE IMPLEMENTATION SUPPORT

There are a number of reasons why implementation levels may be lower when interventions are replicated in community settings. Many of these can be addressed with the provision of adequate support. Structural barriers (e.g., program schedule) sometimes prevent implementers from being able to deliver an intervention regularly. Teachers need help to decide what to prioritize when there are multiple demands on their time, and changes to a program schedule may require administrative approval. This is when it is important for the administration to be involved with the implementation process. Implementation challenges that are identified early and resolved quickly are less likely to undermine morale and quality of delivery. This important role of the administration begins during the adoption phase but continues into the implementation phase. Therefore, it is recommended that administrators attend intervention trainings and develop a way for staff to communicate challenges with implementation as they arise. The administration is also responsible for communicating that an intervention is a priority. This is achieved through the commitment of time and resources, but it also happens in a more meaningful way when the administration adopts a program's philosophy and incorporates the core concepts into their own practice. For example, when the PATHS curriculum is conducted in a school, the principal should hang copies of the posters in his or her office, use the curriculum language when interacting with students and staff, conduct classroom observations of intervention delivery, and publically recognize teachers for high-quality implementation. Universal models are most effective when delivered with a program or schoolwide approach so that the child experiences the core concepts being delivered through the curriculum language and activities across multiple contexts and individuals.

Low levels of implementation quality also may be a function of an implementer's skill level. In these situations, additional training or technical support is often warranted and useful. Advances in the education literature regarding adult learning and professional development are beginning to inform the development of support-system models for social-emotional interventions, particularly those for which the teacher is the delivery agent (Garet et al., 2001; Joyce & Showers, 2002; Putnam & Borko, 2000). Coaching is one approach that has been used successfully in early childhood settings to facilitate the use of evidence-based language and literacy curricula (Domitrovich et al., 2010; Landry et al., 2009; Pianta et al., 2008). In one study, preschool teachers who received individual mentoring in addition to web-based training materials were rated as engaging in higher-quality interactions with students by independent observers compared with those who received access to the web-based training materials alone (Pianta et al., 2008).

Coaching is gaining attention in the early childhood field as a more effective training approach than traditional in-service methods. There is variation in how this approach is used, but typically these individuals are experts in the particular intervention they are supporting. They observe teachers' practices in the classroom, meet outside of class time to discuss and reflect on what was observed, and provide support to promote or refine behaviors in need of further development (Haskins & Loeb, 2007; International Reading Association & National Association for the Education of Young Children, 1998). Research suggests that in order to make meaningful changes to their behavior, teachers need to have opportunities for active learning through observation, meaningful discussion, practice, and reflection (Fishman et al., 2000; Garet et al., 2001; Joyce & Showers, 2002; Putnam & Borko, 2000).

To date, there is very little empirical research on how mentors influence the behavior of the individuals with whom they work. Descriptive studies suggest that teachers value the support and encouragement they experience in relationships with a mentor or coach (Brooks, 1996; Ransford et al., 2009), and in one study, teachers' openness to consultation was associated with high-quality implementation of a comprehensive preschool curriculum (Domitrovich et al., 2009b). In order to help teachers overcome anxiety about starting a new program, manage workplace stress, and disclose problems they are having with implementation, coaches must create a relationship that is characterized by high levels of trust. This is likely to evolve when coaches establish a collegial and professional working relationship and are skilled in the method, content, and timing of their feedback. When teachers are invested in the relationship with their coach, they also may be more positively influenced by social persuasion and reinforcement.

When teachers have difficulty understanding or executing intervention concepts, effective coaches use a variety of strategies, including modeling techniques and providing in vivo support while the intervention is being delivered. In one universal school-based intervention, a comprehensive coaching model was developed that included the use of weekly visits to classrooms, written feedback based on program observations, handouts regarding guidelines for high-quality practice, modeling, and the provision of incentives for high levels of implementation (Pitchford et al., 2010). Research has shown that performance feedback is one of the most effective ways to influence implementer behavior (Leach & Conto, 1999; Noell et al., 2005; Rose & Church, 1998), and in order to really know what teachers are doing in the classroom, coaches actually must observe their practice rather than relying on what teachers report.

Regardless of the techniques used by the coach or the mechanisms through which they influence teachers' behaviors, this type of intensive professional support is expected to cause increases in teacher self-efficacy (Han & Weiss, 2005), which is positively associated with program implementation (Kallestad & Olweus, 2003; Ransford et al., 2009; Rohrbach et al., 1993).

MONITOR IMPLEMENTATION

In order to ensure adequate levels of implementation quality, it is necessary to develop a system to monitor the process (Scott & Martinek, 2006). This type of data collection can be time-consuming and costly, so it may be overlooked, done with poor quality, or given lower priority in community settings, especially if the intervention funding source is focused only on measuring outcomes. Despite these challenges, monitoring implementation is the cornerstone of successful child outcomes. This is so because better implementation quality is associated with more positive outcomes (Durlak & DuPre, 2008), and in the current era of accountability, implementation quality data can be a useful tool in illustrating what was done well during program delivery. The practice of monitoring implementation also may serve to improve quality by those who are delivering the intervention.

As discussed previously, there are a number of dimensions (e.g., fidelity, dosage, and quality of delivery) that can be used to assess the level implementation that is being achieved in a replication. Implementation monitoring requires measures that are tailored specifically for an intervention, so one consideration when choosing a program is whether it provides such tools. There is little empirical work to provide specific guidelines regarding which measures are the most sensitive or relevant to program outcomes, how often implementation should be measured, or who should provide the information (Domitrovich et al., 2010; Durlak,

2010; Institute of Medicine, 2010). The most common source of implementation information is implementers, presumably because ratings from these individual are easy to collect and not very time time-consuming. Dosage usually is most accurately and efficiently reported by teachers, but there is a greater potential for social desirability when implementers rate their own fidelity or quality of delivery. This is particularly true in situations where program implementation is tied to job performance. Observations of fidelity and quality of delivery conducted by trained research assistants, program coordinators, or coaches are the most reliable measures but are less common because they are expensive and time-consuming. At this time, based on what is known within the field of intervention research, communities should use multiple sources (e.g., teacher self-report and observer rating) to collect implementation data and assess multiple dimensions on at least several occasions. The old proviso "What gets assessed, gets addressed" is important here because it is likely that fidelity, dosage, and quality are to be maintained at higher levels if ongoing implementation monitoring becomes systematic and systemic.

LINK IMPLEMENTATION DATA TO QUALITY IMPROVEMENT

Information gathered during the implementation process should be used to make ongoing improvements in the intervention (Scott & Martinek, 2006). To do this, the data must be useful and gathered in a way that they can be accessed and used quickly. It is also important to create an environment in which implementers feel that this information is being used constructively. If a community has the resources to provide coaches to teachers, then these individuals can be used strategically toward this purpose both by collecting the information and by using it for quality improvement. Coaches often function independently of supervisors who evaluate staff. If this is the case, they can deliver feedback to teachers who are implementing the intervention in a way that is likely to be received positively.

Sustainability Phase

Despite the fact that there is an empirical base regarding the effectiveness of prevention programs that target young children, the dissemination of these programs has not been systematic; therefore, they rarely reach a level where they are implemented and sustained with effectiveness over time in community settings. The lack of sustained programs is sometimes a function of how the interventions are financed. If a program is introduced to a community through a research or service grant, once funding ends, the program often fades as well, unless adequate resources can be found to maintain it. However, it also can be a function of factors that operate at the individual and organizational levels, including how the intervention is selected, the characteristics of the model, the quality of implementation when it was first replicated, and whether proper attention has been given to the support system that was necessary to replicate the intervention (Bumbarger & Perkins, 2008). Initiatives designed to promote sustainability of EBIs pay attention to these factors and attempt to work with communities to address them from the beginning of the planning and selection process.

When EBIs are conducted outside the context of research and communities have been able to sustain the use of the intervention over time, one issue that becomes more salient and common is program adaptation. (Dariotis et al., 2008; Dusenbury et al., 2005; Hallfors, Pankratz, & Hartman, 2007). In the field of prevention research, there is a tension regarding whether communities should have the flexibility to adapt or there should be strict adherence to the intervention model (Castro, Barrerra, & Martinez, 2004; Dusenbury & Hansen, 2004). Proponents of adaptations argue that communities need to be able to tailor interventions to the needs of the setting or of participants. This is particularly true when there are cultural differences between those for whom the program was intended originally and the current target audience. Others argue that programs should not be adapted because this may reduce the program's effectiveness (Mihalek et al., 2004). Communities are invested in both these issues, so ideally a balance can be struck such that adaptations to the program are made in a thoughtful way that maintains the core content and process components.

Adaptations are any changes or modifications made to an intervention, and depending on how they are made, they are considered proactive or reactive. *Proactive adaptations* occur as a result of anticipated problems of fit (Kalichman et al., 2007; Kumpfer et al., 2008), whereas *reactive adaptations* occur as a program is being delivered and therefore are unanticipated and less well documented (Galbraith et al., 2009). Problems of fit may be either philosophical or logistic (Elias et al., 2003) and ideally are considered during the adoption process so that any changes to the program can be made before the intervention is started with input from the developer.

When adaptations are made, they alter either the surface or the deep structure of an intervention (Castro et al., 2004; Sussman & Palinkas, 2008). Examples of surface structure changes include alterations made to pictures to match the target audience or language translations of program materials. These types of adaptations should not change the underlying logic model of the intervention or its effectiveness because they maintain the core components. Deep structure changes such as removing, adding, or modifying content are more likely to change the core components of a program and reduce program effectiveness (Galbraith et al., 2009). Deep structure change can happen slowly over time owing to a phenomenon called *program drift* and is an additional reason that a program looses effectiveness (Bumbarger & Perkins, 2008). Over time, small changes take place each time the intervention is delivered until it is no longer delivered as intended, even if the program was delivered initially with quality.

Sustainability strategies have been developed to assist schools and community agencies through the process of adaptation and implementation so that it is done with quality and in a way that can be maintained over time (Devaney et al., 2006). This type of local ownership and empowerment process facilitates the gathering of key stakeholders from a community and provides a structure for identifying the needs of a community, selecting the best EBIs to address those needs, and integrating new and existing intervention efforts so that they are efficient and cost-effective strategies to achieve desired outcomes for children.

Conclusion

Community providers of prevention or intervention services need to have realistic expectations for when child outcomes are expected following the implementation of evidence-based interventions, particularly if they encountered any implementation challenges or were not able to achieve adequate levels of implementation quality during the implementation phase. Picking the right program, setting benchmarks for implementation levels, establishing a monitoring system, and providing support as needed to implementers are all steps that should result in positive outcomes. Once positive outcomes are achieved and the community decides to maintain the intervention over time, steps should be taken to integrate the program more broadly into existing early education and care program structures while maintaining the focus on implementation quality.

References

Atkins, M. S., Frazier, S. L., Leathers, S. J., Graczyk, P. A., Talbott, E., Jakobsons, L., et al. (2008). Teacher key opinion leaders and mental health consultation in low-income urban schools. *Journal of Consulting and Clinical Psychology* 76, 905–8; doi:10.1037/a0013036.

Barnett, W. S., Epstein, D. J., Friedman, A. H., Sansanelli, R., & Hustedt, J. T. (2009). *The state of preschool 2009: State preschool yearbook.* New Brunswick, NJ: National Institute for Early Education Research.

Bierman, K. L. (2004). *Peer rejection: Developmental processes and intervention strategies.* New York: Guilford Press.

Bierman, K. L., & Erath, S. A. (2006). Promoting social competence in early childhood: Classroom curricula and social skills coaching programs. In K. McCartney and D. Phillips (eds.), *Blackwell handbook on early childhood development.* Malden, MA: Blackwell.

Bierman, K. L., Torres, M. M., Domitrovich, C., Welsh, J. A., & Gest, S. D. (2009). Behavioral and cognitive readiness for school: Cross-domain associations for children attending Head Start. *Social Development* 18(2), 305–23; doi: 10.1111/j.1467–9507.2008.00490.x.

Bierman, K. L., Domitrovich, C., Nix, R. L., Gest, S. D., Welsh, J. A., Greenberg, M. T., et al. (2008). Promoting academic and social-emotional school readiness: The Head Start REDI program. *Child Development* 79(6), 1802–17; doi: 10.1111/j.1467–8624.2008.01227.x.

Blair, C. (2002). School readiness: Integrating cognition and emotion in a neurological conceptualization of children's functioning at school entry. *American Psychologist* 57, 111–27; doi: 10.1037//0003–066X.57.2.111.

Bodrova, E., & Leong, D. J. (2007). *Tools of the mind: The Vygotskian approach to early childhood education,* 2nd ed. Upper Saddle River, NJ: Prentice-Hall.

Brooks, V. (1996). Mentoring: The interpersonal dimension. *Teacher Development* 5, 5–10.

Brotman, L. M., Gouley, K. K., Huang, K., Rosenfelt, A., O'Neal, C., Klein, R. G., & Shrout, P. (2008). Preventive interventions for preschoolers at high risk for antisocial behavior: Long-term effects on child physical aggression and parenting practices. *Journal of Clinical Child & Adolescent Psychology* 37, 386–96. doi: 10.1080/15374410801955813.

Bryk, A. S., & Schnieder, B. (2002). *Trust in schools: A core resource for improvement.* New York: Russell Sage.

Bumbarger, B. K., & Perkins, D. (2008). After randomized trials: Issues related to dissemination of evidence-based interventions. *Journal of Children's Services* 3(2), 53–61.

Cameron, C. E., Connor, C. M., & Morrison, F. J. (2005). Effects of variation in teacher organization on classroom functioning. *Journal of School Psychology* 43(1), 61–85; doi:10.1016/j.jsp.2004.12.002.

Cartledge, G., & Kleefeld, J. (1991). *Taking part, introducing social skills to children.* Circle Pines, MN: American Guidance Service.

Castro, F. G., Barrerra, M. J., & Martinez, C. R. (2004). The cultural adaptation of prevention interventions: Resolving tensions between fidelity and fit. *Prevention Science* 5, 41–5; doi:10.1023/B:PREV.0000013980.12412.cd.

Century, J., Rudnick, M., & Freeman, C. (2010). A framework for measuring fidelity of implementation: A foundation for shared language and accumulation of knowledge. *American Journal of Evaluation* 31, 199–218; doi: 10.1177/1098214010366173.

Collaborative for Academic Social and Emotional Learning (2003). *Sage and sound: An educational leader's guide to evidence-based social and emotional learning (SEL) programs.* Chicago: Collaborative for Academic Social and Emotional Learning.

Connell, J. P., & Wellborn, J. G. (1991). Competence, autonomy, and relatedness: A motivational analysis of self system processes. In M. R. Gunnar (ed.), *Self processes and development.* Hillsdale, NJ: Erlbaum.

Curby, T. W., Rimm-Kaufman, S. E., & Ponitz, C. C. (2009). Teacher-child interactions and children's achievement trajectories across Kindergarten and first grade. *Journal of Educational Psychology* 101(4), 912–25; doi: 10.1037/a0016647.

Dane, A. V., & Schneider, B. H. (1998). Program integrity in primary and early secondary prevention: Are implementation effects out of control? *Clinical Psychology Review* 18(1), 23–45; doi:10.1016/S0272–7358(97)00043–3.

Dariotis, J. K., Bumbarger, B. K., Duncan, L. G., & Greenberg, M. T. (2008). How do implementation efforts relate to program adherence? Examining the role of organizational, implementer, and program factors. *Journal of Community Psychology* 36(6), 744–60; doi: 10.1002/jcop.20255.

Denham, S. A., & Almeida, M. C. (1987). Children's social problem-solving skills, behavioral adjustment, and interventions: A meta-analysis evaluating theory and practice. *Journal of Applied Developmental Psychology* 8, 391–409; doi: 10.1016/0193–3973(87)90029–3.

Denham, S. A., & Burton, R. (2003). *Social and emotional prevention and intervention programming for preschoolers.* New York: Springer.

Devaney, E., O'Brien, M. U., Resnik, H., Keister, S., & Weissberg, R. P. (2006). *Sustainable school wide and emotional leraning (SEL): Implementation guide and toolkit.* Chicago: CASEL

Diamond, A., Barnett, W. S., Thomas, J., & Munro, S. (2007). Preschool program improves cognitive control. *Science* 318, 1387–8; doi: 10.1126/science.1151148.

Domitrovich, C., Córtes, R. C., & Greenberg, M. T. (2007). Improving young children's social and emotional competence: A randomized trial of the preschool "PATHS" curriculum. *Journal of Primary Prevention* 28(2), 67–91; doi: 10.1007/s10935–007–0081–0.

Domitrovich, C. E., Greenberg, M. T., Cortes, R., & Kusche, C. (1999). *Manual for the Preschool PATHS Curriculum.* University Park, PA: Pennsylvania State University.

Domitrovich, C. E., Gest, S. D., Gill, S., Bierman, K. L., Welsh, J. A., & Jones, D. (2009). Fostering high quality teaching with an enriched curriculum and professional development support: The Head Start REDI Program. *American Educational Research Journal* 46, 567–97; doi: 10.3102/0002831208328089.

Domitrovich, C. E., Gest, S. D., Gill, S., Jones, D. J., & DeRouise, R. S. (2009). Teacher factors related to the professional development process of the Head Start REDI intervention. *Early Education and Development* 20, 402–30.

Domitrovich, C. E., Gest, S. D., Jones, D., Gill, S., & DeRousie, R. S. (2010). Implementation quality: Lessons learned in the context of the Head Start REDI trial. *Early Childhood Research Quarterly* 25, 284–98.

Domitrovich, C., Bradshaw, C. P., Poduska, J. M., Hoagwood, K., Bucklet, J. A., Olin, S., et al. (2008). Maximizing the implementation quality of evidence-based preventive interventions in schools: A conceptual framework. *Advances in School Mental Health Promotion* 1(3), 6–28.

Driscoll, J. C., & Pianta, R. C. (2010). Banking time in Head Start: Early efficacy of an intervention designed to promote supportive teacher-child relationships. *Early Education & Development* 21, 38–64; doi: 10.1080/10409280802657449.

Dunn, J., Bretherton, I., & Munn, P. (1987). Conversations about feeling states between mothers and their young children. *Developmental Psychology* 23, 132–9; doi: 10.1037/0012–1649.23.1.132.

Durlak, J. A. (2010). The importance of doing well in whatever you do: A commentary on the special section, "Implementation research in early childhood education." *Early Childhood Research Quarterly* 25, 348–57; doi: 10.1016/j.ecresq.2010.03.003.

Durlak, J. A., & DuPre, E. P. (2008). Implementation matters: A review of research on the influence of implementation on program outcomes and the factors affecting implementation. *American Journal of Community Psychology* 41, 327–50; doi: 10.1007/s10464–008–9165–0.

Dusenbury, L., & Hansen, W. B. (2004). Pursing the course from research to practice. *Prevention Science* 5(1), 55–60; doi: 10.1023/B:PREV.00000 13982.20860.19.

Dusenbury, L., Branningan, R., Falco, M., & Hansen, W. B. (2003). A review of research on fidelity of implementation: Implications for drug abuse prevention in school settings. *Health Education Research* 18, 237–56; doi: 10.1093/her/18.2.237.

Dusenbury, L., Brannigan, R., Hansen, W. B., Walsh, J., & Falco, M. (2005). Quality of implementation: Developing measures crucial to understanding the diffusion of preventive interventions. *Health Education Research: Theory and Practice* 20(3), 308–13.

Early, D. M., Maxwell, K. L., Burchinal, M., Alva, S., Bender, R. H., Bryant, D. P., et al. (2007). Teachers' education, classroom quality, and young chidlrne's academic skills: Results from seven studies of preschool programs. *Child Development* 78(2), 558–80; doi: 10.1111/j.1467–8624.2007.01014.x.

Elias, M. J., Zins, J. E., Graczyk, P. A., & Weissberg, R. P. (2003). Implementation, sustainability, and scaling up of social-emotional and academic innovations in public schools. *School Psychology Review* 32(3), 303–19.

Emmer, E. T., & Stough, L. (2001). Classroom management: a critical part of educational psychology, with implications for teacher education. *Educational Psychologist* 36(2), 103–12; doi: 10.1207/S15326985EP3602_5.

Feis, C. L., & Simons, C. (1985). Training preschool children in interpersonal cognitive problem-solving skills: A replication. *Prevention in Human Services* 3, 59–70.

Fishman, B. J., Best, S., Foster, J., & Marx, R. (2000). Fostering teacher learning in systemic reform: A design proposal for developing professional development. Paper presented at the Annual Meeting of the National Association of Research in Science Teaching, New Orleans, LA.

Fixsen, D. L., Noaoom, S. F., Blase, K. A., Friedman, R. M., & Wallace, F. (2005). *Implementation research: A synthesis of the literature* (L. d. l. P. F. M. H. Institute, trans.). Tampa, FL: University of South Florida.

Galbraith, J. S., Stanton, B., Boekeloo, B., King, W., Desmond, S., Howard, D., et al. (2009). Exploring implementation and fidelity of evidence-based behavioral interventions for HIV prevention: Lessons learned from the Focus on Kids diffusion case study. *Health Education and Behavior* 36(3), 532–49; doi: 10.1177/1090198108315366.

Garet, M., Porter, A., Desimone, L., Birman, B., & Yoon, K. S. (2001). What makes professional development effective? Results from a national sample of teachers. *American Education Research Journal* 38, 915–45; doi: 10.3102/00028312038004915.

Gormley, W. T., Gayer, T., Phillips, D., & Dawson, B. (2005). The effects of universal pre-K on cognitive development. *Developmental Psychology* 41, 872–84; doi: 10.1037/0012–1649.41.6.872.

Gottfredson, D. C., & Gottfredson, G. D. (2002). Quality of school based prevention programs: Results from a national survey. *Journal of Research in Crime and Delinquency* 39(1), 3–35; doi: 10.1177/002242780203900101.

Gottman, J., Katz, L. F., & Hooven, C. (1997). *Meta-emotion*. Hillsdale, NJ: Erlbaum.

Greenberg, M. T, & Snell, J. L. (1997). Brain development and emotional development: The role of teaching in organizing the frontal lobe. In P. Salovey and D. J. Sluyter (eds.), *Emotional development and emotional intelligence* (pp. 92–119). New York: Basic Books.

Greenberg. M. T., Kusche, C. A., & Speltz, M. (1991). Emotional regulation, self-control and psychopathology: The role of relationships in early childhood. In D. Cicchetti and S. Toth (eds.), *Internalizing and externalizing expressions of dysfunction: Rochester Symposium on Developmental Psychopathology*, Vol. 2 (pp. 21–55). New York: Cambridge University Press.

Greenberg, M. T., Domitrovich, C., & Bumbarger, B. (2001). The prevention of mental disorders in school age children: Current state of the field. *Prevention and Treatment* 4(1), 1–48.

Greenberg, M. T., Domitrovich, C., Graczyk, P. A., & Zins, J. E. (2005). The study of implementation in school-based preventive interventions: Theory, research and practice. *Promotion of Mental Health and Prevention of Mental Behavioral Disorders* 3, 1–62.

Guglielmo, H. M., & Tryon, G. S. (2001). Social skills training in an integrated preschool program. *School Psychology Quarterly* 16, 158–75; doi: 10.1521/scpq.16.2.158.18701.

Hallfors, D. D., Pankratz, M., & Hartman, S. (2007). Does federal policy support the use of scientific evidence in school-based prevention programs? *Prevention Science* 8, 75–81; doi: 10.1007/s11121–006–0058-x.

Hamre, B. K., & Pianta, R. C. (2007). Learning opportunities in preschool and early elementary classrooms. In R. C. Pianta, M. J. Cox, and

K. Snow (eds.), *School readiness and the transition to school* (pp. 49–84). Baltimore: Brookes.

Hamre, B. K., Justice, L. M., Pianta, R. C., Kilday, C., Sweeney, B., Downer, J. T., & Leach, A. (2010). Implementation fidelity of MyTeachingPartner literacy and language activities: Association with preschoolers' language and literacy growth. *Early Childhood Research Quarterly* 25, 329–47; doi: 10.1016/j.ecresq.2009.07.002.

Han, S. S., & Weiss, B. (2005). Sustainability of teacher implementation of school-based mental health programs. *Journal of Abnormal Child Psychology* 33, 665–79; doi: 10.1007/s10802–005–7646–2.

Haskins, R., & Loeb, S. (2007). *A plan to improve the quality of teaching in American schools. The future of children (policy brief)*. Princeton, NJ: Woodrow Wilson School of Public and International Affairs.

Hoffman, M. L. (1963). Parent discipline and the child's consideration of others. *Child Development* 34, 573–88.

Howes, C., & Smith, E. W. (1995). Relations among child care quality, teacher behavior, children's play activities, emotional security, and cognitive activity in child care. *Early Childhood Research Quarterly* 10, 381–404; doi: 10.1016/0885–2006(95)90013–6.

Howes, C., Burchinal, M., Pianta, R., Bryant, D., Early, D., Clifford, R., et al. (2008). Ready to learn? Children's pre-academic achievement in pre-kindergarten programs. *Early Childhood Research Quarterly* 23, 27–50; doi: 10.1016/j.ecresq.2007.05.002.

Institute of Medicine, National Research Council (2010). *Preventing mental, emotional, and behavioral disorders among young people: Progress and possibilities*, M. E. O'Connell, T. Boat, and K. E. Warner (eds.). Washington: Institute of Medicine.

International Reading Association & National Association for the Education of Young Children (1998). Learning to read and write: Developmentally appropriate practices for young children. *Young Children* 53, 30–46.

Izard, C. E., Trentacosta, C. J., King, K. A., & Mostow, A. J. (2004). An emotion-based prevention program for Head Start children. *Early Education and Development* 15(4), 407–22; doi: 10.1207/s15566935eed1504_4.

Izard, C. E., King, K. A., Trentacosta, C. J., Morgan, J. K., Laurenceau, J., Krauthamer-Ewing, E. S., & Finlon, K. J. (2008). Accelerating the development of emotion competence in Head Start children: Effects on adaptive and maladaptive behavior. *Development and Psychopathology* 20, 369–97; doi: 10.1017/S0954579408000175.

Joseph, G. E., & Strain, P. S. (2003). Comprehensive evidence-based social-emotional curricula for young children: An analysis of efficacious adoption potential. *Topics in Early Childhood Special Education* 23, 65–76; doi: 10.1177/02711214030230020201.

Joyce, B., & Showers, B. (2002). *Student achievement through staff development*, 3rd ed. Alexandria, VA: Association for Supervision and Curriculum Development.

Justice, L. M., & Pullen, P. C. (2003). Promising interventions for promoting emergent literacy skills: Three evidence-based approaches. *Topics in Early Childhood Special Education* 23, 99–113; doi: 10.1177/02711214030230030101.

Justice, L. M., Mashburn, A. J., Hamre, B. K., & Pianta, R. C. (2008). Quality of language and literacy instruction in preschool classrooms serving at-risk pupils. *Early Childhood Research Quarterly* 23, 51–68; doi: 10.1016/j.ecresq.2007.09.004.

Kalichman, S. C., Cherry, C., White, D., Pope, H., Cain, D., & Kalichman, M. (2007). Altering key characteristics of a disseminated effective behavioral intervention for HIV positive adults: The "Healthy Relationships" experience. *Journal of Primary Prevention* 28(2), 145–53; doi: 10.1007/s10935–007–0083–y.

Kallestead, J. H., & Olweus, D. (2003). Predicting teachers' and schools' implementation of the Olweus bullying prevention program: A multilevel study. *Prevention & Treatment* 6.

Kellam, S., & Langevin, D. J. (2003). A framework for understanding "evidence" in prevention research and programs. *Prevention Science* 4(3), 137–53; doi: 10.1023/A:1024693321963.

Knoche, L. L., Sheridan, S. M., Edwards, C. P., & Osborn, A. Q. (2010). Implementation of a relationships-based school readiness intervention: A multidimensional approach to fidelity measurement for early childhood. *Early Childhood Research Quarterly* 25, 299–313; doi: 10.1016/j.ecresq.2009.05.003.

Kontos, S., & Wilcox-Herzog, A. (1997). Influences on children's competence in early childhood classrooms. *Early Childhood Research Quarterly* 12, 247–62; doi: 10.1016/S0885–2006(97)90002–8.

Krevans, J., & Gibbs, J. C. (1996). Parent's use of inductive discipline: Relation to children's empathy and prosocial behavior. *Child Development* 67, 3263–77; doi: 10.2307/1131778.

Kusche, C. A., Riggs, R. S., & Greenberg, M. T. (1999). PATHS: Using analytic knowledge to teach emotional literacy. *The American Psychoanalyst* 33, 1.

Kumpfer, K. L., Pinyuchon, M., deMelo, A. T., & Whiteside, H. O. (2008). Cultural adaptation process for international dissemination of the Strengthening Families Program. *Evaluation and the Health Professions* 31(2), 226–39; doi: 10.1177/0163278708315926.

Ladd, G. W., Herald, S. L., & Kochel, K. P. (2006). School readiness: Are there social prerequisites? *Early Education & Development* 17, 115–50. doi: 10.1207/s15566935eed1701_6.

Landry, S. H., Anthony, J. L., Swank, P. R., & Monseque-Bailey, P. (2009). Effectiveness of comprehensive professional development for teachers of at-risk preschoolers. *Journal of Educational Psychology* 101, 448–65; doi: 10.1037/a0013842.

LaParo, K. M., Pianta, R. C., & Stuhlman, M. (2004). The Classroom Assessment Scoring System: Findings from the prekindergarten year. *Elementary School Journal* 104, 409–26.

Leach, D. J., & Conto, H. (1999). The additional effects of process and outcome feedback following brief in-service training. *Educational Psychology* 19, 441–62; doi: 10.1080/0144341990190405.

Lin, H., Lawrence, F. R., & Gorrell, J. (2003). Kindergarten teachers' views of children's readiness for school. *Early Childhood Research Quarterly* 18, 225–37; doi: 10.1016/S0885-2006(03)00028-0.

Lynch, K. B., Geller, S. R., & Schmidt, M. G. (2004). Multi-year evaluation of the effectiveness of a resilience-based prevention program for young children. *Journal of Primary Prevention* 24(3), 335–53; doi: 10.1023/B:JOPP.0000018052.12488.d1.

Manning, M., Homel, R., & Smith, C. (2010). A meta-analysis of the effects of early developmental prevention programs in at-risk populations on non-health outcomes in adolescence. *Children and Youth Services Review* 32, 506–19; doi: 10.1016/j.childyouth.2009.11.003.

Mashburn, A. J., & Pianta, R. C. (2006). Social relationships and school readiness. *Early Education and Development* 17(1), 151–76; doi: 10.1207/s15566935eed1701_7.

McCall, R. B. (2009). Evidence-based programming in the context of practice and policy. *Social Policy Report* 23(3), 3–18.

Mihalek, S., Irwin, K., Fagan, A., Ballard, D., & Elliott, D. (2004). *Successful program implementation: Lessons from blueprints*. Washington: U.S. Department of Justice, Office of Justice Programs. Retrieved from www.ojp.usdo.gov/ojjdp.

Mize, J., & Ladd, G. W. (1990). Toward the development of successful social skills training for preschool children. In S. R. Asher and J. D. Coie (eds.), *Peer rejection in childhood* (pp. 274–308). New York: Cambridge University Press.

National School Readiness Indicators Initiative (2005). *Getting ready: Findings from the National School Readiness Indicators Initiative*. Providence, RI: Rhode Island Kids Count.

NICHD Early Child Care Research Network (1998). Early child care and self-control, compliance and problem behavior at twenty-four and thirty-six months. *Child Development* 69, 1145–70.

NICHD Early Child Care Research Network (2000a). Characteristics and quality of child care for toddlers and preschoolers. *Applied Developmental Science* 4, 116–35; doi: 10.1207/S1532480XADS0403_2.

NICHD Early Child Care Research Network (2000b). The relation of child care to cognitive and language development. *Child Development* 71, 960–80; doi: 10.1111/1467-8624.00202.

Noell, G. H., Witt, J. C., Slider, N. J., Connell, J. E., Gatti, S. L., Williams, K. L., Koenig, J. L., et al. (2005). Treatment implementation following behavioral consultation in schools: A comparison of three follow-up strategies. *School Psychology Review* 34, 87–106.

Nores, M., & Barnett, W. S. (2010). Benefits of early childhood interventions across the world: (Under) Investing in the very young. *Economics of Education Review* 29, 271–82.

O'Donnell, C. L. (2008). Defining, conceptualizing, and measuring fidelity of implementation and its relationship to outcomes in K–12 curriculum intervention research. *Review of Educational Research* 78(1), 33–84.

Odom, S. L., Fleming, K., Diamond, K., Lieber, J., Hanson, M., Butera, G., Horn, E., Palmer, S., & Marquis, J. (2010). Examining different forms of implementation and in early childhood curriculum research. *Early Childhood Research Quarterly* 25, 314–28; doi: 10.1016/j.ecresq.2010.03.001.

Pankratz, M., Hallfors, D., & Cho, H. (2002). Measuring perceptions of innovation adoption: The diffusion of a federal drug prevention policy. *Health Education Research* 17, 315–26. doi: 10.1093/her/17.3.315.

Parcel, G. S., Ross, J. G., Lavin, A. T., Portnow, D., Nelson, G. D., & Winters, F. (1991). Enhancing implementation of the teenage health teaching modules. *Journal of School Health* 61, 35–38; doi: 10.1111/j.1746-1561.1991.tb07857.x.

Parcel, G. S., Perry, C. L., Kelder, S. H., Elder, J. P., Mitchell, P. D., Lytle, L. A., Johnson, C. C., & Stone, E. J. (2003). School climate and the institutionalization of the CATCH program. *Health Education & Behavior* 30, 489–502; doi: 10.1177/1090198103253650.

Perry, C. L., Murray, D. M., & Griffin, G. (1990). Evaluating the stateside dissemination of smoking prevention curricula: Factors in teacher compliance. *Journal of School Health* 60, 501–4; doi: 10.1111/j.1746-1561.1990.tb05890.x.

Pianta, R. C., LaParo, K. M., & Hamre, B. K. (2008). *Classroom assessment scoring system (CLASS) manual: Pre–K*. Baltimore: Brookes.

Pianta, R. C., Mashburn, A. J., Downer, J. T., Hamre, B. K., & Justice, L. (2008). Effects of web-mediated professional development resources on teacher-child interactions in pre-kindergarten classrooms. *Early Childhood Research Quarterly* 23, 431–51; doi: 10.1016/j.ecresq.2008.02.001.

Pianta, R., Howes, C., Burchinal, M., Bryant, D., Clifford., R., Early, D., & Barbarin, O. (2005). Features of pre-Kindergarten programs, classrooms, and teachers: Do they predict observed classroom quality and child-teacher interactions? *Applied Developmental Science* 9, 144–59; doi: 10.1207/s1532480xads0903_2.

Pitchford, J., Shaffer, K., Becker, K., & Domitrovich, C. E. (2010, May). Supporting an integrated universal intervention: The PATHS to PAX coaching model. Presentation at the International PATHS Conference, Harrisburg, PA.

Putnam, R. T., & Borko, H. (2000). What do new views of knowledge and thinking have to say about research on teacher learning. *Educational Researcher* 29, 4–15.

Ransford, C. R., Greenberg, M. T., Domitrovich, C. E., Small, M., & Jacobson, L. (2009). The role of teachers' psychological experiences and perceptions of curriculum supports on the implementation of a social-emotional learning curriculum. *School Psychology Review* 38, 510–32.

Raver, C. C., Blackburn, E. K., & Bancroft, M. (1999). Relations between effective emotional self regulation, attentional control, and low income preschoolers' social competence with peers. *Early Education and Development* 10, 333–50; doi: 10.1207/s15566935eed1003_6.

Raver, C. C., Jones, S. M., Li-Grining, C. P., Metzger, M., Champion, K. M., & Sardin, L. (2008). Improving preschool classroom processes: Preliminary findings from a randomized trial implemented in Head Start settings.

Early Childhood Research Quarterly 23, 10–26; doi: 10.1016/j.ecresq.2007.09.001.

Raver, C. C., Jones, S. M., Li-Grining, C. P., Zhai, F., Bub, K., & Pressler, E. (2011). CSRP's impact on low-income preschoolers' pre-academic skills: Self-regulation as a mediating mechanism. *Child Development*. 82(1), 362–78.

Raver, C. C., Jones, S. M., Li-Grining, C. P., Zhai, F., Metzger, M., & Solomon, B. (2009). Targeting children's behavior problems in preschool classrooms: A cluster-randomized controlled trial. *Journal of Consulting and Clinical Psychology* 77, 302–16; doi: 10.1037/a0015302.

Rimm-Kaufman, S. E., Pianta, R. C., & Cox, M. J. (2000). Teachers' judgements of problems in the transition to kindergarten. *Early Childhood Research Quarterly* 15, 147–66.

Rimm-Kaufman, S. E., LaParo, K. M., Downer, J. T., & Pianta, R. C. (2005). The contribution of classroom setting and quality of instruction to children's behavior in the kindergarten classroom. *Elementary School Journal* 105, 377–94; doi: 10.1086/429948.

Ringwalt, C. L., Ennett, S., Johnson, R., Rohrbach, L. A., Simons-Rudolph, A., Vincus, A., & Thorne, J. (2003). Factors associated with fidelity to substance use prevention curriculum guides in the nation's middle schools. *Health Education and Behavior* 30, 375–91; doi: 10.1177/1090198103030003010.

Robin, A. L., Schneider, M., & Dolnick, M. (1976). The Turtle Technique: An extended case study of self-control in the classroom. *Psychology in the Schools* 13, 449–53; doi:10.1002/1520-6807(197610)13:4=449::AID-PITS2310130420=3.0.CO;2-W.

Rogers, E. M. (2003). *Diffusion of innovations*, 2nd ed. New York: Free Press.

Rohrbach, L. A., Graham, J. W., & Hansen, W. B. (1993). Diffusion of a school-based substance abuse prevention program: Predictors of program implementation. *Preventive Medicine* 22, 237–60; doi: 10.1006/pmed.1993.1020.

Rose, D. J., & Church, R. J., (1998). Learning to teach: The acquisition and maintenance of teaching skills. *Journal of Behavioral Education* 8, 5–35; doi: 10.1023/A:1022860606825.

Ross, J. G., Luepker, R. V., Nelson, G. D., Saavedra, P., & Hubbard, B. M. (1991). Teenage health teaching modules: Impact of teacher training on implementation and student outcomes. *Journal of School Health* 61, 31–8; doi: 10.1111/j.1746-1561.1991.tb07856.x.

Scott-Little, C., Kagan, S. L., & Frelow, V. S. (2006). Conceptualization of readiness and the content of early learning standards: The intersection of policy and research? *Early*

Childhood Research Quarterly 21, 153–73; doi: 10.1016/j.ecresq.2006.04.003.

Scott, T. M., & Martinek, G. (2006). Coaching positive behavior support in school settings. *Journal of Positive Behavior Interventions* 8, 165–73; doi: 10.1177/10983007060080030501.

Serna, L. A., & Lau-Smith, J. A., (1995). Learning with PURPOSE: Self determination skills for students who are at-risk for school and community failure. An instructor's manual. Unpublished manuscript, Department of Special Education, College of Education, University of New Mexico, Albuquerque.

Serna, L., Nielsen, E., Lambros, K., & Forness, S. (2000). Primary prevention with children at risk for emotional or behavioral disorders: Data on a universal intervention for Head Start classrooms. *Behavioral Disorders* 26, 70–84.

Sheridan, S. M., Knoche, L. L., Edwards, C. P., Bovaird, J. A., & Kupzyk, K. A. (2010). Parent engagement and school readiness: Effects of the Getting Ready intervention on preschool children's social-emotional competencies. *Early Education and Development* 21, 125–56; doi: 10.1080/10409280902783517.

Shonkoff, J. P., & Phillips, D. A. (2000). *From neurons to neighborhoods: The science of early childhood development.* Washington: National Academy Press.

Shure, M. B. (1981). Interpersonal problem solving: A cog in the wheel of social cognition. In D. J. White and M. D. Smye (eds.), *Social competence* (pp. 158–85). New York: Guilford Press.

Shure, M. B., & Spivack, G. (1978). *Problem-solving techniques in childrearing.* San Francisco: Jossey-Bass.

Shure, M. B., & Spivack, G. (1982). Interpersonal problem-solving in young children: A cognitive approach to prevention. *American Journal of Community Psychology* 10, 341–56.

Spoth, R., Guyll, M., Lillehoj, C. J., Redmond, C., & Greenberg, M. T. (2007). PROSPER study of evidence-based intervention implementation quality by community-university partnerships. *Journal of Community Psychology* 35(8), 981–99; doi: 10.1002/jcop.20207.

Sussman, S., & Palinkas, L. A. (2008). Reflections on international translation of evidence-based health behavior programs. *Evaluation and the Health Professions* 31(3), 323–30; doi: 10.1177/0163278708320168.

Sylva, K., Melhuish, E., Sammons, P., Siraj-Blatchford, I., & Taggart, B. (2004). The Effective Provision of Pre-school Education (EPPE) Project: Final report. (Tech. Paper 12, Department of Education and Skills (DfES), London.

Vargas-Barón, E. (2009). *Going to scale: Early childhood development in Latin America.* Washington: The World Bank.

Webster-Stratton, C., & Reid, M. J. (2008). Strengthening social and emotional competence in socio-economically disadvantaged young children: Preschool and kindergarten school-based curricula. In W. H. Brown, S. L. Odom, & S. R. McConnell (eds.), *Social competence of young children: Risk, disability, and intervention* (pp. 185–203). Baltimore: Brookes.

Webster-Stratton, C., Reid, M. J., & Hammond, M. (2004). Treating children with early-onset conduct problems: Intervention outcomes for parent, child, and teacher training. *Journal of Clinical Child and Adolescent Psychology* 33, 105–24; doi: 10.1207/S15374424JCCP3301_11.

Webster-Stratton, C., Reid, M. J., & Stoolmiller, M. (2008). Preventing conduct problems and improving school readiness: Evaluation of the Incredible Years Teacher and child training programs in high-risk schools. *Journal of Child Psychology and Psychiatry* 49(5), 471–88; doi: 10.1111/j.1469-7610.2007.01861.x.

Weisz, J. R., Sandler, I. N., Durlak, J. A., & Anton, B. S. (2005). Promoting and protecting youth mental health through evidence-based prevention and treatment. *American Psychologist* 60, 628–48; doi: 10.1037/0003-066X.60.6.628.

Zins, J. E., Weissberg, R. P., Wang, M. C., & Walberg, H. J. (eds.) (2004). *Building academic success on social and emotional learning: What does the research say?* New York: Teachers College Press.

CHAPTER 13

Framework for Improving the Impact of School-Based Social Competence Programs

Keith J. Topping

Social competence is a very broad term which can mislead schools and other systems. It is the goal of social and emotional learning. However, as we shall see, teachers can have very different ideas about what it constitutes, and students may receive or interpret different ideas from teachers.

The Social Construction of the Concept

How to define *social competence* has been a vexing question for decades. Arguments on the issue are often characterized by a lack of shared vocabulary and conceptual frameworks. Certainly, the whole issue is much more complex than might be assumed by the naive onlooker.

What is attended to in social behavior depends on the characteristics of the model, the characteristics of the situational context, and the characteristics of the observer. Different people implicitly (or occasionally explicitly) choose to see situations completely differently. Having attended an event, whatever meaning is made of the

event may or may not be retained more or less accurately. (The notion has been suggested of a "social memory" to parallel the notion of "social intelligence.") Beyond this, perceiving and recalling a behavior does not enable reproduction of it automatically, especially in a novel context requiring transfer and generalization of learning. Repeated practice may be necessary to achieve any degree of fluency or automaticity, especially when feedback in response to early attempts is mixed. Even if the socially competent behavior is firmly ensconced within the repertoire of the actor, the motivation for its emission may be absent. This again may depend on the actor's perceptions of a particular social context and the rewards and punishments operating within it.

Current conceptions of social competence give equal weight to the behavioral, cognitive, and affective domains. The early emphasis on behavior led to much discussion of "social skills" rather than the broader concept of "social competence." However, even social skills were conceptualized at a molecular level (specific behaviors such as eye contact and voice intonation) and also from a molar perspective (with emphasis on more global behaviors such as assertiveness). Gesten et al. (1987) suggested that *social competence* is "the most general or over-arching term, which represents a summary judgment of performance across a range of interpersonal situations," whereas *social skills* refers to "the highly specific patterns of learned observable behavior, both verbal and nonverbal, through which we influence others and attempt to meet our needs" (p. 27). This suggests that both terms can be used concurrently (with care) to describe different perspectives and levels of analysis of social behavior. It was not until the 1980s that the importance of affect as a major contributor to social behavior was fully recognized. Research identified affective factors that also influenced social behavior, such as anxiety and low self-esteem. There was a growing interest in the emotional functioning of children, specifically in the ability of children to think about emotions and consequently to regulate their emotions.

Thinking has moved from focusing on the acquisition and demonstration of behavioral skills by the individual to placing greater emphasis on the ability to achieve social outcomes. Social outcomes might include peer acceptance, acceptance by significant adults (e.g., parents and teachers), school adjustment, mental health status, and absence of negative contact with the legal system. Signs of successful socialization also have been listed as establishing and maintaining positive social relationships; refraining from harming others; serving as constructive, contributing members of one's peer group, family, school, workplace, and community; engaging in health-enhancing and health-protective behaviors; and avoiding engaging in behaviors that may lead to negative consequences (e.g., substance abuse, unwanted pregnancy, social isolation, AIDS, and dropping out of school) (Consortium on the School-Based Promotion of Social Competence, 1994). However, it is clear that many of these signs reflect the influence of adults rather than the views of students.

Theoretical models that could account for interaction of the cognitive, affective, and behavioral components of social competence were beginning to be constructed. A five-stage social information-processing model was proposed by Crick & Dodge (1994), suggesting a sequence whereby a child is considered to

- Encode cues that are both internal (feelings) and external (observed actions of others)
- Interpret those cues (causal and intent inferences)
- Clarify goals
- Decide on a response
- Enact the behavior

This might be expressed alternatively as perception, analysis, prioritization, and action. The emphasis on the ability to perceive and analyze both internal states and external behavior is useful – in some individuals, the internal capability may operate at a very different level from the external capability.

These models avoid the value issues in relation to outcomes by using words such as *appropriate* that imply (but perhaps unhelpfully do not state) local and specific subjectivity. That social behavior and achievement of social outcomes are only judged to be "competent" according to the prevailing or dominant values and norms of the social environment. This value relativity was expressed eloquently by the Consortium on the School-Based Promotion of Social Competence (1994), asserting that social competence comprised a set of core skills, attitudes, abilities, and feelings given functional meaning by the contexts of culture, neighborhood, and situation. Thus social competence could be viewed in terms of the life skills for adaptation to diverse ecologies and settings. Of course, this means both within school and outside school.

A Definition of Social Competence

Given all these issues, how can we make sense of this area? The definition devised by me is as follows: "Social competence is possessing and using the ability to integrate thinking, feeling and behavior to achieve social tasks and outcomes valued in the host context and culture" (Topping, Bremner, & Holmes, 2000a).

In a school setting, these tasks and outcomes might include accessing the school curriculum successfully, meeting associated personal social and emotional needs, and developing transferable skills and attitudes of value beyond school. However, very different social competencies are required and valued in different contexts. Behaviors that are dysfunctional and disapproved of in one context may be functional and approved of in another. Traditional operational definitions of desirable skills and outcomes are likely to be highly adult-centered and may neglect the child's own objectives. It follows that peer definition and assessment of social competence may be equally or more valid than adult assessment. Similarly, children perceived by adults as having a "poor self-image" within an adult-dominated context may feel very differently about themselves in a peer-dominated context – children have multiple self-concepts as well as multiple intelligences.

The given definition suggests that social competence is not only knowledge- and information-processing capacity but also a set of component skills or procedures applied conditionally, together with a nest of emotional reactions. The skills may include perception of relevant social cues, interpretation of social cues, realistic anticipation of obstacles to personally desired behavior, anticipation of consequences of behavior for self and others, generation of effective solutions to interpersonal problems, translation of social decisions into effective social behaviors, and expression of a positive sense of self-efficacy. Students are learning to think more rationally, so many of their immediate emotional reactions need through learning to be transformed into more explicit behavioral expressions over which they have conscious choice.

A number of the putative components of social competence tend to be expressed negatively, seeking to define social competence as the absence of social incompetence. This highlights the need to term specific behaviors as socially competent or incompetent, not to so label children. Although it might in principle be meaningful to term a person socially competent as a function of the number of social skills he or she possesses, the number of contexts in which the person could demonstrate them, and the number of different objectives the person could thereby achieve, quantifying these performance indicators would prove very difficult.

Why Is Social Competence Important?

School is very much a social environment with many demands on social competence. In schools, young people who cannot get along with their peers in the classroom are likely to be perceived as distractible, if not disruptive; their performance and progress are likely to suffer; and there may be unpleasant aftereffects outside class. In short, you get in trouble, you don't learn, and you get picked on. If your search for a context in which you can feel socially competent and accepted leads you into illegal activities, your social competence in relation to police officers soon might be tested.

Beyond the school years, the world of work also has many social demands. Social competence is one of the transferable skills constantly in high demand from employers. For employers, the important things are not what you know, but what you can do and be quickly trained to do, and the doing almost always will be in a social environment. Social competence is also essential in the successful conduct of everyday life – from minor but high-frequency community activities such as shopping, through establishing and enjoying the support and benefits of friendship and neighborliness, to major but low-frequency home-based activities such as partner bonding and producing children. Relating to the extended family in a large gathering is another example of a situation making considerable demands on social competence. Social competence is also a factor in resilience – those who are socially competent and socially integrated are likely to be more able to withstand the stresses of life and probably more able to withstand temptations to become involved in self-damaging behavior such as drug taking.

What Are the Major Findings on Effectiveness?

Policy and practice in education often have been shaped by what "feels right" to teachers, by contagious fashions that sweep in and then leave without trace, and by the short-term expedients of politicians who feel the need to be seen to be doing something in order to secure votes. However, recent years have seen much talk of a movement to "evidence-based education," effectiveness, and cost-effectiveness.

Topping, Holmes, & Bremner (2000b) systematically reviewed over 700 rigorous research reports of outcome evaluations of school-based programs designed to enhance social competence (www.dundee. ac.uk/eswce/research/projects/socialcompetence). Access to this information was interactive in an electronic bibliographic database, so practitioners could seek answers to questions currently relevant to themselves and their contexts, framed in their own vocabulary and schema. Keywords describing different types of interventions fell into seven categories of intervention: *behavior analysis and modification, counseling and therapeutic, social skills training, peer-mediated, cognitive and self-managed, multiple*, and *miscellaneous*. In addition to considering the contents of the survey, users also should reflect upon what is *not* within it – what methods and programs that are already in use or being promoted do *not* appear to have any satisfactory evidence of effectiveness.

Even where there *is* evidence within the survey of the effectiveness of an approach, that evidence must be interpreted thoughtfully and carefully by users because there are a number of pitfalls. In particular, even if identical programs or methods actually were deployed, the quality of program delivery (or *implementation integrity*) may have been very different in two different sites. Or the programs may have had different objectives, or focused on different age groups, or targeted different types of children, or involved different numbers of children, or had different gender balances among the participants, or were delivered in different locations, or were set in different geographic or socioeconomic areas, or used different measures of effectiveness in different domains (e.g., cognitive, affective, behavioral). Relatively few research reports include information about the generalization of any gains (e.g., to other situations) or the maintenance of any gains (e.g., over time after the end of the program), although both these measures are crucial to estimating practical effectiveness and certainly cost-effectiveness. Regarding the latter, it is relatively unusual to find detailed information about the real total cost of implementing a program, let alone the calculation of unit cost per participant or overall cost-effectiveness.

Behavior analysis and modification–based programs were consistently reported to be effective and robust, especially when used in combination and focused on classroom behavior. However, many studies had small samples, and issues of generalization and maintenance were not ubiquitously addressed. Ease of implementation and durability may be important factors because some research suggests that the quality and consistency of classroom management are more important than its type or style, and the context of implementation may have more effect than the program itself.

Counseling and therapeutic approaches were characterized by very wide variety and very poor quality evaluation research. Lengthy individual professional counseling seems no more effective than brief group counseling by nonprofessionals, although behaviorally oriented methods tend to come out better. One or two forms of therapy have shown some promise.

Social skills training has shown moderate and variable effectiveness, higher for withdrawn children than for those acting out or with learning difficulties. Multimethod approaches involving modeling and coaching that program for generalization over time and contexts tended to be most effective.

Peer-mediated interventions include peer tutoring and peer reinforcement, both of which have been found effective, with potential benefits for the helpers as well as the helped. Peer-mediated conflict-resolution training encompasses various approaches, where implementation integrity is sometimes in doubt and the quality of research variable. Such programs show some evidence of moderate but mixed effectiveness, with very limited information about generalization and maintenance.

Cognitive and self-managed approaches have shown moderate to large effects. More mixed results from small studies and some concern about transfer from knowledge to behavior and maintenance of gains are counterbalanced by large-scale long-term studies that have shown substantial gains maintained over follow-up periods as long as four years. The Spivack & Shure (1974) and Elias & Clabby (1992) programs have proved particularly impressive. Interventions focusing specifically on anger control have shown more mixed results.

Multiple-component broad-spectrum programs to promote social competence have shown some effects, but programs are various and difficult to compare. Overall, outcomes are mixed and moderate and statistical significance not always attained, whereas evidence for generalization and maintenance of gains is limited.

The amount of evaluation evidence on any particular program does not necessarily indicate the extent to which it is used by practitioners. There are a number of programs in widespread use that do *not* have a significant evaluation literature and others that are well evaluated but not particularly well known or widely used. Even for initiatives in categories where high effectiveness has been demonstrated in the research literature, it cannot be assumed that effectiveness in your own initiative will follow automatically.

More Recent Reviews of Effectiveness

From a European perspective, a substantial work is the review of nineteen meta-analyses of 700 studies and further meta-analysis of seventy-six controlled studies (for 1997–2008) of universal socioemotional learning programs carried out by Diekstra (2008). *Universality* implies that the programs were delivered to all pupils, not to a subsection considered especially in need.

From the analysis of meta-analyses, some programs involved purely classroom curricula, whereas others also included activities outside school, such as community service learning (helping others) or varying degrees of parental involvement. There also were differences in the breadth of the programs: Some encouraged very broad socioemotional skills and sought to raise self-esteem, whereas others focused more directly on specific skills (such as refusal skills). The type of professional presenting the program was very diverse, as was the length of the program. Indicators of success or outcome measures also varied widely. Most studies stemmed from the United States, the others largely from the English-speaking world – thus there are issues about appropriateness for other cultures.

The meta-analyses reviewed outcomes of studies in terms of a change in (1) social and emotional skills, (2) attitudes toward self (self-concept) and others (prosocial attitudes), (3) externalizing or behavioral problems and disorders, such as aggressive, disruptive, and violent behavior, (4) antisocial behavior, such as criminal behavior, (5) drug abuse, (6) internalizing or emotional problems and disorders, such as stress, anxiety, depression, and suicidal tendencies, (7) attitudes and behavior toward school (e.g., truancy and absence), and (8) school test scores and school grades.

Overall, the average student who participated in a social-emotional learning (SEL)/SFL program was not only significantly better than before in recognizing and managing emotions, establishing and maintaining positive relationships, communicating with others, and handling interpersonal conflicts effectively, but he or she also was significantly better in these respects than his or her average peer who did not follow such a program. Evidence for SEL programs reducing or preventing externalizing problems and disorders is also extensive and convincing, as is the evidence that such effects are mediated by the improvement of social and emotional skills. Programs that are theoretically consistent and highly interactive and use a variety of didactic or "work" forms are implemented in small groups, cover both general and domain-specific skills (comprehensive life skills programs), and are cast within supporting community or environmental strategies are the most effective. It appears that addressing both general (social and emotional) skills and problem- or disorder-related attitudes and skills (such as drug-refusal skills) within the same program is the most effective way to reduce or prevent problems and disorders as well as to enhance overall development.

Low-socioeconomic-status children profit at least as much and often more from programs than other children. The same is true with regard to ethnicity. Program effects are consistent at all grade levels in primary and secondary school; that is, it is not true that "the earlier the better." There is no evidence that either gender responds more favorably to programs. Regarding program deliverers, programs focusing more on secondary antisocial problems (e.g., drug abuse) were more likely to be delivered by professionals external to the school, and studies were divided on whether teachers and externals were equally competent or peer leaders and/or external professionals were more competent.

The issue of dosage is of relevance (the amount of time spent on the program). Programs of short duration or low intensity (no more than eight to ten sessions or two months' duration) often show considerable smaller or even insignificant effect sizes. Apparently SEL programs, in order to be effective, have to be of a certain length or duration, most probably somewhere between three and six months (with weekly classes). Several meta-analyses suggest that subsequent "booster" sessions may be important.

However, there is still a considerable shortage of studies with longer follow-up periods (i.e., twelve months or more). Some meta-analyses report a decrease in effects over time, but mostly the decrease is not so substantial that the original effects completely dissipate. In the majority of studies, the differences between intervention and control groups at follow-up are still significant. Some other meta-analyses point to stability of effects over time, and others report a so-called sleeper effect (effects at follow-up, six months or longer after termination, are larger than at post-test).

From the new meta-analysis, about a quarter of the results came from continental Europe, and almost half reported follow-up. Programs typically were up to a year in duration and delivered by teachers. A quarter of reported interventions were directed at a change of school culture and climate (the so-called whole-school approach) and often did not have special sessions. More secondary than primary studies were included. Effect sizes in the short term were high for social skills, academic achievement, positive self-image, and prosocial behavior. However, they were low or negative for antisocial behavior, mental disorders, and substance abuse. In middle- to long-term outcomes, academic achievement was the most affected sector, with a moderate effect size. Social skills, positive self-image, and prosocial behavior had low effect sizes. This meta-analysis does raise more questions regarding the longer-term duration of effects from programs, although it is acknowledged that long-term effects may be difficult to measure. Interestingly, it found that short-term programs tended to be more effective than long-term programs. It also found that European programs were no more or less effective than those from North America.

Readers also will wish to consult the Collaborative for Academic, Social, and Emotional Learning (CASEL) website (www.casel.org). Among the wealth of evidence there, the meta-analysis by Payton et al. (2008) is among the weightiest. This report summarizes results from three large-scale reviews of research on the impact of SEL programs on elementary and middle school students. Collectively, the three reviews included 317 studies and involved 324,303 children. SEL programs yielded multiple benefits in each review and were effective in both school and after-school settings and for students with and without behavioral and emotional problems. They also were effective across the kindergarten–eighth grade range and for racially and ethnically diverse students from urban, rural, and suburban settings. SEL programs improved students' social-emotional skills, attitudes about self and others, connection to school, positive social behavior, and academic performance; they also reduced students' conduct problems and emotional distress. Furthermore, school staff (e.g., teachers, student support staff) carried out SEL programs effectively, indicating that they can be incorporated into routine educational practice. In addition, SEL programming improved students' academic performance by 11 to 17 percentile points across the three reviews, indicating that they offer students a practical educational benefit.

The three reviews were as follows: (1) universal review of 180 studies that examined the impact of interventions appropriate for a general student body without any identified behavioral or emotional problems or difficulties, (2) indicated review of eighty studies focused on interventions that worked with students displaying early signs of behavioral or emotional problems, and (3) after-school review of fifty-seven studies of SEL in after-school programs that primarily involved students without identified problems.

Studies that collected data at follow-up indicated that these effects remained over time – although they were not as strong as the results at post-test (i.e., immediately after the intervention). The most common program duration was from one semester to an entire school year, with a mean of forty-five sessions. In two of the reviews (universal and after school), the authors found that interventions using four recommended practices for skill training (termed the SAFE programs) were more effective than programs that did not follow these recommendations. Each letter in the acronym SAFE refers to a recommended practice for teaching skills:

- *Sequenced.* Does the program apply a planned set of activities to develop skills sequentially in a step-by-step fashion?
- *Active.* Does the program use active forms of learning such as role-plays and behavioral rehearsal with feedback?
- *Focused.* Does the program devote sufficient time exclusively to developing social and emotional skills?
- *Explicit.* Does the program target specific social and emotional skills?

However, in the universal review in the short term, only SEL skills yielded a high effect (0.60), whereas attitudes toward self and others, positive social behavior, conduct problems, emotional distress, and academic performance had modest effect sizes (0.23–0.28). At follow-up, again SEL skills had the highest effect size (0.36), with the others varying from 0.12 to 0.17, except for academic skills, which had increased to 0.32. In the review of studies of students with special difficulties, rather better effect sizes were evident (e.g., SEL skills 0.77, others from 0.38–0.50). At follow-up, effect sizes again were relatively larger, ranging from 0.30 to 0.58. After-school programs showed smaller effect sizes to those of both universal and indicated programs.

What Can Teachers Do?

It may be tempting for enthusiastic teachers to search for the most effective program or package to implement. The problem here is that an isolated program may be implemented by a few staff, whereas most other staff carry on with business as usual. A through-going approach to developing social competence considers not only special programs but also the whole way in which day-to-day relationships in the school are conducted. If the two are not in alignment, long-term effects from an isolated program should not be expected.

Recommendations for Whole-School and Programmatic Approaches

Elias (2003) proposed a number of evidence-based goals for teachers wishing to develop social and emotional learning. Most of these are not focused on specific programs but address everyday relationships. First, effective, lasting social-emotional learning is built on caring relationships and warm but challenging classroom and school environments. Thus teachers should try to greet all students by name when they enter the school or classroom; begin and/or end the school day with brief periods of time for students to reflect on what they have learned recently and what they might want to learn next; create rules in the classroom that recognize positive behavior such as cooperation, caring, helping, encouragement, and support; be sure that discipline rules and procedures are clear, firm, fair, and consistent; show interest in their personal lives outside the school; and ask them what kinds of learning environments have been most and least successful for them in the past and use this information to guide instruction.

Second, life skills that promote academic and social-emotional learning must be taught explicitly at every grade level. The following have been proposed: *Know yourself and others:* Identify feelings – recognize and label one's feelings; be responsible – understand one's obligation to engage in ethical, safe, and legal behaviors; and recognize strengths – identify and cultivate one's positive qualities. *Make responsible decisions:* Manage emotions – regulate feelings so that they aid rather than impede the handling of situations; understand situations – accurately understand the circumstances one is in; set goals and plans – establish and work toward the achievement of specific short- and long-term outcomes; and solve

problems creatively – engage in a creative, disciplined process of exploring alternative possibilities that leads to responsible, goal-directed action, including overcoming obstacles to plans. *Care for others:* Show empathy – identifying and understanding the thoughts and feelings of others; respect others – believing that others deserve to be treated with kindness and compassion as part of our shared humanity; and appreciate diversity – understanding that individual and group differences complement one another and add strength and adaptability to the world around us. *Know how to act:* Communicate effectively – using verbal and nonverbal skills to express oneself and promote effective exchanges with others; build relationships – establishing and maintaining healthy and rewarding connections with individual and groups; negotiate fairly – achieving mutually satisfactory resolutions to conflict by addressing the needs of all concerned; refuse provocations – conveying and following through effectively with one's decision not to engage in unwanted, unsafe, unethical behavior; seek help – identifying the need for and accessing appropriate assistance and support in pursuit of needs and goals; and act ethically – guide decisions and actions by a set of principles or standards derived from recognized legal/professional codes or moral or faith-based systems of conduct.

Third, goal setting and problem solving provide direction and energy for learning. Ask students how they calm themselves down when they are very upset; remind them to use this strategy when they get into frustrating or difficult situations, or teach them a self-calming strategy. Have students set goals that include how they will get better at a particular area of study or schooling and how they will make a contribution to the classroom. Teach a problem-solving strategy for understanding fiction, history, or current events that uses frameworks such as those illustrated in the following examples or related ones. Here is an example that can be used for history. It can be adapted easily for discussion of current events.

- What is the event that you are thinking about? When and where did it happen? Put the event into words as a problem or choice or decision.
- What people or groups were involved in the problem? What were their different feelings? What were their points of view about the problem?
- What did each of these people or groups want to have happen? Try to put their goals into words.
- For each person or group, name some different options or solutions to the problem that they thought might help them to reach their goals.
- For each option or solution, picture all the things that might have happened next. Envision both long- and short-term consequences.
- What were the final decisions? How were they made? By whom? Why? Do you agree or disagree? Why?
- How was the solution carried out? What was the plan? What obstacles or roadblocks were met? How well was the problem solved? Why?
- Rethink it. What would you have chosen to do? Why?

Fourth, instruction for academic and social-emotional learning should use varied modalities and approaches to reach the diverse styles and preferences of all learners. Modalities include modeling, role-playing, art, dance, drama, working with materials and manipulatives, and digital media, computer technology, and the Internet. Also important for sound instruction are regular and constructive feedback, discussions that include open-ended questioning, and frequent reminders to use social-emotional skills in all aspects of school life. Vary instruction so that sometimes students are working in a large group, in small groups, in pairs, by themselves, at the computer, or on the Internet working with digital media. Provide opportunities for cross-age tutoring. Allow students to create exhibitions of what they learn in different subject areas that can be shared with other students, parents, and members of the community. Bring in experts and other individuals from the community to share knowledge, skills, customs, and stories with students.

Fifth, effective academic and social-emotional instruction follows from well-planned professional development for all school personnel and a system of support during the initial years of implementation. No lasting success in academic and social-emotional instruction can be expected without ongoing professional development for school personnel and support for their efforts as implementation proceeds. Time should be taken to train staff in children's social-emotional development, modeling and practice of effective teaching methods, multimodal instruction, regular coaching, and constructive feedback from colleagues.

Sixth, evaluation of efforts to promote social-emotional learning is an ethical responsibility that involves ongoing monitoring of implementation, assessing outcomes, and understanding opinions and reactions of those who carry out and receive the efforts. Schools need ways to keep track of student learning and performance in all areas, including the development of social-emotional abilities. Social-emotional learning efforts should be monitored regularly using multiple indicators to ensure that programs are carried out as planned. In addition, ongoing program outcome information and consumer satisfaction measures can be systematically gathered from multiple sources. Instruction must be adapted to changing circumstances. This occurs through examining the opinions of those delivering and receiving social-emotional instruction, documenting ways in which social-emotional programs are implemented and connected with academic instruction, evaluating outcomes observed among various groups of children in one's schools, and monitoring and addressing ongoing new developments, such as changes in district resources, state initiatives, and scientific advances.

School Self-Evaluation

Taking another direction, a framework for school self-evaluation using performance indicators has been devised (Topping & Bremner, 1998). This is intended to help schools undertake an audit of their current approaches to promoting social competence as well as to help schools develop locally relevant means for evaluating the impact of any innovations. It is a flexible framework designed to be fleshed out by negotiation between the main stakeholders who are most familiar with the local needs and ecology, perhaps in the context of staff development meetings.

The framework starts by considering obvious questions, such as What is social competence, and why is it important? Different teachers are likely to offer very different answers. It then encourages teachers to consider clarifying values, assessing ethos, identifying stakeholders and key players (internal and external), and identifying strengths, resources, and support (internal and external). It outlines how to conduct a "social competence audit" covering the purposes of the audit, primary and secondary sector differences, level (i.e., child, class, or schoolwide), specifying observable behavior, performance indicators, and developing more refined indicators.

The major stakeholders are the pupils themselves – How are their views to be heard? This is essential because an attempt to impose a monocultural version of "social competence" from the top down is doomed to failure. Equally, input from all teachers is essential, but in what groupings will you consider them – as attendance registration or form teachers, departmental subject teachers, specialist teachers, senior management, and so on? Some will fall into more than one group, but their grouping may determine how they access communication and consultation processes. What of part-time and temporary teachers and peripatetic teachers who serve several schools? Nonteaching staff, who often make shrewd observations regarding social competence in contexts other than the classroom and also present a role model to pupils, whether intentionally or not, also should be involved in the audit process. Stakeholders external to the school also should be considered. What of the school's advisers, educational or school psychologists, local authority behavior support team, or other relevant professional agents? What of members of the school board or governors, who have a responsibility for communicating with both the school and the community? What of the parents and caregivers of the students? What of local employers, who may have very strong views about which kinds of transferable social competencies make young people more or less employable? Do not view the need to consult with these external stakeholders as a problem because they are also part of the solution.

This leads to identifying areas for improvement and setting objectives and priorities for action at various levels of operation (e.g., child, class, or schoolwide), as well as links to school development plans. This is coupled with identifying resources and support: staff development, processes and packages, resources, support networks and agencies. Of course, alternative frameworks can be found in the literature, but some structure and framework within which to develop and negotiate shared vocabulary and concepts is definitely needed if schools are to move forward constructively in a coordinated and cost-effective way. Nor should this be a one-off exercise but rather a renewing cycle of intervention, evaluation, informed intervention, and so on.

A Systematic Approach

CASEL has produced an "implementation guide and toolkit" (Devaney et al., 2006). CASEL has found two key sets of activities, in combination with the essential element of effective leadership, as important to successful SEL implementation and sustainability. The first set is a series of ten steps that make up a full SEL implementation cycle.

The second set is six sustainability factors that are essential to high-quality, sustainable implementation.

Readiness Phase

Step 1: Principal commits to schoolwide SEL initiative. The principal has reflected on, understands, and accepts the value of SEL as a framework for school improvement and has committed to the effort – including systematic sequenced classroom instruction – required to implement and sustain schoolwide SEL successfully.

Step 2: Principal engages key stakeholders and creates SEL steering committee. The principal has shared information about SEL with key school and community stakeholder groups (e.g., teachers, families, student support personnel, support staff, and community members) and has created an SEL steering committee, consisting of representatives of some or all of those groups, that is authorized to make decisions.

Planning Phase

Step 3: Develop and articulate a shared vision. The steering committee, including the principal, creates a vision of student social, emotional, and academic development and shares that vision schoolwide.

Step 4: Conduct a schoolwide needs and resources assessment. A needs and resources assessment of current SEL programs and practices is conducted: the policy context both locally and statewide, student and staff needs, school climate, readiness to implement SEL as a schoolwide priority, and possible barriers to implementation. The needs assessment creates an understanding of strengths and weaknesses.

Step 5: Develop an action plan for SEL implementation. The steering committee has developed an action plan based on the results of the needs and resources assessment that includes goals, benchmarks, and a timeline for SEL implementation, as well as a plan for addressing the six sustainability factors (below).

Step 6: Review and select evidence-based program(s)/strategies. The steering committee has reviewed and selected evidence-based SEL program(s)/strategies that meet identified SEL goals.

Implementation Phase

Step 7: Conduct initial professional development activities. Trainers from the evidence-based program have provided initial professional development.

Step 8: Launch SEL instruction in classrooms. Teachers have begun to reflect on the instructional and implementation process.

Step 9: Expand classroom-based SEL programming and integrate SEL schoolwide. SEL practices are being integrated into other school activities. Integration and expansion create a consistent environment of support for students' social and emotional development.

Step 10: Revisit implementation activities and adjust for continuous improvement. The steering committee revisits all SEL planning and implementation activities at regular intervals to determine if changes or adaptations are needed to improve programming.

Sustainability Factors

1. *Provide ongoing professional development.* The principal commits resources for ongoing professional development and provides opportunities for reflection and feedback for all school staff (e.g., teachers, support staff, playground monitors, custodians, etc.). Ongoing professional

development and reflection keep SEL instruction and activities fresh and allow for continuous improvement.

2. *Evaluate practices and outcomes for continuous improvement.* The steering committee continually monitors the school's SEL practices and outcomes, making appropriate adaptations and improvements. Regular and ongoing evaluation of practices and outcomes helps to ensure that the school is reaching its goals and implementing programming as intended.

3. *Develop infrastructure to support SEL programming.* The school leader creates an infrastructure, including policies, funding, time, and personnel, to support SEL programming. Establishing an infrastructure for SEL ensures that it remains a visible priority in the school and therefore is more likely to be sustained.

4. *Integrate SEL framework and practices schoolwide.* The steering committee works with staff to review all school activities (e.g., core academic classes, student support services) to maximize the integration of SEL in the school. Integration of SEL into all school activities provides numerous opportunities for students to practice and reinforce the SEL skills they are learning in the classroom.

5. *Nurture partnerships with families and communities.* The steering committee establishes school-family-community partnerships that effectively support and integrate students' social, emotional, and academic development. Family and community partnerships can sustain SEL programming and provide additional support for students to reinforce SEL skills they are learning in school.

6. *Communicate with the entire school community about SEL programming.* The steering committee regularly shares information about the school's SEL programming and celebrates successes with staff, families, students, and community members. Ongoing communication through a variety of means helps to build support and maintain enthusiasm.

An Exemplar Program: PATHS

PATHS (*P*romoting *A*lternative *TH*inking *S*trategies) is a social and emotional learning program for children in kindergarten through sixth grade (http://www.channing-bete.com/prevention-programs/paths/paths.html). It includes parent materials in Spanish. There is also a version for younger children (aged three to five years). PATHS comprises an instructional manual, six volumes amounting to 119 lessons, pictures, and photographs, and additional materials. It has a readiness and self-control unit (using a turtle to invoke student response), three volumes of feeling and relationship units, a problem-solving unit, and a supplementary unit (which includes lessons 90–119). However, there is also a fast-track version of PATHS.

The first unit focuses on introducing PATHS and on helping children gain better self-control. This unit is not necessary for all children, but for those who need it, it is often a prerequisite for being able to attend to the remainder of the curriculum. Teachers or staff would use this unit with children who show significant language and/or cognitive delays or in small classes of children with severe behavior problems. In unit 1, students learn self-control through use of the Turtle Technique. This consists of a series of structured lessons accompanied by a reinforcement program that is individually tailored by each classroom teacher. This technique is unique both because it teaches self-control in interpersonal rather than academic/cognitive domains and because it includes a system for generalization throughout the day. Through a series of lessons, children are told a metaphorical story about a young turtle who has both interpersonal and academic difficulties that arise because he or she does "not stop to think." These problems are manifest in the young turtle's aggressive behaviors (which are related to numerous uncomfortable feelings). With the assistance of a "wise old turtle," the young turtle learns to develop better self-control (which involves going into his or her shell). The script for the turtle story is accompanied by eight drawings that illustrate each section of the story.

The second unit, "Feelings and Relationships," consists of lessons related to emotional and interpersonal understanding. The lessons cover approximately fifty different affective states and are taught in a developmental hierarchy beginning with basic emotions (e.g., happy, sad, angry, etc.) and later introducing more complex emotional states (e.g., jealousy, guilt, pride). Since the ability to label emotional states is a central focus, major emphasis is placed on encouraging such labeling as a precursor for effective self-control and optimal problem resolution. Further, the children are also taught cues for the self-recognition of their own feelings and the recognition of emotions in others, affective self-monitoring techniques, training in attributions that link causes and emotions, perspective-taking skills in how and why to consider another's point of view, empathic realization of how one's behavior can affect other people, and information regarding how the behavior of others can affect oneself. These lessons include group discussions, role-playing skits, art activities, stories, and educational games. An important section is concerned with anger management. In this section, affects such as anger and frustration are discussed, differentiations are made between feelings (all feelings are okay to have) and behaviors (some are okay and some are *not* okay), and modeling and role-play are used to teach children new ways to recognize and control anger. Another method for helping children to calm down and learn better self-control is also introduced in this subunit, which is called the "Control Signals Poster (CSP)."

The third unit teaches interpersonal problem solving. The skills in the preceding domains are all prerequisites for learning competent interpersonal problem solving, so lessons on this topic do not begin until the groundwork has been covered by previous instruction. This content area has been expanded to sequentially cover the following:

STOP – WHAT IS HAPPENING?

1. Stopping and thinking
2. Problem identification
3. Feeling identification

GET READY – WHAT COULD I DO?

1. Deciding on a goal
4. Generating alternative solutions
5. Evaluating the possible consequences of these solutions
6. Selecting the best solution
7. Planning the best solution

GO! – TRY MY BEST PLAN

9. Trying the formulated plan

EVALUATE – HOW DID I DO?

10. Evaluating the outcome
11. Trying another solution and/or plan or, alternatively, reevaluating the goal if an obstacle results in failure to reach the intended goal

Supplementary lessons are also included in the PATHS curriculum. These include optional lessons such as a subunit on teasing, review and extension lessons that can be used to teach PATHS during subsequent years, and advanced lessons such as a subunit on fair/unfair.

PATHS incorporates four major factors: self-control, emotional understanding, problem-solving skills, and creative self-expression. First, children are taught to "Stop and Think," a response that facilitates the development and use of verbal thought. Second, children are provided with enriched linguistic experiences that will help them to mediate understanding of self and others. Third, children learn to integrate emotional understanding with cognitive and linguistic skills to analyze and solve problems. Fourth, and very critically, the development of verbally mediated self-control over behaviors is encouraged.

The PATHS curriculum provides teachers with a systematic and developmental procedure for reducing adverse factors that can negatively affect a child's adaptive behavior and ability to profit from his or her educational experiences. PATHS is designed to help children (1) develop specific strategies that promote reflective responses and mature thinking skills, (2) become more self-motivated and enthusiastic about learning, (3) obtain information necessary for social understanding and prosocial behaviour, (4) increase their ability to generate creative alternative solutions to problems, and (5) learn to anticipate and evaluate situations, behaviors, and consequences. These skills, in turn, increase the child's access to positive social interactions, thus reducing isolation, and provide opportunities for a greater variety of learning experiences. Increasing self-control and reflective thinking skills also contribute to the amelioration of significant underachievement and promote skills that will be beneficial in preventing the genesis of other types of problem behaviors in the future (e.g., alcohol and drug abuse). In addition, as PATHS activities become a regular part of the school day, less instructional time is apt to be used for correcting child behavior problems; in this way, classroom climate can be improved and teacher frustration and "burnout" are reduced.

PATHS has been translated into Dutch, French, and Hebrew. It is used in a variety of schools for normal, deaf, and other special-needs children in The Netherlands, Belgium, Great Britain, Wales, Norway, Canada, Australia, and Israel. In the United States, it is currently being used in sites in Washington State, Texas, Kansas, Illinois, South Carolina, New Mexico, and Pennsylvania.

A recent study of the fast-track version (Bierman et al., 2010) conducted a longitudinal analysis involving 2,937 children of multiple ethnicities who remained in the same intervention or control schools for grades 1, 2, and 3. The study involved a clustered randomized, controlled trial involving sets of schools randomized within three U.S. locations. Measures assessed teacher and peer reports of aggression, hyperactive-disruptive behaviors, and social competence. Beginning

in first grade and through three successive years, teachers received training and support and implemented the PATHS curriculum in their classrooms. The study examined the main effects of intervention as well as how outcomes were affected by characteristics of the child (e.g., baseline level of problem behavior and gender) and by the school environment (e.g., student poverty). Modest positive effects of sustained program exposure included reduced aggression and increased prosocial behavior (according to both teacher and peer reports) and improved academic engagement (according to teacher report). Peer-report effects were moderated by gender, with significant effects only for boys. Most intervention effects were moderated by school environment, with effects stronger in less disadvantaged schools, and effects on aggression were larger in students who showed higher baseline levels of aggression.

Other Resources

In the United Kingdom, Bremner & Topping (1998) collated a "practice and resources guide" giving details of actual implementation of programs in schools. In the United States, CASEL has produced "Safe and Sound" (CASEL, 2003), which includes ratings of many programs under many categories. Both of these are invaluable practical resources for teachers wishing to explore this area.

Conclusion

Defining social competence is problematic because it has behavioral, cognitive, and emotional aspects and also can be conceptualized at the broader or more specific level. The requirements for "social competence" can be defined by a subset of those involved (e.g., teachers) or can be the subject of wider consultation (e.g., with students and parents). Social behaviors that are dysfunctional and disapproved of in one context may be functional and approved of in another. As students learn to think more rationally, many of their immediate emotional reactions are transformed into more explicit behavioral expressions over which they have conscious choice. Becoming socially competent is a dynamic process, so labeling individuals as competent or otherwise is not appropriate. Beyond the school years, the world of work also has many social demands – social competence is a transferable skill in high demand from employers. Those who are socially competent are also likely to be more resilient and able to deal positively with the stresses and temptations of life. Theoretical models have been proposed, but these are diverse in nature, and some programs have no such foundation.

Recent years have seen a movement to "evidence-based education." Social competence (and the social and emotional learning [SEL] that leads to it) is well evidenced. A study in 2000 of 700 programs found that cognitive and self-managed approaches had moderate to large effects. Peer tutoring and peer reinforcement also were effective. Social skills training was variably effective, and behavioral approaches were effective but often lacked information on generalization and maintenance. In 2008, a review of nineteen previous meta-analyses indicated that students gained on a variety of outcome measures. Furthermore, low-socioeconomic-status children did equally well, and neither age nor gender was a significant factor in effectiveness. Longer programs (three to six months) did better. However, follow-up showed a decline in effects (although effects were still statistically significant), and there was a considerable shortage of studies with longer follow-up periods (twelve months or more). A new meta-analysis conducted in 2008 included some studies from outside the United States and found no difference between the United States and other countries. Programs were either whole school–oriented (addressing all interactions in the school) or more specifically program-oriented (addressing interactions mainly within specific sessions) or both. Effect sizes were high for social skills, academic achievement, positive self-image, and prosocial behavior. At follow-up, academic achievement increased, whereas the others decreased, and shorter programs were found more effective than longer ones. Another meta-analysis in 2008 found that "universal" programs (delivered to all children irrespective of need) were effective but less effective than programs delivered to those with special needs in this area. After-school programs were effective but less effective than either of the previous.

Teachers need to consider the nature of day-to-day relationships within school as well as the implementation of specific programs. Goals have been proposed covering both aspects. SEL must be built on caring relationships and warm but challenging classroom and school environments. Then life skills should be taught in the areas of know yourself and others, make responsible decisions, care for others, and know how to act. Goal setting and problem solving should provide direction and energy for learning. Instruction for SEL should use varied modalities and approaches to reach the diverse styles and preferences of all learners. There must be well-planned professional development for all school personnel and a system of support during the initial years of implementation. Lastly, evaluation of efforts to promote social-emotional learning involves ongoing monitoring of implementation, assessing outcomes, and understanding the opinions and reactions of those who carry out and receive the efforts. A framework for school self-evaluation using performance indicators also has been devised, intended to help schools undertake an audit of their current approaches to promoting social competence, as well as help schools to develop locally relevant means for evaluating the impact of any innovations. An "implementation guide and toolkit" also has been produced, containing ten implementation steps (covering readiness, planning, and implementation) and six sustainability factors. An example was given of a particular program – PATHS. This incorporates four factors: self-control, emotional understanding, problem-solving skills, and creative self-expression. A recent randomized, controlled trial of PATHS showed modest effects. Readers were directed to other practical resources.

For the future, clearly more research attention should be given to follow-up studies as well as to measuring quality of implementation in programs that are up-scaled from those delivered by the original researchers. However, there is also a problem of translation into practice – the level of detail found in this chapter makes implementing SEL seem rather difficult, and the lone enthusiastic teacher might feel overwhelmed and unsure where to start. Certainly it is easier when two or more teachers in a school are involved as a team – and from this, wider involvement can grow. The evidence base is strong (although it could be stronger), and this should encourage teachers to pursue ever more substantial implementations in the knowledge that the research is on their side.

References

Bierman, K. L., Coie, J. D., Dodge, K. A., Greenberg, M. T., Lochman, J. E., McMahon, R. J., & Pinderhughes, E. (2010). The effects of a multiyear universal social-emotional learning program: The role of student and school characteristics. *Journal of Consulting and Clinical Psychology* 78(2), 156–68.

Bremner, W. G., & Topping, K. J. (1998). *Promoting social competence: Practice & resources guide.* Edinburgh: Scottish Office Education and Industry Department. Also on CD-ROM.

Collaborative for Academic, Social, and Emotional Learning (CASEL) (2003). *Safe and sound: An educational leader's guide to evidence-based social and emotional learning (SEL) programs.* Chicago, IL: CASEL. Also on CDROM. Retrieved June 1, 2010, from www.casel.org/downloads/Safe%20and%20 Sound/1A_Safe_&_Sound.pdf.

Consortium on the School-Based Promotion of Social Competence (1994). The school-based promotion of social competence: Theory, research, practice and policy. In R. J. Haggerty, L. Sherrod, N. Garmezy, and M. Rutter (eds.), *Stress, risk and resilience in children and adolescents. Processes, mechanisms, and interaction* (pp. 148–62). New York: Cambridge University Press.

Crick, N. R., & Dodge, K. A. (1994). A review and reformulation of social information-processing mechanisms in children's social adjustment. *Psychological Bulletin* 115, 47–101.

Devaney, E., O'Brien, M. U., Resnik, H., Keister, S., & Weissberg, R. P. (2006). *Sustainable schoolwide social and emotional learning (SEL): Implementation guide and toolkit.* Chicago, IL: CASEL.

Diekstra, R. F. W. (2008). Effectiveness of school-based social and emotional education programmes worldwide. In *Social and emotional education: An international analysis* (pp. 255–312). Santander, Spain: Fundación Marcelino Botin.

Elias, M. J. (2003). *Academic and social-emotional learning* (Educational Practices Series No. 11). International Bureau of Education. Geneva: UNESCO-IBE. Retrieved June 1, 2010, from www.ibe.unesco.org/fileadmin/user_upload/archive/publications/EducationalPracticesSeriesPdf/prac11e.pdf.

Elias, M. J., & Clabby, J. F. (1992). *Building social problem-solving skills: Guidelines from a school-based program.* San Francisco: Jossey-Bass.

Gesten, E. L., Weissberg, R. P., Amish, P. L., & Smith, J. K. (1987). Social problem-solving training: A skills-based approach to prevention and treatment. In C. A. Maher and J. E. Zins (eds.), *Psychoeducational interventions in the schools: Methods and procedures for enhancing student competence* (pp. 197–210). New York: Pergamon.

Payton, J., Weissberg, R. P., Durlak, J. A., Dymnicki, A. B., Taylor, R. D., Schellinger, K. B., & Pachan, M. (2008). *The positive impact of social and emotional learning for kindergarten to eighth-grade students: Findings from three scientific reviews.* Chicago: Collaborative for Academic, Social, and Emotional Learning.

Spivack, G., & Shure, M. B. (1974). *Social adjustment of young children: A cognitive approach to solving real-life problems.* San Francisco: Jossey-Bass.

Topping, K. J., & Bremner, W. G. (1998). *Taking a closer look at promoting social competence: Self-evaluation using performance indicators.* Edinburgh: Scottish Office Education and Industry Department.

Topping, K. J., Bremner, W. G., & Holmes, E. A. (2000a). Social competence: The social construction of the concept. In R. Bar-On and J. D. A. Parker (eds.), *The handbook of emotional intelligence: Theory, development, assessment, and application at home, school, and in the workplace* (pp. 28–39). San Francisco: Jossey-Bass.

Topping, K. J., Holmes, E. A., & Bremner, W. G. (2000b). The effectiveness of school-based programs for the promotion of social competence. In R. Bar-On and J. D. A. Parker (eds.), *The handbook of emotional intelligence: Theory, development, assessment, and application at home, school, and in the workplace* (pp. 411–32). San Francisco: Jossey-Bass.

CHAPTER 14

Positive Behavior Support and Young People with Autism

Strategies of Prevention and Intervention

Glen Dunlap, Phillip Strain, and Lise Fox

Children with autism face serious obstacles in virtually all aspects of their development. Most significantly, children with autism have difficulties with their social, communicative, and emotional development, and these difficulties are often punctuated by the presence of challenging behaviors. Common forms of challenging behavior include stereotypic (or "self-stimulatory") and perseverative responding, repetitive and nonsensical noise making, unresponsiveness and noncompliance, and lengthy and sometimes highly disruptive tantrums. Less common but more disturbing forms of challenging behavior includes property destruction, aggression, and self-injury. Regardless of the form, uncontrolled challenging behaviors have the effect of ostracizing the child and often excluding the child from opportunities for social interactions, community participation, and inclusive education.

This chapter provides an overview and discussion of positive behavior support (PBS) as an approach for addressing the challenging behaviors of children with autism. PBS is a well-established framework for preventing and intervening with challenging behaviors

(Bambara & Kern, 2005; Dunlap & Carr, 2007). It is based largely, though not entirely, on the principles and procedures of applied behavior analysis, and it includes a number of key features that, in aggregate, define a collaborative, multicomponent, and multi-tiered approach (Carr et al., 2002; Dunlap et al., 2008). The chapter begins be describing autism and PBS and then introduces a comprehensive, multilayered model for preventing and intervening with challenging behaviors. The final section of the chapter provides a discussion of five guidelines and recommendations regarding PBS and critical issues in the design and implementation of effective supports.

Autism Spectrum Disorders

Autism is a term that refers to a population of individuals with disorders in the development of communication and social behavior. Initially described by Kanner (1943), the phenomenon of autism has commanded an unusual amount of fascination from psychological theorists and therapists, as well as from educators and applied researchers. Different definitions of autism have been advanced, as have educational classifications and interventions. Over the past decade, a consensus has focused on the definition of the American Psychiatric Association's *Diagnostic and Statistical Manual of Mental Disorders* (DSM-IV-TR, 2000). In this definition, a diagnosis of *autistic disorder* requires that a child present with at least (1) some form of qualitative impairment in social interactions, (2) a qualitative impairment in communication, and (3) some type of repetitive and stereotypic pattern of behavior, interests, or activities.

Autism spectrum disorder (ASD) is a term that has become popular in recent years. ASD broadens the conceptualization of autism to include a variety of autistic-like labels such as *Asperger syndrome, Rett syndrome*, and *pervasive developmental disorder – not otherwise specified*. Although ASD is not yet considered a formal psychiatric diagnosis, it is used increasingly as a practical label to describe a broad continuum of individuals with social and communicative disabilities.

The advent of the ASD categorization and, before that, the diagnosis of pervasive developmental disorder may help to explain the dramatic increase in reported prevalence of autism (or ASD) in the population (Goldstein, Naglieri, & Ozonoff, 2009). Over the past 20 to 30 years, studies have reported an increase in prevalence rates from as few as one, two, or possible four per 10,000 to as many as 60 per 10,000 (Fombonne, 2005). Other investigations have reported parent-reported prevalence rates in excess of one per 100 (Kogan et al., 2009), although such extraordinarily high levels have yet to be verified.

Although challenging behaviors per se have never been considered a diagnostic characteristic of ASD, it is true that many children with ASD exhibit behaviors that are disruptive, dangerous, and incompatible with learning and desirable social interactions. Indeed, challenging behaviors are known as the most common and conspicuous reasons for students to be excluded from early intervention, community, and educational programs. Challenging behaviors such as tantrums, aggression, and noncompliance constitute substantial obstacles not only to inclusive education placements but also to most opportunities for peer interaction and social development. Therefore, a high priority for enabling children with autism to benefit from social interactions and therapeutic and educational programs is to develop and implement effective programs of behavior support (Dunlap, Strain, & Ostryn, 2010).

A large variety of interventions for children with ASD have been advanced over the past fifty years, and a good deal of research has been conducted. The data indicate very persuasively that effective strategies are based on educational and behavioral perspectives that are derived from learning principles and from the discipline of applied behavior analysis (Luiselli et al., 2009). In addition, it is important to appreciate that there is nothing especially distinctive about ASD when it comes to the literature on instruction, prevention, and intervention. That is, as far as we know, there is no specific procedure that is effective for children with ASD but not effective for children without ASD, or vice versa. Therefore, when considering effective interventions for children on the autism spectrum, it is reasonable to examine strategies that have been demonstrated to be effective with other children who may share some characteristics with children with ASD, such as the general population of children with developmental disabilities.

Positive Behavior Support

Positive behavior support (PBS) is an approach to intervention based on principles of learning theory, the science of implementation and systems change, and data-based accountability (Carr et al., 2002, Dunlap, 2004). PBS is a pragmatic approach designed to enhance a person's quality of life and reduce challenging behaviors and other challenges of behavioral adjustment. Carr et al. (2002) and Dunlap et al. (2008) identify nine major features as distinguishing the PBS approach from other applied frameworks:

1. A focus on lifestyle change and improved quality of life
2. A commitment to longitudinal lifespan outcomes
3. Intervention strategies that have ecological validity
4. Including principal stakeholders as collaborative partners in the assessment and intervention process
5. An emphasis on the social validity of procedures and outcomes
6. A focus on systems change and multicomponent interventions as being necessary for sustainable outcomes
7. An emphasis on prevention and an appreciation that the most effective procedures occur when challenging behaviors are not present
8. Use of knowledge derived from multiple methodologic practices
9. Incorporation of useful information from multiple theoretical perspectives

Positive behavior support emerged in the middle and late 1980s as a response to growing concern regarding traditional behavior management strategies that relied almost exclusively on the use of consequences to modify behavior. Although contingency management was then and remains now a powerful and valid tool for effecting behavior change, the heavy dependence on the one strategy, in the face of very persistent challenging behaviors, led to the use of increasingly intensive reinforcers to strengthen desirable responding and analogously intensive punishers (i.e., aversive stimuli) to suppress unwanted behaviors. The tendency to use powerful aversives (including painful and noxious stimuli such as water sprays, paddling, and electric shock) in the 1970s and early 1980s provoked strong reactions from advocacy groups. It also was the case that the use of strong and conspicuous consequences was incompatible with the growing movements in favor of deinstitutionalization, community integration, and education in the least restrictive environments (see

Guess et al., 1987; and Repp & Singh, 1990). Together these forces obliged the development of a new and broader approach to behavior management (Horner et al., 1990).

Fortunately, important applied research was being published at the same time that traditional, consequence-based behavior management was being questioned. The basic notion that challenging behavior could be understood as a functional response to environmental contingencies (Carr, 1977) meant that even the most severe and bizarre patterns of behavior could be interpreted as primitive forms of communication, and this realization led to the technologies of functional assessment, functional analysis, and function-based interventions (Carr, 1988; Carr & Durand, 1985; Dunlap et al., 2006; Horner & Budd, 1985; Iwata et al., 1994). This line of research spawned a fruitful industry of interventions involving functional (behavioral) assessments and focused instruction that quickly became one of the essential foundations of PBS.

The second major emphasis that began to emerge in the early and middle 1980s involved antecedent and contextual control over challenging behaviors. The principle involved in this line of research was stimulus control, including the ubiquitous observation that challenging behavior occurs more often in the presence of some stimuli and less often in the presence of others. It also was noted that such antecedent stimulus functions differ across individuals and circumstances but that straightforward processes of functional assessment could identify the relations governing antecedent control for a particular child's responding (Dunlap et al., 1991; Luiselli, 2006). Thus the principles and procedures associated with the manipulation of antecedent variables in the environment became the second technological foundation of PBS.

As stated previously, PBS began to emerge in the middle 1980s, initially in response to the antiaversives and normalization movements, and vitally supported by the behavioral research on functional assessment, function-based interventions, and antecedent manipulations. PBS was established first with individuals with severe disabilities, including ASD. The reason for this is that these were the individuals who tended to display the most severe challenging behaviors and who were subjected to the most extreme aversive treatments, usually in non-public settings such as clinics, hospitals, and self-contained special education programs. The major impetus underlying the earliest work in PBS was to develop and implement effective procedures for producing sustainable improvements in quality of life and challenging behaviors that could be used in any and all settings in the community, schools, and family homes (Horner et al., 1990).

The PBS approach has experienced tremendous growth over the past twenty years. From its beginnings with children with ASD and other severe disabilities, it has expanded to be applied with a large number of populations in a great variety of settings. PBS also was expanded to incorporate larger units of analysis such as classrooms and entire school and preschool programs (Fox & Hemmeter, 2009; Sailor et al., 2009; Sugai et al., 2000). Hundreds of research articles have been published, as have hundreds of manuals, books, videos, and reviews. Importantly, the PBS research that has been published documents powerful effects in terms of reducing challenging behaviors and building functional competencies in children with ASD and related developmental disabilities (Carr et al., 1999; Dunlap & Carr, 2007). The growth of PBS is reflected further by the establishment in 1999 of a scientific journal, the *Journal of Positive Behavior Interventions*, and an international association, the Association for Positive Behavior Support (www.apbs. org), which was formed in 2003.

PBS and Young Children with ASD

Positive behavior support (PBS) embraces a prevention perspective in its approach to challenging behaviors. This has been true in all its applications, and it is increasingly evident in work with young children with ASD. The emphasis is on promoting healthy social-emotional development and arranging the environment to encourage prosocial behaviors and discourage or divert children from engaging in challenging behaviors. If children already engage in patterns of challenging behaviors, the prevention focus of PBS includes procedures to teach skills that are incompatible or inconsistent with problems and to implement antecedent manipulations that evoke desirable responding (Dunlap, Johnson, & Robbins, 1990).

The prevention model being advanced for children with ASD provides for multiple levels of analysis and procedural implementation. The model is based on the three-tiered framework that has been increasingly common in many arenas of social services, including public health and education (e.g., Fox et al., 2003; Simeonsson, 1991; Sugai et al., 2000; Walker et al., 1996). The model begins by defining a target behavior in need of prevention, such as challenging behaviors exhibited by children with ASD. Strategies intended to prevent the occurrence or further development of the target behavior then are categorized along a hierarchy related to the proportion of the population (e.g., children with ASD) for whom the strategy would be pertinent, the intensity of the strategy, and the stage of the target behavior's development. Level 1 strategies are intended for the entire population of interest. The strategies are geared to an early stage of prevention and would be relatively inexpensive and easy to implement. This level is referred to as *primary prevention*, involving universal applications. Universal strategies for children with ASD would be implemented for all children, as young as possible, who are diagnosed or described as having ASD.

Level 2 is referred to as *secondary prevention* and is intended for individuals for whom level 1 is insufficient and who are clearly at risk for or who are already demonstrating early indications of the target behavior. For children with ASD, level 2 might include specific procedures designed to teach appropriate problem solving, self-regulation, and coping and to divert children from using the problem behavior. Level 2 strategies are more focused than level 1, involve a smaller

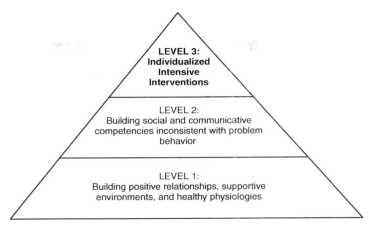

LEVEL 3:
Individualized
Intensive
Interventions

LEVEL 2:
Building social and communicative
competencies inconsistent with problem
behavior

LEVEL 1:
Building positive relationships, supportive
environments, and healthy physiologies

Figure 14.1: Preventing problem behavior in children with ASD.

proportion of the population, and are less intensive and costly than level 3 strategies. Still, for children with ASD, owing to their substantial risk factors, it is likely that a relatively large segment of the population will require and benefit from level 2 strategies.

Level 3 is for individuals who are already displaying the target behavior and require relatively intensive and individualized interventions. This level is referred to as *tertiary prevention*, with individualized, intensive intervention procedures. For children with ASD, level 3 involves individualized assessment and assessment-based interventions that are relatively well represented in the current literature on positive behavior support and applied behavior analysis. These strategies are markedly more expensive in terms of resources and time required than level 1 and 2 strategies. It is important to clarify that level 3 for children with ASD is not just one level of intensity. It is actually a set of procedures on a continuum of intensity that is based on the extent to which the child's problem behaviors are severe, long-lasting, and demonstrably resistant to change. That is, if a child is beginning to display tantrums at school, but the tantrums are limited to one or two classes and have not been exhibited at home or in the community, then the procedures need not be time-consuming or especially effortful (although they still may require individualized assessment and an individualized intervention plan). Similarly,

if the child is only two or three years old with problem behaviors that have functions that are easily understood, then they might call for a relatively straightforward and efficient process of intervention development and implementation (Dunlap & Fox, 1999a; Strain & Schwartz, 2009). On the other hand, if a child has demonstrated severe problem behaviors for several years, and the problems have persisted in many environments despite multiple efforts of remediation, then the level 3 process is likely to require a considerable investment of time and resources to be effective.

The multitiered prevention model is represented in Figure 14.1. The bottom tier, level 1, is intended for all children with ASD, whereas levels 2 and 3 build increasingly focused and intensive supports for children who demonstrate high-risk factors and needs related to social-emotional development and problem behaviors. The following descriptions provide further explanations of the three levels along with examples of intervention strategies.

Level 1 Strategies

Children with ASD have more difficulty in managing their environments than children who are developing typically. As a result, there are more events and circumstances that can be irritants to the child, that can evoke challenging behaviors, and that are not resolved as efficiently as with a typically developing child. Therefore, it is important to reduce potential irritants and to teach the child, from a very early age, that interacting with the social environment is a pleasurable and satisfying enterprise. Level 1 strategies are geared to all children with a diagnosis or likely classification of ASD, and they should be implemented as soon as such a diagnosis or suspected classification is rendered. The strategies are relatively straightforward and may be summarized in the following categories:

1. *Development of positive relationships.* The purpose of this essential category is to teach the child that social contact with parents and other caregivers is the optimal route to obtain nurturance, comfort, pleasure, and guidance. Developing attachments is a challenge for children with ASD, so special efforts are required, even when signs of a child's interest are not apparent. This might require that a parent carefully identify the activities and objects that the child finds pleasurable and use those activities to encourage social interactions. For example, a game of chase might be initiated with a child and then interrupted periodically with the expectation that the child look at the adult or repeat a gesture to continue. Interactions should be pleasurable for the child, and they should be associated with the child receiving input that is consistent with his or her needs and interests. An important outcome of early and ongoing efforts to establish positive bonds is that a relationship is established in which an adult has considerable influence over a child's behavior, and this influence can be essential for the guidance and instruction that the adult must provide on an ongoing basis.

2. *Safe, comprehensible, stimulating, and responsive environments.* Since children with ASD are often limited in their abilities to comprehend their surroundings, it is useful to be sure that clear physical cues are consistently available to help children locate desired items and to make appropriate requests. The understanding of the environment's physical layout, schedule, and expectations can be enhanced through the use of visual supports or object cues that provide the child with information regarding what is expected and how to navigate a social environment (e.g., Dettmer et al., 2000; Olley & Reeve, 1997). In addition, the environment should be set up so that a child's initiations are met with appropriate responses, along with guidance and support to sustain interactions and help to ensure that the child's motivations are fulfilled. Further, a child with ASD should be exposed to a variety of community and social contexts while being supported by assistance and positive guidance to ensure that these experiences are enjoyable and successful for the child. The active engagement of the child within meaningful activities and social interactions is pivotal to the child's overall development and ability to engage comfortably with complex social environments. The comfort that comes with early exposure and active engagement can be instrumental in reducing anxiety and frustration and establish a foundation for healthy social-emotional development.

3. *Physical health.* It is clear that the status of one's physiologic well-being is closely related to the occurrence of challenging behaviors. Therefore, a third level 1 category involves procedures to ensure that the child's physical health is sound, that somatic complaints are understood and addressed, that the child has daily opportunities for vigorous exercise, and that the child consumes food and beverages that are nutritious. The specific relationship between physiologic circumstances and challenging behavior has not yet received extensive investigation, but there is no doubt that the link is a powerful one and that improved medical assessment and care can be a powerful strategy of prevention (Carr & Owen-DeSchryver, 2007).

4. *Communication and other skills.* There is an indisputable connection between communicative competence and the development and occurrence of challenging behaviors. A crucial strategy for all children identified or suspected of having ASD is to help the children acquire the functional communication skills needed to effectively and conventionally control aspects of the environment. For example, even when a child has no other distinguishable language, parents can help toddlers with ASD to use vocalizations or gestures to request or reject objects and activities. Children with ASD who are nonverbal can be provided with instruction to use visuals or objects to ensure their capacity to communicate their needs. Parents should pursue activity-based instruction intentionally and deliberately and, always, with an awareness of what the instruction will do to help the child be an active participant and, to some extent, manager of his or her surroundings. In addition to communication skills, instruction and support will be needed to help the child with ASD to meet other milestones, including play skills, self-care, independence, and some motor skills (e.g., using a crayon or cutting with scissors). Although guidance is important for all children, the child with ASD ordinarily will require more systematic and intensive attention to master important competencies and to sustain engagement with the physical and social environments.

Level 2 Strategies

Level 2 is for children with ASD for whom level 1 is insufficient and who have risk factors that indicate a need for more deliberate and additional strategies. Such risk factors include obvious delays in language development, notable avoidance of social interactions, and a failure to acquire functional skills. In many circumstances, the actual instructional strategies used across levels 1 and 2 may be very similar. The distinguishing differences focus on (1) intensity of intervention, with the expectation being that level 2 strategies will deliver hundreds of intentional learning opportunities across the day, (2) planfulness of intervention, with the assumption being that intervention teams will need to construct daily plans such that domain-specific skill instruction occurs across contexts, materials, and peers, (3) intensity of data collection, with some sort of daily data collection being the norm for the large proportion of level 2 interventions, and (4) intensity of family involvement, with an expectation that level 2 interventions will necessitate programming across home and community environments, with family members being involved in the planning, delivery, and monitoring of interventions.

A notable strategy in the level 2 category was described by Strain and Schwartz (2009) as "appropriate engagement intervention," in which the procedural focus is on increasing children's appropriate engagement with classroom materials and activities. Although not designed explicitly as an intervention for problem behaviors, increases in engagement tend to covary negatively with occurrences of problem behavior, and thus the engagement intervention serves well as a strategy for preventing problems without an intensive behavior intervention plan. Strain and Schwartz also describe inclusive classroom models in which the children's peer social relationships are the fundamental process for promoting social competence and reducing challenging behaviors.

A number of comprehensive programs developed to help young children with ASD have proven effective in building skills and reducing challenging behaviors (e.g., Koegel & Koegel, 2006; Mahoney & Perales, 2003). A well-studied program, *pivotal response treatment* (Koegel & Koegel, 2006), incorporates numerous procedures that are useful for increasing the motivation and engagement of children with ASD. Such variables not only serve to enhance children's academic, communicative, and social development, but they also serve to prevent the occurrence of challenging behaviors. Examples of such procedures are using preferred stimuli, encouraging child initiations, providing clear instructions, reinforcing the child's attempts, teaching within natural contexts, providing choices, varying and interspersing tasks, and using naturally occurring reinforcers. Such procedures involve less effort and intensity than level 3 strategies, yet they can be extremely useful for encouraging social-emotional development and preventing the development or escalation of challenging behaviors.

Level 3 Strategies

Level 3 strategies are intended for children with serious risk factors whose challenging behaviors cannot be resolved satisfactorily with level 1 and 2 procedures. Level 3 involves highly individualized and relatively intensive interventions that are usually preceded by careful planning and assessment, including functional assessment (sometimes referred to as *functional behavioral assessment*). This is the initial level that was defined as *positive behavior support* (Dunlap et al., 2009), although the term is now applied to all levels of the multitiered prevention framework (Sailor et al., 2009). The process of individualized PBS has been researched extensively and is the most well-established and widely accepted approach for addressing serious challenging behaviors, including challenging behaviors of young children with ASD.

The process for implementing individualized PBS strategies generally consists of five steps. As mentioned previously, the degree of precision, intensity, and comprehensiveness with which the steps are implemented will vary from child to child depending on the chronicity and severity of the challenging behaviors. The five steps are as follows:

1. *Teaming.* For individualized interventions, more than one person generally is required for purposes of planning, assessment, and implementation. For young children, one member of the

team is almost always a parent or key family member, and team members also include teachers, aides, therapists, close friends, and, as needed, administrators. It is generally a good idea to include at least one member with knowledge of and experience with applied behavior analysis and PBS. Objectives of the team are to build a unified vision for the coming one to three years and to agree on the child's strengths, resources, and immediate goals. Person-centered planning is a process that has proven to be useful for conducting this kind of process (Kincaid & Fox, 2002).

2. *Functional assessment.* The next step is to use procedures of functional assessment to gain an understanding of how the targeted challenging behaviors are governed by events and circumstances in the environment. Many books and manuals describe the particulars of the functional assessment process (e.g., O'Neill et al., 1997), but they generally boil down to observational and interview methods for answering core questions such as (a) What is the function or purpose of the challenging behavior? (b) Under what specific circumstances is the challenging behavior most likely to occur? and (c) Under what specific circumstances is the challenging behavior least likely to occur? The answers to these questions provide essential guidance for team members in identifying effective and efficient components for an intervention plan.

3. *Developing an individualized intervention plan.* Functional assessment data, as well as information gleaned from the goal-setting and person-centered planning processes, are used to construct an individualized intervention plan. Intervention plans include components from at least three procedural categories. *Antecedent manipulations* (Luiselli, 2006) include changes in the stimuli that are found to precede or evoke challenging behavior. Such stimuli can be removed or ameliorated, whereas stimuli associated with desirable

behavior can be inserted. *Teaching strategies* involve identifying functional alternatives to the challenging behavior and arranging for such alternatives to be systematically prompted and reinforced at times that challenging behaviors otherwise may occur (e.g., Carr & Durand, 2005; Dunlap et al., 2006). *Reinforcement strategies* involve changes in the contingencies that govern the child's challenging behavior. In particular, strategies focus on removing reinforcers that maintain the problem and increasing reinforcers for other behaviors. The intervention plan also includes specific instructions for the adults who will be implementing the plan, including guidance for what to do if the challenging behavior occurs.

4. *Implementation.* Fidelity of implementation is a vital aspect of the PBS process, so it is important to incorporate procedures to help ensure that the plan is implemented as intended. Parents and teachers often benefit from scripts or other prompts to cue them about what to do and when. If evaluation data indicate that anticipated improvements are not occurring, the team can analyze fidelity as one possible reason for inadequate outcomes. Strategies can be included to heighten fidelity, or the plan can be adjusted to include components that will be easier to implement.

5. *Evaluation.* A hallmark of PBS is data-based accountability. All intervention plans require a means for evaluating whether the plan is achieving its intended effects. Data collection should be simple and valid so that all relevant parties can record data without difficulty and so that the data truly reflect the changes that are the purpose of the intervention. Simple evaluation tools include checklists and rating scales (e.g., Dunlap et al., 2010). The point is that some kind of useful evaluation data need to be collected in order for the team to know if the plan is producing benefits as expected or if adjustments to the plan are required.

As indicated previously, the evidentiary database supporting the effectiveness of PBS with young children with ASD and related disabilities is extensive (e.g., Conroy et al., 2005, Dunlap & Fox, 1999a; Dunlap, Strain, & Ostryn, 2010). As testimony, there are hundreds, if not thousands, of articles, books, manuals, and websites devoted to the description and documentation of the PBS process.

Guidelines and Recommendations for Implementation

In this section we identify and discuss five issues that are important for any consideration of prevention and intervention regarding challenging behaviors of young children with ASD. The guidelines and recommendations that follow are based on our collective experiences in implementing strategies designed to improve outcomes for children and their families. The five categories of implementation guidelines are intended as clinical addenda to the framework of PBS described in preceding sections of this chapter.

1. Need to Focus on Family Systems and Family Support

It has been appreciated for several decades that the most important resource available to a young child with ASD is a strong and competent family that includes members who are able to provide the child with time, nurturance, and age-appropriate guidance. Lovaas and colleagues (1973) showed dramatically that children with severe ASD performed much better over time if they were placed in homes with parents who had been trained to carry out behavioral procedures than if they were left in their institutionalized settings. Robbins, Dunlap, & Plienis (1991) provided additional data testifying to the importance of family functioning. In this study, twelve young children with ASD had received one year of relatively intensive training and support in clinic, home, and community settings. At the end of the year, each child was ranked according to the amount of progress made by each child on a standardized index of development. An attempt was made to determine which child, family, or community measures obtained at baseline and over the course of the year would best predict the rate of child improvement over the year. Many variables were examined, including presence of speech and communication, measured IQ, parents' ability to acquire instructional competencies, age at intake, and so on. Interestingly, one measured variable surfaced as the most predictive by far of child outcome. The variable was the amount of stress reported by parents on the Parenting Stress Index (Abidin, 1983) that was unrelated to the child or the child's behavior. This stress presumably derives from discomfort related to finances; social interactions with friends, coworkers, and family; friction with social service agencies; and so on. Of course, the investigation by Robbins et al. is limited in several respects, including its small N and retrospective research design. But the point is nevertheless a very important one: Families that did not report high levels of stress from outside sources had children with ASD who made a great deal of progress during the one-year period of the study. Parents who were more affected by external worries had children with ASD who made less progress.

As a result of these (and many other) early studies, the field has consistently acknowledged the importance of family involvement and family support in the early care and education of young children with disabilities (Guralnick, 2005; Trivette & Dunst, 2005) and especially in early intervention for children with ASD (e.g., Dawson & Osterling, 1997; Dunlap & Fox, 1996; 1999b). Family support can come in many forms, and owing to the individuality of family systems, it is desirable to individualize family support as much as possible. Almost all families need information about ASD, about effective programs and practices, about the availability of helpful resources, and about typical patterns of child development and strategies for helping their child toward an optimally healthy social-emotional (and intellectual)

trajectory. Many families benefit from direct instruction on effective home and community strategies for encouraging prosocial responding, cooperating in home routines, acquiring self-care skills and independence, and reducing challenging behaviors (e.g., Dunlap & Fox, 1999a). Many families also benefit from services such as high-quality respite care, social and emotional support from family group events or counseling, or structured life planning.

Another major area of family involvement and family support involves instruction in how service systems operate and the processes of effective self-advocacy. In most cases, parents will be the principal agent overseeing the longitudinal course of a child's progression through early childhood services, kindergarten and elementary school, and then secondary school and transition to the adult world of work, relationships, and life in the community. This lengthy and vital journey can proceed more effectively and pleasantly if parents are educated about what to expect, how to identify professionals and administrators who are able and willing to endorse and develop high-quality educational and behavioral supports, and, in general, how to advocate most effectively to see that the child experiences the best options available. When parents are effective problem solvers and are competent and comfortable in their ability to work with their child but also with all those who will be responsible for their child's services, the results can be very positive for the child and for all members of the child's family.

2. Need for a Collaborative Approach and Contextual Fit

A distinction that is important in this discussion is between the expert model of consultation and the collaborative model. In the *expert model*, an authority, usually with titles, degrees, and certificates, provides consultative advice that is essentially unilateral. The consultant observes, obtains information from files and conversations, and delivers a technically sound plan (or prescription) to the teachers or parents for solving the problem. But the consultant leaves, and teachers and parents are left with a plan that may or may not make sense in their particular circumstances. A major problem with the consultant model is that the recommendations are rarely implemented or, if implemented, are often implemented with poor fidelity.

The alternative to the expert model is the *collaborative model*, in which the assessments and the plan itself are developed by those who are most involved and invested with the child and with the problem that needs to be solved. The primary agents responsible for conducting the assessments and for developing the plan are the people who will be responsible for the plan's implementation. They may be guided by an expert who has knowledge and experience with the process and the interventions (indeed, in many situations, it may be necessary to have an expert available), but the expert in a collaborative model is a facilitator and not a director of the process. The main individuals who make the decisions about what will be done are the people who actually will conduct the intervention strategies in the class and home settings where the problems actually exist.

The advantages of a collaborative model are numerous. First, the presence of a team of people who know the child well ensures that there will be numerous ideas and perspectives, based on observations, that may prove instrumental in the process of assessment and intervention. Such deep and broad knowledge of a child's learning history, ecology, and preferences can be critical in creating optimally effective intervention components. Second, when people (parents and teachers) offer ideas that are actually included in an intervention plan, there is a real likelihood that the plan will be implemented as intended. This has a great deal to do with the notions of buy-in (Hieneman & Dunlap, 2000) and contextual fit (Albin et al., 1996) that have been prominent in the literature on positive behavior support. These principles suggest that a plan that considers and incorporates the ideas, preferences, routines, and values of the principal

intervention agents is much more likely to be implemented, and implemented with fidelity, than a plan that is simply handed down by a consulting visitor.

Finally, it should be emphasized that the collaborative model has the added benefit of building local capacity to conduct assessment and build and implement a plan. After going through the process with one child, the adult participants are much more likely to engage effectively with the development of a plan for the next child in need of individualized support.

3. *Need for Longitudinal Perspective*

Children are "young" (say, less than five years of age) for a very brief time. They are "older" for a much longer period, and they will be "adults" for the majority of their lives. In a very real sense, the period of early childhood, marvelous as it is, is a time when the foundations for all later learning, socializing, communicating, and loving are being established. This is something that should not be forgotten, but too often curricula for young children with ASD seem to have been designed without regard for this essential reality.

And what are the key foundational competencies that should be the focus of early childhood education, especially for children with ASD? First is communication. The ability and motivation to communicate with others are essential for all aspects of future life. Second and equally important is the ability to get along in the complex social environment in which we live. This includes participating in social interactions, navigating the processes of sharing and simple give and take, and perhaps most important, learning to develop and maintain friendships (Strain & Schwartz, 2009). A third foundation is the ability to manage one's environment without resorting to challenging behavior. This, of course, is closely connected to the first two essentials juat mentioned and is the essential rationale for preventative positive behavior support. There are other very important instructional targets for early childhood, such as learning to do things independently, learning self-care skills (e.g., dressing, toileting), and learning social play repertoires.

But there are many elements of common curricula for young children with ASD that may make little sense from a longitudinal perspective, at least as priority instructional objectives. In comparison with the critical foundational skills, investing precious instructional time to learn discriminations between certain shapes, colors, animals, professions, and so is probably of relatively little importance.

This raises some very important implications. First, the contexts in which the vital foundation skills can be taught best are inclusive classrooms, child-care, and community environments. Inclusion is a requirement for children to learn social skills, friendship skills, and natural communication. Second, it is a good idea to promote inclusive community engagement from an early age because it is only in inclusive educational and community contexts that generalized and functional interactions can be solidly established. Children need to develop and practice adaptive behavioral responses in real social circumstances to the point that challenging behaviors are irrelevant and prosocial behaviors are mastered and generalized. It is this mastery that will yield invaluable benefits from a longitudinal perspective.

4. Issues Concerning Dosage, Intensity, and Engagement

There can be no doubt that achieving quality outcomes is first and foremost on the minds of families affected by ASD. In many situations, and for many years, families and providers have assumed that getting a certain number of hours of direct service or a certain intervention practice is the essential ingredient to achieving quality outcomes. Regretfully, this simple and seductive formula is highly questionable and misleading.

Related to the number of service hours, much of the focus has been on an "estimated" twenty-five hours per week that was part of the National Research Council's

(2001) report on early treatment for ASD. Essentially what the report authors did was add up the hours delivered in eight preschool models with varying efficacy data and then divide by the number of models to yield an average of twenty-five hours. The models in fact ranged in hours from fifteen to forty hours, and the report clearly states that no clear outcome differences were evident across hours. As was true then, it is still the case that there are no credible studies in which the same intervention has been delivered at different levels of intensity. For a variety of ethical and practical reasons, it is doubtful that such research will ever be available.

Similarly, there has been a narrow focus on delivering a singular intervention approach. Some individuals advocate for only pivotal response training, or discrete trial instruction, or incidental teaching, and so on. The problem is that these established interventions vary greatly in their relative efficacy for certain target behaviors. For example, peer-mediated intervention has been shown to be the strongest evidence approach for target behaviors in the social domain. Incidental teaching has been used almost exclusively with verbal language behaviors. Schedules are particularly helpful during transition times, and so on. The point is that no one approach can hope to yield the best outcomes across all the likely goals of any child or family.

If a narrow focus on hours or on getting a certain intervention model is not recommended, then what are the relevant factors? Five evidence-based factors are suggested, as described below:

Factor 1: Intensity. While hours of service may not be a particularly valid measure of intensity, intensity is a highly relevant factor. The alternative view of intensity is based on several decades of research showing that the level of children's active and appropriate engagement in everyday routines is a powerful predictor of developmental growth (McWilliam, Scarborough, & Kim, 2003; Strain & Schwartz, 2009).

That is, when young children are actively and appropriately engaged, one can assume that skill acquisition is occurring. Instead of asking, for example, "How many hours of service are on the individual family service plan (IFSP) or the individualized education plan (IEP)?" the alternative question could be, "Are the IFSP or IEP outcomes, strategies, and corresponding services sufficient to influence the child's engagement across all daily routines (i.e., dressing, eating, play, bedtime, etc)?"

Factor 2: Fidelity of intervention delivery. Selecting an evidence-based intervention does not guarantee that the infant or toddler will receive the intended approach. It is essential to ask what experience providers have with the intervention approach, whether they have a protocol for judging that the intervention is implemented correctly, and what the plans are if the intended outcomes are not forthcoming.

Factor 3: Social validity of goals. Social validity refers to the degree to which there is an immediate impact on the child's quality of life when a particular goal or objective has been met. For example, teaching a toddler to label colors when presented with 3 × 5 cards of different colors would have low social validity compared with teaching the same toddler color recognition when a peer at an art table says, "Do you want some red?" or when his or her mom says, "Want your red or blue pajamas?" In the latter case, the child's new color knowledge can directly control his or her environment and meet immediate needs. Therefore, this teaching goal would have high social validity.

Factor 4: Comprehensiveness of intervention. One of the more clear findings from the last several decades of intervention research on children with ASD is that progress in one domain of performance has a minimal impact on other domains (Lovaas, 1987; National Research Council, 2001; Strain &

Hoyson, 2001). This widely replicated finding necessitates an approach to intervention design that addresses all relevant domains of performance for the child.

Factor 5: Optimal intervention equation. In considering the first four factors, one might pose that the formula associated with quality outcomes is actually multiplicative. That is, the formula is

Intensity × fidelity × social validity × comprehensiveness = quality outcomes

In this formula, the fundamental message is that as any factor approaches a zero value, then the sum or outcome will approach zero as well! The formula also suggests that for many children with ASD, the resulting plan may well involve a large number of hours of direct service. The key difference is that the number of hours should be the product of a carefully designed intervention plan and not determined arbitrarily. Implementation of these guidelines will ensure that more and more children and families affected by ASD will achieve the quality outcomes they desire and deserve.

5. Data-Based Decision Making and Accountability

Children with ASD are different from one another. Their learning, like that of all children, is highly individualized. There is no guarantee that a specific intervention strategy will be effective or that it will be as effective as one might anticipate from reading the literature or observing other children. Also, because the characteristics of ASD present such substantial risks to healthy development, a "wait and see" attitude is not acceptable. Steady and sometimes quite rapid progress is necessary for children with ASD to attain trajectories that will enable them to live satisfying, independent, socially rewarding, and productive lives. Therefore, ongoing data collection and useful data-based decision making must be part of educational and behavioral support plans for all children with ASD.

Some points need to be emphasized. First, it is unnecessary to obtain data on every instructional target on a continuous basis. Ongoing point-by-point and trial-by-trial data collection is wasteful in most cases. Such data can never be used effectively or efficiently. Probe data that are collected, for example, on a weekly basis are usually more than sufficient. Second, data should be obtained in a form that is simple, feasible, valid, and reliable for the purposes for which the data will be used. In most circumstances in homes and classrooms, direct observations (i.e., frequency counts, duration recording, and interval sampling) are simply not feasible; they can distract teachers or parents from other responsibilities, and there are no extra personnel who can serve as data collectors. In such circumstances, simple rating scales that are completed once at the end of a session can be very acceptable alternatives to direct observations (e.g., Chafouleas et al., 2007; Dunlap et al., 2010).

There are two principal purposes for which data are used to make decisions regarding interventions for young children with ASD. The first is for evaluation of progress under a specified intervention, or progress monitoring. In this case, baseline data are obtained for a period of time, usually for at least three days prior to intervention. The data continue to be collected in the same manner while the intervention is implemented. The data should indicate the progress that was anticipated with the intervention. If satisfactory progress is not evident, then the interventionists must determine if the intervention was implemented as planned (if not, the problem may relate to an issue of fidelity) or if the intervention components need to be reconsidered. The second purpose of data collection is to determine fidelity. Fidelity data are often in the form of checklists to determine whether each step of the intervention was implemented at the intended times and places. Fidelity data have become increasingly prevalent as practitioners have come to realize how essential proper implementation is to the effectiveness of intervention.

Summary

Positive behavior support is an approach for building adaptive behavior, improving quality of life, and reducing the occurrences of challenging behavior. In this chapter, we have provided an overview of the approach and some discussion of some key issues related to implementation for young children with autism. Without question, the approach will continue to evolve as its adherents seek better ways to help people affected by maladaptive behavior to obtain richer and more successful lives.

References

Abidin, R. R. (1983). *Parenting stress index – Manual.* Charlottesville, VA: Pediatric Psychological Press

Albin, R. W., Lucyshyn, J. M., Horner, R. H., & Flannery, K. B. (1996). Contextual fit for behavior support plans. In L. K. Koegel, R. L. Koegel, and G. Dunlap (eds.), *Positive behavioral support* (pp. 81–98). Baltimore: Brookes.

American Psychiatric Association (2000). *Diagnostic and statistical manual of mental disorders*, 4th ed., text rev. Washington: American Psychiatric Association.

Bambara, L., & Kern, L. (eds.) (2005). *Individualized supports for students with problem behaviors: Designing positive behavior plans.* New York: Guilford Press.

Carr, E. G. (1988). Functional equivalence as a mechanism of response generalization. In R. H. Horner, G. Dunlap, and R. L. Koegel (eds.) *Generalization and maintenance: Lifestyle changes in applied settings* (pp. 221–41). Baltimore: Brookes.

Carr, E. G. (1977). The motivation of self-injurious behavior: A review of some hypotheses. *Psychological Bulletin 84*, 800–16.

Carr, E. G., & Durand, V. M. (1985). Reducing behavior problems through functional communication training. *Journal of Applied Behavior Analysis 18*, 111–26.

Carr, E. G., & Owen-DeSchryver, L. (2007). Physical illness, pain, and problem behavior in minimally verbal people with developmental disabilities. *Journal of Autism and Developmental Disorders* 37, 413–24.

Carr, E. G., Dunlap, G., Horner, R. H., Koegel, R. L., Turnbull, A. P., Sailor, W., Anderson, J., Albin, R. W., Koegel, L. K., & Fox, L. (2002). Positive behavior support: Evolution of an applied science. *Journal of Positive Behavior Interventions* 4, 4–16.

Carr, E. G., Horner, R. H., Turnbull, A. P., Marquis, J., Magito-Mclaughlin, D., McAtee, M. L., Smith, C. E., Anderson-Ryan, K., Ruef, M. B., & Doolabh, A. (1999). *Positive behavior support for people with developmental disabilities: A research synthesis.* Washington: American Association on Mental Retardation.

Chafouleas, S., Riley-Tillman, T. C., & Sugai, G. (2007). *School-based behavioral assessment: Informing intervention and instruction.* New York: Guilford Press.

Conroy, M. A., Dunlap, G., Clarke, S., & Alter, P. J. (2005). A descriptive analysis of positive behavioral intervention research with young children with challenging behavior. *Topics in Early Childhood Special Education* 25, 157–66.

Dawson, G., & Osterling, J. (1997). Early intervention in autism. In M. J. Guralnick (ed.), *The effectiveness of early intervention* (pp. 307–26). Baltimore: Brookes.

Dettmer, S., Simpson, R. L., Myles, B. S., & Ganz, J. B. (2000). The use of visual supports to facilitate transitions of students with autism. *Focus on Autism and Other Developmental Disabilities* 15, 163–9.

Dunlap, G. (2004). Critical features of positive behavior support. *APBS Newsletter* 1, 1–3.

Dunlap, G., & Carr, E. G. (2007). Positive behavior support and developmental disabilities: A summary and analysis of research. In S. L. Odom, R. H. Horner, M. Snell, and J. Blacher (eds), *Handbook of developmental disabilities* (pp. 469–82). New York: Guilford Press.

Dunlap, G., & Fox, L. (1996). Early intervention and serious problem behaviors: A comprehensive approach. In L. K. Koegel, R. L. Koegel, & G. Dunlap (eds.), *Positive behavioral support: Including people with difficult behavior in the community* (pp. 31–50). Baltimore: Brookes.

Dunlap, G., & Fox, L. (1999a). A demonstration of behavioral support for young children with autism. *Journal of Positive Behavior Interventions* 1, 77–87.

Dunlap, G., & Fox, L. (1999b). Supporting families of young children with autism. *Infants and Young Children* 12, 48–54.

Dunlap, G., Ester, T., Langhans, S., & Fox, L. (2006). Functional communication training with toddlers in home environments. *Journal of Early Intervention* 28, 81–96.

Dunlap, G., Johnson, L. F., & Robbins, F. R. (1990). Preventing serious behavior problems through skill development and early intervention. In A. C. Repp and N. N. Singh (eds.), *Current perspectives in the use of non-aversive and aversive interventions with developmentally disabled persons* (pp. 273–86). Sycamore, IL: Sycamore Press.

Dunlap, G., Strain, P., & Ostryn, C. (2010). Addressing challenging behaviors of young children with autism spectrum disorders. In H. H. Schertz, C. Wong, and S. L. Odom (eds.), *Young exceptional children.* Monograph 12: *Supporting young children with autism and their families* (pp. 54–65). Missoula, MT: Division for Early Childhood.

Dunlap, G., Horner, R. H., Sailor W., & Sugai, G. (2009). Origins and history of positive behavior support. In W. Sailor, G. Dunlap, G. Sugai, and R. H. Horner (eds.), *Handbook of positive behavior support* (pp. 3–16). New York: Springer.

Dunlap, G., Kern-Dunlap, L., Clarke, S., & Robbins, F. R. (1991). Functional assessment, curricular revision, and severe problems. *Journal of Applied Behavior Analysis* 24, 387–97.

Dunlap, G., Carr, E. G., Horner, R. H., Zarcone, J., & Schwartz, I. (2008). Positive behavior support and applied behavior analysis: A familial alliance. *Behavior Modification* 32, 682–98.

Dunlap, G., Iovannone, R., Wilson, K., Kincaid, D., Christiansen, K., Strain, P, & English, C. (2010). *Prevent-teach-reinforce: A school-based model of positive behavior.* Baltimore: Brookes.

Fombonne, E. (2005). Epidemiological studies of pervasive developmental disorders. In F. Volkmar, R. Paul, A Kiln, and D. Cohen (eds.), *Handbook of autism and pervasive developmental disorders*, Vol 1: *Diagnosis, development, neurobiology, and behavior*, 3rd ed. (pp. 42–69). Hoboken, NJ: Wiley.

Fox, L., & Hemmeter, M. L. (2009). A program-wide model for supporting social emotional development and addressing challenging behavior in early childhood settings. In W. Sailor, G. Dunlap, G. Sugai, and R. H. Horner (eds.), *Handbook of positive behavior support* (pp. 177–202). New York: Springer.

Fox, L., Dunlap, G., Hemmeter, M. L., Joseph, G. E., and Strain, P. S. (2003). The teaching pyramid: A model for supporting social competence and preventing challenging behavior in young children. *Young Children* 58, 48–52.

Goldstein, S., Naglieri, J. A., & Ozonoff, S. (eds.) (2009). *Assessment of autism spectrum disorders*. New York: Guilford Press.

Guess, D., Helmstetter, E., Turnbull, H. R., & Knowlton, S. (1987). *Use of aversive procedures with persons who are disabled: An historical review and critical analysis*. Seattle: Association for Persons with Severe Handicaps.

Guralnick, M. J. (2005). An overview of the developmental systems model for early intervention. In M. J. Guralnick (ed.), *The developmental systems approach to early intervention* (pp. 3–28). Baltimore: Brookes.

Hieneman, M., & Dunlap, G. (2000). Factors affecting the outcomes of community-based behavioral support: I. Identification and description of factor categories. *Journal of Positive Behavior Interventions* 2, 161–9.

Horner, R. H., & Budd, C. M. (1985). Acquisition of manual sign use: Collateral reduction of maladaptive behavior, and factors limiting generalization. *Education and Training of the Mentally Retarded* 20, 39–47.

Horner, R. H., Dunlap, G., Koegel, R. L., Carr, E. G., Sailor, W., Anderson, J., Albin, R. W., & O'Neill, R. E. (1990). Toward a technology of "nonaversive" behavioral support. *Journal of the Association for Persons with Severe Handicaps* 15, 125–32.

Iwata, B., Dorsey, M., Slifer, K., Bauman, K., & Richman, G. (1994). Toward a functional analysis of self-injury. *Journal of Applied Behavior Analysis* 27, 197–209 (reprinted from *Analysis and Intervention in Developmental Disabilities* 2, 3–20, 1982).

Kanner, L. (1943). Autistic disturbances on affective contact. *Nervous Child* 2, 217–50.

Kincaid, D., & Fox, L. (2002). Person-centered planning and positive behavior support. In S. Holburn and P. M. Vietze (eds.), *Person-centered planning: Research, practice, and future directions* (pp. 29–50). Baltimore: Brookes.

Koegel, R. L., & Koegel, L. K. (2006). *Pivotal response treatments for autism*. Baltimore: Brookes.

Kogan, M. D., Blumberg, S. J., Schieve, L. A., Boyle, C. A., Perrin, J. M., Ghandour, R. M., et al. (2009). Prevalence of parent-reported diagnosis of autism spectrum disorder among children in the US, 2007. *Pediatrics (online)* 124, 395–413.

Lovaas, O. I. (1973). *Behavioral treatment of autistic children*. Morristown, NJ: University Programs Modular Studies.

Lovaas, O. I., (1987). Behavioral treatment and normal educational and intellectual functioning in young autistic children. *Journal of Consulting and Clinical Psychology* 55(1), 3–9.

Luiselli, J. K. (ed.) (2006). *Antecedent intervention: Recent developments in community focused behavior support*. Baltimore: Brookes.

Luiselli, J. K., Russo, D. C., Christian, W. P., & Wilczynski, S. M. (eds.) (2009). *Effective practices for children with autism: Educational and behavioral support interventions that work*. Oxford, UK: Oxford University Press.

Mahoney, G., & Perales, F. (2003). Using relationship-focused intervention to enhance the social-emotional functioning of young children with autism spectrum disorders. *Topics in Early Childhood Special Education* 23, 74–86.

McWilliam, R. A., Scarborough, A. A., & Kim, H. (2003). Adult interactions and child engagement. *Early Education and Development* 14, 7–27.

National Research Council (2001). *Educating children with autism*, Catherine Lord and James P. McGee, eds. Committee on Educational Interventions for Children with Autism, Division of Behavioral and Social Sciences and Education. Washington: National Academy Press.

Olley, J. G., & Reeve, C. E. (1997). Issues of curriculum and classroom structure. In D. J. Cohen and F. R. Volkmar (eds.), *Handbook of autism and pervasive developmental disorders*, 2nd ed. (pp. 484–508). New York: Wiley.

O'Neill, R. E., Horner, R. H., Albin, R. W., Storey, K., Sprague, J. R., & Newton, J. S. (1997). *Functional assessment of problem behavior: A practical assessment guide*. Pacific Grove, CA: Brooks/Cole.

Repp, A. C., & Singh, N. N. (eds.) (1990). *Current perspectives in the use of non-aversive and aversive interventions with developmentally disabled persons*. Sycamore, IL: Sycamore Press.

Robbins, F. R., Dunlap, G., & Plienis, A. J. (1991). Family characteristics, family training, and the progress of young children with autism. *Journal of Early Intervention* 15, 173–84.

Sailor, W., Dunlap, G., Sugai, G., & Horner, R. (eds.) (2009). *Handbook of positive behavior support*. New York: Springer.

Simeonnson, R. J. (1991). Primary, secondary, and tertiary prevention in early intervention. *Journal of Early Intervention* 15, 124–34.

Strain, P. S., & Bovey, E. (2008). LEAP preschool. In J. Handleman and S. Harris (eds.), *Preschool education programs for children with autism* (pp. 249–81). Austin, TX: Pro-Ed.

Strain, P. S., & Hoyson, M. (2000). The need for longitudinal, intensive social skill Intervention: LEAP follow-up outcomes for children with autism, *Topics in Early Childhood Special Education* 20, 116–22.

Strain, P., & Schwartz, I. (2009). Positive behavior support and early intervention for young children with autism: Case studies on the efficacy of proactive treatment of problem behavior. In W. Sailor, G. Dunlap, G. Sugai, and R. H. Horner (eds.), *Handbook of positive behavior support* (pp. 107–23). New York: Springer.

Sugai, G., Horner, R. H., Dunlap, G., Hieneman, M., Lewis, T. J., Nelson, C. M., Scott, T., Liaupsin, C., Sailor, W., Turnbull, A. P., Turnbull, H. R., III, Wickham, D., Ruef, M., & Wilcox, B. (2000). Applying positive behavior support and functional behavioral assessment in schools. *Journal of Positive Behavior Interventions* 2, 131–43.

Trivette, C. M., & Dunst, C. J. (2005). DEC recommended practices: Family-based practices. In S. Sandall, M. L. Hemmeter, B. J. Smith, and M. E. McLean (eds.), *DEC recommended practices. A comprehensive guide for practical application in early intervention/early childhood special education* (pp. 107–26). Missoula, MT: Division for Early Childhood.

Walker, H. M., Horner, R. H., Sugai, G., Bullis, M., Sprague, J. R., Bricker, D., et al. (1996). Integrated approaches to preventing antisocial behavior patterns among school-age children and youth. *Journal of Emotional and Behavioral Disorders* 4, 194–209.

CHAPTER 15

Implementation of a Family-Centered, School-Based Intervention to Prevent Student Academic and Behavioral Problems

Elizabeth A. Stormshack, Kathryn Margolis, Cindy Huang, and Thomas J. Dishion

Family-centered interventions have been found to reduce the risk of problem behavior developing in youth who are most vulnerable for adjustment problems. In this chapter we describe an ecological approach to treatment called *EcoFit* that was inspired by research suggesting that the most successful integrative interventions are those which target multiple domains (e.g., home, family, peers, and school) of children and families. In addition to describing the intervention model and its effectiveness in decreasing youth problem behavior, we also discuss issues relevant to implementation in the school context.

Students' disruptive behaviors at school can cause serious problems for teachers, parents, and society. Youth who exhibit problem behaviors at school often exhibit a combination of other issues, such as low school attendance, poor academic achievement, anxiety, depression, and substance use. In the school setting, risk for problem behaviors increases as youth aggregate into high-risk peer groups (Dishion et al., 1994). Moreover, the number of children with mental health needs has increased dramatically in the past decade, with some reports estimating as many as one in five children experiencing a mental health problem; worse yet, only 20 percent of these children receive the services they need (Biglan et al., 2003; Katoaka, Zhang, & Wells, 2002). Because academic outcomes are closely linked with emotional and physical well-being, youth mental health concerns pose a significant challenge for schools. Nationwide policies such as the No Child Left Behind Act hold schools accountable for youth academic progress and for overcoming the barriers that impede academic progress among those who don't achieve to their expected levels. However, the No Child Left Behind Act has also compromised broader educational goals, such as social skill development and support for at-risk youth who may have strengths in other areas, such as art or music (Cawelti, 2006). Taken together, these circumstances clearly suggest that schools are an ideal setting for implementing interventions that reduce problem behaviors and prevent academic failure (Greenberg et al., 2003).

Developmental science has accumulated a wealth of information about the etiology of student problem behavior and its associated outcomes, such as later school failure (Conduct Problems Prevention Research Group, 1999; Dishion & Patterson, 2006; Blair & Diamond, 2008). Studies examining the development of problems in youth over time reveal a series of difficulties that often begin in the family and community contexts and eventually lead to problems in the school setting, including the academic and peer arena. We have known for many years that poverty, unsafe neighborhoods, and caregiver mental health problems are associated with student problem behavior and academic failure. Despite these contextual risks and stressors, consistent research suggests that parenting practices, such as family management skills, are linked with reductions in youth problem behavior and improved outcomes (Patterson, Reid, & Dishion, 1992; Gorman-Smith, Henry, & Tolan, 2004). Parenting support and skill training can be effective for reducing risk behavior, even in the context of other risk factors and stressors.

The Home-School Link

Schools traditionally have used individualized education plans (IEPs) or other mandated educational planning to manage students' challenges and follow up with a child-focused, school-based intervention to promote academic success. In addition, educational planning is commonly provided only for youths who are at highest risk. Although successful at one level, these child-focused interventions do not address all the factors that contribute to youth problems and are not reinforced by inclusion of parents and families (Christenson, 2003).

Generally, family-centered interventions and school-based interventions have continued to be separate approaches to managing students at risk for academic failure. School personnel are comfortable implementing programs such as Second Steps and the Promoting Alternative Thinking Strategies

Curriculum (PATHS) to groups of children because they target specific problem behaviors, such as aggression and social skills. These programs may provide youth with crucial skills for succeeding in the school environment, but research has shown that approaches to youth mental health must involve the child and the family to be truly effective (Weisz, Jensen-Doss, & Hawley, 2006). Recent studies suggest that the exclusion of parents from child treatment actually can worsen child problem behaviors (Szapocznik & Prado, 2007). In fact, the success rate of school-based approaches to social skills training is improved when parenting is a component of the curriculum (Lochman & Wells, 2004; Spoth, Redmond, & Shin, 1998).

It is increasingly evident that parenting practices can be a risk factor for the onset and development of youth problem behavior and that a solution is to target parenting in intervention and prevention practices (Dishion & Stormshak, 2007; Spoth, Kavanagh, & Dishion, 2002). Other risk factors also must be considered, especially for low-income children, who may encounter additional barriers that directly affect their academic achievement. As shown in Figure 15.1, indicators of school success (e.g., self-regulation, social competence, and literacy skills) shape problem behavior and academic achievement and are the main targets of school-based interventions. Developmental research implies that this model and its variants are robust and significant across ages and cultural groups (Ackerman, Brown, & Izard, 2004; Raver, Gershoff, & Aber, 2007). Contextual stressors caused by poverty, hardship, and parent mental health problems negatively affect parents' ability to use effective parenting strategies at home and decrease the likelihood of parental involvement in the child's learning. Thus, improving family management skills can decrease the negative influence of contextual stress on youth and improve their school outcomes. Our research has shown that our family intervention is linked with changes in child behavior and emotional control (Fosco et al., forthcoming; Stormshak, Fosco, & Dishion, 2010). We investigated

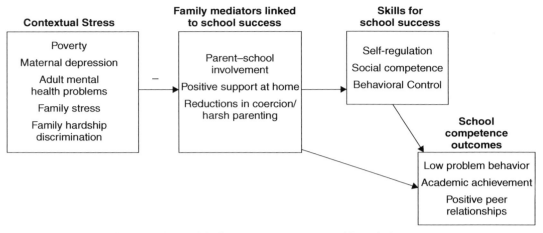

Figure 15.1: A developmental model for intervening in problem behavior to promote school competence.

how the Family Check-Up (FCU; described later in this chapter), a component of EcoFIT designed to enhance family-school partnership to reduce problem behaviors, affected youth self-regulation, depression, and school engagement from the sixth to the ninth grades (Stormshak et al., 2010) and found that it was linked with increased youth self-regulation in seventh grade, controlling for sixth grade levels. In turn, self-regulation was associated with decreased levels of depressive symptoms in eighth grade and increased levels of school engagement in ninth grade. Interestingly, self-regulation was a better predictor of changes in school engagement than was depression, further underscoring the central importance of youth self-regulation processes.

In a second study (Fosco et al., forthcoming), we examined the FCU within a three-wave meditational model of parenting, self-regulation, and antisocial behavior from the sixth to the eighth grades. Consistent with other developmental research results, youth reports of skillful parenting practices were associated with increases in youth self-regulation, which, in turn, were associated with lower levels of antisocial behavior. When intervention effects were added to the model by using an intention-to-treat framework, the findings were similar: Students in the intervention group had greater increases in self-regulation than did those in the control group. Of particular interest, these effects also were true when previous and concurrent levels of parenting practices were accounted for.

Given all the evidence that supports parenting interventions as the most effective means of changing child behavior, it is interesting that family-based interventions are not used more commonly in school settings. School systems have been reluctant to include families in interventions for a variety of reasons, which can be viewed as barriers to effective family-school partnerships (Christenson, 2003). The first barrier is hesitancy on the part of school personnel to get involved with parents about concerns with parenting and family problems. These issues typically are seen as separate from school and therefore should be handled in another context (e.g., mental health agency). The assumption that hard-to-reach families are not invested in education or are somehow unable to support learning at home exacerbates the problem (Mapp & Hong, 2009). Next, schools must deal with budget cuts and the staff's high workload, both of which can prevent involvement with parents and parenting interventions. Last, many of the professionals who work in schools, including school counselors, behavioral support staff, and psychologists, are trained in an individual, child-centered approach to problem reduction and lack the background to work with parents or families. As a result, schools and families have remained separate entities in the treatment of child mental health issues.

The EcoFIT Model

Given the effectiveness of family-centered interventions, the field of family intervention research has shifted its focus to designing intervention programs that are brief, cost-effective, adaptive, and applicable in settings that serve a large number of youth and their families, such as schools (Lochman & van den Steenhoven, 2002; Spoth et al., 2002). The Ecological Approach to Family Intervention and Treatment Model (EcoFIT) surfaced from a series of intervention trials with preschoolers and young adolescents at risk for later problem behavior (Dishion & Kavanagh, 2003; Dishion & Stormshak, 2007; Stormshak et al., 2005).

THE ECOFIT MODEL IS EMPIRICALLY BASED
It is grounded in the developmental research about child and adolescent psychopathology and specifically relevant to behavioral problems (e.g., Dishion & Patterson, 2006; Patterson, Reid, & Dishion, 1992). Parenting practices, especially family management, have been shown to be highly correlated with rates of child and adolescent problem behavior across longitudinal studies examining the etiology of problem behavior (e.g., Loeber & Dishion, 1983). Pertinent to these findings, family management is a central component of the EcoFIT model for effective ecological intervention with children and families.

THE ECOFIT MODEL IS FAMILY-CENTERED
Treatment outcome literature (e.g., Borduin & Henggeler, 1990; Dishion & Patterson, 1992; Eddy & Chamberlain, 2000; Webster-Stratton, 1990) and prevention science research (e.g., Conduct Problems Prevention Research Group, 2002) strongly support the effectiveness of using family-centered strategies

to reduce child and adolescent problem behavior. During the past twenty years, family-centered interventions have shifted from a treatment model that is delivered to clients in clinic settings to an intervention model that recruits parents to proactively engage in interventions that occur in community settings (Stormshak et al., 2005). The EcoFIT approach is designed for implementation in public schools (Dishion & Kavanagh, 2003) and is applicable in various settings, such as preschools and welfare program family services (Shaw et al., 2006).

THE ECOFIT MODEL IS ASSESSMENT-DRIVEN
The intervention is informed by a psychological assessment of children, their families, and their environments (e.g., school, home, and community). The assessments are ecological, comprehensive, and objective, with direct observations playing a critical role in the process. Multimodal, multisource assessments complement clinical impressions and increase the reliability and validity of the case conceptualization. Ecological assessments inform clinical judgment, which improves intervention design and effectiveness.

THE ECOFIT MODEL TARGETS SOCIAL INTERACTIONS IN WHICH MENTAL HEALTH PROBLEMS OF CHILDREN AND ADOLESCENTS ARE EMBEDDED
During the past thirty years, researchers have made great progress in the identification and measurement of the function of relational dynamics between family members and youth and between peers and youth that contribute to mental health concerns for children and adolescents (Dishion & Patterson, 2006). In particular, antisocial behavior correlates with coercive parent-child interactions (e.g., Patterson, Reid, & Dishion, 1992), and interventions that address these dynamics can reduce problem behavior (Dishion, Patterson, & Kavanagh, 1992; Forgatch, 1991; Forgatch & DeGarmo, 2002). An ecological perspective explains individual adjustment in relation to relationship dynamics, and therefore, it is necessary that interventions aiming to strengthen child

adjustment and reduce problem behavior assess and target social interactions.

THE ECOFIT MODEL TARGETS SOCIAL INFLUENCES IN A CHILD'S LIFE BY ADDRESSING PARENTAL MOTIVATION TO CHANGE

The model draws from research about increasing internal motivation to change and assessing readiness to change in its use of motivational interviewing as an effective method (Miller & Rollnick, 2002; Prochaska & Norcross, 1999). Motivational interviewing is used to address parental resistance, which is a common obstacle to change and is related to insufficient family management skills, adult depression, and poor treatment outcomes (Stoolmiller et al., 1993). Providing parents with feedback about the family assessments in a nonconfrontational way helps to engage parents in the intervention for their child.

THE ECOFIT MODEL USES A HEALTH-MAINTENANCE FRAMEWORK

Routine and brief interventions are provided to individuals at key transitional points, and they can be informed by the specific needs of the child (Sameroff & Fiese, 1987). For example, transitional points, such as the shift from elementary to middle school, can present risks for children, who therefore may warrant a brief intervention during that change. In addition, children experiencing contextual risks, such as divorce, may benefit from an intervention timeline that is tailored to their unique individual and family needs. Brief contacts over a long period of time can be used in the treatment, reduction, and prevention of harm relevant to problem behavior and emotional distress in children and adolescents. Integration of the EcoFIT model into a public school or other community setting conforms well with the health-maintenance model because children and families can engage from a setting that has built-in structure and familiarity (Stormshak & Dishion, 2002). For example, schools may find it useful to conduct assessments at the beginning of the year for lower-risk children and at more frequent time points (e.g., weekly, monthly, or quarterly) for higher-risk children.

THE ECOFIT MODEL IS DERIVED FROM A DEVELOPMENTAL-ECOLOGICAL MODEL

As such, the model adaptable to a variety of cultural and contextual factors that may have an impact on child mental health and service delivery. An approach that draws on family strengths ensures that cultural patterns in parenting are integrated into the intervention. In addition, at developmental time periods, such as middle childhood and adolescence, critical attention is given to peer relationships and social interactions because gaining information about these contexts clarifies the protective or risk factors that affect the child's adjustment. Unique cultural values and developmental factors can be incorporated into the model, making EcoFIT an adaptable approach to various cultural groups and families.

Using EcoFIT to Improve Youth Adjustment in School Settings

The critical need to bridge the gap between parents and schools was described earlier in this chapter. The EcoFIT model is a response to that need. The model was designed for implementation in schools and comprises specific components that facilitate parent involvement and family-school connectedness. Components of EcoFIT include the family resource center, the family checkup, and a structured menu of intervention options. Each component is described in the following three subsections.

The Family Resource Center

The *family resource center* (FRC) is a physical location in the school where caregivers can go to access information about resources and supports for their children. The idea has existed since the 1970s and 1980s, when it was used for parents of children with disability status or who were on an IEP, but typically the centers have not been a resource for parenting or for reducing child problem behavior. The FRC is a universal level of intervention in schools that targets children from all risk levels and focuses on parenting and family management skills that can enhance school success. The FRC provides an infrastructure that enables parent-school collaboration, a mechanism for implementation and coordination of family-centered interventions and educational services, and a service for promoting successful adjustment through family management practices that are evidence-based. Essential steps to formation of the FRC include (1) creating a physical space within the school where meetings with parents can be held, (2) integrating the FRC into the existing educational plan (e.g., positive behavior support), (3) identifying a parent consultant or team of trained school staff, and (4) working with school administrators to actively endorse the importance of home-school collaboration.

The FRC should be integrated with existing systems that promote school success, such as School-Wide Positive Behavior Support (SWPBS) (Sprague & Golly, 2005, Sugai et al., 2000, 2001). The FRC is compatible with systems such as SWPBS because it proactively alerts parents to their child's behavior problems at school so that parents can become more actively involved in the remediation of these problems. For example, our research projects have used an ABC report that is sent to parents on a daily (very high-risk students), weekly (at-risk students), or monthly/quarterly basis (all students) (Dishion & Kavanagh, 2003). The ABC report consists of the following components: *A* refers to *attendance* (e.g., excused and unexcused, tardiness), *B* refers to *behavior* (e.g., referrals and teacher reports of students' compliance with behavioral expectations), and C refers to *completion* of academic tasks (e.g., turning in homework, satisfactorily completing courses). Periodic communication such as the ABC reports helps to establish a collaborative home-school link.

After creating the physical FRC space and integrating its services into the existing school behavioral plan, the next step is to *identify a parent consultant*. This person will serve as the parents' ally when they are addressing their child's problem behavior or emotional difficulties. Ideally, the parent consultant is a school staff person, such as the school counselor or vice principal. The consultant acts as a liaison between the school and home; as such, he or she develops behavior plans that work in both settings, coordinates with teachers, communicates with parents, and works with the school system by being involved in system-level planning and change.

It is important that parent consultants are trained to conduct interventions with families and are knowledgeable about school practices. The parent consultant helps to engage parents in a proactive way so that problems can be remediated more effectively. As mentioned previously, an important aspect of remediating problem behavior is supporting parents as they refine their family management skills and motivating parents to change their parenting behaviors. Working with parents to change their parenting practices is a difficult job that requires meeting parents at their stage of change (Prochaska & DiClemente, 1986) and building on their existing skill set. In doing so, it is crucial that the parent consultant is sensitive to parents' struggles with change and can work effectively with resistance to change (e.g., Patterson & Forgatch, 1985). Other necessary skills include building rapport with parents from diverse cultural and contextual backgrounds and collaborating with the student's best interest in mind (Henggeler et al., 1998; Szapocznik & Kurtines, 1989).

After the FRC has become established within the school, parents will begin to use it as a place through which information about their children is disseminated. FRCs in our research project in Portland, Oregon, offer brochures about various aspects of family life and behavior, such as parental monitoring and involvement, limit setting, and completing homework. Our research indicates that parents most often meet with FRC staff about parenting skills and family management, such as limit setting and supervision (41 percent), school problems as identified in the ABC report (25 percent), family problems such as parent distress (e.g., mental health concerns or marital distress) (16 percent); or child adjustment problems, including substance use, depression, and safety (18 percent). It is becoming increasingly clear that the FRC is an important resource for parents in that it supports home-school collaboration and fosters a systemic mechanism for promoting positive youth adjustment and school success.

The Family Checkup

The *family checkup* (FCU) is a selected intervention that can be delivered from the FRC to children and adolescents at higher risk and their families. It offers family assessment, professional support, and motivation to change. The FCU is based on Miller and Rollnick's (2002) motivation-based "drinker's checkup." The FCU accurately assesses the child's risk level relevant to various dimensions, such as home and school behavior, and is followed by a menu of empirically validated interventions. The FCU can be implemented in a public school setting and has been effective in reducing substance use, problem behavior at school, and academic problems in middle and high school, and it effectively enhances parenting skills in early childhood (Dishion et al., 2002; Dishion & Stormshak, 2007).

The FCU consists of three sessions: (1) an initial interview, (2) a comprehensive multiagent, multimethod assessment, and (3) a family feedback session. During the initial meeting, the parent consultant establishes rapport and facilitates discussion about family goals and concerns. This meeting is collaborative and establishes the home-school connection.

The second session involves the integration of diverse ecological perspectives that motivate change in the unique areas of risk for each child and family. During this process, structured reports are gathered from parents, teachers, and the child and are then compared with normative standards. Caregivers who may not be actively involved in the child's life, such as stepparents, are engaged in this process in order to promote collaboration among family members and between the home and the school, which will help to motivate changes in behavior. In addition

to gathering family and teacher reports, the parent consultant or staff member conducts direct observations in the home and at school. Direct observations provide an objective report about family interactions. These diverse perspectives are combined into one family-centered assessment report for which all perspectives are weighed equally and discrepancies in reports can be easily noted and discussed. During the feedback session, this information is presented to parents in a comprehensive format that devotes attention to strengths and areas of concern for the family.

During the third component of the FCU, the *feedback session*, assessment data are communicated in a motivating and strengths-based manner. Information about the parents' and child's areas of risk (e.g., the need to increase parental supervision or child/parent mental health concerns) and the family's areas of strength (e.g., parent-child relationship) are presented through a collaborative process that elicits parents' perceptions relevant to each dimension. Teacher report and observation data are especially useful for providing validation and building motivation because parents repeatedly report feelings of isolation as they manage their child's problem behavior. An essential characteristic of the process is that feedback is delivered in a supportive and motivating way that focuses on family strengths and encourages parent participation. The final part of the feedback session is the collaborative setting of goals by the parent consultant and parents and the provision of a structured menu of intervention options.

Menu of Intervention Options

The FCU enables us to tailor interventions that target the specific goals that parents have identified as necessary areas of growth. Offering a menu of intervention options suggests that a variety of intervention services can be equally effective at reducing problem behavior (Webster-Stratton, Kolpacoff, & Hollingsworth, 1988). This strategy makes it possible to work with parents' readiness to change because parents can proactively select from the various options. For instance, involved parents who may be aware of their child's poor academic performance but know only to criticize the child's poor performance may benefit from a targeted intervention about positive reinforcement. In this case, the FCU would have identified a need for more positive reinforcement and determined that parental involvement was a strength; through motivational interviewing, the caregivers would be encouraged to bolster their skills in involvement by using increased positive interactions.

The intervention menu typically consists of three levels of intervention sessions (Dishion & Stormshak, 2007). The first level provides parents with motivation, support, and the problem-solving skills needed for relatively low-risk problems and issues. For example, after engaging in the FCU, parents may request minimal follow-up telephone calls from the parent consultant that are designed to provide brief, immediate consultation about a problem behavior. These telephone conversations are referred to as *phone check-ins*.

The second level of indicated intervention is referred to as *skill-building interventions*. These interventions help parents to refine skills that are targeted by the FCU as needing improvement, and they closely follow the principles of parental management training (Forgatch, Patterson, & DeGarmo, 2005). Skills that parents often elect to improve through this level of intervention include limit setting, positive reinforcement, parental monitoring, problem solving, and communication. These sessions are conducted either individually with parents or in a group setting with other parents.

The third level of indicated intervention consists of *family adaptation and coping interventions*. Families who experience multiple problems resulting from stressful life events, family disruption such as divorce and remarriage, and potential abuse often struggle to use family management skills because of their emotionally dysregulated environment. Families in this category may benefit from interventions that provide parental support (e.g., individual therapy) and reduce emotional dysregulation (e.g., child or family therapy).

Effectiveness of the EcoFIT Model

Research conducted by means of randomized prevention trials has enabled us to test the effectiveness of EcoFIT by using random assignment of families to receive the FRC and FCU or to receive middle school as usual. Parent consultants were assigned to schools with the task of engaging parents of teacher-identified at-risk youth into the studies. Notable findings for parent engagement and intervention effects were revealed over a ten-year time span.

Engagement

Contrary to common belief that higher-risk families are less likely to seek services, our first research project indicated that parents with higher-risk children were more likely to engage in the FCU. Those who engaged most often were single-parent families, families with students involved in a deviant peer group, and families whose children were rated as highest risk by teachers (Connell, Dishion, & Deater-Deckard, 2006). The second research project actively engaged 40 percent of families in the FCU and revealed that the average number of contacts per family was approximately six, with contacts increasing with child risk level (Dishion et al., 2002). Finally, an effectiveness trial of the EcoFIT that spanned four public middle schools yielded findings that suggested the number of parent contacts in sixth, seventh, and eighth grades was related to reductions in teacher ratings of risk level (Stormshak et al., 2005).

Effectiveness

Three randomized prevention studies have yielded optimistic findings that support the effectiveness of the EcoFIT model for early and middle childhood, preadolescence, and adolescence. In general, random assignment of families to EcoFIT has been found to lower child risk level in terms of reductions in substance use, including marijuana and tobacco use (Dishion et al., 2002); affiliation with deviant peer groups (Dishion, Bullock & Granic, 2002); number of arrests (Connell et al., 2006); and days absent from school (Stormshak, Connell, & Dishion, 2009). The most dramatic effects of assignment to EcoFIT were observed in sixth grade students from the most at-risk families (Connell et al., 2007). For example, reductions in drug use for the highest-risk youth were mediated by changes in observed parental monitoring practices (Dishion, Nelson, & Kavanagh, 2003).

One dimension of antisocial behavior is measured in terms of youth arrest records and school truancy, and assignment to the FCU yielded a dramatic effect on these indicators. Families who engaged in the FCU intervention group evidenced a reduction in the percentage of youth who had been arrested at least once (15 percent arrest record) compared with youth in the control group families who received middle school as usual (100 percent arrest record). Furthermore, sixth graders of families who did not engage in the FCU were six times more likely to be arrested during the next five years than were children of families who received the FCU. In addition to a reduction in arrest frequency, children of families who participated in the FCU attended school more frequently than did those in the control group. Children of families who received the FCU intervention reduced the number of days absent from high school by more than 50 percent from sixth through eleventh grade (Stormshak et al., 2009). Specifically, youth in the control group missed thirty-two days on average compared with thirteen days absent for youth of families who received the FCU. Youth who received the FCU also had higher average grade point averages (GPAs) at high school completion.

These findings indicate that the EcoFIT model successfully reduces substance use, teacher reports of problem behavior, affiliation with deviant peer groups, and days absent from school. Furthermore, the high adaptability of EcoFIT to diverse family and cultural values has yielded high rates of intervention effectiveness across large, ethnically diverse samples from metropolitan areas.

Dissemination of EcoFIT: Considerations for Successful Implementation

Successful dissemination and implementation of an empirically based program are crucial, especially because of growing demands that schools be accountable for students' academic progress. To implement the EcoFIT model successfully, school systems should follow the steps discussed by Flay et al. (2005) for dissemination of evidence-based programs. The first step is that schools must have the resources necessary for successful implementation, including the capability to establish an FRC and provide a school staff person who is able and willing to take on delivery of the intervention.

Next, a training protocol and clearly stated manuals must be disseminated. The training includes specific information about how support for implementation will be provided throughout the school year, how monitoring of school staff will be accomplished, and when consultation with school leaders will occur to evaluate the program's uptake. Intervention manuals that spell out clear content targets and provide multiple tools for targeting each behavior are ideal in a school setting. For example, we focus on three main areas of competence: positive behavior support, limit setting, and family relationships. Teachers, school counselors, and principals can address these areas by using various tools, such as brochures and handouts, that we provide to the school (see Figure 15.2).

The third step is to assess the fidelity of program implementation. Ensuring fidelity of the EcoFIT model requires that descriptive information is made available to staff about how many students are served. It also requires the use of fidelity measurement tools that can be administered quickly. An example of a measurement tool is the Fidelity of Implementation Rating System (FIMP) (Knutson, Forgatch, & Rains, 2005), which is used at the Child and Family Center (CFC) to check fidelity to the EcoFIT model. Preferably, parent consultants in each school provide a videotaped segment of a parent feedback session to the

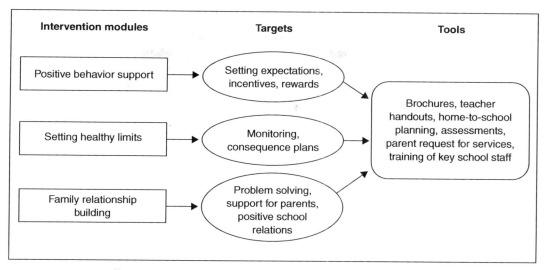

Figure 15.2: Parenting support delivered by school personnel.

CFC, where trained coders use the FIMP to code the tapes and provide feedback to each school about implementation fidelity. This process can be completed online through an interactive website or in person with a consultant to the schools.

We are currently funded to research large-scale evaluation and dissemination of the EcoFIT model. The study will explore factors associated with successful adoption and implementation of the model, such as school environment, school behavioral management practices, and support for staff for implementing the model. This grant project, funded by the Department of Education, will involve random assignment of 44 public middle schools in Oregon to either training and support in the EcoFIT model or school as usual. We will be studying factors that determine successful uptake of the model, such as school-level support, training of staff, and school contact with families. Our current sample of schools already includes very discrepant districts with a wide range of resources for implementation of our project.

Issues for Implementation and Use

Its flexible approach makes the EcoFIT model ideal because interventions can be tailored to meet the individual needs of each

family. However, it is essential for school systems and those implementing the program to be cognizant of barriers that may prevent the EcoFIT model from being successful with some families. Some of these barriers are historical (e.g., past trauma, history of oppression and discrimination), some are contextual (e.g., poverty), and some are chronic (e.g., health and mental health problems, disability). For instance, a family faced with the possibility of becoming homeless may be more concerned with those immediate circumstances than they are about their children completing homework. In this case, the parent consultant's appropriate intervention and support will be to guide the parents to services that will ensure their safety and recovery.

Similarly, ensuring successful adoption and implementation of EcoFIT requires appropriate adaptations of the model for families from diverse cultural groups. As such, the interventions must be consistent with each family's own values in terms of parenting, which often are based in cultural experiences and beliefs (Hill, Bush, & Roosa, 2003). It is critical for the parent consultant and school personnel to work with each family's values and beliefs and still be able to differentiate culturally based parenting practices from ineffective parenting. The

FCU component of the EcoFIT model can be used to address these culturally specific considerations by tailoring the feedback to each family to convey new parenting skills and provide guidance for supportive parenting that is effective in each cultural context.

Conclusion

The EcoFIT model is an effective family-centered, school-based approach to improving youth outcomes in schools and at home. By focusing on parental involvement and addressing parental resistance to change, child problem behaviors and academic concerns are reduced, as evidenced by randomized trials conducted with a diverse population of families. Successful adoption and implementation of the EcoFIT model within schools involves several requisite components, such as school resources and infrastructure, proper training and implementation manuals, and program fidelity checks. Finally, school personnel must be aware of the concerns that may pose a threat to successful implementation, including the context and values of individual families.

Acknowledgments

This work has been supported by Grant 018374 from the National Institutes of Health to the first author and Grant R324A090111 from the Department of Education to the first and fourth authors.

References

Ackerman, B. P., Brown, E. D., & Izard, C. E. (2004). The relations between contextual risk, earned income, and the school adjustment of children from economically disadvantaged families. *Developmental Psychology 40*, 204–16.

Biglan, A., Mrazek, P. J., Carnine, D., & Flay, B. R. (2003). The integration of research and practice in the prevention of youth problem behaviors. *American Psychologist 58*, 433–40.

Blair, C., & Diamond, A. (2008). Biological processes in prevention and intervention: The promotion of self-regulation as a means of preventing school failure. *Development and Psychopathology 20*(3), 899–911.

Borduin, C. M., & Henggeler, S. W. (1990). A multisystemic approach to the treatment of delinquent behavior. In R. J. McMahon and R. D. Peters (eds.), *Behavior disorders of adolescence: Research, intervention and policy in clinical and school settings* (pp. 63–80). New York: Haworth.

Cawelti, G. (2006). The side effects of NCLB. *Educational Leadership 64*, 64–8.

Christenson, S. L. (2003). The family-school partnership: An opportunity to promote the learning competence of all students. *School Psychology Quarterly 18*, 454–82.

Conduct Problems Prevention Research Group (1999). Initial impact of the FAST Track Prevention trial for conduct problems: I. The high-risk sample. *Journal of Consulting and Clinical Psychology 67*, 631–47.

Conduct Problems Prevention Research Group (2002). Evaluation of the first 3 years of the Fast Track Prevention Trial with children at high risk for adolescent conduct problems. *Journal of Abnormal Child Psychology 30*, 19–35.

Connell, A., Dishion, T. J., & Deater-Deckard, K. (2006). Variable- and person-centered approaches to the analysis of early adolescent substance use: Linking peer, family, and intervention effects with developmental trajectories. *Merrill-Palmer Quarterly* [Special Issue] *52*(3), 421–48.

Connell, A., Dishion, T. J., Yasui, M., & Kavanagh, K. (2007). An adaptive approach to family intervention: Linking engagement in family-centered intervention to reductions in adolescent problem behavior. *Journal of Consulting and Clinical Psychology 75*, 568–79.

Dishion, T. J., Bullock, B. M., & Granic, I. (2002). Pragmatism in modeling peer influence: Dynamics, outcomes, and change processes. In D. Cicchetti and S. Hinshaw (eds.), *How prevention intervention studies in the field of developmental psychopathology can inform developmental theories and models. Development and Psychopathology* [Special Issue] *14*(4), 995–1009.

Dishion, T. J., Duncan, T. E., Eddy, J. M., Fagot, B. I., & Fetrow, R. A. (1994). The world of parents and peers: Coercive exchanges and children's social adaption. *Social Development 3*, 255–68.

Dishion, T. J., & Kavanagh, K. (2003). *Intervening in adolescent problem behavior: A family-centered approach*. New York: Guilford Press.

Dishion, T. J., Kavanagh, K., Schneiger, A., Nelson, S. E., & Kaufman, N. (2002). Preventing early adolescent substance use: A family-centered strategy for the public middle school ecology. In R. L. Spoth, K. Kavanagh, and T. J. Dishion (eds.), *Universal family-centered prevention strategies: Current findings and critical issues for public health impact Prevention Science* [Special Issue] 3, 191–201.

Dishion, T. J., Nelson, S. E., & Kavanagh, K. (2003). The FCU for high-risk adolescents: Preventing early-onset substance use by parent monitoring. In J. E. Lochman and R. Salekin (eds.), *Behavior-oriented interventions for children with aggressive behavior and/or conduct problems. Behavior Therapy* [Special Issue] 34(4), 553–71.

Dishion, T. J., & Patterson, G. R. (1992). Age effects in parent training outcome. *Behavior Therapy* 23, 719–29.

Dishion, T. J., & Patterson, G. R. (2006). The development and ecology of antisocial behavior in children and adolescents. In D. Cicchetti and D. J. Cohen (eds.), *Developmental psychopathology*, Vol. 3: *Risk, disorder, and adaptation* (pp. 503–41). New York: Wiley.

Dishion, T. J., Patterson, G. R., & Kavanagh, K. (1992). An experimental test of the coercion model: Linking theory, measurement, and intervention. In J. McCord and R. E. Tremblay (eds.), *The interaction of theory and practice: Experimental studies of interventions* (pp. 253–82). New York: Guilford Press.

Dishion, T. J., & Stormshak, E. (2007). *Intervening in children's lives: An ecological, family-centered approach to mental health care.* Washington: American Psychological Association Books.

Eddy, J. M., & Chamberlain, P. (2000). Family management and deviant peer association as mediators of the impact of treatment condition on youth antisocial behavior. *Journal of Child Clinical Psychology* 5, 857–63.

Flay, B. R., Biglan, A., Boruch, R. F., Castro, F. G., Gottfredson, D., Kellam, S., et al. (2005). Standards of evidence: Criteria for efficacy, effectiveness and dissemination. *Prevention Science* 6, 151–75.

Forgatch, M. (1991). The clinical science vortex: Developing a theory for antisocial behavior. In D. J. Pepler and K. H. Rubin (eds.), *The development and treatment of childhood aggression* (pp. 291–315). Hillsdale, NJ: Erlbaum.

Forgatch, M. S., & DeGarmo, D. S. (2002). Extending and testing the social interaction learning model with divorce samples. In J. B. Reid and G. R. Patterson (eds.), *Antisocial behavior in children and adolescents: A developmental analysis and model for intervention* (pp. 235–38). Washington: American Psychological Association.

Forgatch, M. S., Patterson, G. R., & DeGarmo, D. S. (2005). Evaluating fidelity: Predictive validity for a measure of competent adherence to the Oregon Model of Parent Management Training. *Behavior Therapy* 36(1), 3–13.

Fosco, G. M., Frank, J. L., Stormshak, E. A., & Dishion, T. J. (forthcoming). The family checkup: Evaluating family services delivered in middle schools on youth problem behavior.

Gorman-Smith, D., Henry, D. B., & Tolan, P. H. (2004). Exposure to community violence and violence perpetration: The protective effects of family functioning. *Journal of Clinical Child and Adolescent Psychology* 33(3), 439–49.

Greenberg, M. T., Weissberg, R. P., O'Brien, M. U., Zins, J. E., Fredricks, L., Resnik, H., & Elias, M. J. (2003). Enhancing school-based prevention and youth development through coordinated social, emotional, and academic learning. *American Psychologist* 58, 466–74.

Henggeler, S. W., Schoenwald, S. K., Borduin, C. M., Rowland, M. D., & Cunningham., P. B. (1998). *Multisystemic treatment of antisocial behavior in children and adolescents.* New York: Guilford Press.

Hill, N. E., Bush, K. R., & Roosa, M. W. (2003). Parenting and family socialization strategies and children's mental health: Low-income, Mexican-American and Euro-American mothers and children. *Child Development* 74, 189–204.

Katoaka, S. H., Zhang, L., & Wells, K. B. (2002). Unmet need for mental health care among U.S. children: Variation by ethnicity and insurance status. *American Journal of Psychiatry* 159, 1548–55.

Knutson, N. M., Forgatch, M., & Rains, L. A. (2003). *Fidelity of Implementation Rating System (FIMP): The training manual for PMTO.* Eugene, OR: Oregon Social Learning Center.

Lochman, J. E., & van denSteenhoven, A. (2002). Family-based approaches to substance abuse prevention. *Journal of Primary Prevention* 23(1), 49–114.

Lochman, J. E., & Wells, K. C. (2004). The Coping Power Program for preadolescent aggressive boys and their parents: Outcome effects at the one-year follow-up. *Journal of Consulting and Clinical Psychology* 72, 571–8.

Loeber, R., & Dishion, T. J. (1983). Early predictors of male delinquency: A review. *Psychological Bulletin* 94(1), 68–99.

Mapp, K. L., & Hong, S. (2009). Debunking the myth of the hard-to-reach parent. In S. L. Christenson and A. L. Reschly (eds.), *Handbook on school-family partnerships for promoting student competence* (pp. 345–61). New York: Routledge/Taylor & Francis Group.

Miller, W. R., & Rollnick, S. (2002). *Motivational interviewing: Preparing people for change*, 2nd ed. New York: Guilford Press.

Patterson, G. R., & Forgatch, M. S. (1985). Therapist behavior as a determinant for client resistance: A paradox for the behavior modifier. *Journal of Consulting and Clinical Psychology* 53, 846–51.

Patterson, G. R., Reid, J. B., & Dishion, T. J. (1992). *Antisocial boys*. Eugene, OR: Castalia.

Prochaska, J. O., & DiClemente, C. (1986). Toward a comprehensive model of change. In W. Miller and N. Heather (eds.), *Treating addictive behaviors: Processes of change* (pp. 3–27). New York: Plenum Press.

Prochaska, J. O., & Norcross, J. G. (1999). *Systems of psychotherapy*. Pacific Grove, CA: Brooks/Cole.

Raver, C. C., Gershoff, E. T., & Aber, J. L. (2007). Testing equivalence of mediating models of income, parenting, and school readiness for white, black, and Hispanic children in a national sample. *Child Development* 78(1), 96–115.

Sameroff, A., & Fiese, B. (1987). Conceptual issues in prevention. In D. Shaffer, N. Enzer, & I. Phillips (eds.), *Prevention of mental disorders: Alcohol and other drug use in children and adolescents* (pp. 23–53). Washington: U.S. Department of Health and Human Services.

Shaw, D. S., Dishion, T. J., Supplee, L., Gardner, F., & Arnds, K. (2006). Randomized trial of a family-centered approach to the prevention of early conduct problems: Two-year effects of the FCU in early childhood. *Journal of Consulting and Clinical Psychology* 74(1), 1–9.

Spoth, R. L., Kavanagh, K., & Dishion, T. J. (2002). Family-centered preventive intervention science: Toward benefits to larger populations of children, youth, and families. *Prevention Science* [Special Issue] 3, 145–52.

Spoth, R. L., Redmond, C., & Shin, C. (1998). Direct and indirect latent-variable parenting outcomes of two universal family-focused preventative interactions: Extending a public health oriented research base. *Journal of Consulting and Clinical Psychology* 66(2), 385–99.

Sprague, J. R., & Golly, A. (2005). *Best behavior: Building positive behavior supports in schools*. Longmont, CO: Sopris West.

Stoolmiller, M., Duncan, T., Bank, L., & Patterson, G. (1993). Some problems and solutions in the study of change: Significant patterns of client resistance. *Journal of Consulting and Clinical Psychology* 61, 920–8.

Stormshak, E. A., & Dishion, T. J. (2002). An ecological approach to child and family clinical and counseling psychology. *Clinical Child and Family Psychology Review* 5(3), 197–215.

Stormshak, E. A., Connell, A., & Dishion, T. J. (2009). An adaptive approach to family-centered intervention in schools: Linking intervention engagement to academic outcomes in middle and high school. *Prevention Science* 10, 221–35.

Stormshak, E. A., Dishion, T. J., Light, J., & Yasui, M. (2005). Implementing family-centered interventions within the public middle school: Linking service delivery change to change in problem behavior. *Journal of Abnormal Child Psychology* 33(6), 723–33.

Stormshak, E. A., Fosco, G. M., & Dishion, T. J. (2010). Implementing interventions with families in schools to increase youth school engagement: The family check-up model. *School Mental Health* 2(2), 82–92.

Sugai, G., Sprague, J. R., Horner, R. H., & Walker, H. M. (2000). Preventing school violence: The use of office discipline referrals to assess and monitor school-wide discipline interventions. *Journal of Emotional & Behavioral Disorders* 8(2), 94–101.

Sugai, G., Sprague, J. R., Horner, R. H., & Walker, H. M. (2001). Preventing school violence: The use of office discipline referrals to assess and monitor school-wide discipline interventions. In H. M. Walker and M. H. Epstein (eds.), *Making schools safer and violence-free: Critical issues, solutions, and recommended practices* (pp. 50–7). Austin, TX: PRO-ED.

Szapocznik, J., & Kurtines, W. M. (1989). *Breakthroughs in family therapy with drug-abusing and problem youth*. New York: Springer.

Szapocznik, J., & Prado, G. (2007). Negative effects on family functioning from psychosocial treatments: A recommendation for expanded safety monitoring. *Journal of Family Psychology* 21, 468–78.

Webster-Stratton, C. (1990). Long-term follow-up of families with young conduct problem children: From preschool to grade school. *Journal of Clinical Child Psychology* 19, 144–9.

Webster-Stratton, C., Kolpacoff, M., & Hollingsworth, T. (1988). Self-administered videotape therapy for families with conduct-problem children: Comparison with two cost-effective treatments and a control group. *Journal of Consulting and Clinical Psychology* 56, 558–66.

Weisz, J. R., Jensen-Doss, A., & Hawley, K. M. (2006). Evidence-based youth psychotherapies versus usual clinical care: A meta-analysis of direct comparisons. *American Psychologist* 61, 671–89.

CHAPTER 16

Evidence-Based Reading Interventions

Implementation Issues for the Twenty-First Century

Robert Savage

Overview

This chapter seeks to explore issues in implementation of reading interventions faced by the next generation of researchers and practitioners. Prior to considering implementation, it is argued here that the nature and quality of the basic science need to be considered first. The first part of this chapter considers what we really know with confidence from systematic reviews of intervention experiments on literacy before asking how this then affects the science of implementation. The second part then explores recent work on 'implementation quality' of research undertaken in classrooms exemplification with reference to recent research on the use of literacy technology. I then explore issues concerning the scalability and sustainability of implementations. I illustrate these themes about evidence and research on reading interventions with my own work in the United Kingdom, Australia, and Canada. It is concluded that (1) much work is still needed in the basic science of intervention to support implementation science and (2) teachers and their practice represent

the major focus of implementation and have not been explored sufficiently to date.

What Is Well-Designed Research and What Does It Show?

This chapter forms part of a major text on implementation science. Implementation science is concerned with "the scientific study of methods to promote the systematic uptake of clinical research findings and other evidence-based practices into routine practice" (Implementation Science Journal, 2010). This view strongly suggests, albeit implicitly, that such well-designed research in fact exists, and therefore, we should be concerned about how to mobilize or transfer that knowledge from the clinical trial to the field. In medical research where the discipline of implementation science first emerged, the dominant model of primary research is the clinical trial. Here, 'true' experiments exploring the impact of an independent variable (e.g., a new treatment) on a dependent variable (patient well-being outcomes) are typical. As any student in advanced research methods classes should be able to tell you, such studies typically seek to establish causal links between treatment and outcome in contexts where there are multiple threats to the internal validity of such claims (e.g., Campbell & Stanley, 1963; Gersten et al., 2005). These threats must be protected against by very careful consideration of all aspects of research design. Consequently, the science of clinical trials is well established. The CONSORT group (http://www.consort-statement.org/home/) provides details on all aspects of designing and reporting randomised, controlled trial (RCT) research and criteria for evaluating the quality of such research that should be consulted by anybody interested in evaluating research irrespective of their home discipline [for helpful guidance and a checklist for evaluating research designs in education, see also Gersten et al. (2005)].

A central role in clinical trials is given to well-designed RCTs. RCTs are considered important because in such approaches the chances of each participant being allocated to the intervention or the control are equal. High-quality RCTs provide unique protection that, given a large enough sample, the effects reported are likely to be due to the intervention and not due to chance or a multitude of other extraneous uncontrolled factors. Crucially, however, a strong evidence base for any intervention is built on the multiple replications of such RCT studies by other teams around the world and ultimately on drawing the results of individual RCTs into a pooled study of the impact of all such interventions to determine their overall influence and reliability. Such 'meta-analyses', as they are termed, also can establish which aspects of the trials are most effective. From the perspective of implementation science, they also provide a firm base for policy because if large effects of interventions are evident across many studies, reported patterns are *not* likely to be substantially weakened by the existence of one or two subsequent RCTs that do not replicate original findings [see Savage (2009a) for more details].

Well-executed and well-replicated clinical research trails and the subsequent meta-analyses of such studies may be common practice in the medical sciences. An approach somewhat akin to the clinical trial is evident in some domains of reading research. One is inclined to hear much talk of scientific and evidence-based practice (e.g., McCardle & Chabbra, 2004; McGuinness, 1998). Indeed, I, as well as very many other reading researchers, am a member of a well-established professional society whose main purpose is to undertake 'the scientific study of reading'. Savage & Pompey (2008) thus explored the question, What does the evidence really say about effective literacy teaching? I reviewed a systematic meta-analysis of all RCT design studies on reading available in English. The Savage & Pompey (2008) review explored phonics, text reading comprehension, reading fluency, spelling and educational technologies.

Turning to the first of these domains, phonics, a brief description for the non-expert is first warranted. *Phonics* generally is viewed as the practice of pronouncing individual words from the individual sounds of letters or letter clusters. For example, at the simplest level, the word 'cat' can be assembled from the sounds associated with the letters 'c', 'a' and 't'. Conversely, a child learns to spell words by sounding out the word letter by letter. Such strategies work well in alphabetic systems where words frequently follow letter-to-sound (and sound-to-letter) pronunciation rules. Phonics, however, is controversial in English largely because English, unlike many languages, such as Spanish, German and Dutch, has a complex 'opaque' orthography which admits many exceptions to letter-to-sound and even letter-group-to-sound ('grapheme to phoneme' [GPC]) spelling rules. Indeed, English can be viewed as an 'outlier orthography' compared with most alphabetical writing systems (Share, 2008) owing to the sheer complexity of spelling sound rules and the large number of exceptions to spelling rules [see, e.g., Adams (1990) and Vousden (2008) for reviews and data on the regularity of English spelling].

Observations about the apparent nature of English orthography alone can only take one so far: What does the evidence say on this issue of the efficacy of phonics teaching? Several statistical meta-analytic reviews of well-designed RCTs teaching phonics exist. Among the stronger of these, an extensive systematic review and statistical meta-analysis was undertaken by Bus and van IJzendoorn (1999). This meta-analysis showed that phonic interventions combining phonological-awareness training (the ability to reflect on the sound structure of spoken English) with training of letter-sound knowledge and blending was most effective for reading. Bus & van IJzendoorn (1999) concluded that phonics and phonological awareness are important in English. However, they point out that meta-analysis of joint book reading with pre-school children produces an effect size at least as large as that for early phonic interventions (e.g., Bus, van IJzendoorn & Pellegrini, 1995), so phonics is only one part of the support children need (see also Camilli, Yurecko & Vargas, 2003) for similar methods and conclusions.

A U.S. congress–mandated national research panel (National Reading Panel, 2000) sought to systematically review evidence on early literacy to guide policy. Fifty-two high-quality reading intervention studies exploring the impact of phonological awareness on reading and thirty-eight studies exploring the impact of phonics on reading accuracy were identified. These meta-analyses suggested that the most effective phonics interventions (1) combined phonological skills training with letter-sound knowledge teaching, (2) focussed on one or two reading-related phonological operations (e.g., segmenting and blending all the speech sounds in a word) and (3) were delivered over a relatively short total period of between five and fifteen hours. Systematically delivered explicit instruction was more effective than approaches where phonics was introduced only in the context of story reading or where children were directed only to analyse initial letters

rather than all letters in words. Perhaps most important of all was a fourth point, that *preventative* interventions with children 'at risk' of reading difficulties were identified as being significantly more effective than *remedial* interventions with children already identified as experiencing reading disability. Finally, interventions delivered to small groups of children were at least as effective as one-to-one tutoring.

Critiques of the National Reading Panel (NRP) study have been varied, for example, in being limited to mainly monolingual speakers of English (e.g., Klingner & Edwards, 2006), to being politically naive (Yatvin, 2002) and to have stepped well beyond the evidence base in the recommendations (Allington, 2002). Torgerson, Brooks & Hall (2006) have, however, criticized the NRP meta-analysis directly on methodological grounds. Torgesen, Brooks & Hall (2006) note that the NRP report included both RCT and non-RCT studies. Since RCTs control for the effects of extraneous variables that otherwise might lead to false-positive or false-negative results, additional error may be introduced with the inclusion of quasi-experimental studies. Torgerson, Brooks & Hall (2006) also point out that the NRP report explored only published papers rather than seeking out both published and unpublished papers. The NRP report also generalised control group findings to make desired comparisons. Both approaches may have led to an over-estimation of effect sizes.

Torgesen, Brooks & Hall (2006) carried out a further meta-analysis of the worldwide evidence base for the British government using only RCTs. The results of this analysis confirmed that there was a significant short-term effect of phonics instruction on attainment but that there were no well-designed studies that pursued follow-ups of original intervention programs more than a year or two after the interventions were completed. As a result, there exists no strong evidence on the nature and importance of phonics beyond reception (kindergarten) and years 1 and 2 (grades 1 and 2). Torgesen

Table 16.1. National Reading Panel-Approved Strategies for Reading Comprehension

Strategy	Description
A. Comprehension monitoring. This approach involves the child noting while reading if and how well they understand the text.	Can be assessed by deliberately inserting inconsistencies, e.g., "the *four* billy goats gruff… "
B. Cooperative learning	Help students to work in small groups with discussions of peers views and opinions. In this model, the role of the teacher is to provide 'structure', e.g., to role assignment in groups.
C. Graphic and semantic organizers	The reader graphically represents the meaning and relationship of ideas that underlie words in a text.
D. Story structure	Help children to identify the predictable patterns and 'deep' structure of texts (e.g., in terms of character, plot, etc.) such as 'problem resolution'
E. Question generation (i.e., by a child)	This method involves 'self-directed' speech that is applied to the internal thinking process. Adults may initially scaffold this talk, and children gradually may take it over and externalizing speech and then internalizing speech while reading silently. Meichenbaum & Asarnow (1979) give an example of this:"Well, I have three big things to keep in mind. I ask myself what is the main idea of the story? What is it about? Then what are the main events, and afterwards, what are the characters feeling and why? When I am reading, I should pause sometimes and ask myself what is going on and *listen* to what I am saying to myself, 'Do not worry; keep cool, calm and relaxed.'
F. Question answering	The reader answers high-quality questions posed by the teacher. Higher levels of reading comprehension can be attained if questions posed focus on *processing, analysis,* and *interpretation* rather than only on retrieval of simple factual information.
G. Summarisation	The reader identifies the main or most important ideas from a text among relevant other ideas in the text.
H. Multiple-strategy learning	The judicious combinations of the previous strategies as well as others such as reciprocal teaching and peer-assisted approaches.

Source: National Reading Panel, 2000.

et al. also noted that there was insufficient evidence from studies contrasting different approaches to phonics or from studies systematically varying the length and timing of phonics instruction to draw any reliable particular conclusions about the type of systematic phonics that is necessary or ideal in any reading curriculum, for whom, at precisely what point in their school career, and for what duration. Evidence on how to train teachers to best teach reading also was not available.

If the really high-quality evidence for phonics seems sparse, the evidence base for other aspects of reading is even less strong.

The NRP report of the sub-committee on reading comprehension also explored comprehension, vocabulary and reading fluency. Table 16.1 briefly outlines 'what works' in reading comprehension according the NRP report.

Among these approaches, 'multiple-strategy learning' was deemed the most effective of the reading comprehension strategies by the NRP. Interestingly, it is also the strategy that connected most closely to effective implementation in the classroom (Gersten et al., 2001). In no case was there sufficient evidence to submit data to meta-analyses and to draw conclusions about how best to teach. The NRP also acknowledged that these eight strategies could 'inform practice' rather than be seen as evidence-based approaches as such. Again, as in the review by Torgesen, Brooks & Hall (2006), the NRP committee noted that it is unknown at present how to train teachers to deliver these strategies. Elleman et al. (2009) recently showed from systematic review (of RCTs and quasi-experimental studies) that a reliable overall effect on reading comprehension exists. However, the paper was unable to identify what the most effective vocabulary teaching practice was from a range of approaches documented, leaving implications for implementation unclear.

For reading fluency, only two approaches were considered to have a sufficient evidence base even for a more qualitative review. In the first approach, a cluster of repeated-reading and guided-reading techniques was considered. These techniques focus on reading and re-reading of a given text whilst being given feedback by capable peers or teachers trained in the technique. The second approach simply encourages children to read more widely and consistently during school time. Kuhn & Stahl (2003) point out several limitations to the NRP report on fluency, including the broad diversity of guided-reading techniques used, which only allows for very broad conclusions about what exactly works and concludes that there is not enough strong evidence to support any one specific technique as being superior to others in encouraging children to read more widely.

Beyond the NRP study, it is worth noting how little evidence there is from systematic review or meta-analysis of CT studies for evidence-based practice in just about all other areas of literacy. Savage & Pompey (2008) were unable to locate any systematic reviews of RCTs for spelling or clear evidence from reviews for an impact of technology on literacy (although I will come back to this particular point later). A wider review by Savage (2009b) found that there exists no evidence from RCTs for practices surrounding text composition or writing. There is also relatively little evidence on

multi-lingual practices [there were very few RCTs considered by a subsequent NRP of English as an additional language (August & Shanahan, 2006)]. In my professional education context in Quebec, Canada, the policy of 'French immersion' (also known as 'dual-language system education') involves thousands of children from non-French-speaking backgrounds experiencing their schooling entirely in French. No RCTs of this practice exist either (Genesee & Jared, 2008).

To offset this gloomy picture about RCT research in reading, somewhat more recently, systematic review studies of vocabulary have been published. Mol, Bus & De Jong (2009) and Mol et al. (2008) have shown that a systematic review of RCTs and quasi-experimental studies that shared book reading and dialogic shared book reading interventions in particular measurably improve children's vocabulary, at least when children are very young. There is also a very recent meta-analytical study of studies of morphological awareness training (Bowers, Kirby & Deacon, 2010) showing that it aids reading for young and older typical and atypical readers. Morphemes are the smallest units of meaning within a word (e.g., 'un' – 'help' –'ful' has two 'bound' morphemes at either end and a 'root' morpheme 'help'). Morphological intervention studies seek to help children to identify the shared morphemes in words (e.g., 'nation' and 'national') and thereby support reading, spelling, and vocabulary development. These recent reviews are important contributions to knowledge, showing that intervention here can work. Arguably, these recent studies share with previous work a feature of not leading directly to a recommended practice and did not restrict themselves to RCT studies, so they may inflate effect sizes. Rather, they suggest that a range of practices may be equally efficacious. The key shared elements of such effective interventions remain to be identified. Because of their newness, they also often rely on experimental tasks to assess outcomes which may create larger effect sizes than would be present in age-standardised measures. While clearly efficacious, it is not yet clear that they are effective in real-world classroom teaching contexts.

Conclusion and Implications

This section sought to explore the evidence base for an implementation science of reading. The mini-review suggests that although evidence in support of phonics in reading is in a general sense strong (there are no meta-analytical reviews that have not reported a significant effect and at least three that have), there are, however, very many unanswered questions about phonics concerning the nature, duration, timing and universal suitability of this approach. Arguably the evidence supports prevention over remediation with a limited set of productive strategies such as blending and segmenting. In this sense, there is much agreement that teachers thus should not 'wait for children to fail' before deploying phonics programs. The evidence base takes us only so far, however. It is also far stronger than any other domain of reading research (e.g., comprehension, fluency and spelling to name but a few where there was almost no evidence from series of well-designed RCTs). More generally, the research base is consistent with the work of Seethaler & Fuchs (2005), who noted that in education and psychology, RCTs of reading and mathematics represent substantially less than 5 per cent of all published papers, even in the leading journals in the field, and therefore only be considered a 'drop in the bucket'.

This analysis clearly affects any science of implementation for reading. It is demonstrably wrong to view the state of the literature here as one where the highest-quality research is currently available and awaiting appropriate mobilisation. How might one respond to this state of affairs? One response might be to be guided to a lower level of evidence quality. For example, one might implement 'evidence-based' approaches on the basis of a few reasonably well-designed RCTs rather than systematic reviews of well-designed RCTs. This is a reasonable approach in many senses. Given that there is no strong systematic evidence

base for implementation in many areas of reading research, more detailed investigation of implementation issues for one body of research on technology-based intervention, where a few well-designed RCTs have emerged, is taken up in the second section of this chapter.

The approach of implementing 'evidence-based' approaches on the basis of a few reasonably well-designed RCTs rather than systematic reviews nevertheless requires some caution. More specifically, this approach is simply more fragile than practice based on meta-analyses. The assumptions behind implementations based on a modest base of even well-designed RCTs might be quickly overturned by new evidence from one or two new RCTs in a way that would not be possible with meta-analyses of RCTs. This is most problematical where the new study or studies report large effects in the opposite direction to the previous RCTs. A concrete example of a domain of reading where this may be a risk is the micro-debate concerning the relative efficacy of *synthetic* and *analytical* phonic methods. 'Analytical phonics' is a form of phonics where teachers show children how to deduce the common letter and sound in a set of words which all begin or end with the same grapheme (e.g., *p*et, *p*ark, *p*ush, *p*en). By contrast, in 'synthetic phonics', sounding out of individual grapheme-to-phoneme correspondences (GPCs) is emphasised. For reading, this sounding out is based on the graphemes of printed words and is followed by blending of these sounds to produce a spoken word which the learner should recognise.

This issue of synthetic versus analytical phonics is also raised here as an example of the potential fragility of such evidence-based policy, as well as an example of how relatively modest research evidence and strongly articulated policy sometimes can come to be connected. In this particular case, the Rose review of the teaching of English in England (Rose, 2006) was a government-led review of national reading policy in schools. The conclusions of the report firmly asserted the need for the exclusive use of synthetic approaches in primary (elementary) classrooms. Internationally, the call also has been firmly for synthetic phonics and against analytical (and other) approaches when drawing up recommendations for national or provincial literacy policies [e.g., in Australia, Bowey (2006); in the United States, McGuinness (1998) and National Reading Panel (2000), among many others]. However, the evidence base is modest. With only three RCTs available directly contrasting synthetic and analytical approaches and with very modest differences between the two approaches reported in terms of overall effect size, Torgesen, Brooks & Hall (2006) described the evidence base as 'weak'. New RCT data and new interpretations of the data in the review by Torgesen et al. suggest that at least for some children with English as an additional language, from urban low socio-economic status backgrounds, early intervention in reception (kindergarten) using analytical phonics approaches was more efficacious than synthetic approaches when measured at a one-year follow-up (Di Stasio, Savage & Abrami, 2010).

Given the limited evidence base, one might decide not to use RCTs or not to rely solely on them in implementing evidence-based practice. There are many methodologies in the social sciences, and rightly so given the range and complexity of questions explored in education faculties worldwide. All have a claim to being evidence-based in the general sense. If one relaxes the constraint on using RCTs, one might go a long way by exploring classroom practice and the needs of diverse students (see, e.g., Klingner & Edwards, 2006). One would have to be more circumspect about calling the basis for this policy 'scientific' and 'evidence-based' (in the specific sense used in implementation science), science being based as it is squarely on the experimental method. The opportunity to explore or confirm genuine causal models in the real world is also lost, of course, without RCTs.

It must be noted, of course, that the issues in running RCTs are significant. In terms of cost, commitment, funding, complexity and perhaps ethics, too, where treatments have to be withheld, albeit temporarily, huge additional resources are needed. Intervention research requires exceptional partnerships and trust between teams of researchers and schools and school districts, a shared agenda around improved student outcomes and an understanding of what is and is not possible in classrooms. Such partnerships are, perhaps unsurprisingly, infrequent. Arguably, they are made even harder by the fact that universities and school systems apply different pressures. On the one hand, the pressure to be seen to publish in academia is a pressure that always favours smaller-scale research work. On the other hand, education professionals are inexperienced with a culture of research-based practice and perhaps fear (sometimes rightly!) that approaches used over-simplify professional life, and data might be used in ways that do not benefit teachers and pupils. It is thus understandable that RCTs specifically, and indeed interventions research generally, are rare.

Nevertheless, RCT studies are possible to do well, with genuine partnerships, even at a large scale, as we describe later. A concerted call for some devoted funds in the social sciences to lay a foundation of basic science of intervention and then of implementation is clearly needed. I feel that to be maximally effective, such money should seed collaborative relationships with school professionals to cultivate an embedded culture of evidence-based practice as much as to pay for the running of distinct trials. Arguments based on the long-term value for money are persuasive here. The best evidence-based practice potentially can alter the life paths of millions of children, personally as well as economically. On the other hand, for each child who drops out of high school, the knock-on costs in social services has been estimated as being as high as three million dollars *per* child (Vanderstaay, 2006).

On a different tack, I also would note that even the best-designed RCTs faithfully following CONSORT-type criteria still have much to improve. Practice is constantly evolving. For example, one new direction we would encourage is the *pre*-publishing of research designs and research predictions.

Such approaches require a researcher to say what outcomes are primary and are consulted when a final research paper is submitted to a journal. This practice engenders greater transparency in reporting results and ensures genuine hypothesis testing in interventions, as well as appropriate statistical control for analysis of secondary outcomes. In our own research using an RCT in the Northern Territories, Australia, using the ABRACADABRA web-based reading intervention (described in detail below), we registered the trial with the official RCT clinical trial site in Australia and specified that outcomes in the word recognition and phonological domain would be primary measures. We believe that this is the first educational trial to undertake this step. We suspect that in twenty years such practices will be common in educational research.

Finally, we also should note that nearly all intervention research described here concerns early reading acquisition in English. As Share (2008) has argued, we may wish to view English as an 'outlier orthography' compared with other alphabetical systems. Certainly, the task facing children learning to read in Spanish or German (where reading fluency not accuracy issues may quickly dominate) or Chinese (where morphology may dominate the development of literacy) cannot necessarily be equated with that of English literacy learners (McBride-Chang et al., 2005). It may be that the apparent 'stage' of development in English where reading accuracy requires primary focus is one that simply does not apply (or perhaps applies to nowhere near the same extent beyond grade 1) in languages with orthographies that have consistent GPCs. In this sense, any implementation science in reading will always be orthography-specific.

Implementation Quality: The Case of Technology Integration

The approach of implementing 'evidence-based' approaches on the basis of a few reasonably well-designed RCTs rather than systematic reviews was considered in the first part of this chapter. One domain that Savage & Pompey (2008) found little evidence for was the use of educational technology. Despite the widespread use of technology in schools (e.g., Cuban, 2001), little firm evidence for its efficacy exists from well-designed RCTs. The strongest evidence of intervention effectiveness for information and communication technology (ICT) comes from three comprehensive systematic reviews (see Ehri et al., 2001; Slavin et al., 2008; Torgerson & Zhu, 2004) and a 'tertiary' review in which many systematic reviews are included for a further review (Torgerson, 2007).

Torgerson & Zhu (2004) reviewed the efficacy of the very few ICT-based interventions that used RCT designs. They reported that only small and statistically non-significant effect sizes for interventions were evident across all such studies, suggesting that there is only a modest benefit from the use of ICT in improving spelling and reading ability. Torgerson & Zhu (2004) concluded that teachers should not be persuaded to use technology to teach literacy until several well-designed RCTs with positive effects have been published. Similarly, a systematic review of technology on middle and high school learning by Slavin et al. (2008) found only eight well-designed intervention studies. The mean effect size was a very modest + 0.10, suggesting that computers do not aid literacy in middle schools. It is worth noting that the review by Slavin et al. considered only published papers (and did not seek unpublished reports which often have weaker findings), so the effect size may be inflated by publication bias. The real effect size of computers on literacy could be even nearer to zero.

The National Center for Educational Evaluation and Regional Assistance in the United States evaluated technology-based reading interventions using a range of commercially available ICT products across 33 school districts in 132 schools with a total of 4,389 teachers (Dynarski et al., 2007). Dynarski et al. (2007) used a large-scale RCT design. Their results, however, showed that the mean effect size for interventions was not significantly different from zero on standardised or local provincial tests of reading in either grade 1 or grade 4. Campuzano et al. (2009) followed up this first study in a subset of classrooms and also reported almost no significant effects of technology intervention. One program (of ten) has a significant impact on one type of outcome measure.

It should be noted, however, that a close reading of the study by Dynarski et al. (2007) shows that around a third of teachers did not feel qualified or ready to use the technology after a single day of professional development training given several weeks before the intervention. Perhaps owing to the sheer size of the study, details on the way (or, more realistically, ways) technology was implemented in the classroom were not reported, and it is hard to get a sense of how teachers used technology. In the follow-up study reported by Campuzano et al. (2009), there was no assessment of treatment integrity (whether and how technology actually was implemented in classrooms) owing to project budget cuts. Another limitation of the studies by Dynarski et al. (2007) and Campuzano et al. (2009) is that while they selected technologies that, according to the manufacturers, had been research-validated, there was no independent assessment of the nature and quality of the technology programs used. It may be that the specific programs used were not *efficacious*; that is, they may not have improved literacy even in a perfectly controlled and executed experimental (RCT) intervention study, let alone being *effective* in a field-based implementation study.

According to the classic definition from Cochrane (1971), 'effectiveness trials' seek to explore the impact of interventions under 'real-world conditions'. In the context of educational implementation, 'effectiveness' refers to naturalistic field-based interventions undertaken by briefly trained regular teachers within their regular classrooms and alongside their other regular practices. The key point is that here teachers thus ultimately control the quality of the interventions delivered. Such designs have

maximal external validity (relevance to the real world). In contrast, 'efficacy trials' seek to explore the impact of interventions under optimal conditions of experimental control over variables. In the present context, 'efficacy' refers specifically to significant advantages in reading in experimental trials run by university-based researchers and delivered in ways that are not typical features of regular school settings and practice, such as by extra one-on-one contact or small group support. Here, university-trained researchers ultimately control the quality of the intervention delivered. Such designs have maximal internal validity (the highest chance of demonstrating a causal link between a dependent and independent variable).

On review, the field of educational technology and literacy requires evidence from at least one or two well-executed RCTs that first demonstrate the internal validity of a particular technology, followed by large-scale field-based implementation of that same technology resource to demonstrate its external validity in a second phase. In addition, we know very little about how teachers actually use technology in their classrooms from existing large-scale studies (Campuzano et al., 2009; Dynarski et al., 2007). A third phase of research exploring in detail the processes used by teachers when using technology in different ways would be a useful addition to the field of pure research and to implementation science. We thus describe our programmatic research on the ABRACADABRA web-based literacy resource below.

The ABRACADABRA Web-Based Literacy Program

ABRACADABRA (hereafter ABRA) is an acronym for A Balanced Reading Approach for Canadians Designed to Achieve Best Results for All. ABRA is a completely free-access web-based literacy software for beginning readers. ABRA has four different modules – letters and sounds, reading, comprehension and writing/spelling – that can be used flexibly as required. There is no curriculum or other prescription to follow in using the resource. It currently has a total of thirty-two distinct types of levelled activities and seventeen stories for children, as well as parent and professional development sections and resources and assessment and communication tools for educators.

ABRA development was undertaken by a collaborative multi-university team affiliated to the Centre for the Study of Learning and Performance uniting researchers, instructional and creative designers and educational professionals in a research and development (R&D) team [see, e.g., Abrami et al. (2008) and Hipps et al. (2005) for details on the development of the resource]. ABRA was based on the best-available evidence from previous systematic reviews on effective reading interventions for phonics and letter skills, reading fluency and reading comprehension (e.g., Camilli et al., 2003; National Reading Panel, 2000); Hammill, 2004; Rosenshine & Meister, 1994; Torgerson, Brooks & Hall, 2006; Wolf & Bowers, 1999). ABRA is designed to reflect a balanced literacy approach (e.g., Pressley, 1994) with activities drawn from reviews of effective reading practices (e.g. National Reading Panel, 2000; Rosenshine & Meister, 1994) as well as from review of RCTs. The most recent version of ABRA includes instructional, professional development and parent modules, as well as pupil resources, and can be found at http://abralite.concordia.ca. A version of the tool containing additional assessment and communication modules is also freely available, but given that it can store student records, it must be downloaded and stored on a school board (local education authority) server via http://grover.concordia.ca/abracadabra/.

The Evidence Base for ABRACADABRA

EFFICACY STUDIES

ABRACADABRA is supported by evidence from two RCTs published in high-quality peer review journals. Each study has a post-intervention follow-up. The first RCT evaluation of ABRA contrasted the efficacy of synthetic phonics versus analytical phonics (Comaskey, Savage & Abrami, 2009). ABRA was designed with modules that contain a range of phonic activities that allow the contrast of different approaches to phonics teaching while keeping the activities equivalent on other extraneous features. In this sense, ABRA offers a very fair test of competing phonics theories. The sample was fifty-three children from a disadvantaged low socio-economic status (SES) urban kindergarten where the majority of students experienced English as a second language. Children were exposed to ten to fifteen minutes of ABRA instruction in small groups three times per week for thirteen weeks in a centre-based classroom where children would rotate around the centre, as in 'water play', 'pretend play', and 'ABRACADABRA play' centres. The study was executed and reported following the CONSORT criteria for reporting RCTs. Results suggested that synthetic and analytical programs have qualitatively different effects on children's phonological development. Children exposed to the synthetic phonics approach showed significant improvement in consonant-vowel (CV; e.g., 't' – 'ea') and vowel-consonant (VC; e.g., 'ea' – 't') word blending and the articulation of final consonants, whereas children in the analytical phonics approach showed, as predicted, significant improvements in articulating shared rimes in words (e.g., finding 'ack' in 'back' and 'sack').

Di Stasio et al. (2010) followed up these children in the paper by Comaskey et al. (2009) one year later and reported that results revealed a significant main effect ($p < 0.01$) for the analytical group performing better on a passage reading comprehension task than the analytical phonics group. Modest advantages for children who received the analytical phonics program were evident across other measures too. Di Stasio et al. report an effect-size change in reading standard score that is favourably comparable with other studies, after adjusting for the number of hours of intervention per child (ES = 0.41). Di Stasio et al. concluded that analytical phonics programs may provide modest but significant sustained advantages in literacy for kindergarten children from low SES backgrounds.

Savage et al. (2009) explored the effectiveness of ABRA in 144 typically developing year 1 (grade 1) children using an RCT design. Similar to Comaskey et al. (2009), Savage et al. (2009) contrasted two computer-based interventions: a phoneme-based synthetic phonics and a rhyme-based analytical phonics method. All children in the interventions also received activities to support comprehension and fluency. Unlike Comaskey et al. (2009), in this study, there also was a regular classroom control. Notably, the children were randomised *within classroom* so that intervention and control-group children all received the same regular classroom teaching outside the intervention itself. Children received the intervention in small groups for an average of thirteen hours per child over one term delivered by trained research assistants. Significant differences between treatment and control groups at post-test were evident on phonological awareness, listening comprehension and reading (favouring the synthetic phonics program) and letter-sound knowledge (favouring the analytical phonics program), as well as overall effect sizes that were significantly different from zero at post-test and at delayed post-test eight months after the intervention closed for both interventions in comparison with the controls.

In a related study with the same students, Deault, Savage & Abrami (2009) found that attention predicted significantly more variance in growth in attainment in the control condition, whereas attention no longer predicted growth in reading outcomes in synthetic phonics. That is, children with initially low attention skills in year 1 appeared to find it easier to concentrate and learn more effectively during the synthetic phonics rather than the analytical phonics intervention. Deault et al. (2009) concluded that ABRA can influence the associations between literacy and attention and may support students at risk of reading and attention difficulties. Together these student-delivered efficacy studies with high internal reliability show that ABRA is effective in raising literacy skills of typical and atypical children in kindergarten and grade 1.

EFFECTIVENESS STUDIES

To date, one large-scale effectiveness study has been undertaken (Savage et al., 2010). This study was a large-scale RCT study involving seventy-four classrooms across three provinces (Quebec, Ontario and Alberta) across Canada. Reception (kindergarten) and year 1 and mixed year 1–2 classes were included. Randomisation was undertaken at the classroom level. That is to say, we sought out schools with two classes for each year group and then randomly allocated one classroom to the intervention and one to control conditions. The total sample was in excess of 1,000 children. Intervention over one semester was analysed using hierarchical liner modelling (HLM) techniques that control for pupil-level variance to explore the effects of classrooms (in this case, intervention versus control classrooms) on post-intervention reading skills controlling for pre-test levels on each respective measure. Results showed that children in intervention classrooms made significant growth in standardised measures of phonological blending skills, as well as showing strong effect sizes for improvement across other measures of early reading and related ability. Other field-based RCTs of ABRA are underway at the time of this writing in the Northern Territories of Australia as well as near completion in Alberta, Canada (Piquette-Tomei, Savage & Wesley, 2010). If replicated in these subsequent field-based trials, the study by Savage et al. shows that ABRA is a valuable resource that can be used on the national scale by teachers to improve phonological skills as well as other reading skills.

Studies of Teacher Use of Technology

We know from much previous research that the extent of teachers' computer use at home and their computer training (Wozney, Venkatesh & Abrami, 2006), comfort and confidence with computers (Chen & Chang, 2006), and beliefs related to computers and technology expertise (Chen, 2008; Sang et al., 2010), fear about having to change current teaching methods, as well as anxiety and other emotional reactions towards computers all affect teachers' use of computer technology (see Kay, 2008; Mueller et al., 2008; Wood et al., 2008). We sought to explore when teachers *do* use technology, how does variation in practice affect student outcomes? In this regard, we sought to go beyond traditional notions of treatment integrity, which simply ask, Did the teacher follow the intervention in the prescribed fashion? to explore whether qualitatively different ways of using the technology affected literacy outcomes.

One helpful frame for making sense of teachers use of technology is the work of Sandholtz, Ringstaff & Dwyer (1997). These authors developed a five-stage model of technology use. The first three stages are described below. The first stage is the 'entry stage'. It is characterised by the making of time-consuming mistakes, getting more frustrated, and as a result, ending up making more mistakes, which might cause them to stop using technology altogether (Sandholtz et al., 1997). At this stage, even experienced teachers often can find themselves facing typical problems of novice teachers (Sandholtz et al., 1997) such as executing a lesson plan or leading a session effectively or effectively differentiating or providing sufficient progression of learning for children. As a result, teaching is likely to remain unchanged with technology.

In the next stage – the 'adoption stage' – teachers begin to apply technology in a systematic manner albeit with minimum experimenting. Reflecting, inexperience with the technology, 'teachers attempted to blend its use into the most familiar form of classroom practice: direct instruction' (Sandholtz et al., 1997). Teaching with technology here, however, is marked by generally systematic, well-planned and well-executed lessons. Nevertheless, technology-based learning is not linked well to other forms of learning, such as collaborative or experientially based learning.

In the 'adaptation stage', teachers integrate technology in their instructional designs. This stage is often marked by a realisation of the personal and professional benefits of technology for them and their

students. Transformation of classroom teaching and learning by the use of technology can be seen here. Technology is viewed as a vehicle for achievement of wider learning and is reflected in much broader planning and greater connectivity between all forms of learning in wider learning themes.

Sandholtz's model predicts clear change in student outcomes at different stages of technology use. Much traditional empirical research using treatment integrity measures which documents the differences between what might be seen as ineffective entry-level use and the more effective faithful adoption of innovative interventions on literacy outcomes (e.g., Davidson, Fields & Yang, 2009). However, beyond this advantage for adoption over entry levels of implementation, Sandholtz's model predicts that the adaptation stage will produce large advantages over both the adoption stage and the entry stage. However, these predictions have not been directly tested empirically.

Savage et al. (2010) thus explored how teacher variations in use of a web technology of known effectiveness affected growth in literacy. Teachers used a version of ABRA (http://grover.concordia.ca/abra/version1/abracadabra.html) in grade 1 language arts classes in Canada. Children ($N = 60$) across three classrooms were exposed to ABRA activities, and a control class followed the regular provincial literacy program. Interventions were run by briefly trained teachers for a total of 16 hours. Each teacher chose to use the program in qualitatively distinct ways that corresponded to the first three stages of the technology integration model of Sandholtz et al. (1997), namely: entry, adoption, and adaptation. Growth in literacy between the pre-test and the post-test significant differences associated with technology integration style across all measures of literacy and related language skills. The largest and most widespread effects were evident for the adaptation group that linked technology content to wider learning themes in the classroom. In terms of overall growth in standardized literacy scores across all six such measures used, adaptation proved to be 60 per cent more effective than adoption. Results suggest that explorations of exactly how teachers use technology have important implications for practice as well as for the interpretation of field-based studies of the effectiveness of educational technology.

Effective teaching with ABRA was marked by the teacher's technical competency with ABRA, as well as good pedagogy: Good lesson planning and clear differentiation was observed in the adoption and adaptation classrooms. Effective teaching included attention to both word decoding and text comprehension activities within ABRA rather than a reliance on one aspect of reading over the others. However, the most effective intervention, adaptation, also was marked by a more transformative use of the ABRA system integrated into wider learning, referred to outside of and connected to the non-technological aspects of the language arts curriculum. By contrast, entry-level use of technology was marked by technical issues in delivery and was not well planned, systematic, well differentiated, balanced across text and word-level activities and delivered by the teacher. Teaching with technology of this nature was observed in the entry-level intervention condition and did not yield any significantly greater student literacy learning outcomes whatsoever at post-test than did no exposure to ABRA.

Several other factors may have been important in the effectiveness of ABRA. The most effective teachers used centre-based approaches and small collaborative groups. Teachers provided frequent feedback and acted as facilitators in the intervention which may have mediated learning experiences (Klein, Nir-Gal & Darom, 2000; Willoughby & Wood, 2008). There is also a lot of evidence now that collaborative small-group-based interventions in general can have larger effects than individual interventions and may support the weakest readers most effectively (Foorman & Torgesen, 2001; National Reading Panel, 2000; Nind et al., 2004; Wanzek et al., 2006). Effective teachers also were supported by other school staff, including the school principal, in teaching with technology, suggesting that a collective community role may be important for technology use in schools.

Another fact about implementation that might explain the effectiveness of ABRA is that ongoing support was provided to teachers. Unlike Dynarski et al. (2007) and Campuzano et al. (2009), here, all teachers in the study participated in a training day and also received continuous support when delivering ABRA in their language arts classes. We gave constant support through regular visits, phone and e-mail advice, detailed guidance on pacing the curriculum and feedback on teaching. A subsequent study by Anderson et al. (2010) also explored the impact of support on teachers' use of technology. Ten teachers (four kindergarten, four grade 1 and two grade 1–2 teachers) received just-in-time instructional support over a two and a half month period as they implemented a reading software program as part of their literacy instruction. In-class observations were made of each instructional session. Analysis of the 80 just-in-time support observations indicated that the greatest number of support requests pertained to computer software, followed by computer hardware. A smaller number of requests for support were made regarding classroom management, reading and 'other' issues. As expected, the greatest level of support was required during the initial stages of implementation, with the number of support requests declining over time. Interestingly, the types of support requested remained constant over this extended implementation period, indicating that immediate problems related to software and hardware concerns continue to be the most problematical when integrating technology. The vast majority of problems, however, could be addressed immediately through just-in-time support, allowing the scheduled class to continue as planned. This study provides direct support for just-in-time instruction as an instructional support that can ease the transition to computer integration.

One issue that is worth bearing in mind is the multi-faceted nature of the ABRA intervention. At one level it is an evidence-based literacy resource that can directly affect students if teachers deliver it faithfully. 'Implementation', however, is not a random process but in large part a professional choice. While involving issues of teacher comfort with technology, the decision to implement a study also involves teachers exploring their views of what constitutes good teaching and reflecting on their own knowledge base. On the positive side, if teachers can see the benefit, they sometimes learn about approaches they can incorporate into their practice and even use technology to transform their practice. On the other hand, if a teacher's knowledge or approach is threatened by the technology (or what it might be held to represent), he or she may choose not to become competent in using it or implicitly or explicitly devalue it. This point raises difficult questions about what one is measuring when one looks at implementation here and generally. In implementation science, the decision by a teacher to be involved in a study might be the important focus of research as much as the effects of an intervention itself. In ABRA specifically, there may be a role for exploring through 'thick description' the technology-based and non-technology-based aspects of their classroom teaching before and well after ABRA has been introduced into classrooms.[1]

In Savage et al. (2010), different sources were used to monitor the treatment integrity and quality of the intervention and to identify the distinct ways of ABRA implementation. We have subsequently used this framework to construct a treatment quality indicator for use in other research. This is depicted in Figure 16.1. The first category represents the control condition. The next three categories reflect the entry, adoption, and adaptation stages of technology use from Sandholtz, Ringstaff & Dwyer (1997), and the last category reflects the highest level, involving the transformative teaching of text comprehension as well as word-level skills through technology. Preliminary analyses show that the tool has high inter-rater reliability (in excess of 0.80) for classifying classrooms observed. Classrooms rated as 'adaptive' also were associated with greater gains in phonological blending skills and

text comprehension in our pan-Canadian study reported earlier (Savage et al., 2010). Comparable results have been reported in a recent Australian trial (Wolgemuth et al., 2010).

Some Reflections on Scalability and Sustainability of Interventions

Arguably, the single biggest challenge facing reading researchers, implementation scientists and practitioners in the twenty-first century is the issue of building scalable and sustainable interventions. In one sense, our research using the ABRA resource is one way to do at least some of this because we have demonstrated that it can be used at scale across Canada. Preliminary data suggest that it can be used effectively elsewhere too. ABRA has been embedded within the practice of several school boards and their professional support staff. The use of 'open' free access as opposed closed pay-per-use interventions must aid scalability. One-year follow-ups after the interventions have finished suggest that early advantages from using ABRA are sustained in this specific sense of the word. However, I am under no delusions that sustained change in practice will improve simply as a result of the construction of an accessible web-based resource and dissemination of resource and research findings. Research is also needed on which teachers continue to use ABRA and why and how they do so.

It seems likely that major changes to educational practice and indeed to the whole organisation of school boards might be associated with effective change in intervention research. To take but one example of interventions that seek to change practice, Solity & Vousden (2009) describe major changes in teaching and curricular practices associated with their effective early reading research (ERR) reading intervention in the United Kingdom. Similar findings have been reported in their more recent studies. Shapiro & Solity (2008) asked reception and year 1 teachers to change their practices to use bespoke 'distributed learning' techniques to teach key blending skills to

CONTROL (1)	ENTRY (2)	ADOPTION (3)	ADAPTATION (4)	DIFFERENTIATED ADAPTATION (5)
♦ No implementation ♦ No aspect of ABRA was used	♦ Little to No evidence of teacher planning of ABRA/ELA lessons ♦ Little to No evidence of teacher instructional guidance ♦ Little to No evidence of teacher monitoring students' use of ABRA ♦ No evidence of teacher's awareness of zone of proximal development asstudents instructed to all work on same activity level ♦ Minimal student exposure to ABRA activities ♦ ABRA exposure – mainly unstructured lessons where students choose own activities (play-time /free-time) ♦ Occasional disruption and off-task behaviour of students ♦ Unclear about teacher and student's navigational comfort level with ABRA **OR** ♦ Teacher frustration/discomfort with technology evident	♦ Basic evidence of teacher planning of ABRA lessons ♦ Basic evidence of teacher instructional guidance of ABRA ♦ Basic evidence of teacher monitoring students' use of ABRA ♦ Some evidence of teacher's awareness of zone of proximal development asstudents are instructed to move up task levels if too easy / completed or move back if too hard ♦ ABRA exposure – evidence of structured lessons ♦ Little off-task behaviour of students. ♦ Teacher and students appear comfortable with navigating through ABRA activities ♦ Some evidence of differentiated use of ABRA activities, but mainly within one skill level (i.e. Phonics / Word Level activities).	♦ Clear evidence of teacher planning of ABRA lessons. Teacher links planning and target setting according to students ability level ♦ Clear evidence of teacher providing appropriate instructional guidance / feedback while students on ABRA ♦ Clear evidence of teacher monitoring students' use of ABRA ♦ Clear evidence of teacher's awareness of zone of proximal development as students are instructed to move up task levels if too easy / completed or move back if too hard ♦ ABRA exposure – evidence of structured lessons ♦ Students are clearly engaged in the lesson ♦ Teacher & students are comfort able with navigating through ABRA activities ♦ Extension of ABRA – Some evidence of entry-level activities that extend skills explored in one domain of ABRA, usually Word level (i.e., Rhyme matching game; spelling words or simple sentences; playing BINGO, etc). ♦ Evidence of differentiated use of ABRA activities, at more than one skill level (i.e. Word Level, Text Level or Writing activities). ♦ Evidence of collaborative work & use of collaborative learning opportunities	Criteria as per level four with the addition of the following: ♦ **Extension of ABRA – Clear evidence of extension activities that incorporate higher-level skills (i.e. Comprehension) that extend beyond simple WORD level activities. Examples such as, writing alternate story endings; journal entry reflections on ABRA story; creating a drama skit/puppet show based on ABRA story, etc.** ♦ **Teacher clearly differentiated use of ABRA across ALL FOUR suggested levels of implementation (i.e. Word Level, Text Level, Collaborative Work & Extension Activities)** ♦ **Teacher uses all collaborative learning opportunities – peer supported dialogues, different roles, reciprocal tutoring, etc.**

Original Observer / Class / Date: _____

RATER: _____ DATE: _____ SCORE: ☐

Figure 16.1.

all children in these classes and to replace existing methods. Results showed that intervention-group classrooms substantially outperformed control classrooms in reading at the end of the intervention. Some caution probably is required with these data because the study did not have an RCT design, and there was no direct observation of the practices of the control-group classrooms. Rather dated norms also were used to assess reading. Nevertheless, large gains were observed, and Solity claims that children with reading difficulties were reduced to a mere 1 to 2 per cent compared to up to 20 per cent in the control classrooms.

Our own work in schools training classroom assistants to screen and then deliver reading interventions preventatively (Savage & Carless, 2005; Savage, Carless & Erten, 2009) suggests that improvements in their practice occur over time as teaching skills and confidence in roles are developed. Once classroom assistants are experienced in running such preventative interventions in mainstream year 1 classes, two out of

three below-average readers identified in year 1 reach typical attainment levels by the end of year 2 after early intervention. The approaches described here share a focus on making differentiated teaching in the mainstream classrooms in year 1 as maximally effective as possible [see also Gerber et al. (2004) and Leafsted, Richards & Gerber (2004) for similar approaches for English-language learners, albeit in non-RCT designs]. More generally, Slavin et al. (2008) also note from their systematic review of interventions that the largest improvements in intervention studies involve clear changes in teacher practice rather than changes to curriculum or other features of classroom life.

Another example of how change to teaching practice is central comes from the example of Response-to-Intervention (RtI) initiatives now being implemented worldwide but most fully documented and researched in the United States. The notion that children cannot be allowed to 'wait to fail' has led to the idea that children should receive tiered interventions (often phonics interventions) graded to meet their current needs, with early intensive intervention for children falling behind [see Savage & Deault (2010) for details and a critique of this approach]. In many senses, this model is state of the art and state of the practice currently, justified by some of the evidence described earlier in this chapter. However, the practice steps way ahead of what the research can support and also assumes that 'one size fits all'. Furthermore, the key issue is whether teaching practices have changed for those most needing preventative intervention. Orosco and Klingner (2010) describe in a detailed analysis of one school's implementation of RtI where the majority of children came from low SES Spanish-speaking homes with English as an additional language. Here, observation revealed that alongside limited resources, teaching was mis-aligned with student needs (did not take into account learners' needs for English as an additional language); that, consequently, many teachers' beliefs and models still reflected deficit-based rather than intervention-based approaches; and that special education practices of diagnosis and resource room placement still prevailed over intervention and prevention of reading problems in the underlying school culture. In short, the implementation of a promising and, at least in part, evidence-based policy produced little change for students there because school culture and teaching practice, and the assumptions on which they were based, were essentially unaltered.

Perhaps the clearest example of the scope of change that needs to take place to raise educational attainment is a monograph by Fielding, Kerr & Rosier (2007). These authors describe one U.S. school board's attempt to move towards a 95+ per cent literacy level for all children in the school from a base of 67 per cent literacy. The authors found that this process took ten years of systematic board-, school-, and classroom-level organisational change; multi-level institutional target setting and fundamental alterations of the syllabus and teaching practices. One of the starkest changes was to as much as treble the literacy teaching time available each day for identified struggling readers depending on how far behind their peers they were. The political decision was made to dramatically increase literacy time for struggling readers even at the expense of other aspects of the curriculum on the assumption that literacy was central to the rest of the curriculum.[2] Extensive work with all parties, including labour unions, support staff, parents and others, was required to make these changes. This study of organisational change suggests that it *is* possible to achieve inclusive goals of near-universal literacy. Such fundamental educational change arguably requires joint 'political' vision followed by joint will to achieve such literacy goals as much as further research evidence on literacy practices per se (e.g., Waks, 2007). Meaningful change is likely to be systemic in nature.

Conclusions and Implications

I have used current research on the ABRA reading program by myself and my colleagues to draw some more general themes about implementation science. The first is that emerging evidence-based approaches need to bridge the gap between efficacy studies (with high internal validity) and effectiveness studies (with high external validity). Programmatic studies with well-designed RCTs are needed to make this possible as a basis for truly relevant but evidence-based practice. A second theme is that one needs to explore action in the classroom to understand implementation. Startlingly, some major intervention studies (e.g., Campuzano et al., 2009) do not explore implementation at all, so results tell us very little about an intervention. Elsewhere in reading research, implementation is seen as compliance to a program. I have argued on the basis of my own research that one needs to explore the rich picture of the quality of teaching when exploring implementation A related point is that the best teaching is likely to be complex and connected. It may be hard to identify or isolate the specific elements of success in an expertly taught rich curriculum exactly because the richness and connectivity may be the very reason that it works well. The point here is that the medical model of 'treatment' as applied to education has limitations. A clinical trial model cannot be too rigidly applied and surely will fail completely if one expects to see a pedagogical equivalent of the 'pill' used in medical research. I also have pointed to a range of evidence sources that suggests that an implementation science of reading needs to focus on what teachers do and also why they do and do not do things, as well as on the cultural aspects of the profession as much as on interventions themselves.

Conclusions

This chapter has sought to explore what implementation science might need to grapple with in the twenty-first century by staring with a review of the evidence base for reading research. The first part of this chapter reviewed this evidence and concluded that there is in fact little of the very strongest evidence (meta-analyses of RCTs). Ironically, given its controversial status, the strongest evidence exists for phonics, although a multitude of practically relevant questions about the nature, duration and type of phonics were unknown. Elsewhere, what evidence there is is modest in size and quality, and I use the term 'fragile' to describe it. This evidence base is fragile in the sense that it can be overturned by relatively modest amounts of new evidence. The existing evidence base is also largely drawn from studies of monolingual learners of English. A science of implementation for reading clearly needs more RCT-based primary literature from which to work.

Action cannot, however, wait on such studies. As a result, policy and implementation always will be ahead of what can be justified on the basis of evidence base and often occur in uncharted territory. This is true of RtI model and the use of synthetic phonics, both of which form the staple of many recent policy initiatives in the United Kingdom, the United States, Canada, and Australia. Sometimes one can attempt to use 'fragile' evidence to base principled implementation, as in the case of educational technology, but one will have to be aware of this fragility as well as exploring the nature of implementation very closely on a class-by-class and tool-by-tool basis.

I also have argued that implementation science needs to explore (and encourage) real classrooms change. We cannot expect to see little 'treatments' producing sustained effects. An implementation science of reading will involve exploring relationships amongst teaching, real teacher change and student outcomes over long periods of time. It will require detailed observations and triangulations of these observations and explore professional knowledge and decision making. Student outcomes may serve as markers of the impact of the practices of the teachers observed. In short, I suspect that the teacher and the relationships between the teacher and the school and school board, rather than the student, are likely to become the primary focus of study of implementation science.

Notes

1. I am very grateful to Professor Allyson Hadwin from the University of Victoria, who as discussant of a paper on ABRA research findings at the Canadian Society for the Study of Education meeting in Montreal, in June 2010, stimulated further thinking on this issue.

2. My personal view here of the maximally effective literacy curriculum [for which I note with a due sense of irony that I have no RCT evidence to support (as yet)] is that really good reception and grade 1 teaching for all is crucial. Intervention research generally confirms that post hoc catch-up rarely works, or in rare cases, such as in Fielding, Kerr & Rosier (2007), it is achieved at the expense of other major losses in other parts of the curriculum. It is likely to be most effective to teach the most immediately useful skills together to all children in a way that allows them to get started with reading and experience the bootstrapping effects of early meaningful exposure to varied texts. I am attracted by the notion of a 'rational analysis' of English,

wherein the 100 most frequent words and the 50 most common grapheme-to-phoneme spelling rules allow children to read a majority of words in English (Vousden, 2008). Efficient ways to do this account for the fact that young children have short attention spans, developing memories, and a strong preference for the concrete over the abstract. To avoid alienation of children, teaching in grade 1 also must be rich and always aligned with children's experiences and balance classroom management issues with being welcoming and engaging in atmosphere and supportive and well aligned in instructional terms with students needs. Schools must, of course, sow the seeds of the love of and relevance of texts. If major educational inequalities remain after this sort of experience, one needs to look at what happens before children come to school at age five or six as much as, if not more so than, constructing tiers of intervention that repeat the first two years of literacy teaching for a subset of increasingly isolated and disenchanted children.

References

Abrami, P., Savage, R. S., Wade, A. & Hipps, G. (2008). Using technology to help children to learn to read and write. In T. Willoughby and E. Wood (eds.), *Children's learning in a digital world* (pp. 129–72). Oxford, UK: Wiley-Blackwell.

Adams, M. J. (1990). *Beginning to read: Thinking and learning about print.* Boston: MIT Press.

Allington, R. L. (2002). *Brother and the national reading curriculum: How ideology trumped evidence.* Portsmouth, NH: Heinemann.

Anderson, A., Wood, E., Piquette-Tomei, N., Savage, R. & Mueller, J. (2011). Evaluating teachers' support requests when just-in-time instructional support is provided to introduce a primary level web-based reading program. *Journal of Technology and Teacher Education* 19(4), 499–525. Retrieved from http://www.editlib.org/p/34599.

August, D., & Shanahan, T. (2006). *Developing literacy in second-language learners: Report of the National Literacy Panel on language-minority children and youth.* Mahwah, NJ: Erlbaum.

Bowers, P. N., Kirby, J. R. & Deacon, S. H. (2010). The effects of morphological instruction on literacy skills: A systematic review of the literature. *Review of Educational Research* 80(2), 144–79.

Bowey, J. A. (2006). Need for systematic synthetic phonics teaching within the early reading curriculum. *Australian Psychologist* 41(2), 79–84.

Bus, A. G., & vanIJzendoorn, M. H. (1999). Phonological awareness and early reading: A meta-analysis of experimental training studies. *Journal of Educational Psychology*, 91, 403–14.

Bus, A. G., vanIJzendoorn, M. H. & Pellegrini, A. D. (1995). Joint book reading makes for success in learning to read: A meta-analysis on intergenerational transmission of literacy. *Review of Educational Research* 65, 1–21.

Camilli, G., Vargas, S. & Yurecko, M. (2003). Teaching children to read: The fragile link between science and federal education policy. *Education Policy Analysis Archives* 11(15). Retrieved January 15, 2006, from http://epaa.asu.edu/epaa/v11n15/.

Campbell, D. T., & Stanley, J. C. (1963). *Experimental and quasi-experimental designs for research.* Boston: Houghton Mifflin.

Campuzano, L., Dynarski, M., Agodini, R. & Rall, K. (2009). *Effectiveness of reading and mathematics software products.*(Report NCEE 2009–4042, National Centre for Education Evaluation and Regional Assistance, Institute of Education Sciences). Washington: U.S. Department of Education.

Chen, C. (2008). Why do teachers not practice what they believe regarding technology integration? *Journal of Educational Research* 102, 65–75.

Chen, J., & Chang, C. (2006). Using computers in early childhood classrooms: Teachers' attitudes, skills and practices. *Journal of Early Childhood Research* 4, 169–88.

Cochrane, A. L. (1971). *Effectiveness and efficacy: Random reflections on health services,* 2nd ed. London: Nuffield Provincial Hospitals Trust.

Comaskey, E. M., Savage, R. S. & Abrami, P. (2009). A randomised efficacy study of web-based synthetic and analytic programmes among disadvantaged urban kindergarten children. *Journal of Research in Reading* 32, 92–108; doi: 10.1111/j.1467–9817.2008.01383.x.

Comaskey, E. M., Savage, R. S. & Abrami, P. (2009). A randomized efficacy study of a web-based literacy intervention among disadvantaged urban kindergarten children. *Journal of Research in Reading* [Special Issue on Literacy and Technology] 32, 92–108.

Cuban, L. (2001). *Oversold and underused: Computers in the classroom.* Cambridge, MA: Harvard University Press.

Davidson, M. R., Fields, M. K. & Yang, J. (2009). A randomised trial study of a pre-school literacy curriculum: The importance of implementation. *Journal of Research in Educational Effectiveness* 2, 177–208.

Deault, L., Savage, R. & Abrami, P. (2009). Inattention and response to the ABRACADABRA web-based literacy intervention. *Journal of Research on Educational Effectiveness* 2(3), 250–86.

Dynarski, M., Agodini, R., Heaviside, S. N. T., Carey, N., Campuzano, L., Means, B., et al. (2007). *Effectiveness of reading and mathematics software products: Findings from the first student cohort* (Report to Congress). Washington: National Center for Education Evaluation and Regional Assistance. Available from: ED Pubs, P. O. box 1398, Jessup, MD 20794–1398; tel: 877–433–7827; website: http://ies.ed.gov/ncee/pubs/.

Ehri, L., Nunes, S., Willows, D., Schuster, B. V., Yaghoub-Zadeh, Z. & Shanahan, T. (2001). Phonemic awareness instruction helps children learn to read: Evidence from the National Reading Panel's meta-analysis. *Reading Research Quarterly* 36, 250–87.

Elleman, A. M., Lindon, E. J., Morphy, P. & Compton, D. (2009). The impact of vocabulary instruction on passage-level comprehension of school-age children: A meta-analysis. *Journal of Research In Educational Effectiveness* 2, 1–45.

Fielding, L., Kerr, N. & Rosier, P. (2007). *Annual growth for all students, catch-up growth for those who are behind.* Kennewick, WA: New Foundation Press.

Flay, B. (1986). Efficacy and effectiveness trials (and other phases of research) in the development of health promotion programs. *Preventive Medicine* 15, 451–74.

Foorman, B. R., & Torgesen, J. (2001). Critical elements of classroom and small-group instruction promote reading success in all children. *Learning Disabilities Research & Practice* 16, 203–12.

Genesee, F., & Jared, D. (2008). Literacy development in early French immersion programs. *Canadian Psychology/Psychologie Canadienne* 49(2), 140–7; doi: 10.1037/0708-5591.49.2.140.

Gerber, M., Jimenez, T., Leafstedt, J., Villaruz, J., Richards, C. & English, J. (2004). English reading effects of small-group intensive intervention in Spanish for K–1 English learners. *Learning Disabilities Research and Practice* 19(4), 239–51.

Gersten, R., Fuchs, L. S., Williams, J. P. & Baker, S. (2001). Teaching reading comprehension strategies to students with learning disabilities:

A review of research. *Review of Educational Research* 71, 279–320.

Gersten, R., Fuchs, L. S., Compton, D., Coyne, M., Greenwood, C. & Innocenti, M. S. (2005). Quality indicators for group experimental and quasi-experimental research in special education. *Exceptional Children* 71(2), 149.

Hammill, D. D. (2004). What we know about the correlates of reading. *Exceptional Children* 70, 453–86.

Hipps, G., Abrami, P., Savage, R. S., Cerna, N. & Jorgensen, A. (2005). ABRACADABRA: Research, design, and development of a web-based early literacy software. In S. Pierre (ed.), *Innovations et tendances en technologies de formation et d'apprentissage: Développement, intégration et évaluation des technologies de formation et d'apprentissage* (Vol. Valeurisation de Researches de Québec, pp. 89–112). Québec: Presses Internationales Polytechnique.

Implementation Science Journal (2010). Consort and implementation science. Retrieved February 8, 2008, from http://www.implementationscience.com/.

Kay, R. H. (2008). Exploring the relationship between emotions and the acquisition of computer knowledge. *Computers in Education* 50, 1269–83.

Klein, P. S., Nir-Gal, O. & Darom, E. (2000). The use of computers in kindergarten, with or without adult mediation; effects on children's cognitive performance and behavior. *Computers in Human Behavior* 16, 591–608.

Klingner, J. K., & Edwards, P. A. (2006). Cultural considerations with response to intervention models. *Reading Research Quarterly* 41(1), 108–17.

Kuhn, M. R., & Stahl, S. A. (2003). Fluency: A review of developmental and remedial practices. *Journal of Educational Psychology* 95, 3–21.

Leafstedt, J. M., Richards, C. R. & Gerber, M. M. (2004). Effectiveness of explicit phonological-awareness instruction for at-risk english learners. *Learning Disabilities Research & Practice* 19(4), 252–61.

Meichenbaum, D., & Arsanow, J. (1979). Cognitive behavioral modification and metacognitive development: Implications for the classroom. In P. C. Kendall and S. D. Hollon (eds.), *Cognitive behavioral interventions: Theory, research and procedures.* New York: Academic Press.

McBride-Chang, C., Cho, J. R., Liu, H., Wagner, R. K., Shu, H., Zhou, A., et al. (2005). Changing models across cultures: associations of phonological awareness and morphological structure awareness with vocabulary and word recognition in second graders from Beijing, Hong Kong, Korea, and the United States. *Journal of Experimental Child Psychology* 92(2), 140–60.

McCardle, P., & Chhabra, V. (2004). *The voice of evidence in reading research*. Baltimore: Brookes.

McGuiness, D. (1998). *Why our children can't read and what we can do about it: A scientific revolution in reading*. Harmondsworth, UK: Penguin.

Mol, S. E., Bus, A. G. & deJong, M. T. (2009). Interactive book reading in early education: A tool to stimulate print knowledge as well as oral language. *Review of Educational Research* 79(2), 979–1007.

Mol, S. E., Bus, A. G., deJong, M. T. & Smeets, D. J. H. (2008). Added value of dialogic parent-child book readings: A meta-analysis. *Early Education and Development* 19(1), 7–26.

Mueller, J., Wood, E. & Willoughby, T. (2008). The integration of computer technology in the classroom. In T. Willoughby and E. Wood (eds.), *Children's learning in a digital world* (pp. 272–97). Oxford, UK: Blackwell.

National Institute of Child Health and Human Development. (2000). *Report of the National Reading Panel. Teaching children to read: An evidence-based assessment of the scientific research literature on reading and its implications for reading instruction* (NIH Publication No. 00–4769). Washington: U.S. Government Printing Office.

National Reading Panel (2000). Teaching children to read: An evidence-based assessment of the scientific research literature on reading and its implications for reading instruction (Report of the National Reading Panel). Retrieved January 5, 2010, from http://www.nichd.nih.gov/publications/nrp/report.htm.

Nind, M., Wearmouth, J., Collins, J., Hall, K., Rix, J. & Sheehy, K. (2004). *A systematic review of pedagogical approaches that can effectively include children with special educational needs in mainstream classrooms with a particular focus on peer group interactive approaches* (Research Evidence in Education Library). London: EPPI-Centre, Social Sciences Research Unit, Institute of Education.

Orosco, M. J., & Klingner, J. (2010). One school's implementation of RtI with English language learners: 'Referring into RtI'. *Journal of Learning Disabilities* 43(3), 269–88.

Piquette-Tomei, N., Savage, R. S. & Wesley, D. (2010). Effective literacy research: Collaboration, commitment and a web based tool. In preparation.

Pressley, M. (1994). *Reading instruction that works*. New York: Guilford Press.

Rose, J. (2006). *Independent review of the teaching of early reading: Final report*. London: DfES.

Rosenshine, B., & Meister, C. (1994). Reciprocal teaching: A review of the research. *Review of Educational Research* 64, 479–530.

Sandholtz, J. H., Ringstaff, C. & Dwyer, D. C. (1997). *Teaching with technology: creating student-centred classrooms*. New York: Teachers College Press.

Sang, G., Valcke, M., VanBraak, J. & Tondeur, J. (2010). Student teachers' thinking processes and ICT integration: Predictors of prospective teaching behaviors with educational technology. *Computers & Education* 54, 103–12.

Savage, R. S. (2009a). Methods for understanding literacy improvements. *Encyclopedia of language and literacy development*; retrieved from http://literacyencyclopedia.ca/index.php?fa=items.show&topicId=279.

Savage, R. S. (2009b). What would an evidence-based Canadian literacy strategy look like? In *Paper prepared for the policy committee of the Canadian language and literacy network for consideration by the federal minister of education*. Toronto: University of Toronto Press.

Savage, R. S., & Carless, S. (2005). Learning support assistants can deliver effective reading interventions for 'at-risk' children. *Educational Research* 47(1), 45–61.

Savage, R. S., Carless, S., & Erten, O. (2009). The longer-term effects of reading interventions delivered by experienced teaching assistants. *Support for Learning* 24(2), 95–100.

Savage, R. S., Abrami, P., Hipps, G. & Deault, L. (2009). A randomized, controlled trial study of the ABRACADABRA reading intervention program in grade 1. *Journal of Educational Psychology* 101(3), 590–604; doi: 10.1037/a0014700.

Savage, R. S., Abrami, P., Piquette-Tomei, N., Wood, E. & Delevaux, G. (2010). ABRACADABRA: A study in the development, implementation and effectiveness of a web-based literacy resource. *Journal of Educational Psychology*. Submitted.

Savage, R. S., & Pompey, Y. (2008). What does the evidence really say about effective literacy teaching? [The development of literacy: Implications of current understanding for applied psychologists and educationalists]. *Educational and Child Psychology* 25(3), 21–30.

Seethaler, P. M., & Fuchs, L. S. (2005). A drop in the bucket: Randomized, controlled trials testing reading and math interventions. *Learning Disabilities Research & Practice* 20(2), 98–102.

Shapiro, L. R., & Solity, J. (2008). Delivering phonological and phonics training within whole-class teaching. *British Journal of Educational Psychology* 78(4), 597–620.

Share, D. L. (2008). On the anglocentricities of current reading research and practice: The perils of overreliance on an 'outlier' orthography. *Psychological Bulletin* 134(4), 584–615.

Slavin, R. E., Cheung, A., Groff, C. & Lake, C. (2008). Effective reading programs for middle and high schools: A best evidence synthesis. *Reading Research Quarterly* 43(3), 290–322.

Slavin, R. E., Lake, C., Chambers, B., Cheung, A. & Davis, S. (2009). Effective reading programs for the elementary grades: A best-evidence synthesis. *Review of Educational Research* 79(4), 1391–1466.

Solity, J., & Vousden, J. (2009). Real books vs. reading schemes: A new perspective from instructional psychology. *Educational Psychology: An International Journal of Experimental Educational Psychology* 29(4), 469–511.

Torgerson, C. J. (2007). The quality of systematic reviews of effectiveness in literacy learning in English: A 'tertiary' review. *Journal of Research in Reading* 30, 287–315.

Torgerson, C. J., & Zhu, D. (2004). A systematic review and meta-analysis of the effectiveness of ICT on literacy learning in English. In R. Andrews (ed.), *The impact of ICT on literacy education* (pp. 5–16). London: Routledge Falmer.

Torgerson, C., Brooks, G. & Hall, J. (2006). *A systematic review of the research literature on the use of phonics in the teaching of reading and spelling.* London: DfES Research Report 711.

Vanderstaay, S. L. (2006). Learning from longitudinal research in criminology and the health sciences. *Reading Research Quarterly* 41(3), 328–50.

Vousden, J. I. (2008). Units of English spelling-to-sound mapping: A rational approach to reading instruction. *Applied Cognitive Psychology* 22(2), 247–72.

Waks, L. J. (2007). The concept of fundamental educational change. *Educational Theory* 57, 277–95; doi: 10.1111/j.1741–5446.2007.00257.x.

Wanzek, J., Vaughn, S., Kim, A.-H. & Cavanaugh, C. L. (2006). The effects of reading interventions on social outcomes for elementary students with reading difficulties: A synthesis. *Reading & Writing Quarterly: Overcoming Learning Difficulties* 22(2), 121–38.

Wolf, M., & Bowers, P. G. (1999). The double-deficit hypothesis for the developmental dyslexias. *Journal of Educational Psychology* 91(3), 415–38; doi: 10.1037/0022–0663.91.3.415.

Wolgemuth, J. R., Bottrell, C., Helmer, J., Emmett, S., Harper, H., Lea, T., et al. (2010). Using computer-based instruction to improve indigenous early literacy in northern Australia. Paper presented at the AERA Annual Meeting, Denver, CO.

Wood, E., Specht, J., Willoughby, T. & Mueller, J. (2008). Integrating computer technology in early childhood education environments: Issues raised by early childhood educators. *Alberta Journal of Educational Research* 54, 210–26.

Wozney, L., Venkatesh, V. & Abrami, P. C. (2006). Implementing computer technologies: teachers' perceptions and practices. *Journal of Technology and Teacher Education* 14, 173–207.

Yatvin, J. (2002). Babes in the woods: The wanderings of the National Reading Pan. *Phi Delta Kappan* 83, 364–9.

CHAPTER 17

Summary of Research and Implications for Practice on Reading Interventions for Young English-Language Learners with Reading Difficulties

Colleen K. Reutebuch and Sharon Vaughn

Background and Significance

Background on English-Language Learners with Learning Difficulties/ Disabilities

In the United States, English-language learners (ELLs), estimated to include over 10.8 million students, represent the fastest-growing segment among the school-age population (National Center for Educational Statistics, 2008), with Spanish-speaking students comprising 80 percent of that group (Francis et al., 2006). While preventing reading difficulties in monolingual children has been the focus of research over the past several decades, there is less known about the effectiveness of reading instruction on the literacy and oracy outcomes for ELLs who are experiencing difficulties in learning to read. Although this population is considered heterogeneous owing to individual factors (i.e., educational history, placement and instruction, native and English-language and literacy ability, and sociocultural background) that influence overall academic success (August & Shanahan, 2006), the academic achievement of ELLs on the whole

is low (National Center for Educational Statistics, 2008). Owing to complications with identification of language and disability, students with language and learning difficulties often have been excluded from research studies, so less is known about the academic achievement and outcome of ELLs with specific learning difficulties/disabilities.

Recent legislative and research activities have been aimed at addressing the learning needs of this population. Instructional approaches similar to those used with monolingual students are effective, but research suggests that adjustments are needed to meet the educational demands faced by ELLs (Shanahan & Beck, 2006). English learners face challenges that are compounded by the fact that they enter schools at every grade level and at various times during the academic year with varying levels of language and literacy proficiency in both their native language and English. Students whose first language is other than English who are learning English as a second language or simultaneously often experience difficulties in developing literacy and oracy in the early grades, particularly if there is a lack of established proficiency in either language (Peña & Bedore, 2009).

Miller et al. (2006) have noted that children with better oral language skills progress at a faster pace in acquiring literacy skills throughout elementary schooling and that progress of ELLs in developing oral language may be predictive of later reading disabilities. Furthermore, research suggests that the amount of time of exposure and content of the first and second languages influence acquisition patterns (Bedore & Peña, 2008). Complicating matters are the varying viewpoints among educational leaders, policymakers, and parents about whether and to what extent native-language instruction promotes successful transition of ELLs to English. These issues have become points of contention and confusion for many teachers of ELLs that have driven concerns about the value of providing literacy instruction to students with low oral language development, although some researchers have indicted that early reading instruction does support both reading and language development (Vaughn et al., 2006a, 2006b, 2006c).

Identification of English-Language Learners with Learning Difficulties/ Disabilities

There is limited evidence about the effectiveness of educators in distinguishing difficulties in acquiring English from specific learning/language challenges or learning disabilities and/or inadequate opportunities to learn. Bedore and Peña (2008) assert that children from bilingual backgrounds are sometimes overidentified with language impairment because educators do not have appropriate developmental expectations, whereas in other instances bilingual children are overlooked because educators wait to identify difficulties while the children are learning English. Underachievement of ELLs or their lack of response to classroom instruction is associated with increased referrals for special education (Gyovai et al., 2009). Of ELLs who are identified as having special learning needs, the majority (56 percent) are identified as having learning disabilities, followed by 24 percent served for speech-language impairments (Klingner, Artiles, & Barletta, 2006). Further, the rate of placement into special education appears to be negatively associated with English proficiency levels; notably, as proficiency in English increases, placement rates into special education decrease (Gyovai et al., 2009).

Reading difficulties among ELLs may be more a function of individual differences than language-minority status (August & Shanahan, 2006). A lack of understanding of what distinguishes second-language learning from specific disabilities in acquiring language and literacy has led to a disproportionate representation of minority students in special education in upper elementary grades and late identification in the early grades (Samson & Lesaux, 2009). ELLs with disabilities tend to receive fewer language support services and are more likely to be instructed only in English when compared with ELLs without disabilities (Klingner, Artiles, & Barletta, 2006).

Recent research efforts support a response-to-intervention (RTI) model, with its emphasis on accurate assessment and appropriate and high-quality instruction applied prior to referral for special education and as a means to proper identification of ELLs with learning disabilities (Samson & Lesaux, 2009; Vaughn et al., 2005; Vaughn, Ortiz, & May, 2009; www.rtinetwork.org). With the increasing number of language-minority students enrolling in schools, it is necessary to address the question of whether the lack of English proficiency or the presence of a disability is the impediment to language and literacy acquisition. Additionally, it is clear that there is a need to identify effective reading strategies and interventions for second-language learners that have been empirically validated.

Language and Reading Interventions in the Elementary Grades (1–5)

The research base for effective early literacy instruction and intervention for second-language learners is constructed largely from over thirty years of reading research that has identified effective instruction of monolingual English speakers. Effective practices for teaching early reading to students with reading difficulties includes explicit instruction with opportunities for student to practice with immediate corrective feedback, word-based instruction that includes learning how sounds map to print and how to decode multisyllabic words, opportunities to learn to read for understanding a variety of text genres, and small-group instruction that provides specific instruction to meet students' needs as well as opportunities to discuss text meaningfully (Denton & Mathes, 2003; Swanson, Hoskyn, & Lee, 2000; Torgesen et al., 2001). While considerably more research on effective instructional practices for ELLs with reading difficulties is needed, we can derive instructional practices from the existing research summarized by Goldenberg (2008):

- Use native-language instruction for literacy, and provide instruction for transfer to English-language literacy.
- Teach all the core concepts of reading associated with improved reading outcomes for monolingual students, including phonemic awareness, phonics, vocabulary, comprehension, and writing, knowing that with the exception of phonemic awareness, most of the practices require explicit instruction for transfer to English.
- Encourage reading in English with a focus on developing knowledge and word meaning as well as reading associated with student interests.
- Establish clear instructional goals and learning objectives, and communicate those to students with expectations for how those learning goals can be achieved.
- Provide explicit feedback to students on correct and incorrect responses, reteach instructional areas in which learning is not proficient, and use frequent assessments to determine student progress for reteaching.

- Make instruction clear and meaningful, providing challenging, motivating, and clearly structured content, with appropriate levels of student participation.
- Provide opportunities for students to productively engage with others using discourse and writing; opportunities include student paired learning and cooperative groups.
- Combined approaches that provide direct instruction from the teacher with interaction between teacher and student and among students are effective.
- Design instruction to target both content learning objectives and language objectives.
- Provide organized vocabulary building in all activities, including opportunities to use previously taught words as well as currently taught words orally and in writing.
- Use classroom and language routines that are predictable.
- Provide redundant cues for key information, including pictures, graphs, visual cues, and graphic organizers.
- Consolidate and summarize text and learning through teacher and student paraphrases and summaries.

Adjustments to typical instruction include an emphasis on building oral language as well as taking advantage of a student's native-language proficiency to facilitate learning to read in English.

Primary Interventions for ELLs with Reading Difficulties

There has been much criticism of the "wait-to-fail model" associated with the recognition and remediation of learning difficulties/ disabilities. The No Child Left Behind Act (NCLB, 2002) and the Reauthorization of the Individuals with Disabilities Education Improvement Act (IDEIA, 2004) were instrumental in promoting early detection and prevention strategies that target the instructional needs of struggling students as soon as they exhibit signs of learning difficulty. A series of investigations examined an early identification and prevention approach to remediating reading difficulties with students who were ELLs (Cirino et al., 2009; Vaughn et al., 2006b, 2006c, 2008). The research design screened for struggling readers and provided a supplemental instructional intervention for those at risk for poor learning outcomes in order to accelerate their learning and close the achievement gap before students fell too far behind their peers. Below we describe four randomized, controlled trials (RCTs) including long-term follow-ups designed to evaluate the efficacy of an English and Spanish supplemental intervention (see below for full description) for bilingual (Spanish/English) first graders with reading difficulties. An overview of the English and then Spanish interventions is provided, followed by a summary of the four studies. These studies (two in English for non-English speakers instructed in English and two in Spanish for students who were being instructed in Spanish) were implemented in successive years in Houston, Austin, and Brownsville with four nonoverlapping samples. The studies were conducted as RCTs, and students were randomly assigned to treatment or comparison conditions. Interventionists were hired and trained by the researchers to provide small-group instruction for treatment students. Treatment students received fifty minutes of intervention instruction daily for one year in small groups (i.e., three to five students) as a supplement to their core reading instruction. Intervention was implemented outside the core reading instruction provided in general-education classrooms as in keeping with an RTI approach; supplemental instruction was provided only to students who demonstrate a need to build foundational reading skills based on screening measures or lack of sufficient progress in core classroom instruction. Comparison students typically received business-as-usual instruction, and in some cases, "typical" intervention also was provided by school staff to comparison students (i.e., treatment to comparison students could not be withheld

ethically). At the end of first grade, all four experimental studies reported improved outcomes for intervention students on phonological awareness, word-reading fluency, reading comprehension, and spelling, and these findings were maintained through fourth grade for treatment students.

ENGLISH INTERVENTION

Proactive Reading (Mathes & Torgesen, 2005) was used with researcher-developed English as a second language enhancements to provide intervention (i.e., supplemental instruction) for ELLs receiving reading instruction in English. A version of this early reading curriculum was designed and validated in previous intervention research with monolingual English-struggling readers (Mathes et al., 2005). Proactive Reading was created to be a comprehensive, integrated intervention curriculum that outlined the delivery of explicit phonemic awareness and phonics instruction, how to ensure application of this knowledge to words and text, and the engagement of children in making meaning from what they have read. The research team adapted Proactive Reading in two major ways: by (1) including a story reading with a vocabulary component and oracy supplement (see Hickman, Pollard-Durodola, & Vaughn, 2004) designed to address and promote vocabulary, listening comprehension, and language development for first grade ELLs with reading difficulties and (2) emphasizing appropriate language support activities throughout the instructional sequence based on effective English as a second language practices; such adaptation is necessary given the language needs of these students (e.g., McCardle, Mele-McCarthy, & Leos, 2005). Building on principles of the direct instruction model (Carnine, Silbert, & Kameenui, 1997), activities associated with fluent, meaningful reading were analyzed, and elements were sequenced into a cumulatively building and carefully integrated scope and sequence.

Daily lesson plans consisted of six to ten activities representing five content strands: phonemic awareness, letter knowledge, word recognition, connected text fluency, and comprehension strategies. Scripted lesson plans provided exact wording to ensure that teacher language was clear and focused, and instruction was delivered at a fast pace in which there was constant exchange between the teacher and students. In a typical activity, the teacher asked all students to respond to letters, words, or text in unison, followed by "individual turns," where each child was able to demonstrate his or her understanding of the content. Moreover, the teacher provided lesson activities at a rapid pace. Teachers were required to consistently monitor students' responses, provide positive feedback for correct responses, and scaffold learning as errors occurred. There were 120 lessons of approximately forty minutes each, with ten additional minutes (per lesson) devoted to the oracy and vocabulary component.

Phonemic awareness instruction consisted primarily of two types of activities: phoneme discrimination and phoneme segmentation and blending. Early activities required children to isolate initial sounds in words or to tell if a word started with a particular sound. Later these activities moved to isolating final and medial sounds. Children also were taught how to segment one-syllable words into individual phonemes, as well as to make words from individually spoken phonemes. Oral blending was facilitated though the use of a puppet, whom the children were told could only say words sound by sound, and the students were told to help the puppet say the word at normal speed. *Letter-sound correspondences* were present in all 120 lessons, with a new letter-sound or letter-combination-sound correspondence being introduced every two to three days. Prior to presenting the symbol representing a particular phoneme, that phoneme was manipulated orally during segmenting and blending tasks. The primary objective of the letter-knowledge strand was to develop automatic recognition between a letter symbol and the most common sound it represented. Letter combinations, including diphthongs and vowel teams, were treated in the same manner as single letter-sound correspondences.

Word-recognition tasks included both phonetically regular and irregular/high-frequency words. The actual teaching of word-recognition strategies was accomplished using lists of words that were either presented by the teacher or located in the students' activity books. In terms of reading phonetically regular words, children were taught the sounding-out strategy initially. This process began with simple consonant-vowel-consonant (CVC) words (i.e., closed syllable). Initially, children were given very simple words and extended time to blend the sounds represented by the letters to form words. However, the amount of time allowed to sound out the words was decreased gradually, whereas the complexity of the words was increased gradually. Using progress-monitoring checks, students' mastery of syllable types was recorded, and then these syllable types were included in reading multisyllabic words. Initially, children applied the sounding-out strategy to each syllable, read each syllable "fast," and then read the whole word. The sounding-out step was quickly removed so that children read each syllable part and then read the whole word. Another important aspect of the word-recognition strand was teaching children to be flexible decoders. Children were taught that "sometimes parts of words did not sound out quite right" but that sounding-out usually produced a pronunciation that was close enough to figure out what the word really was. In this way, children were not burdened with being responsible for knowing which words could and could not be sounded out. Instead, they were taught that they could sound out any word they didn't know automatically, but if the resulting word wasn't a "real word," they had to be flexible. Likewise, they were taught that when reading connected text, they were to use context to assist in determining the correct word. Frequent cumulative practice of irregular high-frequency words was another component of most lessons.

In order to facilitate connected text fluency, children were asked to read stories two to three times. These texts were fully decodable, meaning that all phonetic elements and all irregular sight words appearing in the text had been taught previously, and students had already demonstrated mastery of those elements and words. Typically, children read a story in unison on the first reading. On second readings, students read one to two pages of a story individually. The third reading was typically done in pairs, with the teacher pairing up with one child and timing that child's reading rate. Each story had a predetermined fluency criterion. Across both successive readings within a lesson and across lessons over time, the criterion became increasingly faster, even as the text difficulty became increasingly complex.

Beyond word reading and fluency, a major objective for proactive reading was to emphasize comprehension to ensure that children were making meaning as they read. Prior to reading a story each day, teachers engaged in "browsing the story," during which they asked children to look at the pictures in the story and make predictions about the story. With narrative stories, teachers activated prior knowledge by asking students to tell what they already knew about the topic, and over time, children moved from being asked to tell about what they read to eventually being able to sequence only the most important information and identify story grammar elements. With expository stories, children were asked to identify new information learned.

Language support activities (three to eight per lesson) were provided daily throughout the year-long intervention. Each day, students had opportunities to explore the vocabulary, language, and literacy concepts presented in the literacy lessons. Periodic reviews also were included. Additionally, instructional behaviors that have been found to be effective when working with ELLs were embedded in the lessons, including use of visuals, gestures, and facial expressions in teaching vocabulary and clarifying meaning of content; provision of explicit instruction in English-language use; and opportunities to give elaborate responses.

While *oracy and vocabulary development* were integrated into the reading instruction, ten minutes each day was assigned specifically to the development of vocabulary, listening comprehension, and language

development (Hickman et al., 2004). This was accomplished through largely expository English books centered on eight information themes (e.g., pets, bugs, etc.). The only exception was the first theme, which was about "families" and was a narrative theme. Books were selected to be (1) slightly more advanced than the students' listening comprehension, (2) at second- to third-grade reading levels, and (3) aligned with student interests. The researchers selected two to three key vocabulary words each day that corresponded with the text that was being read by the teachers, and teachers taught the meaning of the words and used them in sentences with the students prior to reading the passage from the book to the students. Students were asked questions about the vocabulary and key ideas in stories that were read to them, and teachers used probes to guide students in story retelling, allowing each student to participate.

SPANISH INTERVENTION

For the Spanish intervention, *Lectura Proactiva* (Mathes et al., 2003) was used. This reading intervention followed the same instructional design principles that guided the development of the Proactive program described for struggling native English readers with the exception that the phonics tasks and syllable types reflected the sequence of development of Spanish literacy, and instruction and reading were in Spanish. The result was that the English and Spanish curriculums used in these intervention studies were different in terms of the sequence and focus of instructional content but similar in terms of instructional design and delivery.

The fifty-minute daily lesson plans were organized around seven to ten quick-paced activities that gave students multiple opportunities to respond and receive immediate feedback. During a typical activity, the teacher asked all students to respond to letters or words or read text and provided opportunities for each child to respond to demonstrate knowledge and progress. The teaching routine included modeling new content, providing guided practice, and implementing independent practice. Teachers implemented predetermined lessons and consistently monitored students' responses, providing recognition of correct responses and feedback if an error occurred.

The content strands can be described as emphasizing alphabetic knowledge and skills, connected text fluency, and comprehension. For *alphabetic skills*, students practiced previously taught letter-sound correspondences, including writing these letters, and learned the sound of a new letter. In initial lessons, students were taught to segment words into phonemes and to blend phonemes back into words, and then these skills were used to facilitate understanding of the sounding-out process and as a tool for spelling. Given the syllabic nature of Spanish, teaching students early to read syllables was a focus of instruction so that within a short time students read syllables as a unit rather than phoneme by phoneme. Likewise, teaching students to decode multisyllabic words began almost immediately. The basic strategy was to read an unknown multisyllabic word syllable by syllable and then to put the syllables together to read the whole word. Over time, emphasis was on reading words automatically while the complexity of words increased in terms of both length (i.e., number of syllables) and syllable type (i.e., VCV, CVC, CVV, CCV).

The main objectives were to promote connected text fluency and comprehension. Beginning on the seventh day of instruction, students began reading connected text daily. As with the English intervention, text was decodable, and stories were read repeatedly within a lesson, with an emphasis on fluency. From the beginning, students were asked to make predictions or tell what they knew related to the story before reading (Ogle, 1986). In this procedure, students indentify their background information about a subject ("know"), determine what they might learn from the story ("will"), and then, after reading a story, are asked to retell and sequence events of the story and eventually identify story elements and main idea, identifying what was learned ("learn"). Finally, summarization was introduced using either story grammar for narrative text or simple content webs for expository text.

Researchers also prioritized the development of oracy and vocabulary in Spanish. Teachers providing Spanish intervention spent ten minutes daily doing book reading and vocabulary activities. As was the case with the English intervention, most books were expository and focused on information themes and were selected under similar parameters. Teachers read passages to the students each day and then asked questions about the vocabulary and key ideas, using probes to guide student story retelling, and dialoged with students about the story using complete sentences and new vocabulary terms.

These interventions reflect the theoretical underpinning of effective instructional practices in beginning reading for ELLs, including a strong oracy focus (Gersten & Geva, 2003): (1) explicit teaching, (2) promotion of English-language learning, (3) phonemic awareness and decoding, (4) vocabulary development, (5) interactive teaching that maximizes student engagement, and (6) instruction that promotes opportunities for accurate responses with feedback for struggling readers. Students learning English as a second language, as well as native English speakers, benefit from explicit teaching of the components of literacy (i.e., phonemic/phonological awareness, phonics, fluency, vocabulary, comprehension, and writing), with fluency, vocabulary, and comprehension being crucial to the academic success of ELLs (August & Shanahan, 2006; Francis et al., 2006). National Literacy Panel findings (2006) further supported by Goldenberg (2008) indicated that effective second-language instruction includes explicit teaching that helps students directly and explicitly to learn features of a second language (i.e., syntax, grammar, vocabulary, pronunciation, and norms of social use), along with multiple opportunities to use the second language in meaningful and motivating ways.

Background on English and Spanish Intervention Studies

These studies were conducted over a five-year period and represented four nonoverlapping samples that were followed for three to four years with posttesting again at the end of second grade and then third or fourth grade depending on the sample. Language of instruction for the students was decided by the school district and parents. Thus the determination of whether students were instructed in English or Spanish was not done by the researchers. Instead, we aligned the supplemental intervention with students' primary language of instruction. All students were ELLs representing for the English intervention two sites (one near the border and one high urban) and for the Spanish intervention three sites (one additional urban site). All samples were selected for at-risk status through schoolwide screening and teacher confirmation.

English Interventions for ELLs

STUDY 1: RCT EFFICACY

Study 1 was an experimental study with first grade ELL (English/Spanish) students (n = 48; 24 treatment and 24 comparison) assigned randomly to either the treatment or comparison condition (Vaughn et al, 2006c). Teachers used *Proactive* as a supplemental instructional program daily for fifty minutes for small, homogeneous groups of three to five struggling readers. Treatment students outperformed comparison students on the composite measure of phonological awareness. Treatment students also outperformed comparison students on the Woodcock Language Proficiency Battery–Revised (WPLB-R) English Word Attack subtest (ES = 1.09) and on the WPLB-R passage comprehension subtest (ES = 1.08). This study met the What Works Clearinghouse standards with reservations as a result of minor deviations in the proposed randomization sample.

STUDY 3: RCT EFFICACY

A second RCT experimental study (Vaughn et al., 2006a) considered the effect of the same intervention, *Proactive*, provided to a sample of first grade students (n = 91; 43 treatment and 48 comparison) who were reading below the 25th percentile on the Letter Word Identification subtest of the

WPLB-R and were unable to read more than one word from a standard word reading list. Treatment students received fifty minutes of daily intervention for approximately 115 small-group sessions. Treatment students outperformed students in the comparison group on the phonological awareness composite measure of the Comprehensive Test of Phonological Processing (CTOPP; ES = 0.38) and the English Letter Sound Identification subtest of the CTOPP (ES = 0.36). Students receiving intervention also made greater gains than comparison students on the English Word Attack subtest of the WPLB-R (ES = 0.42). There were no differences on the Passage Comprehension subtest. This study fully met the high standards of the What Works Clearinghouse.

ONE-YEAR FOLLOW-UP TO STUDIES 1 AND 3

A one-year follow-up was conducted on all available participants from studies 1 and 3 (Cirino et al., 2009). Data are reported from fifty-six ELLs in two nonoverlapping studies (study 1, n = 18; study 3, n = 38) with reading difficulties who received supplemental first grade reading intervention (see Vaughn et al., 2006a, 2006c). The comparison sample was composed of fifty-five students (study 1, n = 11; study 3, n = 44). Researchers provided no additional intervention or boosters, so the follow-up at the end of the second grade determined whether students maintained gains in first grade. All outcomes showed main effects of treatment at one-year follow-up, with generally moderate effect sizes on measures of phonological awareness, word attack, word reading, spelling, and passage comprehension (effect sizes of 0.24 to 0.45).

THREE- TO FOUR-YEAR FOLLOW-UP TO STUDIES 1 AND 3

Three- and four-year follow-up data were reported (Vaughn et al., 2008) for the English RCT studies (studies 1 and 3) from fifty ELLs in two nonoverlapping cohorts (study 1, n = 15; study 3, n = 35) with reading difficulties who received supplemental first grade reading intervention (see Vaughn et al., 2006a, 2006c). The comparison sample was composed of fifty students (study 1, $n = 15$; study 3, $n = 35$). Researchers provided no intervention or boosters beyond first grade (study 1 participants were assessed four years after initial intervention; study 3 participants were assessed three years after initial intervention). Results of treatment at three- or four-year follow-up revealed all positive findings in the direction of the treatment group. Although results yielded generally low to moderate effect sizes on measures of phonological awareness, word attack, word reading, spelling, and passage comprehension (effect sizes of 0.03 to 0.45), the findings are a result of no additional treatment for three years. Despite the lack of strong statistically significant effects, the effect size indices in some cases are strong. For example, intervention students outperformed comparison students for English letter-word identification, connected text fluency, listening comprehension, and passage comprehension. The overall effect sizes for these four measures were +0.45, +0.25, +0.24, and +0.25.

Spanish Interventions for ELLs

STUDY 2: RCT EFFICACY

Study 2 was an experimental study with first grade ELL (English/Spanish) students ($n = 80$; 35 treatment and 45 comparison) assigned randomly to either the treatment or comparison condition (Vaughn et al, 2006c). Teachers used *Proactiva* as a supplemental instructional program daily for fifty minutes for small, homogeneous groups of three to five struggling readers. Treatment students outperformed comparison students on the composite measure of phonological awareness. Treatment students also outperformed comparison students on Spanish measures of phonological awareness, letter-sound and letter-word identification, verbal analogies, word reading fluency, and spelling (effect sizes of 0.33 to 0.81).

STUDY 4: RCT EFFICACY

A second RCT experimental study (Vaughn et al., 2006a) considered the effect of the intervention, *Proactiva*, delivered in Spanish.

Sixty-nine students (thirty-five in treatment and thirty-four in comparison) participated in the Spanish study. As with study 3, study 4 treatment students received daily intervention for approximately 115 fifty-minute small-group sessions. There were no differences between the treatment and comparison groups in either Spanish or English on any measures at pretest, but there were significant posttest differences in favor of the treatment group for the following outcomes in Spanish: letter-sound identification ($d = 0.72$), phonological awareness composite ($d = 0.73$), WLPB-R Oral-Language composite ($d = 0.35$), word attack ($d = 0.85$), passage comprehension ($d = 0.55$), and two measures of reading fluency ($d = 0.58$ to 0.75).

ONE-YEAR FOLLOW-UP STUDIES 2 AND 4

One-year follow-up data were reported (Cirino et al., 2009) for the Spanish RCT studies (studies 2 and 4) from 77 ELLs in two nonoverlapping cohorts (study 2, $n = 35$; study 4, $n = 42$) with reading difficulties who received supplemental first grade reading intervention (see Vaughn et al., 2006a, 2006c). The comparison sample was composed of eighty-one students (study 2, $n = 34$; study 4, $n = 47$). Researchers provided no intervention or boosters beyond first grade (study 2 and 4 participants were assessed at the end of second grade, one year after initial intervention).

THREE- AND FOUR-YEAR FOLLOW-UP STUDIES 2 AND 4

Three- and four-year follow-up data were reported (Vaughn et al., 2008) for the Spanish RCT studies (studies 2 and 4) from forty-one ELLs in two nonoverlapping cohorts (study 2, $n = 17$; study 4, $n = 16$) with reading difficulties who received supplemental first grade reading intervention (see Vaughn et al., 2006a, 2006c). The comparison sample was composed of fifty-three students (study 2, $n = 24$; study 4, $n = 29$). Researchers provided no intervention or boosters beyond first grade (study 2 participants were assessed four years after initial intervention; study 4 participants were assessed three years after initial intervention). Results of treatment at

Table 17.1. Summary of Randomized, Controlled Trails Conducted with Bilingual (Spanish/English) First Graders

	English Lang. INT	Spanish Lang. INT	Effect Sizes for Treatment (Language of Instruction)		Follow-up, 1 Year	Follow-up, 3 Years	WWC Standards Met
Study 1			PA	0.46 to 1.24	0.24, 0.43	0.06 to 0.28	*
			Lang.	0.09 to 0.77	0.45	0.25	
			Word attk.	1.09	0.31	0.20	
			Pass. comp.	1.08			
Study 2			PA	0.09 to 0.73	0.04 to 0.64	0.01 to 0.39	**
			Lang.	0.02 to 0.43	0.54	0.14	
			Word attk.	0.85	0.49	0.27	
			Pass. comp.	055			
Study 3			PA	0.02 to 0.36	See	See	
			Lang.	0.11 to 0.22	study 1	study 1	
			Word attk.	0.42			
			Pass. comp.	0.06			
Study 4			PA	0.09 to 0.73	See	See	**
			Lang.	0.02 to 0.43	study 2	study 2	
			Word attk.	0.85			
			Pass. comp.	0.55			

Note: English samples combined for follow-up years 1 and 3; Spanish combined for follow-up: No effects sizes are provided as *d*, and when a range is provided, it represents more than one outcome. INT = intervention; Meas. = measures; PA = phonological processing; Lang. = language; Word attk. = word attack; Pass. comp. = passage comprehension.
* Met What Works Clearing House (WWC) standards with reservations because ten students were unable to be randomized owing to scheduling conflicts.
** WWC does not evaluate intervention studies conducted in languages other than English for ELLs, but both studies meet WWC criteria.

three- or four-year follow-up revealed few significant differences in favor of intervention students on Spanish measures, although effect sizes generally favored this group ($d = 0.33$).

Proactive (English intervention with ELLs) and *Proactiva* (Spanish intervention with ELLs) have demonstrated efficacy in four separate experimental studies as well as follow-up through fourth grade. An important note is that the effect size for reading comprehension, considered to be the most important goal of intervention, ranged from 0.20 three to four years following intervention to 0.49 one year after intervention, favoring treated students in all cases with no boosters or supplements. These findings provide compelling evidence that not only was the treatment effective after the first year of intervention, but the effects also

were maintained on a standardized reading comprehension measure one year and three to four years later (see Table 17.1).

RESPONSE TO INTERVENTION AS TREATMENT MODEL

Response to treatment as a means for identifying students with a reading/learning disability requires teachers to provide early intervention, match instruction to the learning needs of the student, and use data to monitor progress (Vaughn, Linan-Thompson, & Hickman, 2003). RTI is an instructional approach focused on preventing learning difficulties by providing high-quality research-based instruction and interventions that are matched to a student's needs. This process incorporates (1) conducting universal screening to identify students who are at risk of failure,

(2) providing effective instruction grounded in scientifically based instruction to students, (3) providing intervention targeted to meet student needs, and (4) monitoring at-risk students' progress frequently toward grade-level performance goals. Data are collected to examine the students' learning rates over time in order to make appropriate educational and instructional decisions regarding assistance to at-risk students. Students who demonstrate risk are given one or more research-validated interventions, such as *Proactive/Proactiva*. Academic progress is monitored frequently to see if the interventions are sufficient to help students reach the instructional level of their grade. While there is no single model of RTI, the overarching aim is to provide increasingly intensive instruction to children who do not demonstrate progress. RTI has been associated with tiered models of reading instruction and the identification of students with learning disabilities (LDs). In an RTI approach, recognition of students requiring special education is based on the accurate identification of students who do not respond adequately to appropriate instruction. This instructional framework, with its potential for early identification and prevention of reading difficulties, along with its goal of accelerating learning, may hold the key to reducing the disproportion of ELLs identified for special education services. Some researchers question the validity of RTI with culturally diverse learners because the research base on improved outcomes with these students is limited (Klingner & Edward, 2006). Thus issues related to using RTI with ELLs to facilitate movement through the tiers and to make decisions about sufficient levels of core and supplemental instruction that should be provided to prevent further difficulties or to necessitate more extensive interventions or referral for special education are yet to be fully resolved.

Data indicate that many of the interventions to improve early reading for monolingual English speakers are used in classes that include ELLs and that when ELLs are recipients of those same interventions, they tend to respond similarly to non-ELLs (Shanahan & Beck, 2006).

For example, Vaughn, Linan-Thompson, & Hickman (2003) examined a response-to-treatment model with forty-five second graders including fifteen ELLs identified at risk for reading problems who were provided daily supplemental instruction over intervals of ten, twenty, or thirty weeks (students were discontinued at the end of each interval if exit criteria were met) to determine (1) the number of students at risk for LDs who would not meet exit criteria after ten weeks of intervention, (2) the extent to which students who were provided treatment and responded positively would do well in their core reading class once intervention ceased, and (3) the feasibility of using a response-to-treatment model to identify students with LDs by a school or district. Other studies focused specifically on RTI and ELLs, and the incidence of students who do not respond to instruction even after a research-based, intensive, long-term intervention was provided suggests that ELLs require more time to build literacy skills and/or extend their English knowledge through instruction, practice, and experience (Linan-Thompson et al., 2006; Linan-Thompson, Cirino, & Vaughn, 2007).

KEY COMPONENTS OF INSTRUCTION

Researchers have acknowledged elements of effective instruction that serve as the foundation for *all* learners and appear promising for ELLs (i.e., strategy instruction, direct and explicit teaching of vocabulary and comprehension, use of graphic organizers, active engagement, multiple practice opportunities with corrective feedback, and peer pairing) (Francis et al., 2006; Kamil et al., 2008). Effective reading instruction for ELLs builds on the preceding components but also includes targeted instruction in fluency, phonological awareness, instructional-level reading, word study, and writing (Linan-Thompsonet al., 2003). Additionally, Gersten and Geva (2003, p. 47) identify these six successful reading instructional strategies specific for first grade ELLs:

- *Explicit teaching*, including modeling, providing prompts, and adjusting English during lesson (i.e., avoiding use of confusing language such as idioms or figurative language)

- *English learning* with visuals or manipulatives to teach content and use of gestures and facial expressions to teach vocabulary
- *Phonemic awareness and decoding* through systematic instruction in letter-sound correspondence
- *Vocabulary development* built through preteaching and opportunities for students to speak English and to engage in meaningful interactions about text
- *Interactive teaching* to maximize on-task behavior and attention and give students time to respond to questions
- *Instruction geared toward low performers* as a means to achieve a high rate of response accuracy, ensure comprehension, and provide extra instruction, practice, and review

Additional opportunities to extend literacy and oracy skills are critical, which is why many interventions containing components found to be successful with monolingual students necessitate an English as a second language (ESL) supplement (see Hickman et al., 2004; Linan-Thompson et al., 2007). Students learning English as a second language require more time to acquire foundational reading skills and to practice them. Listening to, reading, and writing in English are other essential elements to be included within the instructional plan.

Recommendations and Implications for Practice and Future Research

When additional support for the early literacy skills of second-language learners is needed, educators must make decisions about when to intervene, with what type of intervention, and in what language to do so. Research has demonstrated that as early as kindergarten it is possible to identify ELLs from varying language backgrounds who are at risk for reading difficulties because of underdeveloped phonological awareness skills and/or difficulty learning sound-symbol correspondences (Francis et al., 2006).

Despite the successes of early interventions for at-risk ELLs to acquire basic literacy skills, the documented difficulty for many students to maintain gains without continued supplemental intervention provides insight into the complexity of second-language acquisition and the development of English literacy.

One of the greatest challenges ELLs face is learning English at the same time they are learning and held accountable for grade-level acquisition of content-area knowledge. Once the emphasis shifts from learning to read to reading to learn, ELLs are often described as being able to read words accurately but with little ability to comprehend. Although not entirely clear on what causes these comprehension difficulties in the face of well-developed word-reading skills, there is a working consensus that for many struggling ELLs, their fluency, vocabulary, and other skills specific to comprehension (e.g., background knowledge and strategy use) are insufficient to support the effective understanding of text and its use for learning new content.

Conversely, still lacking is knowledge on effective practices regarding vocabulary and comprehension as they relate to adolescent English learners' content knowledge, as well as effective methods for delivery instructions to ELLs in content-area classes. The Center for Research on the Education and Teaching of English Learners (CREATE), a National Research and Development Center, addresses the critical need to provide effective instruction for English-language students across content areas (Francis & Vaughn, 2009). For example, a multicomponent intervention developed to enhance social studies content-area instruction through the incorporation of literacy instruction included teaching of researcher-designed lessons consisting of the following based on best practices: (1) presentation and review of content and language objectives, (2) a brief overview of the "big idea," (3) explicit vocabulary instruction that integrate paired students' discussion of the word, (4) discussion built around a short video clip (two to four minutes) that complements the daily reading, (5) a teacher-led or paired-student reading assignment followed by generating and answering questions to target comprehension, and (6) a wrap-up activity in the form of a graphic organizer or other writing exercise that serves to review and assess student learning. This instructional intervention has been identified as benefiting all learners while being feasible for implementation into classwide instruction by content-area teachers (Vaughn et al., 2009).

Making appropriate instructional decisions for English learners at risk for reading difficulties depends on (1) the availability of high-quality, effective interventions in the language of instruction and (2) the capacity of the teacher to deliver them effectively so as to ensure that interventions for those learning English as a second language are developmentally and linguistically suitable, as well as adapted to the proficiency levels of the English-language students. There is a growing research base on systematic practices carried out within an RTI framework that demonstrates efficacy with at-risk ELLs. The positive outcomes achieved and sustained over time with evidence-based supplemental interventions implemented within a delivery system that monitors and adjusts instruction based on student responses holds promise. Longer-lasting impact from interventions such as those confirmed with *Proactive/Proactiva* and the ability to use a student's response to intervention as a means to more accurate identification of students for whom it has been difficult to distinguish issues associated with language acquisition from reading difficulties or true disabilities are the likely benefits when research-validated instructional supports are embedded within an RTI framework.

Acknowledgments

First grade research reported here was supported in part by Grants P01 HD39521 and R305U010001, both jointly funded by the National Institute for Child Health and Human Development and the Institute of Education Sciences. Research conducted by the Center for Research on Educational Achievement and Teaching of English Learners (CREATE) was supported by Grant R305A050056 from the Institute of Education Sciences. The attitudes and opinions expressed are those of the authors and do not necessarily reflect those of the funding agencies. The authors wish to thank their many collaborators who made this work possible.

References

August, D. L., & Shanahan, T. (eds.) (2006). *Developing a literacy in a second language: Report of the National Literacy Panel*. Mahwah, NJ: Erlbaum.

Bedore, L. M., & Peña, E. D. (2008). Assessment of bilingual children for identification of language impairment: Current findings and implications for practice. *International Journal of Bilingual Education and Bilingualism* 11(1), 1–29.

Carnine, D. W., Silbert, J., & Kame'enui, E. J. (1997). *Direct instruction reading, 3rd ed*. Upper Saddle River, NJ: Prentice-Hall.

Cirino, P. T., Vaughn, S., Linan-Thompson, S., Cardenas-Hagan, E., Fletcher, J. M., & Francis, D. J. (2009). One year follow-up outcomes of Spanish and English interventions for English language learners at-risk for reading problems. *American Education Research Journal* 46(3), 744–81.

Denton, C. A., & Mathes, P. G. (2003). Intervention for struggling readers: Possibilities and challenges. In B. R. Foorman (ed.), *Preventing and remediating reading difficulties: Bringing science to scale* (pp. 229–51). Timonium, MD: York Press.

Francis, D. J., & Vaughn, S. (2009). Content and strategic interventions for English language learners in the middle grades: An Introduction. *Journal of Research on Educational Effectiveness* 2(4), 289–96.

Francis, D., Rivera, M., Lesaux, N., Kieffer, M., & Rivera, H. (2006). *Practical guidelines for the education of English language learners: Research-based recommendations for instruction and academic interventions* (Under Cooperative Agreement Grant S283B050034 for U.S. Department of Education). Portsmouth, NH: RMC Corporation, Center on Instruction. Available online at www.centeroninstruction. org/files/ELL1-interventions.pdf.

Gersten, R., & Geva, E. (2003). Teaching reading to early language learners. *Educational Leadership* 60(7), 44–9.

Goldenberg, C. (2008). Teaching English language learners. What the research does – and does not – say. *American Educator* 32(2), 7–23, 42–4.

Gyovai, L. K., Cartledge, G., Kourea, L., Yerick, A., & Gibson, L. (2009). Early reading intervention: Responding to the learning needs of young at-risk English language learners. *Learning Disability Quarterly* 32(3), 143–62.

Hickman, P., Pollard- Durodola, S. D., & Vaughn, S. (2004). Storybook reading: Improving vocabulary and comprehension for English-language learners. *Reading Teacher* 57(8), 720–30.

IDEIA (2004). Individuals with Disabilities Education Improvement Act, Public Law No. 108–446 (2004).

Kamil, M. L., Borman, G. D., Dole, J., Kral, C. C., Salinger, T., & Torgesen, J. (2008). Improving adolescent literacy: Effective classroom and intervention practices. A practice guide (NCEE 2008–4027). Washington, DC: National Center for Education Evaluation and Regional Assistance, Institute of Education Sciences, U.S. Department of Education. Retrieved from http://ies.ed.gov/ncee/wwc.

Klingner, J. K., & Edwards, P. A. (2006). Cultural considerations with response to intervention models. *Reading Research Quarterly* 41(1), 108–17.

Klingner, J. K., Artiles, A. J., & Barletta, L. M. (2006). English language learners who struggle with reading: Language acquisition or LD? *Journal of Learning Disabilities* 39(2), 108–28.

Linan-Thompson, S., Cirino, P. T., & Vaughn, S. (2007). Determining English language learners' response to intervention: Questions and some answers. *Learning Disabilities Quarterly* 30(3), 185–95.

Linan-Thompson, S., Vaughn, S., Hickman-Davis, P., & Kouzekanani, K. (2003). Effectiveness of supplemental reading instruction for second-grade English language learners with reading difficulties. *Elementary School Journal* 103(3), 221.

Linan-Thompson, S., Vaughn, S., Prater, K., & Cirino, P. T. (2006). The response to intervention of English Language Learners at risk for reading problems. *Journal of Learning Disabilities* 39(5), 390–8.

Mathis, P. G., & Torgesen, J. K., (2005). *Early interventions in reading, Level 1.* Columbus, OH: SRA/McGraw-Hill.

Mathes, P. G., Linan-Thompson, S., Pollard-Durodola, S. D., Hagan, E. C., & Vaughn, S. R. (2003) Lectura proactiva para principiantes: Intensive small group instruction for Spanish speaking readers. Developed with funds provided by the National Institute of Child Health and Human Development (HD-99–012). Development of English Literacy in Spanish Speaking Children.

McCardle, P., Mele-McCarthy, J., & Leos, K. (2005). English language learners and learning disabilties: Research agenda and implications for practice. *Learning Disabilities Research & Practice* 20(1), 68–78.

Miller, J. F., Heilmann, J., Nockerts, A., Iglesias, A., Fabiano, L., & Francis, D. J. (2006). Oral language and reading in bilingual children. *Learning Disabilities Research & Practice* 21(1), 30–43.

NAEP (2008). *National assessment of educational progress, 2007 – Reading assessments.* Washington: National Center for Educational Statistics, U.S. Department of Education, Institute of Education Science.

NCLBA (2002). No Child Left Behind Act of 2001, Public Law No. 107–110, §2, 147Stat. 1425(2002).

Ogle, D. (1986). K-W-L: A teaching model that develops active teaching of expository text. *The Reading Teacher* 3(6), 564–570.

Peña, E. D., & Bedore, L. M. (2009). Bilingualism in child language disorders. In R. G. Schwartz and R. G. E. Schwartz (eds.), *Handbook of child language disorder* (pp. 281–307). New York: Psychology Press.

Pollard-Durodola, S. D., Mathes, P. G., Vaughn, S., Cardeñas-Hagan, E., & Linan-Thompson, S. (2006). The role of oracy in developing comprehension in Spanish-speaking English language learners. *Topics in Language Disorders* 26(4), 365–84.

Shanahan, T., & Beck, I. L. (2006). Effective literacy teaching for English-language learners. In D. August and T. Shanahan (eds.), *Developing a literacy in a second language: Report of the National Literacy Panel* (pp. 415–88). Mahwah, NJ: Erlbaum.

Samson, J. F., & Lesaux, N. K. (2009). Language-minority learners in special education: rates and predictors of identification for services. *Journal of Learning Disabilities* 42(2), 148–62.

Swanson, H. L., Hoskyn, M., & Lee, C. (1999). *Interventions for students with learning disabilities: A meta-analysis of treatment outcomes.* New York: Guilford Press.

Torgesen, J. K., Alexander, A. W., Wagner, R. K., Rashotte, C. A., Voeller, K. S., & Conway, T. (2001). Intensive remedial instruction for children with severe reading disabilities: Immediate and long-term outcomes from two instructional approaches. *Journal of Learning Disabilties* 43(1), 33–58.

Vaughn, S., & Ortiz, A. (May 2010). Response to intervention in reading for English language learners; available at: www.rtinetwork.org.

Vaughn, S., Linan-Thompson, S., & Hickman, P. (2003). Response to intervention as a means of identifying students with reading/learning disabilities. *Exceptional Children* 69(4), 392–409.

Vaughn, S., Mathes, P. G., Linan-Thompson, S., & Francis, D. J. (2005). Teaching English language learners at risk for reading disabilities to read: Putting research into practice. *Learning Disabilities Research & Practice* 20(1), 58–67.

Vaughn, S., Cirino, P. T., Linan-Thompson, S., Mathes, P. G., Carlson, C. D., Hagan, E. C., & Francis, D. J. (2006a). Effectiveness of a Spanish intervention and an English intervention for English-language learners at risk for reading problems. *American Educational Research Journal* 43(3), 449–87.

Vaughn, S., Linan-Thompson, S., Mathes, P. G., Cirino, P. T., Carlson, C. D., Pollard-Durodola, S. D., & Francis, D. J. (2006b). Effectiveness of Spanish intervention for first-grade English language learners at risk for reading difficulties. *Journal of Learning Disabilities* 39(1), 56–73.

Vaughn, S., Mathes, P., Linan-Thompson, S., Cirino, P., Carlson, C., Pollard-Durodola, S., & Francis, D. J. (2006c). Effectiveness of an English intervention for first-grade English language learners at risk for reading problems. *Elementary School Journal* 107(2), 153–80.

Vaughn, S., Cirino, P. T., Tolar, T., Fletcher, J. M., Cardenas-Hagan, E., Carlson, C. D., & Francis, D. J. (2008). Long-term follow-up for Spanish and English interventions for 1st grade English language learners at risk for reading problems. *Journal of Research on Educational Effectiveness* 1(4), 179–214.

Vaughn, S., Martinez, L., Reutebuch, C. K., Carlson, C., Thompson, S. L., & Francis, D. J. (2009). Enhancing social studies vocabulary and comprehension for seventh-grade English language learners: Findings from two experimental studies. *Journal of Research on Educational Effectiveness* 2(4), 297–324.

What Works Clearinghouse (ed.) (2007). *English language learners. What Works Clearinghouse Topic Report*: Washington, DC: What Works Clearinghouse, Institute of Education Sciences, Department of Education.

CHAPTER 18

Implementing Evidence-Based Leisure Education Programmes during School

Linda L. Caldwell

This chapter will describe two related prevention interventions aimed at middle school youth that focus on an important developmental context: out-of-school or leisure time. The choices young people make during their out-of-school time can have a profound influence on their development, health and well-being. An abundance of research evidences suggests that in healthy leisure activities, adolescents can develop personal skills and attitudes that will help them to become adults who contribute to society, relax and recuperate from stress, and experience identity development through learning about themselves in relation to others, their communities and their societies. Leisure activities are also important avenues of informal learning and contribute to formal academic achievement.

On the other hand, despite all the positive things that can happen through participation in certain out-of-school activities, youth also can engage in addictive and risky behaviours such as substance use or vandalism; experience negative emotional states such as loneliness, stress and boredom; and experience a certain 'lack of authenticity' if

they feel that they are not engaged in self-chosen and interesting activities.

This chapter will discuss the importance of leisure to academic success and healthy adolescent development, define leisure education, describe two school-based leisure education programs, and discuss the issue of implementation fidelity related to leisure education programs. Before proceeding, however, a clarification on the use of terms is needed. The many terms used to refer to 'leisure', including 'recreation', 'free time', 'out-of-school time', 'play', and 'leisure' itself have potentially different meanings. For this chapter, I will use 'free time' or 'out-of-school time' to designate time that could either be used in positive, healthy ways that represent 'leisure' in its purest sense or time that can be used in ways that may present health or other risks to self and/or others. The term 'leisure' will embody the perspective that the engagement is enjoyable, interesting, personally meaningful, self-expressive, self-endorsed, and mostly intrinsically motivated. I will use the terms 'recreation' and 'play' to signify engagement in activity. The challenge in using these terms, however, is that there are no universally agreed-on terms to convey 'leisure' in its broadest sense, and moreover, the terms may hold little relevance to someone from poor or developing countries.

Leisure: A Context of Risk, Protection and Prevention

Leisure is considered to be one of the more 'free' contexts in a person's life and contains a number of health-promoting characteristics. Leisure is a particularly important context for adolescents, who are going through a number of critical bio-psychosocial developmental processes such as autonomy development, identity development, engaging in intimate relationships and puberty. Leisure contexts, activities and experiences all contribute to (and are influenced by) these developmental issues. Moreover, many leisure activities serve to promote educational attainment.

Educational Attainment

There are two major ways leisure can contribute to educational attainment – by influencing academic achievement at school and through informal learning that occurs outside the traditional classroom. With regard to academic achievement, there is fairly consistent evidence that extracurricular activities are associated with educational success (e.g., Darling, Caldwell & Smith, 2005; Mahoney, Cairns & Farmer, 2003), even when controlling for academic ability, family background and other extracurricular activities (Camp, 1990). Likewise, in a meta-analysis of 35 out-of-school programs for at-risk youth, participation was associated with positive reading and math outcomes (Lauer et al., 2006). In a comprehensive review of the literature on activity participation, Feldman & Matjasko (2005) also found evidence that participation has many positive effects on adolescent development and academic achievement, but they suggest that future research needs to take into account both moderators and

mediators of academic success related to activity participation.

Other researchers have suggested that the activity profile of youth is an important contributor (or detractor) from educational attainment. Youth whose out-of-school time participation is characterised by a number of organised or structured activities and fewer passive and unstructured activities have better academic performance compared to those with the opposite profile (Bartko & Eccles, 2003).

A second and often over-looked avenue to increase educational attainment is through informal learning. The C.S. Mott Foundation issued a report from the Time, Learning and Afterschool Task Force that provides numerous examples, data and testimonies of the importance of the various types of learning that take place outside the classroom (Ferrandino, 2007). Moreover, many innovative schools are incorporating multiple avenues to learning that what are typically called 'recreational activities'. For example, in Peekskill, New York, education includes an extended day that includes opportunities to learn leadership through activities such as being an art museum docent or volunteering. Students also learn by performing in the community and participating in the community 'poets' café'. Since the inception of the extended-day program, the school district reported that every year there is an increase in English/language arts proficiency scores as well as fewer reported behavioural problems (Ferrandino, 2007). Another example is the Brooklyn Academy of Science and the Environment. This academy, and other smaller schools in New York City, take education out of the classroom into such places as botanical gardens, museums and other cultural treasures.

This type of informal learning, whether it is associated with formal schooling or taking place outside the school context, is effective because most students are more engaged in these contexts than with typical academic classroom instruction. Having choices and being exposed to different opportunities not only are developmentally appropriate, but they also stimulate passions and allow students to become intensely involved in a project (e.g., Chung & Hillsman, 2005; Dahl, 2004).

Sadly, 'we often disregard the many ways children learn outside of the current school day – from forming cultural bonds to multi-tasking with technology tools' (Ferrandino, 2007, p. 7). Learning can be fun, and recreational activities that are fun do not mean that learning does not occur. Advocating for policies that promote informal learning as a complement to school-based learning would seem to be an important boost for students' academic achievement and in particular for students who are otherwise seemingly disengaged from in-school learning. It also seems important to advocate for leisure education (which will be described subsequently) to provide students (and families) with tools to maximise the informal learning that takes place in leisure.

Health and Development

Most people engage in leisure activities out of some sense of personal choice because the activities are inherently interesting (and therefore intrinsically motivating) or because they serve some future purpose (and are self-endorsed). In turn, intrinsic motivation is associated with health and well-being; at the same time, being non-intrinsically motivated (e.g., by some external reward such as doing something to please someone else or because there is nothing else to do) is associated with negative health outcomes (e.g., Ryan & Deci, 2000). These experiences are not likely to be considered leisure in its true sense. In addition to intrinsic motivation, several other characteristics of leisure make it a unique context of health promotion, human development, and academic achievement. These characteristics include

1. Social support, friendships and social acceptance are endemic to most leisure activities and are important factors in the initiation and maintenance of health behaviours.
2. Competence and self-efficacy are often derived from leisure participation.

3. Leisure provides opportunities for experiences of challenge and being totally absorbed in leisure activity.
4. Leisure provides opportunities for being self-determined and in control.
5. Leisure activities provide a range of many types of opportunities for a number of experiences, including feeling relaxed, disengaged from stress and being distracted from negative life events to being challenged and having high levels of excitement and risk.
6. Nature-based and outdoor recreation experiences promote many forms of health. For example, being close to parks and trails is associated with higher levels of physical activity.

Risk Behaviour and Prevention

Paradoxically, many adolescents (and adults) do not engage in positive free-time experiences and thus do not reap these leisure-related benefits. Even if youth do not engage in risky behaviours such as substance use of violence, it is clear that many do not know how to use their out-of-school time wisely and/or are unaware of various recreational possibilities in their communities. Consequently, youth may watch too much television, spend too much time on the computer, lack physical activity, and/or participate in a number of other less optimal recreation activities. Educational efforts that can lead adolescents to more productive and fulfilling use of out-of-school time are necessary and have been referred to as 'leisure education'.

Leisure education is a useful way to help youth learn to take responsibility for finding or creating stimulating and productive things to do in free time that are possible in their communities. Important to adolescent development, if youth develop interests and learn to take charge of their free-time experiences in positive ways, they are less likely to be at risk for engaging in socially maladaptive and unhealthy behaviours. Moreover, facilitating the development of interest and involvement in positive recreational activities early in a young person's life is critical because leisure interests developed in childhood set a solid foundation for healthy use of leisure time throughout adulthood; in fact, about 50 per cent of the activities a youth is involved in during childhood and adolescence are carried on to adulthood (Iso-Ahola, 1980).

Leisure education with adolescents is also biologically important. Recent research indicates that the adolescent brain is primed for developing enduring interests because it is easily shaped by social learning through experience, direct interaction, self-reflection, education and interaction with adults and peers (Dahl, 2004). Goal-directed behaviours intensify during this time and are often manifested by developing passions in music, art and hobbies. Thus exposure to a variety of new recreation experiences and opportunities likely will lead to early activation of leisure-related interests and passions that will contribute to positive adolescent development and may turn into life-long interests and passions.

On the other hand, changes in the adolescent brain also predispose adolescents to increased sensation-seeking that can promote risk-taking or other potentially dangerous behaviours (Dahl, 2004). Executive functioning skills such as good decision making and problem solving evolve a bit after the emotion centre in the brain is highly activated. The mismatch in development of emotional regulation and executive functioning explains to some degree why youth often make poor judgements in emotionally charged situations and why they are prone to risk behaviours with peers.

What Is 'Leisure Education'?

'Leisure education' is the process of educating adolescents about healthy use of out-of-school time through recreation. Two of these processes are important to highlight. First, 'education through leisure' is what individuals learn about themselves and their world through participation in recreation. In other words, recreation pursuits lead to discovery, understanding and growth. This type of leisure education tends to be informal and personal and can occur in natural (e.g., parks) or built environments (e.g., teen centres). For example, a teenager may learn rock-climbing skills on a climbing wall and learn that she has personal tenacity that may apply in other realms of her life.

A second way to view leisure education is 'education for leisure'. In this case, one learns to be prepared to participate in leisure through skill building (e.g., learning to play chess), knowledge acquisition (e.g., learning a bus route), and attitude development (e.g., valuing leisure or understanding the benefits of participation in healthy leisure pursuits). Formal programs that teach youth activity or leisure skills such as painting and music are examples of education for leisure. Education for leisure also can occur as part of a formal program designed to teach youth about how to use their leisure in personally fulfilling and responsible ways. This form of leisure education tends to be curriculum- or program-based and provided in schools or as part of an after-school program.

Leisure Education: A Brief History

Leisure education is not a new concept and dates back to the early Greeks. The Latin word 'scholè' essentially means 'employment of leisure time to study and learn'. The English words 'school' and 'scholar' are derived from 'scholè'. In 1916, John Dewey wrote about the need for schools to educate youth for the wise use of leisure time. Shortly thereafter, in 1918, the U.S. Cardinal Principles of Secondary Education were issued by the Commission on the Reorganisation of Secondary Education (see Table 18.1 for the wording of the principle) (Department of the Interior, Bureau of Education, 1928). Although between 1910 and 1930 there was a flurry of leisure education activity by schools that established extracurricular activities and programs, including sports, publications, hobbies, and social- and academic-related experiences, those efforts largely went by the wayside during the 1930s.

Table 18.1. Cardinal Principle 6: Worthy Use of Leisure

Education should equip the individual to secure from his (or her) leisure the recreation of body, mind and spirit and the enrichment and enlargement of his (or her) personality. This objective calls for the ability to use the common means of enjoyment, such as music, art, literature, drama and social intercourse, together with the fostering in each individual of one or more special vocational interests.

Heretofore, the high school has given little conscious attention to this objective. It has so exclusively sought intellectual discipline that it has seldom treated literature, art and music so as to evoke right emotional response and produce positive enjoyment. Its presentation of science should aim, in part, to arouse a genuine appreciation of nature.

The school has failed also to organise and direct the social activities of young people as it should. One of the surest ways in which to prepare pupils worthily to use leisure in adult life is by guiding and directing their use of leisure in youth. The school therefore should see that adequate recreation is provided both within the school and by other proper agencies in the community. The school, however, has a unique opportunity in this field because it includes in its membership representatives from all classes of society and consequently is able through social relationships to establish bonds of friendship and common understanding that cannot be furnished by other agencies. Moreover, the school can so organise recreational activities that they will contribute simultaneously to other ends of education, as in the case of the school pageant or festival.

Source: Commission on the Reorganization of Secondary Education, Department of the Interior, Bureau of Education, 1928.

It wasn't until the 1960s that interest in leisure education was once again strongly advocated. Charles K. Brightbill's book, *The Challenge of Leisure*, contained a chapter on leisure education. In 1966, Brightbill wrote *Educating for Leisure-Centered Living*, which extended his earlier ideas about the importance of education for leisure. Another response to the interest in leisure education was the National Recreation and Park Association's Leisure Education Advancement Project (LEAP, 1970). This project led to the development of a comprehensive curriculum for youth in kindergarten through grade twelve and was designed to be infused into the existing curriculum for that grade (Lancaster & Odum, 1976).

Recent Leisure Education Efforts Related to Prevention

Although historically leisure education has been considered important, few programs have persisted over time. In part, this has been because the general public has not understood why leisure education is important, particularly during times when science and math subjects have taken precedence over 'life skills' activities. Another reason may be that there have been no evidence-based leisure education programs that have been based on solid theory and conceptualisation.

The two related leisure education programs described here were both rooted in the desire to prevent risky substance use and sexual risk behaviour using a prevention curriculum designed to decrease related risk factors and increase leisure-based protective factors. Thus our research team has developed, implemented and evaluated two related school-based universal primary preventive interventions: TimeWise: Taking Charge of Leisure Time and HealthWise: Life Skills for Adolescents. Both these interventions address risk behaviours by educating youth to make healthy and good choices in their leisure time. TimeWise has been implemented in rural and urban Pennsylvania, and HealthWise, which used TimeWise as a basis but includes more focus on health behaviours and facts, was implemented and evaluated in Cape Town, South Africa. In general, both prevention programs were developed based on the leisure characteristics previously noted that connect to positive health and adolescent development. Both these interventions have been funded by the National Institutes of

Health/National Institute on Drug Abuse. A unique aspect of both these programs is that they take a positive approach to prevention (increasing positive behaviours) rather than a problem-focussed approach (decreasing negative or risky behaviours). These interventions and a brief report on the outcomes are provided next.

TimeWise: Taking Charge of Leisure Time Evaluation

The primary objective of the TimeWise efficacy trial was to compare TimeWise to a no-intervention group in an attempt to decrease rates of substance-use initiation or substance use. Our hypothesis was that leisure-related outcomes would mediate decreases in substance use/initiation. Nine schools were recruited to participate. Four were randomly assigned to the experimental group and five to the comparison group. All schools were in rural school districts in Pennsylvania (United States) and were chosen to represent relatively poor, small (i.e., fewer than 1,000 students) school districts. In each school, approximately one-third of the students received free or reduced-price lunches. The TimeWise core curriculum was implemented in the four experimental condition school districts in the spring of 2001 to 634 seventh grade students (315, or 49.7 per cent, were female, and 95 per cent were European Americans). In the springs of 2002 and 2003, three-period booster sessions were administered (students then were in the eighth and ninth grades). Students were from rural backgrounds; 30.4 per cent of the students lived in a rural area, 25 per cent lived in a neighbourhood but not 'in a town', 25.2 per cent lived in a town, and 6.9 per cent lived on a farm. They also were from low-socioeconomic-status areas; 56.7 per cent bought their own lunch, 20.8 per cent received free lunches, and 11.8 per cent were eligible for reduced-cost lunch.

A number of leisure-related theories were used in creating the TimeWise curriculum. Ecological systems theory (e.g., Bronfenbrenner, 1994) was the over-arching basis for the development of TimeWise.

This theory suggests that in order to understand or influence an individual, several factors must be considered, including personal characteristics (e.g., personality, gender and age), social factors (e.g., parents, peers, teachers and other important adults), community factors (e.g., quality of schools and presence of parks and trails) and larger cultural factors (e.g., community values and ethnic and/or racial issues). Within the context of ecological systems theory, leisure-related theories were used to help the curriculum developers understand personal, social and community-wide factors that were important to incorporate into the TimeWise curriculum. These theories included self-determination theory (e.g., Ryan & Deci, 2000), development as action in context (Silbereisen & Todt, 1994), constraints theory (Jackson, 2005), optimal arousal theory (Mannell & Kleiber, 1997), boredom and interest development (Hunter & Csikszentmihalyi, 2003) and flow theory (Csikszentmihalyi, 1990).

Based on these theories, TimeWise is comprised of six core and five additional lessons. In the manual, each lesson is broken into two core activities that take about 30 to 40 minutes to implement in a structured classroom setting. The six core lessons focus on teaching students to

1. Determine personally satisfying and meaningful leisure activities and interests
2. Understand the benefits of participating in healthy leisure
3. Understand how one's motivation affects one's experience and participation in healthy behaviours
4. Alleviate boredom and increase optimal experience in leisure time
5. Learn how to take responsible action to participate in desired activities
6. Identify and overcome constraints that get in the way of participation in desired activities

The additional lessons include

1. Educating others about leisure
2. Making decisions and taking risks

3. Achieving flow
4. Managing stress and becoming mindful
5. Friendships and leisure
6. Leisure and change

Selected TimeWise Results

Results from the TimeWise intervention are promising (e.g., Caldwell et al., 2004). We found that those who received TimeWise had greater interest in activities and lower rates of boredom. TimeWise students also reported lower levels of amotivation (i.e., doing things because there is nothing else to do and lack of self-regulation) and greater levels of initiative (e.g., taking charge and pursuing an interest) and the ability to restructure activities. Youth who had the TimeWise program also were more aware of leisure opportunities in the community and reported being better able to make plans and decisions in their leisure time. Regarding substance use, the results were promising, but given the very low rate of substance use among this rural sample, it was difficult to detect differences between experimental and comparison groups. TimeWise youth did, however, report lower rates of use of marijuana and inhalants, particularly for males. This effect was more pronounced at the end of ninth grade.

Implementation Issues and Lessons Learned

When we delivered the program ourselves (i.e., with members of the research team), we were able to have complete control over the content and delivery. We also were content experts. This control and expertise allowed us to be very efficient and effective in the delivery of the program. After the initial delivery of TimeWise, we worked with teachers in an urban school district to deliver the program to middle school youth. Although there was a great deal of enthusiasm for the content and manual, it proved very challenging for these teachers (mostly health and physical education teachers) to incorporate the program into their existing day and requirements. We did map

TimeWise activities and content onto the state's educational standards, but it was still difficult to squeeze TimeWise into the day.

Feedback from teachers indicated that part of the program was that middle school students get such a limited time for physical activity as it is that to take time away from physical activity to incorporate more classroom-based activities was ill-advised. Given this situation, which is likely the case in many school districts, we advise a closer content integration within physical activity, whereby students learn life-long leisure skills. We also advise providing structured TimeWise after-school programs to bring to life the material in the curriculum and provide students with opportunities to explore new activities and develop skills. The other issue raised by teachers is that it took them longer to teach the lessons than we anticipated. In retrospect, this makes sense. When we delivered it, given our content and delivery expertise, we were not faced with a timing problem. However, it is quite understandable that as teachers learn the material themselves and follow the script in the manual, content delivery would take more time.

HealthWise South Africa: Life Skills for Young Adults

HealthWise (Caldwell et al., 2004) was developed in response to a request from colleagues in South Africa who were interested in youth risk reduction and health promotion through leisure. HealthWise emanated from TimeWise but included a stronger focus on sexual risk reduction, substance use and the co-morbidity of the two. It also included a stronger emphasis on general life skills, such as anger and anxiety management. HealthWise was pilot tested in 2001–2, modified, and then evaluated over five years beginning in 2003.

Nine high schools in Mitchell's Plain, South Africa, were recruited to participate in the study; students in four schools received HealthWise, and five schools served as comparisons. Overall, 6,050 youth participated. We collected data every six months on three

Table 18.2. HealthWise Lessons

Grade 8 lessons:
1. Self-awareness
2. Managing anxiety
3. Managing anger
4. Exploring free time
5. Free time in my community
6. Beating boredom and developing interests
7. Overcoming roadblocks
8. Decision making
9. Managing risk
10. Avoiding sexual risk behavior
11. Myths and realities of drug use
12. Avoiding and reducing risk

Grade 9 lessons:
1. Review of HealthWise grade 8
2. Leisure motivation
3. Community connections
4. Planning and managing leisure
5. Relationships and sexual behavior
6. Conflict resolution

sequential eighth grade cohorts through grade ten. Mitchell's Plain was established as a township for people of mixed-race backgrounds (i.e., coloured) during the apartheid era. People in this region are generally poor, unemployment is high and most schools are in need of repair. Based on students' self-reports, 86 per cent of the study population were mixed race, 9 per cent were black and the remainder either Indian or white.

The HealthWise curriculum included seventeen lessons, with each requiring two to three lesson periods (see Table 18.2 for a listing of the lessons). Figure 18.1 depicts the risk and protective factors targeted along with the corresponding lessons. The overall goals of the HealthWise curriculum were to (1) reduce the sexual risk, (2) reduce drug abuse and (3) increase positive use and experience of free and leisure time. The program was designed to provide a sequential set of activities to teach youth

1. How to use their free time in ways that will be beneficial to themselves, their families and friends and their community;

2. Specific inter- and intra-personal skills to make good decisions, control their emotions such as anger and anxiety, resolve conflicts and overcome boredom in free time;

3. Specific facts about the causes and effects of drug use and sexual risk-taking behaviors;

4. Specific ways to avoid peer pressure and to take responsible action in their free time; and

5. How to interact with and access community resources.

The latter point, interacting with community resources, was critical. Being located in an economically deprived and under-resourced area, we were very concerned about youth being able to access adequate health services as well as leisure resources. Thus we built this element into the curriculum, and it evolved over the five years of the study. One of the initial innovations made to implementation of the curriculum (based on the pilot study) was to hire two youth development specialists (YDSs). Their role was to support the teachers in curriculum implementation, particularly around the leisure-related topics and sexuality lessons. Both of these areas were relatively new to the teachers, who expressed discomfort with being able to teach the lessons. One of the reasons teachers initially had a difficult time with the leisure lessons was because they, themselves, had impoverished leisure, and they did not understand the importance of healthy leisure in their own or their students' lives. Because of this, we developed better training modules for the leisure and sexuality lessons and hired the YDSs.

The addition of the YDSs resulted in a number of important and exciting innovations. These included networking with non-governmental organisations and recreational resources as well as building and strengthening relationships between universities and schools, developing needs-specific alternative after-school leisure programs, strengthening existing organisations and clubs in schools and linking projects so that students acquire

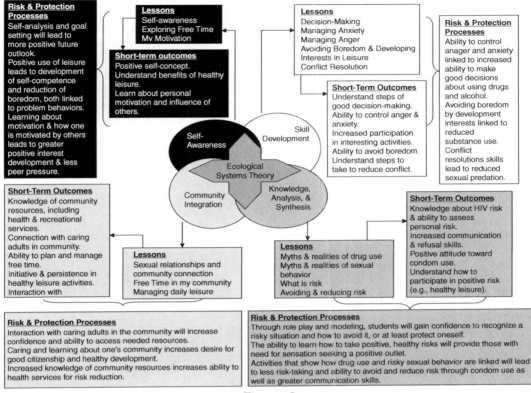

Figure 18.1.

skills progressively as they progress through projects (e.g., from swimming to surfing to lifesaving). The YDSs also started the Youth Adult Partnership (YAP) program which brought together parents, teachers and students to participate in group activities that facilitated leadership skills and relationship building. Through the YAP program, students also learned financial skills by raising funds for individual projects and advocating for incorporating after-school programs in yearly budgets.

One of the more sustainable and effective secondary effects of the HealthWise program was the Brown Paper Performing Arts Project (BPPAP). In this project, drama students from the nearby University of the Western Cape would come into the schools during the after-school period and work with the middle school youth to learn drama techniques. They met two afternoons a week over a period of seven months

(Wegner et al., 2008). The primary goal was for learners to explore the different facets of and participate in performing arts as a leisure activity. Learners had opportunities to develop a range of skills in script writing, acting, reading, speaking, listening, assertiveness and decision making.

During the BPPAP, a portion of time was devoted to allowing time to talk with the youth about issues in their lives, ranging from relationship issues to trouble with parents, teachers or others. In addition, BPPAP activities were aimed at promoting healthy development of the adolescents, such as self-esteem and self-awareness.

Selected HealthWise Results

From an outcomes perspective, of particular interest was to understand the relation between boredom in leisure and leisure motivation and substance use and sexual risk behaviours. In one set of analyses using seven waves of HealthWise data, the strongest leisure-related predictors of using substances both between and within subjects were greater leisure boredom, too much perceived parental control and poor, unhealthy leisure choices (Sharp et al., 2006). Furthermore, youth who *became more bored* in their leisure between the eighth and tenth grades had the highest odds of smoking and use of alcohol and marijuana. A one-unit increase in leisure boredom from the beginning of eighth grade to the beginning of tenth grade was associated with increased odds of using alcohol, cigarettes and marijuana (14, 23, and 36 per cent, respectively) (Sharp et al., 2006). Researchers also found that those with high levels of leisure-related intrinsic motivation had the lowest odds of smoking and use of alcohol, marijuana and inhalants (Caldwell et al., 2010).

Researchers also were interested in youth's experiences within activities. Therefore, they asked youth about specific activities in which they participated as well as levels of motivation and boredom for each specific activity. They found that compared with youth who participated in one or more leisure activities but were motivated and interested, youth who participated in several leisure activities but were unmotivated and bored in all of them had the highest likelihood of alcohol and tobacco use (Tibbits et al., 2009). Furthermore, females who only spent leisure time in social activities and were unmotivated and bored while doing so had a much higher likelihood of alcohol and tobacco use than females who only spent time in social activities but were interested and motivated. Additional analysis suggested that spending time with friends positively predicted lifetime alcohol use, whilst participating in hobbies and music and singing activities negatively predicted lifetime alcohol use. Spending time with friends (for everyone) and reporting high levels of boredom in leisure (for girls) also predicted lifetime marijuana use (Tibbits et al., 2009).

The BPPAP was evaluated using qualitative evaluation methods. Students and facilitators participated in focus groups, digital story-telling methods were used with students and teachers were interviewed (Lesko, Bosman & Wegner, 2006). Findings showed that students found the program interesting, fun and meaningful. In addition, they reaped a number of benefits. One of the boy participants said, 'We do drama, singing and acting. It is nice, very nice. Instead of doing drugs, we do drama'. Along those same lines, another boy stated

> I would like to do something like this in our communities because there are a lot of children who need this because they are 'tikking' [methamphetamine use] and drinking and doing drugs, and I can count on my hands how many of them are still in school. All of the girls there they have babies and stuff like that, and I think if they have something like this to keep them busy, they won't be doing other things because if like we do the show in other areas then we could maybe even inspire them.

There was clear evidence of social emotional learning because one of the themes dealt with learners' personal growth and development, an increase in self-confidence and the acquisition of new skills. A girl participant said

> I was shy, I could never look somebody in the eye or talk to them, but after I came here, we played this game that I just loved, the game called 'eye contact' – something we do each time when we start. Before, we looked at each other, but we didn't really make eye contact. Here they taught us to look into the next person by looking in his eyes or her eyes.

Another benefit was the development of new peer relationships and promotion of intercultural understanding. During the BPPAP, students reported getting to know each other on a more personal level, which promoted respect and understanding of one another. For example, one of the boys said

> I am talking about the multi-cultural things, and I, yes and me as a person, I wouldn't go to their group because I feel like I wouldn't fit in, but now they talk about something and I wouldn't understand, but now when we in drama class we all friends. When they talk about something, then we

ask them now what does that mean, and
so we learn their language as well.

Summary

So far this chapter has described the importance of leisure in healthy adolescent development, the role of leisure education, and has reviewed two leisure education programs that provide promising evidence of their ability to promote healthy adolescent development and reduce risk behaviour. Much more research is needed in terms of effective leisure education programs for different populations and for different purposes. For example, leisure education also could be effective in promoting physically active leisure or in reducing the stressors on military families with loved ones away from home. The appropriate age for leisure education is unknown – if there is even an appropriate age. It may be a better question to ask what types of leisure education are most effective for what ages? As seen in this section, it is also important to pursue cultural issues regarding leisure and leisure education for different groups. In the next section, the issue of implementation fidelity is discussed.

Implementation Quality Issues and Future Research

The TimeWise study was an efficacy trial, which meant that members of the research team taught the lessons. Thus, as noted previously, we had complete control over the content and delivery of the curriculum, and issues around implementation quality were not as salient. In the HealthWise study, however, issues surrounding implementation quality were very important. In both interventions we collected process-evaluation data. In TimeWise, we asked implementers from our research team to complete a daily log after each time they implemented a lesson. These logs assessed how much time was spent on each activity and what per cent of the intended content actually was covered and asked a few questions about students'

reactions to the lessons. We also surveyed about 25 per cent of the youth who were in the program to ask them their thoughts about the program.

In the HealthWise study, we also collected similar process-evaluation data. This was very important because it was an effectiveness trial, which meant that we trained the teachers to deliver the program. This gave us far less control over implementation fidelity. Because we found some differences between school sites in some of the outcomes, we used the process-evaluation data to help us better understand these differences. For example, we found that the strongest effects on increases in leisure-related intrinsic motivation and stable identified motivation, as well as decreases in introjected motivation and amotivation, occurred in the school where teachers had high levels of implementation quality (Caldwell et al., 2008, 2010).

The essential question to be addressed was whether the program was ineffective for some youth or whether lack of effects was due to poor implementation quality. Anecdotally and through observation (from numerous visits to the study sites and in discussion with our South African research colleagues, teachers and principals), we suspected that there was one school that outperformed the others. The data supported this conjecture. This finding prompted us to compete for a third HealthWise grant, this time focusing on implementation quality. We are grateful to the National Institute of Drug Abuse (NIDA) for funding this next study, which we are currently in the process of planning and will begin early in 2011. In this study, fifty-six schools from the Cape Town Metro South Education District will be randomly assigned to one of eight experimental groups. This study will allow us to make conclusions about which factors or combination of factors best promotes implementation fidelity.

There has been a great deal of recent attention in the scientific community to better understand factors related to implementing an evidence-based intervention (EBI) with quality and fidelity (e.g., Ginexi & Hilton,

2006). This type of research is often called 'translational' or 'type 2'. Recently, for example, two notable journals, *Evaluation and the Health Professions* and the *American Journal of Community Psychology*, devoted special issues to the topic of translation research (2006 and 2008, respectively). Furthermore, in response to the Society for Prevention Research's concern about conducting studies on type 2 translational research (T2TR), a task force was formed and a research agenda was proposed on the topic at the society's 2008 annual meeting (Spoth et al., 2008). In particular, the task force called for research that systematically studies how EBIs are incorporated into existing systems (e.g., a school district), the degree to which EBIs are implemented with fidelity and factors that influence the integration and successful implementation of EBIs (Spoth et al., 2008).

From a simplistic perspective, there are two main issues surrounding T2TR. As outlined by Spoth et al. (2008), the life cycle of an EBI (i.e., once it has been deemed effective) consists of adoption, effective implementation and sustainability. Thus the first main issue is at the implementation level, that is, actually *doing* the EBI in practice. The second main issue is the *science* behind the doing (e.g., Ginexi & Hilton, 2006; Rohrbach et al., 2006; Wandersman et al., 2008). Rogers' (1995) 'diffusion of innovation theory' has been widely used as a starting point to understand the science behind T2TR. This theory describes the stages an innovation goes through from creation to use but does not provide guidance for a more nuanced understanding of that process. Thus there has been little systematic theory building that helps prevention science understand how and why adoption, effective implementation and sustainability occur outside of a randomised, controlled study (Botvin, 2004; Ginexi & Hilton, 2006). One notable recent exception is the 'interactive systems framework for dissemination and implementation' developed by Wandersman et al. (2008) that focuses on research to practice models

within a community context in an attempt to address the dearth of T2TR.

Although specific plans are still under way in our new HeathWise implementation fidelity study, some of the ideas on which we will base our study are presented next. Adherence and adaptation with fidelity are particularly relevant when interventions are implemented in contexts or conditions that differ from where they were tested. The initial implementation of HealthWise occurred in four mixed-race (also called 'coloured') schools, whereas in the upcoming study, youth in black, white and mixed-race neighbourhoods will receive the intervention. Lack of adherence and adaptation without fidelity (however unintentional) can lead to program drift and a loss of effectiveness. The issue of adaptation may be particularly important to more comprehensive interventions such as HealthWise or to interventions that target specific risk factors that may be more or less culturally sensitive, such as HIV/AIDS risk (e.g., Harshbarger et al., 2006). For example, modifications are often made owing to personal discomfort with the content (e.g., discussion of sexuality), method of teaching (e.g., interactive style) or because teachers anticipate misbehaviour of students (Fagan et al., 2008). Others have found that modifications are made to adapt to local needs and incorporate local talent and individual strength (Backer, 2001). Modifications can increase implementers' ownership of the intervention (Harshbarger et al., 2006) as well as increase the relevance of the program for different populations; apply new examples, situations, and exercises; and shorten the length of or consolidate the number of sessions (Buston et al., 2002; Kelly et al., 2000). Other research has concluded that many adaptations are reactive in response to barriers and other local challenges rather than deliberate innovation (Bumbarger & Perkins, 2008). Despite the attention to adherence and adaptation, there is little empirical knowledge about what influences program adaptations that either add to or detract from implementation fidelity when programs go to scale.

Factors that Influence Implementation Fidelity

In their review paper, Dusenbury et al. (2003) identified key elements that promote high-quality fidelity of implementation in efficacy studies. These elements include teacher training, program characteristics, teacher characteristics, and organisational characteristics. While the work of Dusenbury et al. was based on an extensive review of the literature across several fields of prevention, Ringwalt et al. (2003) conducted one of the few studies to specifically examine factors that promoted implementation fidelity. The two strongest predictors of implementation fidelity in their study were teacher training and the degree to which teachers perceived that they had autonomy in terms of implementing the program. Another study on implementation fidelity conducted by Payne et al. (2006, p. 235) concluded that 'schools that engage in local program selection and high-quality training, that have supportive principals, that are better organised to implement programs, that integrate programs into normal school activities, and that use standardized programs demonstrate higher intensity of program implementation'.

In response to the need to better understand factors that combine to promote implementation fidelity, Domitrovich et al. (2008) developed a conceptual framework that addresses three spheres of influence on implementation fidelity: macro, school and individual. We will specifically focus on the school and individual levels in our study (although we must consider macro-level factors in any overall conclusions). Thus, in consideration of the literature as well as the local conditions in which school district operates, we choose three factors hypothesised to influence implementation fidelity for our study – teacher training; teacher structure, support and supervision and enhanced school environment. In addition, we will include teacher characteristics in the analyses either as explanatory or control variables. Our primary research goal is

to be able to directly assess the individual importance of each factor on implementation fidelity and student outcomes, as well as the interactive effect of each of these on the outcomes. This will enable us to be able to provide very specific advice as to the best method or combination of methods to produce the most impact with the HealthWise intervention.

Teacher training is an effective component of preparing implementers to deliver an intervention with quality and fidelity (e.g., Dusenbury et al., 2003, 2005; Ennett et al., 2003; Fagan et al., 2008; Gager & Elias, 1997). Although studies examining the relationship between teacher training and fidelity have shown a positive association, the relationship is weaker than might be expected (e.g., Gottfredson & Gottfredson, 2002). Thus it is possible that in certain environments or under certain conditions, training is not the most effective method of giving knowledge about the intervention. This is a critical question to the school district because teacher training is a major component of their culture, especially around topics that are sensitive. As well, South African teachers are historically less well trained to deliver these important health lessons and need a great deal of support.

Some form of technical assistance or teacher support/coaching on an on-going basis is important to fidelity of implementation (e.g., Fagan et al., 2008; Harshbarger, et al., 2006), although there are mixed results about coaching (Giles et al., 2008). Others have indicated that some form of supervision and feedback, even at a global level, may be important to quality of implementation (Domitrovich et al., 2008; Weist, 2008). After discussions with school district personnel, we decided that a more appropriate and sustainable path to take was providing structure, support and supervision (SSS). This condition will be aimed at monitoring and supporting the timing, frequency, duration and mode of delivery of the HealthWise lessons (e.g., Domitrovich et al., 2008). It is motivated by the observation that the teachers with whom we work responded well to structure and guidance but needed flexibility.

At the school level, there are numerous factors that may influence implementation fidelity and prevention outcomes. The culture or climate of the environment in which an intervention takes place can be an important factor in promoting implementation fidelity (Bradshaw et al., 2008; Gottfredson & Gottfredson, 2002; Payne et al., 2006), although it is often overlooked in the dissemination process (Adelman & Taylor, 2003; Burns & Hoagwood, 2005; Dusenbury et al., 2003; Greenhalgh et al., 2005; Rohrbach et al., 2006; Wandersman et al., 2008). Other factors, such as having the curriculum integrated into normal school operations, affect teacher enthusiasm and commitment, thus also affecting implementation fidelity (Gottfredson & Gottfredson, 2002).

Enhancing the school environment is particularly relevant for our study because the school district (as is all of South Africa) is beginning to adopt the Health Promoting Schools Framework (HPSF), which is based on empowerment and including a more comprehensive community approach to education. Previous work by our research team (Lazarus, 2007) clearly indicated that HealthWise fits well within that framework in general. Although it is beyond the scope of this grant to fully implement an HPSF, we will use several principles associated with HPSF. For example, we will form a steering group of teachers and parents to determine how best to promote health and well-being of students, teachers, principals and parents using HealthWise as an organising framework. Also, we will cultivate leadership within the schools and parents to promote aspects of HealthWise on a school-wide basis.

Summary

The research community has a great deal to learn about the development, implementation, evaluation and sustainability of school-based interventions. Implementation fidelity and appropriate adaptations are particularly important issues to our work in

part because the concepts of leisure and leisure education are new to most people. As we experienced with the HealthWise program, this lack of experience with leisure-related constructs resulted in some teachers not adhering to the material as it was meant to be covered. Although not discussed in this chapter, another group of colleagues and I experienced a similar phenomenon in working with inner-city school teachers when they tried to implement TimeWise to a group of urban youth. Although they were in a chaotic administrative situation and little time was given to them to devote to any 'health-promotion and physical activities', we found that a lack of understanding about the importance and benefits of leisure also prevented them from implementing the program as developed. Any school-based program that is out of the ordinary should be given careful attention with regard to support of teachers. We are hopeful that our upcoming study may contribute to some ways in which this support may be provided most effectively.

Concluding Remarks

The focus of this chapter has been to offer a discussion and scientific evidence about the importance of leisure and leisure education interventions as part of the school curriculum. I have provided a description of two related studies that have provided some compelling evidence, when taken together, of the need for leisure education as a means of health promotion and risk reduction. Finally, I described preliminary plans for a future study that will provide insight into promoting implementation fidelity. There is still much more to learn and do, however. This is particularly important given that although school-based leisure education has a long history, it is not a curriculum focus that has been sustainable.

Given the content of this chapter, it is natural to conclude that parents and teachers should advocate for a leisure education–type program to be part of the school curriculum. I recognize from working with teachers and school administrators that this is an uphill battle and unlikely to succeed. Perhaps, however, with mounting research evidence, this case will be easier to make. My colleagues and I have focused primarily on the important health and developmental benefits of leisure and leisure education. A similar case needs to be made for the importance of leisure on academic performance because this is the educational mandate, and thus more research is needed in this area.

A final thought is the need to focus on college students for two reasons. First, they also could benefit from leisure education as they transition from high school to university life, filled with more freedoms and temptations than high school. Many college students seem ill-prepared to deal with these freedoms and temptations. A second reason, however, and more germane to this chapter, is to educate future middle and high school teachers about the importance of leisure. They can learn to become good role models to their students through personally meaningful leisure. Furthermore, even if leisure education is not formalised as part of the curriculum, with a strong background and understanding of the importance of leisure to adolescent health and development, new teachers can informally promote positive leisure among their students. After-school programs, health classes or even science classes that focus on a leisure topic could be incorporated into the school day.

References

Adelman, H. S., & Taylor, L. (2003). On sustainability of project innovations as systemic change. *Journal of Educational and Psychological Consultation* 14, 1–25.

Backer, T. E. (2001). *Finding the balance: Program fidelity in substance abuse prevention. A state-of-the-art review.* Rockville, MD: Substance Abuse and Mental Health Services Administration, Center for Substance Abuse Prevention.

Bartko, W. T., & Eccles, J. S. (2003). Adolescent participation in structured and unstructured activities: A person-oriented analysis. *Journal of Youth and Adolescence* 32, 233–42.

Botvin, G. J. (2004). Advancing prevention science and practice: Challenges, critical issues, and future directions. *Prevention Science* 5, 69–72.

Bradshaw, C. P., Reinke, W. M., Brown, L. D., Bevans, K. B. & Leaf, P. J. (2008). Implementation of school-wide positive behavioral interventions and supports (PBIS) in elementary schools: Observations from a randomized trial. *Education and Treatment of Children* 31, 1–26.

Brightbill, C. K. (1960). *The challenge of leisure.* Englewood Cliffs, NJ: Prentice-Hall.

Brightbill, C. K. (1966). *Educating for leisure-centered living.* Harrisburg, PA: The Stackpole Company.

Bronfenbrenner, U. (1994). Ecological models of human development. In *International encyclopedia of education*, Vol. 3, 2nd ed. (pp. 1643–7). Oxford, UK: Elsevier Sciences.

Bronfenbrenner, U., & Morris, P. A. (1998). The ecology of developmental processes. In R. M. Lerner (vol. ed.) and W. Danon (series ed.), *Handbook of child psychology*, Vol. 1: *Theoretical models of human development* (pp. 993–1028). New York: Wiley.

Bumbarger, B. K., & Perkins, D. F. (2008). After randomised trials: Issues related to dissemination of evidence-based interventions. *Journal of Children's Services* 3(2), 55–64.

Burns, B. J., & Hoagwood, K. (eds.) (2005). Evidence-based practices. II. Effecting change. *Child and Adolescent Psychiatric Clinics of North America* 14(2), xv–xvii.

Buston, K., Wright, D., Hart, G. & Scott, S. (2002). Implementation of a teacher-delivered sex education programme: Obstacles and facilitating factors. *Health Education Research* 17, 59–72.

Caldwell, L. L. (2004). *TimeWise: Taking charge of leisure time curriculum for middle school students.* Scotts Valley, CA: ETR Associates.

Caldwell, L. L., Baldwin, C. K., Walls, T. & Smith, E. A. (2004). Preliminary effects of a leisure education program to promote healthy use of free time among middle school adolescents *Journal of Leisure Research* 36, 310–35.

Caldwell, L., Patrick, M., Smith, E., Palen, L. & Wegner, L. (2010). Influencing adolescent leisure motivation: Intervention effects of HealthWise South Africa. *Journal of Leisure Research* 42(2), 203–20.

Caldwell, L. L., Younker, A., Wegner, L., Patrick, M., Vergnani, T., Smith, E. A. & Flisher, A. (2008). Understanding leisure-related program effects by using process data in the HealthWise South Africa project. *Journal of Park and Recreation Administration* 26, 146–62.

Camp, W. G. (1990). Participation in school activities and achievement: A covariance structural analysis. *Journal of Educational Research* 83, 272–8.

Chung, A., & Hillsman, E. (2005). *Evaluating after-school programs: The School Administrator*. Arlington, VA: American Association of School Administrators.

Csikszentmihalyi, M. (1990). *Flow: The psychology of optimal experience*. New York: Harper & Row.

Dahl, R. (2004). Adolescent brain development: A period of vulnerabilities and opportunities. *Annals of New York Academies of Science* 1021, 1–22.

Dane, A. V., & Schneider, B. H. (1998) Program integrity in primary and early secondary prevention: Are implementation effects out of control? *Clinical Psychology Review* 18, 23–45.

Darling, N., Caldwell, L. L. & Smith, R. (2005). Participation in school-based extracurricular activities and adolescent adjustment. *Journal of Leisure Research* 37, 51–77.

Department of the Interior, Bureau of Education (1928). Bulletin, 1918, No. 35: *Cardinal principles of secondary education: A report of the commission on the reorganization of secondary education*. Appointed by the National Education Association. Washington: US Government Printing Office. Accessed May 24, 2010, at http://www.oise.utoronto.ca/research/edu20/moments/1918cardinal.html.

Dewey, J. (1916). *Democracy and education: An introduction to the philosophy of education*. New York: The Free Press.

Domitrovich C. E., Bradshaw, C. P., Poduska, J. M., Hoagwood, K., Buckley, J. A., Olin, S., Romanelli, L. H., Leaf, P. J., Greenberg, M. T. & Ialongo, N. S. (2008). Maximizing the implementation quality of evidence-based preventive interventions in schools: A conceptual framework. *Advances in School Mental Health Promotion* 1(3), 6–28.

Durlak, J. A., & DuPre, E. (2008). Implementation matters: A review of research on the influence of implementation on program outcomes and the factors affecting implementation. *American Journal of Community Psychology* 41, 327–50.

Dusenbury, L., Brannigan, R., Falco, M. & Hansen, W. B. (2003). A review of research on fidelity of implementation: Implications for drug abuse prevention in school settings. *Health Education Research* 18, 237–56.

Dusenbury, L., Brannigan, R., Hansen, W. B., Walsh, J. & Falco, M. (2005). Quality of implementation: Developing measures crucial to understanding the diffusion of preventive interventions. *Health Education Research* 20, 308–13.

Elliott, D. S., & Mihalik, S. (2004). Issues in disseminating and replicating effective prevention programs. *Prevention Sciences* 5, 47–53.

Ennett, S. T., Ringwalt, C. L., Thorne, J., Rohrbach, L. A., Vincus, A., Simons-Rudolph, A. & Jones, S. (2003). A comparison of current practice in school-based substance use prevention programs with meta-analytic findings. *Prevention Science* 4, 1–14.

Fagan, A. A., Hanson, K., Hawkins, J. D. & Arthur, M. W. (2008). Bridging science to practice: Achieving prevention program implementation fidelity in the community youth development study. *American Journal of Community Psychology* 41, 235–49.

Feldman, A. F., & Matjasko, J. L. (2005). The role of school-based extracurricular activities in adolescent development: A comprehensive review and future directions. *Review of Educational Research* 75, 159–210.

Ferrandino, V. L. (2007). *A new day for learning*. Report from the Time, Learning and Afterschool Task Force, funded by C.S. Mott Foundation. Available at www.edutopia.org/anewdayforlearning.

Fixsen, D. L., Naoom, S. F., Blasé, K. A., Friedman, R. M. & Wallace, F. (2005). *Implementation research: A synthesis of the literature* (FMHI Publication 231). Tampa: University of South Florida, Louis de la Parte Florida Mental Health Institute, The National Implementation Research Network.

Gager, P. J., & Elias, M. J. (1997). Implementing prevention programs in high-risk environments: Application of the resiliency paradigm. *American Journal of Orthopsychiatry* 67, 363–73.

Giles, S., Jackson-Newsom, J., Pankratz, M. M., Hansen, W. B., Ringwalt, C. L. & Dusenbry, L. (2008). Measuring quality of delivery in a substance use prevention program. *Journal of Primary Prevention* 29, 489–501.

Ginexi, E. M., & Hiton, T. F. (2006). What's next for translation research? *Evaluation & the Health Professions* 29, 334–7.

Gottfredson, D. C., & Gottfredson, G. D. (2002). Quality of school-based prevention programs:

Results from a national survey. *Journal of Research on Crime and Delinquency* 39, 3–35.

Greenberg, M. T., Domitrovich, C. E., Graczyk, P. A. & Zins, J. E. (2005). *The study of implementation in school-based preventive interventions: Theory, research and practice.* Rockville, MD: Substance Abuse and Mental Health Services Administration, Center for Substance Abuse Prevention.

Greenhalgh, T., Robert, G., Macfarlane, F., Bate, P., Kyriakidou, O. & Peacock, R. (2005). *Diffusion of innovations in health service organizations: A systematic literature review.* Oxford, UK: Blackwell.

Harshbarger, C., Simmons, G., Coelho, H., Sloop, K. & Collins, C. (2006). An empirical assessment of implementation, adaptation, and tailoring: The evaluation of CDC's national diffusion of VOICES/VOCES. *AIDS Education and Prevention* 18(Suppl. A), 184–97.

Hunter, J. P., & Csikszentmihalyi, M. (2003). The positive psychology of interested adolescents. *Journal of Youth and Adolescence* 32, 27–35.

Iso-Ahola, S. E. (1980). *The social psychology of leisure and recreation.* Dubuque, IA: Wm. C. Brown.

Jackson, E. L. (ed.) (2005). *Constraints to leisure.* State College, PA: Venture.

Kelly, J. A., Heckman, T. G., Stevenson, L. Y., Williams, P. N., Ertl, T., Hays, R. B., et al. (2000). Transfer of research-based HIV prevention interventions to community service providers: Fidelity and adaptation. *AIDS Education and Prevention* 12(Suppl. A), 87–98.

Lancaster, R. A., & Odum, L. L. (1976). LEAP: The leisure education advancement project. *Journal of Health, Physical Education, Recreation, and Dance* 47, 47–8.

Lauer, P. A., Akiba, M., Wilderson, S. B., Apthorp, H. S., Snow, D. & Martin-Glenn, M. L. (2006). Out-of-school time programs: A meta-analysis of effects for at-risk students. *Review of Educational Research* 76, 275–313.

Lazarus, S. (2007). HealthWise research project: Sustainability of the HealthWise intervention. Unpublished technical report.

Lerner, R. M., Freund, A. M., DeStefanis, I. & Habermas, T. (2001). Understanding developmental regulation in adolescence: The use of the selection, optimization, and compensation model. *Human Development* 44, 29–50.

Lesko, I., Bosman, V. & Wegner, L. (2006). Evaluation of the Healthwise Brown Paper Performing Arts Project at Glendale High School. Unpublished research report, University of the Western Cape, South Africa.

Mahoney, J. L., Cairns, B. D. & Farmer, T. W. (2003). Promoting interpersonal competence and educational success through extracurricular activity participation. *Journal of Educational Psychology* 95(2), 409–18.

Mannell, R. C., & Kleiber, D. A. (1997). *A social psychology of leisure.* State College, PA: Venture.

Mihalic, S., Irwin, K., Fagan, A., Ballard, D. & Elliott, D. (2004). *Successful program implementation: Lessons learned from Blueprints.* Washington: US Department of Justice, Office of Justice Programs. Retrieved from www.ojp.usdo.gov/ojjdp.

Payne, A. A., Gottfredson, D. C. & Gottfredson, G. D. (2006). School predictors of the intensity of implementation of school-based prevention programs. *Prevention Science* 7, 225–37.

Ringwalt, C. L., Ennett, S., Johnson, R., Rohrbach, L. A., Simons-Rudolph, A., Vincus, A. & Thorne, J. (2003). Factors associated with fidelity to substance use prevention curriculum guides in the nation's middle schools. *Health Education and Behavior* 30, 375–91.

Rogers, E. M. (1995). *Diffusion of innovations*, 2nd ed. New York: The Free Press.

Rohrbach, L. A., Grana, R., Sussman, S. & Valente, T. W. (2006). Type II translation: Transporting prevention interventions from research to real-world settings. *Evaluation and the Health Professions* 29, 302–33.

Ryan, R. M., & Deci, E. L. (2000). Self-determination theory and the facilitation of intrinsic motivation, social development, and well-being. *American Psychologist* 55, 68–78.

Sharp, E., Caldwell, L., Graham, J. & Ridenour, T. (2006). Individual motivation and parental influence on adolescents' experiences of interest in free time: A longitudinal examination. *Journal of Youth & Adolescence* 35(3), 340–53; doi: 10.1007/s10964-006-9045-6.

Silbereisen, R. K., & Todt, E. (1994). *Adolescence in context: The interplay of family, school, peers, and work in adjustment.* New York: Springer-Verlag.

Spoth, R., Rohrbach, L., Greenberg, M., Hawkins, J. D., Pentz, M., Roberstson, E. & Sloboda, Z. (2008). Lost in translation? – Mapping advances and opportunities in type II translational research. Presented at the Society for Prevention Research Conference, San Francisco, CA, May 30, 2008.

Tibbits, M., Caldwell, L. L., Smith, E. A. & Wegner, L. (2009). The relation between leisure activity participation profiles and substance use among South African youth. *World Leisure 51*, 150–9.

Wandersman, A., Duffy, J., Flaspohler, P., Noonan, R., Lubell, K., Stillman, L., Blachman, M., Dunville, R. & Saul, J. (2008). Bridging the gap between prevention research and practice: The Interactive Systems Framework for dissemination and implementation. *American Journal of Community Psychology 41*, 171–81.

Weist, M. (2008). Enhancing implementation quality. *Advances in School Mental Health Promotion 1*, 2–5.

Wegner, L., Evans, I., September, X., Jacobs, J., Lesko, I. & Bosman, V. (2008). 'Instead of doing drugs we do drama': Health promotion through leisure. Paper presented at the 18th World Congress of the International Association for Child and Adolescent Psychiatry and Allied Professions, Istanbul, Turkey, April 31–May 3, 2008.

Part V

IMPROVING THE IMPLEMENTATION OF EVIDENCE-BASED PROGRAMMES AND INTERVENTIONS VIA STAFF SKILLS, ORGANISATIONAL APPROACHES, AND POLICY DEVELOPMENT

CHAPTER 19

Key Features of Promoting Collaborative Dialogue in the Classroom

Robyn M. Gillies

Introduction

Co-operative learning is widely accepted as a pedagogical practice that can be employed in classrooms to stimulate students' interest in learning through collaborative interaction with their peers. When children work co-operatively, they learn to listen to what others have to say, give and receive help and discuss different ideas, and in so doing, they learn to develop mutual understandings of the topic at hand. In fact, talk is so important that it now recognised as more than a means of sharing thoughts. It is also a social mode of thinking and a tool for the joint construction of knowledge and new learning (Mercer, 1996). Students who co-operate show increased participation in group discussions, engage in more useful help-giving behaviours and demonstrate more sophisticated levels of discourse than students who do not work co-operatively with their peers (Gillies, 2003, 2004). The result is that children who work co-operatively tend to perform better academically (Johnson & Johnson, 2002), and are more motivated to achieve than

children who have not had these experiences (Johnson & Johnson, 2008).

However, whilst co-operative learning provides opportunities for students to dialogue, concern has been expressed about the quality of the discourse that often emerges if students are left to engage in discussions without training in how to interact with others. Meloth and Deering (1999) found that task-related talk about facts, concepts and strategies only appears with low frequency when left to emerge as a by-product of co-operative learning, whilst Chinn, O'Donnell & Jinks (2000) found that children only used high-quality discourse when they were required to discuss reasons for their answers. Similarly, Rojas-Drummond & Mercer (2003) reported that although children do not initially use talk to explore and investigate issues when they work collaboratively together, they can be taught to do so, and this has a positive effect on their thinking and reasoning. In short, all these authors believe that direct intervention by teachers to facilitate discussions is warranted if children are to learn to dialogue effectively with each other.

Teacher's Role in Promoting Effective Small-Group Discourse

Although the benefits of children's discussion in co-operating groups is acknowledged (King, 2002; Gillies, 2003), little research has examined the role teachers play in promoting interaction among students. This is a concern because there is no doubt that teachers play a critical role in inducting children into ways of thinking and learning by making explicit how to express ideas, seek help, contest opposing positions and reason cogently and to do so in socially appropriate ways. Given the widespread benefits attributed to co-operative learning, neglecting to document the role of the teacher is unusual. This may have happened because teachers have been encouraged to act as facilitators, encouraging children to use each other as a resource rather than rely on outside help (Hertz-Lazarowitz & Shachar, 1990), so the focus has been on the benefits that accrue to children from interacting with others (Webb & Farivar, 1999) rather than on the role teachers play in the learning process.

One early study that did examine teachers' discourse as they interacted with their classes in traditional, whole-class and small-group settings was conducted by Hertz-Lazarowitz and Shachar (1990), who found that the organisational structure of the classroom affected how teachers interacted with students. In whole-class instruction, teachers spent more time directing, instructing, questioning and disciplining students, and their language, in turn, was more authoritarian and impersonal. In contrast, when teachers established co-operative learning, their language was more pro-social, encouraging and supportive of students' endeavours. Hertz-Lazarowitz and Shachar argued that when teachers establish co-operative learning where they have to work with a number of small groups rather than one large one, they become engaged in a complex process of linguistical change as well, so their language becomes more friendly and personal.

In a study that built on this research, Gillies (2006) investigated whether there were differences in the language secondary school teachers used who implemented co-operative learning as opposed to small-group learning. The distinction in grouping students is important because it is argued that small-group work has many of the characteristics of whole-class instruction, where students may sit together but actually work individually on tasks to achieve their own goals (Galton et al., 1999). This is in contrast to co-operative groups, where tasks are established so that students are linked interdependently and must work together to solve problems, promote each other's learning, contribute to the group's discussion, share resources and resolve conflicts (Johnson & Johnson, 2003).

The Gillies (2006) study was conducted in four high schools and involved 26 teachers and 303 students from grades seven through nine. All teachers agreed to embed co-operative learning pedagogy into a unit of work once a term for four to six weeks for three school terms. Prior to commencement of the study, all teachers had participated in a two-day workshop designed to help them to embed co-operative learning into their classroom curricula. This included information on establishing co-operative learning as proposed by Johnson & Johnson (1990), including how to

- Establish positive task interdependence so that all group members were required to complete a part of the larger group task;
- Negotiate the social skills needed to ensure that the group members listened to the ideas of others, contributed to the discussion, resolved conflicts and engaged in democratic decision making;
- Ensure that all students were accountable for the work they produced;
- Promote student interaction and
- Ensure that opportunities were provided for group members to reflect on their group's progress (i.e., what the group had achieved and what it still needed to achieve)

The results showed that when teachers did use co-operative learning, 18.2 per cent of their total language involved interactions where they mediated the children's thinking to promote learning, 20.5 per cent involved questioning behaviours (i.e., asking open and closed questions), and 6.3 per cent involved disciplinary comments (i.e., reprimands). This was in contrast to the teachers who implemented small-group work, where only 12.5 per cent of their total interactions involved mediating students' learning, 13.7 per cent involved questioning behaviours, and 12.9 per cent involved disciplinary comments.

Teachers' Discourse during Co-operative and Small-Group Learning: Study 1

Given that Gillies (2006) and Hertz-Lazorowitz and Shachar (1990) were able to demonstrate that when teachers embed co-operative learning pedagogy into their classroom curricula, they engage in more facilitative interactions than teachers who implement whole-class instruction or small-groups only, the purpose of the Gillies and Boyle (2008) study reported here is to provide a detailed analysis of the discourse teachers use when they implement co-operative learning. It is important to understand the types of discourse that teachers use because Gillies (2006) demonstrated that students' discourse is affected by the types of group experiences they have. For example, the students in the classrooms where their teachers implemented co-operative learning provided nearly twice as many elaborative or helping responses, and they were more verbally active, recording nearly twice as many task-related interactions (i.e., all interactions excluding 'interruptions') as the students in the small-group-only groups. Importantly, it is these interactions that have been shown to contribute to enhanced learning outcomes (Cohen, 1994; Cohen et al., 2002).

Seven teachers who participated in the co-operative condition in the Gillies (2006) study (described earlier) participated in the Gillies and Boyle (2008) study described later. Two of the teachers were male and five were female, and they all taught English or arts and technology courses for students in junior high school.

Procedure

All the teachers were audiotaped twice during lessons in which they had agreed to embed co-operative learning activities, and these audiotapes provided the data that that enabled the mediated-learning behaviours (discourse) to be identified and coded according to the prescribed categories discussed later. Samples of the students' language from two small groups in each classroom also were collected by placing the audiocassette on the desk for the duration of the small-group activity.

Coding

Teachers' discourse was coded by categories originally developed by Hertz-Lazarowitz and Shachar (1990) and modified by Gillies (2004). Although the Gillies (2006) study, from which these data are derived, found that both mediated-learning and questioning behaviours were significant, this chapter focuses on the mediated-learning behaviours rather than the questioning behaviours. This is so because many of the questions the teachers used required only short, unelaborated answers; hence their contribution to scaffolding students' learning is less clear and therefore not examined.

The mediated-learning behaviours from the teachers' transcripts were coded initially, and they included the following verbal behaviours: challenging basic information, using cognitive and meta-cognitive reasoning, prompting, focusing on issues, asking open questions (i.e., questions that required students to generate an elaborated response) and validating and acknowledging students' efforts.

Results

Types and examples of the mediated-learning behaviours that the teachers demonstrated during their lessons are outlined

Table 19.1. Types and Examples of Mediated-Learning Behaviour

Mediated-Learning Behaviours	Examples
Challenges Teacher 4 (The grade 10 students were deconstructing an advertisement for a car with a model lying across the bonnet in a tightly fitted, sexually appealing red dress.)	*What was the piece of vocabulary you'd associate with red? Why was that?*
Cognitive (reasons are required) Teacher 3 (The teacher directs the students to discuss the elements that are crucial to a good story and are found in the story the students have just read.) Teacher 6 (Grade 8 students are sharing ideas on the fire ant menace in preparation to writing a group essay on this topic.)	*I'm going to ask you (group) to tell us why you've weighted the elements (of good story writing) the way you have and give us a justification of why you have.* *Fire ants can be a real menace. What does 'menace' mean? How are they going to be a menace?*
Meta-cognitive (thinking about thinking) Teacher 5 (Grade 9 students have been discussing issues of racism and prejudice.)	*Think about this picture. This nice-looking lady holding the baby.... What do you think this picture is saying?*
Prompts Teacher 2 (Grade 8 students have been discussing different characters in a novel they have read.)	*What kinds of characteristics do you think this person has?*
Focuses on issues Teacher 1 (This is an art lesson on the different techniques that can be used to design a picture – colour, texture, presentation.)	*Amy, would you like to choose another colour paper, and we'll do this one as well?*
Asking open questions Teacher 7	*What was the technique I wanted you to use with the clips? Who can tell us about it?*
Validating and acknowledging students' efforts Teacher 7 (This is an art and technology class where the students are designing kitchen utensils as co-operative teams.)	*Let's have a look. Looks good.* Tom, your team's working a lot better today.... you're showing other people and giving everyone a hand.

in Table 19.1. These included behaviours that challenged students to think about their actions through to asking cognitive and meta-cognitive questions that required them to provide reasons or reflect on their thinking. The teachers also used prompts to scaffold students' learning and questions to get them to focus on specific issues whilst simultaneously validating and acknowledging their efforts with the task at hand.

To elucidate the types of mediated-learning behaviours used, a vignette is provided

of the discourse of one teacher as she interacted with her students during their small-group activities. The vignette is followed by an extract of the students' dialogue in one group from her classroom.

In this vignette, the teacher is helping her grade ten English students to deconstruct a picture of an advertisement that the group are reviewing by using different discourses such as gender, class and technology to unpack the messages that are communicated by advertisers. The signifiers that the students are focusing on are colour, gesture, culture and specific words in the written text that will help them to identify the discourses that are being used. The students have been asked to read the text both literally and inferentially to identify the discourses. In the following vignette, the students are deconstructing a picture of an advertisement for perfume involving a young woman holding a clear and sleek bottle of perfume with a red plunger in it whilst a young man looks longingly into her eyes. The teacher begins by briefly illustrating examples of the terms signifier, connotation (denotation had been discussed previously) and discourse – terms the students need to be familiar with if they are to successful deconstruct the advertisement and identify the message or messages it conveys. The purpose of this activity is to understand the subtleties of the message in the advertisement the students are learning to critique.

Teacher Vignette

1. T: *If you're looking at stove, that's the signifier, but the connotation is that the 'woman's in the kitchen', so the discourse is gender?* (Teacher prompts students to identify the type of discourse in the advertisement.)
2. S: *Gender.*
3. T: *Is that right? You got it.*
4. S: *Yep!* (Students agree.) (Teacher acknowledges and validates student's response.)
5. T: *What's the first signifier? What do you see first of all?* (Teacher prompts students to direct their attention to the advertisement and identify what attracts their attention.)
6. S: Bottle
7. T: *What's its denotation?* (Teacher checks understanding of a key term.)
8. S: *A container.*
9. T: *And its connotation is?* (Teacher prompts students to think more carefully about the concept.)
10. S: *In this particular case it holds a quality perfume.*
11. T: *Look at the subtext here. Look at the fire and ice and the text, and we can go back to the bottle. What do you notice about this part of the bottle?* (Teacher prompts students to focus on part of the bottle to identify a signifier.)
12. S: *About what? Its shape or what?*

13. T: *Its shape, its colour. What do you think it's telling us?* (Teacher challenges students to think about the subtleties of the message.)
14. S: *It's clear. It's white.*
15. T: *Yes, it's clear. It's white. Okay, so it's going to fit with the ice. OK? ... Here you've got the clear white bottle just like ice with a red plunger just like fire. You've got two signifiers working here. What's the connotation of that?* (Teacher scaffolds students' understanding to help them connect the signifiers.)
16. S: *Fire and ice. Fire will melt it. The connotation would be opposites attract. Opposites contrast?*
17. T: *So what's your discourse?* (Teacher challenges the students to think about the discourse the advertisement is using.)
18. S: *Gender? It's perfume being sold, so we're trying to attract the opposite sex.*
19. T: *Yes, it's gender slash sex. You need to mention the discourse by looking at the signifiers.... Yes, in this case, it holds a quality perfume.* (Teacher acknowledges students' suggestion.)

In this vignette, the teacher provides the students with examples of a signifier and a connotation (turn 1). It is important that the students can distinguish between these two terms because they need to be able to use them to deconstruct the message that the advertisement conveys. When a student responds that the discourse is 'gender' and the other students concur, the teacher acknowledges and validates their response (turn 3). This is then followed by a prompt (turn 5) to focus the students' attention on the first signifier that attracts their attention. The questions that follow (turns 7 and 9) check students' understanding of key terms such as 'denotation' (turn 8) and 'connotation' (turn 10), understandings that are needed to help them deconstruct the advertisement. The remainder of the interaction with the students involves the teacher prompting, challenging and checking to ensure that the students have a clearer understanding of the messages that are being transmitted (turns 11 and 15) and ways they can build connections between the subtleties expressed (turns 17 and 19). It should be noted that the teacher had very good rapport with her students because her interactions were positive, and she made every effort to ensure that the students understood the task at hand. In turn, the students were open to including her in their group discussions as she moved around the room and monitored their work, intervening when she believed that it was appropriate to do so.

In order to understand what the students were doing in their small groups, the following vignette is presented of one small group's discussion of the advertisement they are deconstructing. This vignette was chosen at random from one of two groups that were audiotaped during the preceding lesson. The discussion occurred after the teacher's interaction, reported earlier, with another group. In this vignette, the students began by examining an advertisement for a new car with a female model leaning across the bonnet (different advertisement from the one the teacher discussed with the earlier group). The students' discussion focused on the key signifiers, such as colour, alcohol and the representation of different facial features on the model because their task was to try to deconstruct this advertisement using different discourses such as gender, class and the dominance of technology to determine the subtle messages conveyed. The students begin by brainstorming different messages, such as connotations and discourses that they believe the advertisement conveys.

Student Vignette

1. S: *It's sex. Female sex.*
2. S: *Seduction?*
3. S: *Female dominance?*
4. S: *What about you, Damian?* (S. seeks ideas.)
5. S: *Male submission, I think?*
6. S: *Jewellery.*
7. S: *Okay! What's that mean – Hands on boob?*
8. S: *Sexy.*
9. S: *Okay! What else has that got?* (S. challenges others to further examine the 'sexy' connotation.)
10. S: *Male sex, female sex.*
11. S: *Gender bitch.*
12. S: *Gender discourse?*
13. S: *The colour red – emphasises sex.*

14. S: *What else does that tell us? What do you think?* (S. seeks additional information and ideas from others.)
15. S: *Technology. We use technology to get our messages across. Look at the light and the colours in the picture.* (S. provides explanation for the discourse he's suggested.)
16. S: *Maybe it's 'class' because she's gotten dressed up?* (S. suggests 'class' as another discourse and provides an explanation for that suggestion.)
17. S: *Gender game. The discourse is gender.* (S. suggests another type of discourse the advertisement conveys.)
18. S: *So what do we have? Gender dominance? Class?* (S. challenges others to identify the discourses that are relevant.)
19. S: *What about the colour? What does that signify?* (S. challenges others to elaborate on their understanding of the colour in the advertisement.)
20. S: *Red is a warm colour. Comfort?*
21. S: *It also signifies she's a 'red hot bitch'.*
22. S: *More sexy.*
23. S: *Cosmetics. Look at what she's wearing.*
24. S: *Class (dominance) because its (alcohol) in a glass and not a bottle. It's sophisticated. It's aimed at middle to working class.*
25. S: *Yep! That's part of the message.* (S. acknowledges and validates student's response.)
26. S: *Gender?*
27. S: *Does this picture reinforce the notion as women as objects of beauty?* (S. challenges others to affirm or disaffirm her proposition.)
28. S: *Why's she looking at him and he's looking at her? Isn't that because of the boobs?*
29. S: *Yes. Look at the hair.*
30. S: *Is that a denotation?* (S. seeks clarification on a denotation from others.)
31. At this point, the teacher wanders over to the group and makes the following comment:
32. T: *Denotation … you're not going to refer specifically to a denotation in your essay. You could talk about the hair being long, straight, shiny and hanging across the eyes, but all that comes into connotations doesn't it?*

In this vignette, the students used some of the mediated-learning behaviours they heard their teacher model. These included soliciting ideas from others, challenging others' opinions or ideas, clarifying understandings and acknowledging and validating others' efforts. Given that these students were never taught specifically to focus on using these types of mediated-learning behaviours to interrogate the messages in the advertisement, it could be that they either had been exposed to this type of discourse previously or may have appropriated it from their teacher as she interacted with the groups in their classroom.

Summary of Study 1

This study describes the types of mediated-learning behaviours seven high school teachers demonstrated when they were trained to embed co-operative learning pedagogy into their curricula. The mediated-learning behaviours the teachers used were designed to challenge students' understanding and encourage them to think more deeply and reflectively about the issues under discussion. They did this by asking more cognitive and meta-cognitive questions, where students were expected to provide reasons for their answers, connect their ideas to previous learning and justify their conclusions. King, Staffieri & Adelgais (1998) found that students engage in higher-order thinking and learning when they are trained to ask cognitive and meta-cognitive questions that challenge their partners to think about the information they are learning and connect new information to what they already know. Similarly, Palinscar & Herrenkohl (2002) found that students engage more effectively in scientific argumentation when they are taught how to think about the material presented, relate it to theories and predictions and pose questions that challenge others' perspectives of the information presented. In short, both King, Staffieri & Adelgais and Palincsar & Herrenkohl demonstrated that students learn more when they relate new information to prior knowledge and understandings.

The teachers in this study modelled how to think about the information under discussion through the mediated-learning behaviours that they demonstrated

as they interacted with students in their groups. These behaviours included not only challenging students' perspectives and asking cognitive and meta-cognitive questions but also using other supportive discourse patterns that reflect scaffolding and acknowledge students' efforts at learning – discourses that Turner et al. (2002) maintain build students' sense of competence and help them to accept more responsibility to learn. Moreover, by encouraging students to share their ideas with their peers, clarify their misconceptions and work together to construct new understandings, the teachers provided opportunities for students to use the mediated-learning discourses they had demonstrated.

Teachers' Discourse during Co-operative Learning and Communicative Skills Training: Study 2

In a study that built on the findings of the previous study that showed that there are clear differences in the mediated-learning discourses of teachers in the co-operative or small-group condition, this study by Gillies & Haynes (2010) sought to compare the effects of training teachers in specific communication skills designed to promote thinking and scaffold learning on teachers' and students' discourses during co-operative learning. This study was necessary because Gillies & Khan (2008) had previously investigated the effects of teacher discourse on student discourse, problem solving and learning during co-operative (co-operative + communication skills condition & co-operative condition) and small-group learning and found that children whose teachers had been taught specific communication skills to challenge their thinking engaged in significantly more elaborative and help-giving behaviours with group members and demonstrated better reasoning and problem-solving skills than peers whose teachers had not received this training. The results from this study, though, were somewhat inconclusive because whilst the teachers in the co-operative and communications skills–trained condition demonstrated significantly more challenging and scaffolding behaviours than the teachers in the group-work–trained condition, they did not differ significantly from their colleagues in the co-operative condition. Gillies and Khan suggested that one explanation for the lack of significance between the teachers in the two co-operative conditions (co-operative + communication training condition and co-operative condition) may have been the e-mail newsletters that all teachers received which provided information on different strategies teachers could use to promote co-operation, thus unintentionally sensitizing teachers in the co-operative condition to the importance of promoting discussion during co-operative experiences.

The Gillies & Haynes (2010) study built on the research that indicated that teachers play a key role in promoting discourses that challenge children's thinking and scaffolding their learning. The study did this by seeking to determine whether teachers who receive training in explicit questioning strategies demonstrate more verbal behaviours that mediate children's learning than teachers who have not participated in this training. It also sought to determine whether students who received training in explicit questioning strategies demonstrate more explanatory behaviours than their untrained peers and, as a consequence, whether they demonstrate more advanced reasoning and problem-solving skills on follow-up learning activities.

Communicative Skills Training

Thirty-one teachers and 615 children from grades six through eight participated in this study. The teachers agreed to incorporate co-operative learning pedagogy into a unit of work once a term for four to six weeks for two school terms. All teachers participated in a two-day workshop to provide them with the background knowledge and skills to help them establish small, co-operative group activities in their classrooms. In addition to this information, one cohort of teachers

(co-operative + strategic questioning condition) received additional training in specific communication skills that promote meaningful discussion within groups. Because of the wide variability in students' capacities to engage in discussions, the teachers were introduced to three different linguistic tools that could be used to help students to ask and answer questions.

The first tool, collaborative strategic reading (CSR) (Vaughn et al., 2001), is designed to enhance students' understanding of text by teaching them to use four strategies that successful readers use to comprehend text. These strategies include

- The preview strategy (predicting what the passage is about);
- The click and clunk strategy (clicks represent words students recognise, and clunks are unknown words);
- The get the gist strategy (identifying the main idea in the passage) and
- The wrap-up strategy (students summarise the main theme in the passage).

Teachers introduced each strategy one and a time, modelled it and then provided opportunities for students to practice it. The students also were given prompt cards to help them remember the sequence of questions.

The second tool, Ask to think-tel why (King, 1997), teaches students to ask a sequence of questions that are designed to promote higher-level thinking and complex learning. The five types of questions that students are taught are

- Review questions (*'Describe in your own words …'*);
- Probing questions (*'Tell me more about …'*);
- Hint questions (*'Have you considered …'*);
- Intelligent-thinking questions (*'How are … and … the same and different?'*) and
- Self-monitoring questions (*'Have we covered all the ideas we want to?'*).

The teachers modelled these questions so that the students understood how they could use them to obtain different types of information. The students were given prompt cards to help them remember the different types of questions they could ask.

The final tool to helping students ask questions was an adaptation of the 'cognitive tools and intellectual roles approach' that Palincsar & Herrenkohl (2002) used to promote student engagement and collaboration during inquiry-based science lessons. By using a variation of the reciprocal teaching strategies of predicting, questioning, clarifying and summarising (Brown & Palincsar, 1988) to help students develop explanations about scientific phenomena, Palinscar & Herrenkohl constructed a set of audience roles designed to promote discussion during the whole-class reporting-back stage. In the Gillies & Haynes (2010) study, these roles were adapted so that some groups in the audience were responsible for checking on the clarity of the presentation, others were responsible for commenting on the group's summary of the findings or potential solutions and others focused on the relationship of the group's presentation of the topic and the summary of the findings or potential solutions. In essence, the children in the audience were actively involved in thinking about the presentation and commenting on it. Examples of the roles and the language the students in the audience used include

- Clarity of the presentation: *'I liked the way you presented ... but can you tell us why you did/did not ... ?'*
- Summary of findings and solutions: *'The findings were ... presented, but we're unsure what you were saying about.... Can you explain that again?'*
- Relationship of group's presentation to the findings: *'The link between what you presented and your findings is.... Have you considered other ways in which you could have presented this information?'*

Procedure

As with study 1, all teachers were audiotaped once a term for two terms during lessons in which they had agreed to embed co-operative learning pedagogy. Additionally, two groups of students in each teacher's class were concurrently audiotaped, and all audiotapes were coded according to prescribed categories outlined below.

Coding

Both the teachers' and the students' discourses were coded according to schedules used by Gillies (2006). All discourses were coded according to frequency across recorded class sessions.

TEACHERS' DISCOURSE

This schedule identified six categories of teacher verbal behaviour that capture the range of behaviours that teachers demonstrate during co-operative learning. These behaviours include demonstrates control (i.e., instructs, directs), disciplines (i.e., reprimands); mediates learning (i.e., paraphrases, prompts, challenges, scaffolds, summarises); encourages questions (i.e., generates a short response); and maintains learning (i.e., helps students, refers to technical issues).

STUDENTS' DISCOURSE

This schedule identified five categories of verbal behaviour that students typically use during their small-group discussions. These behaviours include elaborations (i.e., detailed help); questions (i.e., open and closed); short responses; engages with others on a topic (i.e., extends discussion); and directs (i.e., gives directions).

Results and Discussion

The results show that when teachers are trained to use specific communication skills during co-operative learning (co-operative + strategic questioning condition), 39.2 per cent of their total discourse involved interactions that mediate learning, 1.0 per cent involved disciplinary comments and 2.7 per cent involved comments that maintained learning. This was in contrast to the co-operative learning group only, where 25.3 per cent of their total discourse involved mediated learning, 3.6 per cent involved disciplinary comments and 3.8 per cent involved maintaining learning. (There were no significant differences between control, encourages, and questions in the two conditions.) The study also showed that 32.1 per cent of the total discourse of the children in the co-operative and strategic questioning condition involved providing elaborative help. This was in contrast to the co-operative learning group, where 20.1 per cent of their total discourse involved providing elaborative help. Given the important role Webb (2009) argues that elaborative talk plays in the development of problem-solving and reasoning abilities, it was not surprising that the children in the co-operative and strategic questioning condition obtained higher learning outcomes on the follow-up reasoning and problem-solving tasks.

In order to illustrate how the teachers mediated the children's learning, the following vignette is provided of one teacher as she moved around the small groups in her room prompting, challenging, and scaffolding the children's understanding of the task, in this case, making a board game that teaches players about three-dimensional shapes. This is a topic the class was learning about in the mathematics curriculum.

Teacher Vignette

Group 1
1. S: *Every shape has faces, so we should go with faces.*
2. T: *That's all right. Have you thought about maybe having more than just one focus? Instead of just faces, you could incorporate a few.* (T. challenges children to consider different foci.)
3. S: *On another one, we could do edges and faces on another one.* (S. elaborates on possibilities.)
4. T: *Are you going to be writing the questions on here?* (T seeks clarification.)
5. S: *On the spinner. So you spin it, and if it lands on a cube, you have eight faces, so you move eight places.* (S. elaborates on possibilities.)
6. T: *Oh right. So what would be the thing you would be teaching them?*
7. S: *How many faces are on the different shapes?*
8. T: *So that's going to be a very specific thing, isn't it? How could you make it a bit broader rather than just faces?* (T. challenges children to consider different possibilities.)

9. S: *Er. Um.*
10. T: *Think about it. Maybe you could incorporate some question cards as well.* (T. prompts.)
11. S: *Yes. If you answer it, you go forward one space. If you don't answer it, you go back one.* (S. elaborates on possibilities.)
12. T: *So, you might want to look into your pack and see if there's some other things in there that might give you some ideas.* (T. prompts children to consider other possibilities.)

Group 2
1. T: *Have you worked out what your focus is going to be?* (T. prompts.)
2. S: *It is 3D shapes.*
3. T: *Okay. Don't forget that the idea of this game is that by the end of playing the game, the people playing it will have learned something about 3D shapes and their properties.* (T prompts.)
4. S: *What we're going to do is have a couple of questions. If you get one right answer, then you get five bucks. That would be easy, that one would be hard and that would be harder.* (S. elaborates.)
5. T: *So, you are levelling your questions? As you get closer and closer to the end?* (T. probes.)
6. S: *Yes, you get more money.*
7. T: *That's a good idea. So, on your game board, how are you going to indicate that?* (T. challenges.)
8. S: *What do you mean?*
9. T: *Well, how will the person know? Maybe at the start it might have just a one dollar sign, and as it's getting harder and harder, they can earn more and more money. How could you indicate that it's going to get harder? Or are you just going to put that in the rules?* (T. challenges children to consider how they are going to communicate their ideas.)
10. S: *Put it in the rules.* (S. elaborates.)
11. T: *Sometimes a visual.... Like, if you picked up this game and hadn't read the rules yet, what would you like to see on the game board that would get you excited about trying to get to the end?* (T. challenges children to think about the clarity of their information.)
12. S: *Maybe a colour code.* (S. elaborates.)
13. S: *Maybe light blue, then dark blue and getting darker and darker.* (S. elaborates on possibilities.)
14. T: *And also, if it involves money, how might you indicate that?* (T. prompts.)
15. S: *Use dollar signs.*

16. T: *Yes. These first ones might only have $1 signs on them, and as they move along, you get $2 or $3 signs on them. And maybe by the time you get to the end, there are $5 signs. So the very last question is going to be really difficult. That's a good idea, levelling your questions. And, in that pack you might find some things that will help you. (T. prompts)*

In this vignette, it is interesting to note how the teacher mediates the children's learning as she moves around the groups. In the first group, she challenges and prompts the children to help focus their attention and consider different possibilities (turns 2, 4 and 10), and in all instances, the children respond with an elaborated response (turns 3, 5 and 11). Similarly, when she prompts, probes and challenges students in the second group (turns 3, 5, 9 and 11), the children respond with elaborations (turns 4, 6, 10, 12 and 13). When interacting with both groups, the teacher posed questions that encouraged the children to think and reflect on their responses, and this, in turn, helped them to generate more detailed and elaborative replies.

Summary of Study 2

The study demonstrates that when teachers are provided with the linguistic tools (i.e., CSR, Ask to think-tel why, and cognitive tools and intellectual roles) that illustrate how to ask and answer questions, they, in turn, demonstrate more mediated-learning behaviours where they challenge and scaffold children's learning than their peers who have not been systematically taught to use these tools. This finding is consistent with a previous study by Gillies & Khan (2009), who found that when teachers are trained in specific questioning skills designed to teach children how to ask and answer questions, they also engage in more discourses that mediate children's learning than peers who have not participated in such training. Interestingly, the children whose teachers had been provided with the linguistic tools provided more elaborative responses in their

discussions than their peers whose teachers did not use these tools. It appears than when children are exposed to questions that challenge their thinking and scaffold their learning, it sensitises them to the importance of responding with more detailed and elaborative responses than they may have given previously.

Theoretical and Practical Implications

There are both theoretical and practical implications that emerge from the studies described herein. At the theoretical level, the two studies illustrate the key role that teachers play in the social construction of knowledge at both the inter- and intra-personal level. The mediated-learning interactions that the teachers used were designed not only to scaffold the students' learning but also to prompt meaningful cognitive and meta-cognitive thinking about the problem-solving activities (King, 1999; Palincsar, 1998). Because the teachers' language was both tentative and inviting, they were able to scaffold or mediate potential learning whilst also challenging the children's thinking and encouraging them to consider alternative points of view (King, 2002). In so doing, they were introducing the students not only to new patterns of thought but also to new ways of learning how to reach consensus about what they were thinking and how that information may be used to resolve the problem at hand (Damon, 1984; Palincsar & Herrenkohl, 2002).

It has been argued that it is through repeated exchanges with adults or peers in mutually co-operative interactions that students' thinking becomes influenced by these communicative exchanges and they begin to adopt them as their own (Damon, Shachar & Sharan, 1994). The responses expected from this type of discourse appear to create an expectation in recipients to reconcile or justify their perspectives with those of others, clarify misunderstandings and provide responses that others will accept as valid. Furthermore, these discourses, coupled with the intimacy of the co-operative small group, may have provided a psychological environment that motivated the students to be more willing to reconcile contradictions between themselves and others, test out their ideas and work to co-construct new knowledge (Johnson & Johnson, 2003; Gillies, 2003).

At the practical level, both studies provide examples of how students may use some of the mediated-learning interactions their teachers used to scaffold learning and challenge their thinking. This is particularly interesting given that the students had not been trained to use these specific verbal behaviours, so it can only be assumed that they learned them in the context of the co-operative environment and their teachers' discourse to determine the relevance of these mediated-learning behaviours to their needs. Given that students are often more aware of what their peers do not understand and will provide help to clarify their understanding, training teachers to use good communication skills is critically important if students, in turn, are to use effective helping discourses when they work in co-operating groups.

The studies described herein provide unique insights into how teachers can use language to promote collaborative dialogue in the classroom during co-operative learning. They do this not only by challenging students' perspectives and asking cognitive and meta-cognitive questions but also by using other supportive discourse patterns that scaffold students' learning and validate their efforts. These discourses, it is argued, build students' sense of competence with using language and motivate their learning. Moreover, when students are encouraged to share their ideas with their peers, clarify their misconceptions and work together to construct new understandings, teachers provide opportunities for students to appropriate and use the language they have demonstrated, and it is these language discourses that promote learning.

References

Brown, A., & Palincsar, A. (1988). Guided, cooperative learning and individual knowledge acquisition. In L. Resnick (ed.), *Cognition and instruction: Issues and agendas*. Hillsdale, NJ: Erlbaum.

Chinn, C., O'Donnell, A. & Jinks, T. (2000). The structure of discourse in collaborative learning. *Journal of Experimental Education* 69, 77–89.

Cohen, E. (1994). Restructuring the classroom: Conditions for productive small groups. *Review of Educational Research* 64, 1–35.

Cohen, E., Lotan, R., Abram, P., Scarloss, B. & Schultz, S. (2002). Can groups learn? *Teachers College Record* 104, 1045–68.

Damon, W. (1984). Peer education: The untapped potential. *Journal of Applied Developmental Psychology* 5, 331–43.

Galton, M., Hargreves, L., Comber, C., Wall, D. & Pell, T. (1999). Changes in patterns of teacher interaction in primary classrooms: 1976–1996. *British Educational Research Journal* 25, 23–37.

Gillies, R. (2003). The behaviours, interactions, and perceptions of junior high school students during small-group learning. *Journal of Educational Psychology* 95, 137–47.

Gillies, R. (2004). The effects of communication training on teachers' and students' verbal behaviours during co-operative learning. *International Journal of Educational Research* 41, 257–79.

Gillies, R. (2006). Teachers' and students' verbal behaviours during co-operative and small-group learning. *British Journal of Educational Psychology* 76, 271–87.

Gillies, R., & Boyle, M. (2008). Teachers' discourse during cooperative learning and their perceptions of this pedagogical practice. *Teaching and Teacher Education* 24, 1333–48.

Gillies, R., & Haynes, M. (2010). Increasing explanatory behaviour, problem-solving, and reasoning within classes using cooperative group work. *Instructional Science* 39(3), 349–66; doi: 10.1007/s11251-010-9130-9.

Gillies, R., & Khan, A. (2009). Promoting reasoned argumentation, problem-solving and learning during small-group work. *Cambridge Journal of Education* 39, 7–27.

Gillies, R., & Khan, A. (2008). The effects of teacher discourse on students' discourse, problem-solving and reasoning during cooperative learning. *International Journal of Educational Research* 47, 323–40

Hertz-Lazarowitz, R., & Shachar, H. (1990). Teachers' verbal behaviour in cooperative and whole-class instruction. In S. Sharan (ed.), *Cooperative learning: Theory and research* (pp. 77–94). New York: Praeger.

Johnson, D., & Johnson, R. (1990). Cooperative learning and achievement. In S. Sharan (ed.), *Cooperative learning: Theory and research* (pp. 23–37). New York: Praeger.

Johnson, D., & Johnson, R. (2002). Learning together and alone: Overview and meta-analysis. *Asia Pacific Journal of Education* 22, 95–105.

Johnson, D., & Johnson, R. (2003). Student motivation in cooperative groups: Social interdependence theory. In R. Gillies and A. Ashman (eds.), *Cooperative learning: The social and intellectual outcomes of learning in groups* (pp. 136–76). London: Routledge Falmer.

Johnson, D., & Johnson, R. (2008). Social interdependence theory and cooperative learning: The teacher's role. In R. Gillies, A. Ashman and J. Terwel (eds.), *The teacher's role in implementing cooperative learning in the classroom* (pp. 9–36). New York: Springer.

King, A. (2002). Structuring peer interaction to promote high-level cognitive processing. *Theory into Practice* 41, 33–40.

King, A. (1999). Discourse patterns for mediating peer learning. In A. O'Donnell and A. King (eds.), *Cognitive perspectives on peer learning* (pp. 87–116). Mahwah, NJ: Erlbaum.

King, A. (1997). Ask to think-tel why: A model of transactive peer tutoring for scaffolding higher level complex learning. *Educational Psychologist* 32, 221–35.

King, A., Staffieri, A. & Adelgais, A. (1998). Mutual peer tutoring: Effects of structuring tutorial interaction to scaffold peer learning. *Journal of Educational Psychology* 90, 134–52.

Meloth, M., & Deering, P. (1999). The role of the teacher in promoting cognitive processing during collaborative learning. In A. O'Donnell and A. King (eds.), *Cognitive perspectives on peer learning* (pp. 235–55). Mahwah, NJ: Erlbaum.

Mercer, N. (1996). The quality of talk in children 'collaborative activity in the classroom. *Learning and Instruction* 6, 359–77.

Palinscar, A. (1998). Keeping the metaphor of scaffolding fresh: A response to C. Addison Stone's 'The metaphor of scaffolding: Its utility for the field of learning disabilities'. *Journal of Learning Disabilities* 31, 370–3.

Palinscar, A., & Herrenkohl, L. (2002). Designing collaborative contexts. *Theory into Practice* 41, 26–35.

Rojas-Drummond, S., & Mercer, N. (2003). Scaffolding the development of effective collaboration and learning. *International Journal of Educational Research* 39, 99–111.

Shachar, H., & Sharan, S. (1994). Talking, relating, and achieving: Effects of cooperative learning and whole-class instruction. *Cognition and Instruction* 12, 313–53.

Turner, J., Midgley, C., Meyer, D., Gheen, M., Anderman, E. & Kang, Y. (2002). The classroom environment and students' reports of avoidance strategies in mathematics: A multilevel study. *Journal of Educational Psychology* 94, 88–106.

Vaughn, S., Klingner, J. & Bryant, D. (2001). Collaborative strategic reading as a means to enhance peer-mediated instruction for reading comprehension and content-area learning. *Remedial and Special Education* 22, 66–74.

Webb, N. (2009). The teacher's role in promoting collaborative dialogue in the classroom. *British Journal of Educational Psychology* 79, 1–28.

Webb, N., & Farivar, S. (1999). Developing productive group interaction in middle school mathematics. In A. O'Donnell and A. King (eds.), *Cognitive perspectives on peer learning* (pp. 117–50). Mahwah, NJ: Erlbaum.

CHAPTER 20

Practical Applications of a Fidelity-of-Implementation Framework

Mollie Rudnick, Cassie Freeman, and Jeanne Century

Introduction

Educational practitioners are regularly faced with a variety of expectations from inside and outside the educational system about what should happen in the classroom. These expectations are expressed in curricular programs, policy mandates, and research-based recommendations. Many of the expectations for classroom practice involve having teachers closely follow the programs they are given with fidelity. Despite expectations to follow the program exactly as written, teachers may enact them in very different ways with varying levels of fidelity. Because exact implementation is not a given, and because there may be great variation throughout a school, it is difficult for school leaders to know exactly what is happening in their buildings. Nevertheless, it is because of this variation that it is so important for school leaders to know what is happening so that they can provide appropriate supports for improving teaching and learning.

Fidelity-of-implementation (FOI) measures have been lauded recently as a necessary part of rigorous efficacy and effectiveness studies. In such studies, FOI measures confirm that the presumed treatment sufficiently differs from the control so that researchers can confidently describe how well the treatment works. However, because there has been so much focus on using FOI measures this way, they have been overlooked as a valuable source of information for other audiences and purposes. When program implementation data are collected and analyzed with appropriate measures and approaches, they can yield valuable insights for practitioners, and school and district leaders can use them to inform decisions about professional development, in-school supports, and guidance for program use in classrooms.

When researchers and reform leaders discuss implementation with school leaders and teachers, they often focus on achieving a high FOI. This emphasis is based on an assumption that once there is empirical evidence to show that an innovation is effective, the way to replicate that effectiveness is to implement the program exactly as written. Although understandable, the logic behind this point of view is faulty. As mentioned previously, it is generally recognized that teachers never enact a program exactly as written. While some of these changes can adversely affect student outcomes, teachers can and should make what some refer to as "acceptable adaptations." These are changes to programs that accommodate the particular contexts and conditions of their classrooms and students. Rather than compromise program effectiveness, these adaptations can improve it.

For this reason, it is critical to obtain accurate information about how programs are actually implemented behind the closed doors of each classroom. There is little doubt that practitioners can benefit from using programs that have been proven effective in other settings, but because teachers adapt those programs, leaders should work with them to ensure that these adaptations are thoughtful, rigorous, and appropriate. Thus, rather than focus on achieving full FOI and measuring "how much" of a program teachers implement, this chapter discusses tools for measuring implementation that provide data that specifically describe *how* teachers are using programs. Knowing this, school leaders can understand which elements of a program are used and the nature of that use so that they can provide appropriate supports for improving teaching and learning.

Our intention here is to demystify the notion of FOI by demonstrating its use for practitioners who have both large- and small-scale questions to answer. FOI begins with articulating the program model so that users know what is or is not being enacted and in what ways it is being enacted. While articulating a program model is a basic evaluation concept, it is key to understanding what is going on in any classroom, school, or district regardless of the purpose. This understanding was at the heart of our efforts to create FOI instruments.

Conceptual Framework

The Center for Elementary Mathematics and Science Education (CEMSE) at The University of Chicago set out to create

instruments that would aid district and school personnel, as well as researchers, in the endeavor of measuring FOI. The three-year project, funded by the National Science Foundation, developed a suite of instruments for rigorously measuring the FOI of reform-based science and mathematics instructional materials[1] at the K–8 level, as well as a *User's Guide* that describes procedures for using those instruments and adapting them for use with other instructional materials.

At the outset of the project, we conducted a thorough review of the literature on FOI not only in education but also in other fields such as health and business. We found that while there is general consensus about what FOI is, there is not agreement in these fields about how to describe or define FOI at any level of detail. For this reason, we determined that we would need to create our own working definition of FOI, as well as a conceptual framework that would allow us to create the instruments to measure FOI across several programs. We chose to word a general definition as follows: *The extent to which an enacted program is consistent with the intended program model.* While this definition closely resembles others' work (Bodzin, Cates, & Price, 2003; Lewis & Seibold, 1993; Ruiz-Primo, 2005), we deliberately chose the words *enacted* and *intended program model* because they lent themselves to a wide range of educational interventions and thus provided a broad starting point for developing a conceptual framework that could support FOI measurement for both reform-based mathematics and science programs and other programs as well.

We began our framework development with a well-recognized work by Dane & Schneider (1998), who reviewed studies of prevention programs for measures of what they refer to as "program integrity" (what we call FOI). They found that the authors of the studies in their review defined FOI along at least one of five "dimensions": adherence, exposure, quality of delivery, participant responsiveness, and program differentiation. Dane & Schneider (1998) recommended that in the future, all five dimensions be measured in order to gain a better understanding of program integrity and that there be standardized definitions of these dimensions to help promote comparisons across studies. Even though others had used these dimensions as a starting point for FOI work, we felt that because they did not yet have standardized definitions, and because we felt that they were incommensurate in scope and specificity, we would account for them but not use them as a foundation for our framework.

Other influential work came from those who used two approaches: identification of what we call "critical components" of the programs and the organization of those components into two categories: "structure" and "process." Wang et al. (1984), for example, identified "critical program dimensions" (what we refer to as *critical components*) in two categories: those relating to the provision of adaptive instruction (*structure*) and those relating to support of effective implementation of adaptive instruction (*process*). Mowbray et al. (2003), on the other hand, discussed "fidelity criteria" (*critical components*) and organized them by "framework for service delivery" (*structure*) and "the ways in which services are delivered" (*process*). These approaches seemed to fit with other work in health and education that had measured FOI by identifying program components that were more and less critical for achieving desired outcomes (Bond et al., 2000; Ruiz-Primo, 2005), giving us reassurance that they could be a sound approach for our framework. Thus, building on this earlier work, we used a combined structure/process and critical-component approach for our framework development.

Critical components, more explicitly defined, are the elements of a program model that are essential to its implementation. Consistent with our decision to use this approach, we operationalized our FOI definition by rewording it as *the extent to which the critical components of an intended program are present when that program is enacted*. We currently have a set of forty critical components common to both mathematics and science programs that we have accounted

for in our framework. These critical components were revised and refined over two years during an instrument pilot and field test (described in greater detail later).

The Framework

Throughout the framework development process, we were guided by our goal of providing useful measurement categories in a sound organizational structure. After several iterations, we defined two broad organizational categories: (1) structural critical components and (2) instructional critical components. *Structural critical components* reflect the developers' decisions about the design and organization of the physical program materials and fall into two subcategories: (1) procedural and (2) educative. *Structural-procedural critical components* are the elements of the program that communicate to the teacher in the simplest sense *what to do*. While some might argue that all parts of a program might implicitly or explicitly suggest what the teacher should do, the critical components in this category focus on the basic steps of the lesson and the ways the intervention is physically organized to communicate intentions to the teacher. *Structural-educative critical components* represent the developers' expectations for what the teacher needs to *know* to enact the program as intended. Thus they are analogous to built-in professional development or training and reflect the developers' intentions about how to structure and organize that information for the users.

Instructional critical components represent the actions, behaviors, and interactions that the teacher and students are expected to engage in when enacting the intervention. These components are not tied to specific sections of a lesson but can occur at any time during the enacted instruction. *Instructional-pedagogical critical components* focus on the teacher's actions, behaviors, and interactions. *Instructional-student engagement critical components* focus on the students' actions, behaviors, and interactions with the content, the teacher, and one another.

CATEGORIES OF DIFFERENTIATION	FOI OF INSTRUCTIONAL MATERIALS			
	CATEGORIES OF CRITICAL COMPONENTS			
	Structural Critical Components		Instructional Critical Components	
	Procedural	Educative	Pedagogical	Student Engagement
Common to Mathematics and Science Programs				
Common to Mathematics Programs				
Common to Science Programs				
Program Specific				

Figure 20.1. FOI Conceptual Framework.

As we developed the FOI framework, we also identified critical components in each of the programs we wanted to measure. During this iterative process, we placed each critical component in the appropriate cell in the framework. As we did so, we saw that while many of the critical components were common across programs, some were unique to specific programs, and we needed to develop a way to represent that in our framework. As a result, we decided to add an element to the framework that we call *categories of differentiation* (see Figure 20.1). This element allowed us to distinguish programs' shared (e.g., common to mathematics and science programs) and unique (e.g., program-specific) critical components.

Instrument and Item Construct Matrices

As we developed the framework, we conducted an extensive review of the instructional materials to identify a set of critical components for each. We also consulted with developers from each program and asked them, with no guidance from us, to identify what they considered the critical components of their programs. Then we reviewed their lists and used them to confirm the critical components we had identified and to help us identify critical components we may have overlooked. We later approached the developers again, providing them with our revised list and asking them to review it, confirm that each critical component listed was in fact a part of their program, and rank the relative importance

of each. In addition to our work with developers, we asked teachers with experience teaching each of the programs to list the components they felt to be critical. The current list of critical components in the framework is given in Figure 20.2.

After the framework and initial critical component list were drafted, we began to create a suite of instruments to measure the presence of each critical component. The final suite of instruments consists of a classroom observation protocol, a teacher instructional and attitude questionnaire, a school leader questionnaire, teacher logs, a schoolwide observation protocol, and school leader and teacher interview protocols.

Once we had arrived at a solid set of critical components, our first task was to determine the best way to measure them across the suite of instruments. To facilitate this process, we developed a matrix (see Figures 20.3 and 20.4) with each critical component in its own column and each instrument listed in its own row. Most critical components could be measured in a variety of instruments, so we decided to measure each critical component in at least two instruments and to consider the best fit among critical component, item, and instruments. Among the considerations we had to account for were the time required for instrument administration, the level of detail we could obtain in one instrument compared with another, the appropriateness of the instrument for the construct (e.g., it was not appropriate to measure "duration of unit" in an observation protocol), and the practical limitations of administration and expense. As we made decisions about the best approach for

FOI OF INSTRUCTIONAL MATERIALS

	Structural Critical Components		Instructional Critical Components	
	Procedural	Educative	Pedagogical	Student Engagement

Common to Matematics and Science	1. Duration of unit
	2. Time spent on instruction
	3. Lesson order
	4. Order of segments and parts within lesson
	5. Inclusion of all essential segments within lesson
	6. Inclusion of all essential lessons within lesson
	7. Lesson overview
	8. Lesson preparation
	9. Materials
	10. Writing structures
	11. Readings
	12. Assessments and assessment tools
	13. Content of lesson
	  a. Facts
	  b. Procedures
	  c. Concepts
	  d. Process
	14. Class structures
	15. Instructional delivery formats
	16. Projects*
	17. Extensions*
	  a. Discipline related
	  b. Non-discipline related
	18. Additional resources*
	19. Homework*
		1. Content background information
		2. Pedagogy background information
		3. National standards and benchmarks information*
		4. Lesson notes
			1. Teacher facilitation of small group work
			2. Teacher facilitation of student discussion
			3. Teacher facilitation of students doing potentially intellectually challenging work
			4. Teacher facilitation of student autonomy
			5. Teacher facilitation of student taking risks
			6. Teacher facilitation of student interest
			7. Teacher facilitation of materials, manipulatives, and tools use
			8. Teacher use of assessment to inform instruction
			9. Teacher use of differentiation
				1. Students contribute to small group work
				2. Students engage in discussion
				3. Students engage in potentially intellectually challenging work
				4. Students demonstrate autonomy
				5. Students take risks
				6. Students do/complete essential activities
				7. Students do/complete optional or non-essential activities

Common to Science		A. Safety	A. Teacher facilitation of student data collection	A. Students collect data
Common to Mathematics	A. Unit Order		A. Teacher supports multiple solution strategies	A. Students use multiple solution strategies

Figure 20.2. Critical Components in FOI Framework.

	Structural-Procedural																				Math	Structural-Educative			Science
	Math and Science																								
	Duration of Unit	Time Spent on Instruction	Lesson Order	Order of Segments and Parts within Lesson	Inclusion of All Essential Segments within Lesson	Inclusion of All Essential Lessons	Lesson Overview	Lesson Preparation	Materials Presence	Writing Structures	Readings	Assessment and Assessment Tools	Content of Lesson	Class Structures	Instructional Delivery Formats	Projects*	Extensions*	Additional Resources*	Homework*	Unit Order	Content Background Information	Pedagogy Background Information	National Standards and Benchmarks Information	Lesson Notes	Safety
Teacher Questionnaire	▓		▓		▓	▓			▓			▓				▓		▓	▓						▓
School Leader Questionnaire	▓																			▓					
Teacher Interview	▓				▓							▓											▓		▓
School Leader Interview									▓																
Classroom Observation		▓					▓		▓	▓	▓	▓	▓	▓											
School-wide Observation											▓				▓										
Teacher Log	▓	▓	▓	▓	▓	▓				▓	▓	▓	▓	▓	▓	▓	▓	▓	▓	▓				▓	▓
Teacher Attitude Questionnaire									▓																

Figure 20.3. Instrument-Construct Matrix for Structural Critical Components.

	Instructional Pedagogical										Math	Science	Instructional Student Engagement						Math	Science
	Math and Science												Math and Science							
	Teacher Facilitation of Small Group Work	Teacher Facilitation of Student Discussion	Teacher Facilitation of Students Doing Potentially Intellectually Challenging Work	Teacher Emphasis on Types of Content	Teacher Facilitation of Student Autonomy	Teacher Facilitation of Students Taking Risks	Teacher Facilitation of Student Interest	Teacher Facilitation of Materials, Manipulatives, and Tools Use	Teacher Use of Assessment to Inform Instruction	Teacher Use of Differentiation	Teacher Supports Multiple Solution Strategies	Teacher Facilitation of Student Data Collection	Students Contribute to Small Group Work	Students Engage in Discussion	Students Engage in Potentially Intellectually Challenging Work	Students Demonstrate Autonomy	Students Take Risks	Students Do/Complete Essential Activities	Students Do/Complete Optional or Non-Essential Activities*	Students Use Multiple Solution Strategies	Students Collect Data
Teacher Questionnaire	▓	▓	▓	▓	▓	▓	▓	▓	▓		▓		▓	▓	▓	▓	▓	▓		▓	▓
School Leader Questionnaire	▓		▓					▓													
Teacher Interview	▓			▓									▓								
School Leader Interview	▓		▓										▓								
Classroom Observation	▓	▓	▓	▓	▓	▓	▓	▓	▓	▓	▓	▓	▓	▓	▓	▓	▓	▓	▓	▓	▓
School-wide Observation	▓	▓	▓	▓	▓	▓	▓		▓		▓	▓	▓	▓	▓	▓	▓	▓	▓	▓	▓
Teacher Log	▓	▓	▓	▓	▓	▓	▓	▓	▓	▓	▓	▓	▓	▓	▓	▓	▓	▓	▓	▓	▓
Teacher Attitude Questionnaire																					

Figure 20.4. Instrument-Construct Matrix for Instructional Critical Components.

measuring each construct, we filled in that cell in the matrix.

After completing the instrument-construct matrix, we used it as a starting point for an item-construct matrix by populating the cells for each critical component-instrument combination with items that could comprise the instruments. During this process, we ensured that the same items in the critical-component cells were present across instruments and made appropriate adjustments based on the specific instrument. For example, for the teacher questionnaire, we decided not to ask the teachers to rate themselves in terms of "quality" of a critical component but rather decided to ask them to describe the "quantity" of a critical component, reserving the quality determination for an objective observer. To illustrate, on the teacher questionnaire, one of the items measuring the presence of "Teacher Facilitation of Potentially Intellectually Challenging Work" reads, "How often do you provide an opportunity for students to make predictions?" and is rated on a five-point scale from very rarely to very often. The comparable item in the observation protocol reads, "The teacher provides an opportunity for students to make predictions" and is rated on a three-point scale, where observers have coding notes to guide their ratings.

We felt that asking in these two ways would allow us to gather data on two different aspects of this the critical component of interest using the approach and instrument that would yield the most useful and reliable information. This approach also reflected our understanding that it is not likely to be feasible for practitioners or even researchers to use the whole suite of instruments owing to time and resource constraints. Thus the redundancy of some items allows users to still gather meaningful data on critical components of interest even if they do not use every instrument in the suite. See the summary in Figure 20.5 for information on the subjects and approaches used for each instrument.

FOI Instruments and Use Scenarios

The instruments were pilot tested in thirteen schools and then field tested in thirty-nine schools. Because we recognized that the needs and amount of time and resources of potential users of the instruments would vary, we created three levels of data collection for the pilot and field tests that reflected instrument-use scenarios that potential users might follow.

The level-one schools, as we called them, were the sites of the most intensive data-collection efforts. We might expect a user who is interested in a very robust data set on program use in a school to use a similar strategy. This use scenario consisted of (1) all teachers in the school completing the teacher instructional questionnaire, (2) the school leader completing the school leader questionnaire and participating in an interview, (3) observations of at least two teachers in each grade during two of their science (or mathematics) lessons and interviews with those teachers, (4) after the second observation, those teachers completing six instructional logs (one log for each of six class sessions including the class session observed), and (5) a schoolwide observation protocol for the school.

The level-two scenario focused on using the instruments that required teachers to spend minimal time outside the regular working day to participate in data collection. Users who are interested in information across the schools but don't have the resources to collect as much data as in a level-one school might use a similar design. It included the following: (1) All the teachers in the school complete a teacher instructional questionnaire, (2) the school leader completes the school leader questionnaire and participates in an interview, (3) at least one teacher in each grade for science or mathematics instruction is observed, and (4) a schoolwide observation protocol is created for the school.

The level-three scenario focused less on the school as a whole and more on individual teachers. A user interested in learning about how a specific teacher or a group of teachers uses the program might use this scenario. While we did not have any level-three schools for the pilot test, we did for the field test. In these schools, we worked with one teacher per grade band (K, 1–2,

Instrument	Subject	Completion Time	Sample Item	Sample Item CC
Teacher Questionnaire	Teacher	20 minutes	How often do you follow the order of the lessons in the unit? *Rated on a 5-point scale of "Very Rarely" to "Very Often.*	SP3: Lesson Order
School Leader Questionnaire	Person most knowledgeable about mathematics instruction at the school (e.g., principal, mathematics specialist)	15 minutes	How often do most teachers at your school do the following: Facilitate group work (e.g., encourage group members to actively participate, address guidelines for group interaction, ensure all students understand the task at hand)? *Rated on a 5-point scale of "Very Rarely" to "Very Often."*	IP1: Teacher Facilitation of Group Work
Teacher Interview	Teacher	30 minutes to conduct interview; 30 minutes for data entry	Where does your understanding of the teaching strategies covered in the program come from? Have you consulted the general information from the materials about teaching strategies? Where in the materials did you find this information?	SE2: Pedagogy Background Information
School Leader Interview	Person most knowledgeable about mathematics instruction at the school (e.g., principal, mathematics specialist)	30 minutes to conduct interview; 30 minutes for data entry	How do the teachers in this school assess student progress? What tools or sources of student data do they use? How often do they use these strategies?	IP9: Teacher Use of Assessment to Inform Instruction SP12: Assessments and Assessment Tools
Classroom Observation	Teacher	Observation of full lesson; 30-45 minutes for data entry	Conceptual content is consistent with the instructional materials. *Rated on a 3-point scale.*	SP13: Content of lesson
School-Wide Observation	Sample of teachers	10-minute observations of multiple classes in the school	Rate how many students did the following: Try new things. *Rated on a 4-point scale.*	ISE5: Students take risks
Teacher Log	Teacher	15 minutes	Please check all that you did during today's session: Asked students to apply knowledge to new settings/scenarios	IP3: Teacher Facilitation of Students Doing Potentially Intellectually Challenging Work
1st log	Teacher	15 minutes	Are there any lessons you do not plan to teach? What lessons do you not plan to teach?	SP6: Inclusion of All Essential Lessons
Teacher Attitude Questionnaire	Teacher	15 minutes	There is enough time each week to teach science.	Moderating variable: Time

Figure 20.5. FOI Instrument Overview.

	Teacher Questionnaires	Teacher Observations	Teacher Interviews	Teacher Logs	School Leader Interview	Leader Questionnaire	School-wide Observation Protocol
Level 1	x	x	x	x	x	x	x
Level 2	x	x			x	x	x
Level 3	x	x	x	x		x	

Figure 20.6. Instruments by Level.

3–5, 6, and 7–8). Data collection included the following: (1) Each teacher completes the teacher instructional questionnaire, (2) two observations of the teacher's science or mathematics instruction, (3) each teacher completes six instructional logs (one log for each observed class session and each consecutive class session until a total of six logs are completed), and (4) each teacher participates in an interview. The only school-level data collected in this scenario was a school leader questionnaire that could be completed any time during the data-collection period.

A summary of the pilot- and field-test designs and instruments associated with each level is provided in Figure 20.6.

School Reports

Following the pilot and field tests, we provided each of the participating schools with a report detailing the presence of the critical components in their school's data set (we made it clear that while still potentially useful, the data were gathered using instruments that were not yet validated). We shared the reports with school leaders (i.e., principals, assistant principals, and subject-area specialists) but recommended that the reports not be shared schoolwide in that form because we were concerned that staff would receive a document that they might interpret inappropriately. The school reports were tailored to each school; we reported on critical components for which we had sufficient data and that we believed would be of interest to the school. Each of the reports was organized by the different categories of critical components (i.e., structural-procedural, structural-educative, instructional-pedagogical, and instructional-student engagement), and the findings were compared for critical components across instruments.

On reviewing the reports, most of the school leaders indicated a desire to use the data to plan future professional development around a subset of key areas that coincided with the critical components that needed attention (e.g., teacher facilitation of student discussion); one even indicated an interest in using the information in the report to guide observations of teachers, focusing on critical components such as facilitation of group work. Further, many of the school leaders asked if they could be trained on the use of the instruments once they were validated so that they could continue using implementation data.

Applications and Key Considerations for Instrument Use

Although our instrument-development work focused on developing instruments for measuring use of particular mathematics and science programs, throughout our project, we began to discover that our approach to measuring implementation – identifying critical components, using the FOI framework, and measuring critical components with a suite of instruments – could be adapted to other curricula, subject areas, and reforms. On several occasions we had an opportunity to work with developers who were interested in using our instruments to measure use of their programs; in two other cases, we adapted the instruments to use as tools for the evaluation of broader reforms (e.g., a biotechnology professional development program). As we worked with these groups, we codeveloped a process that can be applied to other research endeavors. Key considerations that may be encountered during the process are described below, followed by illustrations of five different use cases at various levels of the school system. It is important to note that the process and considerations outlined below has proven to be iterative, requiring adjustments and revisions as the process continues.

First, users should determine their question(s) of interest about the use of an innovation. Research question considerations include both the area of interest within FOI (e.g., teacher instructional practices, use of program structures, use of multiple programs, etc.) and the unit of analysis of implementation (e.g., teacher, specific grade level within a school, school, district, etc.). Also, users should determine who will use the findings and for what purposes. The research questions should prove to be informative for the specific audience and their needs. Moreover, not all audiences will require the same degree of statistical rigor depending on how they intend to use the data. For instance, a research question need not explore causal relationships but may merely seek to yield descriptive information about practice in an instructional environment.

Additionally, it is important to consider whether users are interested in *use* or *fidelity*. A use perspective will focus on understanding what teachers are doing in the classroom, whereas a fidelity perspective will be focused on how that use aligns with the intended program enactment. While our instruments are applicable to both scenarios, decisions about the use or fidelity frame of reference will inform the research questions and ultimately the type of data analysis users choose. For example, from a use perspective, the research question might be: To what extent are the teachers enacting practices that support intellectually challenging work? On the other hand, a fidelity perspective would lead to a research question such as: Are teachers skipping key parts of the lessons?

Generally, users have existing general questions or interests that lead them to be interested in the FOI instruments. This part of the process, then, is about clearly articulating these questions and ensuring that they are appropriate for users' needs.

Once users have determined their research question(s), they can begin to identify more specifically their critical components of interest. Users can use the critical-component framework (in Figure 20.2) as a starting point. Depending on the research question(s), users might not be interested in gathering information on all the critical components. For example, a user might be interested only in the use of the instructional elements of the program and therefore not collect information on the structural elements.

Users also may want to collect more specific information on one particular critical component or a set of critical components. In such cases, additional items could be created to collect more in-depth information on those critical components. In one instance, for example, we worked with the developers of the elementary mathematics curriculum *Mathematics Trailblazers*, who were mainly interested in how teachers were using assessment in a new field-test version and older editions of their program. We worked with them to customize the instruments to include more specific indicators of the critical components SP12, "Assessments and Assessment Tools," and IP9, "Teacher Use of Assessment to Inform Instruction." In other cases, users might find that their programs have elements that are unique and thus will require adding a critical component with accompanying items. For example, we worked with developers of *3D-VIEW* and *ACES* (two science programs) to customize the instruments

for use in an evaluation of their programs. Each program had elements that were not already captured in the instruments, including the use of three-dimensional technology and computer simulations. In both cases, we added program-specific critical components and worked with the developers to determine where and how to measure those components.

After determining the research question(s) and critical component(s) of interest, users will need to identify which instruments they would like to use, as well as the research design (e.g., how many questionnaires, observations, and logs are needed). The item-construct matrix described earlier (see Figures 20.3 and 20.4) illustrates which instruments are available to measure each critical component. In instances where critical components were added, users have to decide which instruments are the best fits for measuring those new critical components. During this process, users should strike a balance between considering their resources and making sure that the instruments sufficiently answer their research questions. More specifically, users should ask themselves if they have the time, money, and human resources to implement the instruments. At the same time, it is important to realize that certain instruments yield different types of information from others. For example, while observations and interviews may give more in-depth information than questionnaires, they are much more costly and time-intensive. The use cases in the next section illustrate some of the possible instrument combinations that can be used to answer particular questions given particular constraints.

The plan for data analysis is an iterative process that will be informed by the research questions and the design. During development of the research questions, users need to consider developing a question that can be analyzed using appropriate methods with which they are familiar. Additionally, users will need to determine how they are going to represent the data. Representations might include scaled reporting of critical components (i.e., structural-procedural components are represented as the percent enacted of the total), binary (i.e., if each component is present or not), or as an index (i.e., related instructional-procedural critical components are combined into a composite score). Additionally, we suggest that it is inappropriate to combine the data on all critical components into a single scaled score because it does not take advantage of the specificity provided by the FOI framework. In other words, measuring enactment in categories allows users to focus on the particular areas of concern and have a more descriptive understanding of program implementation and use.

Use Cases

To better illustrate the process and provide potential ideas on the process of using the FOI instruments, five use cases are illustrated below.

1. A district administrator is interested in tailoring future mathematics professional development efforts to the needs of the teachers in the district and must determine what those needs are.
2. A principal is at a school that has been using reform-based science materials for five years, yet test scores are not improving. This principal would like more information to help explain why the test scores are not improving.
3. A science specialist at a school with no coherent science curriculum wants to know what exactly teachers are doing and what materials they are using to teach science.
4. A teacher has been given a new mathematics program to implement and yet has had no professional development on the program. He would like to find out if he is "on target" in how he is using the program.
5. A grade-level group of teachers has been using a specific curriculum for three years and would like to learn more from each other and make their practice more consistent.

District Administrator

For the district administrator who is interested in knowing the needs of teachers so that she can tailor future mathematics professional development, the research question is: In which areas do most teachers need additional support to meet expectations for teaching and learning for our mathematics curricula? Her district's large size (400 schools) means that she (or even a team of people working on this effort) cannot physically observe every teacher, nor is she likely to even be able to observe a teacher from every school in the short time period in which she has to gather information. Because of this, she has to compromise and decides to select three teachers from each school to observe. In doing so, she assumes that the teachers within a school are similar enough to each other that she can observe a subset of the teachers and they will be a reasonable representation of the school. Additionally, the administrator is not certain about which of the five sanctioned curricula schools are using.

After assessing her needs in terms of the research question and available resources, the administrator works with other district personnel to consult the five curricula to determine their structural and instructional expectations for teaching mathematics and compare them with the critical components already included in the FOI instruments. After confirming that all the critical components are already represented in the instruments, she consults the instrument-construct matrix and her budget to determine which instruments to use. She decides on the teacher instructional questionnaire, school leader questionnaire, and teacher logs. All instruments will be electronic so that the district will not have to use its paper budget and the administrator can instantly know which teachers and school leaders have completed the instruments. The teacher and school leader questionnaires will be administered first, followed by the five teacher logs.

After gathering all the data, the administrator makes a report identifying the structures and instructional practices being used in the classrooms. Because her audience consists of other personnel in her office, she decides to report on each critical component aggregated across classrooms and schools and then create critical-component profiles for each school. She then groups the schools into types of instructional implementation and will use those types to develop specific professional development for the areas in which groups of schools need the most help.

Principal

The principal interested in understanding why test scores have not improved may need to develop more pointed research questions. First, she wants to understand how the science program is being used in each classroom. Since she does not have a science leader in her school and does not feel confident about her own understanding of the science curriculum, she decides to ask the district science coordinator to help her inventory the program critical components to determine their fit with the FOI instrument critical components. Once identified, she can then determine the extent to which the critical components are present in each classroom in her school. Therefore, her question is: To what extent are the critical components from our school science program present in individual classrooms in my school?

After meeting with the district science coordinator to identify the program's critical components, she consults the instrument-construct matrix to determine which instruments she will use to collect her data. Since the principal regularly visits classrooms, she decides that she will participate in training for and use the classroom observation protocol for all her science teachers and observe them each three times in one month. Additionally, she will ask the teachers to complete the teacher instructional questionnaire so that she can get a better idea of how they are implementing the science curriculum over time. The principal will ask teachers to complete the questionnaire during a regularly scheduled staff meeting so that she can be sure to get timely responses.

After the principal has finished collecting data, she decides to represent the extent to which each critical component is present in each classroom by averaging the ratings of items from the three observations and considering them with the responses from the questionnaire to create critical-component scores for each teacher. Then she correlates the critical-component scores with each teacher's average for student test scores to see if there seems to be a trend. She also plans to meet with the district science coordinator and personnel from the district office of data and reporting to discuss the correlations and examine other correlations between individual critical components and the teachers' average student test scores. The data will be used to help the principal offer each teacher specific ideas for improving practice and to point teachers to professional development experiences that address their specific needs.

Rather than create a formal report, the principal decides to keep track of the science teachers' curricular enactment by using the same observation protocol at another time period during the school year and then again during the next school year to see if there have been any changes in enactment. These data will remain in each teacher's personnel file so that the principal can revisit them during evaluation meetings.

Science Specialist

The science specialist who wants to get a better idea of what teachers are doing during science and what materials they are using would be best served by looking at the classroom level (individual teachers) as the unit of analysis. He knows that teachers are not all using the same programs or materials and therefore is framing his research in terms of use rather than fidelity. In other words, he is using the framework and critical components to tell him about teachers' use of science materials as opposed to telling him about fidelity to a specific program.

He has decided that he will use the information primarily to inform how he supports teachers and decides that initially he will only look at what structures teachers are using and will explore looking into instructional strategies in the future. He decides that his research questions are: What structures (borrowing from our FOI framework language) are teachers using during science? and What materials are teachers using to teach science?

After framing his research questions, the science specialist begins to look at our critical-component framework. He takes the fact that not all teachers are using the same program or materials into consideration when deciding on which critical components to focus on. Because he wants to know what teachers are teaching (i.e., content), the basic materials teachers are using (e.g., writing structures, readings, materials, assessments, projects, homework, etc.), and how the science instruction is set up (e.g., time spent on instruction, duration of unit, use of class structures, and use of instructional delivery formats), he decides to include the majority of the structural-procedural critical components. However, because he is more interested in use than in fidelity, he decides not to include critical components that are more directly related to specific programs (e.g., inclusion of all essential lessons and lesson segments, order of lessons and lesson segments, etc.). Because he is focusing initially on what teachers are using and doing structurally, he only includes the structural-procedural critical components.

After choosing his critical components of interest, he looks at the instrument-construct matrix to determine which instruments he will administer to teachers. As he does so, he also considers his research design and how many times he might administer each instrument. As he is doing this, he considers his time and resources; he has one hour of "release time" each day when he can work with teachers, as well as a 45-minute planning meeting twice a week with all eight science teachers. He decides that he will first administer the teacher questionnaire to all teachers to get a general idea of what they

are doing. He will give them time to complete the questionnaire during their weekly planning meeting to ensure that they all respond. Since the questionnaire will give him a better idea of how frequently teachers are using critical components over time, he decides that he also wants to know what teachers are doing from day to day. Because he has an hour of release time each day and wants to have more of a presence in classrooms during science, he will observe each teacher at least once. Given his past experience, he realizes that he will not always have a full hour to observe teachers. Thus, to gather more information about what teachers are doing on a day-to-day basis, he will ask teachers to fill out logs for two weeks. Again, he will provide teachers with time during the group planning meetings to fill out the logs.

Finally, he decides what the analysis and reporting will look like. He decides to create summary statistics for each critical component (e.g., percent of teachers using writing structures or using different class structures or instructional delivery formats) because he feels that he can easily do this sort of analysis, and it will allow him to get a quick overview of the status of science at the school. Additionally, he can use those data to inform decisions about supports the school might provide (e.g., how teachers can incorporate student writing/journals into their practice) and what materials might be ordered in the future (e.g., teachers are not doing hands-on activities because they lack the materials or teachers are all using a set of books they found at the library). He also spends time summarizing the data by each instrument so that he can compare his single-lesson observations with what teachers report they are using in a single lesson (logs) and throughout a unit (teacher questionnaire).

Teacher

A teacher who is teaching a new mathematics program without the benefit of any professional development decides to look at his own practice in-depth to figure out if he is on the right track. Because he is not sure that he has all the pieces and materials from the program (e.g., supplemental books, student journals, student books, and manipulatives), he is going to look at both the structures of the program and the instructional side of the program. After coming across our initial FOI framework, he decides the instruments could help him. His research question, then, is: To what extent am I implementing the program structures and instructional strategies in a manner consistent with the intended program? Unlike the other scenarios, the teacher is doing this more informally and will not be reporting to others. Thus this use case is much less formal than the others.

Since the teacher wants an overall picture of his implementation, he decides to look at structural-procedural, instructional-pedagogical, and instructional-student engagement. He decides that he is not as interested in his use of the educative pieces because he has a solid background in both content and pedagogy related to the program.

Since he does not have many resources at his disposal, he decides that he will use the teacher logs to track his practice for six weeks or one entire math unit. While he does not have a great amount of time, he feels that tracking his practice in this way not only will inform his research questions but also will help him be more reflective about his practice. He also will ask the mathematics specialist at his school to come into his classroom and observe his instruction using the classroom observation protocol three times throughout this period. Since the specialist has years of experience with the program and has provided professional development on the program in the past, he thinks that she will know what the program should look like. She has been asking teachers for ideas about additional ways to support them, so he thinks that she will be receptive to this idea.

Because he is informally exploring these questions for himself, the teacher does not plan on creating a formal report. However, he decides to create tables with summary and descriptive statistics of each of the critical components from the log. He then will look at each of the components to determine which ones he is consistently implementing and which ones he needs to focus on. Additionally, he will meet with the specialist and share the log data with her. They can compare what he reported in the logs with what she observed. With her past experience, she also can provide him with benchmarks for implementation and let him know which parts of the program he is implementing in a manner consistent with the program model.

Grade-Level Group of Teachers

This group of five teachers from the same grade level has three years of experience implementing the program and decides that they would like to work together and learn from each other's practice. As with the teacher scenario, this is an informal, small-scale project. And as with the science specialist, these teachers are more interested in their use of the program as opposed to their fidelity of implementation. After initial conversations, the teachers come to the conclusion that they are generally using the structures of the program in the same way but are unsure of which instructional strategies they are and are not using consistently. Thus they decide on the following research questions: Which instructional strategies (or critical components) are we implementing with the same frequency? Which instructional strategies (or critical components) are we using in the same ways?

As with the individual teacher scenario, these teachers recognize that they have limited time and resources to answer these research questions. After consulting the instrument-construct matrix, they decide that they will use the teacher questionnaire and observations. They will initially complete the teacher questionnaire to get an idea of how often they each use the different instructional strategies (e.g., give students an opportunity to make predictions or encourage unsure students to ask questions). Then, over a one-month time period, each teacher will observe the other four teachers. After talking with their principal and looking at their schedules, they decide that they have enough flexibility to arrange the observations during the other teachers' preparation periods.

Much like the specialist and individual teacher scenario, the grade-level group of teachers does not need a formal report, nor are they reporting the results beyond their own group. Therefore, they create a report with each instructional strategy, the frequency with which each teacher reports using it, and a summary of the observation ratings for each item. Because they are interested in making their own practice consistent, they summarize the findings by each teacher. This allows them to look at each strategy and determine who is implementing it in a way they wanted, who is not, and how the former could support the latter.

Conclusion

Like many processes in schools, understanding program enactment and fidelity is complicated. When we set out to create this suite of instruments, we wanted to make them broadly applicable for use with a number of programs and a number of different audiences. The FOI work presented herein is not about using someone's research in your school but rather what you can do with the instruments to affect the practices where you are. Given the right tools, the concept of fidelity and measuring program use can help practitioners to learn more about their own practice and learn what is and is not working.

Given the flexibility of the FOI conceptual framework and instruments, it is our hope that practitioners with any amount of time, resources, or research experience will be able to use these instruments to further their understanding of and improve their practice. Our goal is to remove the artificial boundaries between researchers and practitioners and help all interested parties work together to share information and shape change. We encourage any reader to contact us for more information on these tools and ideas on how we might work together to understand FOI in their settings.

Notes

1. *FOSS, STC, Science Companion, IES, SEPUP,* and *Everyday Mathematics.*

References

Bodzin, A. M., Cates, W. M., & Price, B. (2003). Formative evaluation of the exploring life curriculum: Year two implementation fidelity findings. Paper presented at the meeting of the National Association for Research in Science Teaching (NARST), Philadelphia, PA.

Bond, G., Williams, J., Evans, L., Salyers, M., Kim, H., Sharpe, H., & Leff, H.S. (2000). *Psychiatric rehabilitation fidelity toolkit.* Cambridge, MA: Human Services Research Institute.

Dane, A. V., & Schneider, B. H. (1998). Program integrity in primary and early secondary prevention: Are implementation effects out of control? *Clinical Psychology Review* 18(1), 23–45.

Lewis, L. K., & Seibold, D. R. (1993). Innovation modification during intraorganizational adoption. *Academy of Management Review* 18(2), 322–54.

Mowbray, C. T., Holter, M. C., Teague, G. B., & Bybee, D. (2003). Fidelity criteria: Development, measurement, and validation. *American Journal of Evaluation* 24(3), 315–40.

Ruiz-Primo, M. A. (2005). A multi-method and multi-source approach for studying fidelity of implementation. Paper presented at the Annual Meeting of the American Educational Research Association, Montreal, Canada.

Wang, M. C., Nojan, M., Strom, C. D., & Walberg, H. J. (1984). The utility of degree of implementation measures in program implementation and evaluation research. *Curriculum Inquiry* 14, 249–86.

CHAPTER 21

Increasing Student Voice in School Reform

Building Partnerships, Improving Outcomes

Dana T. Mitra

Introduction

Adolescents frequently describe their school experiences as anonymous places in which they have no voice and no one cares about them (Earls, 2003; Heath & McLaughlin, 1993; Pope, 2001). In fact, alienation results in two-thirds of students being disengaged from high schools (Cothran & Ennis, 2000). Disengaged students attend school less, have lower self-esteem, achieve less academically, and are more likely to drop out of school (Fullan, 2001; Noguera, 2002). To help remedy the alienation of young people and to strengthen school improvement efforts overall, a growing effort is focusing on increasing *student voice* in schools. The current concept of student voice describes the many ways in which youth have opportunities to share in the school decisions that will shape their lives and the lives of their peers (Fielding, 2001; Levin, 2000; Mitra, 2003). Research has described similar processes as pupil *participation, active citizenship, youth leadership,* and *youth empowerment.*

Student voice activities can take a variety of forms. At the simplest level, student voice can consist of young people sharing their opinions of school problems with administrators and faculty. Student voice initiatives also can become extensive when young people collaborate with adults to address the problems in their schools – and in rare cases with youth assuming leadership roles in change efforts (Mitra, 2005). Whether young people are sharing their opinions or leading change efforts, it is important to emphasize that student voice efforts are categorically different from traditional student roles in school (e.g., planning school dances and holding pep rallies).

At their best, student voice efforts can serve as a means to conceptualize and implement educational change. In student voice initiatives, students have the agency to participate in discussions about the core operations of schools, including teaching and learning and schoolwide decision-making practices. Student voice efforts therefore provide opportunities not only to prepare students for a democratic society but also to transform schools into democratic settings in which young people can gain the necessary skills in understanding how to participate in pluralistic communities (Gutmann, 1987).

The developing concept of *student voice* remains undertheorized in educational research. Yet student voice activities fit well within the broader definition of *youth-adult partnerships*, which are defined as relationships in which both youth and adults have the potential to contribute to visioning and decision-making processes, to learn from one another, and to promote change (Jones & Perkins, 2004). With appropriate guidance and coaching by adults (Camino, 2000), collaboration consists of creating a learning environment in which individuals come together in groups with the willingness to share authority, accept responsibility, and highlight individual members' abilities and contributions (Panitz, 1996). Student voice initiatives therefore can be considered school-based forms of youth-adult partnerships.

Improving School Reform Efforts

A growing body of research being conducted in the United States, the United Kingdom, Australia, and Canada has examined the purpose and outcomes of student voice initiatives. These studies have found that student voice can greatly affect high schools, including providing important leverage for conceptualizing and implementing change. Table 21.1 summarizes the ways in which student voice activities have been found to influence high schools. The remainder of this section details these findings.

Improve Positive Youth Development

Student voice initiatives also can yield great improvements in positive youth development outcomes. Youth development is a process that prepares young people to successfully navigate the transition to adulthood. By understanding the developmental needs of adolescents and how institutions and organizations might meet those needs, the intention of a youth development perspective is to focus researchers,

Table 21.1. Ways in Which Student Voice Initiatives Can Influence Schools

- Improve positive youth development
- Strengthen strategic planning, decision making, and training
- Improve quality and scope of implementation
- Strengthen classroom practice
- Improve school culture

policymakers, and practitioners on youth preparation (Villarruel et al., 2003). In my previous research I have identified a series of assets that are the most salient outcomes of youth participation in student voice initiatives—agency, belonging, and competence (Mitra, 2004, Mitra et al., 2007).

Agency in a youth development context indicates the ability to exert influence and power in a given situation. It connotes a sense of confidence, a sense of self-worth, and the belief that one can do something, whether contributing to society writ large or to a specific situation (Heath & McLaughlin, 1993). Research conducted with middle school students in the United States also found that students valued their schooling the most when their teachers heard their voices and "honored" them (Mitra, 2004; Oldfather, 1995). Student voice initiatives also can lead to an increase in youth leadership and empowerment (Larson, Walker, & Pearce, 2005), which can be a source of social capital for youth that can yield opportunities for further education, employment, and other enrichment opportunities (O'Connor & Camino, 2005). Student voice initiatives also provide legitimate opportunities for youth to take on meaningful roles (Camino, 2000), including opportunities to be change makers in their schools and communities so that they can experience making a difference—and especially by helping others in need (Mitra, 2004).

The concept of *belonging* in a youth development frame consists of developing relationships consisting of supportive, positive interaction with adults and peers and of opportunities to learn from one another (Costello et al., 2000; Goodenow,

1993; PISA, 2003; Roeser, Midgley, & Urdan, 1996). Student voice activities have been found to increase students' attachment to their peers, their teachers, their school, and their broader community (Mitra, 2003; Mitra et al., 2007), including seeking out and building on the strengths of diverse groups of people (Camino & Zeldin, 2002). When students believe that they are valued for their perspectives and respected, they begin to develop a sense of ownership and attachment to the organization in which they are involved (Atweh & Burton, 1995). Most notably, scholars have found that an adolescents' belonging to her school is positively related to academic success and motivation (Goodenow, 1993; Ryan & Powelson, 1991).

Competence in a youth development context consists of the need for youth to develop new skills and abilities, to actively solve problems, and to be appreciated for one's talents (Villarruel & Lerner, 1994). Student voice initiatives also often provide a rare opportunity to value a diverse range of talents and leadership styles (Camino & Zeldin, 2002; Denner, Meyer, & Bean, 2005; Sanders et al., 2007), including being a critical thinker, teacher, anchor, peacemaker, and supporter (Larson, Walker, & Pearce 2005; Perkins & Borden, 2003; Zeldin et al., 2002). Student voice initiatives also offer opportunities to learn a broad range of competencies, including physical, intellectual, psychological, emotional, and social skills (Camino, 2000). Specifically, student voice initiatives increase the ability of young people to identify problems and develop action plans to address them, to facilitate conversations with adults and youth, and to speak publicly to diverse audiences (Mitra, 2004).

Strengthen Decision Making, Strategic Planning, and Training

Research from student voice efforts as well as from youth involvement in nonprofit and after-school programs finds that youth input can improve organizational visioning and strategic planning (Kirshner, O'Donoghue, & McLaughlin, 2003; Eccles & Gootman, 2002; Zeldin, 2004; Zeldin, Camino, & Mook,

2005). In particular, young people often are willing to raise issues that adults might not see or might avoid. Students not succeeding in the current system, including those failing subjects or at risk of dropping out, can offer particularly insightful advice on problems with school structure and culture (Mitra, 2001; Smyth, 2007). Struggling students tend to cite structural and classroom procedures that hamper learning, the lack of opportunities to build caring relationships with adults, and blatant discrimination as being the actual problems (Colatos & Morrell, 2003; Mitra, 2001; Nieto, 1994; Soohoo, 1993). Student voice efforts can lead to increased interest in institutionalizing student input into the decision-making process, including the development of standing committees on curriculum planning, staff development, and discipline committees (Fielding, 2001; Mitra, 2004). Young people also have served as researchers and witnesses documenting school policies that exacerbate achievement gaps and identify ways in which detrimental school conditions can adversely affect students' psychological, social, and academic well-being (Fine et al., 2007).

Student input also has led to changes in preservice teacher training and ongoing staff development. Alison Cook-Sather's (2001, 2002) research, for example, has examined ways for student voice to inform the practice of teachers in training, including encouraging teachers to rethink who is an authority of educational practice. When teachers and teachers-to-be learn how to listen to their students, teachers began to remove the stereotypes and labels that can be so easily attached to students.

Improve Quality and Scope of Reform Implementation

Involving young people also can improve the quality of implementation of reform efforts. Students can serve as important sources of information that otherwise are not available regarding implementation and experiences of educational change (Kushman, 1997; Rudduck, Day, & Wallace, 1997; Thorkildsen, 1994). Student information can be particularly useful for reshaping reform efforts when they are slowly or shallowly implemented (Yonezawa & Jones, 2007).

Since effective implementation of reform benefits from participation by and acceptance from those most affected (Elmore, 1983; McLaughlin, 1991), efforts to actively involve students can lead to improved student understanding of the educational changes in their schools (Mitra, 2004). Students also can help to mobilize teachers and parents in support of change (Levin, 2000). Young people also can serve as a bridge of communication and explanation between the school and families reluctant to interact with school personnel. One initiative in northern California focused on mobilizing the parents of first-generation Latino families to take a more active role in interacting with the high school and demanding quality educational services (Mitra, 2006). While the effort was designed as a parent mobilization initiative, the adult organizer soon learned that the parents lacked capacity and interest in participating in such an initiative. Instead, the students proved to be the actors who could articulate the concerns of their families and increase communication and understanding between their families and schools.

Strengthen Classroom Practice

A large body of research documents the value of student voice initiatives improving classroom practice (including Cushman, 2000; Daniels, Deborah, & McCombs, 2001; Kincheloe, 2007; Thorkildsen, 1994). Often, this form of student voice is termed *consultation*, which is defined as teachers partnering with students to discuss teaching and learning, including inviting students to provide feedback on instructional styles, curriculum content, assessment opportunities, and other issues in the classroom (McIntyre & Rudduck, 2007; Rudduck, 2007). Research has found that students can improve academically when teachers construct their classrooms in ways that value student voice – especially when students are given the power to work with their teachers

to improve curriculum and instruction (Oldfather, 1995; Rudduck & Flutter, 2000). Consultation can increase the relevance of the curriculum, including self-directed learning opportunities for students, the need to explore connecting students' part-time jobs with their coursework, and the desire to engage in less specialized coursework in their final years of high school so that they have a wider range of postsecondary options (Lee & Zimmerman, 1999; Rudduck, 2007; Soohoo, 1993). Consultation also can provide better metacognitive understanding of students' own learning, including helping students to gain a stronger sense of their own abilities and educating students about the differences between learning styles, multiple intelligences, and emotional intelligence (Lee & Zimmerman, 1999; Johnston & Nicholls, 1995; Mitra, 2004). Researchers have found that an increase in a teacher's focus on student experiences and learning styles also can increase student interest in schoolwork and learning (Daniels, Deborah, & McCombs, 2001).

Improve School Culture

In addition to improvements at the classroom level, student voice efforts also have led to improvements in the culture of high schools. When asking student opinions, a common theme across several studies is students' desires for positive, strong relationships with their teachers as opposed to the isolation and lack of respect and appreciation that students reported they often feel (Lynch & Lodge, 2002; Phelan, Davidson, & Cao, 1992; Poplin & Weeres, 1992; Yonezawa & Jones, 2007). Student voice initiatives therefore tend to highlight the importance of teacher-student relationships and the overall culture of a school. Often student input can lead to an increased focus on improving school climate, such as improvements in advisory period structures and life-skill curricula (Fielding, 2001). Students at Whitman High School in northern California, for example, took teachers on tours of their neighborhood, including where they lived, worked, and hung out on street corners and where gangs staked out their territories (Mitra, 2003). Students felt that they truly did come to know their teachers better, and they believed that their teachers came to better understand them as well. Teachers and students reported that they found the experience valuable, commenting that they developed a better understanding of student experience.

Conditions that Enable and Sustain Student Voice Initiatives

Given the potential challenges of designing and implementing student voice initiatives, understanding what conditions enable and sustain student voice initiatives is critical. The stark differences in traditional roles of young people and adults in schools require intentional efforts to create a new set of working conditions that include new norms, relationships, and organizational structures (Della Porta & Diani, 1999; Oakes & Lipton, 2002). Table 21.2 summarizes the enabling conditions discussed in this section, and the remainder of this section details those conditions.

Securing Sustainability by Partnering with an Intermediary Organization

While research is increasingly pointing to the need to think of change as not being feasible unless it is implemented and sustained schoolwide (Datnow, Hubbard, & Mehan 2002) and increasingly if it is not supported and sustained at the district level as well (Berends, Bodily, & Kirby, 2002; Florian 2001; McLaughlin & Mitra, 2004), research suggests the need to think more intentionally, School change needs to be conceptualized as a process that involves not only the school system but also a broader cast of actors engaged in providing supporting roles such as coaching, professional development, provision of funds, creation of reform visions (Mitra, 2009a). In an environment in which administrators are expected to pay attention to several initiatives at once, including ever-present concerns about test scores, fostering

Table 21.2. Conditions that Enable and Sustain Student Voice Initiatives

- Securing sustainability by partnering with an intermediary organization
- Sending signs that the youth-adult partnership is not "business as usual"
- Emphasizing respect and trust among group members
- Creating meaningful but not equal roles
- Creating visible victories
- Providing dedicated time and space for collaboration
- Building the capacity for youth and adults to fulfill their roles

youth-adult partnerships can fall to the wayside, even when administrators value their importance. Outsourcing some of the support and technical assistance needed for youth-adult partnerships can help to keep the idea alive but relieve administrators of some of the burdens of ensuring the success of youth-adult partnerships.

This outsourcing of technical assistance for youth-adult partnerships has been demonstrated to be one of the strongest common threads among sustainable youth-adult partnerships. A strong affiliation with an *intermediary organization*—usually a nonprofit focused on youth activism and community justice issues (Mitra, 2006, 2009a)—can lead to stability for youth-adult partnerships. The concept of intermediary organizations as important players in educational reform efforts is fairly new (Honig, 2004), yet researchers of education change have emphasized similar concepts of outside organizations providing important information and bridging communication between schools and with other organizations.

Intermediary organizations have been found to mediate four needs—vision, leadership, funding, and knowledge sharing (Mitra, 2009a). They provided training for adults and young people to learn how to work together. In school settings, fostering collaboration between youth and adults requires the intentional creation of new roles other than "teacher" and "student." Learning how to support youth to assume more leadership is particularly challenging in school settings where teachers are often used to being in control. Because institutional norms of schools define the roles of teachers and students, becoming a partner with youth requires adults to step out of teacher mode. Instead, they must learn to be a coach who provides meaningful leadership opportunities and fosters the skills of youth to be able to assume these positions (Camino, 2000; Denner, Meyer, & Bean, 2005). Intermediary organizations can provide adults with strategies and support for adjusting their roles in youth-adult partnerships.

Youth participating in partnerships also need to learn specific skills, including communication with others and organizational skills. While adults have a responsibility to encourage shared leadership with youth, they often bear the ultimate responsibility for keeping the youth moving forward in a positive direction, which includes helping the youth get "unstuck" when a sense of being overwhelmed or a lack of skill paralyzes a group. Getting unstuck includes learning specific technical skills, including facilitation, planning projects, preparing press releases, and oral presentations (Camino & Zeldin, 2002).

In addition to providing training and visioning support, intermediary organizations also help with identifying and seeking funding (Mitra, 2007; Honig, 2004). Without dedicated staff working on finding ongoing resources, youth-adult partnerships tend to falter over time. By working with intermediary organizations to secure ongoing funds, the youth-adult partnerships in northern California could focus their vision for change rather than worrying about their ongoing survival. Intermediary organizations overall had greater capacity in terms of staff and technical expertise to secure ongoing financial support. Intermediary organizations also provided for a permanent staff member whose job was to serve as an advisor for group activities. Their staff members could focus their time and energies on applying for grants from foundations, cultivating private donors, and working hard to ensure long-term financial support from school district officials.

Affiliation with an intermediary organization not only can provide monetary support but also can provide access to an outside network of information and knowledge transfer (Seely-Brown & Duguid, 2000). According to one youth organizer in California, "One of the key things that I think you need to do to survive in this field is outreach to others, like the California Association of Student Councils and others. They may know of a couple of groups and schools, and then you can really get yourself out there. You need to expand your connections with other organizations" (Mitra, 2009a, p. 1855). Such support allowed students to collaborate with other schools. Some intermediary organizations also can provide access to a network of other youth-adult partnerships so that groups could share ideas and learn from one another. Other advisors seek support beyond their intermediary organization by looking for regionwide conferences and meetings for adults working as advocates for youth. For example, an intermediary organization in the San Francisco Bay Area hosted an annual "youth-organizing exchange retreat" intended to provide opportunities for adult advisors to learn from one another (Mitra, 2009a, p. 1856).

SENDING SIGNS THAT THE YOUTH-ADULT PARTNERSHIP IS NOT "BUSINESS AS USUAL"

Within school settings, successful youth-adult partnerships require an intentional effort to send the message to youth and adults that the student voice initiative is not a traditional relationship between teachers and students. In all youth-adult partnerships, adults must learn to be a coach who provides meaningful leadership opportunities and fosters the skills of youth to be able to assume these positions (Camino, 2000; Denner, Meyer, & Bean, 2005). Learning how to enable youth to assume more leadership is particularly challenging for teachers because they are often used to being in control. When adults are effective at stepping out of their teacher personas, youth in such collaborations overwhelmingly speak of being able to see the human side of adults. Words such as *friendship*, *trust*, *role model*, and *counselor* emerged again and again in research data (Mitra, 2006). Research has found that youth-adult partnerships fail if they do not provide sufficient focus and attention to the development of trust and building of community among group members (Camino, 2005; Friedman & Duffett, 2000; Schön & McDonald, 1998; Zeldin, Camino, & Mook, 2005). The creation of a safe space and open lines of communication must be given priority in the work of student voice initiatives.

EMPHASIZING RESPECT AND TRUST AMONG GROUP MEMBERS

Often in student voice initiatives, groups are so anxious to make change that little time is devoted to building the capacity of the group members and the overall identity of the group. In such cases, adults and youth may complete a specific project successfully, but without a broader vision and collective purpose, the group disbands and often even the accomplished activities disappear as well. Yet a growing body of research that indicates that youth-adult partnerships need to *establish respect and trust among group members* aligns with similar themes in research on community-based youth-adult partnerships (Mitra, 2009b; Zeldin, Camino, & Mook, 2005).

CREATING MEANINGFUL BUT NOT EQUAL ROLES

Adults and youth need opportunities to share what they have learned based on their experiences and their beliefs. A sense of shared ownership grows when student voice initiatives encourage group members to experiment with a variety of roles, including being a critical thinker, a teacher, a learner, a peacemaker, a supporter, a facilitator, and a documenter (Denner, Meyer, & Bean, 2005; Zeldin et al., 2002). Successful student voice initiatives therefore require a clear understanding of what roles each individual plays within the group (Mitra, 2005). They do not create an expectation of equal roles but instead foster equal responsibility and respect through mutual understanding.

Youth-adult partnerships are much different from the common misconception that an increase in youth leadership means that adults simply must "get out of the way" (Camino, 2005). This assumption suggests that power is a zero-sum game. Instead, research has found that the more empowered adults are, the more they can enable power in others, including youth (Camino, 2000; Ginwright, 2005; McQuillan, 2005). Nevertheless, in instances such as the formation of youth-adult partnerships, where the imbalance of power among group members is extreme, adults often had to make explicit gestures that signaled their stepping back in order to create a space in which youth could have a shared responsibility for group decision making. Such a process does not entail handing over control to youth per se but instead consists of creating a space in which all group members—youth and adults—could develop a common vision for their collective, could carve out an important and meaningful role for themselves in the activities, and could share responsibility for decisions and accountability for group outcomes (Mitra, 2005).

CREATING VISIBLE VICTORIES

As an adult-youth partnership begins working on a collective activity, the legitimacy and importance of the group need to be shored up quickly through an accomplishment that is both meaningful to youth and sufficiently impressive to adults (Mitra, 2009a). This process creates credibility for group activities and a sense of common identity and confidence among group members. A project that is fairly straightforward yet meaningful to the group members can yield a "visible victory" (McLaughlin, 1993) that can boost group morale and also establish credibility of the group with the broader school and community. Such an exercise is particularly important in school settings because achieving legitimacy is such a great challenge given the institutionalized roles of youth as students and adults as teachers and administrators. Creating smaller goals both helps to retain the youth involved and also allows for the assimilation of new members each semester as new phases of a project begin.

In school settings, visible victories must occur within a fast time frame. Time for youth in schools tends to be broken into school years and sometimes even semesters, not to mention that youth are only in the school settings for three to four years overall. Sustaining youth morale and participation in an adult-youth partnership includes creating initiatives, or "campaigns" according to some groups, that are short enough in duration to achieve some clear goals, such as by the end of a semester (Zeldin et al., 2002). Yet such activities must be authentic and meaningful to the group members in an adult-youth partnership (Mitra, 2004; Denner, Meyer, & Bean, 2005; Perkins & Borden, 2003). An essential part of youth culture is "being real." It is such an essential part of youth culture to be authentic and honest that the youth in these cases strongly expressed that their work in the group needed to have importance and value, or they would not continue to participate.

PROVIDING DEDICATED TIME AND SPACE FOR COLLABORATION

Successful school-based youth-adult partnerships not only created an informal tone but also often rearranged the physical space of a classroom during their meetings to establish a more equitable form of interaction (Krueger, 2005; Mitra, 2009b). Such altered arrangements included circling desks and, in some groups, even the permanent insertion of couches and more comfortable forms of seating. In addition to the size of the room, the size of the school overall also appears to have an impact on the ability of school-based youth-adult partnerships to accomplish their goals and to continue to work together after their seed funding ended, with smaller schools appearing to help to form student voice initiatives (Mitra, 2009b).

Finding a common meeting time for group activities is also critical, but it can be a challenge for young people. Meetings might occur before or after school, during lunch, and even during the school day if the work of the group can be incorporated into an official school course (Mitra, 2007). Each choice faces problems in terms of conflicting with school work and with

the many extracurricular and employment commitments of young people today. An extracurricular model can become a problem for school-based youth-adult partnerships when some of the youth in the group are not performing well in school because school-based administrations can place constraints on participation in such activities. Some student voice initiatives resolve the problem by paying the youth for their participation in the group so that they do not need to find additional time to get a part-time job. Others resolve the problem by developing an official course focusing on student voice issues. Such an arrangement solved the problem of competing activities and extracurricular regulations, but it required students to find time in their academic schedules, and it can create a potentially awkward dynamic in which the youth in the partnership must be evaluated as a part of the course. Ultimately, the adult in the room must pass judgment on all group members on a regular basis to fulfill school grading requirements.

BUILDING THE CAPACITY FOR YOUTH AND ADULTS TO FULFILL THEIR ROLES

Often adults are reluctant to share power until they have assurance that youth possess the skills and confidence to assume leadership (Muncey & McQuillan, 1991; Zeldin, 2004; Zeldin, Camino, & Mook, 2005). While partnerships should capitalize on the assets and talents that youth and adults bring to a group (Camino, 2000; Perkins & Borden, 2003), research has indicated that adults and youth both need specific skill development to serve as contributing members in their youth-adult partnerships (Mitra, 2004, 2005).

While all groups reported greatly benefiting from the external trainings from partner intermediary organizations and other sources, internal coaching also is needed to distribute leadership among many group members (Mitra, 2009b). This need for internal coaching emphasizes previous research findings that youth leaders and adults need to learn how to be coaches who enable youth to assume leadership roles (Camino 2000; Denner, Meyer, & Bean 2005). Adults in particular therefore need support and learning opportunities for partnerships to thrive. Previous research suggests that this knowledge includes developing an understanding of youth developmental needs and cultural contexts so that they are able to act with intention as they foster youth leadership (Camino & Zeldin 2002). In addition to learning how to enable youth leadership, adults in particular need to learn how to safely step out of "teacher mode," including distributing the balance of decision making and roles among youth and adults.

Youth need to develop the capacity to participate in youth-adult partnerships. They need to develop an understanding of effective communication in adult contexts and specific skills such as time management, planning, and learning to resolve differences among group members (Mitra, 2004). Building understanding of the perspectives of the other in the partnership can help the group to forge a more equitable form of interaction.

Improving Implementation of Student Voice Efforts

The early findings from the research reviewed in this chapter demonstrate the ways in which including student voice could strengthen the implementation of educational change, increase attention to equity and personalized environments, improve civic engagement, and strengthen developmental outcomes for youth. The inclusion of students in the reform process therefore provides many potential benefits with little additional cost. Increasing student voice more broadly requires caution, however. Surface-level implementation could create greater alienation among young people by offering insincere gestures rather than authentic partnership. As with any educational change, the quality of implementation will prove to be as important as the merit of the idea itself.

References

Atweh, B., & Burton, L. (1995). Students as researchers: Rationale and critique. *British Educational Research Journal* 21(5), 561–75.

Berends, M., Bodilly, S., & Kirby, S.N. (2002). *Facing the challenge of whole-school reform: New American Schools after a decade.* Santa Monica, CA: Rand Corporation.

Camino, L. A. (2000). Youth-adult partnerships: Entering new territory in community work and research. *Applied Developmental Science* 4, 11–20.

Camino, L. (2005). Pitfalls and promising practices of youth-adult partnerships: An evaluator's reflections. *Journal of Community Psychology* 33(1), 75–85.

Camino, L., & Zeldin, S. (2002). From periphery to center: Pathways for youth civic engagement in day-to-day life of communities. *Applied Developmental Science* 6(3), 213–20.

Carver, R. L. (1997). Theoretical underpinnings of service learning. *Theory into Practice*, 36(3), 143–9.

Coburn, C. E. (2005). The role of nonsystem actors in the relationship between policy and practice: The case of reading instruction in California. *Educational Evaluation and Policy Analysis* 27(1), 23–52.

Colatos, A. M., & Morrell, E. (2003). Apprenticing urban youth as critical researchers: Implications for increasing equity and access in diverse urban schools. In B. Rubin and E. Silva (eds.), *Critical voices in school reform: Students living through change.* London: Routledge/Falmer.

Cook-Sather, A. (2002). Authorizing students' perspectives: Toward trust, dialogue, and change in education. *Educational Researcher* 31(4), 3–14.

Cook-Sather, A. (2001). Between student and teacher: Learning to teach as translation. *Teaching Education* 12(2), 177–90.

Costello, J., Toles, M., Spielberger, J., & Wynn, J. (2000). History, ideology and structure shape the organizations that shape youth. In *Youth development: Issues, challenges, and directions* (pp. 185–231). Philadelphia: Public/Private Ventures.

Cothran, D., & Ennis, C. (2000) Building bridges to student engagement: Communicating respect and care for students in urban high school settings. *Journal of Research and Development in Education* 33, 106–17.

Cushman, K. (2000). Students solving community problems: Serious learning takes on a new look. *Challenge Journal: The Journal of the Annenberg Challenge* 4(1).

Daniels, D. H. K., Deborah, L., & McCombs, B. L. (2001). Young children's perspectives on learning and teacher practices in different classroom contexts: Implications for motivation. *Early Education and Development* 12(2), 253–73.

Datnow, A., Hubbard, L., & Mehan, H. (2002). *Extending educational reform: From one school to many*. London: Routledge/Falmer.

DellaPorta, D., & Diani, M. (1999). *Social movements: An introduction*. Malden, MA: Blackwell.

Denner, J., Meyer, B., & Bean, S. (2005). Young women's leadership alliance: Youth-adult partnerships in an all-female after-school program. *Journal of Community Psychology* 33(1), 87–100.

Earls, F. (2003). *Age segregation and the rights of children*. Ann Arbor, MI: Society for Research in Child Development.

Eccles, J., & Gootman, J. A. (2002). *Community programs to promote youth development*. Committee on Community-Level Programs for Youth, Board on Children, Youth, and Families, Commission on Behavioral and Social Sciences Education, National Research Council and Institute of Medicine. Washington: National Academies of Science.

Elmore, R. F. (1983). Complexity and control: What legislators and administrators can do about implementing public policy. In L. S. Shulman and G. Sykes. (eds.), *Handbook of Teaching and Policy*. New York: Longman.

Fielding, M. (2001). Students as radical agents of change. *Journal of Educational Change* 2(2), 123–41.

Fielding, M. (2004). Transformative approaches to student voice: Theoretical underpinnings, recalcitrant realities. *British Educational Research Journal* 30(2), 295–311.

Fine, M. (1991). *Framing dropouts: Notes on the politics of an urban high school*. Albany, NY: State University of New York Press.

Fine, M., Torre, M. E., Burns, A., & Payne, Y. A. (2007). Youth research/participatory methods for reform. In D. Thiessen and A. Cook-Sather (eds.), *International handbook of student experience in elementary and secondary school* (pp. 805–28). Dordrecht, The Netherlands: Springer.

Flanagan, C., & Faison, N. (2001). *Youth civic development: Implications of research for social policy and programs*. Ann Arbor, MI: Society for Research in Child Development.

Florian, J. (2001). *Sustaining education reform: Influential factors* (ERIC Document Reproduction Service No. ED453583). Aurora, CO: Mid-Continent Research for Education and Learning.

Friedman, W., & Duffett, A. (2000). *Getting by: What American teenagers really think about their schools*. Washington: Public Agenda Foundation.

Fullan, M. G. (2001). *The new meaning of educational change*, 3rd ed. New York: Teachers College Press.

Ginwright, S. A. (2005). On urban ground: Understanding African-American intergenerational partnerships in urban communities. *Journal of Community Psychology* 33(1), 101–10.

Goodenow, C. (1993). Classroom belonging among early adolescent students: Relationship to motivation and achievement. *Journal of Early Adolescence* 13(1), 21–43.

Gutmann, A. (1987). *Democratic education*. Princeton, NJ: Princeton University Press.

Heath, S. B., & McLaughlin, M. W. (eds.) (1993). *Identity and inner-city youth*. New York: Teachers College Press.

Honig, M. I. (2004). The new middle management: Intermediary organizations in education policy implementation. *Educational Evaluation and Policy Analysis* 226(1), 65–87.

Johnston, P. H., & Nicholls, J. G. (1995). Voices we want to hear and voices we don't. *Theory into Practice* 34(2), 94–100.

Jones, K., & Perkins, D. (2004). Youth-adult partnerships. In C. B. Fisher and R. M. Lerner (eds.), *Applied developmental science: An encyclopedia of research, policies, and programs*. Thousand Oaks, CA: Sage.

Kincheloe, J. (2007). Clarifying the purpose of engaging students as researchers. In D. Thiessen and A. Cook-Sather (eds.), *International handbook of student experience in elementary and secondary school* (pp. 745–74). Dordrecht, The Netherlands: Springer.

Kirshner, B., O'Donoghue, J. L., & McLaughlin, M. W. (eds.) (2003). *New directions for youth development: Youth participation improving institutions and communities*. San Francisco: Jossey-Bass.

Krueger, M. (2005). Four themes in youth work practice. *Journal of Community Psychology* 33(1), 21–9.

Kushman, J. W. (ed.) (1997). *Look who's talking now: Student views of learning in restructuring schools*, Vol. ED028257. Washington: Office of Educational Research and Improvement.

Larson, R., Walker, K., & Pearce, N. (2005). A comparison of youth-driven and adult-driven youth programs: Balancing inputs from youth and adults. *Journal of Community Psychology* 33(1), 57–74.

Lee, L., & Zimmerman, M. (1999). Passion, action and a new vision for student voice: Learnings from the Manitoba School Improvement Program. *Education Canada* 39(2), 34–5.

Levin, B. (2000). Putting students at the centre in education reform. *International Journal of Educational Change* 1(2), 155–72.

Lynch, K., & Lodge, A. (2002). *Equality and power in schools: Redistribution, recognition and representation.* London: Routledge/Falmer.

McIntyre, D., & Rudduck, J. (2007). *Improving learning through consulting pupils.* London: Routledge.

McLaughlin, M. W. (1993). Embedded identities: Enabling balance in urban contexts. In S. B. Heath and M. W. McLaughlin (eds.), *Identity and inner-city youth* (pp. 36–68). New York: Teachers College Press.

McLaughlin, M. W. (1991). The Rand change agent study: Ten years later. In A. R. Odden (ed.), *The evolution of education policy implementation* (pp. 143–56). Albany, NY: State University of New York Press.

McLaughlin, M., & Mitra, D. (2002). Moving deeper and broader with theory-based change. *Journal of Educational Change* 3(1), 301–23.

McQuillan, P. J. (2005). Possibilities and pitfalls: A comparative analysis of student empowerment. *American Educational Research Journal* 42(4), 639–72.

Mitra, D. L. (2009a). The role of intermediary organizations in sustaining student voice initiatives. *Teachers College Record* 7, 1834–68.

Mitra, D. L. (2009b).Collaborating with students: Building youth-adult partnerships in schools. *American Journal of Education* 15(3), 407–36.

Mitra, D. L. (2007). Student voice in school reform: From listening to leadership. In D. Thiessen and A. Cook-Sather (eds.), *International handbook of student experience in elementary and secondary school* (pp. 727–44). Dordrecht, The Netherlands: Springer.

Mitra, D. L. (2006). Youth as a bridge between home and school: Comparing student voice and parent involvements as strategies for change. *Education and Urban Society* 38(4), 455–80.

Mitra, D. L. (2005). Adults advising youth: Leading while getting out of the way. *Educational Administration Quarterly* 41(3), 520–53.

Mitra, D. L. (2004). The significance of students: Can increasing "student voice" in schools lead to gains in youth development. *Teachers College Record* 106(4), 651–88.

Mitra, D. L. (2003). Student voice in school reform: Reframing student-teacher relationships. *McGill Journal of Education* 38(2), 289–304.

Mitra, D. L. (2001). Opening the floodgates: Giving students a voice in school reform. *Forum* 43(2), 91–4.

Mitra, D., Sanders, F., Movit, M., & Perkins, D. F. (2007). Examining ways in which youth conferences can spell out gains in positive youth development. Paper presented at the Annual Meeting of the American Educational Research Association, Chicago, IL.

Muncey, D., & McQuillan, P. (1991). Empowering nonentities: Students in educational reform (working paper 5). School Ethnography Project, Coalition of Essential Schools, Brown University, Providence, RI.

Nieto, S. (1994). Lessons from students on creating a chance to dream. *Harvard Educational Review* 64(4), 392–427.

Noguera, P. (2002, December). Joaquin's dilemma: Understanding the link between racial identity and school-related behaviors. *In Motion Magazine* 12(4), 290–1. Retrieved April 29, 2004, from http://www.inmotionmagazine.com/er/pnjoaq2.html.

Oakes, J., & Lipton, M. (2002). Struggling for educational equity in diverse communities: School reform as a social movement. *Journal of Educational Change* 3(3–4), 383–406.

O'Connor, C., & Camino, L. (2005). *Youth and adult leaders for program excellence: Youth Participation in Research and Evaluation: Outcomes for Youth.* Madison, WI: Community Youth Connection, University of Wisconsin Extension.

Oldfather, P. (1995). Songs "come back most to them": Students' experiences as researchers. *Theory into Practice* 34(2), 131.

Panitz, T. (1996). A definition of collaborative vs. cooperative learning. Available online at http://www.lgu.ac.uk/deliberations/collab.learning/panitz2.html.

Perkins, D., & Borden, L. (2003). Positive behaviors, problem behaviors, and resiliency in adolescence. In R. M. Lerner, M. A. Easterbrooks, and J. Mistry (eds.), *Handbook of psychology*, Vol. 6: *Developmental psychology*. Hoboken, NJ: Wiley.

Phelan, P., Davidson, A. L., & Cao, H. T. (1992). Speaking up: Students' perspectives on school. *Phi Delta Kappan*, May, 695–704.

PISA – Program for Internal Student Assessment (2003). *Student engagement at school: A sense of belonging and participation* (Survey). Washington: Organization for Economic Co-Operation and Development.

Pope, D. C. (2001). *"Doing school": How we are creating a generation of stressed out, materialistic, and miseducated students.* New Haven, CT: Yale University Press.

Poplin, M., & Weeres, J. (1992). *Voices from inside the classroom.* Claremont, CA: Institute for Education in Transformation at the Claremont Graduate School.

Roeser, R. W., Midgley, C., & Urdan, T.C. (1996). Perceptions of the school psychological environment and early adolescents' psychological and behavioral functioning in school: The mediating role of goals and belonging. *Journal of Educational Psychology* 88(3), 408–22.

Rudduck, J. (2007). Student voice, student engagement, and school reform. In D. Thiessen and A. Cook-Sather (eds.), *International handbook of student experience in elementary and secondary school* (pp. 587–610). Dordrecht, The Netherlands: Springer.

Rudduck, J., & Flutter, J. (2000). Pupil participation and perspective: "Carving a new order of experience." *Cambridge Journal of Education* 30(1), 75–89.

Rudduck, J., Day, J., & Wallace, G. (1997). Students' perspectives on school improvement. In A. Hargreaves (ed.), *Rethinking educational change with heart and mind* (The 1997 ASCD Year Book). Alexandria, VA: Association for Supervision and Curriculum Development.

Ryan, R. M., & Powelson, C. L. (1991). Autonomy and relatedness as fundamental to motivation and education. *Journal of Experimental Education* 60(1), 49–66.

Sanders, F., Movit, M., Mitra, D., & Perkins, D. F. (2007). Examining ways in which youth conferences can spell out gains in positive youth development. *LEARNing Landscapes* 1(1), 49–78.

Schmuck, P., & Schmuck, R. (1990). Democratic participation in small-town schools. *Educational Researcher* 19(8), 14–19.

Schön, D., & McDonald, J. (1998). *Doing what you mean to do in school reform: Theory of action in the Annenberg Challenge.* Providence, RI: Annenberg Institute for School Reform.

Seely-Brown, J., & Duguid, P. (2000). *The social life of information.* Cambridge, MA: Harvard Business Press.

Smyth, J. (2007). Toward the pedagogically engaged school: Listening to student voice as a positive response to disengagement and "dropping out." In D. Thiessen and A. Cook-Sather (eds.), *International handbook of student experience in elementary and secondary school* (pp. 635–58). Dordrecht, The Netherlands: Springer.

SooHoo, S. (1993). Students as partners in research and restructuring schools. *The Educational Forum* 57(Summer), 386–93.

Thorkildsen, T. A. (1994). Toward a fair community of scholars: Moral education as the negotiation of classroom practices. *Journal of Moral Education* 23(4), 371–85.

Villarruel, F. A., & Lerner, R. M. (eds.). (1994). *Promoting community-based programs for socialization and learning.* San Francisco: Jossey-Bass.

Villarruel, F. A., Perkins, D. F., Borden, L. M., & Keith, J. G. (2003). *Community youth development: Practice, policy, and research.* Thousand Oaks, CA: Sage.

Yonezawa, S., & Jones, M. (2007). Using students' voices to inform and evaluate secondary school reform. In D. Thiessen and A. Cook-Sather (eds.), *International handbook of student experience in elementary and secondary school* (pp. 681–710). Dordrecht, The Netherlands: Springer.

Zeldin, S. (2004). Youth as agents of adult and community development: Mapping the processes and outcomes of youth engaged in organizational governance. *Applied Developmental Science* 8(2), 75–90.

Zeldin, S., Camino, L., & Mook, C. (2005). The adoption of innovation in youth organizations: Creating the conditions for youth-adult partnerships. *Journal of Community Psychology* 33(1), 121–35.

Zeldin, S., Camino, L., Calvert, M., & Ivey, D. (2002). *Youth-adult partnerships and positive youth development: Some lessons learned from research and practice in Wisconsin.* Madison, WI: University of Wisconsin Extension.

CHAPTER 22

Coaching for Instructional Improvement

Conditions and Strategies that Matter

Barbara Neufeld and Morgaen Donaldson

Introduction[1]

Seeking to improve instructional practice and ultimately student learning, districts across the United States have embraced an old idea and given it a new application. Taking their cue from athletics, where coaches enable football and tennis players to succeed by helping them strengthen their skills, districts have adopted coaching as a model for the professional development of teachers. Coaching, they believe, will help educators to increase their ability to make informed decisions about instruction that will increase students' learning.

No one as yet has proven that coaching contributes significantly to increased student achievement. Indeed, there are scant studies of this form of professional development and how it influences teachers' practice and students' learning.[2] However, in light of current knowledge about what it takes to change a complex practice such as teaching, there are reasons to think that coaching, in combination with other professional development strategies, is a plausible way to increase teachers'/schools' instructional capacity.[3]

In this chapter we begin by reviewing the rationale for implementing coaching as a key form of teacher professional development. By focusing on coaching, however, we do not suggest that one reject all other opportunities and structures for teacher learning. There are good reasons for having large-group professional development that introduces teachers to a new concept or activity. There are great benefits to intensive summer institutes that focus on content as well as pedagogy. There are many good reasons for teachers to broaden the array of people with whom and from whom they learn. But improving teachers' learning – and, in turn, their practice and students' learning – requires professional development that is closely and explicitly tied to teachers' ongoing work and that supports them in taking what they have learned and using it well in their classrooms.

After presenting the rationale for coaching, we turn to a description of Collaborative Coaching and Learning (CCL), a model of coaching developed and implemented in the Boston Public Schools (BPS). CCL was designed to support teachers in developing new pedagogical knowledge and skill in the context of collaborative, instructionally-focused professional development. Then we describe the impact of CCL on teaching and learning in Boston Public Schools and consider the factors that affected whether and how the model was implemented in those settings. Finally, we discuss what has been learned about the strengths, demands, and limitations of this model and therefore the implications for implementation and impact in a wide range of schools.

The Rationale for Coaching

Coaching is a natural response to changes in how we define student learning and what it means for students to learn and know something. Student learning, given the demands of the twenty-first century, is defined as much more than remembering and repeating what the teacher has said; it includes the capacity to use what has been learned in traditional and novel ways, the capacity to make connections between new knowledge and old. To accomplish learning of this sort, schools must provide students with opportunities to solve problems and come to understand academic content in more complex ways than were required in the past.

This vision of student learning casts teachers as guides or coaches who facilitate learning by "posing questions, challenging students' thinking, and leading them in examining ideas and relationships."[4] These activities are considered essential because, as Cohen, McLaughlin, & Talbert (1993) write, "What students learn has to do fundamentally with how they learn it." Teachers need opportunities in which to learn to teach in ways that enable them to add coaching to their pedagogical repertoire in order to encourage students to learn and understand in more complex ways.

The implications of these ideas for schools, students, and teachers are significant. Schools and classrooms need to become places in which teachers coach and guide as well as directly instruct children, places in which students approach academic content

through assignments that involve problem-solving, critical-analysis, and higher-order-thinking skills. Classrooms need to be places in which students puzzle over problems and material as they develop meaningful understanding of content and analytical processes. Teaching that includes all these components is known as *teaching for understanding.*

Coaching: Professional Development that Supports Teaching for Understanding

To teach for understanding, most teachers need new knowledge and skill.[5] But traditional approaches to professional development are not designed in ways that are likely to help teachers learn what they need to know to teach this way. This is so because traditional forms of professional development do not rest on recent research on learning.

> *It is still widely accepted that staff learning takes place primarily at a series of workshops, at a conference or with the help of a long-term consultant. What everyone appears to want for students – a wide array of learning opportunities that engage students in experiencing, creating, and solving real problems using their own experiences, and working with others – is for some reason denied to teachers when they are learners. In the traditional view of staff development, workshops and conferences conducted outside the school count, but authentic opportunities to learn from and with colleagues inside the school do not.*[6]

During the fifteen years since Lieberman's article appeared, there have been myriad cries to change the traditional organization and content of professional development so that it better addresses teachers' learning needs as suggested by cognitive psychology.[7] Reformers continue to argue that professional development of the sort needed to help teachers teach for understanding requires both new ideas about what counts as professional development and new policies that provide the framework within which professional development can occur.

Ideas about the essential features of teacher professional development have not changed in the last fifteen years.

- It must be grounded in inquiry, reflection, and experimentation that are participant-driven.
- It must be collaborative, involving a sharing of knowledge among educators and a focus on teachers' communities of practice rather than on individual teachers.
- It must be sustained, ongoing, intensive, and supported by modeling, coaching, and the collective solving of specific problems of practice.
- It must be connected to and derived from teachers' work with their students.
- It must engage teachers in concrete tasks of teaching, assessment, observation, and reflection that illuminate the process of learning and development.
- It must be connected to other aspects of school change.[8]

Reorganizing professional development along these lines has led to great interest in coaching as a critical component of teachers' opportunities to learn because coaching, at its best, embodies the features just identified. It is grounded in inquiry, sustained, connected to and derived from teachers' work with their students, and tied explicitly to improving practice.

At this point in time, however, coaching is a promising rather than a research-proven practice.[9] As suggested earlier, it is a response to (1) the failure of more traditional stand-and-deliver professional development programs that have demonstrated scant transfer of any pedagogical improvements to classrooms and (2) the demand for teachers who can develop students' higher-level-thinking skills as well as their content knowledge.

Why are there so few studies of coaching? First, coaching is not one kind of professional development. It is not a "unitary construct, the effects of which can be studied like a vaccine or fertilizer."[10] Coaches have different roles across settings, and they may be trying to influence very different kinds of instructional practices. The

school contexts within which coaches work also differ substantially and influence their role and potential impact. Similarly, coaches' professional development varies, as does their need to shift their coaching focus to respond to pressures provided by state accountability systems. Coach selection, preparation, and supervision – processes that differ sometimes even within the same system – will influence how and how well coaches implement their roles. These realities, plus the unlikely chance of developing studies based on the random assignment of coaches, teachers, and students to treatment groups, make designing research studies that focus on "coaching" across sites extremely difficult.[11] Furthermore, for all the reasons identified earlier, it is difficult, perhaps impossible, to parse out the influence of coaching alone on student achievement.

Nonetheless, coaching models have proliferated over the last ten years, with research suggesting that coaches, for the most part, work one on one with teachers in their classrooms even if they also foster small-group professional development sessions. Most models do not include joint observations and collaborative discussions of colleagues' observed teaching. In many schools and school districts, therefore, coaching has lacked the collaborative component recommended by those who have studied professional development.

This was the case in Boston as well, where the BPS, in collaboration with the Boston Plan for Excellence (BPE), had supported on-site coaching since the 1996–7 school year. Generally speaking, coaches in Boston worked in schools once a week, helping individual teachers and providing small-group literacy professional development. Although teachers and principals valued the coaches' work, the coaches were frustrated by challenges that were associated with the organization of the role, namely, the one-day-per-week, one-teacher-at-a-time model. Overall, coaching was not reaching enough teachers, it was not contributing to teachers' collaborative opportunities to learn, and it was not reducing teacher isolation. Thus, beginning in the 2000–1 school year, the BPE redesigned its coaching model to remedy the problems identified in its initial coaching model and thereby better support improved teaching and learning.

Boston's Coaching Model[12]

The new model, Collaborative Coaching and Learning (CCL), began in late June 2001 when the Boston Plan for Excellence (BPE), Boston's public education fund, wrote a memo to a small set of Boston schools with which it had been working for five years to improve teaching and learning. The memo identified the basis on which the BPE had developed a new coaching model.

> The most important finding [from our five years of work] is that for a school to accelerate and deepen the implementation of best practices across all grades, teachers must have numerous on-site opportunities to learn together. Collaborative learning enables teachers to share best practices and to inquire into their own practices to generate new learning. We will thus be working with EP [effective practice][13] schools to create a collaborative coaching structure in each school.[14]

CCL is a coaching model that includes all the recommended elements of high-quality professional development.

Design of the Model

The BPE stated, "The aim of Collaborative Teaching and Learning (CCL) is just that – to reduce isolation and to encourage a culture in which teachers visit each other's classrooms to observe, participate in, and share best practices." With its collaborative design and literacy focus, during the 2001–2 school year, CCL supported schools in deepening teachers' knowledge and use of Readers' and Writers' Workshop.[15] To accomplish this, coaches were assigned to schools two days each week for eight weeks at a time to work with a set of teachers working at the same grade level or, in the middle and high schools, in the English language arts department. Each eight-week period was called a

cycle.[16] Each CCL cycle during that first year included the following components designed to support collaborative learning focused on Readers' and Writers' Workshop:

1. Demonstration of key teaching points done in the teachers' own classrooms – the lab sites
2. Reading of professional literature tied to implementation of Readers' and Writers' Workshop;
3. engagement with colleagues in inquiry groups around the professional reading;
4. use of observation, practice, and reflection to improve instruction.

According to the BPE's description of the model in *Straight Talk About CCL: A Guide for School Leaders*, the inquiry component of a cycle should last for sixty minutes per week and was described as follows: "Working with the literacy or math coach, a team of teachers chooses a course of study about which they need to learn more based on their student performance data. The team, which may include teachers of ELL [English language learners] and special needs students, meets weekly to discuss and reflect on readings and research related to their course of study."[17]

The classroom-based work associated with a cycle, the lab site, has three components: the preconference, a demonstration/observation lesson, and debrief. Designed to last for ninety minutes per week, "Each week's lab-site begins with a preconference in which the team reviews the purpose of the lesson and agrees on what to watch for. Then, the teachers, coach and principal/headmaster observe a demonstration lesson in a host classroom and analyze the strategy's effectiveness in a debrief. During a cycle of eight weeks, they take turns doing the demonstration, using strategies they have studied in their inquiry."

Finally, each cycle was to include a component in which "teachers set goals for their own implementation of the strategies they studied together. During the cycle and between cycles, the coach and/or members of the teacher team make visits to individual classrooms to support teachers as they make new strategies a regular part of their classroom practice." During and after the cycle, then, the coach was to help individual teachers as they implemented the strategies that were the focus of the inquiry and had been modeled in the demonstration lessons. Coach support was to be individualized in light of teachers' and students' needs.[18]

CCL was implemented at first in the 2001–2 school year in a small set of BPS, with the BPE providing technical support for the model. These schools had conditions in place likely to support the model. Principals were strong instructional leaders and had been effective in implementing other components of the district's whole-school improvement agenda. Teachers had participated in the collaborative work required by their instructional leadership teams (ILTs) and "Looking At Student Work" (LASW) groups.[19] The overall social context of their schools supported collaborative teacher work or, at the very least, was moving in that direction.

One year later, at the start of the 2002–3 school year, CCL was adopted as the literacy-focused coaching model for all of Boston's schools.

Impact of the Model

Without question, CCL fundamentally changed coaching as professional development in the BPS and led to far more collaborative learning in the district's schools than had been in place prior to its implementation.

At the end of year 1, it was clear that CCL involved more teachers in the coaching process than did the previous one-on-one model and required teachers to practice and learn in the view of their colleagues. This was often difficult for teachers who had worked privately with a coach in the past; it was particularly daunting to those who had resisted coaching or who had never participated at all. And yet teachers experienced the risks and benefits of learning collaboratively and determined, for the most part, that the risks were worth the benefits.

Some schools, by the end of the year, had more demand for CCL coaching than they could provide.[20]

In fact, the data suggest that years 1 and 2 of CCL yielded quite positive results. To begin, teachers in all seven of the Effective Practice Schools (EPS) cycles we observed identified significant advantages of the CCL model.[21] They noted that the model required them to define a focus for their learning and a strategy for getting there. The focus, combined with professional reading, the lab-site work, and the support of the coach created intentional professional reflections on teaching. Teachers reported having richer conversations in their lab-site groups than they had ever had with one another or in one-on-one conversations with coaches. Not all the teachers in our sample had positive lab-site experiences, but even those who were not satisfied with the overall CCL experience still valued the collaborative aspect of the model and its potential for improved professional development. The cycles were described as "intense," and yet teachers with all levels of experience and with more and less familiarity and comfort with Readers' and Writers' Workshop found them valuable.

In addition to the value of the lab-site design, teachers valued the fact that the coach was on-site more of the time and able to assist teachers in their own rooms as well as in the lab sites. Although teachers who participated in lab sites realized that they had not learned all that they needed to know about teaching with the workshop model, at the end of the first year of CCL, most reported being more comfortable with the model and having more confidence in their ability to use Workshop as a strong instructional strategy.

CCL provided teachers with the opportunity to practice in front of their colleagues as well as observe their colleagues' practice, which was a considerable departure from many teachers' past experiences. With some exceptions, teachers appreciated the opportunity to observe the coach as well as their colleagues' teaching.[22] Teaching in front of the coach and colleagues was a hurdle for most teachers. Initially, coaches had to nudge, prod, and assign teachers to this role. In the long run, however, no one with whom we talked regretted doing a demonstration lesson. Many teachers seemed proud that they had made their practice public and said that they would be willing to try it again. They valued the coach and colleague feedback they had received.

Although it was daunting at times to participate in the lab sites, teachers reported that they were grateful for the opportunity to engage in this learning opportunity. First, the lab sites involved authentic work, concrete activities done in classrooms, in the places where teachers work. Second, the coach was on-site with the teachers to observe the teaching and offer feedback in the form of questions and/or comments. Third, as a result of observing, teaching, and getting feedback, teachers learned Workshop strategies that they could try in their own classrooms. The lab sites were the places where all the reading – the *theory*, as teachers often called it – was turned into practices. And it is practices that teachers want to learn and improve.

After 2002, the BPS continued to implement CCL as its primary approach to the improvement of teaching and learning in English language arts. CCL cycles continued to focus on data-driven needs at the schools, and for the most part, teachers reported that (1) CCL was a positive experience, and (2) they used what they were learning in their classrooms.[23]

For example, at the end of the 2004–5 school year, the BPS identified independent reading as an area in need of improvement in twelve of the district's elementary schools that had begun using a new, federally funded reading program. In one of the elementary schools in our continuing study of CCL, teachers reported that the new program's demands left them with little time to help students choose books on an appropriate level, read them independently, and respond to their reading in journals. Based on these concerns, the coach created a CCL cycle to help teachers strengthen their skills in these areas. Teachers in the CCL saw a

clear benefit in their classrooms. First, they had a practical source of information to support implementation of independent reading. Second, CCL served as an opportunity for teachers to hear and discuss ideas that came from a number of their colleagues who were struggling with the same issues. The teachers and the coach felt that the impact of this CCL cycle could be seen directly in their classrooms. They reported that students began to know themselves as readers, choosing books independently at their level.

In a middle school in our sample, one CCL cycle focused on improving reading comprehension in nonfiction texts. The coach and the principal selected this focus because the seventh grade English language arts (ELA) teachers were implementing a nonfiction unit in their classrooms, and this was an area that state and local data indicated was challenging for students. According to the coach, principal, and teachers, this CCL cycle had a positive impact on teachers' thinking and instructional practice, as well as on student learning. From the coach's perspective, the cycle enabled most of the teachers to go deeper with work they had begun the previous school year on a topic of great importance to increasing student achievement. In the process, the coach reported, teachers were changing their thinking as well as their practice in ways likely to help them teach their students. Teachers agreed with the coach's assessment of the impact of this CCL cycle.

CCL, like any instructional improvement program, was not implemented fully as designed initially. It took several years for BPE and BPS to increase the fidelity with which each of the components was implemented and to institutionalize the coaching model in a set of schools. Furthermore, as the district increased, the number of schools in which the model was implemented beyond the initial set of effective practice schools, it became clear that certain challenges arose repeatedly. These challenges, some of which were related to the demands of the model itself, some to the organization and culture of the schools, and some to district-based factors, weakened CCL's potential to improve instruction unless principals and coaches were able to overcome them. Their success in addressing them influenced the extent and quality of CCL implementation. We turn next to a discussion of the factors that influenced schools' ability to overcome these challenges.

Factors that Matter in Implementing CCL[24]

As Boston's schools worked to implement CCL, the factors that influenced their success included (1) principal leadership, (2) coach knowledge and skill, (3) teachers' attitudes, knowledge, and skill, (4) the social context/climate of the school, (5) school organization and size, and (6) district support. We elaborate these factors and then discuss the ways in which adaptations to the model, made in response to these factors, influenced the fidelity and quality of CCL implementation. We stress fidelity and quality because, without them, teachers were unlikely to have the learning opportunities they needed to improve their practice and thereby students' achievement.

Principal Leadership

Principals played a pivotal role in the successful implementation of CCL. No matter how well CCL was designed, no matter how willing the teachers and how talented the coaches, without the principals' skill and commitment, there would have been little implementation of this model and scant impact. Principals contributed substantial time to scheduling, designing, and participating in lab sites. Some even took the risk of demonstrating a workshop strategy by teaching in front of their teachers. They supported the coaches while they reinforced the district's emphasis on Readers' and Writers' Workshop. Principals worked as part of a team with teachers, coaches, and the BPE to make CCL successful.

Implementing CCL requires principals to make decisions about (1) the order in which

cycles will be implemented, (2) the teachers who will be involved in each cycle, (3) how to provide reliable and consistent substitutes or other coverage for teachers when needed, (4) how to arrange schedules so that the participating teachers are available to do their CCL work, and (5) what role they should take in each of the cycles. Although some of these decisions can be made in collaboration with the coach or other school units, such as teams or departments, in the end it is the principal who determines how this model of coaching will be implemented in each school.

To maximize CCL's benefits to teachers and students, principals needed to think carefully about the order in which the cycles would be scheduled across the school year. Principals considered a number of factors that influenced the order and timing of the cycles in their schools. For example, if a group of teachers wanted to "launch" a new practice, it might make sense to have their CCL group early in the school year. In contrast, if a group of teachers wanted to go more deeply into a practice they had begun previously, it would not be problematic to schedule their CCL later in the school year. Or if a group of elementary teachers was required to participate in professional development in another content area, then it would make sense to schedule their CCL cycle so that it did not occur at the same time. When principals were successful in developing a schedule of CCL cycles that made sense in light of teachers' schedules and schools' goals, then it had the potential to be a meaningful and productive learning opportunity for teachers. This was not always easy.

Especially in the first few years of implementation, principals strove to ensure that the members of each CCL group would work collaboratively and therefore benefit from CCL as a joint learning process as well as from the study of specific content. Toward this end, principals sometimes shaped CCL groups so that they included, for example, a minimum number of resistant teachers. They had learned that such teachers, even if they voluntarily agreed to participate in a cycle, might be detrimental to a group's inquiry and lab-site work and create undue stress for coaches. In some cases, principals feared that such teachers' attitudes might even create a negative climate for CCL at the grade- or whole-school levels. Therefore, principals gave careful thought to whether and how to include resistant teachers in CCL groups. At the same time, principals knew that they could not simply ignore or set aside the teachers who resisted the coaching model and/or Workshop. Therefore, while they tried to ensure compatibility in CCL groups, principals looked for ways to encourage positive participation from resistant teachers.

Principals also made tactical decisions about how to allocate their own time to the CCL groups in light of a number of factors related to the group itself. Especially in the early years of the model, principals participated in groups that might not have made progress without the implicit accountability provided by the principal's attendance. Some groups included several teachers who had not had much Workshop professional development and/or were not convinced that CCL would be valuable to them. Principals participated with these CCL groups in order to ensure (1) that the groups stayed on task and (2) that they had a worthwhile experience that would enhance their knowledge and skill with CCL and Workshop strategies. Coaches in our sample were grateful for this kind of principal support and believed that the principals' presence in certain CCL groups had a positive impact on teachers' learning.

Once the cycles were under way, principals in schools with high-quality implementation met regularly as well as on an ad hoc basis with coaches to find out how the work was going, identify problems, and support the coach in implementing the CCL model.

As we have described, principals had essential roles in creating a schedule for lab sites, providing teachers with time for their CCL work, monitoring the composition and content focus of the groups, keeping track of their progress, and stepping in when help

was needed.[25] Principals were engaged with CCL as facilitators, advisors, and, when necessary, "nudgers" who could persuade teachers to take a chance and host a lab site. They helped to establish the school culture in which CCL could flourish. CCL did not thrive without such principal supports.

These efforts on the part of principals whose schools demonstrate high-quality CCL implementation reflect a deep understanding about how to use their schools' available resources to meet their long-term goals. The level of thoughtful, detailed planning that went into each cycle was critical for maximizing teachers' opportunities to learn from the coach and from each other.

Coach Knowledge and Skill[26]

Coaches had responsibility for making CCL work in their school contexts. To succeed, they needed principal support, sufficient time, and an appropriate group of teachers with whom to work. They also had to know how to coach and work within the structure of the model. What did this entail?

Coaching, like teaching, is not a routine activity. It must be focused on instructional goals and planned, but it also must be responsive to the needs of the learners and the exigencies of specific classroom situations. Coaches need a repertoire of interpersonal as well as technical coaching skills if they are to succeed in using CCL (or any coaching model) to advantage. They must know how to gain and sustain the trust of the teachers and the principals with whom they work, including those who demonstrate some resistance to lab sites and/or individual coaching. They need to be fully versed in all aspects of the reform they are helping teachers to implement. If they do not know what high-quality instruction looks like, they will be poorly situated to coach teachers toward it. Teachers simply will not find their coaches credible. And coaches need to understand the design and rationale for CCL and how each of its components can be used to increase teachers' knowledge and skill with the instructional reform in order to implement the model with fidelity.

More specifically, given the design of CCL, coaches need to know how to use school data to formulate an inquiry into the focus area of the cycle. If teachers need to strengthen their ability to teach comprehension or inference skills, coaches must know which articles or other resources to share with teachers to increase their knowledge. And, having provided the resources, they must know how to facilitate a research-based conversation with teachers.

With respect to the lab site, coaches need to understand the implications of having different teachers demonstrate a lesson at different points in the cycle. They must know how much support demonstrating teachers need prior to the demonstration. Coaches, in other words, need to be able to assess the teachers' instructional skill in the cycle and make informed judgments about how to proceed. In this regard, coaches also need to know how to deal with resistant as well as reluctant participants.

Coaches also needed to provide teachers with specific directions regarding how the demonstration relates to the cycle's focus and what teachers should notice while observing. When the coach did not guide the teachers in what to attend to in observing the demonstration lesson or connect the lesson to the CCL cycle's larger focus, the ensuing debriefs were too general and could not lead to deep teacher learning.

One of the most difficult tasks facing a CCL coach is facilitating high-quality debriefs. Coaches needed to help teachers learn to provide constructive feedback to one another in contexts when the observed lesson was excellent or when it might have missed the mark or raised questions. Without this ability, there will be scant learning from the lab-site component of the model. Yet the prevailing culture in schools presses against teachers asking "hard" questions of one another. Indeed, we found that even coaches had difficulty raising issues they thought needed attention. Coaching is supposed to be supportive; hard questions and critical feedback can make it feel negative and evaluative. For many of the coaches, facilitating debriefing discussions proved to be a problematic and difficult departure from their previous coaching work.

During debriefs in the first two years of CCL, teachers tended to praise the demonstrations implemented by their colleagues regardless of the quality of the observed instruction. Coaches withheld critical comments, fearing that they would antagonize teachers and lose their trust. As a result, coaches realized that they were unable to push teachers to deeper levels of reflection about their teaching. In subsequent years, many coaches continued to report that they still found it difficult to provide thought-provoking feedback to teachers during debriefs because they feared alienating teachers by appearing to be evaluating their work.

School-level and teachers' conceptions of their roles also can bring challenges to coaches. For example, when supporting implementation of Readers' and Writers' Workshop in elementary schools, coaches worked with teachers who expected to be teaching reading and writing. In contrast, when supporting the implementation of Readers' Workshop in high schools, coaches worked with English teachers who had never considered themselves reading teachers. Encouraging high school teachers to add the teaching of reading to their curriculum could be challenging for coaches and for teachers. Coaching teachers to include reading across the curriculum, a popular strategy in low-achieving middle and high schools, similarly posed challenges for teachers and coaches who were not familiar with teaching reading in a range of content areas, for example, science and mathematics. Some CCL cycles included multiple-content-area teachers. Forging a collaborative group across content areas required new knowledge and skill for coaches. Regardless of school level, providing skillful coaching for teachers who worked with students who had special needs and/or those who taught English language learners similarly required coaches to have learned how to support a wide range of teachers and their diverse students.[27]

Coaches, in light of the demands of their job, require specialized knowledge and skill that they do not always have when they first take on this new role. To gain this knowledge, coaches, like their teacher counterparts, need professional development that is ongoing, addresses their specific learning needs, and responds to the wide range of teachers with whom and conditions in which they work. Professional development therefore was a key factor in creating coaches who had the capacity to support teachers in changing their practice using the structure provided by CCL. Coaches in Boston participated in targeted professional development for a full day twice each month. They had a forum thereby in which to share "best CCL practices" with their colleagues, learn new strategies, and be coached to improve their own practice.

Teachers' Attitudes, Knowledge, and Skill

Teachers' attitudes, knowledge, and skill played a major role in the implementation of CCL cycles we observed. Teachers' attitudes toward CCL and Readers' and Writers' Workshop varied. Although most teachers we interviewed participated fully in their CCL cycle, there were teachers who refused. A few refused because they objected to the Workshop approach; they did not think this strategy was the way to help their children read effectively. In other cases, as the model was scaled up to all the district's schools, a substantial minority of teachers remained unwilling to demonstrate their instruction in front of colleagues. In fact, teacher resistance led to a successful effort by the Boston Teachers' Union to protect teachers' right to refuse the demonstration. Although some teachers who were initially unwilling to host a lab site were persuaded to take on this role subsequently, many of them reported that demonstrating was not a valuable experience. Strong resistance to demonstrating continued in some lab sites despite the coaches' and principals' best efforts to encourage teachers to participate. Resistance seriously impeded coaches' ability to implement CCL as it was designed.

Teacher knowledge and skill also affected the degree to which CCL was implemented successfully. When there were very few teachers in a lab-site group who felt comfortable with their instruction and confident about demonstrating in front of their peers, it was sometimes difficult for the lab-site group to make real progress using the CCL model. Lab-site groups needed at least a few teachers who were knowledgeable and bold enough to help spearhead the work that must take place if this approach to professional development is to succeed. They needed the intellectual capital and positive example that such teachers provided. However, relying on only one knowledgeable and willing participant to do multiple demonstration lessons, a strategy attempted in a few schools, proved an unproductive strategy that often led to teacher burnout with respect to further participation in CCL.

Teacher efficacy also shaped the implementation of CCL through the quality of instruction. Some CCL groups included new teachers who were enthusiastic about the model but struggled to implement the strategies the group had devised because of their novice teacher challenges. In particular, teachers who struggled with classroom management and basic instructional techniques focused on surmounting these challenges, leaving little room for experimenting with new Workshop strategies. It is important to note, however, that although this sometimes meant that CCL was not implemented as planned, it likely did play an important role in setting these teachers on the path to improvement.

The Social Context/Social Climate of the School

The Effective Practice Schools in which CCL was first attempted had, for the most part, collaborative, instructionally-focused contexts and cultures. Although these schools still might have a grade-level team or department that had not yet coalesced, they could implement CCL successfully by focusing early cycles on units that had already developed collaborative cultures. Principal leadership in such schools supported CCL implementation.

CCL implementation, by contrast, was weak or nonexistent in schools that lacked collaborative, instructionally-focused contexts and cultures. Our data led us to conclude that CCL's fate was strongly linked to these features of schools' social contexts. CCL might become part of a range of efforts designed to establish a more supportive school culture, but the coaching model by itself did not have the power to overcome strong countervailing social contexts. In our view, this finding does not minimize the value of CCL as a coaching model. Rather, it reminds us that most instructional programs cannot be used to solve noninstructional problems.

Collaborative school cultures are characterized by constructive professional relationships among teachers and between teachers and administrators. Educators within a school do not need to be personal friends, but they need to be able to keep the ultimate goal, student learning, in mind and work together for the good of the students. We found that teachers with unresolved disputes with principals or colleagues were likely to bring "hard feelings" to their CCL work. This tended to interfere with the development of trust that must accompany CCL if teachers are going to demonstrate instructional strategies in front of one another.

The negative feelings that surface among members of a CCL can make it almost impossible for coaches to do their work. In such contexts, coaches reported that they spent considerable time mediating disputes between teachers and between teachers and their principals at the expense of time spent on improving instruction. When the disputes involved long-standing teacher-principal interaction patterns, coaches reported that they generally were unsuccessful in (1) resolving the underlying issues, (2) changing the social context of the school, and therefore, (3) implementing CCL.

School Organization and Size

Another key factor contributing to CCL implementation was school organization and size. Very small schools, regardless of level, and high schools, whether large or small, presented particular challenges to

implementing CCL. These challenges were related to decisions about how to constitute and schedule CCL groups.

Very small elementary schools faced challenges if they had only one teacher at each grade level; very small high schools faced the same challenges when they had only one English teacher per grade. At the elementary level, CCLs sometimes were organized with grade K–3 teachers and 4–6 teachers, but the variation in children's reading levels and the content of the curriculum across multiple grades reduced the impact of CCL as professional development. Small high schools developed cross-content-area CCL cycles that focused on reading strategies across the curriculum in response to the challenges posed by size. These approaches seemed to become more successful over time.

At the middle school level, schools that were organized with teams of teachers faced some challenges. The principal could organize CCL with grade-level English language arts teachers from multiple teams or with the existing multidisciplinary teams that were then asked to focus on reading across the curriculum. Because middle schools often scheduled time for teams to meet, it was usually easier for principals to find time for multidisciplinary team-based CCL than it was to find CCL time for English teachers across teams.

High schools posed challenges when they were large owing to the need for same-grade/same-subject teachers to have common planning periods in which teachers could meet in CCL groups. The "small learning community (SLC) organization" of some high schools presented principals with the same scheduling challenges found in middle schools.[28] One SLC-organized high school used creative scheduling, videotaping of teachers' demonstration lessons, and after-school CCL professional development to implement a set of productive CCL cycles.[29]

District Support

Although it may seem to go without saying that districts must support the implementation of CCL (or any coaching model), given the array of changing policies that can impinge on a district from states and the federal government, we think it is worth noting what a district, in this case the BPS, needed to do in order to support CCL implementation so that it maximized teachers' and thereby students' opportunities to learn.

First, coaching is an expensive approach to professional development, and its feasibility depended in large part on a Boston's economic status. For a number of years, grant funds supported Boston's intensive coaching effort. However, even prior to the current national recession, the BPS had faced budget cuts that reduced overall financial support for coaching. The result was somewhat of a triage system in which most schools had to select a half-time literacy or a half-time mathematics coach. While the need for cost cutting was understandable, it reduced the potential impact of the professional development, leaving multiple schools without any coaching support for literacy.[30]

Second, a district's response to a state's accountability system can undermine the quality of CCL. If a school is not meeting its target for growth in student achievement, a district can pressure a principal to have the coach focus teachers' professional development on the knowledge and skill tested and the form of test questions rather than on an overall improvement of reading instruction.[31] When this happened in the BPS, as it did in one high school included in our study of high school reform, the result was CCL cycles that ran counter to the model's emphasis on teacher inquiry, including teachers' authority to choose a focus based on their analysis of data. As such, it led to decreased teacher buy-in and to perversion of the district's instructional goals.

Third, the BPS needed to ensure that principals understood the coaching model and encouraged its effective implementation in their schools. To do this, the district provided them with professional development in CCL and in Readers' and Writers' Workshop. Principals, for the most part, understood the model. However, given school size, school climate, and principals' own preferences for teacher professional development, they varied in the extent to which they fully supported its implementation.

In some schools, when principals found themselves unable to put the requisite conditions in place so that CCL could happen, district administrators were not on hand to help them. The BPS varied considerably in its efforts to assist principals who found it challenging to implement CCL. In addition, when principals did not support the coaching model, the district did not always determine whether principals were correct in rejecting the model for their schools.[32] In theory, if the principals were correct, then the district needed to support the principals in developing an alternative strategy for teachers' professional development. If, however, the principal was deemed to be incorrect, then the district needed to hold the principal accountable for implementing CCL. At times, the BPS seemed to adopt a laissez-faire approach to implementing CCL, thereby undermining the model they professed to support.

Fourth, the district needed to make sure that the process by which coaches were selected, prepared for their roles, and assigned to schools was rigorous, fair, and responsive to the schools' needs. To this end, a highly skilled administrator was given responsibility for these functions. Without attending to these processes, coaches might not have the skills, credibility, and/or support they needed to do their work well.[33] In the BPS, principals and teachers rarely remarked negatively about their literacy coaches.

Adaptations to CCL

As noted earlier, we found that schools often made changes to the CCL cycle while implementing it. Adaptations were based on a combination of coaches' and principals' informed professional judgment in light of challenges at their schools. Some adaptations proved essential for furthering the larger goal of improving teachers' instruction and students' learning opportunities. Others proved "lethal," seriously undermining the progress of CCL implementation and thereby thwarting improvements in teachers' practice.

When adaptations occurred, cycles rarely excluded components of the model. However, adaptations led to variations in the *extent* to which cycles demonstrated specific high-functioning characteristics. For example:

- Some coaches reduced the amount of professional reading they discussed with teachers and focused more on looking at student work and discussing the teachers' instruction. Several coaches did not assign professional reading outside the CCL sessions, although the BPS has concluded that CCL is more likely to be highly functioning when teachers voluntarily read outside sessions.

- None of the sites in the study completed in February 2006 had more than four demonstration lessons in the eight-week cycle, and two CCL cycles included only three.[34] Furthermore, there were a number of ways in which the demonstration aspect of these CCL cycles was not likely to maximize teacher learning. *First*, in several sites, teachers were not deeply involved in planning demonstration lessons. Instead coaches planned them. *Second*, poor substitute coverage sometimes made attendance at demonstrations inconsistent. *Third*, at one school the coach planned and implemented all the demonstration lessons, although the BPS has found that demos that are planned collaboratively and conducted at least some of the time by teachers characterized high-functioning CCL cycles

- Cycles varied considerably in the amount of individual coach follow-up that was available to teachers. At the extremes, one school created a schedule of cycles that allowed a great deal of individual coaching, whereas another had a schedule that impeded individual follow-up from the coach.

Adaptations varied in the extent to which they strengthened or weakened CCL in light of its conceptual underpinnings, formal design, and goals. Thus, while some modifications/adaptations were consistent with the CCL model, others contradicted recommendations by the BPS and BPE and appeared to lead to weaker implementation of the cycles.

Implications

In studying CCL over a period of years and identifying its strengths as well as its challenges for schools, we remain convinced that the model has the potential to increase the quality of teachers' pedagogy. We think CCL can do this (1) by focusing teachers and their coaches on implementing a coherent, evidence-based approach to reading and writing instruction whether or not it is Readers' and Writers' Workshop and (2) by creating and sustaining a professional, instructionally-focused learning community within schools. Nonetheless, as we have noted, there are challenges to implementing the model. Schools varied in their capacity to use CCL as it was designed and to make adaptations that maintained its strengths while increasing its feasibility for their settings.

A number of factors influenced how CCL was implemented in Boston's schools. These included principals' understanding of the model, as well as their support for it; coaches' knowledge and skill; teachers' attitudes and aptitudes; school culture, organization, and size; and district support. When these factors worked in concert with the structures and processes of CCL, the model could be well implemented. When one or more factors stymied principals, coaches, or teachers, the model could not be implemented as intended. As a result, they sought ways to modify it in light of conditions at the schools and the goal of instructional improvement. Some adaptations, as we have noted, were more in line with CCL's underlying theory of professional development than were others.

Given these findings about CCL, as well as the findings from implementation studies of other instructional improvement programs that include coaching, what are the questions districts or schools need to ask themselves if they want to include CCL or coaching more broadly defined in their repertoire of professional development options?[35]

- *Do we know what we want the coaching program to achieve?* With respect to literacy, the BPS was clear that it was using CCL to support the implementation of Readers' and Writers' Workshop. This clarity provided parameters for the coaches' work and indicators of desired teacher practices.
- *Do principals have the capacity and will to support CCL?* Principals played a critical role in CCL implementation. They needed to attend to the logistical necessities of CCL as well as shaping a culture conducive to collective inquiry and deprivatized instructional practice. Not all principals had the capacity to think creatively about time and resources, and even fewer knew how to develop positive collaborative school cultures. Yet CCL's success depended on the skill and commitment of school leaders.
- *Will we be able to hire and train a knowledgeable and skillful group of coaches?* How will we allocate them to schools for maximum impact? Assuming that competent principal leadership is in place, CCL's success depends on the knowledge and skill of coaches. Therefore, districts that wish to transform teaching and learning through CCL must think carefully about who will fill coaching positions, how they will be trained, who will train them, and how they will be deployed to make the largest impact on classrooms.
- *Do the schools in which we want to implement the model have an adult culture that will facilitate teachers demonstrating their teaching in front of each other?* If the answer is "No," what will we need to do to foster such a culture? The BPE and BPS worked diligently to convince teachers that they could not learn to teach using a new pedagogy without practicing and that it would be far more beneficial to practice

in the company of others. Nonetheless, in the early years, many teachers were extremely fearful about demonstrating their teaching. CCL, a very different form of professional development than traditional workshops, challenged the traditional private culture of teaching.

- *Do the schools in which we want to implement the model have a culture and climate that support collaborative practice – or at least does not work against it?* This is a very different question from the one we just posed. With this question, we remind readers that CCL by itself cannot turn around a negative school culture. It can help to develop a collaborative culture in a school that has a positive but private teacher culture. It is, however, the wrong intervention for a school in which teachers are antagonistic to one another and/or to the principal.[36]
- *Do we have/do we want to develop schools in which teachers have a significant voice in their own professional development?* In order for CCL to become an effective, sustainable in-house professional development, teachers must develop ownership of and responsibility for their learning and for that of their colleagues. This requires a commitment on the part of district and school leaders to allow teachers to make instructional decisions in response to their analysis and interpretation of the data. Coaches have a role in shaping teachers' analyses, to be sure, but CCL's success rested on teachers' authentic decision making. If school and district leaders are reluctant to give teachers this authority, CCL will not flourish.
- *How will the district office support the coaching model so that it is well-enough implemented to provide teachers with genuine opportunities to significantly and meaningfully improve their teaching?* CCL has great potential, but when schools adapt it in ways that minimize teachers opportunities to learn by (1) eliminating or giving short shrift to the inquiry component, (2) reducing the time spent on practicing new teaching strategies, (3) failing to skillfully debrief the observed teaching,

and/or (4) reducing the time available for one-on-one follow-up coaching, then the model cannot lead to improved teaching and thereby to improved student learning. The BPS, like many other districts, appeared to lack the will and capacity to make some of the structural and functional changes in its way of management that were needed to increase the quality with which CCL was implemented at the high schools in particular.[37] Without the willingness and capacity to make requisite changes, however, CCL and other coaching models will fail to reach their potential because, in effect, they will not be implemented.[38]

Despite the urgency of improving teaching and learning, the reality is that it takes several years for teachers to master what are fundamentally new and different instructional strategies, even when those teachers are eager to implement what they are learning and even when they are supported by strong coaches.[39] It is important to keep in mind the challenge of changing instructional practices so as to give the intervention time to have an impact. By letting urgency lead to rushing, districts and schools can put impossible expectations and demands on teachers and principals to raise instructional quality in a short time and to conclude, too soon, that the coaching program has failed.

Finally, is CCL worth the effort? Our detailed discussion of the factors that matter in implementing CCL may lead some to throw up their hands and declare that coaching cannot be worth this level of effort. But we believe that CCL as a model of coaching, although difficult to implement, is worth trying.

First, most of the implementation issues and challenges we have raised accompany any professional development strategy. If district and school-level administrators are not knowledgeable about what they ask schools to do, they cannot support implementation. If the district neither supports nor holds principals and others accountable, no program will be implemented effectively. If principals lack the knowledge, skill, and

commitment to a professional development strategy, then they likely will not give it the support it needs. And although some of the challenges associated with CCL may be more daunting than those associated with the implementation of other instructional reforms, there is no school reform program that is challenge-free.

Second, coaching shows great promise for changing the professional culture in which teachers work. Teaching has been described as an isolated profession in which individuals work in private. CCL aims explicitly to change this culture. There is reason to think that teachers working collaboratively to improve their practice over time and with the support of a knowledgeable coach can accomplish much more than has been accomplished to date with professional development that sustains isolated practice.

Finally, the goal of improving teaching is improved student learning. Coaching, organized as CCL, holds out the promise of achieving this goal by fundamentally reforming teaching as a culture as well as a skilled practice. If changes to instruction are to be deep and lasting, this cultural reform is likely essential.

Appendix A

Components of a High-Functioning CCL (Developed by the BPS)

- All components of CCL are implemented. When modifications are necessary, they are thoughtfully planned.
- A year-long schedule for CCL is in place at the site.
- Time allotted: At least forty-five minutes for inquiry and lab/debrief.
- Coverage for teachers for lab is in place.
- Readings presented to course of study participants are timely and related to the focus of the cycle.
- Scope of the cycle is thoughtfully planned.
- Active participation by group members occurs.
- Teachers voluntarily read outside of CCL time.

- Data are used to inform course of study.
- Inquiry drives the lab demonstrations.
- Demonstration lessons are planned collaboratively.
- Lessons are based on research evidence from professional texts.
- Coach is knowledgeable about CCL content and theory.
- One-on-one visits are scheduled with teachers in the course of study.
- Coach has an off-cycle plan.
- Coach sets expectations for classroom implementation of learning.
- Coach uses skillful facilitation to engage all participants and to keep the group focused.
- Coach regularly documents their work through logs and the CCL binder.
- Principals are aware of the course of study and the participants.
- Administrators actively participate in at least one cycle.
- Principal actively supports teachers' implementation through classroom observations of CCL participants.
- Assessments and samples of student work are used as evidence of student learning.
- Teacher and student goals are set at the start of the course of study and are revisited throughout the cycle.
- Participants reflect on their learning at the end of the cycle and create a plan for continuing their learning when they are off-cycle.

Notes

1. The introduction to this chapter is adapted from Neufeld, B., & Roper, D., Coaching: A strategy for developing instructional capacity, promises, and practicalities. The Aspen Institute Program on Education and the Annenberg Institute for School Reform, June 2003. Available at www.annenberginstitute.org.
2. Walpole, S., & McKenna, M. C. (2009). Everything you've always wanted to know about literacy coaching but were afraid to ask: A review of policy and research. In K. M. Leander, D. W. Rowe, D. K. Dickinson, R. T. Jimenez, M. K. Hundley, and V. J. Risko (eds.), Fifty-ninth yearbook of the National Reading Conference (pp. 23–33). Milwaukee, WI: NRC; Walpole, S., & Blamey, K. L.(2008). Elementary literacy coaches: The reality of dual roles. The Reading Teacher 62(3), 222–31.
3. Annenberg Institute for School Reform (2004). Professional development strategies that improve instruction: Instructional coaching. Providence, RI: AISR.
4. Cohen, D. K., McLaughlin, M. W., & Talbert, J. E. (eds.) (1993). Teaching for understanding: Challenges for policy and practice. San Francisco: Jossey-Bass.
5. See Windschitl, M. (2002). Framing constructivism in practice as the negotiation of dilemmas: An analysis of the conceptual, pedagogical, cultural, and political challenges facing teachers. Review of Educational Research 72(2), 131–75, for a detailed analysis of the demands of this kind of teaching.
6. Lieberman, A. (1995). Practices that support teacher development: Transforming conceptions of professional learning. Phi Delta Kappan 76(8), 591.
7. Annenberg Institute for School Reform. (2004). Professional development strategies that improve instruction: Instructional coaching. Providence, RI: AISR.
8. This list (with changes from the original order) is from Darling, Hammond, & McLaughlin (1995). See also Miller, L. (1995). The old model of staff development survives in a world where everything else has changed. The Harvard Education Letter 11(1), 1–3; Garet, M. S., Porter, A. C., Desimone, L., Birman, B. F., & Yoon, K. S. (2001). What makes professional development effective? Results from a national sample of teachers. American Educational Research Journal 38, 915–46; and Barr, K., Simmons, B., & Zarrow, J. (2003). School coaching in context: A case study in capacity building. Paper presented at the American Educational Research Association Annual Meeting, Chicago.
9. Joyce, B., & Showers, B. (2002) Student achievement through staff development. Association for Supervision and Curriculum Development, Alexandria, VA; Poglinco, S., Bach, A., Hovde, K., Rosenblum, S., Saunders, M., & Supovitz, J. (2003). The heart of the matter: The coaching model in America's choice schools. Philadelphia: Consortium for Public Policy Research in Education, University of Pennsylvania.
10. See Walpole and McKenna (2009, footnote 2). See also Poglinco et al. (2003) for a discussion

of variation in coaches' roles even within one reform model, in this case, America's Choice.

11. See Walpole and McKenna (2009, footnote 2) for a synthesis of recent research on coaching plus an elaboration of themes related to the design of coaching models and factors that influence how they are implemented.

12. This description of the evolution of CCL is adapted from Donaldson, M., & Neufeld, B. (2006). Collaborative Coaching and Learning in literacy: implementation at four Boston public schools. Available at www.edmatters. org.

13. The Effective Practice Schools were 26 Boston public schools that had demonstrated (a) high levels of implementation of some of the essentials of whole-school improvement and (b) strong principal leadership for instruction. These schools were recognized for their accomplishments in a public ceremony at the end of the 2000–1 school year. They had in place conditions conducive to taking the step of testing a more collaborative, focused, and intense approach to coaching.

14. BPE memo sent to Principals-Headmasters, Effective Practice Schools, June 28, 2001. This memo was cosigned by Dr. Thomas Payzant, Superintendent of Schools.

15. Workshop is a set of strategies that reflect the fact that students must actively create understanding and that instructional strategies should be designed to enable students who do this work. As a result, Workshop (a) has a structure: minilesson, independent work, and sharing; (b) provides opportunities for teachers to work directly with every student in the class through conferencing and small-group target instruction; (c) gives students the opportunity to read, write, talk, think, and construct their knowledge as part of the instructional process; and (d) gives students a "voice" in a community of learners.

16. In the first year, cycles lasted for six weeks. However, coaches and teachers requested a longer time period for their work, and the cycles were lengthened to eight weeks beginning in the second year of implementation.

17. *Straight Talk* is available at www.bpe.org.

18. A very small number of schools selected mathematics as their area of instructional focus and therefore had math rather than literacy coaches. This chapter focuses on CCL as it was used in literacy.

19. ILTs are comprised of teacher and administrator representative who are charged with identifying an instructional focus for the school and selecting ways to address that focus through professional development and other activities. ILT meeting agendas are shaped by teachers' and administrators' concerns and questions with respect to the school's instructional focus. LASW groups are developed as grade-level or team groups and are intended to help teachers use their students' work to make informed decisions about their instruction. Meetings are structured by the use of a protocol that directs teachers' attention to (a) the students' work (rather than the students themselves), (b) the standards to be addressed by the assignment, (c) the quality of the students' work considered against a rubric reflecting those standards, and (d) what needs to happen next in the classroom if the work is to improve.

20. Neufeld. B., & Roper, D. (2002). Off to a good start: Year 1 of Collaborative Coaching and Learning in the Effective Practice Schools. Available at www.edmatters.org.

21. *Ibid.*; and Neufeld, B., & Roper, D. (July 2003). Year 2 of Collaborative Coaching and Learning in the Effective Practice Schools: Expanding the work. Available at www. edmatters.org.

22. In a few lab sites, the demonstrations were of poor teaching quality, and teachers who observed them did not value spending their time in this way. We discuss this issue later in the chapter.

23. Donaldson, M., & Neufeld, B. (2006). Collaborative Coaching and Learning in literacy: Implementation at four Boston public schools. Available at www.edmatters.org.

24. The findings in this section are based on a series of evaluation studies conducted by Education Matters over a five-year period that began in the 2001–2 school year and concluded in the 2005–6 school year. Some of the studies focused primarily on CCL. Others, for example, Education Matters' study of high school reform, included CCL as one aspect of the larger high school reform program.

25. Principals needed to be able to "cover" teachers' classes when they were participating in CCL. This required the use of substitutes or other available personnel if teachers' students were not scheduled to be with other teachers for art or music, for example, in elementary schools. Coverage issues in middle and high schools could be quite complicated despite the departmentalized organization of those schools.

26. See Borman, J., & Feber, S., (2006). *Instructional coaching: Key themes from the literature* (pp. 9–11). Providence, RI: The Education Alliance: Brown University, for a review focused on what coaches need to know and approaches to their professional development; see also Neufeld & Roper (2003).

27. Education Matters' studies of the development of the professional developer role in the San Diego city schools first led us to understand the critical need for coach professional development. See Neufeld, B., Kuwahara, Y., & Swanson, J. (2000). Update report: Implementing standards-based reform in San Diego city schools; and Neufeld, B. (2000). Implementing standards-based reform in San Diego city schools: Update report, August 22, 2000. For additional detail on coach professional development needs, see Neufeld & Roper (2002, 2003). All reports are available at www.edmatters.org.

28. Neufeld, B., & Levy, A. (2005). High school renewal in the Boston public schools: Focus on organization and leadership. Available at www.edmatters.org.

29. See Donaldson, M. (2006). Launching independent reading at the secondary level: An English CCL at Morrison High School. In Donaldson & Neufeld (2006).

30. Neufeld, B. (2007). Instructional improvement in the Boston public schools: The limits of focus and stability. In *A decade of urban school reform: Persistence and progress in the Boston public schools.* Cambridge, MA: Harvard University Press.

31. We have this shift in the emphasis of coaching in Boston and in other states. For an example from Kentucky, see Kannapel, P. J., & Moore, B. D. (2009). Adolescent Literacy Coaching Project (ALCP) year 3 evaluation report: A report prepared for the Collaborative Center for Literacy Development (CCLD). Available at http://www.kentuckyliteracy.org/.

32. Some high school principals, called *headmasters* in Boston, rejected CCL because small school size made it virtually impossible for them to create and schedule CCL cycles with appropriate groups of same-subject teachers, and cross-content groups of teachers were not deemed to be effective.

33. See Neufeld & Roper (2003) for additional thoughts about the role of school districts in supporting coaching.

34. This is a significant finding in light of the fact that the schools for this study were chosen by the district because they were considered to be high implementers.

35. We have not included any estimates of the cost of coaching in this chapter, although we noted that it was expensive. It goes without saying that districts/schools need sufficient funding for multiple years to implement a strong coaching program.

36. Research presented at the Annual Meeting of the American Educational Research Association, May 2010, identified school culture as one of the factors correlated with better implementation of instructional coaching. See Coaching of teachers linked to stronger gains in reading. *Education Week* 29(31), 6–7, May 12, 2010.

37. Hubbard, L. (2010). Research to practice: A case study of Boston public schools, Boston Plan for Excellence, and Education Matters. In C. E. Coburn and M. K. Stein (eds.), *Research and practice in education: Building alliances, bridging the divide.* New York: Roman & Littlefield.

38. See Viadero (2010) for initial results of a recent study of coaching and the factors that were associated with improving student's reading.

39. Garet, M. S., Porter, A. C., Desimone, L., Birman, B. F., & Yoon, K. S. (2001). What makes professional development effective? Results from a national sample of teachers. *American Educational Research Journal* 38, 915–46.

References

Annenberg Institute for School Reform (2004). *Professional development strategies that improve instruction: Instructional coaching.* Providence, RI: AISR.

Barr, K., Simmons, B., & Zarrow, J. (2003). School coaching in context: A case study in capacity building. Paper presented at the American Educational Research Association Annual Meeting, Chicago.

Birman, B. F., & Yoon, K. S. (2001). What makes professional development effective? Results from a national sample of teachers. *American Educational Research Journal* 38, 915–46.

Borman, J., & Feber, S., (2006) *Instructional coaching: Key themes from the literature.* Providence, RI: Education Alliance, Brown University.

Coburn, C. E., & Stein, M. K. (2010). *Research and practice in education: Building alliances, bridging the divide.* New York: Roman & Littlefield.

Cohen, D. K., McLaughlin, M. W., & Talbert, J. E. (eds.) (1993). *Teaching for understanding: Challenges for policy and practice.* San Francisco: Jossey-Bass.

Darling-Hammond, L., & McLaughlin, M. W. (1995). Policies that support professional development in an era of reform. Phi Delta Kappan 76(8), 642–50.

Donaldson, M. (2006). Launching independent reading at the secondary level: An English CCL at Morrison High School. In Donaldson, M., and Neufeld, B. (eds.), *Collaborative coaching and learning in literacy: Implementation at four Boston public schools.* Available at www.edmatters.org.

Donaldson, M., & Neufeld, B. (2006). Collaborative coaching and learning in literacy: Implementation at four Boston public schools. Available at www.edmatters.org.

Garet, M. S., Porter, A. C., Desimone, L., Birman, B. F., & Yoon, K. S. (2001). What makes professional development effective? Results from a national sample of teachers. *American Educational Research Journal* 38, 915–46.

Joyce, B., & Showers, B. (2002). *Student achievement through staff development.* Alexandria, VA: Association for Supervision and Curriculum Development.

Kannapel, P. J., & Moore, B. D. (2009). Adolescent Literacy Coaching Project (ALCP) year 3 evaluation report. A report prepared for the Collaborative Center for Literacy Development (CCLD). Available at http://www.kentuckyliteracy.org/.

Lieberman, A. (1995). Practices that support teacher development: Transforming conceptions of professional learning. *Phi Delta Kappan* 76(8), 591.

Miller, L. (1995). The old model of staff development survives in a world where everything else has changed. *The Harvard Education Letter* 11(1), 1–3

Neufeld, B. (2007). Instructional improvement in the Boston public schools: The limits of focus and stability. In *A decade of urban school reform: Persistence and progress in the Boston public schools.* Cambridge, MA: Harvard University Press.

Neufeld, B. (2000). Implementing standards-based reform in San Diego city schools: Update report. Available at www.edmatters.org.

Neufeld, B., & Levy, A. (2005). High school renewal in the Boston public schools: Focus on organization and leadership. Available at www.edmatters.org.

Neufeld, B., & Roper, D. (2003a). Year 2 of collaborative coaching and learning in the effective practice schools: Expanding the work. Available at www.edmatters.org.

Neufeld, B., and Roper, D. (2003b). Coaching: A strategy for developing instructional capacity, promises, & practicalities. Aspen Institute Program on Education and the Annenberg Institute for School Reform, June. Available at www.annenberginstitute.org.

Neufeld. B., & Roper, D. (2002). Off to a good start: Year 1 of collaborative coaching and learning in the effective practice schools. Available at www.edmatters.org.

Neufeld, B., Kuwahara, Y., & Swanson, J. (2000). Update report: Implementing standards-based reform in San Diego city schools. Available at www.edmatters.org.

Poglinco, S., Bach, A., Hovde, K., Rosenblum, S. L., Saunders, M., & Supovitz, J. (2003). *The heart of the matter: The coaching model in America's choice schools.* Philadelphia: Consortium for Public Policy Research in Education, University of Pennsylvania.

Viadero, D. (2010). Coaching of teachers linked to stronger gains in reading. *Education Week* 29(31), 6–7.

Walpole, S., & Blamey, K. L. (2008), Elementary literacy coaches: The reality of dual roles. *The Reading Teacher* 62(3), 222–31.

Walpole, S., & McKenna, M. C. (2009), Everything you've always wanted to know about literacy Coaching but were afraid to ask: A review of policy and research. In K. M. Leander, D. W. Rowe, D. K. Dickinson, R. T. Jimenez, M. K. Hundley, and V. J. Risko (eds.), *Fifty-ninth yearbook of the National Reading Conference* (pp. 23–33). Milwaukee: NRC.

Windschitl, M. (2002). Framing constructivism in practice as the negotiation of dilemmas: An analysis of the conceptual, pedagogical, cultural, and political challenges facing teachers. *Review of Educational Research* 72(2), 131–75.

CHAPTER 23

The Use of Evidence-Based Programs and Quality Child Care

Anne Michelle Daniels

Introduction

The use of evidence-based practices or programs has been completed in several different professional fields (Dunst, Trivette, & Cutspec, 2002). Although this includes social fields such as social services (Gambrill, 1999) and education (National Research Council, 2002), there is some question as to what exactly this means for the researcher, practitioner, and policymaker. One reason for this confusion is that in a social field such as child care, questions of what an evidence-based program looks like and how it becomes dignified as an evidence-based program are unanswered. These questions are hard to answer because evidence-based practices have not been well defined in the literature (Dunst, Trivette, & Cutspec, 2002). Another reason may be that the reality of research to practice is often a very wide fissure. A rationale for this problem is that research is not often written in a user-friendly format for practitioners such as child care providers (Snap Shot, 2006). Another explanation is the type of research

that needs to be conducted to reach evidence-based status. For example, often the "gold standard" of research is the experimental model with randomized, controlled trials that can be replicated (Cutspec, 2007). However, in education, there are many research methods that inform the researcher in a more meaningful way. These include action research and ethnography (Willinsky, 2001). However, according to Cutspec, (2007), *Evidence-Based Education UK* (E-BE UK) indicates that there are three key techniques that could be used for education to become more evidence-based. First, it is important to develop evidenced-based policies that could be addressed and used. Evidence-based practices also should be created and standardized. Finally, an evidenced-based "environment" should be designed to not only promote the need for evidence-based policies and programs but also to have them accepted. This chapter discusses the importance of quality child care in South Dakota and South Dakota's statewide attempt to create evidenced-based policies and programs. Specifically, the creation of the South Dakota's Infant/ Toddler Professional Development System will be used as a case study of how to get a state ready to complete evidence-based research.

Child Care: Present Need and Economic Impact on South Dakota

Child care has a great economic impact on the state of South Dakota, as evidenced by the sheer number of South Dakotan children enrolled in paid child care and by the overall contribution of child-care facilities to the global economy of the state. South Dakota has the highest percentage of women with children under the age of six in the workforce in the United States, and recent data indicate that over 75 percent of South Dakota's mothers of preschool children are working outside the home. Additionally, 47 percent of South Dakotan children under the age of six are enrolled in paid child care compared with the national average of only 26 percent. Furthermore, over 70 percent of South Dakotan children under the age of six have both parents working outside the home.

In light of these statistics, it is hard to recognize the child-care business as anything less than an economic powerhouse in South Dakota. In 2000, licensed and registered child care generated over 4,300 jobs and over $100.6 million in gross annual receipts. Additionally, South Dakota leverages more than $11.4 million in federal funds at a $2.82-to-$1.00 ratio by investing in child care. These data clearly show the need for child care in South Dakota and how imperative the industry is to the state's economy. Although this is important information, it should be noted that this field also has a national turnover rate of 33 percent. Notwithstanding, South Dakota's child-care turnover rate is above average at 36 percent (Child Care and Early Education Workforce Survey, 2004). This number obviously has an impact on the quality of care as well as research implications.

Quality Child Care: Importance, Benefits, and Future Implications

With almost half the South Dakotan population under age six presently enrolled in paid child care, it is paramount that the focus is not just about meeting the demands for enrollment but also providing the utmost *quality* of care possible – particularly since the quality of child care is linked to such elements as brain development, learning ability, and emotional security of children. Quality of care, of course, is imperative for the individual child, but it subsequently influences the future communities and workforce of South Dakota. Unfortunately, almost half the infant-toddler programs in the nation have been considered to be of poor quality (Helburn et al., 1995). Notwithstanding, in 2004, nationally, only 8 percent of licensed child-care centers were accredited by the National Association for the Education of Young Children, and South Dakota had less than 2 percent (Surr, 2004).

About 85 percent of the foundations of human brain development are formed by age three (Lally and Mangione, 2008), and children's early relationships in child care can have a profound impact on their developing brains (Shonkoff & Phillips, 2000). Case in point: Several researchers have related high-quality care to positive child development within several developmental areas, including social-emotional and attachment (Elicker et al., 1999; Howes et al., 1992; Howes & Smith, 1995), language and literacy (Burchinal et al., 1996), cognitive achievement (Burchinal et al., 1996), peer relations (Holloway & Reichart-Erickson, 1988; Howes et al., 1992; Kontos & Wilcox-Herzog, 1997), and later school success (U.S. General Accounting Office, 2002).

Furthermore, specific to infants/toddlers, care that facilitates the growth of secure relationships can have a long-lasting positive impact on young children's development, learning abilities, and emotional regulation (NICHD, Early Child Care Research Network, 1996). It should be noted that quality is more highly correlated with child outcomes in the moderate- to high-quality range (Love, 2010).

High-quality care also has been shown to be especially effective in promoting positive development in low-income and at-risk children (National Research Council, 2000). This is extremely important in a state such as South Dakota because the state currently has 21.1 percent of children under the age of four living in poverty and over 20 percent of children under the age of six living in poverty (NCCP, 2009). [Please note that for the year 2009, the federal poverty level for a family of four is $22,050 (NCCP, 2009).]

Defining Quality Child Care: Overview of Practical Issues and Research Obstacles

As the research in the preceding section indicated, the lack of quality child-care facilities does not just affect the individual child – which is a tragedy in itself – but it also affects the global well-being of South Dakota in the future. This alone warrants additional research and the use of evidence-based programming in the area of quality child care.

In order to develop the most sound research plan and evidence-based programming, the current obstacles to such an endeavor must be understood. First, there is a very serious problem with research pertaining to quality: There is a lack of common agreement among researchers as to how to define *quality* child care. This failure to define quality child care is partially due to the varying care needs of children in relation to age. For example, *quality* has been used to "describe features of program environments and children's experiences in these environments that are presumed to be beneficial to children's well-being" (Love, Schochet, & Meckstroth, 1996, p. 4). Ways of defining *quality* for infants and toddlers include "positive relationship between knowledgeable, responsive caregivers and the infants in their care" (Vanell & Wolf, 2000) and "the relationships between the non-parental caregiver and the child's parents" (Howes, 1999).

Further muddling the definition of *quality* in reference to child care are the various concepts developed to understand and describe quality. In the 1980s, researchers started using the concepts of "process" and "structural" dimensions to express child-care quality (Abbott-Shim & Sibley, 1992; Arnett, 1989; Goelman & Pence, 1985; Harms & Clifford, 1980; Howes, 1990). Although differing from each other, these studies demonstrated two common features in conceptualizing quality in child-care programs: (1) There is a distinction between the dynamic (process) and static (structural) features of the classroom, and (2) the larger social context found outside the classroom is an important determinant of the quality of children's classroom experiences (Love et al., 1996).

Child Trends (2009, p. 2) summarized the definitions of structural and process measures of child-care quality that recurred in the child-care literature in the past decade:

> *Quality in early care and education can be measured in different ways: through structural measures (measures of group size, ratio, and caregiver education), through process measures (measures that focus on environmental supports and/or interactions, like the extent and quality of caregiver-child interaction), and through global measures (measures that rate both physical features and routines in the care setting as well as interactions). Process measures of quality appear to be most directly linked with child outcomes, though the associations are small. Structural measures are also linked with child outcomes, but they appear to be connected through the way they increase or decrease the likelihood of stimulating and supportive interactions.*

In another analysis, Lamb (2006, p. 968) gave a slightly different definition of process and structural measures of quality:

> *Process measures are observational measures of the settings and interactions between care providers and children.... and the structural indices are measures of teacher training and experience, group size, teacher-child ratios, crowding, staff turnover, and the like. Conceptually, structural and process measures differ to the extent*

that factors indexed by the structural measures potentiate high-quality interaction and care but do not guarantee it, whereas process measures try to quantify the actual care received by children.

Now it is obvious that even the elements derived to conceptualize quality child care are beginning to lose concise meaning as researchers try to broaden the breadth of the concepts to fully describe all child care situations.

South Dakota has adopted the terms as indicated by Child Trends (2009) to operationally define

- *Structural measures* – measures of group size, ratio, and caregiver education
- *Process measures* – measures that focus on environmental supports and/or interactions, such as the extent and quality of caregiver-child interaction
- *Global measures* – measures that rate both physical features and routines in the care setting as well as interactions

This distinction is imperative. In order to help design research methodology, an operational definition must be apparent in order to have reliable and valid measures. Additionally, any evidence-based programming should address these definitions individually as well as collaboratively.

Child Care and Standardizing Professional Development

Zaslow et al. (2007) indicated one purpose of measuring quality in child-care settings is to help individual caregivers and programs increase quality. Thus the importance to professional development and how it is best implemented in order to increase individual caregivers/teachers' skills must be explored. According to Caulfield (1997), both children and caregivers can benefit from a heightened awareness in professionalism. *Professionalism* involves "the utilization of specialized knowledge and adherence to professional standards in a particular occupation in order to achieve desirable outcomes"

(Caulfield, 1997, p. 261). Although there seem to be some core components within early care and education professionalism, this concept is by no means standardized. Caulfield (1997) simply summarizes professionalism as having elements of appropriate knowledge of child development, an ability to work positively with families, understanding observation and documentation, and adhering to a code of ethics. However, many other researchers indicate that professionalism is often misunderstood and is much more complicated owing to the lack of operational definitions and standardized, reliable, and valid measurements. Moreover, the vastness of the early childhood workforce and its unique characteristics (Zaslow et al., 2007) can cause confusion. This confusion can hamper informed policymaking and funding decisions and increasing quality care. Additionally, it stands to reason that if South Dakota cannot operationally define its professional development, then how is it possible to measure its effectiveness? Thus one of the first steps in creating a system that can promote quality and provide valid and reliable measurement was for South Dakota to create an Infant/Toddler Professional Development System.

Professional development needs to have clear and consistent definitions, with valid and reliable measurements that are cohesive with those definitions (Child Trends, 2005). Zaslow et al. (2007) reported that terms such as *formal education* often can be problematic and should no longer be considered a status variable. The term *formal education* can be applied to the level of education, the type of education, whether it was knowledge-based or application-based, such as a practicum, and even the amount of hours/credits. Furthermore, a content analysis of course work may need to be completed pursuant to the Early Childhood Professional Development Registries. Additionally, the Child Trends white paper indicated that "training" should be explored within the scopes of (1) auspice (i.e., the trainers' qualifications and whether the training meets the needs of regulating and certifying committees), (2) the format and if it is stand-alone

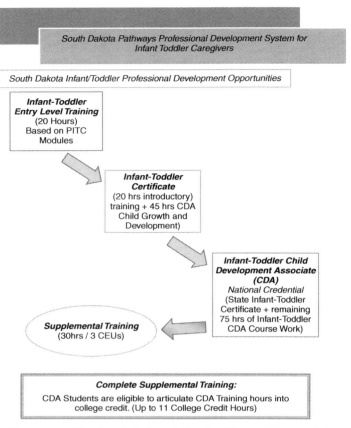

Figure 23.1. The South Dakota infant/toddler training model.

or series training, (3) the mode of delivery, which explains whether training is conducted face to face or via technology, such as the World Wide Web, (4) the content, which indicates whether it resonates with the Child Development Association content or meets the components of National Association of the Education for Young Children standards, (5) the extent, which refers to how much professional development is completed, and (6) recency, which defines when and how long ago the training was completed (Zaslow et al., 2007).

Other terms that are often interchanged and confused include *credential, certificate,* and *license.* Kreader, Fergurson, & Lawrence (2005) also report that the terms *technical assistance* and *mentoring* often can be perplexing. This confusion of terms can cause frustration. Caregivers and directors can become frustrated because they do not

understand what they need to complete to meet regulatory requirements. Likewise, policymakers and funders can become frustrated owing to the lack of standardized information that can be compared and aggregated in order to make informed decisions. Finally, researchers are often at a loss when looking at the effectiveness or quality of child care when there is no standardization across the programs.

In order to decrease frustration and increase quality, as well as provide an important step to a research environment, Figure 23.1 shows the South Dakota infant/toddler training model.

This model indicates the professional development levels and amount of training that needs to be done for an individual to be considered entry level and acquire a certificate or credential. Thus it effectively operationally defines the levels of an infant/toddler child-care provider. It also addresses the National Council of Professional Recognition's Child Development Associate (CDA). The CDA is a standardized credential that is recognized throughout the states. It is, however, a long process that often is not completed owing to the high turnover in the field.

In order to further standardize and promote quality care across the state, South Dakota also has created a professional career lattice – South Dakota Pathways to Professional Development (Pathways) (South Dakota Department of Social Services, Division of Child Care, 2010). Pathways is a statewide project recognizing those who work in child care serving the needs of children and families. The project is designed for child-care providers, educators, trainers, directors, administrators, and advocates of children – those with entry-level education or advanced degrees. The goal of the Pathways project is to support those who actively pursue ongoing educational opportunities and professional commitments to the field. The project also supports the development of a network of qualified trainers. These trainers are committed to providing adult learning experiences that promote quality care for children. The Career Lattice helps to provide fidelity to the training and to how the information is to be implemented. This is imperative in evidence-based programming and must be addressed at the very beginning of program introduction.

The Career Lattice defines seven levels of professional achievement. Each level includes training, education, and experience requirements. The Career Lattice can be used to chart a course for career development and recognition for education and professional achievements. By developing a knowledgeable and skilled workforce, the lattice can lead to an increase in the number of quality programs for children in South Dakota. Currently, there are approximately a thousand child-care providers/teachers in the program. (See Table 23.1 for the number of providers within each level.)

Additionally, the lattice has a professional trainer registry. The overall purpose of the

Table 23.1. South Dakota Pathways to Professional Development Career Lattice

Pathways Level	Number of Providers
Level 1: Introductory informal education	294
Level 2: Advanced informal education	178
Level 3: Professional credential	95
Level 4: Apprentice or higher-education course work	39
Level 5: Early childhood associates degree	44
Level 6: Baccalaureate degree	190
Level 7: Masters or doctoral degree	19

trainer registry is to develop a network of trainers who are committed to providing quality adult learning experiences for individuals who work with children and families in South Dakota (South Dakota Department of Social Services, Division of Child Care, 2010). Again, the registry is also used to promote fidelity in the trainings.

Objectives of the trainer registry include

- To enhance availability of professional training for trainers based on core knowledge and competencies (skills) individuals should have in order to provide quality adult education experiences. By using the core competencies, reliable and valid measures can be employed to assess the effectiveness of the trainings.
- To recognize individuals who complete specialized training and work experiences promoting their ability to provide quality professional development experiences for adults.
- To maintain records of training sessions conducted by registered trainers in conjunction with the Career Lattice.

Each trainer must complete an application process, which includes three steps. The first step includes the regional Early Childhood Enrichment Program (ECE) or the Child Care Resource and Referral (CCR&R) program. Each application is

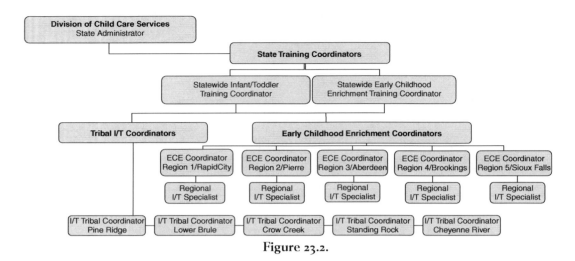

Figure 23.2.

sent to the appropriate regional early childhood enrichment program. Second, the program staff will contact the trainer to set up a meeting for special instruction and to receive applicable trainer materials. Finally, the trainer is notified of the trainer registry level he or she has attained and is provided with a Pathways certificate. By standardizing the trainers' levels, this helps researchers across the state to have an operationally defined training level within the research. Consequently, the confusion of who is doing the training and their qualifications and what type of training has been eliminated.

The certificate is ongoing, and trainers are encouraged to actively pursue additional education in the core areas of knowledge (skills). Trainers also must register training sessions or events at least four weeks in advance with the regional Early Childhood Enrichment office and complete tracking forms correctly. Each trainer must adhere to the standardized core knowledge and competencies as outlined in the "South Dakota Pathways to Professional Development Core Competencies" guide.

In order to offer statewide high-fidelity professional development programs and to improve the quality of infant/toddler child care in South Dakota, the Department of Social Services, Division of Child Care Services, created a statewide child-care resource and referral system known as the Early Childhood Enrichment programs (ECEs). The ECEs were developed to coordinate and provide early childhood and school-age training, technical assistance, and child-care referral (see Figure 23.2).

South Dakota's ECEs offer services to improve the quality and retention of caregivers, teachers, and others involved in the day-to-day care of children in the child-care setting. Funding for the state's ECEs is through regional contracts granted to the state through the Administration of Child and Families Child Care and Development block grants.

During state fiscal year 2009, a wide variety of training and technical assistance activities was offered to regulated child-care programs:

- 5,328 unduplicated child-care providers received services through the ECE system.
- 1,331 unduplicated child-care programs of 1,345 state-registered and -licensed programs were served through training and technical assistance.
  - 231 of these programs were child-care centers.
  - 876 of these programs were family child-care homes.
- 249 Child Development Associate (CDA) classes were held, reaching 238 unduplicated child-care providers in 107 child-care programs.

- 276 unduplicated child-care providers took advantage of Continuing Education Units (CEU) training hours available through the ECE system.
- According to the 2009 South Dakota Market Rate Survey of all regulated child care programs:
  - Of the 209 Child Care Center and Group Family Child Care programs responding, 91 percent had used or participated in ECE training and services.
  - Of the 647 Family Child Care providers responding, 81 percent had used or participated in ECE training and services.

Eleven percent of the preceding professional development opportunities were targeted for infant/toddler caregivers. In fact, as indicated in Figure 23.1, there are several different infant/toddler training programs. The Infant/Toddler Entry Level twenty hours of professional development opportunities are based the Program for Infant/Toddler Care (PITC). The PITC program has been authored by Drs. J. Ronald Lally and Peter L. Mangione. This internationally recognized philosophy promotes responsive, caring relationships for infants and toddlers, thus promoting high-quality care. Currently, over thirty states are using it in their states' training programs. The PITC philosophy promotes the credence that infant/toddler care is " different from preschool care" and must address the unique needs of infant and toddlers. PITC maintains that quality care hinges on the caregiver's ability to recognize and respond to those needs. Thus the focus of the philosophy is the relationships involved in infant/toddler care. There are six primary training areas that are divided into four modules. They include primary care, small groups, continuity, individualized care, cultural responsiveness, and inclusion of children with special needs. PITC has been used in South Dakota for over ten years, and South Dakota currently has over one-hundred PITC trained professional development trainers. Over 2,100 trainings have been conducted in fifty-six of sixty-six South Dakota counties and ninety communities since 1999.

While the average length of trainings is 2.5 hours, it should be noted that all four PITC modules have been used in twenty hours of trainings.

In order to measure actual knowledge change, *before* and *after* assessments were administered to the participants of the professional development opportunities. The before and after assessments included ten questions that were specifically designed to evaluate participant knowledge related to a particular infant/toddler training topic. Participants received one point for each question they answered correctly. A score of 10 indicated a perfect score on the assessment. The mean after scores in all areas were found to be *significantly higher* than the mean before scores. Overall, the results of the before and after assessments completed during the ten years of the program clearly revealed that participants increased their knowledge in quality infant/toddler care by completing the trainings. This important information indicates that child-care providers are better equipped to create an environment and to provide quality care within an infant/toddler classroom. However, it does not indicate that the needed transfer of knowledge to practice is occurring. However, the knowledge information may be a primer for a random control trial of behavior change within classrooms with teachers who have attended the infant/toddler professional development opportunities.

In 2006, research pertaining to behavior change and infant/toddler teachers' effectiveness based on PITC practices in the classroom was conducted in South Dakota. This two-year-long research project, the Partnership Initiative for Enhancement (PIE), was a coordinated effort between the South Dakota Division of Child Care Services, Early Childhood Enrichment programs (ECEs), South Dakota State University, and the Bush Foundation. A randomized, controlled trail was completed in order to assess teacher effectiveness in applying PITC practices in the classroom. The control group did not receive the twenty hours of entry-level training, whereas the treatment group did complete the twenty hours of training.

Trained observers used two reliable and valid environmental rating scales to assess the quality of care in thirty child-care centers across state before the treatment group attended the trainings. These scales assessed global, structural, and process quality within the classroom. After child-care providers in the treatment group received the training, both groups were reassessed after a six-month time period. Results indicated that indeed in several areas (specifically in structural and process quality), there was a significant difference in quality behavior indicators and the teachers' ability to apply those behaviors within the classroom. Thus the treatment (in this case, the standardized, research-based professional development opportunities) improved quality. Currently, a manuscript pertaining to the PIE data has been submitted, and the principle investigators are procuring funding for replication of the project.

Although the PIE project cannot specify PITC or South Dakota's trainings as being evidence-based as of yet, it does indicate that the infant/toddler professional development opportunities are effective, but more information is needed. Thus caregivers, researchers, and policymakers need to explore the future needs of the state's programs and policies. Case in point: Although quality child care has been shown to positively affect child development in areas such as speech and language, literacy, and school readiness, there is very a limited amount of evidence-based research on the curricula needed to promote those benefits (Cutspec, 2007). With several different child-care and out-of-school care programs currently being used within the state, there are five recommendations that should be considered. These recommendations will help to save money on ineffective programs (if any) and possibly increase funding for evidence-based programs and research. The recommendations are

- Money and time should be spent on promoting and explaining the importance of evidence-based policies and programs statewide. This promotion should target parents, caregivers, researchers, and policymakers.
- More programs should be standardized statewide in order to create a "research-to-practice-friendly environment." It is hard to complete and replicate meaningful research if terms such as *quality* or types of programs are not operationally defined. Additionally, the research should be disseminated in a user-friendly format.
- Research should be conducted on why South Dakota's child-care turnover is so high and how the state can decrease that turnover. Turnover not only affects the quality of care but also affects the quality of research because of attrition.
- Policymakers, funders, and practitioners should be educated on the importance of an evidence-based programs as well as the fidelity of presenting and using the programs. (Turnover also affects the fidelity of the programs.)

References

Abbott-Shim, M., and Sibley, A. (1992). *Assessment profile for early childhood programs: Research manual*. Atlanta: Quality Assist.

Arnett, J. (1989). Caregivers in day-care centers: Does training matter? *Journal of Applied Developmental Psychology 10*, 541–52.

Burchinal, M. R., Roberts, J. E., Nabors, L. A., & Bryant, D. M. (1996). Quality of center child care and infant cognitive and language development. *Child Development 67*, 606–20.

Caulfield, R. (1997). Professionalism in early care and education. *Early Childhood Education Journal 24*(4), 261–3.

Child Care and Early Workforce Survey (2004). *Who cares for the children in South Dakota*. Vermillion, SD: University of South Dakota School of Education.

Child Trends (2005). Draft of summary of themes: Workshop on defining and measuring professional and training of the early childhood workforce. Washington: Child Trends, Inc.

Child Trends (2009). What we know and don't know about measuring quality in early childhood and school-age care and education settings (Publication 2009–12). Washington: Child Trends, Inc.

Cutspec, P. A. (2007). Bridging the research-to-practice gap: Evidence-based education. *Winterberry Research Perspectives* 1(4).

Dunst, C., Trivette, C. M., & Cutspec, P. A. (2002). Toward an operational definition of evidence-based practices. *Winterberry Research Perspectives* 1(1).

Elicker, J., Fortner-Wood, C., & Noppe, I. C. (1999). The context of infant attachment in family child care. *Journal of Applied Developmental Psychology* 20(2), 319–36.

Gambrill, E. (1999). Evidence-based practices: An alternative to an authority-based practice. *Families in Society: The Journal of Contemporary Human Services* 80, 341–50.

Goelman, H., & Pence, A. (1985). Toward the ecology of day care in Canada: A research agenda for the 1980s. *Canadian Journal of Educators* 10(4), 323–44.

Harms, T., & Clifford, R. M. (1980). *The early childhood environment rating scale*. New York: Teachers College Press.

Helburn, S., Culkin, M. L., Morris, J., Mocan, N., Howes, C., Phillipsen, L., Bryant, D., Clifford, R., Cryer, D., Peisner-Feinberg, E., Burchinal, M., Kagan, S. L., & Rustici, J. (1995). *Cost, quality, and child outcomes in child care centers: Public report*. Denver: University of Colorado, Department of Economics. Available at www.childcareresearch.org/location/ccrca1459.

Holloway, S. D., & Reichhart-Erickson, M. (1998). The relationship of day care quality to children's free play behavior and social problem-solving skills. *Early Childhood Research Quarterly* 3, 39–53.

Howes, C. (1999). Attachment relationships in the context of multiple caregivers. In J. Cassidy and P. R. Shaver (eds.), *Handbook of attachment: Theory, research, and clinical applications*. New York: Guilford Press.

Howes, C. (1990). Can the age of entry into child care and the quality of child care predict adjustment in kindergarten? *Developmental Psychology* 26(2), 292–303.

Howes, C., & Smith, E. W. (1995). Relations among child care quality, teacher behavior, children's play activities, emotional security, and cognitive activity in child care. *Early Childhood Research Quarterly* 10, 381–404.

Howes, C., Phillips, D. A., & Whitebrook, M. (1992). Thresholds of quality: Implications for the social development of children in center-based child care. *Child Development* 63, 449–60.

Kreader, J. L., Ferguson, D., & Lawrence, S. (2005). Impact of training and education for caregivers of infant and toddlers. *Child Care & Early Education-Research Connections* 3, 2–7.

Kontos, S., & Wilcox-Herzog, A. (1997). Influences on children's competence in early childhood classrooms. *Early Childhood Research Quarterly* 12, 247–62.

Lally, J. R., & Mangione, P. L. (2008). The program for infant/toddler care. In *Approaches to early childhood education*, 5th ed. Englewood Cliffs, NJ: Prentice-Hall.

Lamb, M. E., & Ahnert, L. (2006). Nonparental child care: Context, concepts, correlates, and consequences. In K. Renninger et al. (eds.), *Handbook of child psychology*, 6th ed., Vol. 4: *Child psychology in practice*. (pp. 950–1016). Hoboken, NJ: Wiley.

Love, J. M. (2010) Are they in any serious danger? What quality in early childhood programs is and why it is important. Investment in Early Learning: Making an Impact, Panel 3, First 5 California Conference.

Love, J. M., Schochet, P. Z.; & Meckstroth, A. (1996). *Are they in any real danger? What research does – and doesn't – tell us about child care quality and children's well-being*. Plainsboro, NJ: Mathematica Policy Research.

National Center for Children in Poverty (NCCP) (2009). South Dakota: Demographics of children. Retrieved May 30, 2010, from http://www.nccp.org/profiles/SD_profile_7.html.

National Research Council (2000). *Eager to learn: Educating our preschoolers*. Washington: National Academy Press.

National Research Council (2002). *Scientific research in education*. Washington: National Academy Press.

NICHD, Early Child Care Research Network (1996). Characteristics of infant CC: Factors contributing to positive caregiving. *Early Childhood Research Quarterly* 11, 269–306.

Shonkoff, J. A., & Phillips, D. (2000). *From neurons to neighborhoods: The science of early childhood development*. Washington: National Academy Press.

Snap Shot. FPG Child Development Institute, University of North Carolina at Chapel Hill (2006). Evidence-based practice empowers early childhood professionals and families. Snap Shot Research Summary No. 33, September, pp. 1–2.

South Dakota Department of Social Services, Division of Child Care (2010). http://dss.sd.gov/childcare/.

Surr, J. (2004). Who's accredited? What and how the states are doing on best practices in child care. *Child Care Information Exchange* March–April, 14–22.

U.S. General Accounting Office (2002). *Child care: States have undertaken a variety of quality improvement initiatives, but more evaluations of effectiveness are needed.* Washington: United States General Accounting Office (GAO-02-897), 2002; available at http://www.gao.gov/new.items/do2897.pdf.

Vanell, D. L., & Wolfe, B. (2000). Child care quality: Does it matter and does it need to be improved? Available at http://aspe.hhs.gov/hsp/ccquality00/index.htm.

Willinsky, J. (2001). Extending the prospects of evidence-based education. *InSights* 1(1), 23–41.

Zaslow, M., Halle, T., McNamara, M., Weinstein, D., & Dent, A. (2007). Working towards a recommended common core of measures of early childhood professional development: Issues and preliminary recommendations. White paper (draft). Child Trends, Inc., Washington.

CHAPTER 24

Action Research: Reshaping Practice Through Assessment and Critical Reflection

Violet H. Harada and Joyce Yukawa

Introduction

Today's educators strive to improve teaching and learning conditions in an increasingly challenging and constantly shifting environment, where they face mounting demands for accountability. *Action research* is a "paradigm for change" that "responds to global educational reforms towards privatization and high-stakes accountability of processes and outcomes" (Orland-Barak, 2009, p. 114). It provides a "valuable means for enhancing and sustaining a motivated professional community that can stand up to these pressures and challenges" (Orland-Barak, 2009, p. 114).

Lytle and Cochran-Smith (1992) define *action research* as "a way of generating both local knowledge and public knowledge about teaching, that is, knowledge developed and used by teachers for themselves and their immediate communities, as well as knowledge useful to the larger school and university communities" (p. 450). It is done for themselves by teachers, administrators, and other educators with a vested interest in the teaching and learning process (Mertler,

2006). Whether individuals, small teams, or a schoolwide group conducts the research, the endeavor focuses on educators "investigating a question and devising an informed response to meet the challenges within their classrooms and schools" (Seider & Lemma, 2004, p. 220). Action research builds on a foundation of critical inquiry that requires a systematic collection of data and maintenance of written documentation (Stenhouse, 1985). Conceived as a spiraling process of planning, acting, developing, and reflecting, action research is not a spontaneous activity but a deliberate and purposeful enterprise.

Action research is empowering and powerful as an approach to professional, personal, educational, and social change (Kemmis, 2009; McKernan, 1996; Noffke, 1997a; Rearick & Feldman, 1999). While action research can be applied to "questions ranging from individual teachers trying to solve very specific teaching and learning problems to collaborative research on larger pedagogical or school organizational issues," it targets two fundamental goals: creating deeper understandings about the processes of teaching and learning while bringing about change and bridging research and practice (Carson, 1990, p.167).

By engaging practitioners in sustained and explicit forms of inquiry, action research affords a structure to identify problematic areas, collect evidence using both qualitative and quantitative methods in naturalistic settings, and analyze and apply evidence to improve teaching and learning (Gordon, 2009; Baumfield, Hall, & Wall, 2008). According to Ball & Cohen (1999), action research situates learning in "concrete tasks and artifacts of practice" and "creates new capacity for professionals to learn from one another, capitalize on existing capability, and break down the traditional isolation of teachers' work and broaden their opportunities to learn" (p. 17).

In this chapter we begin with a brief description of the evolution of action research in the last half-century, followed by an examination of the characteristics of action research with particular attention to the importance of critical reflection in the inquiry process. We proceed with a summary of the methods and approaches used in designing and implementing action research and conclude with examples of studies that represent the diverse body of practitioner research. We use the terms *practitioner researcher* and *practitioner inquiry* as well as *teacher researcher* and *teacher inquiry* synonymously with *action research*.

Evolution of Action Research

Action research draws on the traditions of qualitative research in anthropology, education, and social work (McFarland & Stansell, 1993; Eisner & Peshkin, 1990). McKernan (1996) indicates that the origins of action research as a method of inquiry can be traced to "the Science in Education movement of the late nineteenth century" (p. 8).

Kurt Lewin (1946), one of the pioneers of modern social, organizational, and applied psychology, is generally credited with coining the term *action research* and constructing a theory of action research in the 1940s that integrated social theory and social action (Masters, 1995). His formulation of action research focused on action cycles to institute change, that is, taking actions, carefully collecting information on their effects, and then evaluating them (Adelman, 1993; Lewin, 1946). According to Lewin, action research gave "credence to the powers of reflective thought, discussion, decision and action by ordinary people participating in collective research on private troubles that they have in common" (Adelman, 1993, p. 8). He also emphasized the need for collaboration and group inquiry in collecting information about social issues and solving sociological problems (Lewin, 1946).

John Dewey's work in experimentalist and progressive education provided a theoretical framework for action research (Watson, 1949). In his laboratory school in Chicago, Dewey stressed the importance of teachers reflecting on their practices (Mayhew & Edwards, 1936). Dewey's emphasis on the need to define the educational problem and the inclusion of a hypothesis contrasted with Lewin's model, which seemed to focus more attention on the action steps. It was Dewey's version of the process, combined with Lewin's understanding of group dynamics in a democracy, that gradually emerged as a paradigm for action research in the post–World War II years (Noffke, 1997b).

Action research gained a critical niche in education through the Horace Mann–Lincoln Institute at Teachers College, Columbia University (McFarland & Stansell, 1993, p. 14). Founded in 1943, the institute became a research laboratory striving to effect curriculum changes and serving as a link between Teachers College and the schools. The institute focused on "school-based curriculum development, the need for a closer knowledge-practice connection, and the benefits of field research" (Noffke, 1997b, p. 9). Study committees were established for the in-service education of teachers. They emphasized curriculum change and the implications of child development for the curriculum (Horace Mann–Lincoln Staff, 1945). The overall goal was "educating persons who were socially sensitive, creative, and self-directing" (Goodson, 1946, p. 42).

Stephen Corey (1953) and Gordon MacKenzie, key leaders of the institute, viewed action research as a legitimate research form. Like Lewin, Corey emphasized the need for researchers and teachers to collaborate in conducting research (McFarland & Stansell, 1993). While experts might be called in to consult, Corey maintained that practitioner researchers were responsible for the implementation of the research. He also believed that the quality of the research by teachers would improve gradually as they gained experience.

Action research gained further legitimacy when distinguished educators such as Hilda Taba advocated for this form of research in the late 1950s. She identified two basic purposes for action research: (1) to produce evidence needed to solve practical problems and (2) to help those who are doing the action research to acquire more adequate perspectives regarding their problems, to deepen their insights as to what is involved in their task, and to extend their orientation toward children (Taba & Noel, 1957, p. 2).

Action research lost ground in United States during the 1960s because "its methodology was questioned by the scientific establishment" and researchers criticized it as "quantified common sense rather than as a form of scientific, empirical research" (Hodgkinson, 1957, p. 146). The decline was "directly related to the split between science and practice ... and to the shift towards the establishment of expert educational research and development laboratories" (McKernan, 1996, p. 10).

In the 1970s, however, action research in education resurfaced in Britain (Smulyan, 1984). Lawrence Stenhouse's (1975, 1985) collaborative work with British educators in both lower and higher education emphasized the value of teachers grappling with issues of classroom practice. In 1974, Stenhouse's associate, John Elliott (1991), founded the Cambridge Institute of Education, and after a decade of research, he and his colleagues concluded that classroom action research "does not provide generalizable empirical

research findings" as much as it helps "teachers generate and examine explanations for their own teacher behavior" (McFarland & Stansell, 1993, p.16). Its appeal today is the "promise inherent in action research to build the capability of individuals and organizations to move beyond current cognitions and practice" (Calhoun, Allen, & Halliburton, 1996, p. 5). McFarland and Stansell (1993) maintain that action research is no longer "just another movement on the fringes of the profession.... it has become in recent years a worldwide activity that makes major contributions to both knowledge and practice" (p. 17).

Characteristics of Action Research

The goal of action research is "changing practitioners' practices, their understanding of their practices, and the conditions in which they practice" (Kemmis, 2009, p. 463). Kemmis refers to action research as a "meta-practice" that shapes other practices in which the doing, thinking, and relating form a "unitary praxis of morally committed action oriented and informed by traditions of thought that emerge and develop in relation to one another" (Kemmis, 2009, p. 465). It is holistic, interpretative, and explanatory rather than prescriptive. Researchers construct meaning out of the events and phenomena they encounter in the workplace. Since meanings derived are not always predictable, researchers do not work with a totally predetermined research design (McCutcheon & Jung, 1990). In addition, action research must be sensitive to the cultural and social positioning of both researcher and researched (Radford, 2007).

Mohr et al. (2004) identify the following as defining characteristics of action research:

- *Intentional purpose.* The researchers commit to a focus for their investigation and determine how best to collect and analyze the data. While the researchers cannot predict the outcomes of their investigations, they approach the challenge with the intent to gain critical insights into their teaching and students' learning. Since the teacher's formative evaluation interacts in a cyclic fashion with the research, deliberate scrutiny becomes a regular part of the teaching process (Seider & Lemma, 2004, p. 221).

- *Systematic process.* To gain a deeper and more accurate view of the teaching-learning context, researchers employ strategies to document assumptions, collect both quantitative and qualitative data, and give voice to findings and implications.
- *Public perspective.* By engaging in action research, practitioners shift "from a private perspective to a more open, public one in order to encourage challenges to their understanding" (Mohr et al., 2004, p. 24). They frequently share findings with school colleagues and extend beyond their schools to wider arenas of dissemination through publications and conference presentations.
- *Ethical considerations.* Researchers obtain permission to quote students or use work samples, and they are careful to protect information that might compromise the privacy of their students, community members, or colleagues.
- *Contextual impact.* Action research "both shapes and is shaped by its context" (Mohr et al., 2004, p. 25). That is, the researchers attempt to identify and better understand the assumptions underlying the contexts in which they operate, strive to uncover the relationships and tensions at work, and make changes for the better.

Dimensions of Action Research

Although various models of action research exist (Mills, 2007; Rearick & Feldman, 1999), all models address three dimensions: (1) theoretical orientation, (2) purpose, and (3) reflection among participants (Rearick & Feldman, 1999). The first dimension, *theoretical orientation*, focuses on technical, practical, and emancipatory stances. From a technical stance, problems are defined at the outset, and solutions are grounded in experiences and observations (Grundy, 1987). A practical stance emphasizes action "with"

rather than "upon" the environment, with solutions grounded in fuller understanding as well as better technique. The emancipatory perspective seeks to uncover the societal structures that enhance or inhibit freedom (Bustingorry, 2008). The goal is "empowerment to engage in autonomous action arising out of authentic, critical insights into the social construction of human society" (Grundy, 1987, p. 19).

The second dimension of purpose centers on "personal growth, professional understanding that goes beyond the personal, thereby adding to the knowledge base for teaching, or expansion to a political awareness of the need for social action" (Rearick & Feldman, 1999, p. 335; see also Noffke, 1997a). The third dimension points to types of reflection – autobiographical, collaborative, or communal. While the researcher is the focus of autobiographical reflection, in collaborative and communal reflections, the questioning goes beyond the self to ever-widening contexts. Both collaborative and communal reflections involve dialogue about actions and ideologies and move beyond "subjective experience to a social construction of self and the system within a larger interpersonal context" (Rearick & Feldman, 1999, p. 336).

An additional dimension discussed by Elliott (2007) is locus of control as a defining feature. On one end of the spectrum is externally mediated research controlled by an outside researcher. In contrast, experimental teaching places teachers in control of the data-gathering process, analysis of the findings, and interpretation of the results. On the other end of the spectrum, networked learning communities involve groups of practitioners who open their work to peer scrutiny. This enables professional communities to work together in identifying common problems across a range of situations and to collectively solve problems and share understandings.

Critical Reflection in Action Research

Reflection is an essential element of action research (e.g., Carr & Kemmis, 1986; Chiu,

2006; Elliott, 2007; Kraft, 2002; McKernan, 1996; Rearick & Feldman, 1999; Ward & McCotter (2004); Watts & Lawson, 2009). While diverse models of reflection have been proposed (Chiu, 2006), much of the literature on reflection in action research begins with Dewey's (1933) definition of reflection: "An active, persistent and careful consideration of any belief or supposed form of knowledge in the light of the grounds that support it and the further conclusions to which it tends" (p. 6). In response to the limits of technical rationality and the view that scientific methods should be the primary means of problem solving in professional practice, Schon (1983) emphasized the importance of tacit knowledge as applied to practice in the moment (reflection-in-action), augmenting Dewey's view of reflection as a conscious, deliberate activity. Boud, Keogh, & Walker (1985) added to Dewey's cognitive definition an attention to feelings in the reflection process. To Dewey's primarily individualistic view, others have added the importance of the dialogic and discursive dimensions of the process (e.g., Mezirow, 1998).

Recent literature presents reflection as developmental, based on Van Manen's (1977) model of the three stages of reflection: technical, practical, and critical (e.g., Hatton & Smith, 1995; Rearick & Feldman, 1999; Ward & McCotter, 2004; Watts & Lawson, 2009). In studies of preservice teachers, Larrivee (2000, 2008) builds on these stages and adds a fourth (prereflection):

1. *Prereflection:* "Teachers react to students and classroom situations automatically, without conscious consideration of alternative responses" (2008, p. 342).
2. *Technical reflection:* "Teachers' reflections focus on strategies and methods used to reach predetermined goals. Teachers are concerned with what works rather than any consideration of the value of goals as ends in themselves" (2008, p. 342–3).
3. *Pedagogical reflection:* "Practitioners apply the field's knowledge base and current beliefs about what represents quality practices ... [and] teachers reflect on educational goals, the theories

underlying approaches, and the connection between theoretical principles and practice" (2008, p. 343).
4. *Critical reflection:* "Teachers reflect on the moral and ethical implications and consequences of their classroom practices on students. Critical reflection involves examination of both personal and professional belief systems. Teachers who are critically reflective focus their attention both inwardly at their own practice and outwardly at the social conditions in which these practices are situated. They are concerned about issues of equity and social justice that arise in and outside the classroom and seek to connect their practice to democratic ideals" (2008, p. 343).

Each form of reflection is valuable and can be built on to encourage teachers to move to other forms of reflection because they meet the goal of action research to improve in three areas – execution of practice, understanding of the practice, and the situation in which the practice takes place (Carr & Kemmis, 1986).

Critical reflection generally involves three broad stages regardless of when reflection occurs in the action research process: (1) a critique of assumptions that involves consideration of the ethical dimensions of practice, (2) facing challenging emotions, and (3) transforming perspectives and changing practice. The critical examination of assumptions and the attempt to surrender familiar assumptions lead to struggle, conflict, and often fear and doubt. The ability to face uncertainty and chaos during this process leads to a deeper understanding, a shift in perceptions, and engagement in new patterns of thinking and action that allow more appropriate responses to classroom situations and educational circumstances (Larrivee, 2000, p. 305).

Benefits of Action Research

The benefits of action research include the democratization of the research process by envisioning teachers as researchers rather than as the researched. Action researchers examine ways in which they implement daily practice (Esposito & Evans-Winters, 2007; Mertler, 2006; Cochran-Smith & Lytle, 1993). Knowledge gained can "liberate students, teachers, and administrators and enhance learning, teaching, and policy making" (Mills, 2007, p. 8). By democratizing the process, action research also challenges assumptions about the relationship between theory and practice. For this reason, O'Connell (2009) maintains that action research is boundary-crossing, that is, bridging the gap between academic research and knowledge derived from practice. Similarly, Somekh & Zeichner (2009) single out the "discursive power" of action research and its capacity to challenge "the normative values of two distinct ways of being – that of the scholar and the activist" (p. 5). They contend that the intertwining and reflexive activities of action and research erode the boundaries between action and knowledge generation, allowing it to be appropriate for "generating and sustaining social transformation … a particularly well-suited methodology for educational transformation in the twenty-first century" (Somekh & Zeichner, 2009, p. 6).

Action research also raises critical questions about the traditional roles of university researchers in relation to school practitioners. Cochran-Smith & Lytle (1993) believe that "teacher researchers are uniquely positioned to provide a truly emic perspective that makes visible the ways students and teachers together construct knowledge" (p. 448). "By drawing upon their own histories and classroom practices, teacher researchers alter the relationship between knower and known," thereby obviating "the necessity of translating findings in the conventional sense, and moving teacher research toward praxis, or critical reflection on practice" (Cochran-Smith & Lytle, 1993, p. 448).

On the long-term professional development effects of action research, Seider & Lemma (2004) conducted a study to investigate the extent to which teachers who had engaged in action research as a capstone to their master's program subsequently sustained practices of reflection, analytic

introspection, and viewing student data sources for decision making. Among their findings were the following: (1) Teachers sustained the "inquiry mind-set" gained while learning the processes associated with conducting action research and continued using aspects of the process; however, conducting new projects was less likely; (2) teachers' sense of professional efficacy was enhanced, even after many years had intervened; (3) action research had immediate benefits for students, but long-range benefits were not determined; (4) although challenging, teachers perceived that conducting action research was professionally valuable; and (5) teachers described school environments conducive to conducting action research as those which provide structures for teams to work on mutual goals supported by strong administrative leadership (p. 219).

Methodology

In contrast to more traditional research methodologies, action research relies on the "analytical and interpretative expertise of the teacher-researcher in terms of research design, implementation, and evaluation" (Armstrong & Moore, 2004, p. 11). The process requires reflexivity – becoming aware of one's perceptual biases – and an understanding of the dialectic relationship between the various aspects of the workplace context (Winter, 1996). Researchers assume a collaborative stance that acknowledges the views of multiple participants. This leads to the development of diverse critiques rather than a single authoritative interpretation (Armstrong & Moore, 2004).

Rigor and Ethics

Action research uses both qualitative and quantitative data-collection methods based on a flexible rather than dichotomous relationship between the two approaches. Whether the research is published or unpublished, researchers must ensure the quality of their work. While there is debate about the value of applying concepts of validity, reliability, and generalizability to qualitatively oriented action research, "teacher-researchers must understand the meanings of these terms to produce results that are trustworthy and persuasive" (Mills, 2007, p. 84). According to Guba (1981), trustworthiness of qualitative inquiry must address credibility, transferability, dependability, and confirmability. *Credibility* refers to the researcher's ability to account for the complexities present in a study and to explain emerging patterns based on such activities as "prolonged participation at the site, peer debriefing, and member checks to test the overall report with the study's participants" (Mills, 2007, pp. 86–7). Triangulation, resulting from a variety of data sources and collection methods, allows for cross-checking data. *Transferability* requires collection of detailed descriptive data so that the audience for the work "can see the setting for themselves" (Mills, 2007, p. 86). The stability of the data, or *dependability*, calls for overlap methods where two or more methods are used so that the weakness of one is compensated by the strength of the other (Guba, 1981). Finally, *confirmability* of the data refers to the objectivity of the collected data. This is addressed by triangulation and researcher reflexivity (e.g., keeping journals) that reveals underlying biases and assumptions (Mills, 2007, p. 87).

The issue of generalizability is not usually applicable to action research because its goal is to understand "what is happening in a specific school or classroom rather than arriving at generalized conclusions about other classes and programs" (Mills, 2007, pp. 96–7). While the research may have high validity for the specific classroom or school, its transferability can be questioned. For this reason, partnerships may be crucial to help "teachers develop a professional discourse about learning and provide opportunities for the sharing of ideas across different institutional contexts" (Baumfield, Hall, & Wall, 2008, p. 10).

Ethical considerations are particularly challenging for teacher-researchers because of the "intimate and open-ended nature of action research where there is little distance between the researcher and subjects" (Mills,

2007, p. 107). Informed consent ensures that all subjects retain autonomy and the ability to judge for themselves what risks are worth taking for the purpose of furthering scientific knowledge (Mills, 2007). However, fully informed consent is often difficult to obtain because the direction of the research is frequently unpredictable and evolves as the study progresses. Dissemination of findings also should respect the privacy of participants. Furthermore, confidentiality and anonymity should be extended to how the data are stored. Finally, researchers must make a commitment to communicate findings to the participants, thereby honoring the contributions made (Baumfield, Hall, & Wall, 2008).

Beyond these methodologically based ethical considerations, action research is also centrally concerned with ethical commitments to equity, social justice, and empowerment (Kemmis, 2009).

Elements and Phases of the Research Process

Regardless of the theoretical perspective assumed, action research envisions theory and practice as complementary phases of the change process. It begins with a deep self-questioning process to identify a researchable question. Denscombe (2003) suggests the following types of questions to aid teacher-researchers in pondering the viability of tackling specific issues and problems that exist within the larger contexts in which they work:

- Does the research address a concrete issue or practical problem?
- Is there a clear view of how the findings will feed directly into practice?
- Is there participation by the practitioner at all stages of the project?
- Have grounds for partnership between the practitioner and outside expert been explicitly negotiated and agreed?
- Is the research part of a continuous cycle of development?
- Will the research be manageable with a routine workload?

Action research in school contexts might focus on an individual subject (What is the most effective approach to working with student X?), a group of subjects (What are the needs of the special education students in this inclusion classroom?), a curriculum area (What might be the most effective interventions for teaching mathematical probability to middle school students?), or a larger social issue (How can girls feel empowered to enroll in advanced science and math courses?).

Mertler (2006) categorizes the various elements in the action research process as four interwoven phases – planning, acting, developing, and reflecting. These phases focus on the intention of the inquiry and the impetus for the investigation, the tools employed as well as the analytic process used, and the audience and community with whom the results are shared.

The *planning phase* involves identifying and limiting the topic, reviewing the related existing literature, and developing the framework of a research plan. Johnson (2005) advises that the topic selected should be manageable as well as one of genuine interest to the researcher. The literature review aids the teacher-researcher to make informed decisions about the focus and the research design (Parsons & Brown, 2002) and might include a needs assessment to provide documented evidence of a perceived problem or situation. In developing a research plan, the researcher must identify factors or variables that are central to the investigation and decide on procedures for data collection and analysis.

In the *acting phase*, teacher-researchers implement the plan, collect the data using a broad range of collection tools, and analyze the data. This may involve qualitative, quantitative, or mixed methods for data collection depending on the research question and the intended audience. To ensure triangulation, researchers use multiple methods to collect evidence (Baumfield, Hall, & Wall, 2008). Examples of common collection tools include interviews, questionnaires, checklists, attitude scales, sociograms, field notes, and observations. Readily available school data might include individual education plans, attendance records, and test scores. Other data sources are artifacts produced in the classroom, for example, student work samples, learning logs, and peer observations. In quantitative studies, analysis usually occurs following the completion of all data collection. In qualitative studies, however, analysis is typically performed during the data-collection process to identify emerging themes, patterns, and categories (Mertler, 2006). Throughout a qualitative study, "feedback loops are crucial in promoting a sustained dialogue about learning and teaching with subjects" (Baumfield, Hall, & Wall, 2008, p. 59).

The *developing phase* moves into formulating a proposed strategy for implementing the results (Cresswell, 2005). The action plan centers on a specific and tangible approach to trying out a new solution to the original problem. This is the "ultimate goal of any action research study – it is the 'action' part of the research" (Mertler, 2006, p. 28). As the plan is implemented, it is critical to continue monitoring and evaluating the effectiveness of the implementation. As mentioned earlier, the plan may focus on an individual subject, a group of subjects, or a schoolwide/district situation. With plans that extend beyond a single classroom, more formal written reports may be required that describe the context for the work, the rationale and need for it, the implementation and assessment process, and a summary of the results as well as implications for future practice (Baumfield, Hall, & Wall, 2008).

The *reflecting phase* ultimately spirals into another cycle of planning, reviewing, and doing. Teacher-researchers share and communicate the results with school colleagues and with the larger educational community. Dissemination of findings assumes many forms ranging from presentations at faculty meetings to reports shared with parents as well as school and district administrators. Researchers also may publish their studies in professional and scholarly journals and speak at local and national conferences. Importantly, they reflect on what has been done, determine its effectiveness, and make

Table 24.1. Key Elements of Action Research and Related Questions

Key Elements	Related Questions
Formulation of idea	What are my underlying assumptions and visions? What will I try to improve my practice? What will be the observable change from this proposed innovation or intervention?
Exploration of idea	How can my assumptions and visions be placed in the context of the school? What do others know about this proposed innovation? What has been published? How do I know whether my actions in this situation will have the outcome I intend? Will my questions be answerable within the complexities and realities of the class/school context?
Planning the research	How do I involve pupils and colleagues in the study? How can I develop benchmarks to guide my progress? How might this change be measured or observed? What data would be most appropriate to collect? How will I document the process? How will I verify that my judgments are credible? Is what I am doing ethical?
Implementation of plan	What does the data gathered tell me about the situation to be changed? Was my research design appropriate for what I wanted to address with my questions? Did the data that I collected enable me to answer my research questions? Why do I think the change is an improvement?
Communication of findings	Who are my primary audiences? How will I portray what I have learned and make it public?

decisions about possible changes for future implementations (Mertler, 2006).

It is critical to also recognize that reflection is an ongoing activity throughout action research. Mills (2007) states that researchers should regularly "pause in gathering data and reflect on what they have thus far collected. Questions that need to be asked: Is the research question still answerable and worth answering? Are the data-collection techniques catching the data needed and filtering out the data that are irrelevant?" (p. 121). Persistent questioning underscores the importance of reflection that not only improves practice but also extends and deepens the researcher's understanding of a rationale or philosophy of practice (Baumfield, Hall, & Wall, 2008; McCutcheon & Jung, 1990; Carr & Kemmis, 1986; Elliott, 1991; Zeichner & Noffke, 2001; Ponte et al.,

2004; Mertler, 2006; Arhar, Holly, & Kasten, 2001). Table 24.1 presents examples of reflective questions that might be asked throughout the research process. By seeking answers to these questions, teacher-researchers continually examine their own assumptions and practices through the lenses of other stakeholders in the educational community.

Action Research in Action

In this last section we briefly describe examples of action research to suggest the diversity of topics and analytic perspectives it encompasses. The examples represent studies conducted in K–12 and university classrooms and research involving preservice teachers as well as in-service professionals. The studies were drawn from academic and professional journals as well as books on teacher action research written in English over the last two decades. A large body of work on teacher action research exists in other languages (Noffke, 1997a) but was not reviewed for this chapter.

All studies reflect the voices of teacher-researchers on the multiple interpretations and practices of action research. They address the relationships between research, knowledge creation, and action that intertwine personal, professional, and political concerns. They show practitioners questioning the basis of their work. Many of the studies involve collaboration, and some involve the creation of communities that address common concerns, attempt to achieve mutual understanding and a common position, and work to effect change. The studies are organized by three orientations to action research (Noffke, 1997a): (1) professional orientation: knowledge production and professional development; (2) personal orientation: self-awareness and identity; and (3) political orientation: social change. Each section is introduced with a brief description of the salient features of the orientation.

Professional Orientation: Knowledge Production and Professional Development

In the following studies of action research with a professional emphasis, research is done as "a professional, neutral process of knowledge accumulation … [and] bridges the traditional theory-practice, knowledge-action gap" (Noffke, 1997a, p. 306). The studies range from those which aim to improve the means to predetermined ends (meeting curriculum standards), to research on questions arising from classroom experience, and finally, to a questioning of the connection between theoretical principles and practice. A wide variety of quantitative and qualitative data-collection and analysis methods are used. The reflection methods used are predominantly technical and pedagogical (Larrivee, 2008), whether they are done individually or collaboratively.

STANDARDS-BASED CURRICULUM CHANGE

In supporting standards-based curriculum change, teachers are concerned with what works rather than any consideration of the value of the goals as ends in themselves (Larrivee, 2008, pp. 342–3). They use technical reflection that focuses on strategies and methods used to reach predetermined goals, exemplified here by curriculum standards.

Performance in Reading. Matt Wayne (2003), a middle school teacher in New York, wondered how he might help struggling sixth grade students achieve performance standards in reading. As part of the requirements, the students were expected to read at least twenty-five books by different authors and from different genres within the year. Wayne conducted observations and audiotaped interviews to study the reading habits and book selections of his students. He noted that struggling students were selecting books beyond their reading levels and not actually reading them. To help students choose more appropriate books, Wayne redesigned his classroom library so that books were arranged according to four major reading levels, and the spines of books were color coded to match the levels. He also encouraged students to consider books at their reading levels by placing corresponding colored stickers in their journals. He examined circulation statistics to gauge the effectiveness of this particular intervention. Wayne also substituted written log reports with taped book conversations between pairs of students. To determine the students' progress, he compared their reading scores on the quarterly reading progress indicator tests administered by the school and found that the class a whole "registered a 3 percent increase in scores over the year" (Wayne, 2003, p. 31). On the statewide reading test, Wayne reported that "our class average of 40.6 percent was the highest average among the fifth, sixth, and seventh grade classes in our school" (Wayne, 2003, p. 31).

Performance in Speaking and Listening. Working with sixty-six second-language learners in Manhattan's Chinatown, Lara Goldstone (2003) discovered that most of the sixth grade students were not meeting the state performance standards for speaking and listening. Approximately 80 percent of the students were Chinese; the other 20 percent were Puerto Rican, Ecuadorian, African American, and Caucasian. To achieve the standards, students had to participate actively in group discussions and encourage other students to offer their opinions. They also had to clarify and expand on their own contributions to discussions. Recognizing that speaking out in public might be in conflict with the cultural norms of the community, Goldstone decided to focus on more explicit communication with parents about the rationale behind the performance standards. She reasoned that greater awareness of the speaking standards might encourage parents to support their children in achieving these standards. Gladstone had the standards translated for various language groups and extended the time and availability of parent-teacher conferences. A bilingual school aide and several seventh-grade students served as translators at parent-teacher conferences where the conversations focused on students' scores on discussion activities, the importance of this skill, and ways that parents might help their children improve. In her action research, Goldstone collected and analyzed assessments of in-class discussions, notes from parent conferences, and survey responses from students and parents. Results of the student surveys reflected a "growing awareness of the criteria for good speaking and how the students measure up to the standard" (Goldstone, 2003, p. 70). Surveys of the parents also showed "growing agreement about the importance of speaking" (Goldstone, 2003, p. 71). By using a scoring grid to assess the audiotaped discussions, Goldstone was able to identify specific criteria being met by the students. Her findings indicated that by the third quarter, all but four students were "participating significantly" (Goldstone, 2003, p. 70). She also identified three major obstacles to successful communication with parents: "limited access to translators, limited access to translated materials regarding the standards, and cultural barriers that made it difficult

for some parents to practice discussions about academic topics with their children" (Goldstone, 2003, p. 77).

Classroom-Based Inquiry

The studies in this section describe action research to answer questions arising from classroom experiences. These teacher-researchers aim to better understand their students, themselves, and their educational context in order to act more wisely and effectively. They use primarily qualitative methods, as well as pedagogical reflection, to examine the connection between principles and practice (Larrivee, 2008).

INFLUENCE OF CLASS SIZE
Based on her concerns as a high school mathematics teacher, Nathasha Warikoo (2003) explored the following research question: Does class size make a difference in students' classroom experience? By studying the existing research on this topic, she discovered that a majority of the published literature on class size focused on elementary grades rather than high school (Finn, 1998). She decided to document her teaching methods as well as methods employed by a colleague in working with classes ranging from twelve to twenty-four students. She videotaped a series of classes and analyzed how she spent her time with students. She also had peers observe her and made time logs of her class sessions. Additionally, she documented students' perceptions of their learning experiences through journals, surveys, and interviews. In larger classes, Warikoo discovered that there were more whole-class discussions instead of group work supported by teacher assistance. Student responses indicated that a majority favored smaller classes, where they might receive greater individual guidance from the teacher. On one of the survey questions, for example, almost half the students indicated that they "concentrated more during individual time with the teacher than when working independently" (Warikoo, 2003, p. 105). Similarly in the interviews, the students said that they appreciated smaller

classes during "cooperative learning not only because they could work with their peers but also because the teacher had more time to spend with them individually" (Warikoo, 2003, p. 107). Based on the videotapes and observations, Warikoo also noted that there was increased teacher attention paid to low-achieving students in smaller classes. Her research prompted her to suggest two policy recommendations: implementation of class size reduction in schools and provisions for professional development targeting effective teaching methods that leverage the benefits of small class sizes.

MAKING HISTORY RELEVANT
"Why do I have to know this stuff?" This constant question from her ninth grade world history classes became the research question for Maryann Byrne's (2009) examination of strategies to make history more relevant for her students. She invited her students to be coresearchers, as individually and together they defined relevance for themselves. The class explored ways to test and evaluate beliefs and assumptions through surveys, discussions, and classroom activities that examined the impact of historical events on life today. Byrne noted

> Our classroom has become a site that embodies a number of theories of why the study of history is relevant ... as crucial in promoting democratic citizenship [and] as essential for promoting empathy and a sense of social justice.... Finally, most of the students have come to realize that history is not a collection of old facts about people long gone, but an ongoing, unfinished story of the human condition in which we all play a role [p. 312].

One salutary effect of the collaborative research was an atmosphere of openness and engagement:

> I hope I can continue to establish a beneficial level of discourse and classroom structure, open to negotiation, that will allow my students to feel empowered as active participants in their own education. I was pleasantly surprised at how this approach positively impacted classroom management

> issues and would like to look more deeply into how increased student autonomy influences student behaviors [p. 314].

Theory into Practice

The studies in this section show teacher-researchers taking inquiry to a more theoretical level using primarily qualitative methods. They generally use pedagogical reflection – applying "the field's knowledge base and current beliefs about what represents quality practices" and reflecting on "educational goals, the theories underlying approaches, and the connection between theoretical principles and practice" (Larrivee, 2008, p. 343).

METACOGNITION AND WRITING
As an elementary school literacy paraprofessional, Jody McQuillan (2009) investigated the relationship between self-assessment, metacognition, and writing. Through studying the research on writing and self-assessment, she identified key elements for self-assessment and created a tool to promote student self-reflection. Over a period of eight weeks, she worked with small groups of fifth grade students on writing activities that began with minilessons on topics determined by student needs. The students kept notes of the minilessons, created graphic organizers prior to writing, and used McQuillan's self-reflection tool as well as a more structured rubric before, during, and after they had completed their writing. An important component was peer assessment through discussion using the rubric. Collaboration among students, classroom teachers, and literacy specialists also was a critical part of the research. McQuillan explained the importance of self-assessment to students and solicited student feedback on the rubrics. She worked with classroom teachers to collect writing samples and observations of the students in class. She also worked with literacy specialists to identify self-assessment across different grade levels. When McQuillan analyzed data from these multiple sources, she discovered that

students were initially uncritical about their own writing, giving themselves high marks, but after discussing with their peers, self-assessment scores dropped. She concluded

> Students' self-assessment of their own writing pieces makes them more active learners, and it enhances their own learning. While developing students' metacognitive skills about writing could improve future writing pieces, I also think that these skills can be empowering for students, and they are critical for learning across the curriculum and even in life [p. 329].

Doing this research also helped McQuillan to unite theory with practice:

> After researching different forms of self-assessment, I integrated a self-assessment tool into the writing lessons, and I continually reflected on the process and the product. The processes of researching and reflection ultimately bridged the gap between theoretical research and classroom practice [p. 329].

BRAIN RESEARCH AND FOREIGN-LANGUAGE TEACHING

Emmerich Koller (2001) had used a sequential lecture approach to teach German and was concerned that some students were unengaged or slow learners. He examined his own perceptions and paradigms against the results of brain research applied to foreign-language teaching. Based on his findings, he changed his teaching methods to include preparing mind maps, acting out parts of the story, and writing poems and songs for lists of various grammar structures. Student interest increased markedly, and some students raised their grades significantly. His reflection on his struggles and successes indicate the emotional dimensions of action research:

> As I struggled to put theory into practice, I found the challenges formidable but not insurmountable. My transformation was a gradual, sometimes painful, sometimes exhilarating process that continues today and may never be completed. Therein lies not only the challenge but also the reward for daring to do something new, because success lies in the journey, not in the destination [pp. 140–1].

RESEARCH IN READING AND WRITING IMPROVEMENT

Vida Schaffel (2001), elementary reading teacher in a multicultural urban public school, changed the way she taught reading through research on the connection between reading and writing. Studying the research in the field strengthened her desire to move from basal texts and drill to a more interactive combination of listening, reading, and writing centered on giving her students the means to explore the meaning of their past experiences. She allowed students to work individually at their own levels and paces. Free journal writing was an important component. Her work was rewarding for her students and herself:

> Children who had trouble reading texts had no trouble reading their own writing.... I see myself more now as a facilitator rather than the purveyor of knowledge. I am constantly collecting data in my classroom while I analyze my own teaching and learning. I view children in a more holistic and developmental way than I did previously. I am more conscious of "process" and see "product" as being multidimensional and multifaceted [pp. 259–60].

For Schaffel, who was pioneering new teaching methods in her school, the support of other teachers was essential:

> It is difficult to be the only one in the workplace trying out new ideas. Even though I felt what I was doing was right, it still didn't make the task any easier. What did keep me going was the support and encouragement of a group of teacher researchers from the suburbs that I met with once a month [p. 259].

These studies of standards-based curriculum change, classroom-based inquiry, and theory-based practice are a sampling of the numerous teacher action research projects that emphasize the professional dimension. These research projects were rooted in the teacher-researchers' desire to answer questions arising from their classroom experiences and systematically conducted to improve practice, gain a deeper and more accurate view of the educational context, and bridge the gap between theory and practice. We now turn to studies that emphasize the personal dimension, with a focus on self-awareness and professional identity.

Personal Orientation: Self-Awareness and Identity

The following studies of action research focus on "greater self-knowledge and fulfillment in one's work, a deeper understanding of one's own practice, and the development of personal relationships through researching together" (Noffke, 1997a, p. 306). These teacher-researchers experience a process of personal transformation through the examination of practice and self-reflection (Noffke, 1997a, p. 329). In these studies, teacher-educators play a key role in encouraging critical reflection when teachers challenge assumptions, link theory to practice, and examine personal and professional belief systems (Larrivee, 2008, p. 343).

TEACHER DIALOGUE IN PROFESSIONAL DEVELOPMENT

Nancy Kraft (2002) studied the role of teacher dialogue and collaborative inquiry in a professional development course on improving elementary science instruction through action research. Eight elementary teachers met for one week during the summer and then monthly during the fall semester to present research and best practices in science, share reflections and progress on their research projects, and dialogue about issues and questions they encountered. Course facilitators assisted the teachers in questioning their beliefs, assumptions, and practices regarding teaching, learning, knowledge, and curriculum, as well as helping them deepen their understanding of science and how to operationalize the science standards in their own classrooms. Among the key themes that arose in the discussions were power relationships in schools between administrators and teachers and between teachers and students, ways to engender teacher ownership over curricular matters, and how to increase student ownership and voice in the classroom.

Collaborative inquiry enabled the teachers to question belief systems and understand the relationship between beliefs and classroom practices. Critical reflection enabled them to examine classroom practices in light of the larger context that often limited the potential of their work. Kraft concluded that the study "establishes teacher research as a viable tool for teachers to reclaim their authority and take control of their lives as professionals" (p. 189).

TEAMED APPROACH TO STUDENT TEACHING

J. Kay Fenimore-Smith (2004) participated in collaborative action research of a teamed approach to student teaching that tested three myths commonly held by novice teachers: "Everything depends on the teacher," "The teacher is the expert," and "Teachers are self-made" (p. 227). The research team consisted of a teacher-educator/researcher, a fourth grade teacher, and a student teacher. Data were collected through formal interviews, classroom observations, conferences, weekly inquiry sessions, student-teacher seminars, and the individual journals of each participant. As the student teacher progressed through her student teaching, she became aware of the fluidity of the learning process and the need for flexibility in the planned curriculum. As a result, she drew increasingly on her students' knowledge and backgrounds to develop learning activities. For example, she deviated from the state-mandated social studies curriculum to do a unit on Mexico to enhance learning opportunities for the Hispanic and white students in her class. Through adaptation and reflection, she moved from an unquestioned belief in the teacher as expert to an awareness of the complexities of learning situations and the need for flexible responses. Critically assessing her own instruction led to the ability to be critical about teaching in general. The team approach provided "a dialogic framework that helped to broaden student-teacher understanding of teaching as a process rather than an established paradigm" and "created space for multiple perspectives and voices" (p. 237). The action research dialogue also helped to democratize the relationship between the classroom teacher and university educator through "active, critical examination of the power relations and structures that produce teachers (and cultural myths)" (p. 238).

COLLABORATIVE RESEARCH

Sonia Bustingorry (2008) reported on the development of teacher autonomy through action research undertaken by high school science teachers in poor communities in Chile. The schools in these communities were characterized by high rates of poverty, a large indigenous population, and low rates of academic success. The teachers learned with each other and received guidance and support through collaborating with university researchers. Over a period of four years, the teachers moved from technical rationality to reflective teaching. One participating teacher confirmed the value of collaboration:

> I have had the opportunity to exchange ideas with other specialist colleagues and this does not happen at small schools such as ours.... [W]e have lent each other materials, we have consulted a lot. I also find it very positive that our students are changing and they have various contributions and life experiences and I think this has been very enriching [p. 414].

Bustingorry concludes that conducting action research was empowering:

> The constant practice of action research cycles – planning, action, observation, and reflection – made in individual form and shared with his/her [peers], around their pedagogical practice, influenced positively the development of the professional autonomy of the teachers involved in the research [p. 418].

These example studies show teachers questioning their professional identities and assumptions about teaching and gaining greater self-awareness and autonomy through collaboration with their peers and teacher-educators. The action research process is one of personal transformation enabled through interpersonal dimensions such as dialogue, interaction, and awareness of multiple perspectives and contextually shaped meanings. For some, this leads to an emphasis on the political dimension and social change, to which we now turn.

Political Orientation: Social Change

The following studies of action research show teachers struggling to identify structures that inhibit freedom and justice and taking action. These teacher-researchers critically reflect on the moral and ethical implications of their classroom practices on students and examine personal and professional belief systems. They are concerned about issues of equity and social justice that arise in and outside the classroom and seek to connect their practice to democratic ideals (Larrivee, 2008). Research methods are based on a critical, interpretive approach used to search out meanings and organize action to overcome constraints. The result is democratization of the research process and empowerment of participants.

RACE AND ETHNICITY

In a middle school of predominantly high-ability white students that had recently made efforts to diversify racially and ethnically, Kathryn Herr and colleagues sought to raise awareness throughout the school and the community of the experiences of students of color and to acknowledge "that there is power in the social construction and meaning attached to race and ethnicity" (Anderson, Herr, & Nihlen, 2007, p. 97). Over a three-year period, they conducted tape-recorded group interviews with students at lunch time, asking one main question: "Tell me what it's like being a student of color here" (p. 97). Herr notes, "What began as a fairly typical research interview study grew into more of a collaborative, action-oriented effort involving the students, my fellow research colleague[s], and me" (p. 98). Students began to meet together on their own time, apart from the structure of the group interview, to continue discussing the ideas brought up in the group. The group was called the Minority Awareness

Committee, later changing its name to the Humanity Interaction Team (HIT) after a series of threats to individuals and the school. The research project evolved into research embedded in praxis around the theme of racism:

> The original research was conceptualized to improve practice ... its actual evolution, including the sense of empowerment of the students, expanded the research agenda to one where research and action became a single process. Rather than the change effort following a linear equation where the data are gathered and then are applied to problem solving, the research question acted as a catalyst, generating a theme – racism – for further exploration and education [p. 118].

In assessing the rigor of the study, Gary Anderson, the outside researcher, identified four types of validity: (1) outcome validity: "established through the continual rethinking of the dilemmas presented, which ultimately resulted in a permanent student diversity organization" (p. 119); (2) process validity: "ongoing learning was established through the continuation of the HIT, which indicates that the learning will continue" (p. 120); (3) catalytic validity: increased consciousness level of students both in the majority and in the minority, and to some degree among the school administrators and teachers; and (4) dialogic validity: "achieved through collaboration between colleagues" (p. 120). Anderson also experienced his own struggles and transformation through action research:

> I had not anticipated that moving into an action research framework would feel so uncomfortable, that I would need to speak in the forums offered to me while feeling that I myself only had partial knowledge. I longed for the mythology of a cleaner research project, where I would speak from a safe, distant place about my data, and the change effort would carefully flow in a systematic way, informed by the power of the research results. I had not expected the reality to be so much messier than the research I had done in other sites where, as an outsider, I entered the research site and studied it but was not intimately involved in it [p. 115].

PEACE EDUCATION

Terry Carson's (1990) study of a critical action research group that included Carson provided insights on the challenging nature of critical/emancipatory action research. Eight elementary, junior high, and high school teachers in public and private schools formed a critical action research group with the goal of implementing peace education in their schools. Their vision of peace education encompassed rejection of militarization, a concern for structural inequalities, promotion of human rights, development of intercultural trust, and attention to questions of personal peace (e.g., alienation, substance abuse, and family violence). Within the context of their own institutions, the goals were to better understand the meaning of peace education, to develop the practice of peace education, and to help to transform their schools into structures respectful of human rights and nonviolent conflict resolution.

The group met every three weeks; conversations were tape-recorded and analyzed. Each participating teacher faced a different challenge. When his students planned a fundraising project for foster children in India, one teacher was conflicted over his view of charity as creating unhealthy relationships of dependence versus the desire to support his students' need to take positive action. Another teacher, whose class paired with another class in Indonesia, was gratified that her students became aware of both the economic disparities and the fundamental similarities between youth in the two countries. Others in the group faced the loss of a sense of community within their schools when their peace interests alienated fellow teachers. As a whole, the group moved toward a deeper appreciation of diverse dimensions of peace education, especially the ambiguity and difficulty of peace education concepts in practice: "Peace education casts politics, pedagogy, and what it means to be a teacher in a different light.... The point of peace education is learning to relate to one another and to the world differently" (p. 171).

These example studies reveal teachers grappling with the challenging issues of racism and violence as they examine the moral and ethical implications of their belief systems and practices. They struggle both internally and externally to create conditions that are more harmonious, just, and equitable. Critical reflection is a powerful element in this process, involving a critique of assumptions, confronting challenging emotions, and transforming perspectives and practice. Through the unity of research, practice, and imperatives for social change, politically oriented educational action research can enable professional, personal, and social transformations.

Conclusion

This chapter has provided an overview of the evolution, characteristics, methodology, and practice of action research with particular attention to the importance of critical reflection. As the example studies make clear, teacher-researchers draw on a wide range of action research philosophies, theoretical and professional orientations, and methodological concepts and tools as they engage in systematic processes to improve practice, understand teaching and learning in context, and change the ideological, educational, and social structures that are injurious to a "humane, just, equitable, fulfilling life for the students" (Rearick & Feldman, 1999, p. 336).

We began this chapter with the recognition that in the past decade educational policy has responded to global economic challenges by mandating student achievement focused on labor-market competitiveness rather than education for participation in just and equitable societies. Through the words of Orland-Barak (2009), we suggested that action research is a powerful paradigm for change that can help to sustain professional communities capable of standing up to these pressures. Orland-Barak's (2009) vision of action research as a practice of variety is a means for conceptualizing how this is possible through the unique forms of knowledge produced by teacher-researchers,

which could only be sampled in this chapter. Through inclusiveness and knowledge dissemination across educational communities, a rich body of knowledge that is extensive and deep, practical and theoretical, professional and social, scholarly and emancipatory, local and global, and attendant to classroom practice as well as educational policy can be amassed to support growth, choice, change, and dialogue that strengthen individuals and communities.

References

Adelman, C. (1993). Kurt Lewin and the origins of action research. *Educational Action Research* 1(1), 7–24.

Anderson, G. L., Herr, K., & Nihlen, A. S. (2007). Empowerment and practitioner action research: An example. In G. L. Anderson (ed.), *Studying your own school: An educator's guide to qualitative practitioner research* (pp. 95–121). Thousand Oaks, CA: Corwin Press.

Arhar, J. M., Holly, M. L., & Kasten, W. C. (2001). *Action research for teachers: Traveling the yellow brick road.* Upper Saddle River, NJ: Merrill Prentice-Hall.

Armstrong, F., & Moore, M. (2004). *Active research for inclusive education: Changing places, changing practice, changing minds.* London: Routledge Falmer.

Ball, D. L., & Cohen, D. K. (1999). Developing practice, developing practitioners: Toward a practice-based theory of professional education. In L. Darling-Hammond and G. Sykes (eds.), *Teaching as the learning profession: Handbook of policy and practice* (pp. 11–32). San Francisco: Jossey-Bass.

Baumfield, V., Hall, E., & Wall, K. (2008). *Action research in the classroom.* Thousand Oaks, CA: Sage.

Boud, D., Keough, R., & Walker, D. (1985). *Reflection: Turning experience into learning.* London: Kogan Page.

Bustingorry, S. O. (2008). Towards teachers' professional autonomy through action research. *Educational Action Research* 16(3), 407–20.

Byrne, M. (2009). Appendix A: Examples of teacher action research projects. Example 2: Why do I have to know this stuff? In G. J. Pine (ed.), *Teacher action research: Building knowledge democracies* (pp. 299–314). Thousand Oaks, CA: Sage.

Calhoun, E. F. (1994). *How to use action research in the self-renewing school.* Alexandria, VA: Association for Supervision and Curriculum Development.

Calhoun, E. F., Allen, L., & Halliburton, C. (1996, April). A report on the implementation of and results from schoolwide action research. Paper presented at the annual meeting of the American Educational Research Association, New York.

Carr, W., & Kemmis, S. (1986). *Becoming critical: Education, knowledge and action research.* Philadelphia: Falmer Press.

Carson, T. (1990). What kind of knowing is critical action research? *Theory into Practice* 29(3), 167–73.

Chiu, L. F. (2006). Critical reflection: More than nuts and bolts. *Action Research* 4(2), 183–203.

Cochran-Smith, M., & Lytle, S. L. (1993). *Inside/outside: Teacher research and knowledge.* New York: Teachers College Press.

Corey, S. M. (1953). *Action research to improve school practices.* New York: Teachers College Press.

Cresswell, J. W. (2005). *Educational research: Planning, conducting, and evaluating quantitative and qualitative research.* Upper Saddle River, NJ: Merrill Prentice-Hall.

Denscombe, M. (2003). *The good research guide,* 2nd ed. Berkshire, UK: Open University Press.

Dewey, J. (1933/1997). *How we think.* Mineola, NY: Dover Publications.

Eisner, E. W., & Peshkin, A. (eds.) (1990). *Qualitative inquiry in education: The continuing debate.* New York: Teachers College Press.

Elliot, J. (1991). *Action research for educational change.* Bristol, PA: Open University Press.

Elliott, J. (2007). Assessing the quality of action research. *Research Papers in Education* 22(2), 229–46.

Esposito, J., & Evans-Winters, V. (2007). Contextualizing critical action research: Lessons from urban educators. *Educational Action Research* 15(2), 221–37.

Fenimore-Smith, J. K. (2004). Democratic practices and dialogic frameworks: Efforts towards transcending the cultural myths of teaching. *Journal of Teacher Education* 55(3), 227–39.

Finn, J. D. (1998). *Class size and students at risk: What is known? What is next?* Washington: National Institute on the Education of At-Risk Students.

Goldstone, L. (2003). The mother tongue: The role of parent-teacher communication in helping students reach new standards. In E. Meyers and F. Rust (eds.), *Taking action with teacher research* (pp. 63–78). Portsmouth, NH: Heinemann.

Goodson, M. R. (1946). Charting a course for educational progress. *Teachers College Record* 48(1), 35–60.

Gordon, Carol A. (2009). An emerging theory for evidence based information literacy instruction in school libraries. 1. Building a foundation. *Evidence Based Library and Information Practice* 4(2), 56–77.

Grundy, S. (1987). *Curriculum: Product or praxis.* New York: Falmer Press.

Guba, G. (1981). Criteria for assessing the trustworthiness of naturalistic inquiries. *Educational Communication and Technology* 29(2), 75–91.

Hatton, N., & Smith, D. (1995). Reflection in teacher education: Towards definition and implementation. *Teaching and Teacher Education* 11(1), 33–49.

Hodgkinson, H. L. (1957). Action research: A critique. *Journal of Education Sociology* 31(4), 137–53.

Hollingsworth, S. (ed.) (1997). *International action research: A casebook for educational reform* (pp. 49–59). London: Falmer Press.

Hollingsworth, S., Dodds, M., & Miller, J. (1997). The examined experience of action research: The person within the process. In S. Hollingsworth (ed.), *International action research: A casebook for educational reform* (pp. 49–59). London: Falmer Press.

HoraceMann-Lincoln Institute of School Experimentation Staff (1945). Departmental notes. *Teachers College Record* 46(4), 275–6.

Johnson, A. P. (2005). *A short guide to action research,* 2nd ed. Boston: Allyn & Bacon.

Kemmis, S. (2009). Action research as a practice-based practice. *Educational Action Research* 17(3), 463–74.

Koller, E. (2001) Overcoming paradigm paralysis: A high school teacher revisits foreign language education. In G. Burnaford, J. Fischer, and D. Hobson (eds.), *Teachers doing research: The power of action through inquiry,* 2nd ed. (pp. 129–42). Mahwah, NJ: Erlbaum.

Kraft, N. P. (2002). Teacher research as a way to engage in critical reflection: A case study. *Reflective Practice* 3(2), 175–89.

Larrivee, B. (2008). Development of a tool to assess teachers' level of reflective practice. *Reflective Practice* 9(3), 341–60.

Larrivee, B. (2000). Transforming teaching practice: Becoming the critically reflective teacher. *Reflective Practice* 1(3), 293–307.

Lewin, K. (1946). Action research and minority problems. *Journal of Social Issues* 2(4), 34–46.

Lytle, S. L., & Cochran-Smith, M. (1992). Teacher research as a way of knowing. *Harvard Educational Review* 62(4), 447–74.

Masters, J. (1995). The history of action research. In I. Hughes (ed.), *Action research electronic reader.* Sydney, Australia: University of Sydney. Accessed January 18, 2010, at http://www.behs. cchs.usyd.edu.au/arow/Reader/rmasters.htm.

Mayhew, K. C., & Edwards, A. C. (1936). *The Dewey school: The laboratory school of the University of Chicago.* New York: Appleton-Century.

McCutcheon, G., & Jung, B. (1990). Theory into practice. *Teacher as Researcher* 29(3), 144–51.

McFarland, K. P., & Stansell J. C. (1993). Historical perspectives. In L. Patterson, C. M. Santa, K. G. Short, and K. Smith (eds.), *Teachers are researchers: Reflection and action* (pp. 12–18). Newark, DE: International Reading Association.

McKernan, J. (1996). *Curriculum action research. A handbook of methods and resources for the reflective practitioner,* 2nd ed. London: Kogan Page.

McQuillan, J. (2009). Appendix A: Examples of teacher action research projects. Example 2: What happens to students' writing when I add a self-assessment component to each writing activity? In G. J. Pine (ed.), *Teacher action research: Building knowledge democracies* (pp. 315–31). Thousand Oaks, CA: Sage.

Mertler, C. A. (2006). *Action research: Teachers as researchers in the classroom.* Thousand Oaks, CA: Sage.

Mezirow, J. (1998). On critical reflection. *Adult Education Quarterly* 48(3), 185–98.

Mills, Geoffrey E. (2007). *Action research: A guide for the teacher researcher,* 3rd ed. Upper Saddle River, NJ: Pearson Merrill/Prentice-Hall.

Mohr, M., Rogers, C., Sanford, B., Nocerino, M. A., MacLean, M., & Clawson, S. (2004). *Teacher research for better schools.* New York: Teachers College Press.

Noffke, S. E. (1997a). Professional, personal, and political dimensions of action research. *Review of Research in Education* 22, 305–43.

Noffke, S. E. (1997b). Themes and tensions in US action research: Towards historical analysis. In S. Hollingsworth (ed.), *International action research: A casebook for educational reform* (pp. 2–16). London: Falmer Press.

O'Connell, F. R. (2009). Teacher research and the problem of practice. *Teachers College Record* 111(8), 1882–93.

Orland-Barak, L. (2009). Unpacking variety in practitioner inquiry on teaching and teacher education. *Educational Action Research* 17(1): 111–19.

Parsons, R. D., & Brown, K. S. (2002). *Teacher as reflective practitioner and action researcher.* Belmont, CA: Wadsworth/Thomson Learning.

Ponte, P., Ax, J., Beijaard, D., & Wubbels, T. (2004). Teachers' development of professional knowledge through action research and the facilitation of this by teacher educators. *Teaching and Teacher Education* 20(6), 571–88.

Radford, M. (2007). Action research and the challenge of complexity. *Cambridge Journal of Education* 37(2), 263–78.

Rearick, M. L., & Feldman, A. (1999). Orientations, purposes and reflections: A framework for understanding action research. *Teaching and Teacher Education* 15(4), 333–49.

Schaffel, V. (2001). Shifting gears: An urban teacher rethinks her practice. In G. Burnaford, J. Fischer, and D. Hobson (eds.), *Teachers doing research: The power of action through inquiry,* 2nd ed. (pp. 253–60). Mahwah, NJ: Erlbaum.

Schon, D. A. (1983). *The reflective practitioner.* New York: Basic Books.

Seider, S., & Lemma, P. (2004). Perceived effects of action research on teachers' professional efficacy, inquiry mindsets and the support they received while conducting projects to intervene into student learning. *Educational Action Research* 12(2), 219–38.

Smulyan, L. (1984, April). Collaborative action research: Historical trends. Paper presented at the Annual Meeting of the American Educational Research Association, New Orleans, LA.

Somekh, B., & Zeichner, K. (2009). Action research for educational reform: Remodeling action research theories and practices in local contexts. *Educational Action Research* 17(1), 5–21.

Stenhouse, L. (1975). *An introduction to curriculum researcher and development.* London: Heinemann.

Stenhouse, L. 1985. *Research as a basis for teaching.* London: Heinemann.

Taba, H., & Noel, E. (1957). *Action research: A case study.* Washington: Association for Supervision and Curriculum Development.

VanManen, V. (1977). Linking ways of knowing with ways of being practical. *Curriculum Inquiry* 6(3): 205–28.

Ward, J., & McCotter, S. (2004). Reflection as a visible outcome for preservice teachers. *Teaching and Teacher Education* 20(3), 243–57.

Warikoo, N. (2003). Outcomes of reduced class size in high school math classrooms. In E. Meyers and F. Rust (eds.), *Taking action with teacher research* (pp. 96–113). Portsmouth, NH: Heinemann.

Watson, G. (1949). What are the effects of a democratic atmosphere on children? *Progressive Education* 17(5), 336–42.

Watts, M., & Lawson, M. (2009). Using a meta-analysis activity to make critical reflection explicit in teacher education. *Teaching and Teacher Education* 25(5), 609–16.

Wayne, M. (2003). Our unfinished story: Rising to the challenge of high standards. In E. Meyers and F. Rust (eds.), *Taking action with teacher research* (pp. 17–40). Portsmouth, NH: Heinemann.

Winter, R. (1996). Some principles and procedures for the conduct of action research. In O. Zuber-Skerritt (ed.), *New directions of action research* (pp. 13–14). London: Falmer Press.

Zeichner, K. M., & Noffke, S. E. (2001). Practitioner Research. In V. Richardson (ed.), *Handbook of research on teaching* (pp. 298–330). Washington: American Educational Research Association.

CHAPTER 25

Measuring Child Well-Being in Schools

How Robust Outcome Data May Inform the Selection, Design, and Implementation of Evidence-Based Programmes

Tim Hobbs and Tamsin Ford

Introduction

The purpose of this chapter is to provide a non-technical introduction about why data on the well-being of children are critical to the design and implementation of services for children in schools and to show how these data may be collected and interpreted for this purpose. Concepts of child well-being are introduced and the case made for why schools should be interested in measuring it. A methodology for assessing the nature and distribution of children's well-being using robust standardised measures is then described. The chapter then goes on to illustrate the types of data that may be generated from the use of standardised measures in schools. It introduces data related to the well-being of the average child in a given school, coupled with how those data may be used to estimate the proportions and distribution of children with likely impairments to their health and development. Finally, the ways in which these data may be used to inform the design and implementation of strategies and services to improve children's well-being are described.

The Broadening Remit of Schools: Moving beyond Educational Attainment

In the past, the primary focus of schools was to develop children's cognitive skills, particularly reading, writing, mathematics, science and critical and creative thinking. The goal was for children to pass examinations and to gain qualifications. This, of course, remains true and is further entrenched in a growing climate of school measurement and performance accountability, emphasised, for example, by the requirement of state and district report cards in the United States and the 'league tabling' of schools by academic performance in the United Kingdom.

However, there is 'another side to the report card' that is often neglected by policy-makers: the non-cognitive development, skills and assets of children (Elias et al., 2002). These may be broadly defined in terms of children's mental health and social and emotional skills. Mental health comprises not only the absence of impairments to emotional health or adaptive behaviour (such as anxiety, depression, disorders of conduct,

423

or attention-deficit/hyperactivity) but also subjective well-being more broadly encapsulated by a realisation of potential and the ability to cope with common challenges and adversity (World Health Organization, 2005). Social and emotional skills thus are a central component of broader definitions of well-being and comprise a range of facets reflecting self- and social awareness, self-regulation and management, responsible decision making and effective relationship and communication skills (CASEL, 2003; Elias et al., 1997; Greenberg et al., 2003). Taken together, mental health and social and emotional skills provide the foundation or necessary components for more positive and expansive definitions of well-being (Seligman & Csikszentmihalyi, 2000), the attainment of which many argue represents a fundamental aim in its own right for schools and other children's service agencies.

A growing number of reviews and meta-analyses of experimental evidence strongly indicate that it is possible to improve the mental health and social and emotional skills of children and that this may lead to marked improvements in other school-related outcomes (CASEL, 2008; Catalano et al., 2002; Durlack & Wells, 1997; Greenberg, Domitrovich & Bumbarger, 2001; Wang, Haertel & Walberg, 1997; Wilson, Gottfredson & Najaka, 2001).

To take just one compelling example, Durlack et al. (2011) report, in a meta-analysis of 213 programmes designed to foster social and emotional skills of school-age children, that these interventions were not only highly successful in improving these specific outcomes (reflected by a mean effect size of 0.57) but also positively affected children's academic performance (reflected by a mean effect size of 0.27). Put another way, even though it was not the explicit focus of these interventions, a child at the 50th percentile in terms of academic performance (i.e., performing better than 50 per cent of children in his or her school) would move up to about the 61st percentile following intervention (i.e., performing better than 61 per cent of children) (Durlack et al., 2011).

It is thus increasingly argued that as well as developing children's cognitive skills, schools also should teach and equip children with non-cognitive developmental assets not only to enhance well-being per se but also to enable them to engage successfully in society and the workforce (DeFries et al., 1990; Elias et al., 1997; Jackson & Davis, 2000; Kolbe, Collins & Cortese, 1997; Roeser, Eccles & Samaroff, 2000). Whilst schools often must do this in the context of limited resources, it is argued that improvements in children's non-cognitive assets and mental health will reap returns not only in children's immediate academic achievement but also in their longer-term economic and societal benefits (Heckman & Masterov, 2007).

If non-cognitive assets and mental health are essential for children's health and development, it follows that accurate measurement and monitoring of these dimensions are essential if schools are to design and implement services to improve outcomes for children. This chimes with a growing awareness across all agencies that measuring child well-being is an important basis for the planning of children's services, for making tough decisions about the allocation of limited resources, monitoring change and charting their impact on outcome (Axford & Hobbs, 2010; Ben-Arieh & George, 2006; Bradshaw, 1994; Costello, Foley & Angold, 2006; Ford, 2008; Gould, 2001; Rutter & Stevenson, 2008).

Additionally, schools are increasingly required to monitor and report on the well-being of children (in addition to academic performance) as part of their own statutory self-assessment, reflecting the growing prominence of the 'other side of the report card'. This, coupled with the large captive audience, makes schools an ideal place in which to collect data on children's well-being.

If data are to be used to underpin important decisions regarding services for children, then we must have faith in what these data are telling us. Despite this, the nature and quality of assessment of children's non-academic outcomes in schools vary considerably; in accord with children's services more broadly (Axford et al., 2009), schools typically have little data on children's health and development outcomes. That which is available varies greatly in quality; too often these data stem from bespoke questionnaires administered to unrepresentative sub-sections of the school population.

Standardised Measures

In order to provide accurate and reliable data to aid the implementation of interventions and programmes, we argue that schools should rely, where possible, on 'standardised measures'. These are questionnaires developed by experts on measurement; tested extensively and proven to be valid, reliable and sensitive to change; and supplemented by robust comparison data.

A *valid* measure is one that measures what it claims to measure. For example, a measure of hyperactivity should identify issues related to inattention, concentration and restlessness but not necessarily antisocial or aggressive behaviour.

A *reliable* measure is one that consistently produces the same results assuming that no change has occurred. For example, two different teachers administering the same questionnaire to the same children should get the same results. Similarly, a measure should show the same situation over time if no change has occurred; for example, if a child completes a questionnaire about how much exercise he or she does, and this does not change over a six-month period, then the results of the questionnaire should be similar throughout.

A measure that is *sensitive to change* is one that is able to detect real changes when they occur. Thus, if a child's level of hyperactivity or exercise changes over time or following an intervention, then the instrument should be able to detect accurately the magnitude of that change.

Finally, it is also essential that there is some basis for comparison; for example, relatively speaking, is an average score of 2.9 out of 10 good or bad? Similarly, if 8 per cent of a school population report being bullied,

is this figure high or low? The availability of appropriate comparison data helps to inform such judgements. A robust standardised measure will have comparable data available, ideally from diverse, nationally representative samples (referred to as 'norm data' in the literature).

The Strengths and Difficulties Questionnaire (SDQ)

To illustrate the potential application and value of the routine use of standardised measures of well-being in schools, we describe one particular tool designed to assess the mental health and social relationships of school children: the Strengths and Difficulties Questionnaire (SDQ) (Goodman, 1997, 2001). The principles and illustrations described in this chapter can be applied equally to other robust standardised measures assessing varying dimensions of children's well-being. (A non-exhaustive list of other potential measures is provided in Appendix A.)

The SDQ measures the mental health of children aged three to sixteen years and is built on the foundations of earlier work by Michael Rutter et al. (1967). It is a brief questionnaire comprising twenty-five items and can completed by the child, parent or teacher or a combination of these respondents. There are slightly different versions of the questionnaire for each respondent group. Parents and teachers may complete the questionnaire on behalf of children aged three years and upwards, and a child self-report has been developed and tested for children over ten years old (although some have cautiously suggested that it may be used by younger children aged seven or older) (Mellor, 2004; Muris et al., 2004). A validation and reliability study is underway in the United States (Angold, personal communication) in which the SDQ is being used in children aged two and compared with another validated measure used for this age group.

The SDQ has been used widely in Europe, North America and many other countries and has been translated into over

60 languages. It can be downloaded from the Internet free of charge for non-commercial purposes (www.sdqinfo.com).

The SDQ contains the following five sub-scales, each containing five questions, assessing the following dimensions:

- *Conduct problems:* disruptive or aggressive behaviour
- *Emotional symptoms:* anxiety and depression
- *Hyperactivity/inattention:* poor concentration and hyperactive behaviour
- *Peer relationship problems:* initiation and reciprocation of peer friendship
- *Pro-social behaviour:* kindness to and consideration of others

Each sub-scale generates a score between 0 and 10. Higher scores relate to greater problems in each area, except for pro-social behaviour, where higher scores relate to more pro-social behaviour. The first four of these sub-scales also can be summed to generate a 'total difficulties score' ranging from 0 to 40, thus providing an indication of the overall mental health of the child or population.

In addition to the total difficulties score and five sub-scales, there is also an optional impact supplement. Whereas the SDQ records the presence or absence of mental health problems, the impact supplement assesses the extent to which these problems can cause distress and impair the child's development or the well-being of those around him or her. It also asks if the child has a significant problem with his or her emotions, concentration and behaviour and about the chronicity of these difficulties.

The SDQ also fulfils the criteria of standardised measure by being valid, reliable and sensitive to change. In terms of validity, the SDQ has been demonstrated to effectively discriminate, with reasonable accuracy, between children with and without a likely mental health disorder (Goodman et al., 2000; Goodman, Renfrew & Mullick, 2000). Completion of the questionnaire by a child, parent and/or teacher increases the accuracy of such judgements. Furthermore, the SDQ

also demonstrates a high level of concurrent validity with the well-established Rutter questionnaires (Elander & Rutter, 1996) and the Child Behaviour Checklist (Achenbach & Rescorla, 2000; Goodman & Scott, 1999). Reliability and sensitivity to change are also well documented (Goodman, 1997, 2001; Ford et al., 2009). The SDQ has British norms taken from a large national study (Ford, Goodman & Meltzer, 2003; Green et al., 2005), as well as norms for some of the translations of the SDQ, including the U.S. version (www.sdqinfo.com).

Epidemiology: Administering Standardised Measures in Schools

The methodology for understanding patterns of disease and illness within a population is referred to as 'epidemiology'[1]. The same principles are being used increasingly to understand the prevalence and distribution of impairments to children's psychosocial functioning within large populations of children (Costello & Angold, 2006; Costello, Egger & Angold, 2005; Costello et al., 2003). It follows that the same methodology can be applied in individual schools.

As well as focussing solely on impairments to children's health and development, these methods also may be used to understand how positive or protective aspects of children's health and development may be distributed within a population. It is not the purpose of this chapter to describe in detail the specific methodological dimensions of this work; suffice to say that representative proportions of children (or teachers completing measures on behalf of representative proportions of children) should complete the administered standardised measures. In schools, it is typically most efficient and practical to adopt a child self-report census approach (i.e., all children in the school complete the measure or at least all children from selected grades/year-groups). At least 75 per cent response rates, ideally those nearer 90 per cent, are necessary to give a reasonably accurate picture of the psychological and developmental needs

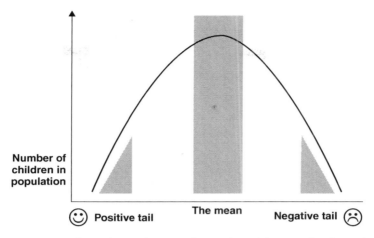

Number of
children in
population

☺ Positive tail   The mean   Negative tail ☹

Figure 25.1. Hypothetical Distribution of Mental Health in a School Population.

of the children because children who do not complete the questionnaire are likely to differ in systematic ways from the children who do. Attaining the highest possible response rate and comparing responders and non-responders on known characteristics are important to minimize the impact of selection bias on your findings.

Distributions of Well-Being within a Population

So what might epidemiological data from the SDQ, for example, tell us about the well-being of children in schools, and how might these data be used to aid the implementation of programmes designed to improve child outcomes?

Let us take behaviour as an illustration. Like most outcomes, behaviour is not equally distributed across the population; as such, there are numerous ways in which the behaviour of the population may be assessed. Consider Figure 25.1, an illustrative distribution from one hypothetical school. The horizontal x axis represents behaviour across a scale ranging from good to poor behaviour. The vertical y axis of the graph plots the number of children in the population on this scale of mental health.

To the far left of the distribution is a relatively small proportion of children who have no behaviour problems, and to the far right,

a similar proportion who have very poor behaviour that likely would meet a clinical diagnosis for a conduct disorder. These two ends of the population distribution, respectively, may be referred to as the positive and negative and 'tails' of the distribution.

The majority of children fall somewhere between these two extremes. This is referred to as the 'mean' of the distribution. Of course, in reality, outcomes very rarely form a perfectly symmetrical distribution such as this (referred to in statistics as a 'normal distribution'). The shape of the curve depends on the outcome being measured, the tool used to measure the outcome and the population being assessed. Nonetheless, this illustration introduces two concepts central to this chapter: the negative tail of the distribution and the well-being of the average child within a population.

Comparing the Well-Being of the Average Child across Schools

The SDQ lends itself well to considering both the well-being of the average child within a population and the proportion of children with likely impairments to their well-being[2]. The former is now considered.

Across each sub-scale of the SDQ, the scores of the average child in a class or school may be compared with the scores of the average child in wider populations, such as city, county, state or country. So

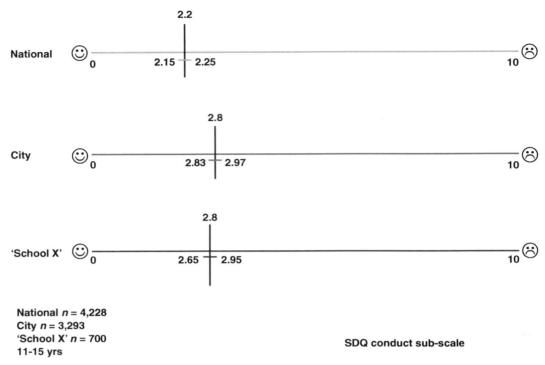

National *n* = 4,228
City *n* = 3,293
'School X' *n* = 700
11-15 yrs

SDQ conduct sub-scale

Figure 25.2. Comparing the Mental Health of the Average Child.

what might this tell us about the well-being of children in any given school? Consider the data on children's behaviour from the conduct problems sub-scale of the SDQ in Figure 25.2[3]. The behaviour of the average child aged 11 to 15 years in 'School X' is compared with the behaviour of the average child of the same age in that city as a whole and with the national picture. On the behaviour sub-scale of the SDQ, scores run from 0 to 10, with higher scores indicating poorer behaviour. Mean scores are indicated by the short vertical lines and figures dissecting the longer horizontal lines representing School X and the city and national pictures.

The average child in School X, indicated by the bottom line in Figure 25.2, scores 2.8, meaning that the behaviour of the average child in that school is marginally better than that of the average child in the city as a whole (who score 2.9). The 95 per cent confidence interval error bars around these mean scores (indicated by the short horizontal lines around mean scores) overlap, indicating

that these differences are not likely to be significant. The average child's behaviour in School X is therefore broadly comparable with that of the city as a whole.

However, the behaviour of the average child in School X and the city as a whole appears to be worse than the behaviour of the average child from the national picture (who, in this case, scores 2.2). The 95 per cent confidence interval range of the national average does not overlap with the School X and city as a whole, indicating that these scores are likely to be significantly different. The same principles may be applied to compare mean scores on various instruments across many schools.

Comparing the Proportions of Children with Likely Impairments with Development across Schools

A strength of the SDQ is that scores also may be used to calculate the proportion of children with likely significant impairments related to each sub-scale and to the total

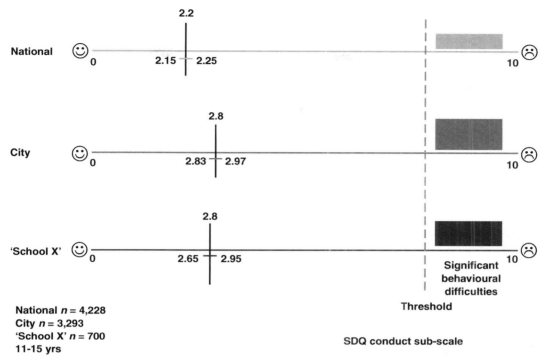

Figure 25.3. Comparing the Mean and Size of the Negative Tail.

score – referred to previously as the 'negative tail' of the tail of the distribution.

For example, a child scoring 20 or above on the self-reported total difficulties scale is likely to meet a clinical diagnosis for a mental health disorder if he or she were to be assessed by a psychiatrist. As with the mental health of the average child, the size of the negative tail of the distribution within a school may be compared with other populations, such as the national picture. These data may be further mapped onto mean score data, as illustrated in Figure 25.3.

In this case, we can see that the proportion of children with likely impairments to behavioural functioning (what may be classified by a psychiatrist as a likely conduct or oppositional-defiant disorder) in School X is 17 per cent compared with 21 per cent in the city as a whole. By comparing this figure with the national picture of 11 per cent, we can see that the rates of disruptive behaviour in this individual school and the city as a whole are elevated: Almost twice as many children in the city are likely to have

impairments to their behaviour when compared with the national average. It is also of note that poorer behaviour of the average child appears to be associated with a greater proportion of likely impairments (discussed further later in this chapter).

Disaggregating Data at the School Level

As well as providing an overall picture of the well-being of the average child and the proportion of those at the tail of the distribution, data from standardised measures may be disaggregated – that is, separated into their constituent components – in order to provide a more fine-grained analysis of well-being in school. For example, mean and tail data may be compared for boys and girls; in most cases, boys exhibit more behavioural problems than girls, whilst girls report greater difficulties in emotional well-being – but closer inspection of the data may identify exceptions to this pattern.

The well-being of children also may be plotted across age or grades within schools.

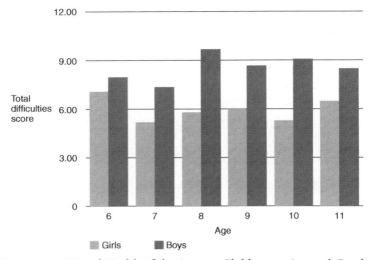

Figure 25.4. Mental Health of the Average Child across Age and Gender.

Data disaggregated in this way may identify particular ages at which children have the most difficulty. For example, Figure 25.4 displays mean teacher-reported SDQ total difficulties scores (a general indicator mental health) across grades in elementary/primary schools within one local authority in the United Kingdom (Hobbs, Little & Kaoukji, 2007). These data demonstrate that boys in these elementary schools have higher levels of difficulties than girls. However, in the participating local authority, girls enter primary school with relatively higher levels of difficulty than boys do, but there are improvements in later years. These data demonstrate that although boys in the local authority started primary school with relatively fewer problems compared with later years, there were marked increases from age eight upwards. Patterns such as these are likely to vary within and across schools and thus will inform intervention efforts.

Provided that each sub-group contains a sufficient number of children, data also may be used to identify disparities and inequalities in well-being across different sub-populations, for example, children with fewer financial resources (indicated by the receipt of free of subsidised school meals), different ethnic or racial groups, those with special educational needs, or those looked after by the local authority.

How might these data be used to inform the design and implementation of services or programmes designed to improve the well-being of children in schools? There are at least seven ways introduced below.

1. Data to Prioritize Outcomes to be Improved

Too often schools try or are required to do too much with limited resources. Often decisions to implement services to improve the well-being of children are made in the absence of robust outcome data; instead, schools are left to rely on streams of administrative data (such as rates of absenteeism, punitive measures taken by staff and academic performance) and staff and parent perceptions of need.

Collection of robust outcome data, focusing on intrinsic aspects of children's health and development using standardised measures such as the SDQ, represents a fundamental shift in assessment of need and planning of services for schools. Instead of making decisions in the dark or from limited administrative data, schools can prioritise the design and implementation of services that match the needs of the children.

The use of robust standardised instruments to assess a range of outcomes, along with appropriate banks of comparison or

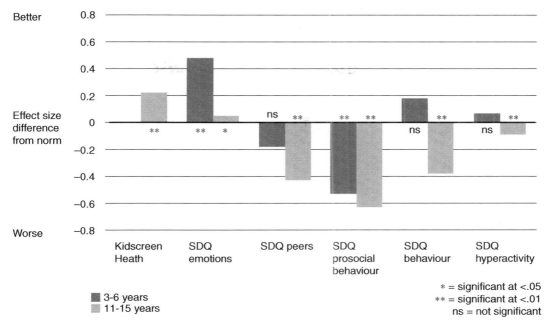

Figure 25.5. Prioritizing Outcomes: Effect-Size Differences from the Norm.

norm data, facilitates the processes of prioritising outcomes. Data may indicate particular aspects where children are developing on par or better than comparison data; on the other hand, they may highlight areas that are cause for concern and where efforts to improve outcome may be focussed. As such, these data may encourage schools to do fewer programmes but ensure that the programmes implemented are evidence-based.

To illustrate this, Figure 25.5 draws attention to those areas in which the average child within a number of schools in a U.K. local authority are doing relatively well or poorly compared with national norm data (Hobbs et al., 2010). The SDQ is supplemented with data from the physical health sub-scale of another standardised measure, *Kidscreen-52*. Data are reported for both parent-report SDQ for children aged zero to six years and child self-report measures for children aged eleven to fifteen years. The bars reaching upwards indicate that the average child in the local authority is doing better than the average child nationally, whilst bars falling below the central line indicate that children

are doing worse. The magnitude of these positive or negative relative differences are indicated by effect-size differences from the norm; effect sizes in the region of 0.2 typically are considered small, with those around 0.5 considered to be moderate.

In the example in Figure 25.5, children's physical and emotional health is relatively good compared with norm data, whilst hyperactivity and behaviour present a mixed or broadly comparable picture. On the other hand, these data indicate that both younger and older children's social functioning is a cause for concern and prioritisation for improvement [which in this particular group of schools helped inform the implementation of school-based programme called *Promoting Alternative THinking Strategies* (PATHS)] to improve the social and emotional literacy of children (Greenberg & Kusch©, 2002).

2. Data to Identify Populations for Targeted Intervention

Naturally, policy-makers and school leaders want to reduce harm and suffering of those with the worst outcomes – those at the negative tail of the distribution. To this end, many intervention efforts are targeted to work directly with this relatively small and often hard to treat population. Treatment interventions seek to bring children 'back over the threshold' to a place where their psychosocial functioning is deemed healthier.

Outcome data from standardised measures can provide information on the size and composition of the tail of the distribution in order to help inform the selection, design and implementation of treatment intervention efforts or programmes for those with likely impairments to their health and development.

Interventions are more effective when they are tightly focussed and aligned with the target population they were designed to serve. The use of robust outcome data, particularly when related to the negative tail of the distribution, therefore may be used in order to match the needs of specific populations with programmes or interventions specifically designed to address the identified problems for those specific populations. For example, disaggregated data may identify that economically disadvantaged males of a particular age show markedly elevated rates of impairment and thus would benefit from targeted treatment efforts. Outcome data thus help to inform decisions regarding what approaches are best suited for a specific school population or sub-population.

3. *Data to Encourage a Shift towards Prevention and Early Intervention*

The theoretical, moral, economic and empirical case for prevention and early intervention has been made many times over (see, e.g., Adelman & Taylor, 2000; Heckman & Masterov, 2007; Little & Mount, 1999). However, the availability of local data related to a specific school or children's service setting is invaluable and creates a firm basis for important decisions about the allocation of resources. For example, data from Figure 25.4 may stress to local decision makers that intervention in the early stages of the development of problems could help to prevent

or reduce difficulties later on. Similarly, all relatively poor outcomes presented in Figure 25.5 are worse for older children than for younger children, suggesting that problems become more exaggerated as children develop. Whilst longitudinal data would be required to confirm this, these data point towards the potential benefits of preventative and early intervention approaches.

Similar to identification of the size and composition of the tail of the distribution, disaggregated outcome data also may help to identify children most *at risk* of developing specific impairments to their health and development (such as those categorised as 'borderline' by the SDQ) and thus the potential size and composition of potential target groups for early intervention services. Alternatively, data may indicate the value of universal prevention programmes, in which all children within a school or classroom receive an intervention in an effort to reduce risks or enhance protective factors to obviate future problems.

The availability of local robust outcome data therefore may bring arguments for prevention and early intervention to life within schools and create an authoritative catalyst for change. To illustrate this, robust outcome data using the SDQ and other standardised measures were instrumental in policy-makers' decisions to invest £42 million in prevention and early intervention within children's services, including schools and education, within the United Kingdom's largest local authority (Birmingham City Council, 2007). These data also have helped estimate the size of target populations for a range of evidence-based early intervention efforts.

4. *Data to Inform Radical Approaches to Improvement of Well-Being of All Children*

Thus far the potential uses of outcome data from standardised measures has focussed largely on reducing the negative tail of the distribution (in terms of preventative or targeted intervention). However, using data related to the well-being of the average child in schools (demonstrated in Figures 25.2 and 25.3) also can pave the way for radical intervention efforts in schools, namely, public health approaches.

The premise of a public health approach is the improvement of the well-being of *all* children, not just those at the negative tail of the distribution. There are a number of expositions on the theory[4], but Rose's (1992) strategy of preventative medicine is the most elegant. It works on the premise that populations (be they school populations or society as a whole) are not just a collection of individuals but part of a collective distribution (demonstrated in the hypothetical distribution of mental health in Figure 25.1). As such, the health and behaviours of individuals 'are profoundly influenced by … collective characteristics and social norms' (Rose, 1992, p. 62).

Herein lies the public health potential: The attitudes and behaviours of individuals are intrinsically linked to the rest of the population; the majority of us basically like to be like everyone else. A public health approach seeks to harness this phenomenon and improve the behaviour of the average person, thus shifting the whole distribution in a positive direction. Therefore, rather than focussing on those at the negative tail of the distribution, a public health approach in school will target the average child, promoting positive change in everyone. It follows that over time, a shift in the distribution of the whole population also will drag the negative tail in a positive direction, reducing the number with impairments to their health and development.

Public health ideas are well accepted in relation to some physical health outcomes or risks, such as salt intake and alcohol consumption (Rose & Day, 1990). In order to demonstrate and test these ideas in relation to children's psychosocial outcomes in school, it is essential that data are available not only related to the tail of the distribution but also regarding the well-being of the average child. Standardised measures, such as the SDQ, thus offer the opportunity for schools to collect both forms of data and thus test these ideas.

5. Data for Screening Individual Children

As well as using aggregated (and therefore potentially anonymous) data to identify the broad target groups for intervention and estimating the size of these populations, data from standardised measures also may be used to identify specific individuals with likely impairments who could benefit from further assessment or targeted treatment intervention: this is referred to as 'screening'[5]. Although less common in practice but identified as a major priority for future development in a recent Institute of Medicine report on preventing mental health disorders in children and adolescents, screening also can be used to identify those most *at risk* of developing impairments, thus informing early intervention and prevention efforts (National Research Council and Institute of Medicine of the National Academies, 2009). The purpose of screening is distinct from the aggregated methods described previously and, as such, carries with it a distinct set of ethical and practical considerations.

Brief standardised questionnaires can be used to screen for children at risk of serious psychopathology and identify those requiring an intervention. For example, SDQ responses from children, parents and teachers can be combined using a computer algorithm (see www.sdqinfo.com) to give a rating (e.g., unlikely, possible, probable) of how likely the child is to have a psychiatric disorder (Goodman, 2001). This probability varies for the precise population studied. For example, in the general population, 50 per cent of children with a probable disorder according to the SDQ algorithm had a psychiatric disorder on detailed assessment compared with 75 per cent of children who were looked after by the local authority (i.e., in foster care or children's homes) (Goodman et al., 2004). No measure is 100 per cent accurate at detecting disorder, and screening measures may miss some children with impairing psychopathology and misidentify others as having it. The SDQ screening measure therefore is insufficient on its own to assign a diagnosis and should be backed up with a thorough clinical assessment where difficulties are suspected, and staff should refer any children whom they think may have serious difficulties, regardless of what the screen suggests.

A study in the United Kingdom is investigating the use of the SDQ backed up by a detailed validated assessment of mental health among children coming into the care of the state. The carers, teachers and young people (if aged eleven+) are invited to complete the SDQ after the child has remained in care for four months. Responses are collated using the diagnostic algorithm, and children with possible or problem disorders are invited to complete the more detailed Development and Well-Being Assessment (DAWBA) (see www.dawba.com: Goodman et al., 2000). Should the assessment identify a disorder, children are accepted by the relevant mental health service, with the detailed DAWBA assessment going with them to provide a foundation to their clinical assessment. This protocol proved feasible and acceptable to young people, carers, teachers and mental health practitioners and has led to the development of a pre-school version and deployment of the original protocol in other areas of the United Kingdom (Newlove et al., forthcoming).

Screening, however, presents a range of additional methodological and ethical hurdles over and above other forms of anonymised or aggregated data collection in schools. It is beyond the scope of this chapter to deal with these in depth, but the following issues are critical. The interested reader is directed to a special edition on screening in schools of the *Journal of School Psychology* (Albers, Glover & Kratochwill, 2007).

First, it is essential that screening measures demonstrate high degrees of predictive validity and sensitivity to change (Glover & Albers, 2007). Measures must be able to identify, with high degrees of precision, those with or at risk of developing impairments to health and development. Poor sensitivity may mean that the instrument

could underestimate the number children who are at risk of or suffer a likely impairment. Similarly, a poor instrument also may over-identify those with or at risk of developing impairments. Screening instruments also should be equally accurate and unbiased across different sub-populations, such as race/ethnicity, gender and socioeconomic status. As described earlier, the SDQ had better sensitivity among groups at high risk of psychopathology (Goodman et al., 2004).

Second, screening instruments must be practical, economical and accepted and used by stakeholders (Glover & Albers, 2007). The costs of administration and infrastructure needed to screen must not out-weigh the benefits, and screening methodologies and instruments must be quick and easy to implement. School staff also must see the potential benefits of screening, and concerns about reduced staff discretion must be considered (Elliot, Huai & Roach, 2007; Levitt et al., 2007).

Third, the ethical issues regarding screening and the ability and resources of schools to provide adequate services must be carefully considered. Active parent and child informed consent always should be a prerequisite of screening, meaning that both parents and children understand and explicitly agree to the purpose and possible consequences of taking part. In addition, if a school is screening for impairment or risk, are the resources in place to deal with identified need? For example, if the SDQ and DAWBA were used in a large high school and indicated that 20 per cent of children had high levels of need requiring service provision, would the school and associated children's services agencies be able to provide adequate services once need was identified? Similarly, unintended consequences and stigmatisation of those (accurately or inaccurately) identified during screening must be carefully avoided (Levitt et al., 2007). Effective screening programmes in schools thus need to be developed in collaboration with local mental health services.

6. Data to Evaluate Programme Impact on Child Outcomes

Standardised measures may be used as a 'before and after' tool to evaluate the effectiveness of interventions, specifically in terms of impact on children's well-being. Used in this way, they also may help to understand issues critical to the implementation and subsequent refinement of programmes to improve the well-being of children.

For the purpose of evaluating outcome, it is especially important that standardised measures are sensitive to change – that they can detect improvements or deterioration in outcomes over time. Measures that are very general and can be used in a wide range of children are likely to show smaller changes than measures that are specific to a particular sub-group – children with obsessive-compulsive disorder, for example (Lee et al., 2005). The SDQ and a follow-up version of the questionnaire have been demonstrated to be fit for this purpose and have been used to evaluate the impact of various programmes and interventions on children's mental health (including many within schools) (Mathai, Anderson & Bourne, 2003).

The most rigorous form of evaluation for estimating the impact of programmes designed to improve the well-being of children is experimental methods, namely, randomised, controlled trials (RCTs) and quasi-experimental designs (QEDs) (Rossi, Lipsey & Freeman, 2004; Torgerson & Torgerson, 2008). In an RCT design, children (or schools) are *randomly* allocated to two groups, one group receiving an intervention (the experimental group) and one typically receiving services as usual (the control group). In a QED design, children or schools are not randomly allocated, but experimental and control groups are matched across dimensions such as need and key demographic variables. An RCT design is more rigorous because it reduces the potential bias of matching, although it is not always possible or ethical to implement.

Prior to randomisation or matching and the provision of the new service, all children (and/or parents or teachers of children) typically complete one or a number of standardised measures to assess specific aspects of children's well-being prior to intervention. Standardised measures then typically are administered to both experimental and control groups during and/or immediately following intervention and ideally on a number of further occasions post-intervention (i.e., six months, a year, and possibly longer). It is then possible to determine what, if any, impact the intervention has on children's outcomes over and above 'services as usual'.

A step-wedge design can be used where a trial seems unethical or when practical restraints prevent all children, classes or schools from receiving the intervention simultaneously. In this design, all participants receive the intervention, but the order in which they do is randomly assigned across participants (at the level of the child, class or school as appropriate). Measures are taken before and after each intervention point from all participants so that those waiting comprise a control group.

However, many schools are not in the position to be able to evaluate the impact of interventions experimentally, and even when evaluation is considered, schools often fall back on simple pre- and post-intervention assessment of well-being without using a control group. Such a strategy seriously risks over-estimating the impact of change for three reasons. First, childhood psychopathology fluctuates, and by definition, young people are presented for intervention when their difficulties are in a bad phase; in all likelihood, outcomes would improve (a little) without any intervention, although not to the level of children without psychiatric disorders. Second, a phenomena called 'regression to the mean' is likely, meaning that children scoring particularly high (or low) will be likely to score nearer average on the second measurement. Third, another epidemiological phenomenon, 'attenuation', means that people tend to report less the second time that they complete a questionnaire.

In an attempt to circumnavigate these issues, the SDQ has an *added-value score* (Ford et al., 2009). Parental SDQ data from children who either had a psychiatric disorder or whose parents had talked to a primary-care physician or their teacher about their child's mental health in the 2004 British Child Mental Health Survey (Green et al., 2005) were used to empirically derive an algorithm for comparing observed parental SDQ scores from interventions with the expected parental SDQ scores from the epidemiological sample. The epidemiological sample thus functions as a proxy control group. A positive added-value score suggests that the children's parental SDQ scores have improved *more than would be expected*, whilst a negative SDQ score suggests a *less than expected* improvement or deterioration. When used in the control and intervention groups of children participating in an RCT of the Incredible Years Parenting Program, the SDQ added-value score was able to reflect accurately the change detected in the original trial (Ford et al., 2009).

The value-added score is calibrated for use with children at risk of significant clinical psychopathology and therefore is suitable for use only in targeted and indicated interventions. It would over-estimate change in universal interventions. Similarly, it is based on British children, and empirical work is required to test whether it can function in other populations. However, the use of epidemiological data as a proxy control group is a promising method for schools and others to evaluate their interventions where larger studies are unwarranted or unfeasible.

7. Data to Monitor Changes in Outcome over Time and Contribute to a School's Own Self-Assessment

In addition to experimental methods, standardised measures also may be used to monitor broad changes in the well-being of children in schools over time. This use of data is distinct from and not an appropriate alternative to evaluation. Nonetheless, the methods and resulting data described in this chapter can be used to take a 'snapshot' of need at a particular point in time. These snap-shots of need result in what are referred to as 'cross-sectional data' because they provide a profile of the population at one point in time. These methods can be repeated at regular intervals (e.g., year on year) to provide an indication of trends in the well-being of children in school over time. It follows that data may not necessarily be collected from the same children at each point in time (e.g., new children enter schools, older children leave school and children may or may not be present at school during data-collection times). It is therefore critical that data are collected from representative and broadly comparable populations at each time point in order to allow meaningful comparisons to be made.

Another way of monitoring changes in outcomes is to collect data from the *same children* over a period of time, thereby creating a 'moving picture'. This allows the establishment of typical developmental profiles of well-being over the course of children's development and promotes an understanding of services, policies and practices that may alter these trajectories. Whilst snap-shot pictures of need may be collected using anonymous data, the creation of 'moving pictures' – what are referred to as 'longitudinal data' – requires the collection of identifying information (such as name and date and birth) that allows linkage of data on individual children collected at different times.

Repeated cross-sectional or longitudinal data are no substitute for experimental evaluation. If school leaders want to know whether an intervention works in improving children's outcomes, then an experimental evaluation is necessary. Without a control group, this is not possible to ascertain. However, snap-shots or moving pictures may provide school leaders with useful data on broad trends in outcome over time. These data also may be used to compile individualised school reports providing a snap-shot of children's well-being and thus informing the 'other side of the school report' and satisfying part of the school's own statutory self-assessment requirements.

Conclusions

This chapter has introduced concepts and methodologies for understanding and measuring children's well-being and illustrated how these data may be used to inform the design and implementation of services and programmes for children in school. These data provide an objective base on which to make important decisions about service delivery which, too often, are made in the absence of any data at all. It is argued that collection of high-quality epidemiological data on the well-being of children may represent the 'other side of the report card' and can equip school leaders and practitioners with valuable information to inform radical innovations that may improve broader outcomes of children and, as a consequence, potentially enhance children's academic performance.

When epidemiology is well conducted, these promises may be fulfilled. However, decisions based on data will only be as strong as the data on which they are based. This chapter has not discussed in any detail many of the technical methodological requirements that must be fulfilled if a high-quality piece of epidemiological work is to be undertaken: These include, for example, robust sampling strategies to ensure that data are representative of the school population as a whole, how to handle and account for missing data, how to weight data statistically in order to ensure greater representativeness and what tests of statistically significant differences and effect size are best suited to the types of data obtained[6]. Similarly, epidemiological work within schools requires that strict ethical, informed consent and data security procedures are followed. Technical assistance thus often will be required to help schools ensure that data are robustly and ethically collected.

It follows that schools have much to gain by collaborating with other establishments in the collection of high-quality data on child well-being, either via informal networks of schools or orchestrated by school district leaders or governing local authorities. Not only will richer data sets be generated, allowing schools to compare various aspects of well-being within and between schools, but efficiencies also will be made in the engagement of required technical assistance to ensure that the data are robust.

Data on school children's well-being also will be highly beneficial to other children's service agencies outside education. When orchestrated at the school district or local authority level, data also may be linked to existing administrative data and may be used to help inform strategic development and service delivery across multiple children's service agencies (see Axford & Morpeth, Chapter 26 of this volume).

Collection of data, in of itself, will not improve child well-being. It is not sufficient just to understand the nature and distribution of well-being in a school. Rather, robust data can provide decision makers with a firm foundation on which to make evidence-informed decisions regarding the design and implementation of effective services for children.

Appendix A

A short and non-exhaustive list of standardized instruments that may be used in schools to measure varying dimensions of children's mental health is provided below. Some are freely available, and others are copyrighted and must be purchased.

Further scales assessing children's mental health also may be found at: http://www2.massgeneral.org/schoolpsychiatry/screeningtools_table.asp. For measures that assess other social and emotional dimensions of children's well-being, see http://casel.org/assessment/needs.php.

Name	Description	Reference
Strengths and Difficulties Questionnaire (SDQ)	A 25-item instrument for parents, teachers or children aged 11+ broadly assessing psychopathology in children aged 3–16.	Goodman (1997); www.sdqinfo.com
Child Behavior Checklist (CBCL)	A 120-item instrument for parents, teachers of children aged 11+ broadly assessing psychopathology in children aged 6–18.	Achenbach & Rescorla (2001); www.aseba.org
Warwick-Edinburgh Mental Well-being Scale (WEMWBS)	A 14-item child self-report instrument assessing children's positive mental health (positive thoughts and feelings); adapted from the adult version for children aged over 12 years.	Clarke et al. (2010); www.healthscotland.com/ understanding/population/ Measuring-positive-mental-health.aspx
Social Skills Rating System (SSRS)	A set of standardised questionnaires assessing positive and problem social behaviors for children aged 8–18. These may be completed by children, parents or teachers.	Gresham & Elliot (1990); www.psychcorp; pearsonassessments.com
Kidscreen-52	A 52-item parent or child self-report measure assessing subjective quality of life of children aged 8–18.	The Kidscreen Group Europe (2006); www.kidscreen.de
The Conner's Rating Scales (CRS-R)	A 26- to 28-item parent, teacher or child self-report instrument assessing hyperactivity, inattention and conduct problems for children aged 3–17.	Conners et al. (1998); www.psychcorp; pearsonassessments.com
Child Depression Inventory (CDI)	A 27-item child self-report instrument (or 10 item shorter version) used to assess depression in children aged 7–17 years.	Kovacs (1980/1); www.psychcorp pearsonassessments.com
Beck Depression Inventory-II (BDI-II)	A 21-item child self-report instrument assessing the presence and severity of depressive symptoms for children aged 13 and above.	Beck, Steer & Brown (1996); www.psychcorp; pearsonassessments.com
Mood and Feelings Questionnaire (MFQ)	A self-report instrument that helps children aged 13–18 describe their moods, emotions and feelings. Short and long versions of the questionnaire are available (13 and 33 items, respectively).	Angold et al. (1995); http://devepi.duhs.duke.edu/ mfq.html
Revised Children's Manifest Anxiety Scale	A 37-item child self-report instrument for children aged 6–19 measuring emotional and social dimensions of anxiety.	Reynolds & Richmond (1978); www.proedinc.com
The Child Aspergers Syndrome Test (CAST)	A 39-item parent-report instrument assessing likelihood of an autistic spectrum disorder in children aged 5–11 years.	Williams et al. (2005); www.autismresearchcentre.com

Notes

1. For an accessible introduction, read *Epidemiology for the uninitiated*, by Coggon, Rose & Baker (1993).
2. Whilst the SDQ was specifically designed to measure the negative tail of the distribution, it also has been demonstrated to function well across the population distribution; however, other tools, such as the WEMWBS, described in the appendix, offer a more focused assessment of positive dimensions of mental health.
3. Adapted from Hobbs, Axford & Jodrell (2010).
4. For an introduction, see Detels et al. (2004).
5. A distinction must be made between screening and other forms of assessment or diagnosis (Glover & Albers, 2007). Screening is typically conducted with *all* students within a specified population (be this a classroom, school or district) in order to identify those with or at risk of developing impairments. Specific diagnostic assessments, on the other hand, are undertaken with individuals previously identified as requiring further assessment owing to concerns raised about their well-being. They are conducted by specifically trained professionals, typically using in-depth quantitative and qualitative interview techniques, in order to make diagnoses based on these enquiries.
6. For an introduction to these issues, see Coggon et al. (1993), Last (1995), and Lohr (1999).

References

Achenbach, T. M., & Rescorla, L. A. (2000). *Manual for the ASEBA preschool forms and profiles*. Burlington, VT: University of Vermont Department of Psychiatry.

Adelman, H. S., & Taylor, L. (2000). Moving prevention from the fringes into the fabric of school improvement. *Journal of Education and Psychological Consultation* 11, 7–36.

Albers, C. A., Glover, T. A. & Kratochwill, T. (2007). Editorial: Introduction to the special issue: How can universal screening enhance educational and mental health outcomes? *Journal of School Psychology* 45, 113–16.

Angold, A., Costello, E. J., Messer, S. C., Pickles, A., Winder, F. & Silver, D. (1995). The development of a short questionnaire for use in epidemiological studies of depression in children and adolescents. *International Journal of Methods in Psychiatric Research* 5, 237–49.

Axford, N., Green, V., Kalsbeek, A., Morpeth, L. & Palmer, C. (2009). Measuring children's needs: How are we doing? *Child and Family Social Work* 13, 243–54.

Axford, N., & Hobbs, T. (2010). Getting the measure of child health and development outcomes (1): A method for use in children's services settings. *Child Indicators Research* 4(1), 81–100.

Beck, A. T., Steer, R. A. & Brown, G. K. (1996). *Manual for the Beck Depression Inventory II*. San Antonio, TX: Pyschological Corporation.

Ben-Arieh, A., & George, R. M. (eds.) (2006). *Indicators of child well-being: Understanding their role, usage and policy influences*. Dordrecht, The Netherlands: Springer.

Birmingham City Council (2007). *The brighter futures strategy*. Birmingham, AL: BCC.

Bradshaw, J. (1994). The conceptualisation and measurement of need. In J. Popay and G. Williams (eds.), *Researching the people's health*. London: Routledge.

Breslau, J., Lane, M., Sampson, B. A. & Kessler, R. C. (2008). Mental disorders and subsequent educational attainment in a US national sample. *Journal of Psychiatric Research* 42, 708–16.

CASEL (2003). *Safe and sound: An educational learner's guide to evidence-based social and emotional (SEL) programs*. Chicago: University of Illinois.

CASEL (2008). *Connecting social and emotional learning with mental health*. Chicago: University of Illinois.

Catalano, R., Berglund, M. L., Ryan, J. A. M., Lonczak, H. S. & Hawkins, J. D. (2002). Positive youth development in the United States: Research findings on evaluations of positive youth development in programs. *Annals of the American Academy of Political and Social Science* 591, 98–124.

Clarke, A., Putz, R., Friede, T., Ashdown, J., Adi, Y., Martin, S., Flynn, P., Blake, A., Stewart-Brown, S. & Platt, S. (2010). *Warwick-Edinburgh Mental Well-being Scale (WEMWBS) acceptability and validation in English and Scottish secondary school students (The WAVES Project)*. Edinburgh: NHS Scotland.

Coggon, D., Rose, G. & Baker, D. (1993). *Epidemiology for the uninitiated*, 3rd ed. London: BMJ Books.

Conners, K. C., Sitarenios, G., Parker, J. A. & Epstein, J. N. (1998). The Revised Conners'

Parent Rating Scale (CPRS-R): Factor structure, reliability, and criterion validity. *Journal of Abnormal Child Psychology* 26(4), 1573–2835.

Costello, E. J., & Angold, A. (2006). Developmental epidemiology. In D. Cicchetti and D. J. Cohen (eds.), *Developmental psychopathology*. Vol. 1: *Theory and Method*. Hoboken, NJ: Wiley.

Costello, E. J., Egger, H. & Angold, A. (2005). 10-Year research update review: The epidemiology of child and adolescent psychiatric disorders. I. Methods and public health burden. *Journal of the American Academy of Child and Adolescent Psychiatry* 44, 972–86.

Costello, E. J., Foley, D. L. & Angold, A. (2006). 10-Year research update review: The epidemiology of child and adolescent psychiatric disorders 2. Developmental epidemiology. *Journal of the American Academy of Child and Adolescent Psychiatry* 45, 8–25.

Costello, E. J., Mustillo, S., Erkanli, A., Keeler, G. & Angold, A. (2003). Prevalence and development of psychiatric disorders in childhood and adolescence. *Archives of General Psychiatry* 60, 837–44.

DeFries, J. C., Crossland, C. L., Pearson, C. E., & Sullivan, C. J. (1990). Comprehensive school health programs: Current status and future prospects. *Journal of School Health* 60, 127–90.

Detels, R., McEwen, J., Beaglehole, R. & Tanaka, H. (eds.) (2004). *Oxford textbook of public health*. Oxford, UK: Oxford University Press.

Durlack, J. A., Weissberg, R. P., Dymnicki, A. B., Taylor, R. D. & Schellinger, K. B. (2011). The impact of enhancing student's social and emotional learning: A meta-analysis of school-based universal interventions. *Child Development* 89(1), 405–32.

Durlack, J. A., & Wells, A. M. (1997). Primary prevention mental health programs for children and adolescents: A meta-analytic review. *American Journal of Community Psychology* 25, 115–52.

Elander, J., & Rutter, M. (1996). Use and development of the Rutter parents' and teachers' scales. *International Journal of Methods in Pyschiatric Research* 6, 63–8.

Elias, M. J., Wang, M. C., Weissberg, R. P., Zins, J. E. & Walberg, H. J. (2002). The other side of the report card: Student success depends on more than test scores. *American School Board Journal* 189, 28–30.

Elias, M. J., Zins, J. E., Weissberg, R. P., Frey, K. S., Greenberg, M. T., Haynes, N. M., et al. (1997). *Promoting social and emotional learning: Guidelines for educators*. Alexandria, VA: Association for Supervision and Curriculum Development.

Elliot, S. N., Huai, N. & Roach, A. T. (2007). Universal and early screening for educational difficulties: Current and future approaches. *Journal of School Psychology* 45, 137–61.

Ford, T. (2008). Practitioner review: How can epidemiology help us plan and deliver effective child and adolescent mental health services? *Journal of Child Psychology and Psychiarty* 49, 900–14.

Ford, T., Goodman, R. & Meltzer, H. (2003). The British Child and Adolescent Mental Health Survey 1999. *Journal of the American Academy of Child and Adolescent Psychiatry* 42, 1203–11.

Ford, T., Hutchings, J., Bywater, T., Goodman, A. & Goodman, R. (2009). Evaluation of the Strengths and Difficulties Questionnaire Added Value Score as a method for estimating effectiveness in child mental health interventions. *British Journal of Psychiatry* 194, 552–8.

Glover, T. A., & Albers, C. A. (2007). Considerations for evaluating universal screening assessments. *Journal of School Psychology* 45(2), 117–35.

Goodman, R. (1997). The Strengths and Difficulties Questionnaire: A research note. *Journal of Child Psychology and Psychiatry* 38, 581–6.

Goodman, R. (2001). Psychometric properties of the Strengths and Difficulties Questionnaire (SDQ). *Journal of the American Academy of Child and Adolescent Psychiatry* 40, 1337–45.

Goodman, R. & Scott, S. (1999). Comparing the Strengths and Difficulties Questionnaire and the Child Behaviour Checklist: Is small beautiful? *Journal of Abnormal Child Psychology* 27, 17–24.

Goodman, R., Ford, T., Corbin, T. & Meltzer, H. (2004). Using the Strengths and Difficulties Questionnaire (SDQ) multi-informant algorithm to screen looked after children for psychiatric disorders. *European Child and Adolescent Psychiatry* 13, 25–31.

Goodman, R., Ford, T., Gatward, R. & Meltzer, H. (2000). Using the Strengths and Difficulties Questionnaire (SDQ) to screen for child psychiatric disorders in a community sample. *British Journal of Psychiatry* 177, 534–39.

Goodman, R., Ford, T., Richards, H. & Meltzer, H. (2000). The Development and Well-being Assessment: Description and initial validation of an integrated assessment of child and adolescent psychopathology. *Journal of Child Psychology and Psychiatry* 41, 645–57.

Goodman, R., Renfrew, D., & Mullick, M. (2000). Predicting type of psychiatric disorder from Strengths and Difficulties Questionnaire (SDQ) scores in child mental health clinics in London and Dhaka. *European Child and Adolescent Psychiatry* 9, 129–34.

Gould, N. (2001). Developing an approach to population needs assessment in English social services. *Social Work and Social Sciences Review* 9, 22–35.

Gowers, S. G., Harrington, R. C., Whitton, A., Lelliott, P., Beevor, A., Wing, J. & Jezzard, R. (1999). Brief scale for measuring the outcomes of emotional and behavioural disorders in children: The Health of the Nation Outcome Scales for Children and Adolescents (HoNOSCA). *British Journal of Psychiatry* 174, 413–16.

Green, H., McGinnity, A., Meltzer, H., Ford, T. & Goodman, R. (2005). *Mental health of children and young people in Great Britain, 2004*. London: TSO.

Greenberg, M. T. (2006). Promoting resilience in children and youth: Preventative interventions and their interface with neuroscience. *Annals of the New York Academy of Sciences* 1094, 139–50.

Greenberg, M. T. & Kusché, C. A. (2002). *Promoting alternative thinking strategies: Blueprint for violence prevention (Book 10)*, 2nd ed. Boulder, CO: Center for the Study and Prevention of Violence.

Greenberg, M. T., Domitrovich, C. & Bumbarger, B. (2001). The prevention of mental disorders in school-aged children: Current state of the field. *Prevention and Treatment* 4, 1–61.

Greenberg, M. T., Weissberg, R. P., O'Brien, M. U., Fredericks, L., Resnick, H. & Elias, M. J. (2003). Enhancing school-based prevention and youth development through coordinated social and emotional learning. *American Psychologist* 58, 466–74.

Gresham, F. M., & Elliot, S. N. (1990). *Social skills rating system*. Circle Pines, MN: American Guidance Service.

Heckman, J. J. & Masterov, D. M. (2007). The productivity argument for investing in young children. *Review of Agricultural Economics* 29(3), 446–93.

Hobbs, T., Axford, N. & Jodrell, D. (2010). Getting the measure of child health and development outcomes (2): The picture for a local authority in England. *Child Indicators Research* 4(1), 81–100..

Hobbs, T., Little, M. & Kaoukji, D. (2007). Using the Strengths and Difficulties Questionnaire (SDQ) to measure the behavior and emotional health of children in schools in the UK. *International Journal of Child and Family Welfare* 10, 150–64.

Jackson, A. W. & Davis, G. A. (2000). *Turning points 2000: Educating adolescents in the 21st century*. New York: Teachers College Press.

Kessler, R. C., Foster, C. L., Saunders, W. B. & Stang, P. E. (1995). Social consequences of psychiatric disorders. I. Educational attainment. *American Journal of Psychiatry* 152,1026–32.

Kolbe, L. J., Collins, J. & Cortese, P. (1997). Building the capacity for schools to improve the health of the nation: A call for assistance from psychologists. *American Psychologist* 52, 256–65.

Kovacs, M. (1980/1981) Rating scales to assess depression in school-aged children. *Ada Paedopsychiatna* 46, 305–15.

Lee, W., Jones, L., Goodman, R. & Heyman, I. (2005). Broad outcome measures may underestimate effectiveness; an instrument comparison survey. *Child and adolescent Mental Health* 10, 143–4.

Levitt, J. M., Saka, N., Romanelli, L. H. & Hoagwood, K. (2007). Early identification of mental health problems in schools: The status of instrumentation. *Journal of School Psychology* 45, 163–91.

Little, M., & Mount, K. (1999). *Prevention and early intervention with children in need*. Aldershot, UK: Ashgage.

Lohr, S. L. (1999). *Sampling: Design and analysis*. Pacific Grove, CA: Brooks/Cole.

National Research Council and Institute of Medicine of the National Academies (2009). *Preventing mental, emotional, and behavioral disorders among young people: Progress and possibilities*. Washington: National Academies Press.

Mathai, J., Anderson, P. & Bourne, A. (2003). Use of the Strengths and Difficulties Questionnaire as an outcome measure in a child and adolescent mental health service. *Australasian Psychiatry* 11, 334–7.

Mellor, D. (2004). Furthering the use of the Strengths and Difficulties Questionnaire: Reliability with younger child respondents. *Psychological assessment* 16, 396–401.

Muris, P., Meesters, C., Eijkelenboon, A. & Vinken, M. (2004). The self-report version of the Strengths and Difficulties Questionnaire: Its psychometric properties in 8- to 13-year-old non-clinical children. *British Journal of Clinical Psychology* 43, 436–88.

Newlove, T., Leach, J., Murphy, E. & Ford, T. (forthcoming). Evaluation of a pilot project for the mental health screening of children who are looked after.

Reynolds, C. R., & Richmond, B. O. (1978). What I think and feel: A revised measure of chilren's manifest anxiety. *Journal of Abnormal Psychology* 6, 271–80.

Roeser, R., Eccles, J. & Samoroff, A. J. (2000). School as a context of early adolescents' academic and social-emotional development: A summary of research findings. *Elementary School Journal* 100, 443–71.

Rose, G. R. (1992). *The strategy of preventative medicine*. Oxford, UK: Oxford University Press.

Rose, G. R., & Day, S. (1990). The population mean predicts the number of deviant individuals. *British Medical Journal* 301, 1031–4.

Rossi, P. H., Lipsey, M. W. & Freeman, H. E. (2004). *Evaluation: A systematic approach*, 7th ed. London: Sage.

Rutter, M. (1967). A children's behaviour questionnaire for completion by teachers: Preliminary findings. *Journal of Child Psychology and Psychiatry* 8, 1–11.

Rutter, M., & Stevenson, J. (2008). Using epidemiology to plan services: A conceptual approach. In M. Rutter, D. Bishop, D. Pine, S. Scott, J. Stevenson & E. Taylor (eds.), *Rutter's*

child and adolescent psychiatry. Oxford, UK: Blackwell Publishing.

Seligman, M., & Csikszentmihalyi, M. (2000). Positive psychology: An introduction. *American Psychologist* 55, 5–14.

Torgerson, D. J., & Torgerson, C. J. (2008). *Designing randomised trials in health, education and the social sciences*. Basingstoke, UK: Palgrave Macmillan.

Wang, M. C., Haertel, G. D. & Walberg, H. J. (1997). Toward a knowledge base for school learning. *Review of Educational Research* 63, 249–94.

Williams, J. S. F., Allison, C., Bolton, P., Baron-Cohen, S. & Brayne, C. (2005). The CAST (Childhood Asperger Syndrome Test): Test accuracy. *Autism* 9(1), 45–68.

Wilson, D. B., Gottfredson, D. C. & Najaka, S. S. (2001). School-based prevention of problem behaviors: A meta-analysis. *Journal of Quantitative Criminology* 17, 247–72.

World Health Organization (2005). *Promoting mental health: Concepts, emerging evidence, practice*. Geneva: World Health Organization.

CHAPTER 26

The Common Language Service-Development Method

From Strategy Development to Implementation of Evidence-Based Practice

Nick Axford and Louise Morpeth

Introduction

Much more is known today than twenty years ago about what works (and what doesn't) in improving child well-being. But simply amassing this knowledge does not translate into action or tangible benefits: A recent review of implementation research concluded that 'It has been well documented in many disciplines that major gaps exist between what is known as effective practices (i.e., theory and science) and what is actually done (i.e., policy and practice)' (Fixsen et al., 2005, p. 2). A powerful manifestation of this problem is the low use of evidence-based programmes in children's services in the United States and in particular the United Kingdom (Fixsen & Blasé, 2006; Klett-Davies et al., 2008; Bumbarger & Perkins, 2009).

This feeble market penetration reflects a wider difficulty in children's services, namely, getting research into practice. Innovations to strengthen the connection include re-packaging complex studies into more digestible chunks, synthesising findings from similar studies and creating databases of effective programmes. The Social Research Unit at Dartington Hall, Dartington, Devon, United Kingdom, has long maintained that these are necessary but not sufficient activities because the model of change and the assumptions underpinning it are simplistic (Millham, 1993; Bullock et al., 1998; Bullock, 2006). Policy-makers, managers and practitioners cannot be expected to incorporate research into decision making simply because research findings are made accessible. Numerous factors mediate the link between significant scientific research findings and changes in what is done with and for children and families.

Over a number of years, the unit therefore has developed an alternative approach. Common Language offers a series of inter-related concepts and a set of resources, including practice tools, training, data sources and a service-development method. It was created specifically for children's services and seeks to reduce impairment to children's health and development. Its name alludes to the need to facilitate conversations between different stakeholders in children's services, all of whom tend to have their own language; it is designed to connect the different professions, agencies and disciplines that need to come together to improve child well-being.

The field of research utilisation elaborates on a number of different mechanisms through which individuals and organisations use research to inform decision making at the individual case and aggregate or planning levels (Nutley et al., 2007; Chaskin & Rosenfeld, 2008). A particularly helpful analysis of activities to promote research use in U.K. social care identified three models (Walter et al., 2004), all of which have been incorporated into Common Language (Axford et al., 2006). Thus it encourages the use of research-based materials in routine practice through practice tools ('embedded research') and requires practitioners and managers to identify and use research themselves ('research-based practitioner'). It also seeks to develop appropriate structures, processes and cultures within service agencies through strategy development and service design ('organisational excellence'). Specifically, *Common Language* incorporates a structured service-development method, or what is increasingly referred to as an 'operating system' – the analogy referring to the way in which such a package can facilitate a range of possible programmes, just as a computer operating system such as Microsoft Vista supports Excel, Word, Access and so on (Fagan et al., 2008). This is the focus of this chapter.

Operating systems represent attempts to connect prevention science and community engagement (Weissberg & Greenberg 1998; Spoth & Greenberg 2005). The best-known approaches are Communities that Care (Hawkins & Catalano, 2002), Results-Based Accountability (Friedman, 2005) and Getting to Outcomes (Chinman et al., 2004). Each one offers procedures to help communities and/or service agencies to improve child outcomes by developing (or selecting), implementing and then evaluating prevention, early intervention and treatment activities (Renshaw, 2008). They usually require analysing the needs of children and families and then selecting which

outcomes to focus on before identifying or designing the activities that will produce those outcomes and, finally, implementing services with support for the practitioners concerned. Some require a higher scientific standard of evidence of need than others, typically captured through epidemiological studies, and some stipulate that participants select from a menu of evidence-based practices (EBPs), whilst others encourage innovation. The amount of implementation support they offer varies.

So how does Common Language measure up in terms of these features?

How the Common Language Operating System Works

The Common Language operating system was developed in two phases. In the first phase (1995–2002), a method for achieving a better match between the needs of children and services received (Little et al., 1999) was applied in numerous local authorities and children's services agencies, mainly in the United Kingdom but also in some areas of continental Europe and the United States (Little et al., 2002b; Tunnard, 2002; Melamid & Brodbar, 2003; Johnson & Sawbridge, 2004; Taylor, 2005). The approach focused exclusively on children served by service agencies and often looked at particular sub-groups, such as children in care or those who are disabled. It involved collecting qualitative data from agency case files and using these as the basis for designing needs-led services. In the second phase (2003–present), the method evolved to cover all children and incorporated a more detailed and sophisticated set of procedures for using the data to help improve outcomes. Services better matched to need are more likely to be developed if data are gathered from all children in the community rather than from service populations only because it cannot be assumed that all children in need are known to agencies. This version has been used in Ireland, Birmingham, U.K., and Atlanta, GA, USA.

The Common Language operating system has five stages. The first, strategy

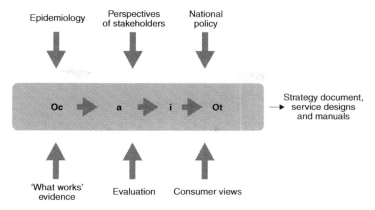

Figure 26.1. The Strategy-Development Process[1].

development, involves setting out in broad terms the desired outcomes to be achieved and how they will be achieved. The second stage is service design and entails specifying the nature of the services to be implemented as part of the strategy. Third, a detailed manual is prepared for each service design, setting out exactly what will be delivered and how. It serves as a handbook for those implementing the services. The implementation stage comes fourth and is supported with training and technical assistance to ensure quality and fidelity of service delivery. Fifth, the service is evaluated for its impact, implementation and cost-effectiveness.

The aim of strategy development is to secure consensus amongst a group of service leaders about the outcomes they want to achieve for children, the types of activities that will be implemented to secure them and the investment – in terms of money, staffing, goodwill, premises and so on – needed to enable these. The product is a concise document describing the investment strategy in a language that is easily understood. This work is not undertaken in isolation; the leaders are exposed to high-quality data about all children in the area concerned, gathered using an epidemiological survey (see below), as well as research evidence about 'what works' and national policy and stakeholder perspectives (Figure 26.1). The strategy-development process combines facilitation and training. An experienced

facilitator leads the group through a series of exercises to help form a consensus and also defines key concepts to help structure the conversations.

The investment strategy is typically translated into a number of 'service designs', which, like the strategy, are developed in collaboration with representatives of service agencies and the community. Each design sets out precisely and succinctly the outcomes to be achieved over a specified period, the target group of children or families, the essential service components (what is actually delivered), the logic model or programme theory (to explain how the service components contribute to the outcomes) and demand (a realistic estimation of the number of potential and likely service users). The service design then is worked up into an implementation manual, which adds details: the research background to the service and the need it is addressing; the selection, training and supervision of staff and clients; staffing structure, roles and responsibilities; expectations regarding time allocation; resource materials; the nature of training and technical assistance; ethical standards and what the evaluation comprises. The manual complements any programme materials to be delivered, such as lesson plans. It serves as the blueprint for implementation and also is intended to make the evaluation more straightforward.

The Common Language operating system focuses on any age group in the 0- to 25-year range and concerns both children and their families. It is used, in part, to develop universal services, namely, those aimed at *all* children; some of these adopt a 'public health' approach, in that they intend to shift the mean of the distribution on a particular outcome in order to improve the situation of the worst off over time (see Rose, 1992; Axford & Little, 2009). Common Language is also used to develop services targeted at children with identified actual or likely impairments on given outcomes – for example, children with diagnosed behaviour or mental health problems. Thus the strategies developed using Common Language often include a mix of public health and targeted services.

The process is driven by a focus on outcomes, defined in terms of children's health and development. The selection of outcomes is first step in the strategy-development stage, and considerable time is usually allocated to this aspect. This is so because the modus operandi in many children's services organisations has been to focus on what can be done with available inputs – money, staff, buildings and so on – and to measure success in terms of output indicators – how much service is provided, what processes are completed, which administrative categories children fall into and so on. Outcomes and their measurement traditionally have been an after-thought. Several factors shape which outcomes service leaders prioritise, including the scale of the problem, the cost to service agencies and wider society of acting or not acting, the evidence on what can be achieved, political priorities and available funding streams.

High-quality epidemiological data on children's health and development and influences on them – including environment, socio-economic status and family relationships – provide the platform for the work. Critically, they inform the selection of desired outcomes in the strategy-development stage. The data are generated using two instruments that comprise valid and reliable standardised scales for measuring child well-being. These are delivered, respectively, to parents or carers of children aged zero to

six years via a self-completion instrument administered in a household survey [Health and Development Outcomes of Children in the Community (HDOC)] and to children aged seven to eighteen years in school settings via an on-line audio computer-assisted personal interviewing (ACAPI) format [Health and Development Outcomes of Children in School (HDOS)]. Robust sampling procedures are used to ensure that the samples are representative of the population concerned, and statistical weighting is applied to correct any slight imbalances in, say, the gender, age or ethnic distribution (Hobbs, 2009). The results are presented in terms of the average and cut-off (indicating significant concern) scores for each scale and considered in relation to comparison (where possible, normative) data from other studies to help service leaders judge how well children in the sample are doing (Hobbs et al., 2010).

These data are powerful because they paint a picture of all children and come directly from children and families. However, to ensure that other perspectives are taken into account, and to cover outcomes not addressed by the epidemiological survey, they are supplemented by data from other sources. These include administrative information on need and demographics as well as quantitative and qualitative findings from other research studies, for example, concerning the relationship between influences and outcomes. A brief analysis of service use helps with detecting significant gaps in provision.

The Common Language operating system can be driven by policy-makers in service systems or by the community. Ideally, both sets of stakeholders will be involved. Thus the Social Research Unit's work in several communities in Ireland was led by community activists who formed consortia comprising residents and representatives of local statutory and voluntary service providers (e.g., Zappone, 2007). In Birmingham, by contrast, the director of children's services took the initiative by convening the directors of the city's main statutory and voluntary agencies for an intensive strategy-development process over six days. This can appear very 'top-down', so counterbalancing efforts entail consulting extensively with practitioners and children and families about priorities or the shape of the services being designed.

Irrespective of whether the approach taken is more top-down or more bottom-up, Common Language encourages the involvement of a diverse group of stakeholders. This invariably spans the ranks of seniority, from service leaders and managers to frontline practitioners. It includes professionals and non-professionals, be they service users or other members of the community. And it cuts across professions and disciplines, taking in social work, health, education and police and youth justice personnel from the statutory and non-statutory sectors. The rationale for this expansive approach is that the resulting services are more likely to work if those charged with delivering them and those for whom they are intended understand and have some sense of ownership of them. There is no blueprint for engaging these constituencies, so creativity is encouraged.

Some operating systems encourage 'bluesky thinking' from participants in the form of inventing 'new' services, whilst others require those involved to select exclusively from a menu of programmes that meet a prescribed standard of evidence of effectiveness. Common Language, by contrast, has explicitly encouraged both innovation *and* the adoption and adaptation of existing programmes. In the case of designing brand-new services, it has provided a process for sketching links between risk factors identified in the epidemiological study and considering what activity could break the chains of risk that lead to poor outcomes. Increasingly, agencies are urged to pursue the evidence-based programme option first rather than opt to start with innovation.

The use of high-quality research evidence is encouraged in every aspect of Common Language. In addition to requiring the collection of robust data on children's health and development outcomes, as outlined earlier, the method seeks to connect decision makers with scientific evidence about the aetiology of problems in children's lives because this highlights suitable points of intervention and about 'what works' to prevent or treat those difficulties. Participants in the method are sign posted to the 'model' and 'promising' programmes listed in various databases of effective interventions, but efforts are also made to ensure that decisions are grounded in an understanding of what different standards of evidence mean (e.g., Social Research Unit, 2010). There is a particular emphasis on programmes that have been through several real-world randomised, controlled trials and found consistently to produce statistically significant effects (e.g., Mihalic et al., 2002).

The evidence is brought to the attention of participants in various ways, including expert presentations to service leaders, directed reading and study tours to observe evidence-based programmes in action and meet with their developers, implementers and evaluators. A summary of the evidence supporting the service designed or selected is required in every implementation manual.

All innovations and adaptations of existing programmes that emerge from the process are evaluated rigorously. Ideally, each evaluation will examine the impact of the service on outcomes, the extent to which it is implemented with quality and fidelity (i.e., consistent with the service design), how satisfied service users are with their experience, and finally, whether and how far the service is cost-effective. Experimental evaluation is recommended unless it is impractical or unethical because this will provide the strongest evidence of impact (Torgerson & Torgerson, 2008). It is assumed that services found to be cost-effective will be scaled up and that those which are ineffective will be stopped or amended to address any weaknesses identified. It is vital that evaluation requirements be taken into account early in the design stage because they affect delivery decisions – for example, regarding referral procedures or the number of children who need to receive the service over a specified period.

Common Language is underpinned by a conceptual framework that rests on the concepts of outcomes, activities, investments and outputs. It is informed by the disciplines of prevention and implementation science, developmental psychopathology and organisational and management studies. In order to help the service-design process to run smoothly and to generate 'buy-in' amongst stakeholders, service-design group members and other senior staff are invited to take part in a fifteen-day training programme that covers core concepts and procedures.

Finally, unlike some operating systems, Common Language involves providing concerted support for practitioners implementing the services developed or adopted through the process. Thus the service-design group plans implementation requirements such as staff recruitment, training, supervision, coaching, technical assistance and the engagement of users. These issues are covered in a dedicated chapter of the manual. In the event of an existing programme being implemented, its dedicated support package tends to be adopted (if it has one), although care is needed to ensure that this is sustainable in a regular service system.

Applications of the Common Language Operating System

Among the areas where the Common Language operating system has been implemented are the United Kingdom and Ireland. These applications are now described.

Atlantic Philanthropies is a multinational grant-making organisation. In 2004, it decided to invest $200 million in the Republic of Ireland and Northern Ireland in what became known as the Disadvantaged Children and Youth Programme (DCYP) (Paulsell et al., 2009). The Common Language operating system was used to help develop and structure the over-arching logic model for the investment and was adopted by most grantees to help develop their strategies. The goal of the programme is, over a ten-year period, to secure demonstrable gains in children's health, educational achievement and sense of belonging to the communities in which they live (Little & Abunimah, 2007; Axford et al., 2008).

Two types of investment have been made to support this goal. 'Community Engagement' sites are economically disadvantaged areas with a child population of between 3,000 and 7,000. They have used Common Language to develop strategies comprising between five and ten services and ideas for integration. Average investment per site is about 5 million euros per annum, with each strategy designed to improve outcomes over a ten-year period. In 'Innovation Sites', a community or voluntary organisation uses Common Language to design a new service or adapt an evidence-based programme with the goal of improving outcomes for children across a wide geographical area. The work is normally expected to take three to five years to complete, including evaluation, and investment is about 1 million euros each year per site. The nature of all sites is discussed in more detail elsewhere (Paulsell et al., 2009), so two examples are summarised here.

Tallaght West, a Community Engagement site, lies at the foot of the Wicklow mountains, thirteen kilometres southwest of Dublin City. Despite a rich community life, with many strong and deeply rooted voluntary organisations, it remains one of the most disadvantaged areas of Ireland. In this context, a consortium of people living and working there formed the Childhood Development Initiative (CDI)[2] and, using Common Language, created a ten-year strategy to improve the health, safety and learning of local children and to strengthen their sense of belonging in that community (CDI, 2005).

This strategy has three elements: (1) creating new exemplar services, including an early childhood care and education service and after-school services to promote literacy and pro-social behaviour, respectively; (2) enhancing the quality and integration of existing local services, including more coordinated planning to identify and address gaps in service delivery; and (3) creating and sustaining an improved neighbourhood environment, such as through a community safety contract developed among residents, the police and the local authority. The strategy was based on extensive and in-depth use of epidemiological and other research evidence; consultation with children, parents and other local stakeholders; reference to national policy and international literature and expertise regarding what works in prevention and early intervention (see Zappone, 2007).

Archways[3], by contrast, is a non-profit organisation established in 2007 to promote the use of evidence-based programmes for children and young people in the Republic of Ireland who are experiencing social, emotional and behavioural difficulties. It seeks to promote the roll-out and evaluation of the Incredible Years (IY) series of programmes designed to reduce children's aggression and behaviour problems and increase social competence at home and at school (Webster-Stratton et al., 2001). This includes delivering the IY programmes to parents, teachers and children; providing service providers with on-going training, materials and consultation; supporting group leaders to maintain programme fidelity and attain accreditation and managing quality research to evaluate programme implementation and outcomes. Archways received funding from Atlantic Philanthropies early in its development stage, and an IY implementation manual was prepared using Common Language to help strengthen fidelity and assist with integrating the intervention into mainstream provision.

Although robust, it was always recognised that the new service designs in the DCYP only represent a series of hypotheses about the best way to improve child outcomes. Community Engagement and Innovation sites therefore are required to commission high-quality evaluations as part of the work. For example, the CDI asked the Centre for Social and Educational Research (CSER), based in the Dublin Institute of Technology (DIT), and the Institute of Education (IoE), University of London, to assess the impact of its early years programme, whilst Archways asked a team led by the National University of Ireland, Maynooth, to evaluate IY (see McGilloway et al., 2009). Both studies are

employing randomised, controlled trial (RCT) designs over three years. Prior to the Atlantic programme, there were barely a handful of experiments in children's services on the island, with only one published (Johnson et al., 1993).

Meanwhile, Birmingham is a large, multicultural city in the heart of England. It has a population of just over 1 million, a quarter of whom are under eighteen years of age. A former industrial centre, the city experiences higher than average levels of unemployment and poverty. Expenditure on children's services is approximately £1.3 billion per year, and an estimated 50,000 people work face to face with children. The project there had an unconventional start. The City Council's director of children's services attended one of the Social Research Unit's study tours in the United States. This was at a time when national legislation and policy guidance (DfES, 2004) demanded better joined-up services and the production of a children's plan stating what services would be put in place to meet identified need. After spending four days learning about Common Language and meeting with researchers, community leaders and practitioners implementing and evaluating evidence-based programmes, the director decided to use the Common Language operating system to shape the development of the city's children's services.

Once home, the director secured the support of elected members and his senior team and became the champion for what become known as 'Brighter Futures' (BCC, 2007). He appointed a member of his senior team to lead the work. She convened a one-day meeting of the leaders of children's services from across the city and, through that, secured their commitment to participate in the strategy-development process, which required them to commit to attend six planning days over four months. A series of consultation events was arranged so that the decisions and ideas emerging from the leadership group could be tested with large groups of managers and practitioners.

In preparation for the first strategy-development day, surveys were conducted – using the instruments discussed earlier in this chapter – to provide a reliable picture of the well-being of a representative sample of children aged zero to eighteen years across the city. The data that emerged were complemented by information from a systematic trawl and synthesis of administrative data and local needs assessment reports. The data were presented to the leadership group in a style that enabled them to decide their priorities for children. For instance, it became clear that Birmingham's children had significantly elevated rates of conduct disorder compared with children of the same age in the United Kingdom as a whole (Hobbs et al., 2010). Since the mental health of young people in the United Kingdom was known to be poor compared with previous decades and many other Western developed countries (Layard & Dunn, 2009), this finding led to behaviour being selected as one of six priority outcomes.

The leadership group were guided through the strategy-development process outlined earlier and produced the Brighter Futures strategy. This enshrined a commitment to focus on six priority outcomes: physical health, literacy and numeracy, social literacy, emotional health, behaviour and job skills. Children were to be maintained at home, in school and out of the criminal justice system wherever possible. All investments in services would need to demonstrate how selected activities logically would result in the chosen outcomes. Services would be planned for 'all children' and for 'children in need' according to their developmental stage. The portfolio would include a balance of prevention, early intervention and intervention activity (see Little & Mount, 1999) with a gradual decommissioning of activity that had no evidence base and an investment in programmes, polices and practices with a robust evidence base.

The publication of Brighter Futures coincided with the local authority using a method called 'business transformation' to improve services. Ordinarily, this involves investing in processes to find savings in the long term, for example, by introducing a computer system that will reduce the administrative burden, so requiring fewer administrative staff. The Children's Directorate were able to make a case for investing in prevention and early intervention services on the premise that this would result in a reduced need in the future for expensive 'heavy-end' interventions. They secured an investment of £42 million (~$60 million) over five years with an expected return of £100 million (~$140 million) over fifteen years. This was based on estimates that drew on the work of the Washington State Institute of Public Policy (see below).

As part of Brighter Futures, Birmingham is implementing and rigorously evaluating four evidence-based programmes: Family Nurse Partnership (Olds et al., 1998), Promoting Alternative Thinking Strategies (PATHS) (Greenberg et al., 1998), Incredible Years (Webster-Stratton et al., 2001) and Triple P (Prinz et al., 2009). It also plans to introduce four more in the near future. Since the selected programmes have been subjected successfully to several RCTs outside of the United Kingdom, the evaluations in Birmingham are effectively 'replication studies' – seeking to replicate the findings from elsewhere using similar and, where possible, simplified methods. If the programmes prove to be effective, cost-beneficial and feasible, they will be rolled out across the city. If this works, Birmingham could become the first city to take evidence-based programmes to scale in a children's services system.

Lessons for Future Applications

The Common Language operating system has not been evaluated formally in terms of its capacity to encourage evidence-based practice and improve child outcomes. It is hoped to undertake rigorous studies of process and impact using both qualitative and quantitative methods, as has been done for Communities that Care (e.g., Crow et al., 2004; Hawkins et al., 2008a, 2008b) and, to a lesser degree, Results-Based Accountability (Utting et al., 2008). Besides the experimental evaluations of discrete interventions introduced in Ireland and Birmingham, there is a series of reflective commentaries by different stakeholders on the implementation of Common Language in Ireland (Little & Abunimah, 2007; Langford, 2007; Keenan, 2007; Zappone, 2007), an independent evaluation of the Ireland programme (Paulsell et al., 2009), an independent qualitative analysis of the views of stakeholders involved in that process (Renshaw, 2009) and an evaluation of one aspect of the service-development method, namely, study tours (Axford et al., 2010). These and our own experience of applying the method over several years now can be drawn on to identify some key lessons for future applications of Common Language and other operating systems.

It is worth saying at the outset that the Common Language operating system has been applied in different geographical and administrative contexts, suggesting that it is relevant in different settings. Investors in children's services, including government departments and philanthropy, as well as the recipients of investments, such as not-for-profit organisations, have used the approach.

It is also fair to say that Common Language improves on standard methods of needs assessment used in service-commissioning models in children's services. An analysis of two contrasting local authorities in the United Kingdom suggests that large-scale quantitative surveys using standardised measures with representative samples to gauge the well-being of children compared with normative data are rare relative to small-scale qualitative analyses of service users' 'felt' needs (Axford et al., 2009). The Social Research Unit previously developed quantitative and qualitative methods to help policy-makers and managers to determine rapidly and for little cost the needs of children and families in their area (Little et al., 1999, 2002), but these, too, have important limitations, not least their focus on service populations (Axford, 2010). Fortunately, the methods for collecting quality data on the well-being of *all* children have become more sophisticated in recent years, enabling inter-area comparisons and the monitoring

of trends (Bradshaw et al., 2007; Collishaw et al., 2004), and Common Language draws on these developments (see Axford & Hobbs, 2010).

Common Language also invariably generates considerable energy and enthusiasm amongst participants. It reminds many participants why they chose a career working with children and helps others to clarify what needs to be done. However, the challenge of converting this into real change should not be underestimated. When reports about child well-being and need sit on shelves gathering dust, it is often not because the desire for change is lacking but rather because those involved do not have the methods to act on the information. Common Language, therefore, treats data collection as the first of several steps in a process rather than as an end in itself.

Even so, progress often can be frustratingly slow. This is partly a side effect of working collaboratively but also due to the inertia to change that seems to be endemic to most large public-service organisations. The strategy-development process – including the community and school surveys – was completed in six months in the Atlanta project in the state of Georgia in the United States. Since the context there was auspicious, with generous support from the funder and the city's education department, it would be hard to envisage completing the process more quickly. In Ireland and Birmingham, where the use of Common Language helped to secure large investments, the majority of services remain unchanged several years on; business as usual has survived largely intact. Why is this? What are some of the challenges that have been encountered?

To start with, while the exhortation to 'work together' in children's services is common, it is deceptively hard to do in practice (Anning et al., 2006). Through the Common Language work, we have encountered at least five barriers. First, although people working with children often use the same words, such as 'risk', 'outcome' and 'prevention', they often mean different things by those words. Failure to secure a common understanding results in conversations at crossed purposes.

Second, not all partners are equal. In the United Kingdom, a psychiatrist has a higher status than a social worker; a lawyer commands more authority than a teacher. These differentials in power and status can lead to certain perspectives being over-represented. Third, although unified by an interest in children's development, each profession assigns different importance to understanding normal and abnormal development. By virtue of their training, the average health visitor, for example, will be better versed in developmental milestones than will an average teacher, and one agency's serious case is routine for another. Fourth, each profession looks at children through a different lens and has different explanations for the causes and solutions to children's problems. For example, health professionals may encourage the medical management of child hyperactivity, whereas teachers may seek behavioural management solutions. Fifth, there are diverse interpretations of what counts as good-quality evidence. Medicine, for example, has an accepted hierarchy of standards of evidence that accords RCTs a higher status than other methods. This influences decisions about funding for different treatments. In other professions, such as social work, this approach meets strong resistance (Gray et al., 2009). Common Language tries to take these differences in language, status, ways of knowing and views on evidence into account.

Another challenge has been getting the right people involved in strategy development. It is now common knowledge that it is impossible to introduce significant innovations in services successfully without the support of the person at the top, whether this is in a school, a not-for-profit organisation or a government department. With change comes the risk of failure, and in order to take that risk, individuals need to have the support of their leaders. The individuals facilitating the use of Common Language therefore seek to build strong, trusting relationships with those leading the changes. However, this is double edged: If a leader moves on, support for the project can evaporate. Common Language arguably has been more successful when it is not championed solely by one charismatic individual. The work in Birmingham, for instance, has a number of champions, and the approach is embedded in organisational processes, which means that it is more likely to survive changes in personnel.

A further challenge is ensuring that those who lead the more detailed service design and implementation process understand and support the methods used. To this end, one of the resources accompanying Common Language is a training programme. It comprises 14 modules, each of which addresses either a concept (e.g., 'Outcome') or a method (e.g., 'How to evaluate an outcome'). According to the review by Fixsen et al. (2005) of implementation research, the training in itself is unlikely to foster evidence-based programmes, but if it runs in parallel with the service-design work and is supported by expert advice and coaching, it is more likely to be effective.

The next challenge is a side effect of an otherwise positive development. As the number of programmes to address children's problems has increased, so too have the number of on-line databases of programmes. These are developed with the noble intention of making it easier to find effective programmes, but they have several weaknesses. One is that there are too many of them (at least twenty). Another problem is that they apply different criteria and confuse the user. Thus a programme that qualifies as 'effective' according to one database will fall short in another. Further, the databases tend not to be built with policy-makers or funders in mind; information on costs, cost benefit and implementation requirements and supports is often absent or incomplete, hindering the task of deciding whether a programme is a good and feasible investment.

It is particularly curious that the databases contain such sparse data about cost because this is arguably the most potent information when seeking to influence decision makers. The Washington State Institute for Public Policy (WSIPP) in the United States produces the type of analysis that can help policy-makers make objective and well-informed judgements about potential investments (see Aos, 2004). It provides a framework in which programmes can be compared for their effect, cost and long-term benefit, so making it easier to determine a balanced and cost-effective portfolio of programmes. Its work was sufficient to persuade the state legislature to decide not to build a planned prison and instead to invest the money in prevention and early intervention that would avert the need for such institutions. Since many of the assumptions underpinning the WSIPP model apply to Washington state or the United States, work is now under way to adapt it for use in the United Kingdom.

Inevitably this kind of work leads to questions about the value of services that already exist. Yet while Common Language sparks interest in commissioning and funding new activity, unsurprisingly, this is rarely matched by enthusiasm for decommissioning services. Adding is easy, but taking away is hard. In a context of the global economic crisis and shrinking public-sector budgets in most Western developed countries, policy-makers will have to grapple with this thorny issue. They have two options: progressively slice budgets and expect more of the same to be done for less money or decide the activity that will, according to the evidence, deliver the best results and decommission that which does not meet the standard (Little & Axford, 2010). The application of Common Language in a recession requires the identification of disinvestments before investments.

Some challenges to progress are also bound up in evidence-based programmes themselves. Common Language offers a system-level approach to improving outcomes, which includes promoting the greater use of such programmes. As service systems have tried to introduce such programmes, it has become clear that this is not an easy marriage. Programmes are not developed with systems in mind, and systems do not readily accommodate programmes (Little, 2010). For example, it is generally accepted that programmes get the best results when delivered with fidelity, but achieving fidelity

requires an infrastructure comprising training, coaching, supervision and monitoring, none of which is routinely organised and funded within a system. Equally, few evidence-based programmes could sustain a large-scale roll-out; most are developed and tested by academics who generally lack the skills to 'take a product to the marketplace' and make it widely available. Until these issues are addressed, the introduction of evidence-based programmes in existing systems is likely to remain a marginal activity.

If strategy development and service design are to translate more easily into changed practice on the ground, there is also a need for more attention to organisational readiness. Some of the main factors that affect the success of any new service initiative have been identified (Donnermeyer et al., 1997; Lehman et al., 2002; Chilenski et al., 2007). These may be categorised in different ways, but typically they cover the following: whether individuals and groups perceive that the current situation needs to change ('motivational readiness'); whether the organisation has suitable material and staff resources to implement change ('institutional resources"); whether staff have the required experience, skills, attitudes and self-belief to effect change ('staff attributes') and whether the organisation and individuals within it function well ('organisational climate'). In aspects of the projects discussed earlier, participants have paid insufficient attention to these factors, and programme implementation has suffered as a result. There have been cases, for example, of children's centres having insufficient staff or space to run new groups or head teachers proving reluctant to try something new and even of persistent ideological doubts amongst policy-makers about the value of evidence-based programmes. It is not suggested here that only 'perfect' sites be selected: They do not exist. It is possible, however, to assess readiness and identify what extra support will be needed and where.

The final challenge comes from the wider policy context. Over the past thirteen years, the U.K. government has been inconsistent in its commitment to evidence-based practice in children's services (Rutter, 2007). There has been a very modest investment in implementing and evaluating a handful of evidence-based programmes, but simultaneously, there have been over 1,000 pilot projects and a massive investment in untested programmes. Given public-sector cuts, it is arguable that there will be heightened interest in the cost and effectiveness of programmes and that evidence-based programmes will be implemented more widely.

Where Next?

There is a growing knowledge of the factors that are known to influence the adoption, quality implementation and sustainability of evidence-based programmes (Rogers, 1995; Fixsen et al., 2005; Bumbarger & Perkins, 2008). In the pre-adoption phase, for example, it helps to analyse need and demand for services and to engage stakeholders from various constituencies. Adoption by individuals or institutions is more likely if information about the programme in question is packaged and transmitted helpfully and if efforts are made to ensure organisational readiness and sufficient financial resources. Quality implementation only happens if leaders are supportive of the work and practitioners receive adequate training and technical assistance, and the work will only be sustained longer-term if proper infrastructure and funding are put in place.

Thus the implementation challenge includes but is about more than bridging the gap of knowledge between research and practice. It is bound up with issues concerning resource allocation, priorities, ethical considerations and the distribution of power among politicians, administrators, professional groups and client groups (Johansson, 2010). These demand proper reflection, and much-neglected research from the public administration field could help in this respect (e.g., Hill & Hupe, 2005). This should not be interpreted as an invitation to make system-level changes at the expense of changing what is actually provided for children

because in isolation, they are unlikely to affect outcomes (Bickman et al., 1995; Bickman & Fitzpatrick, 2002). Experience to date shows that Common Language and the systems in which it works need to address both issues.

Meanwhile, no one suggests that Common Language is a panacea. Like other operating systems, it has strengths: keeping a focus on child well-being through the use of empirical data, fostering a common understanding across different stakeholders, negotiating change within the systems, orienting people towards costs and benefits, connecting people with the 'what works' literature, and shifting the balance towards investment in prevention. But it also has weaknesses, as shown earlier. Securing a demonstrable improvement in child well-being will require other technologies alongside Common Language: It is only part of the solution.

Notes

1. The meaning of the abbreviations is as follows: Oc = outcome; A = activities; I = investments; Ot = output.
2. http://connect.southdublin.ie/cdi/index.php.
3. www.archways.ie.

References

Anning, A., Cottrell, D., Frost, N., Green, J. & Robinson, M. (2006) *Developing multiprofessional teamwork for integrated children's services.* Maidenhead: Open University Press.

Aos, S., Lieb, R., Mayfield, S., Miller, M. & Pennuci, A. (2004) *Benefits and costs of prevention and early intervention programs for youth.* Olympia, WA: Washington State Institute for Public Policy.

Axford, N. (2010). Conducting needs assessments in children's services. *British Journal of Social Work* 40(1), 4–25.

Axford, N., & Hobbs, T. (2010). Getting the measure of child health and development outcomes (1): A method for use in children's services settings. *Child Indicators Research* 4(1), 59–80; doi: 10.1007/s12187-010-9074-2.

Axford. N., & Little, M. (2009). How to win friends and influence people. *Journal of Children's Services* 4(2), 2–3.

Axford, N., Berry, V., Little, M. & Morpeth, L. (2006). Developing a common language in children's services through research-based, inter-disciplinary training. *Social Work Education* 25(2), 161–76.

Axford, N., Morpeth, L., Little, M. & Berry, V. (2008) Linking prevention science and community engagement: A case study of the Ireland Disadvantaged Children and Youth Programme. *Journal of Children's Services* 3(2), 40–54.

Axford, N., Green, V., Kalsbeek, A., Morpeth, L. & Palmer, C. (2009). Measuring children's needs: How are we doing? *Child & Family Social Work* 14(3), 243–54.

Axford, N., Jonas, M., Berry, V., Green, V. & Morpeth, L. (2010). Can study tours help promote evidence-based practice in children's services? *European Journal of Social Work* 13(4), 523–43; doi: 10.1080/13691450903471237.

Birmingham City Council (BCC) (2007). *The Brighter Futures strategy*. BCC.

Bickman, L., Guthrie, P. R., Foster, E. M., et al. (1995). *Evaluating managed mental health services: The Fort Bragg experiment*. New York: Plenum.

Bickman, L., & Fitzpatrick, J. L. (2002) Evaluation of the Ft. Bragg and Stark County systems of care for children and adolescents: A dialogue with Len Bickman. *American Journal of Evaluation* 23(1), 69–80.

Bradshaw, J., Hoelscher, P. & Richardson, D. (2007). An index of child well-being in the European Union. *Social Indicators Research* 80, 133–77.

Bullock, R. (2006). The dissemination of research findings in children's services: Issues and challenges. *Adoption & Fostering* 30(1), 18–28.

Bullock, R., Gooch, D., Little, M. & Mount, K. (1998). *Research in practice: Experiments in development and Information Design*. Aldershot, UK: Ashgate.

Bumbarger, B., & Perkins, D. (2008). After randomised trials: Issues related to the dissemination of evidence-based interventions. *Journal of Children's Services* 3(2), 55–64.

Chaskin, R. J., & Rosenfeld, J. M. (eds.) (2008). *Research for action: Cross-national perspectives on connecting knowledge, policy and practice for children*. Oxford, UK: Oxford University Press.

Chilenski, S. M., Greenberg, M. T. & Feinberg, M. E. (2007). Community readiness as a multidimensional construct. *Journal of Community Psychology* 35(3), 347–65.

Chinman, M., Imm, P. & Wandersman, A. (2004). *Getting to Outcomes 2004: Promoting accountability through methods and tools for planning, implementation, and evaluation*. Santa Monica, CA: Rand Corporation.

Collishaw, S., Maughan, B., Goodman, R., & Pickles, A. (2004). Time trends in adolescent mental health. *Journal of Child Psychology and Psychiatry* 45(8), 1350–62.

Crow, I., France, A., Hacking, S. & Hart, M. (2004). *Does Communities that Care work? An evaluation of a community-based risk prevention programme in three neighbourhoods*. York, UK: Joseph Rowntree Foundation.

Department for Education and Skills (DfES) (2003). *Every child matters: Change for children*. London: DfES.

Donnermeyer, J. F., Plested, B. A., Edwards, R. W., Oetting, G. & Littlethunder, L. (1997). Community readiness and prevention programs. *Journal of the Community Development Society* 28(1), 65–83.

Fagan, A. A., Hanson, K., Hawkins, D. J. & Arthur, M. W. (2008). Bridging science to practice: Achieving prevention program implementation fidelity in the Community Youth Development Study. *American Journal of Community Psychology* 41, 235–49.

Fixsen, D., Naoom, S. F., Blasé, K. A., Friedman, R. M. & Wallace, F. (2005). *Implementation research: A synthesis of the literature*. Tampa, FL: University of South Florida.

Friedman, M. (2005). *Trying hard is not good enough: How to produce measurable improvements for customers and communities*. Victoria, BC: Trafford Publishing.

Gray, M., Plath, D. & Webb, S. A. (2009). *Evidence-based social work: A critical stance*. Abingdon, UK: Routledge.

Greenberg, M. T., Kusché, C. & Mihalic, S. F. (1998). *Promoting Alternative Thinking Strategies (PATHS): Blueprints for violence prevention (Book Ten)*. Blueprints for Violence Prevention Series (D. S. Elliott, Series Editor). Boulder, CO: Center for the Study and Prevention of Violence, Institute of Behavioral Science, University of Colorado.

Hawkins, J. D., & Catalano, R. F. (2002) *Communities that Care – Tools for community leaders: A guidebook for getting started*. South Deerfield, MA: Channing-Bete.

Hawkins, J. D., Catalano, R. F., Arthur, M. W., Egan, E., Brown, E. C., Abbott, R. D. &

Murray, D. M. (2008a). Testing Communities that Care: The rationale, design and behavioral baseline equivalence of the Community Youth Development Study. *Prevention Science* 9(3), 178–90.

Hawkins, J. D., Brown, E. C., Oesterle, S., Arthur, M. W., Abbott, R. D. & Catalano, R. F. (2008b). Early effects of Communities that Care on targeted risks and initiation of delinquent behavior and substance use. *Journal of Adolescent Health* 43, 15–22.

Hill, M., & Hupe, P. (2005) *Implementing public policy: Governance in theory and in practice.* London: Sage.

Hobbs, T. (2009). Looking for a grand view: Introducing concepts of robust sampling to policy makers and practitioners engaged in measuring the well-being of children at the local authority levels. *International Journal of Social Research Methodology* 13(5), 383–93; doi: 10.1080/13645570903354294.

Hobbs, T., Axford, N. & Jodrell, D. (2010). Getting the measure of children's health and development outcomes (2): The picture for a local authority in England. *Child Indicators Research* 14(1), 81–100.

Johansson, S. (2010). Implementing evidence-based practice and programmes in the human services: Lessons from research in public administration. *European Journal of Social Work* 13(1), 109–25.

Johnson, R., & Sawbridge, P. (2004). Family placements: matching needs and services. In V. White and J. Harris (eds.), *Developing good practice in children's services.* London, Jessica Kingsley Publishers.

Johnson, Z., Howell, F. & Molloy, B. (1993). Community mothers programme: Randomised controlled trial of a non-professional intervention in parenting. *British Medical Journal* 306, 1449–52.

Keenan, O. (2007). The evolution of children's services in Ireland and prospects for the future: A personal perspective. *Journal of Children's Services* 2(4), 71–80.

Klett-Davies, M., Skaliotis, E. & Wollny, I. (2008) *Mapping and analysis of parenting services in England.* London: Family & Parenting Institute.

Langford, S. (2007). People, relationships and power struggles: The view from the director-general of the Irish office of the minister for children. *Journal of Children's Services* 2(1), 67–75.

Layard, R., & Dunn, J. (2009). *A good childhood: Searching for values in a competitive age.* London: Penguin.

Lehman, W. E. K., Greener, J. M., & Simpson, D. (2002). Assessing organizational readiness for change. *Journal of Substance Abuse Treatment* 22(4), 197–209.

Little, M. (2010). *Systems and outcomes: Making evidence-based programmes and other proven practices systematic.* London: Demos.

Little, M., & Abunimah, A. (2007). Improving outcomes for children in the island of Ireland: The role of philanthropic investment. *Journal of Children's Services* 2(2), 60–7.

Little, M., & Axford, N. (2010). Subtract ... be incisive – Here, borrow my knife. *Journal of Children's Services* 5(1), 2–3.

Little, M., & Mount, K. (1999). *Prevention and early intervention with children in need.* Aldershot, UK: Ashgate.

Little, M., Axford, N. & Morpeth, L. (2002a). *Aggregating data: Better management information and planning in children's services.* Dartington, UK: Warren House Press.

Little, M., Bullock, R., Madge, J. & Arruabarrena, I. (2002b). How to develop needs-led evidence-based services. MCC *Building Knowledge for Integrated Care* 10(3), 28–32.

Little, M., Madge, J., Mount, K., Ryan, M. & Tunnard, J. (1999). *Matching needs and services,* 2nd ed. Dartington, UK: Dartington Academic Press.

McGilloway, S., Bywater, T., Ní Mháille, M., et al. (2009). *Proving the power of positive parenting: An evaluation of Incredible Years Ireland.* Dublin: Archways.

Melamid, E., & Brodbar, G. (2003). Matching needs and services: An assessment tool for community-based service systems. *Child Welfare* 82(4), 397–412.

Mihalic, S., Ballard, D., Michalski, A., Tortorice, J., Cunningham, L. & Argamaso, S. (2002). *Blueprints for violence prevention, violence initiative: Final process evaluation report.* Boulder, CO: University of Colorado.

Millham, S. (1993). *An embarrassment of riches or a rich embarrassment? Four decades of social policy research – An inaugural lecture.* Dartington, UK: Social Research Unit, University of Bristol.

Nutley, S. M., Walter, I. & Davies, H. T. O. (2007). *Using evidence: How research can inform public services.* Bristol, UK: Policy Press.

Olds, D., Hill, P., Mihalic, S. & O'Brien, R. (1998). *Nurse-family partnership: Blueprints for violence prevention (Book Seven).* Blueprints for Violence Prevention Series (D. S. Elliott, Series Editor). Boulder, CO: Center for the Study and Prevention of Violence, Institute of Behavioral Science, University of Colorado.

Paulsell, D., DelGrosso, P. & Dynarski, M. (2009) *The Atlantic Philanthropies' disadvantaged children and youth program in Ireland and Northern Ireland: Overview of program evaluation findings – Final report.* Princeton, NJ: Mathematica Policy Research.

Prinz, R. J., Sanders, M. R., Shapiro, C. J., Whitaker, D. J. & Lutzker, J. R. (2009). Population-based prevention of child maltreatment: The US triple P system population trial. *Prevention Science* 10, 1–12.

Renshaw, J. (2008). *Tools for improving outcomes and performance: Comparing six different approaches.* London: IdEA.

Renshaw, J. (2009). Common Language in Ireland: The view from stakeholders. Unpublished paper.

Rogers, E. M. (1995). *Diffusion of innovations.* New York: Free Press.

Rose, G. (1992). *The strategy of preventive medicine.* Oxford, UK: Oxford University Press.

Rutter, M. (2007). Sure Start local programmes: An outsider's perspective. In J. Belsky, J. Barnes, and E. Melhuish (eds.), *The national evaluation of Sure Start: Does area-based early intervention work?* Bristol, UK: Policy Press.

Social Research Unit (2010). *Standards of evidence of effectiveness.* London: GLA.

Spoth, R. L., & Greenberg, M. T. (2005). Toward a comprehensive strategy for effective practitioner-scientist partnerships and larger-scale community health and well-being. *American Journal of Community Psychology* 35(3–4), 107–26.

Taylor, K. (2005). Understanding communities today: Using matching needs and services to assess community needs and design community-based services. *Child Welfare* 84 (2), 251–64.

Torgerson, D. J., & Torgerson, C. J. (2008). *Designing randomised trials in health, education and the social sciences.* Basingstoke, UK: Palgrave Macmillan.

Tunnard, J. (2002). Matching needs and services: Emerging themes from its application in different social care settings. In H. Ward and W. Rose (eds.), *Approaches to needs assessment in children's services.* London: Jessica Kingsley.

Utting, D., Painter, A. & Renshaw, J. (2008). *Turning the curve stories.* Nottingham, UK: Department for Children, Schools and Families Publications.

Walter, I., Nutley, S., Percy-Smith, J., McNeish, D. & Frost, S. (2004). *Improving the use of research in social care* (Knowledge Review 7). London: Social Care Institute for Excellence and the Policy Press.

Webster-Stratton, C., Mihalic, S., Fagan, A., Arnold, D., Taylor, T. & Tingley, C. (2001). *The Incredible Years: Parent, teacher and child training series. Blueprints for violence prevention (Book Eleven).* Blueprints for Violence Prevention Series (D. S. Elliott, Series Editor). Boulder, CO: Center for the Study and Prevention of Violence, Institute of Behavioral Science, University of Colorado.

Weissberg, R. P., & Greenberg, M. T. (1998). Prevention science and collaborative community action research: Combining the best from both perspectives. *Journal of Mental Health* 7(5), 479–92.

Zappone, K. (2007). Freedom and prevention: Developing effective children's services in Tallaght, Ireland. *Journal of Children's Services* 2(3), 64–73.

Part VI

SIGNPOSTS TOWARD EFFECTIVENESS

CHAPTER 27

Key Themes and Future Directions for Implementation Science and Psychology in Education

Barbara Kelly

This book is a resource for those applying psychology in educational contexts. Its aim is to offer information about implementation science which describes ways in which psychology can be made more effective and successful in real-world contexts. The book covers an extensive range of topics reflecting the comprehensive and diverse nature of implementation science. However, a number of key themes emerge from the chapters which have implications for narrowing the gap between science and practice and for future directions of the application of implementation science to the psychology of education (concepts, theories and underlying epistemology); using implementation science to create successful interventions; practitioner involvement and training; and finally, contextual, organizational and policy issues.

Concepts, Theories and Underlying Epistemology

A number of chapters point to the need for a new *conceptual* focus on the type of scientific

approach to be adopted in supporting and measuring psychological interventions in the real world. In particular, chapters in Parts I and II highlight the importance of multi-method approaches to the design of interventions in the real world. These ideas are pertinent to the understanding of *evidence-based* interventions which authors highlight as containing paradoxes and unhelpful assumptions about the nature of science in practice. Several chapters in Part II highlight the need for a differentiation of the evidence we gather to help implement effectively and introduce the idea of using alternative epistemology to link traditional, empirical approaches to the key social and interpersonal processes involved in successful implementation in dynamic, real ecologies. Chapters 2, 7, 11 and 26 describe frameworks which very successfully incorporate interventionist steps reflecting the key elements identified by implementation science as central to success. These frameworks capture and address the complexity of the multi-level work required to influence and support the transfer of effectiveness. They are highly adaptable and may play a formative role in supporting academic research and in engaging stakeholders in understanding and adopting a common shared language, both conceptual and practical.

Using Implementation Science to Create Successful Interventions

Much of the work covered offers careful analysis of what contributes to failure in applying psychology, and some responses and remedies are readily inferred, allowing applied practitioners to develop ameliorative approaches directly from the evidence. In addition, many chapters outline in considerable detail the type of practice and specific interventions which will support effectiveness. In Part III, authors offer a range of in-depth accounts covering, for example, how to measure practitioner readiness for evidence-based interventions and implementation, how to consult specifically to focus on changes in practice and how to incorporate implementation epistemology within key executive steps to promote effective practitioner support of interventions. However, responses to some very complex findings are less clear and need exploration and adaptation of information emerging both in the implementation field itself and in other intervention contexts. For example, the need to *promote* readiness for intervention in schools and other educational contexts is central across the implementation science evidence base but provides a good example of a very complex challenge. Chapter 8 makes us aware of the factors, characteristics and attributes of the practitioner and of ecological features which indicate *lack of readiness* for supporting interventions effectively, but we need to transform this information to develop the means to actively and effectively promote readiness. This type of interpretative work is provided by themes and evidence across many chapters not necessarily linked directly to implementation science at present (but they may play a significant role in the future). This very fact suggests that an important task may be to identify where implementation

information and evidence already exists and to link it actively and directly to the developing implementation science evidence base. Chapter 9 on organizational consultation and Chapter 15 on the background and development of the Ecofit Program are good examples of evidence-based improvement of intervention readiness. Chapter 9 contributes to the development of effective implementation strategies from existing work on the engagement of institutions in the change process, and Chapter 15 draws heavily on existing research on the relative success of designing and incorporating multi-strand as opposed to single-strand interventions to target change. In these instances, implementation science offers an evidence-based *directive* on which aspects of these approaches need to be strengthened to support strategy and delivery of programmes and on which are most likely to influence effectiveness. Implementation expertise and evidence already exist which can be adopted in an evidence-based way by researchers and practitioners.

Practitioner Involvement and Training

Much of the evidence from implementation science places practitioners at the centre of intervention, particularly their preparation and training to apply interventions. The chapters in this volume identify the practitioner-related implementation processes which need to be in place across a range of very different educational needs and contexts to boost the effectiveness of interventions. For those involved directly in supporting the implementation of interventions and programmes, this information has *precise implications* for the preparation of staff and practitioners, their initial selection, the type and level of training and skill development needed and for the monitoring and evaluation of outcomes. Research justifies the conclusion that in many instances the practitioner is more important than the intervention itself. The practitioners' influence seems to be linked at a fundamental level to a range of very individual factors, for example, their views, attitudes, skills, knowledge and even style of delivery. High-quality delivery leading to positive outcomes from psychology-related programmes and interventions is linked, in turn, to positive and receptive views about the intervention or programme, constructive attitudes towards its implementation, appropriate skills, understanding of the theory and purpose of the intervention and enthusiastic and confident delivery. In the context of what might be termed 'training for implementation', several chapters explore how this might be tackled across contexts with highly specific requirements. In Chapter 22, for example, different types of training are considered in relation to their effectiveness in ensuring that the required skills for successful implementation are embedded. Timing of training is crucial; training needs to be embedded *before* the intervention begins and reviewed, supported and sustained during the intervention. In Chapter 23, the implications of this are highlighted and extended in relation to studies reviewed concerning improving the quality of training and skills offered by teachers and child-care workers generally. This effectively illustrates a key point – that implementation science has implications for all *teaching and caring contexts*. Existing research on the effectiveness of teaching and training methodology has much to offer implementation science and is a major evidence-based resource in helping to boost knowledge on effective intervention.

Contextual, Organizational and Policy Issues

Implementation science has a central role to play in the overall development of schools and wider educational contexts, for example, in relation to creating effective policy and organisational ethos, both of which may affect the effectiveness of any psychological intervention. Chapters 2, 7, 25 and 26, as well as many others, endorse an ecological approach to exploring the nature of

problems to be addressed by interventions. In various ways, they highlight the need for in-depth and highly collaborative forms of organisational consultation in both initial identification of problems and delivering interventions. Most effective is the supported purchase or customised development and delivery of programmes via carefully developed needs analyses to provide a good contextual/intervention match; stepped, collaborative planning with those who will deliver the programme around resources – human-, resource- and time-related – and built-in evaluation and reflection. Researching the nature of the problem or issue to be addressed as a collaborative process is described and substantiated by a number of chapters using shared frameworks for practice in applying psychology. On a large scale, the use of the Strengths and Difficulties Questionnaire described in Chapter 25 is an example of the innovative application of an evidence-based instrument to support the detailed direction, implementation and evaluation of well-being programmes in schools.

Some of the intricacies of implementation are embedded in difficult-to-access areas. In some studies, highly individual characteristics are implicated in invisible processes of disruption. The skilled development of relationships which foster and promote progress and change seem to offer one, almost therapeutic avenue for improving successful positive change.

Implementation science is essential to the development of effective support for children and young people in education worldwide. It is indispensable to the usefulness and effectiveness of psychology in education, offering a wide-ranging evidence base outlining fundamental requirements for the success of interventions. The guidance it provides on effective change has far-reaching implications. The extensive and impressive evidence outlined is emerging as a distinctive, coherent and comprehensive scientific approach and gaining recognition as it provides answers to long-standing riddles of contextual influences on the process of change.

Concluding Comment

In conclusion, implementation science offers more than might have been anticipated initially in building a much-needed expanded perspective and complementary paradigm for applied science. In term of ethics, accountability and cost-effectiveness, empiricism needs to answer real-world problems more effectively. Implementation science redefines concepts of real, scientific, evidence-based and effective built on an expanded epistemology and methodology which sits comfortably alongside the traditional perspectives offered by empiricism. Implementation science offers organising evidence-based principles and re-focussing frameworks which create a more clearly defined role for professionals delivering psychology in education. Importantly, it also can underpin any activity in education, including teaching and organisation, ethos development, fostering of well-being, measurement of impact and effective collaboration by providing direction for those investing in progressive change.

Index

educational policy and programs (*cont.*)
  full implementation procedures for, 20–1
  future research issues in, 463
  initial implementation stage for innovations in, 19–20
  instructional practices, improvement of, 373–87
  leisure education programmes, evidence-based prevention interventions, 313–27
  organizational characteristics in, 167–70
  reading interventions and collaboration with, 277–84
  research to policy to practice paradox in, 133–4
  school readiness interventions, 184–98
  scientific paradigm and, 5
  social competency programs, 230–45
  staff selection process for, 23–4
  student engagement in school reform proposals, 361–9
  systematic reviews of, 94
educational psychology. *See* school psychology services
educative critical components, social-emotional interventions for young children and role of, 215–17
Effectiveness and efficiency: random reflection on the health services (Cochrane), 93
effectiveness studies
  ABRACADABRA reading intervention program, 287
  EcoFit model, student academic and behavior interventions, 271–2
  effect size, 47–8
  Implementation Science and, 70–1
  of intervention outcomes, 46–50
  of intervention protocols, 7
  number-needed-to-treat analysis, 48–9
  organizational consultation, 166–70
  problem formation in, 76, 80
  of process outcomes, 45–6
  programme evaluations using, 37
  research synthesis concerning, 71–2
  school psychology services, 114–16
  social competency programs, 233–6
  social-emotional interventions for young children, 209–11, 217
  technology integration in reading programs, 285
Effective Practice Schools, Collaborative Coaching and Learning (CCL) model and, 376–9, 389n.13
effect size
  coding of, 77, 81–2
  disaggregation, 78

experimental design case study, 58–61
meta-analytic syntheses, 73–4
randomised controlled trial analysis, 47–8
reading intervention analysis, 278–80
in science teaching, systematic review of, 97–8
technology integration in reading programs, evaluation of, 284–93
efficacy studies
  ABRACADABRA reading intervention program, 286–7
  of English interventions for learning-disabled ELL students, 305–6
  Implementation Science, 70–1
  problem formation, 76, 80
  research synthesis, 71–2
  of Spanish interventions for learning-disabled ELL students, 306–9
  technology integration in reading intervention, 284–93
  TimeWise: Taking Charge of Leisure Time program, 317–19
efficiency studies
  Implementation Science and, 70–1
  problem formation in, 76, 80
  syntheses in, 71–2
electronic reference databases, relevant study identification, 76, 80
Elias, M., 18
Elleman, A. M., 280–1
Elliott, John, 405
Elmore, R. F., 167–70
emotion modeling
  child well being measurements and, 423–5
  social-emotional interventions for young children and characteristics of, 211–14
emotion supports, social-emotional interventions for young children and, 211–14
empathy, in social competency programs, 237–8
English as Additional Language/English language learners (ELLs)
  ABRACADABRA reading intervention program and, 286–7
  action research concerning, 412–13
  reading intervention effect on, 281
  summary of research and practice in reading interventions for, 306–9
English supplemental intervention
  efficacy and follow-up studies of, for learning-disabled ELL students, 305–6
  learning-disabled English language learners, 299–304
  research methodology in studies of, 304–5

Printed in Great Britain
by Amazon